BOLLYWOOD

THE FILMS! THE SONGS! THE STARS!

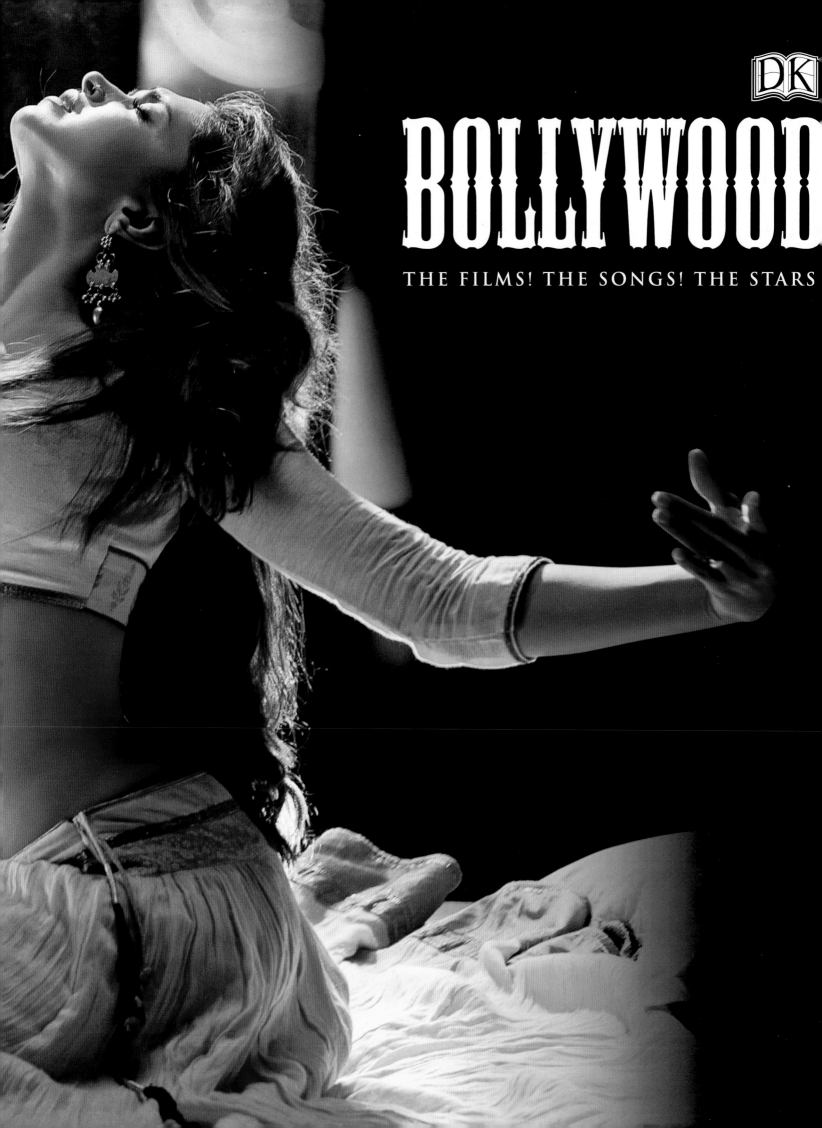

BOLLYWOOD

THE FILMS! THE SONGS! THE STARS

First American Edition, 2017
Published in the United States by DK Publishing
345 Hudson Street, New York, New York 10014

Copyright © 2017 Dorling Kindersley Limited
DK, a Division of Penguin Random House LLC
17 18 19 20 21 10 9 8 7 6 5 4 3 2 1
001–300182–Sept/2017

CONTRIBUTORS

- **S. M. M. Ausaja** A film historian and memorabilia archivist based in Mumbai, India, Ausaja is the Vice President at Osians Connoisseurs of Arts, a premier auction house for art and cinema in Mumbai. He has authored the book *Bollywood in Posters* and his next book, *The Bachchans*, a coffee-table project, is due in October 2017.

- **Karan Bali** A writer and filmmaker based in Mumbai, India, Karan is the co-founder of *Upperstall.com*, a website on contemporary and classic Indian cinema. He has also directed various documentaries, and was an Assistant Director on *Everybody Says I'm Fine!* and *Matrubhoomi*.

- **Aseem Chabbra** A New York-based freelancer who focuses on films and arts, Aseem has been published in *The New York Times*, *The Boston Globe*, *The Philadelphia Inquirer*, *Time Out*, *New York*, *Mumbai Mirror*, *The Hindu* and *Rediff.com*. He's the author of *Shashi Kapoor: The Householder, The Star*.

- **Rajesh Devraj** A screenwriter and researcher based in Mumbai, India, Rajesh has co-authored the book *The Art of Bollywood* and has written the screenplay for movies such as *The Fakir of Venice, Arjun: The Warrior Prince, Quick Gun Murugun,* and *Positive*.

- **Juhi Saklani** A freelance writer and photographer based in New Delhi, India, Juhi was a travel writer and editor for *Outlook Traveller Guidebooks* for more than a decade. A Hindi film lover, she is the author of Lonely Planet's *Filmi Escapes: Travel with the Movies*, and writes on films for her blog *Laughter Memoirs*. She has also authored Times Books' *Delhi by Metro* and DK's *Eyewitness Gandhi*.

- **Suparna Sharma** A journalist based in Delhi, India, Suparna Sharma is a film critic for *The Asian Age* newspaper. She is currently working on a book on India's first gossip writer, Devyani Chaubal.

- **Tanul Thakur** A National Award-winning film critic and independent journalist based in Mumbai, India, Tanul's articles have been published in *Caravan, Open, Fountain Ink, GQ, Yahoo! India, The Wire, Firstpost,* and *OZY,* among others.

ADDITIONAL CONTRIBUTORS

- **Kajori Aikat**
- **Alexandra Black**
- **Iain Ball**
- **Laura Buller**
- **Esther Ripley**
- **Alison Sturgeon**

CONTENTS

THE AGE OF BIG MONEY
2000–PRESENT

TAAL

BAJIRAO MASTANI

FOREWORD

I abhor the title of this book. The Indian Film Industry is what I shall always refer to as Cinema in India. We are an independent creative industry and not a derivative; any attempt to imply otherwise, shall not find favor with me.

But the absence of any kind of film documentation is another malaise that has been of great concern to me; one that I lament greatly. To find a global publishing house now wanting to tap into "the increasing interest in the Hindi film industry from national and international quarters" is indeed most laudable.

Hindi cinema, indeed the entire cinema in India, is the largest film-producing unit in the world. To me it has always played the role of a unifier, an integrator. When we sit inside that darkened hall we never ask who the person sitting next to us is—his or her caste, creed, color, or religion. Yet we enjoy the same story, laugh at the same jokes, cry at the same emotions, and sing the same songs. In a world that is disintegrating around us faster every day, where can one find a better example of national integration than within those hallowed portals of a cinema hall? There are not many institutions left that can boast or propagate such unity.

I once asked a Russian gentlemen in Moscow what it was that attracted him to Hindi cinema. He replied: "When I come out of the theater after watching a Hindi film, I have a smile on my face and a dry tear on my cheek!" There can be no better assessment of our films than this—and that too from an individual who was not an Indian. But my father, the great poet and litterateur, Harivansh Rai Bachchan, summed it all up most succinctly. On asking him one day what Hindi cinema meant to him, he said: "I get to see poetic justice in three hours! You and me shall not see this in a lifetime … perhaps several lifetimes!"

SMM Ausaja, a friend and a passionate film admirer, curator, and journalist, contributes to a section of this book. My wishes to him and to the publication.

Amitabh Bachchan

► **Bowled over by Bollywood**
Paying homage to an integral and inherently Indian experience, artists perform on a Bollywood-themed tableau at the Commonwealth Games held in New Delhi on October 3, 2010.

INTRODUCTION

Heartrending stories, hair-raising action, dynamic heroes, passionate heroines, and a glorious visual aesthetic that makes everything seem larger than life—the Bollywood film can transport its audience to a world where anything is possible, and where dreams really can come true. Song and dance are part of the escapism, together with energetic performances, vibrant costuming, and a rich sentimental seam that plays on the emotions of the viewer and overwhelms the senses. It is no surprise that Bollywood has entranced Indian cinemagoers for more than a century, and that India's unique approach to filmmaking has been a major influence in Hollywood and beyond.

From its beginnings in 1913, Hindi cinema certainly proved an incredibly versatile medium for expressing the passions, obsessions, and fears of the nation. In the darkness of the cinema, all Indians could share the same jokes, emotions, and dreams. The silent films of the early years seduced audiences with their lively, mostly all-male casts, establishing Hindi cinema as a potent form of entertainment for the people. By the 1930s and the advent of sound technology, the industry was turning out more than 200 films a year. Indian independence in 1947 heralded the beginning of a golden age. A prolific outpouring of films during the 1950s and 1960s helped to forge a new national identity, both reflecting and influencing the hearts and minds of the Indian people. In the 1970s, the term "Bollywood" was born, combining the words Bombay and Hollywood—the same decade also saw India overtake the US as the world's biggest film producer.

Right from the start, song and dance was an integral part of the Bollywood film. Originally influenced by the rich tradition of folk theater, choreographed musical sequences serve an important purpose—providing a transition between events and helping to reinforce the emotions underlying each scene. Music and dance are an indispensable feature of many Bollywood genres, from action and romance to historical epic.

Bollywood films form a phenomenal tribute to the creative talents of India. As the following pages reveal, some films are unabashed expressions of love, friendship, and good times; others deal with contemporary social issues in a sensitive way, broaching difficult subjects such as religious division and gender inequality. Whatever the subject, Hindi film conveys an emotional energy and visual brilliance that is unrivaled in international cinema. This book is by no means an encyclopedia of Bollywood; rather it is a celebration of some of the highlights, milestones, and surprise hits of more than a century of artistry and innovation in Indian cinema.

Picture perfect
Painted across 6 m (20 ft) of wall in Mumbai's posh suburb of Bandra, this mural of Nandlal Jaswantlal's *Anarkali* (1953), by the Bollywood Art Project initiative, is an ode to the vibrant history of popular Hindi cinema.

THE BEGINNING

1913–1950

As the nation struggled for freedom, studios took the fledgling film industry from silence to sound, creating a new language of cinema to reflect the changing sociopolitical reality.

THE BEGINNING

The first decades of Indian cinema saw pioneering efforts to help Indian film find its feet, lay down its technical foundations, and create its own cinematic language.

India got its first look at moving pictures as early as July 7, 1896, when films made by the Lumière Brothers of France were screened at the Watson Hotel in Mumbai. Through the early efforts of pioneers, Indian cinema began to slowly find its roots: H.S. Bhatvadekar filmed some of the earliest film footage in India, while showmen such as J.F. Madan and A. Esoofally organized "bioscope" shows, an early form of film projection, in tents. In another early venture, Dadasaheb Torne filmed a Marathi play, *Pundalik*, released in 1912.

However, Indian cinema was formally born in 1913, with the release of *Raja Harishchandra* by Dadasaheb Phalke (see pp. 16–17), the tale of a king tested by the gods for his commitment to the truth. For the first time, Indian audiences saw an Indian story, enacted by homegrown actors and shot by an Indian crew, on the nation's screens.

Early films by Phalke and other new filmmakers were largely based on mythological stories, as Indian audiences were familiar with them and held them in reverence. However, the 1920s saw an expansion into more varied genres. In addition to mythological and devotional films, movies based on social themes and action stunts began to gain in popularity. This decade saw the first generation of indigenous film stars

▲ **Changing times**
In an era when theaters only screened plays and foreign films, Dadasahib Torne created a film out of a play, *Pundalik*. This 1912 advertisement, published in *The Times of India*, announced the film's first screening in Mumbai.

such as Patience Cooper, Sulochana, Gohar, Master Vithal, and Zubeida. It is ironic that many of them were women, considering how difficult it was to get actresses to work in films, due to the dubious reputation of the industry in the early years. Indeed, Phalke had to cast a man for the role of the heroine in *Raja Harishchandra*.

UNIQUE IDENTITY

The 1930s witnessed major technical breakthroughs for Indian filmmaking. With the release of India's first talkie *Alam Ara* (see p. 20), it was the decade in which Indian films began to talk and sing. Song and dance (see pp. 272–73) became an integral part of all mainstream films, helping Indian cinema to create a unique cinematic identity, which the industry holds on to even today. It was a time of singing stars—Master Nissar, Jahanara Kajjan, Kanan Devi, and K.L. Saigal. The arrival of "playback" revolutionized the industry, pioneered by the Bengali film *Bhagya Chakra* (1935) and its Hindi remake *Dhoop Chhaon* (1935): with songs now recorded separately from filming, better voices could be used to help actors who could not sing. This was also the era of the earliest Indian films in color: an early effort, *Sairandhari* (1933), was shot in color but its processing was unsuccessful, so in 1937 *Kisan Kanya* became India's first "color talkie." Perhaps it is fitting

◀ **Women on screen**
An Anglo-Indian from Kolkata, Patience Cooper paved the way for Indian women in the film industry. With her global looks and local appeal, she played lead roles for more than a decade.

► **Bringing film to the masses**
India's first centrally air-conditioned cinema, Mumbai's Regal Theatre, was built by film exhibitor Framji Sidhwa. The first film to be aired at the theater was Laurel and Hardy's *The Devil's Brother* in 1933. Before the flowering of Indian cinema, the theater used to show only English films.

that these innovations came at a time when Indian filmmaking was becoming more organized—the era of the studios (see pp. 28–29), not unlike the studio system in Hollywood. Some of Indian cinema's early classics such as *Devdas* (see p. 22), *Achhut Kanya* (see p. 23), *Sant Tukaram* (1936), and *Duniya na Mane* (see p. 26) emerged in this period, proving that social commitment, art, and commerce could go hand in hand. With the wider outreach of the Hindi language across India, the Hindi film business became the country's premier film industry.

TIMES OF CENSORSHIP

The 1940s was a dramatic decade. During the war years, profiteering black marketeers turned to the glamour of the film world. With the growing popularity of actors, stars were weaned away from their studios on huge, per picture payments instead of contracted monthly salaries. With wartime restrictions on raw stock, the self-sufficient studios found it impossible to sustain high overhead costs and slowly began shutting down.

This was also a time when India's struggle for freedom had entered its last phase. Ruffled by the uprisings all over the country, British censors clamped down on films supporting the Indian cause. Films addressing India's freedom had to resort to indirect means to do so. *Kismet* (see pp. 30–31) accomplished this by superficially invoking Germany and Japan—Britain's adversaries in World War II—in the song "Door Hato Aye Duniya Walon, Hindustan Hamara Hai" (Go Away Foreigners, India Is Ours).

POST-PARTITION UPHEAVAL

Indian independence in 1947, along with the Partition of the subcontinent, meant India forgoing one of its major filmmaking centers—Lahore—to West Pakistan, while Bengali cinema lost a chunk of its market to East Pakistan (now Bangladesh). However, the inherently secular and flourishing film industry saw most of its Muslim talent stay back in India. Some prominent artists who did leave for Pakistan included singing star Noor Jehan, actress Swarnalata and her actor-filmmaker husband Nazir, writer Saadat Hasan Manto, and composer Ghulam Haider. On the other hand, actor Pran (see p. 125), and filmmakers Dalsukh Pancholi and Roop K. Shorey were among those who left Lahore for Mumbai.

After India's independence, it became possible to portray India's fight for freedom on celluloid. *Shaheed* (1948) saw

Dilip Kumar (see pp. 48–49) play a freedom fighter sacrificing his life for the country. *Lahore* (1949) depicted the Partition and its aftermath, with Nargis playing an abducted woman in Lahore. And in *Samadhi* (1950), Ashok Kumar portrayed a brave soldier of Subhash Chandra Bose's Indian National Army.

As the newly formed nation offered millions a better future, the migration rate from villages to cities increased sizably, leading to more films with an urban backdrop. Mehboob Khan's love triangle, *Andaz* (1949), centered on the urban rich, influenced many films in subsequent years, such as Raj Kapoor's (see pp. 44–45) masterpiece *Awaara* (see pp. 40–43). Most importantly, though, the 1940s saw a huge influx of some truly incredible talent into all departments of the film industry. With their coming to full bloom the following decade, Indian cinema's golden age was inevitable.

► **Patriotism in the movies**
A major box office hit, Ramesh Saigal's patriotic spy thriller *Samadhi*, starring actors Ashok Kumar and Nalini Jaywant, became the highest grosser of 1950.

► **Pioneering voice**
A phenomenal singing star in the 1930s and 1940s, K.L. Saigal is said to be the first male superstar of Indian cinema. The Indian film studio, New Theatres, is credited with discovering Saigal and shaping his music.

"Till the 1940s, Bombay filmmakers frequently addressed issues pertaining to social injustice ... region, and religion."

ENCYCLOPEDIA OF HINDI CINEMA, ENCYCLOPEDIA BRITANNICA, 2003

DADASAHEB PHALKE

DIRECTOR **1870–1944**

Widely known as the father of Indian cinema, Dadasaheb Phalke fought against all odds to make the first Indian film, laying the foundations of the industry.

I t was around the Christmas of 1910 that Dhundiraj Govind Phalke attended a film screening of Alice Guy's 1906 French film *The Life of Christ*. The film inspired Phalke greatly, and he decided to foray into the field of filmmaking, choosing his subjects from Indian mythology and culture. From this small seed, the Indian film industry would eventually flower to become the world's largest "Institute of the Imaginary."

Phalke was born on April 30, 1870, in the town of Trimbakeshwar in Nashik, Maharasthra. His father, a Sanskrit scholar, was a teacher at

Elphinstone College in Mumbai. Following high school, Phalke joined the prestigious Sir J.J. School of Arts in Mumbai, where he trained in various arts, including photography.

After this, Phalke dabbled in various jobs—portrait photographer, stage makeup man, assistant to a German illusionist, and even a short stint as a magician himself. His penchant for entrepreneurship didn't end there— when he decided to start a printing press, he found backers willing to pay for his trip to Germany to acquaint himself with the latest printing processes. Even though he remained with the press for some time after his return, by then Phalke had realized that a career in printing was not his true calling. It was around this time that he saw *The Life of Christ*.

THE GAME CHANGER
Since his childhood, Phalke had been brimming with ideas for narrating Lord Krishna's various exploits, and now he was keen to translate them into film. He took his wife Saraswatibai to another

screening of *The Life of Christ* to illustrate his vision, after which she understood his dream. Despite disapproval from various relatives— some who even considered Phalke mad—she stood by him; in time, Saraswatibai would become his strongest collaborator.

To realize his plan, Phalke pledged his life insurance policy in addition to raising a loan from an old friend, and set sail for England on February 1, 1912. He returned to India with a Williamson camera, a perforating machine, developing and printing equipment, and some raw stock. But he still needed money to make films. To impress Yeshwant Nadkarni, Phalke's financier, he called on his past as an illusionist to make a "trick" film: intermittently shooting the growth of a pea plant to make it seem like it was growing before the audience's eyes.

THE FIRST INDIAN FILM
By now, Phalke had decided to push back the film on Lord Krishna and to instead tell the story of Harishchandra, a king in Hindu mythology revered for his commitment to the truth. The result would be the first-ever feature film with a fully Indian cast and crew and completely produced in India, *Raja Harishchandra* (1913).

However, it was no easy task. No respectable woman was willing to act in the film as Harishchandra's wife

◄ Pioneer of Indian cinema
Inspired by great names like Cecil Hepworth, one of the founders of British cinema, Phalke introduced filmmaking to India.

KEY WORKS

Raja Harishchandra, 1913

Mohini Bhasmasur, 1913

Satyavan Savitri, 1914

Lanka Dahan, 1917

Shri Krishna Janma, 1918

Kaliya Mardan, 1919

Bhakta Prahlad, 1926

Nala Damayanti, 1927

 First film for Indian audiences
The first Indian film, *Raja Harishchandra*, brought a popular folk tale about a noble king to the screen.

announced his retirement from filmmaking in the late 1920s. However, the call of celluloid was too powerful to ignore, and Phalke made a comeback with *Setu-Bandhan* (1932). Sadly for him, the sound era had arrived and though he tried to post-synchronize the film with dialogue, it sank at the box office. His final effort, *Gangavataran* (1937), did not find an audience, and Phalke died in obscurity in Nashik on February 16, 1944.

PHALKE'S LEGACY
It is only due to the efforts of archivist and director of the National Film Archive of India (NFAI), P.K. Nair, that Phalke is remembered as the founder of the Indian film industry. Today, the most prestigious award of Indian cinema, the Dadasaheb Phalke Award, is named after him.

Taramati. Phalke even approached prostitutes to act in the film but they also refused. Finally, Phalke convinced a male restaurant cook with feminine features and long slender fingers, Anna Salunke, to play his heroine. So Indian cinema's first heroine was played by a man, in a similar fashion to how early theater productions in England used men to enact women's roles.

Raja Harischandra is the tale of a righteous ruler who sacrifices his kingdom and family to abide by his principles of honesty and truth. The gods testing him are impressed by his idealism and restore him to his former position. Audiences were thrilled to see a familiar story enacted by Indian actors. *Raja Harischandra* was released at the Coronation Theatre in Mumbai, and brought rich returns for Phalke. He had to remake the entire film in 1917 when the only surviving prints caught fire.

TASTE OF SUCCESS
Phalke soon moved his entire setup to Nashik, Maharashtra. He introduced India's first actresses, Kamlabai Gokhale and Durgabai Kamat, in his next film, *Mohini Bhasmasur* (1913). The movie also gave him ample scope to try his hand at special effects and animation. Phalke's film company in Nashik grew into a large team of artists and technicians, most of whom lived on the premises like a large communal family.

Phalke's films show us that he had a strong visual sense coupled with technical resourcefulness quite like the pioneering French illusionist and filmmaker, Georges Méliès. He reached the peak of his career with *Lanka Dahan* (1917), *Shri Krishna Janma*

(1918), and *Kaliya Mardan* (1919), a film in which his daughter, Mandakini, acted as little Krishna. During screenings of these films, when the actors playing Lord Rama or Krishna appeared on screen, the impact was so great that audiences prostrated themselves before the characters in order to seek their blessings.

These three films were overwhelmingly successful and Phalke himself would often travel across the country on a bullock cart with a projector, a screen, and his films. The revenue was mostly in coins, and their weight on his return journeys was enormous.

FADING GLORY
By the 1920s, a distressed Phalke found that the film world was becoming too focused on money. Feeling like an outsider in the very industry he helped to create, he

▲ Dedicated to the art
Driven by his passion, Phalke paid great attention to every element of his films—from cast selection to the more technical aspects of production.

"I … saw the film [The Life of Christ] again … I felt my imagination taking shape on the screen."

D.G. PHALKE, *ESSAYS ON THE INDIAN CINEMA*

TIMELINE

- **April 30, 1870** Born in Trimbakeshwar in Nashik District, Maharasthra.

- **1885** Studies at J.J. School of Arts, Mumbai, Maharashtra.

- **1890** Learns three-color block making, photolithography, and ceramics at Ratlam, Madhya Pradesh.

- **1908** Establishes Phalke's Art Printing & Engraving Works, later called Laxmi Art Printing Works, at Lonavala.

- **1909** Sails to Germany to acquaint himself with the latest printing processes.

- **1910** *The Life of Christ* inspires Phalke to get into filmmaking.

- **1912** Travels to London to acquire cinema equipment. Meets British pioneer Cecil Hepworth, who tutors him at Walton Studios. Returns to establish Phalke Films in Dadar, Mumbai.

- **1913** *Raja Harishchandra* is the first feature film to be fully produced in India. Phalke undertakes another trip to England to organize trade shows. Returns to India despite being given job offers in Europe.

- **1913** *Mohini Bhasmasur* stars India's first actresses, Kamlabai and Duragbai.

- **1917** Phalke's documentary, *How Films Are Made*, demystifies the filmmaking process.

- **1917–18** Publishes several essays on cinema, *Bharatiya Chitrapat*, in film magazine *Navyug*.

- **1918** Sets up Hindustan Cinema Films.

- **1922** Resigns briefly from Hindustan Cinema Films to spend time in Varanasi writing a play, *Rangbhoomi*.

- **1932** Returns to cinema post-retirement to make *Setu-Bandhan*. The film flops.

POSTER OF *SETU BANDHAN* (1932)

- **1937** Phalke's final film, *Gangavataran*, is a debacle.

- **February 16, 1944** Dies in Nashik, Maharashtra.

HEROINES
IN TIMES OF
TABOO

The women who worked in early films broke through rigid social barriers to do so, despite the risk of being ostracized.

▶ **Life mirroring cinema**
Jawani ki Hawa (1935) starred Devika Rani (center) and Najmul Hasan, who—just like their characters in the movie—eloped.

Acting was a profession that women did not dare consider in the early days of Indian cinema. The pioneering filmmaker Dadasaheb Phalke (see pp. 16–17) had to cast a man, Anna Salunke, as his heroine in *Raja Harischandra* (1913). Although Phalke managed to convince two women, Durgabai Kamat and her daughter Kamlabai, to act in his next film, *Mohini Bhasmasur* (1913), Salunke continued playing female roles as women still shied away from performing in front of the camera.

WORKING WOMEN
More liberal than their traditional Indian counterparts, women from the Jewish and Anglo-Indian communities slowly made their way into films. Patience Cooper, an Anglo-Indian from Kolkata, is widely considered to be the first Indian female film star. Many actresses had to take on "Indian" screen names to fit in, such as Renee Smith, who became Seeta Devi, and Ruby Myers, who went by Sulochana, and who became the biggest female film star of her time. She commanded a salary higher than the Governor of Bombay (now Mumbai).

Eventually, Indian women began entering the film world. The heroine of *Alam Ara* (see p. 20), Zubeida, and her sisters, Sultana and Shehzadi, were stars of the silent film era; their mother, Fatma Begum, was also one of India's earliest women directors. Gohar Mamajiwala, who came from a well-to-do Muslim family, entered the film industry after her father's business failed. She would go on to be both a successful actress and a partner in one of India's biggest filmmaking companies, Ranjit Movietone, in the days of the big studios (see pp. 22–23).

But if one actress truly broke taboos at the time, it was Durga Khote. Coming from a respectable Hindu family, she was a mother of two young children when she entered films in the early years of the talkies.

Although audiences soon came to accept actresses on screen, they were largely restricted to stereotypical "suffering women" roles. Films that went against the grain saw the woman pay for being a rebel or finding redemption by returning to society's fold. Ironically, it took a blonde, whip-wielding actress called Fearless Nadia (see p. 21) to take on Indian society's patriarchal norms and succeed.

> *"In those days, women from good families and films did not go together."*
>
> **DURGA KHOTE,** *I, DURGA KHOTE,* 2006

ALAM ARA

1931

The first Indian talkie, *Alam Ara* also introduced many motifs of commercial Hindi cinema, such as the use of songs within the narrative and the theme of lost and found characters.

Watching the Hollywood musical *Show Boat* (1929) at the Excelsior Theatre in Mumbai, Ardeshir M. Irani, founder of the Imperial Film Company, felt so inspired that he decided to make an all-talking, all-singing feature film set in India.

▼ First Indian talkie
The movie poster played up the talking and singing aspects of the film to entice Indian audiences into cinemas.

Wanting to be the first producer to make an Indian talkie, Irani kept the work under wraps until its completion.

For the story, Irani decided on *Alam Ara*, a play about royal intrigue by the famed Mumbai dramatist Joseph David. The plot revolves around a king's court. Adil, the army chief, spurns the advances of the evil queen, Dilbahar. She gets him imprisoned and banishes his pregnant wife to the jungle. Adil's wife dies giving birth to a girl, Alam Ara, who is brought up by nomads. Upon learning the truth about her father, she travels to the palace to free him. There, she falls in love with the prince.

OBSTACLES AND CHALLENGES
Irani faced many challenges during the making of the film. First and foremost, there was the issue of sound. With the help of Wilford Deming, who taught him the basics of sound recording, he installed the Tanar system that enabled the capture of sound while filming. Songs had to be performed live by actors in front of the camera. The set was close to a noisy railway line, so the film had to be shot when the trains were not running.

The leading actress of the time, Sulochana was an obvious choice for the female lead—but since she could not speak Urdu or Hindustani well, she lost the role to Zubeida. For the lead actor, Irani decided to go for a well-known name and signed Master Vithal, India's top stunt hero. Vithal had to break his contract with Sharada Studio for the film. A court case ensued; Irani successfully won with the help of top legal expert Muhammad Ali Jinnah, who would go on to become Pakistan's first Governor-General. Despite all this effort, it was later found that Vithal couldn't speak Hindi properly, so the script had to be altered to make him magically dumb—effectively ending his career as a leading man in Hindi films.

SUCCESSFUL RECEPTION
Despite the film's production problems, it was a huge hit on its release. Police had to be summoned to control crowds outside theaters. According to the film magazine *Indian Talkie*, tickets were on sale for 15 to 20 times their usual cost.

The film's songs became popular, too, especially "De De Khuda Ke Naam Pe Pyare," sung and enacted by Wazir Mohammed Khan. *Alam Ara* heralded a tradition where songs would become an integral part of Indian cinema.

CAST AND CREW

★ **Zubeida** Alam Ara
  Master Vithal Prince
  Prithviraj Kapoor General Adil

🎬 **Director** Ardeshir M. Irani
🏠 **Producer** Imperial Film Company
🎵 **Music composers**
  Ferozshah M. Mistri, B. Irani
📖 **Scriptwriters** Joseph David,
  Munshi Zaheer
🎥 **Cinematographer** Adi M. Irani

▲ A love story
The film was a tale of love between a prince and a gypsy girl, Alam Ara. It was based on a Parsi play written by dramatist Joseph David, who went on to become a Bollywood screenwriter.

HIT SONGS

De De Khuda Ke Naam Pe Pyare
(Spare Me Change in the Name of God)
🎤 **Singer** Wazir Mohammed Khan

HUNTERWALI

1935

Hunterwali introduced audiences to India's first-ever female stunt star, "Fearless Nadia" (Mary Ann Evans). An instant hit, the film ran for 25 weeks in cinemas.

CAST AND CREW

★ **Fearless Nadia** Princess Madhuri/ Hunterwali
Boman Shroff Jaswant
Jaidev Cunnoo

🎬 **Director** Homi Wadia
⬠ **Producers** Wadia Movietone, J.B.H. Wadia
♫ **Music composer** Master Mohammed
♪ **Lyricist** Joseph David
📖 **Scriptwriters** Homi Wadia, Joseph David, J.B.H. Wadia
🎥 **Cinematographer** Balwant Dave

Loosely based on the popular American series *The Perils of Pauline*, and inspired by the daring fight sequences of the swashbuckling Hollywood star, Douglas Fairbanks, *Hunterwali* (A Woman with a Whip) sees the blonde, blue-eyed Evans play a princess as well as a tough, masked vigilante in disguise. She fights for the poor before ultimately defeating the film's villain, the evil Minister, who has kidnapped her father with an eye on the throne.

FEARLESS NADIA

The shoot began with a stunt that required Evans to beat up bodyguards and leap off a high roof. After some initial hesitation, she performed the stunt effortlessly. Overjoyed by his heroine's feat, producer J.B.H Wadia labeled her "Fearless Nadia," an epithet that became Evans' screen name. Thrilled by her abilities, J.B.H. and his younger brother Homi, became more adventurous, upping the ante of her action sequences. The Wadia brothers also increased the budget of the movie, which they used to add in romantic sequences and songs to make the film even more entertaining.

However, shooting came to an abrupt halt when Nadia injured herself while performing a stunt. She could not move for the next three days and had to rest for several weeks. But she was back on set for more daredevilry as soon as the doctor declared her fit.

ANOTHER HURDLE

Despite the Wadias' confidence that they had a winner on their hands, when it came time to distribute the movie, no buyer was willing to take it, and *Hunterwali* lay in its cans for months. Distributors were scared that audiences would react in fury to a white female lead in revealing costumes beating up Indian men.

Finally, the Wadias released *Hunterwali* themselves after building a successful marketing campaign around their exotic star. The film was a smash hit right from its premiere. Audiences were as amazed by Nadia's cartwheels, splits, and fights as they were by her hot pants and boots. The scene where she declares herself "Hunterwali" to fight social injustice drew loud claps and whistles from awestruck cinemagoers.

Whips, masks, and miniature "Hunterwali" pictures soon went on sale everywhere. More importantly, the film gave Indian cinema a sensational and fearless new star.

◄ The caped crusader
With her mask, whip, and cape, as well as her good looks and daredevil persona, Fearless Nadia became an instant sensation.

MARY ANN EVANS (1908–96)

Australian-born Mary Ann Evans, better known to the world as "Fearless Nadia," was perhaps Indian cinema's first feminist, championing women's causes. Trained in horse riding and ballet, and with a background as a circus performer, she could effortlessly swing from chandeliers, balance atop hurtling trains, crack a whip, and throw punches on set—breaking many gender stereotypes of the time. Eventually married to Homi Wadia, Nadia was a major stunt star between the 1930s and 1950s, in a career spanning about 50 films.

DEVDAS

1935

Taking a major step forward in the art of storytelling, *Devdas* attempted to move away from the theatricality that was prevalent at the time, and adopt a more realistic style.

Published in 1917, Sarat Chandra Chattopadhyay's iconic Bengali novel was first adapted as a silent film in 1928, well before New Theatres studio remade it in Bengali and Hindi in 1935. P.C. Barua directed both of these versions and also played the lead role in the Bengali film. The Hindi adaptation, however, saw Kundan Lal Saigal as the doomed hero Devdas, unable to marry his childhood sweetheart, Parbati, who is forced to wed another man. Despite the best efforts of the courtesan Chandramukhi, whom he visits to get over losing Parbati, Devdas continues to wallow in self pity.

The film's rich cinematic treatment and eloquent dialogue established Barua as one of the best filmmakers in India.

SINGING SUPERSTARS

The film also made Saigal into a major star. His brooding looks, with the lock of hair falling across his forehead, and his voice full of love and despair, sent audiences into a frenzy. Ironically, Saigal had a sore throat at the time of recording the songs for *Devdas*, forcing him to sing in a softer voice, which matched Barua's naturalistic treatment of the story perfectly. Saigal's singing in *Devdas* was ultimately recognized as some of the best of his career.

Before selecting Jamuna Barua to play Parbati, the director had originally wanted the top singer and actress Kanan Devi to play the part, but her studio, Radha Films, refused to give her permission. Devi later found out that her contract had already expired and that Radha Films had conveniently kept silent about it. She subsequently signed up with New Theatres and went on to make some of her best films with the studio.

INSPIRED ADAPTATIONS

Over the years, the character of Devdas, the ultimate romantic, has continued to fascinate filmmakers. Hindi cinema saw Dilip Kumar play the tragic hero in a 1955 film, directed by Bimal Roy. Shah Rukh Khan took on the role in Sanjay Leela Bhansali's epic 2002 interpretation, while Anurag Kashyap gave the tale a unique dark spin in *Dev.D* (2009), starring Abhay Deol. Earlier, in the 1970s, filmmaker Gulzar had begun a version with Dharmendra, but it was never finished.

CAST AND CREW

★ **Kundan Lal Saigal** Devdas
   Jamuna Barua Parbati
   Rajkumari Chandramukhi

🎬 **Director** P.C. Barua
⬭ **Producer** New Theatres Ltd
🎵 **Music composer** Timir Baran
𝄪 **Lyricist** Kidar Sharma
▭ **Scriptwriters** P.C. Barua, A.H. Shore, Kidar Sharma
🎥 **Cinematographer** Bimal Roy

◀ **True to life**
The simple costumes worn by the lead characters in the 1935 adaptation of *Devdas* made them look more real and credible.

KUNDAN LAL SAIGAL (1904–47)

A former railway timekeeper and typewriter salesman, Jammu-born K.L. Saigal went on to become a superstar of Hindi cinema. He mesmerized audiences with his magical voice and was a top singing star for much of the 1930s and 1940s. Saigal worked at the New Theatres film studio, Kolkata, from 1932–40 before shifting base to Mumbai. Dependence on alcohol destroyed his health, and despite a final attempt at going clean, he passed away in Jalandhar at just 42 years old. Singers, such as Mukesh (see p. 43) and Kishore Kumar (see pp. 100–101), were heavily influenced by his voice before carving out distinct singing styles of their own.

ACHHUT KANNYA

1936

Achhut Kannya speaks out against the evils of the Hindu caste system, using the language of a typical song-and-dance commercial film to make its point.

◀ **Iconic song**
Rani and Kumar were not proficient singers, so music composer Saraswati Devi taught them to sing the lyrics for "Main Ban Ki Chidiya" syllable by syllable.

CAST AND CREW

★ **Devika Rani** Kasturi
 Ashok Kumar Pratap
 P.F. Pithawala Mohan
 Kamta Prasad Dukhia

 Director Franz Osten
 Producer Himansu Rai
 Music composer Saraswati Devi
 Lyricist J.S. Casshyap
 Scriptwriters Niranjan Pal, J.S. Casshyap
 Cinematographer Josef Wirsching

and their love scenes have a charming innocence about them. It has to be said, though, Kumar looks and acts quite babyish in the film, and Rani, with her perfectly shaped eyebrows and impeccable makeup, is hardly the realistic village maiden. However, the luminosity she brings to the film is undeniable, also creating a prototype for Bollywood's rendition of a village belle.

FEMALE MUSIC COMPOSER
The film's music composer, Saraswati Devi, was a Parsi and one of the first female music directors to work in Indian cinema. However, she faced strong disapproval from the Parsi community, which considered working in the film industry as indecent, especially for a woman.
 Her song "Main Ban Ki Chidiya" (I Am a Bird of the Forest), sung by Rani and Kumar as they sit on the branch of a tree, cooing sweet nothings to each other, has gained an iconic status down the years.

GREAT RECEPTION
Achhut Kannya was filmed and edited in just eight weeks and proved to be a smash hit at the box office. Also, the film—and

Rani's performance in particular—garnered great praise from both audiences and critics.
 Among the luminaries who saw the film were poet and politician Sarojini Naidu and the first prime minister of India, Jawaharlal Nehru, who came to Mumbai specifically for a screening of the film at the Roxy Cinema.

The 1936 film *Achhut Kannya* is among the early films by Bombay Talkies, which set the trend of how mainstream cinema would deal with serious social issues. Even as these films would raise probing questions about the wrongs in society, they would sugar-coat the issues within the guise of popular entertainment. In any case, the early Bombay Talkies films were known for their largely cosmopolitan narratives, glossy appearance, and technical virtuosity. An early effort by the studio to film a rural story, *Achhut Kannya* is

based on writer Niranjan Pal's story *Level Crossing*. The film questions the caste system through the doomed love story of Pratap, an upper-caste Brahman boy, and Kasturi, an untouchable, low-caste girl.
 The film also explores issues such as modern medicine versus traditional medicine, state law versus village justice and—through the character of Pratap's broad-minded father—questions the general moral code of the time.
 The lead pair of Devika Rani (see pp. 24–25) and Ashok Kumar (see p. 31) share an easy, amicable camaraderie,

▲ **Poster with a message**
This film was one of the first Indian films to address the social evil of untouchability, setting the trend for many later films.

"Easily the best Devika Rani film to date ... "

THE HINDU, 1937

DEVIKA RANI

ACTRESS–PRODUCER 1908–94

Known as the "first lady of the Indian screen," Devika Rani acted in some of Hindi cinema's earliest classics, produced at the legendary Bombay Talkies film studio.

Reacting to the leading lady of an English film set in India, *Karma* (1933), London newspaper *The Star* wrote, "Go and hear English spoken by Miss Devika Rani. You will never hear a lovelier voice or diction or see a lovelier face. Devika Rani has a singular beauty, which will dazzle all London."

However, the British response to the film, which was based on the love story of a prince and a queen from a neighboring state, was indifferent. This led the actress and her producer–director–actor husband, Himansu Rai, to turn their attention away from making films for the West about "exotic" India and to focus on the developing film industry back home.

REFINED LINEAGE

Rani was the grandniece of poet and Nobel laureate Rabindranath Tagore, and daughter of the first Surgeon-General of Chennai. As was the custom with the privileged class, she was sent to England for her education, where she studied at South Hampstead High School. She later got a scholarship to study at the Royal Academy of Dramatic Art (RADA) in London, and also studied architecture and décor and design in England.

Despite her various talents, Rani was still unclear about her future. While working in textile design to support herself, she met lawyer turned filmmaker Himansu Rai at a party in London. He persuaded her to work

▲ **The show begins**
This Bombay Talkies production, directed by Franz Osten in 1936, was one of the first of a series of films with Devika Rani as the lead actress.

in films with him, and she began by assisting Rai's cousin Promode Nath in art direction for his film *A Throw of Dice* (1929).

THE BIRTH OF BOMBAY TALKIES

Rani's experience at the UFA Studios in Berlin, where *A Throw of Dice* was edited, was life-changing. Training in different departments of filmmaking, she came into contact with iconoclastic director G.W. Pabst and actors such as Emil Jannings and Marlene Dietrich. Fluent in German, she also trained

◄ **Remarkable actress**
Devika Rani is best known for her exceptional acting skills. Spirited and charismatic, she made it possible for girls from respectable families to work in film.

KEY WORKS

Jeevan Naiya, 1936

Achhut Kannya, 1936 (see p. 23)

Janma Bhoomi, 1936

Jeevan Prabhat, 1937

Izzat, 1937

Vachan, 1938

Nirmala, 1938

Durga, 1939

Anjan, 1941

Hamari Baat, 1943

> "*Devika Rani ... puts the stereotyped charms of Hollywood blondes completely in the shade.*"

DAILY DISPATCH, MANCHESTER, ENGLAND

under theater director Max Reinhardt and assisted with makeup and costumes on film sets.

By the time Rai and Rani—now husband and wife—made *Karma*, the Nazi party in Germany was on the rise and bringing drastic changes across Europe. The couple decided to return home, taking with them the Hindi version of *Karma*, called *Nagan ki Ragini*, and a strong German crew to make state-of-the-art films.

Their company, Bombay Talkies, established in 1934, debuted in 1935 with the film *Jawani ki Hawa*, a thriller set aboard a train. It starred Rani, with Najmul Hasan as the leading man. The two became romantically involved during the making of the film and eloped while filming the studio's next production, *Jeevan Naiya*. A distraught Rai tracked them to the Grand Hotel in Kolkata and persuaded Rani to come back, but dropped the hero. Bombay Talkies was now in need of a new leading man when Rai's eye fell on his young laboratory assistant, whom he launched in *Jeevan Naiya*, opposite Rani. This young man was Ashok Kumar (see p. 31).

LEADING LADY
In 1936, Rani and Kumar made their most popular film, *Achhut Kannya*, based on the story of doomed love between an untouchable girl

▶ Blockbuster pairing
Devika Rani and Ashok Kumar starred together in *Nirmala*, in 1938, to critical and commercial acclaim.

and an upper-caste Brahman boy. Critics went into raptures over Rani's sensitive portrayal of the young lower-caste girl, even if she looked much too urban and sophisticated in the role. *The Times of India* described Rani's acting as "a performance never seen or equalled on the Indian screen."

By then, Bombay Talkies had settled into regular production, with all their early female-centric films revolving around Rani. Most film historians agree that with her stunning beauty and magnetism, Rani was the dominant film actress in the first decade of talkies in India.

METAMORPHOSIS
In 1940, the untimely death of Rai left Bombay Talkies rudderless. Determined to keep his dream alive, Rani courageously took charge of the film company. As Controller of Production, she bankrolled hits like *Basant* (1942) and *Kismet* (see pp. 30–33), the studio's most

successful film. However, due to an internal rift, a rival group led by Kumar and Sashadhar Mukerji broke away to form another company, Filmistan in 1943. This coupled with changes in the studio system and huge overhead costs made it extremely difficult for Rani to continue running the company.

Rani's last film as an actress was *Hamari Baat*. At this stage she was disillusioned by the overtly commercial shape the Indian film industry was taking, and was finding no backers for her future plans for Bombay Talkies.

A NEW LIFE
In 1945, Rani bid adieu to filmmaking and married Svetoslav Roerich, son of Russian painter Nicholas Roerich. The couple settled in Manali, Himachal Pradesh where, it is said, she dabbled in making documentaries on wildlife. Rani later acquired land on the outskirts of Bangalore, in southern India, where she managed an export company.

Though retired from the film industry, she organized the first ever Film Seminar on behalf of a group of filmmakers and the Indian government in 1955, which was addressed by India's first prime minister, Jawaharlal Nehru.

Rani was subsequently awarded the Padma Shri for her services to Hindi cinema, and on November 21, 1970, she became the first recipient of the highest cinematic award in the country—the Dadasaheb Phalke Award. She passed away in Bangalore, proud and undeterred, at the age of 85.

◀ The risk-taker
A versatile actress, Devika Rani handled varied roles at Bombay Talkies with relative ease. Here she plays an adolescent girl living with her aged mother in the rural melodrama *Durga* (1939).

POSTER FOR THE FILM *ANJAN*, 1941

DUNIYA NA MANE

1937

The first in V. Shantaram's remarkable trilogy at Prabhat Films, *Duniya na Mane* explores a woman's staunch refusal to accept her marriage to a much older man.

CAST AND CREW

★ **Shanta Apte** Nirmala
Keshavrao Date Keshavlal
Vimala Vasistha Chachi
Shakuntala Paranjpye Sushila
Raja Nene Jugal

🎬 **Director** V. Shantaram
⌂ **Producer** Prabhat Film Company
🎵 **Music composer** Keshavrao Bhole
🅰 **Lyricist** Munshi Aziz
📖 **Scriptwriters** Narayan Hari Apte, Munshi Aziz
📷 **Cinematographer** V. Avadhoot

Also called *The Unexpected*, *Duniya na Mane* (Society Doesn't Approve) is the Hindi version of a Marathi–Hindi bilingual production by the Prabhat Film Company. One of the finest films to come out of the studio system, this movie was based on Narayan Hari Apte's controversial Marathi novel, *Na Patnari Goshta*. Way ahead of its time, the novel denounced arranged marriages that ignored the rights of women. When Shantaram decided to make a film of this book, his partners at Prabhat Films were apprehensive about how it would be received by a traditional Indian audience. He went ahead with the film's production anyway, and was vindicated when *Duniya na Mane* became a commercial and a critical success.

NIRMALA'S PLIGHT
The film follows the plight of Nirmala, an orphan, who is tricked into marrying an elderly widower, Keshavlal, a lawyer old enough to be her father. Keshavlal has a son, Jugal, and a daughter, Sushila, who is a widow and social reformer of Nirmala's age, if not older. Nirmala refuses to be browbeaten by her sham marriage and bravely stands up to every obstacle she encounters. These include the unwanted attentions of her stepson Jugal and the constant criticism and interference of her husband's aunt, or Chachi.

INGENIOUS DIRECTION
Duniya na Mane reaffirms Shantaram's status as one of India's greatest directors. The film is multi-layered and makes heavy use of symbolism and metaphors to tell its story. In particular, a striking analogy is drawn at regular points throughout the film between a decrepit old wall clock and Keshavlal's advanced age and increasing frailty.
    The brooding music for the film was written to match *Duniya na Mane*'s stark, realistic tone. Although there is no background music, every time Nirmala sings, she plays a gramophone record to provide an accompaniment to her song.

FIRM SPIRIT
One of the highlights of the film is Shanta Apte's spirited performance of Nirmala, especially when she sings an English song that sums up the heroine's bravery and resolve not to be disheartened by her situation. She tellingly sings from American poet

▲ **Making use of time**
This movie uses a number of common household objects, such as this wall clock, to symbolize themes that are central to the story.

H.W. Longfellow's combative poem, *Psalm of Life*—"In the world's broad field of battle/In the bivouac of life/Be not like dumb, driven cattle/Be a hero in the strife!"—cleverly summing up the central theme of this daring and revolutionary film.

> ## "It's not merely a picture—but hard and cruel life on celluloid with a theme that frightens one with its reality."

FILMINDIA

▲ **Memorable performance**
The film's poster features Shanta Apte, whose fiery portrayal of Nirmala, the reluctant wife, was well ahead of its time.

SIKANDAR

1941

Sikandar is one of the most striking historical dramas of Indian cinema. Its lavish sets and epic war scenes more than equaled the best of Hollywood at the time.

CAST AND CREW

★ **Prithviraj Kapoor** Sikandar
Vanmala Rukhsana
Sohrab Modi King Puru
Zahur Raja Amar

🎬 **Director** Sohrab Modi
🎞 **Producer** Minerva Movietone
🎵 **Music composers** Meer Saheb, Rafiq Ghaznavi
🎵 **Lyricist** Pandit Sudarshan
📖 **Scriptwriter** Pandit Sudarshan
🎥 **Cinematographer** Y.D. Sarpotdar

Arguably Sohrab Modi's finest film, *Sikandar* confirms his status as one of Hindi–Urdu cinema's leading filmmakers. Indeed, few can match him in creating historical epics such as *Pukar* (1939), *Prithvi Vallabh* (1943), *Jhansi ki Rani* (1953), and, of course, *Sikandar*.

The film, presented as "A Gold Leaf from Ancient History," is set in 327 BCE. Having conquered Persia, Alexander the Great, or Sikandar, falls in love with a beautiful Persian woman, Rukhsana. He goes against the advice of his mentor, Aristotle, who warns him not to let a woman distract him from his dream of conquering the world. Bowing to his teacher's request, Alexander leaves Persia to vanquish India and reaches the Hydaspes, or the river Jhelum. Crossing the Jhelum, he clashes, both verbally and in battle, with Indian King Puru, also known as King Porus, in his attempt to annex the subcontinent, before finally returning home to Greece.

A BRILLIANT DIRECTOR

With support from the Maharani and state officials of Kolhapur for creating the spectacular battle scenes, Modi was able to combine thrilling action with high drama, influenced by the traditons of Parsi theater. This was hardly surprising, considering that Modi had been involved with Parsi theater before he entered the film world. Also, as a Shakespearean stage actor, he was noted for his declamatory style of delivery. It is said that even the blind came to "see" Modi's films, just to hear his masterly vocal delivery. In fact, the confrontations between Prithviraj Kapoor as Sikandar and Modi as Puru, deserve a special mention for their highly charged dialogue.

However, the true spectacle of *Sikandar* lies in its outdoor scenes and in the brilliant execution of the war sequences with thousands of extras and innumerable horses and elephants. The strong impact of these scenes is greatly aided by Y.D. Sarpotdar's sweeping camerawork, which makes innovative use of dramatic camera movements and dynamic compositions.

PATRIOTIC FERVOR

Sikandar was released at a time when Britain's involvement in World War II was at its height. In India, too, the political atmosphere was highly charged. The film cleverly portrayed Sikandar as a ruthless foreign invader and King Puru as a true patriot, fighting to save the motherland. This aroused strong national sentiment among many cinemagoers, just as India's struggle for independence was gaining momentum.

Sikandar remained popular for years. It was later dubbed in Persian and also saw a revival in Delhi in 1961, during the annexation of Goa.

PRITHVIRAJ KAPOOR (1906–72)

Born in Samundri, Punjab, in British India, he is regarded as the "founder" of India's first film family—the Kapoors. Prithviraj arrived in Mumbai in the late 1920s and began his career with silent films. He became an actor at the New Theatres studio in Kolkata in the 1930s, after which he returned to Mumbai, enjoying a successful career as a leading man well into the 1940s. Prithviraj founded Prithvi Theatres in 1944 and kept it going untill 1960. He was awarded the Padma Bhushan in 1969 and the Dadasaheb Phalke Award (posthumously) for his contribution to Indian cinema.

▼ **Breathtaking cinematography**
Sweeping outdoor shots with thousands of extras in richly detailed costumes helped create the film's spectacular battle scenes.

PIONEERING STUDIOS

The days of the big studios of the 1930s and 1940s represent a period of film-making when art, social commitment, and commerce went hand in hand.

The Indian film industry—like Hollywood in its golden period—found a semblance of organization in the days of large filmmaking companies calling the shots. This was a period when scripting, filming, laboratory work, distribution, and exhibition were all overseen by well-equipped management. Each studio had its own personnel, a laboratory, and studio buildings, and some were tied with theaters to screen their films. Although some actors became stars, they still worked as employees of the studio.

Important studios of the time included Bombay Talkies, New Theatres, Prabhat Film Company, Ranjit Movietone, Minerva Movietone, and Wadia Movietone, with each having its own distinct identity. If Bombay Talkies was known for its films with high, technical standards, Prabhat stood out for its devotional and social films shot on impeccable sets. And where Wadia depended on the swashbuckling stunt films of Fearless Nadia, New Theatres became renowned for its adaptations of Bengali literature. Perhaps it's fitting that two major technical innovations—the coming of sound (1931) and the invention of the playback method (1935)—both came in this highly creative era. Small wonder, then, that some of the early classics of Indian cinema, such as *Devdas* (see p. 24) or *Duniya na Mane* (see p. 28) came out of the studio system.

TIMES OF CHANGE

By the end of the 1930s, the studios were established entities with seemingly secure futures. But by 1940, the film business was prosperous enough to attract new entrepreneurs, many of whom had made their money in the black market during World War II. Such producers lacked infrastructure, so they just rented or purchased what they required when the need arose, making lucrative offers to popular stars on a per-picture basis. As a result, actors, directors, and technicians began to leave the studios when they realized that they could make more money on a single picture than in a year with a studio. Additionally, with a restriction on the import of raw stock due to the war, production in the studios reduced drastically, even as fly-by-night operators purchased stock in the black market. The studios, lying idle for long periods of time, found their self-sufficiency ebbing, and many shut down. By the mid-1950s, the major studios had all but closed, thus bringing down the curtain on Indian cinema's first true Golden Age.

◀ **Studio employees**
Prabhat studios boasted excellent in-house facilities. Their art department was famous for its realistic set construction.

"The competition among the studios brought added attention to the visual quality of the films."

GOVIND NIHALANI, *ENCYCLOPAEDIA OF HINDI CINEMA*, 2003

KISMET

1943

One of the earliest blockbusters of Hindi cinema, *Kismet* ran for more than three and a half years at the Roxy Cinema in Kolkata.

CAST AND CREW

★ **Ashok Kumar** Shekhar/Madan
  Mumtaz Shanti Rani
  Chandraprabha Leela
  Shah Nawaz Inspector
  Kanu Roy Mohan

🎬 **Director** Gyan Mukherjee
🎞 **Producer** Sashadhar Mukerji
🎵 **Music composer** Anil Biswas
♪ **Lyricist** Kavi Pradeep
📖 **Scriptwriters** P.L. Santoshi, Shahid Lateef
🎥 **Cinematographer** R.D. Pareenja

The legendary film studio Bombay Talkies divided into two rival power centers in 1940. Devika Rani, its controller of production, and director Amiya Chakrabarty led one group while the other included producer S. Mukerji, actor Ashok Kumar, and director Gyan Mukherjee.

It was this latter "rebel" group that would eventually split from Bombay Talkies to form a new film company Filmistan in 1943, but not before presenting Bombay Talkies with the best farewell present possible—*Kismet* (Destiny). To date, this film remains one of the biggest hits in the history of Hindi cinema.

PUSHING BOUNDARIES

Kismet is a landmark film. Besides its record-breaking performance at the box office, it also popularized various themes of mainstream Indian cinema. While other films before it, such as *Alam Ara* (see p. 20), had sporadically used the lost-and-found theme (see p. 92), the concept caught on in a big way after *Kismet,* and continued to fascinate filmmakers including Nasir Hussain and Manmohan Desai right through to the 1980s.

Kismet also pushed other boundaries. Its hero Shekhar grows up to become a petty criminal on the streets—an anti-hero. What's more, the film throws in the daring issue of premarital sex and the stigma of unwed motherhood through a sub-plot involving Leela, the sister of the heroine, Rani.

In fact, *Kismet* packs in a lot of what are now seen as plot clichés—including the pickpocket who tries to reform due to the heroine's love for him; him stealing for the last time to pay for an operation to cure her bad leg; a lost son who ran away as a child, an old locket containing his mother's photo and a tattoo on his forearm with his name that form the clues to his identity; a climactic song that brings all the characters together; and, of course, a big happy family reunion at the end—all brought about by destiny.

▲ **Special bond**
The love between Rani and Shekhar, framed by social injustice, is a central element in this Bombay Talkies production.

MARION TO THE RESCUE

Kismet is surprisingly well-paced for its time, and is crafted more like a Hollywood film. Ashok Kumar recalled years later that, while discussing the film's story with Gyan Mukherjee and S. Mukerji, they lamented the fact that Indian movies were not as gripping as those made in Hollywood. The reason for this, they concluded, was the lack of good writing in India. Subsequently, through a friend based in the US, they got hold of a book by Frances Marion on screenplay writing, which analyzed various Hollywood classics such as *Ben Hur: A Tale of the Christ* (1925) and *The Champ* (1931) in minute detail. The book advocated logic and concise writing, the importance of every scene taking the film's narrative forward, and also gave valuable tips on how to develop a scene while establishing character. According to Kumar, *Kismet* owed a lot to Marion.

CONCEALED PATRIOTISM

Kismet was released at a time when the country's freedom movement was in full swing, with the Quit India Movement of 1942 still fresh in the public mind. While the film's main plot has nothing to do with India's fight for independence, it nevertheless reflects nationalist sentiment through its music. In a stage show, Rani performs a song with the refrain "Door Hato Aye Duniya Walon Hindustan Hamara Hai" (Move Away Outsiders, India is Ours). Normally, the British would have never allowed such words. However,

◄ **Less is more**
This poster of *Kismet* draws attention to its main characters, Shekhar and Rani, and also reflects the somber tone of the film.

> # "It is apparent that the man ... had a panache and vision for the art of storytelling."
>
> **A.P.S. MALHOTRA**, ON GYAN MUKHERJEE IN *THE HINDU*, 2016

► **Seasoned thief**
Ashok Kumar plays the con man Shekhar with sophistication. His simple attire, along with the ubiquitous cigarette, is integral to his character's personality.

lyricist Pradeep, who had to go into hiding to avoid being arrested, cleverly added references to Japan and Germany, Britain's adversaries in World War II, as enemies of the nation, and so the Censor Board had no choice but to permit its inclusion.

The war also saw the British government put a restriction on the import of raw stock, and limit the final length of a film to not more than 11,000 ft (3,350 m), or about 122 minutes of running time. However, thanks to his "special contacts," one of the film's producers, Rai Bahadur Chunilal, also a member of the Censor Board, obtained an exemption for the film. This helped tremendously during filming because comedian V.H. Desai was notorious for bungling his lines, and once took a mind-boggling 124 takes for a single shot where he had to say just three words—"Kya mila, partner?" (Got anything, partner?).

THE CRITIQUE

Kismet had its fair share of detractors, who felt the film glorified crime and portrayed objectionable morals. Seeing the hero, a pickpocket, rewarded with a family, fortune, and the hand of the heroine at the end of the film, Baburao Patel asked, "Which young man would not like to be a criminal and a pickpocket after seeing Ashok Kumar get all this glory and popularity in *Kismet*?" in his acidic review of the film in *Filmindia* magazine. However, cinemagoers, particularly young audiences, felt that Shekhar was an appropriate hero in times of economic sanctions, scarcities, and emerging black markets. It was also Kumar's natural and charming performance that made audiences root for him.

Despite its fair share of criticism, *Kismet* can be seen as one of the first megahits that Bollywood saw. Its popularity with audiences resulted in its long run at the cinemas; this record was broken 32 years later by *Sholay* (see pp. 134–37), which achieved a longer run, playing for more than five years at Bombay's Minerva Theater.

ASHOK KUMAR (1911–2001)

Bhagalpur-born Kumudlal Ganguly became a star quite by accident. A laboratory assistant at Bombay Talkies, he was spotted by director Himansu Rai during the filming of *Jeevan Naiya* (1936) and was cast opposite the "first lady of Indian cinema," Devika Rani. Adopting the screen name Ashok Kumar, he went on to become one of Bollywood's leading actors. With a hugely successful career spanning more than six decades, Kumar developed a natural and understated style of acting by absorbing and learning from the Hollywood performances of the time. Having started out as a clean-cut young hero singing his own songs, he went on to play leading roles for nearly three decades before taking on character roles, both positive and negative, in a career spanning well over 300 films. Kumar was awarded the Dadasaheb Phalke Award at the 36th National Film Awards for his service to Indian cinema.

STORYLINE

Shekhar, a petty thief, is released from his third stint in prison. He soon meets Rani, a disabled dancer who is in huge financial debt. Moved by her troubles, Shekhar resolves to help her and presents her with a stolen pearl necklace. His thievery is discovered and Rani feels betrayed. However, Shekhar has fallen in love with her, and steals again to pay for surgery that will cure Rani's disability. In the grand finale, Rani performs on stage, in the presence of all the film's protagonists.

MUMTAZ SHANTI
AS RANI

PLOT OVERVIEW

THE ANTIHERO

Shekhar, a petty pickpocket, is released from prison. He spots another thief stealing a gold chain off an old man. Shekhar steals it back from the thief. The old man wanted to sell the chain to go to the theater. Amused, Shekhar takes him there to see the show **❶**.

At the theater the old man reveals that the performer, Rani, is his daughter. She has been disabled since childhood. He also tells Shekhar that he used to own the theater, but is now in debt to the new owner, Indrajit Babu, once his servant. Rani spots her father sneaking away and pursues him, nearly falling under a car. Shekhar saves her life.

A NECKLACE STOLEN

In the crowd, Shekhar steals a pearl necklace belonging to Indrajit's wife. The police are nearby so he hides it in a violin case in a tonga (horse-drawn vehicle). The police search Shekhar and find nothing. Meanwhile, the tonga leaves. Shekhar finds it and makes the driver go back to where he took his previous passenger.

RANI SAVES SHEKHAR

On reaching the tonga's last destination, Shekhar breaks into a house and retrieves the necklace. He tries to escape but is caught by the police. Rani comes to his rescue. She and her sister, Leela, live in the house with their teacher, Panditji **❷**. Rani is in debt to Indrajit, having undertaken to pay what her father owes. Shekhar moves in as a tenant to help Rani.

THE SONGS

Aaj Himalay Ki Choti Se
(From the Tip of the Himalayas)
Singers: Amirbai Karnataki, Khan Mastana
❶ Picturized on Rani

⭐ *This song, arousing strong nationalist sentiments at the time of India's freedom struggle, was written by lyricist Pradeep, earning him the label "patriotic poet."*

Dheere Dheere Aa Re Badal
(Emerge Slowly O Cloud)
Singer: Amirbai Karnataki
❷ Picturized on Rani and Leela

RANI SINGS "AAJ HIMALAY KI CHOTI SE" ON STAGE

> "*... this movie retains a freshness and an innocence which is utterly wonderful.*"

GRETA KAEMMER, MEMSAABSTORY.COM, 2012

SHEKHAR SAVES RANI FROM
FALLING UNDER A CAR

TWO LOVE STORIES

The inspector investigating the lost necklace finds out that Indrajit's elder son, Madan, left the house years ago after a fight with his father and never returned. Indrajit's younger son, Mohan, meanwhile, is involved in a love affair with Leela. In the meantime, Shekhar pawns the necklace to pay off Rani's debts ❸. Shekhar and Rani fall in love with each other.

THE TRUTH COMES OUT

Discovering that Rani owned the necklace as a child, Shekhar gets it back and gives it to her ❹. A doctor tells Shekhar that Rani could be cured with an operation. Leela insists Rani wear the necklace to the theater for her show. Indrajit's wife notices it. Shekhar admits he stole the necklace and gave it to Rani. He confesses to being a thief and is arrested ❺.

A FINAL CRIME

Shekhar escapes from police custody. Leela reveals to Rani she is pregnant by Mohan ❻. Rani beseeches Indrajit to allow Mohan to marry Leela, but he refuses because of Leela's poverty. Meanwhile, Shekhar steals money for Rani's operation from Indrajit's house accidentally leaving his locket behind. Indrajit recognizes the locket.

Shekhar gives the money to the doctor, but requests him to keep the payment anonymous. Rani's operation is successful. She later finds out it was Shekhar who paid for her operation. Panditji informs Rani that Leela has run away from home ❼. A desolate wandering Leela reunites with her father by accident.

FAMILIES UNITED

Indrajit announces a grand show with Rani, hoping to catch Shekhar. Everybody attends the theater, including Mohan, Leela and her father, Indrajit and his wife, and the police ❽. Shekhar is arrested after the show. It is revealed through the locket and a tattoo that Shekhar is Madan, Indrajit's long lost son. Indrajit agrees to the marriages of his sons to Rani and Leela.

---

❸ ⦁ ❹ ⦁  ❺ ⦁ ❻ ⦁ ❼ ⦁ ❽

**Ab Tere Siwa Kaun Mera
Krishan Kanhaiya
(Who Do I Have Apart
From You, Lord Krishna)**
Singer: Amirbai Karnataki
☺ *Picturized on Rani*

**Hum Aisi Kismet Ko
(This Unpredictable Destiny)**
Singers: Amirbai Karnataki, Arun Kumar
Picturized on Rani and Panditji ☺

**Papiha Re
(O Cuckoo, Go Tell My Love)**
Singer: Parul Ghosh
Picturized on Leela ☺

**Ghar Ghar Mein Diwali
(Lights in Every Other House)**
Singer: Amirbai Karnataki
Picturized on Rani ☺

**Dheere Dheere Aa Re Badal
(Emerge Slowly O Cloud)**
Singers: Amirbai Karnataki, Ashok Kumar
☺ *Picturized on Rani and Shekhar*

**Tere Dukh Ke Din Phirenge
(Your Days of Sorrow Will Wane)**
Singer: Arun Kumar
☺ *Picturized on Panditji*

★ *Ashok Kumar sang this song with Amirbai Karnataki in the film, but his voice was replaced by that of Arun Kumar in the recorded version.*

RANI IS HAPPY TO WEAR
THE PEARL NECKLACE
GIVEN TO HER BY SHEKHAR

NEECHA NAGAR

1946

Neecha Nagar is an early example of a socially realistic Indian film. It was awarded the Grand Prix at the Cannes Film Festival in 1946—the first Indian film to receive this honor.

CAST AND CREW

★ **Rafiq Anwar** Balraj
Uma Anand Maya
Kamini Kaushal Rupa
Rafi Peer Sarkar
S.P. Bhatia Sagar
Zohra Sehgal Bhabi
Mohan Segal Raza
Hamid Bhatt Yaqoob Chacha

Director Chetan Anand
Producer Rashid Anwar
Music composer Ravi Shankar
Lyricists Vishwamitra Adil, Manmohan Anand
Choreographer Zohra Sehgal
Scriptwriter Hayatullah Ansari
Cinematographer Vidyapati Ghosh

The film *Neecha Nagar* (Lowly City) marked the directorial debut of Chetan Anand. After his graduation from the Government College in Lahore, Anand worked with the BBC in England, then taught at the Doon School in Dehradun, Uttarakhand. He arrived in Mumbai in the 1940s, where he became involved with the progressive, left-leaning Indian People's Theatre Association (IPTA). It was this link with the IPTA that led to him directing *Neecha Nagar*.

Actress Kamini Kaushal and musician Ravi Shankar also launched their cinematic careers with this film.

SOCIAL DRAMA

The film, with contributions from fellow IPTA member K.A. Abbas, takes its inspiration from Russian writer Maxim Gorky's play *The Lower Depths* (1902), as well as being heavily influenced by German master Fritz Lang's silent film, *Metropolis* (1927). It depicts the worlds of the rich and poor on different land levels—the wealthy live up high on a mountain, while the poor live down below on the plains.

Water is used as a weapon to control the residents of the city on the lower level—"Neecha Nagar." The rich villain cuts off the supply of fresh water to this city in the plains, and diverts dirty drainwater into the houses there. By doing this, he plans to bring disease and death to it, driving the poor from their homes so that he can buy their land cheaply. The smartly dressed villain is called Sarkar, meaning Master or Government—almost certainly hinting at the callous attitude toward the poor of many wealthy capitalists.

INTERNATIONAL SUCCESS

Though realistic in theme, the styling of *Neecha Nagar* borrows liberally from expressionism, as it innovatively combines elements from the world of theater with offbeat camera angles, dramatic plays of light and shade, and effective use of montage. A version was sent to the Cannes Film Festival in 1946, with a song and all of the dance sequences cut to make it more palatable for an international audience. It was one of 11 films at the festival to be awarded the Grand Prix prize.

Sadly, despite the critical acclaim outside the country, *Neecha Nagar* made little impact back in India. It would take Chetan Anand quite some time to release his next production, *Afsar* (1950), which was only made thanks to Dev Anand (see pp. 88–89), Chetan's brother and the film's leading man, who had by then become a major star. *Afsar* was the first film to come out of the siblings' own production company, Navketan.

◀ **The unfortunate**
Kamini Kaushal and Rafiq Anwar play the roles of two siblings, Rupa and Balraj, in the film. They are the poor, exploited residents of Neecha Nagar.

CHANDRALEKHA

1948

With its excellent on-screen narration and magnificent sets, *Chandralekha* was a big breakthrough for a Chennai production into the pan-Indian market of Hindi cinema.

In its time, *Chandralekha* was the most expensive bilingual Bollywood film to date, made in Tamil and Hindi at a cost of ₹4.3 million (about ₹240 million/$4 million today). However, it was the film's director, S.S.Vasan, who had the last laugh financially. The film did so well that by the end of 1949, the two versions of *Chandralekha* had collectively grossed over ₹15.5 million (about ₹845 million/$13 million today),

with Vasan himself taking away a share of ₹7.4 million (about ₹404 million/$6.5 million today).

A SHOT IN THE DARK

The making of *Chandralekha* was just as epic as the film itself. In 1943, Vasan heard a story by Gemini Studios' Story Department about a tough heroine, Chandralekha. He rejected the tale, but found that the character's name stuck with him. He announced his intention to make a film of this name, although he

still had no story in place. Three months later, with still no clear plot, Vasan contemplated shelving *Chandralekha*. Instead, he gave the writing team a final week to come up with something. In this time, one of the writers came across British author George W.M. Reynolds' 1839 novel *Robert Macaire*. An incident in the opening chapter gave him an idea, and so *Chandralekha* took off.

MAMMOTH UNDERTAKING

The film, a swashbuckling costume drama, features two princes who are brothers—one good (Veer Singh) and one evil (Shashank)—who not only fight each other for control of the kingdom, but also for the love of a feisty young woman, Chandralekha. Spectacular circus sequences were added after filming had begun, with the plot being changed to include them. In one particularly thrilling scene, Chandralekha rescues Veer Singh from a cave with the help of several circus elephants.

◄ **Stunning showmanship**
Brilliantly choreographed, the extravagant drum-dance sequence, depicted in the film poster, involved some 400 dancers and was filmed with four cameras capturing the action.

While the public was stunned by the dazzling horsemanship, eye-popping trapeze stunts, and the tuneful music, the highlight of *Chandralekha* was a magnificent drum dance just before the climactic sword fight—one of the longest sword fights in Indian cinema.

For the Hindi remake Vasan kept the same lead players, but replaced some Tamil actors with Hindi artists.

Vasan believed that after having "put up with many insipid war propaganda pictures," what the Indian cinemagoer needed was escapist pageantry, and the huge success of *Chandralekha* vindicated this opinion. What's more, the movie's popularity gave Vasan an entry into the Hindi film industry, with the legitimate status of a showman in his own right.

S.S. VASAN (1903–69)

The owner of Gemini Studios, S.S. Vasan, believed that films were meant to be easy entertainment. Colossal production costs, gigantic sets, sensational dances, and hair-raising action were the hallmarks of his films. Always one for spectacular "items" and unusual casting coups, he recruited Hindi cinema's top stars, Dev Anand (see pp. 88–89) and Dilip Kumar (see pp. 48–49), for *Insaniyat* (1955), and also set up two of India's best dancers, Vyjayanthimala (see p. 94) and Padmini, for a memorable dance-off in *Raj Tilak* (1958).

He served as President of the Film Federation of India for two terms, and was awarded the Padma Bhushan in 1969.

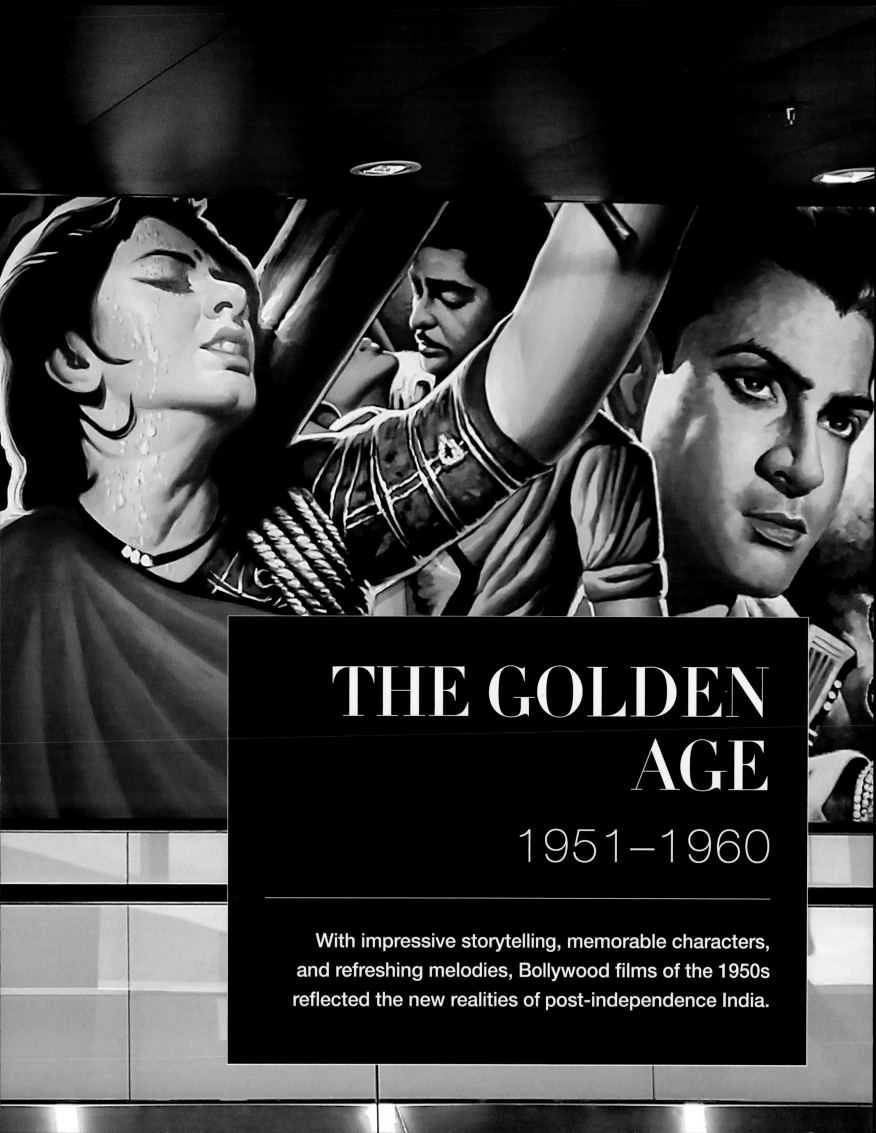

THE GOLDEN AGE

1951–1960

With impressive storytelling, memorable characters, and refreshing melodies, Bollywood films of the 1950s reflected the new realities of post-independence India.

THE GOLDEN AGE

In a newly independent India, Hindi cinema cinema evolved into a golden age, witnessing the rise of a new wave of talented actors, directors, and singers.

▲ **Evolution of cinema**
Films of the 1950s such as *Awaara* (1951) made use of the Mitchell camera. The era saw the rise of notable cinematographers such as V.K. Murthy and Radhu Karmakar.

The 1950s are often referred to as the Golden Age of Hindi cinema, and with good reason. While the importance of the studio era (see pp. 28–29) cannot be denied, the fact remains that its best films seem dated to contemporary viewers. The classics of the 1950s, however, are still watched widely. Their melodies are sung on television shows, and their acting styles are much admired; the themes they explored are still relevant, and their storytelling continues to exert a huge influence on filmmakers. For example, the opening scene of *Lagaan* (see pp. 266–69) is reminiscent of the coming of the rains in *Do Bigha Zamin* (see p. 50), while *Om Shanti Om* (see pp. 292–95) demonstrates how a plot twist borrowed from the 1950s can still shock today's audiences.

INDEPENDENT PRODUCERS
In terms of film production, the era represented a break from the past. The black marketeers who had thrived during World War II lured stars and directors with their illicit money and broke the hold of the studio system. By the beginning of the 1950s, the great studios—Bombay Talkies, Prabhat Film Company, New Theatres—had all fallen, paving the way for a new generation of independent producers. Many of these were Punjabi migrants who had arrived in Mumbai after the partition of the country in 1947. Before this decade, Hindi films were being made in Lahore, Kolkata, and Pune as well, but now the action shifted entirely to Mumbai, which became the sole production centre for Hindi cinema.

◀ Setting the scene
Lovers Raj Kapoor and Nargis share an umbrella in the rain: this scene from the memorable song "Pyaar Hua Ikraar Hua Hai" in Raj Kapoor's *Shree 420* (1955) has become an iconic image of Indian cinema.

This was truly the birth of Bollywood In this melting pot of an industry, a typical recording session could involve a refugee Punjabi music director directing a Bengali singer to sing the verse of an Urdu poet. The arranger for this might be a Goan jazz bandleader who had been forced by Prohibition to work in the movies. Such creative confluences played a significant role in shaping the movies that came out of Mumbai. In a nation obsessed with caste and religious identities, Mumbai's cinema belonged nowhere and everywhere.

THE NEW TRENDS
Such a mongrel approach naturally found no favor with the authorities. There were those who believed that the culture of the newly independent nation should be "pure" and purged of all hybrid elements—B.V. Keskar, the country's Minister of Information and Broadcasting at the time, went as far as to ban Hindi film music completely from the airwaves. Under these watchdogs of Indian culture, censorship was the strictest it has ever been in the country—as the censor records of this period demonstrate, even innocuous romantic scenes could be hacked for showing "amorous tendencies" or "undue proximity."

Despite these challenges, or perhaps spurred by them, the cinema of the 1950s continued to scale new heights. Behind this creative leap were some remarkable individuals—directors such as Bimal Roy and Guru Dutt (see pp. 66–67), and the three megastars

◀ Bollywood's big three
Dilip Kumar (left), Raj Kapoor (center), and Dev Anand (right) are credited with cementing the star system—their strong personalities shaped their films.

Raj Kapoor (see pp. 44–45), Dilip Kumar (see pp. 48–49), and Dev Anand (see pp. 88–89). In film music, too, a new sound would be defined by a host of talented composers, as well as singers Lata Mangeshkar (see pp. 60–61), Asha Bhonsle, Mukesh (see p. 43) and Mohammad Rafi, who came into their own in this decade.

SHAPING A BETTER INDIA
The films these individuals made, reflected the independent nation's search for an identity. The cinema of this time shared the dream of building a new and better India, but it did not ignore the harsh realities. Many of the notable writers and directors of this period had socialist leanings, some of whom were members of the leftist Indian People's Theater Association (IPTA). They brought to their work a questioning spirit that went beyond empty slogans; looking unflinchingly at India's grim reality of poverty, unemployment, and social injustice. The reformist strain they introduced would eventually run through popular entertainment as well as more serious cinema. It deepened

◀ Classical composition
The story of a musician who challenges Mughal Emperor Akbar's court musician Tansen, Vijay Bhatt's *Baiju Bawra* (1952) boasts a brilliant classical soundtrack composed by Naushad.

into cynicism and disillusionment as the decade wore on—a change reflected in Sahir Ludhianvi's (see p. 147) lament "Jinhe Naaz Hai Hind Par Woh Kahan Hain?" (Where Are Those Who Are Proud of India?), which signals the end of the idealism of the 1950s.

PAVING THE WAY
The showmen in the Hindi film industry would have scoffed at Sahir's question: praising the splendors of the Indian past paid off well at the box office, as S.S. Vasan's *Chandralekha*

▲ Tuneful two
Singer Geeta Dutt (left) sang a large number of duets—more than 150—with another 1950s singing superstar, Mohammed Rafi (right).

(see p.35) proved in 1948. Through the 1950s, Hindi cinema emulated Vasan's "pageants for the peasants" in big-budget spectaculars, such as *Aan* (see pp. 46–47). The apogee of this trend was *Mughal-e-Azam* (see pp. 68–71), made at the end of the decade. These lavish films represented a counter strand in the cinema of the 1950s; instead of facing up to a grim present or uncertain future, one could always retreat into the fantasy of a glorious past. In a black-and-white era, color extravaganzas, such as V. Shantaram's kitschy *Jhanak Jhanak Payal Baaje* (1955), showed what lay ahead for Hindi cinema. In the coming decade, it would turn away from the poetic realism of the 1950s to a cinema of spectacle and colorful diversions.

AWAARA

1951

Regarded as one of India's finest films, Raj Kapoor's *Awaara* proved popular throughout Asia and the USSR, and opened horizons for Bollywood movies outside India.

CAST AND CREW

★ **Prithviraj Kapoor** Judge Raghunath
Nargis Rita
Raj Kapoor Raj Raghunath
Leela Chitnis Leela Raghunath
K.N. Singh Jagga
Shashi Kapoor Young Raj Ragunath

🎬 **Director** Raj Kapoor
🎭 **Producer** Raj Kapoor
🎵 **Music composers** Jaikishan D. Panchal, Shankar S. Raghuwanshi
🎵 **Lyricists** Hasrat Jaipuri, Shailendra
🕺 **Choreographers** Madame Simkie, Krishna Kumar, Surya Kumar
📖 **Scriptwriters** K.A. Abbas, V.P. Sathe
🎥 **Cinematographer** Radhu Karmakar
👕 **Costume designers** Om Parkash, Madame Chorosch

Released four years after India's independence, *Awaara* (Tramp) was the third film directed by Raj Kapoor (see pp. 44–45) following *Aag* (1948) and *Barsaat* (1949). The film came out during a period of great change with large-scale migrations to cities—a subject Indian filmmakers were keen to explore.

Awaara was part of a wave of films that cast a spotlight on the harsh realities of urban life. The film addresses issues of class divide, exploitation, poverty, sleaze, and crime, drawing stylistic influences from the film noir tradition of post-war Hollywood, to reveal the grim underbelly of city life.

▼ **Sensual pair**
Raj Kapoor and Nargis starred in several films together. Their on-screen chemistry caught the imagination of youth in India and abroad.

SOCIAL MESSAGE

Awaara's overarching theme is that of nature versus nurture. Raj Kapoor directed himself in the lead role of a lovable tramp—a character clearly influenced by Charlie Chaplin's film persona. Like Chaplin's hapless hero, Kapoor, too, plays a kindhearted vagabond (also named Raj) living by his wits in a cruel world. However, in *Awaara*, the character overtly expresses his yearnings for a better world, even if the message is sugarcoated in a mix of drama, action, and song-and-dance (see pp. 272–73) sequences.

▲ **A difficult childhood**
Young Raj Raghunath, played by Raj Kapoor's younger brother, Shashi Kapoor, is constantly mocked and bullied by neighborhood kids.

ALL IN THE FAMILY

A major reason for the film's success was its casting, which caught the public's imagination. The film features several members of the Kapoor family. *Awaara* was originally meant to be directed by Mehboob Khan, but a disagreement over the casting led writers K.A. Abbas and V.P. Sathe to seek an alternative director. The writers were committed to the idea that a real-life father and son—Prithviraj and Raj Kapoor—should play the two main roles, as opposed to

Khan's preferred choice Dilip Kumar (see pp. 48–49). The screenplay was then handed to Raj Kapoor and became the first film to be shot at his newly founded R.K. Studios. Besides Raj Kapoor's father Prithviraj, the film also features his younger brother Shashi as the young Raj, while his young son Randhir appears in the film's opening credits. Basheshernath, Raj's grandfather, also makes a cameo role, and his brother-in-law Premnath appears in a song sequence. Nargis, who was said to be romantically involved with Raj Kapoor at the time, was cast as the love interest, further blurring the line between the real and the on-screen world. The chemistry between the pair is electric—particularly in the song

"The … romance between Nargis and Raj Kapoor offscreen gave them an electrifying screen presence."

GANESH ANANTHARAMAN, *BOLLYWOOD MELODIES: A HISTORY OF THE HINDI FILM SONG,* 2008

PRITHVIRAJ
NARGIS
RAJ KAPOOR

RAJ KAPOOR'S
AWĀRA
Music: SHANKAR JAIKISHAN

◄ **Ahead of its time**
The posters for *Awaara*, showing
Raj Kapoor planting a kiss on Nargis's
bare shoulders, was bold for the times
in which the movie was released.

filmed over three months, the
song was skilfully choreographed by
French dancer Madame Simkie and
shot on several grand sets constructed
by art director M.R. Achrekar. In
fact, the sequence was not part of the
original screenplay, but was added later
to increase the film's popular appeal.

FOREIGN FAME
Besides the film's huge popularity in
India, *Awaara* is notable for its success
abroad. The film and its title song, in
particular, swept through Asia with
record-breaking runs in the Middle
East, making Raj Kapoor and Nargis
superstars. It was dubbed in Persian,
Turkish, and Arabic, achieved success in
China, and was showcased at the 1953
Cannes Film Festival. Released in the
former Soviet Union as *Bradyaga* (1954),
the film made such an impression that
when the two leads visited the country,
they were repeatedly mobbed by fans;
bands greeted them at airports with
renditions of *Awaara Hoon;* and in true
homage, a Russian puppeteer featured
puppets of the two as part of his show.
In 2012, *Awaara* appeared in *TIME*
magazine's list of the 100 greatest
films made since 1923.

K.A. ABBAS
(1914–87)

Journalist, playwright, novelist,
screenplay writer, and filmmaker,
the Panipat-born Khwaja Ahmad Abbas'
association with films began when he
worked at *The Bombay Chronicle*.
Proficient in English, Urdu, and Hindi,
his involvement with the left-leaning
Indian People's Theatre Association
ensured his films had foundations in
the socialist-realist mode. His prominent
films include *Anhonee* (1952) and *Do
Boond Pani* (1971).
He launched
actor Amitabh
Bachchan (see
pp. 126–27)
with *Saat
Hindustani*
(1969).

"Dam Bhar Jo Udhar" in which she
seductively dances around Raj in the
moonlit night, or in the highly charged
scene in which Raj slaps her when she
calls him a savage. Nargis's portrayal of
the heroine was ahead of its time, both
resolute as the voice of Raj's conscience,
and non-traditional—she even appears

in one scene in a swimsuit, baring
more skin than most actresses would
have dared to at the time.

DREAMY TRACKS
True to any R.K. Studios films, the
music is an obvious highlight of
Awaara. The show-stopping musical

set-piece is arguably the nine-minute
dream sequence. Set amid swirling
clouds, the sequence symbolizes the
hero's tormented state of mind as he
is caught between a duty to serve the
criminal boss and the pressure to listen
to the voice of conscience and do the
right thing. Thought to have been

STORYLINE

Judge Raghunath's wife is kidnapped. The kidnapper, Jagga, eventually releases her, but she is pregnant when she returns home. The judge suspects the child's paternity and throws his wife out of the house. The child, Raj, grows up on the streets, mentored into a life of crime by Jagga, who wants to prove to Raghunath that it is environment rather than heredity that forms character. Years later, when Raj finds out the truth about the past, he kills Jagga. Charged with murder, he appears in court, where Raghunath is presiding.

RAJ AND JAGGA
DISCUSS BUSINESS

COURT CASE

THE FACTS OF THE CASE

PLOT OVERVIEW

A young man, Raj, is brought to trial for the attempted murder of Judge Raghunath. A young lawyer, Rita, offers to defend Raj. She then calls the judge to the witness box and asks him to state the circumstances in which he turned his wife, Leela, out of the house.

RAGHUNATH DEFIES SOCIETY
BY MARRYING A WIDOW

Raghunath had married Leela, a widow, against the wishes of his family ❶. Jagga kidnaps Leela, seeking revenge against Raghunath for sentencing him on the basis of his criminal heredity—even though he was innocent. On discovering she is pregnant, Jagga releases her. When she returns home, Raghunath is unconvinced of his wife's virtue and the paternity of the unborn child. He turns Leela out into the streets ❷.

Leela moves to Bombay with her young son. Living in abject poverty, she toils and sends him to school, where he finds solace with a classmate, Rita. Bullied and beaten by other street kids, Raj grows up to be a petty criminal working for Jagga and is in and out of jail ❸.

Raj lies to his mother, explaining away jailtime absences as traveling for business trips ❹. Raj meets a young woman by accident when he steals her purse.

Escaping from the police, Raj runs into Judge Raghunath's house, where he meets the young woman again, who turns out to be Rita, now a ward of the judge ❺. They rekindle this childhood relationship, which blossoms into love ❻.

THE SONGS

THREADBARE CLOTHES
OF THE "TRAMP"

❶ **Zulam Sahe Bhari** (Suffering Great Injustice)
Singer: Mohammed Rafi
😊 *Picturized on Leela*

Naiyya Teri Majhdhar (Your Boat Is Midstream)
Singer: Mohammed Rafi
Picturized on Raghunath
😊 *and Leela*

❷ **Awaara Hoon** (I Am a Vagabond)
Singer: Mukesh
😊 *Picturized on Raj*

⭐ *The song's immense popularity led to local versions being recorded in Greece, Turkey, Russia, China, and Romania.*

❸ **Ek Do Teen** (One Two Three)
Singer: Shamshad Begum
😊 *Picturized on Raj*

❹ **Jab Se Balam** (Ever Since the Beloved)
Singer: Lata Mangeshkar
😊 *Picturized on Rita*

Dam Bhar Jo (Even for a Moment)
Singers: Mukesh, Lata Mangeshkar
Picturized on Rita and Raj 😊

> "[Awaara] *was a neat package that stood out for its entertainment and a social message that holds true even today.*"

VIJAY LOKAPALLY, SENIOR JOURNALIST, *THE HINDU*, APRIL 23, 2010

RAJ AND RITA DURING
THE BIRTHDAY PARTY

MUKESH (1923–76)

Born in Delhi, Mukesh Chand Mathur came to Mumbai under actor Motilal's patronage in the early 1940s. Before discovering his own style, Mukesh was influenced by playback singer K.L. Saigal. Mukesh's first break as a singer came in the year 1945. Mukesh went through a serious lull in the mid-1950s when his acting career failed to take off. Following the failure, he returned to singing full time and never looked back. His voice was particularly well suited for melancholic songs. Mukesh became particularly successful as the voice of Raj Kapoor and Manoj Kumar from the 1950s to 1970s. He died of a sudden heart attack during a concert tour in Detroit on August 27, 1976.

THE VERDICT

Torn between his love for Rita and his loyalty to Jagga, Raj has a dream where Rita offers him heaven and Jagga hell **7 8 9**. Raj decides to reform but finds the going difficult with his past record **10**.

On her birthday, Raj gives Rita a necklace he stole from Judge Raghunath. Rita realizes he is a thief **11**. She goes to meet Leela and hears Raj's story **12**. Rita then meets Raj and tells him she will support him in getting his life back on track. However, Raghunath turns down Raj when he asks for Rita's hand in marriage.

Following a botched bank robbery, Jagga hides out in Leela's house. When she recognizes him, he attacks her. Raj kills him in self-defense. He goes on trial where Raghunath is the presiding judge. Rita convinces Leela to come to court to give her statement. She realizes the judge is her husband and is hit by a car while chasing him.

Before dying, Leela gives her statement and tells Raj that Raghunath is his father. Angered at the misery his mother has suffered, Raj escapes from custody to try to kill the judge but is unable to do so.

Flashback over, Rita declares this is Raj's full story in court, and blames the judge equally. Raj speaks out against the system and for the dispossessed. Judge Raghunath finally accepts Raj as his son. Raj is sentenced to jail for three years. Rita promises to wait for him.

7 **8** **9** **10** · **11** **12** ·

Yeh Nahin Hain Zindagi
(This is Not a Life
Worth Living)
Singer: Manna Dey
Picturized on Raj

Tere Bina Aag Ye Chandni
(Without You, the Moonlight
Seems Like Fire)
*Singer: Lata Mangeshkar
and chorus*
Picturized on Rita

Ek Bewafa Se Pyar Kiya
(I Have Loved a Betrayer)
Singer: Lata Mangeshkar
Picturized on Rita and Raghunath

Ab Raat Guzarne Wali Hai
(The Night Shall Pass)
Singer: Lata Mangeshkar
Picturized on Rita

Ghar Aaya Mera Pardesi
(My Beloved Is Home)
Singer: Lata Mangeshkar
Picturized on Rita

Hum Tujhse Mohabbat Karke
(By Falling in Love with You)
Singer: Mukesh
Picturized on Raj and Rita

RITA PINES FOR RAJ

ELABORATE DREAM SEQUENCE IN WHICH THE FORCES
OF GOOD AND EVIL COMPETE FOR DOMINANCE

RAJ KAPOOR

Hailed as the "greatest showman of Indian cinema" for more than half a century, the modest Raj Kapoor saw himself as simply one of many.

Ranbir Raj Kapoor was born to be in the movie business. The eldest son of theater and film actor Prithviraj Kapoor, he was born in Peshawar (now in Pakistan). When Raj was still very young, his father moved the family to Mumbai to pursue his career in films. Kapoor performed poorly in his exams; he knew where his heart lay. Taking the job of a studio assistant, Kapoor started his training early on with several leading directors at the Bombay Talkies Studio. The work was hardly glamorous in the beginning. He served as a clapper boy and even had to mop floors at the studio. However, the hard work paid off as the young boy gained hands-on experience of show business. One of the first films Kapoor worked on was *Jwar Bhata* (1944), which marked the debut of actor

◄ R.K. icon
The R.K. Films logo immortalized a pose from *Barsaat*, where Kapoor firmly holds Nargis, a violin in his hand.

Dilip Kumar. Kapoor's own acting debut was at the tender age of 11 in *Inquilab* (1935), but his big break *Neel Kamal* (1947) didn't arrive for another 12 years.

THE R.K. BANNER
Determined to make it to the top, Raj Kapoor set up his own film studio, R.K. Films, in 1948. The first film to come out under the R.K. banner was *Aag*, which launched Kapoor as a producer–director. The film, which was based on the life of a dreamer who opts out of a career in law to follow his love for theater, failed to set the box office on fire. However, the film did

► The vagabond
With worn-out shoes, rolled-up trousers, and wide-eyed innocence, Kapoor's vagabond character highlighted the social and economic gaps in India. The character appeared in several films.

mark the first of Kapoor's 16 performances opposite legendary actress Nargis. The dream cast of Nargis, Dilip Kumar, and Raj Kapoor thrilled cinemagoers in Mehboob Khan's 1949 love triangle *Andaz*. It was the first and last time the three stars appeared on screen together. Although a success, *Andaz* faced tough competition from *Barsaat*, a film directed and produced by Kapoor, and released the

KEY WORKS

Andaz, 1949

Barsaat, 1949

Awaara, 1951 (see pp. 40–43)

Shree 420, 1955

Jaagte Raho, 1956

Sangam, 1964 (see pp. 80–81)

Anari, 1959

Jis Desh Mein Ganga Behti Hai, 1960

Mera Naam Joker, 1970

Bobby, 1973 (see p. 118–19)

Prem Rog, 1982

Ram Teri Ganga Maili, 1985

◄ Star trio
The beautifully filmed love triangle between Nargis, Dilip Kumar, and Raj Kapoor in *Andaz* was outstripped at the box office by Kapoor-directed *Barsaat* due to the latter's greater popular appeal.

same year. The film overtook *Andaz* at the box office to become the top grossing film of 1949.

THE SHOWMAN

Raj Kapoor's next triple triumph as actor, producer, and director was *Awaara* (Vagabond), in 1951. With *Awaara,* Kapoor achieved the rare feat of directing a classic at the young age of 26. The film attained cult status for creating a character who was down but never out, surviving in a hostile world through his wits and guile. He became immensely popular for imitating Charlie Chaplin's "Little Tramp" persona. Nargis also gave a showstopping performance, which thrilled critics as well as cinemagoers. Movie reviews commented on the crackling on-screen chemistry between the pair, and there was speculation about an affair between the two. Kapoor, who had married his cousin Krishna Malhotra in 1946, denied having a relationship with Nargis. In an interview, he said that he had a real wife and a screen wife, and that they were two separate things. The hit pair came out with a number of films during the 1950s, including *Shree 420, Chori Chori* (1956), and *Jis Desh Men Ganga Behti Hai*, which was nominated for a Filmfare Award.

A MAN OF SIMPLE TASTE

Kapoor's star status grew both as an actor and as a filmmaker within India and beyond. The showman enjoyed great popularity in countries such as the USSR and China. However, fame did not change his down-to-earth personality: he still preferred to sleep on the floor even when staying in fancy hotels and chose home-cooked food over elaborate meals in restaurants.

► The great filmmaker
Raj Kapoor preferred to be behind the camera, directing his sons, introducing new stars, and creating strong female characters.

He was known to go for a simple meal of fried eggs after returning from a long shoot. Kapoor's acting fame faltered slightly in the mid-1960s. His first color film, *Sangam*, did well, but later films made little impact. In 1970, Kapoor invested all his financial resources in making *Mera Naam Joker*. This semi-autobiographical, comic-tragic tale of the life of a clown took six years to make. While he described it as his favorite film, at the time, audiences were not impressed, finding it too lengthy and emotionally draining.

THE CORLEONES OF BOLLYWOOD

Taking the director's chair for much of the rest of his career, Kapoor handed over the family acting legacy to his sons Randhir and Rishi. Commenting on the family tradition, Randhir Kapoor said, "We are like the Corleones in *The Godfather*." In 1988, Raj Kapoor suffered a severe asthma attack during an award ceremony and died soon after.

▲ No laughing matter
Now considered one of Raj Kapoor's finest works, *Mera Naam Joker* is also one of the longest Indian films ever made. Critics have called it a "misunderstood masterpiece."

> *"I want my audience to not just see romance but to feel it."*

RAJ KAPOOR, CITED IN *MUMBAI MIRROR*, 2013

TIMELINE

December 14, 1924 The eldest of six children, Raj Kapoor is born to Prithviraj Kapoor and Ramsarni Devi Kapoor.

1947 Appears in his first leading role in *Neel Kamal* opposite another newcomer, Madhubala.

1948 Founds a production company named R.K. Films. With its first release, *Aag*, Kapoor becomes one of the youngest film directors in India.

1951 Starring Nargis and Kapoor, *Awaara* becomes a box office sensation. Kapoor's father makes an appearance in the film.

1960 Directed by his long-time cinematographer Radhu Karmakar, *Jis Desh Mein Ganga Behti Hai*, starring Kapoor, sweeps the Filmfare Awards.

1970 *Mera Naam Joker* is released to a dismal reception. With a five-hour duration, it is the longest Indian film to date. A shortened version later finds critical success.

1971 Receives Padma Bushan, the third-highest civilian award, to celebrate his contribution to the arts.

1982 Makes his last major film appearance, in *Vakil Babu*.

1987 Receives the prestigious Dadasaheb Phalke Award for his contribution to Indian cinema.

RAM TERI GANGA MAILI WAS RAJ KAPOOR'S LAST FILM

1988 Dies in hospital following an asthma attack. The hospital is flooded with sobbing fans.

2012 His performance in *Awaara* is ranked as one of the top 10 greatest performances of all time by *TIME* magazine.

AAN

1952

The first Indian film to reach an international audience across the US, the UK, other parts of Europe, and Africa, this superb epic helped to establish Indian cinema worldwide, and introduced color to Bollywood.

◀ Box office gold
The star-studded spectacle *Aan* was the biggest blockbuster in India of 1952. It set the box office on fire, earning back more than four times its filming budget within three years.

A dashing swordsman, a scheming prince, a proud princess, and a headstrong village maiden: the key characters in director Mehboob Khan's epic adventure tale *Aan* (Pride) are certainly colorful ones. Yet, it is another kind of color that makes this film groundbreaking. *Aan* was the first Indian film to be filmed in Technicolor, enabling viewers to revel in vivid orange sunsets and breathtaking landscapes on screen. Khan used this relatively new technology to craft a visual spectacle, and its popularity

with audiences helped to convince other Indian film-makers and cinematographers finally to embrace color.

PRINCESS AND A PAUPER
Aan's plotline echoes that of the play *The Taming of the Shrew* by English playwright William Shakespeare. However, there is a hint of revolution alongside the romance, as rulers trade places with the ruled. *Aan's* dashing hero is Jai Tilak, a village leader in a clan ruled by the kind-hearted and fair King Murad. The king has two siblings: the cold-hearted princess Rajshree and her cunning brother Shamsher Singh. Jai first clashes with the royal siblings when he tames Rajshree's wild stallion in a contest. Blades aloft, Shamsher then battles Jai in a dramatic fencing match. Jai lets the prince win but loses his heart to the arrogant princess. Meanwhile, the king decides to give up his throne and hand over power to the people. This infuriates Shamsher, who has his henchmen kill the king in his sleep in a bid to seize the throne.

The focus now shifts to the new ruler, Shamsher. Cruising through the village in a swanky Cadillac, he spots Mangala, a village maiden. Mangala is in love with her childhood friend Jai, but he does not reciprocate her feelings. Determined to have her, Shamsher kidnaps Mangala and imprisons her in his lavish palace in an attempt to make her love him. A heartbroken Mangala commits suicide.

Jai avenges her death by attacking and mortally injuring Shamsher. Jai kidnaps Rajshree when she attempts to avenge her brother. He is determined to make her live the life of a poor villager so she may appreciate their plight better. Just when Rajshree begins to realize she has feelings for Jai, Shamsher, who was thought to be dead, returns to get his revenge. As kings return from the dead, the proud relent, and the righteous rebel, this epic reaches its dramatic conclusion.

BIG-BUDGET BLOCKBUSTER
No expense was spared in the making of this film. Khan and Faredoon A. Irani, his cinematographer, set out to film in as many outdoor locations as possible. Mostly shot in rural Maharashtra, the results are enchanting, with waterfalls that cascade down mountainsides, beautiful flowers and lush greenery, and sunrises and sunsets—all drenched in color. The elaborate outdoor sets, such as the palace games arena, are equal to those of any Hollywood epic of the time.

The palace interiors are fantastic as well. Opulent fabrics, over-the-top furniture, and incredible art fill the rooms. Fanciful sculptures surround lush fountains, while stone pillars and staircases add an imposing touch.

The colorful costumes range from the humble sari to swaths of rich fabric complete with spakling embellishments. The music,

too, reflects the grandeur of the film, with composer Naushad hiring a 100-piece orchestra to perform his lilting compositions.

WILD AND EXOTIC
A distinct animal theme runs through the film. Animal sculptures of a variety of creatures from fish to elephants, some gilded and painted, adorn the palace rooms. The film features a zooful of real animals, too. When Shamsher flips a giant switch, an actual lion stalks out of his dungeon. A herd of camels stampede across the

▶ A rogue and a royal
Dilip Kumar was already a hugely popular actor when he signed up for *Aan*. Cast in the role of the princess wooed by Kumar's peasant, Nadira was a newcomer to the screen, replacing established star Nargis, who withdrew from the film due to other commitments.

> "[Aan] *shows the tremendous potential of India motion pitures for securing the world market...*"

CECIL DEMILLE, AMERICAN FILM DIRECTOR, IN A LETTER TO
MEHBOOB KHAN, 30 OCTOBER 1952

screen, and horses thunder through the landscape in a thrilling chase. *Aan* was one of the first Indian movies to have an animal coordinator on board to supervise these exciting scenes.

STAGGERING RECEPTION

Despite mixed critical reviews, *Aan* had moviegoers flocking to the cinema in droves. They went to see Dilip Kumar (see pp. 48–49), who was box office gold at the time, and actors Nimmi and Prem Nath, who were also big stars.

HIT SONG

**Dil Mein Chhupake
Pyar ka Toofan**
(Hiding a Storm of Love
in My Heart)
🎤 **Singer** Mohammad Rafi

In July 1952, *Aan* had its world gala premiere in London, UK. Renamed *The Savage Princess* for the international market, the film became the first Indian-made feature to be widely screened in cinemas throughout Europe and the US. The international version of the movie was shorter by about an hour.

Its global commercial breakthrough was an important first for Indian cinema, and with its familiar themes *Aan* was a strong choice to introduce Indian movies into the world market. Mehboob's gift for storytelling and his extraordinary creative vision for *Aan* gave his filmmaking career a huge boost. In 1957, he made *Mother*

India (see pp. 56–59), a film now regarded as his best work. But with *Aan* he achieved two significant firsts: he brought color to Bollywood, and brought Bollywood to the world.

▲ **The versatile actor**
In this swashbuckling epic, Dilip Kumar, the actor dubbed the "King of Tragedy," played a lighter role. He relished playing Jai—the sword-fighting, princess-chasing, romantic rogue.

NADIRA (1932–2006)

Born Farhat Ezekiel Nadira to a Baghdadi Jewish family in Bombay (now Mumbai), she made her box office debut in *Aan* at the age of 19. Known in the film industry simply as Nadira, she landed leading roles throughout the 1950s and 1960s and won an award for Best Supporting Actress for *Julie* (see p. 131). Her bold personality, distinctive features, and European looks made her uniquely suited for the role of a vamp. In her later years, she became a leading character actor, playing the role of a mother, aunt, or older woman. Nadira married twice, both marriages ending in divorce. She died at the age of 73 after a prolonged illness.

DILIP KUMAR

One of Indian cinema's greatest stars, Dilip Kumar continues to be considered the benchmark for aspiring actors seeking excellence in their craft.

Mention the word thespian in India and the first name that comes to mind is Dilip Kumar. A method actor in the early days of Indian cinema, he has given some of the most iconic performances ever in Hindi films.

Born Yousuf Khan in Peshawar in undivided British India, Dilip Kumar moved with his family to Mumbai in the mid to late 1930s. While still in his teens, a disagreement with his father led him to move to Pune, where he worked as an assistant manager in a military canteen. On returning to Mumbai, a family associate took him to the movie studio Bombay Talkies— where he met the actress Devika Rani (see pp. 24–25)—and they saw potential in the young man and signed him on for a princely monthly salary of ₹1,250 (about ₹2,05,000/$3,200 today).

KEY WORKS

Andaz, 1949

Deedar, 1951

Aan, 1952 (see pp. 46–47)

Devdas, 1955 (see p. 333)

Naya Daur, 1957 (see p. 55)

Mughal-e-Azam, 1960 (see pp. 68–71)

Gunga Jumna, 1961

Ram Aur Shyam, 1967

Terribly scared of his father, he did not want to reveal to him that he had joined the film industry, so he took on the screen name Dilip Kumar.

A TOUGH START

The beginning, however, was tough. The *Filmindia* review of his first film, *Jwar Bhata* (1944), declared that his acting effort in the film amounted to nil. *Pratima* (1945) and *Milan* (1946), also produced by Bombay Talkies, made no impact either. Kumar finally tasted success with *Jugnu* (1947), an ill-fated romance where he acted opposite singing star Noor Jehan. He then went from strength to strength, scoring particularly well in tragedies such as *Shaheed* (1948) and *Mela* (1948). He finally became a top star with Mehboob Khan's memorable love triangle *Andaz* (1949),

◀ **Reel to real life**
Dilip Kumar and Saira Banu acted together in five films, including *Gopi* (1970). Banu's two wishes were to become a movie star and Mrs. Dilip Kumar. She got both.

▶ **King of actors**
With his handsome looks, intense acting, and inimitable style, Dilip Kumar won audiences' hearts as a brooding Rochester in *Sangdil* (1952)—an adaptation of Charlotte Bronte's classic novel *Jane Eyre*.

◄ **An actor par excellence**
For many, Kumar's portrayal of the alcoholic, lovelorn Devdas in the 1955 film *Devdas*, is a masterclass in acting and a role tailor-made for the "tragedy hero."

Following *Bairaag* (1976), in which he played a triple role, Dilip Kumar took time off from acting.

CHARACTER ROLES
Dilip Kumar returned to films playing character roles, beginning with *Kranti* (1981). His work in Ramesh Sippy's *Shakti* (1982), and his collaborations with Subhash Ghai in films such as *Vidhaata* (1982), *Karma* (1986), and *Saudagar* (1991), stand out as superb examples of his craft. In *Shakti*, Dilip Kumar played an honest police officer estranged from his criminal son, and won his eighth and final Filmfare Award for Best Actor. During the 1990s, he also tried his hand at directing with *Kalinga*, but the film remains unfinished to date. On the personal front, Dilip Kumar was said to

- **December 11, 1922** Born in Peshawar, Dilip Kumar is the son of Mohammad Sarwar Khan.

- **1944** Begins his cinematic journey with *Jwar Bhata*, directed by Amiya Chakrabarty.

- **1947** Release of his breakthrough film, *Jugnu*, opposite Noor Jehan.

- **1949** Reaches dramatic star status as a tragic hero in love triangle in *Andaz*.

- **1954** Wins the first ever Filmfare Award for Best Actor, playing an alcoholic, for *Daag* (1952).

- **1957** Records his own playback in *Musafir* for the song "Laagi Nahi Chhute" with Lata Mangeshkar.

- **1961** Produces and acts in *Gunga Jumna*, one of his finest films.

- **1966** Marries actress Saira Banu.

- **1980** Becomes the Sheriff of Bombay.

- **1981** Returns to the screen with the film *Kranti*.

DILIP KUMAR APPEARED IN A CHARACTER ROLE AFTER A LONG BREAK

co-starring Nargis and Raj Kapoor. This time *Filmindia* magazine gushed that he had improved beyond recognition under Mehboob's direction.

PRINCE BECOMES KING
The 1950s saw Dilip Kumar rule the Hindi film industry along with actors Dev Anand and Raj Kapoor, each of whom had their own distinct identity. "Dilip Kumar's silent, self-effacing minimalism stood out boldly against the backdrop of Raj Kapoor's boisterous excesses and Dev Anand's exaggerated stylishness," observed film writer Kamlesh Pandey.

Around this time, filmmaker K. Asif resumed work on *Mughal-e-Azam* (see pp. 68–71), a film for which he had previously rejected Kumar. Asif changed his mind and cast the now established star to play the Mughal prince, Salim.

The first half of the decade saw a series of Dilip Kumar starrers—*Jogan* (1950), *Babul* (1950), *Deedar* (1951), *Shikast* (1953), and *Devdas* (1955)—where Dilip Kumar, tousled hair and all, played the tragic lover leading him to be labelled the "King of Tragedy."

While his performances were impeccable, acting such heavy roles took their toll on him. He was advised by doctors to take on some lighter characters. Heeding the counsel, he went on to perform in some frothy entertainers, such as *Azaad* (1955), *Kohinoor* (1960), and *Ram aur Shyam* (1967), displaying razor-sharp comic timing. Showing the versatility of his style of acting, he won the Filmfare Award for Best Actor for all three films. He reached the peak of his career with a film he produced himself, *Gunga Jumna* (1961). Said to be ghost-directed by Dilip Kumar, the classic features the actor and his

younger brother Nasir Khan playing the role of brothers on opposite sides of the law. Dilip Kumar's role is also notable for its usage of the Bhojpuri dialect.

THE SECOND INNINGS
After *Gunga Jumna*, however, Kumar's films started to get a lukewarm reaction at the box office, with *Leader* (1964)

"I have either been dubbed a tragedian or a comedian ... I think I'm a bit of everything."

DILIP KUMAR, *FILMFARE,* 1994

and the *Wuthering Heights*-inspired *Dil Diya Dard Liya* (1966) both proving to be major disappointments. While Dilip Kumar did bounce back temporarily with *Ram aur Shyam*, the dip in his success continued with *Sunghursh* (1968) and *Aadmi* (1968).

be involved with the actresses Kamini Kaushal and Madhubala (see pp. 72–73) before marrying Saira Banu in 1966. There was a small scandal when he married socialite Asma Rehman in the early 1980s. He split from Rehman within two years and reunited with Banu.

A much-lauded actor, Dilip Kumar has been imitated by many but matched by few.

◄ **Back with a bang**
After a five-year hiatus, Dilip Kumar returned to the screen in 1991 with another veteran actor, Raaj Kumar, in Subhash Ghai's *Saudagar*.

- **1983** Gets his last Filmfare Award for Best Actor for his role in *Shakti*.

- **1991** Is honored with the Padma Bhushan, India's third-highest civilian award.

- **1994** Gets the Dadasaheb Phalke Award for his contribution to Indian cinema.

- **1998** Receives the Nishan-e-Imtiaz, one of the highest civilian awards in Pakistan.

- **1998** Appears in his last film, *Qila*.

- **2015** Is honored with the Padma Vibhushan, India's second-highest civilian award.

DO BIGHA ZAMIN

1953

Bimal Roy's classic is the moving tale of a farmer's struggle to save his land from the clutches of a landlord.

CAST AND CREW

★ **Balraj Sahni** Shambhu Mahato
Nirupa Roy Parvati (Paro) Mahato
Rattan Kumar Kanhaiya Mahato
Murad Thakur Harnam Singh
Jagdeep Laloo Ustad
Nana Palsikar Dhangu Mahato
Meena Kumari Thakurain

🎬 **Director** Bimal Roy
⬠ **Producer** Bimal Roy
♫ **Music composer** Salil Chowdhury
A♪ **Lyricist** Shailendra
📖 **Scriptwriter** Salil Chowdhury
🎥 **Cinematographer** Kamal Bose
👔 **Costume designers** John, Dhanji Mistry

For many Indian film directors of the Golden Age, 1952 was the year that changed everything. It was in this year that the International Film Festival of India was inaugurated in Mumbai, which opened their eyes to a cinema beyond Bollywood and Hollywood. One film in particular proved to be hugely influential—Italian director Vittorio De Sica's *Bicycle Thieves* (1948), which inspired director Bimal Roy to set up his own production company and shoot a story on the streets of Kolkata. The result was *Do Bigha Zamin* (Two Acres of Land), a critically acclaimed film that went on to win several prizes at international film festivals such as Cannes and Karlovy Vary.

REALISTIC MELODRAMA
Despite its nod to Italian neorealism—a film movement characterized by stories set among the poor and filmed on real locations—the film is a solidly Indian melodrama that borrows something from the Leftist theatre of the times. Salil Chowdhury, an IPTA (Indian People's Theatre Association) music composer who made his Mumbai debut with *Do Bigha Zamin*, wrote the story, which observes an India struggling against its feudal past to move toward an uncertain industrial future. The film shows the plight of a poor peasant, Shambhu, whose land is being taken over by a landlord to build a factory. In a bid to raise money to save his land, he moves to Kolkata to work as a rickshaw puller, while his son Kanhaiya becomes a shoeshine boy. Though the two find some support and friendship on the city's streets, their trials and tribulations do not cease. The story follows their struggle as they try to hold on to their humanity and integrity, even as the odds against them become unsurmountable.

THE CRUEL CITY
Internationally released with the title *Calcutta: The Cruel City*, the film is also a portrait of Kolkata through the eyes of a migrant. The city's misty mornings and watered streets stand in contrast to the harsh reality faced by Shambhu, who is treated callously as a human carthorse. Roy brings his audiences heart-breakingly close to his characters in the harrowing rickshaw race which pushes Shambhu to a breaking point. The scene also reveals the immense dignity and truth of Balraj Sahni's performance, one of the finest ever for a Hindi film.

▲ **A political statement**
The film's promotional booklet is reminiscent of the nation's socialist phase. The characters' worn-out clothes were said to have been bought from Mumbai's Chor Bazaar—a secondhand market.

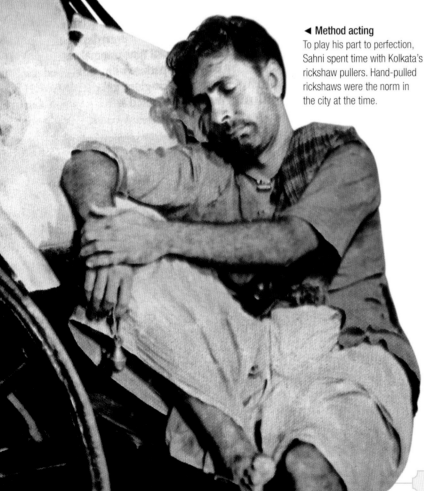

◄ **Method acting**
To play his part to perfection, Sahni spent time with Kolkata's rickshaw pullers. Hand-pulled rickshaws were the norm in the city at the time.

BALRAJ SAHNI
(1913–73)

Balraj Sahni worked as a teacher at Santiniketan and a journalist before he moved to Mumbai. His socialist beliefs led him to join the Indian People's Theatre Association (IPTA); his acting in their productions led to his first film role in K.A. Abbas' (see p. 41) *Dharti ke Lal* (1946). A well-read, sophisticated actor, Sahni trained hard to play the rustic rickshaw puller in *Do Bigha Zamin*. His dedication to his craft is apparent in films such as *Kabuliwala* (1961) and *Garm Hava* (see p. 129). The latter film featured his moving portrayal of an old-world Muslim figure in post-Partition India.

C.I.D.

1956

The quintessential 1950s Bollywood thriller, this Dev Anand vehicle is as memorable for its suspenseful plot as it is for its hummable melodies.

Helmed by director Raj Khosla, *C.I.D.* has the stamp of its producer Guru Dutt (see pp. 66–67), who perfected the breezy blend of music, comedy, romance, and suspense seen here, in a delicately "soft-boiled" approach to a crime film. The film borrows some noir inflections from contemporary Hollywood, but ultimately it works as a star vehicle for lead actor Dev Anand (see pp. 88–89), and Hindi-film debutante Waheeda Rehman (see p. 85), whose role as the vamp with a heart of gold established her as an actress of uncommon grace and skill.

MURDER MYSTERY
The film opens with the murder of a righteous newspaper editor who is on the verge of exposing a corrupt public figure. The killer is identified in a lineup by a petty thief named Master, and is arrested by Inspector Shekhar. A mysterious woman named Kamini warns Shekhar against pursuing their investigation; he is intrigued when she is later introduced to him as a friend of his superior's daughter, Rekha. Determined to solve the puzzle and identify the mastermind behind the crime, Shekhar persists in his mission but is framed on a charge of police brutality when his suspect dies in jail. In an attempt to prove his innocence, Shekhar runs from the law. With the help of Kamini, he finally manages to reveal the true culprit.

A COMMENTARY ON THE TIMES
C.I.D.'s joys lie primarily in its star turns and a O.P. Nayyar's score, whose sensuous *sarangi* lines and jaunty rhythms enliven the song sequences choreographed by Zohra Sehgal. As a thriller, *C.I.D.* has perhaps far too many diversions to be effective. The film is not really a whodunit as its villain is seen and identified early on in the film as a prominent member of the society.

As in post-Independence films with socialist leanings, Inder Raj Anand's screenplay takes the side of the common man against the capitalist class. Following the trend set by Guru Dutt's own films, *C.I.D.* revels in the depiction of low-life characters, represented here by the pickpocket Master, who presents a caustic vision of a Mumbai where the homeless are mocked and harassed as vagrants, while those who cut people's throats are acclaimed as businessmen. Fittingly, the song "Ae Dil Hai Mushkil Jeena Yahaan/Ye Hai Bombay Meri Jaan" (Oh Heart, It's Hard To Survive Here/For This Is Bombay, My Dear) has since become an unofficial anthem for the city.

> "*While taking on some ... trappings of American film noir, C.I.D. remains a commercial Hindi film.*"
>
> **COREY CREEKMUR,** INSTITUTE FOR CINEMA AND CULTURE, UNIVERSITY OF IOWA

CAST AND CREW

- ★ **Dev Anand** Inspector Shekhar
  Waheeda Rehman Kamini
  Shakila Rekha
  Johnny Walker Master
  Mehmood Sher Singh

- 🎬 **Director** Raj Khosla
- 🎞 **Producer** Guru Dutt
- 🎵 **Music composer** O.P. Nayyar
- 🎵 **Lyricists** Majrooh Sultanpuri, Jan Nisar Akhtar
- 💃 **Choreographer** Zohra Sehgal
- 📖 **Scriptwriter** Inder Raj Anand
- 🎥 **Cinematographers** V.K. Murthy, Anwar Pabani
- 👔 **Costume designer** Bhanu Athaiya

▼ **The city of darkness**
Fitting the Bombay noir genre, *C.I.D.* explores the dark side of the city and has all the elements of an urban suspense thriller.

MASTERS
OF MUSIC

The 1950s saw Hindi film music reach its pinnacle, as lyricists, singers, and composers came together to create some of the most unforgettable songs of all time.

From India's first talkie, *Alam Ara* (1931), songs have played a critical role in Indian films. The simple tunes of the first film songs were probably composed to accommodate singing actors, most of whom did not have the range of trained singers. The advent of playback in 1935, in which a song was first recorded in the studio and then "played back" at the shooting location, became a turning point. Film songs evolved into increasingly complex compositions now sung by trained vocalists, who could do justice to the composer's work. By the 1950s and 1960s, Hindi film music had improved by leaps and bounds.

THE GAME-CHANGERS

Composers began combining Indian classical music with folk, Western pop, jazz, and rock 'n' roll beats. Music directors, with the help of specialist arrangers, began utilizing more Western instruments—the saxophone, trumpet, harmonica, drums, and even guitar—creating songs with their own unique identity. From Rabindra Sangeet to semiclassical and classical, Punjabi folk to early Western influences, musicians had begun to borrow and assimilate from everywhere.

The popularity of film songs often became the means for second-grade movies to overcome flimsy plots and tacky production values to achieve commercial success. Songs added "repeat value" to a film, as sometimes audiences returned just to see a particular song in the movie. The 1950s also saw the formation of teams of composers, singers, and lyricists, some of whom became lifelong collaborators. Shankar–Jaikishan's music for *Awaara* (see pp. 40–43) cemented their partnership with singer Mukesh, the lyricists Shailendra and Hasrat Jaipuri, and actor-director Raj Kapoor (see pp. 44–45). The song "Awaara Hun" (I Am a Vagabond) became a superhit in the Soviet Union and China. The team would go on to collaborate for several more films.

Lyricists with a strong background in Urdu literature and poetry conveyed a rich philosophy of life even as they explored a wide range of emotions through their wordplay. Music directors, such as S.D. Burman, reigned supreme collaborating with singers Geeta Dutt, Mohammed Rafi, Asha Bhosle, and Kishore Kumar (see pp. 100–101), to create immortal melodies. Playback singers became stars in their own right and the songs were lapped up by the masses. C. Ramchandra's "Eena Meena Dika" from *Asha* (1957), and O.P. Nayyar's "Jaata Kahan Hai" (Where Are You Going) from *C.I.D.* (see p. 51) were adopted by a new generation of fans when they were remixed for the films *Shaandaar* (2015) and *Bombay Velvet* (2015).

▶ **Making sweet music**
The sounds of the 1950s continued into the 1970s with composers such as R.D. Burman (far right), seen here with singers Mohammed Rafi (second from right) and Asha Bhosle (far left).

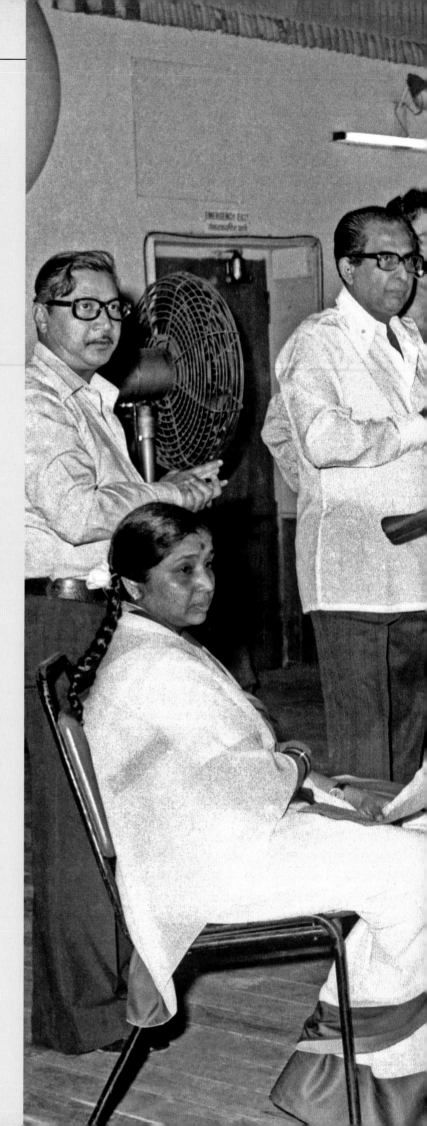

"The singers and writers in our time made the songs immortal."

KHAYYAM, IN AN INTERVIEW WITH HINDUSTAN TIMES, APRIL 2, 2016

PYAASA

1957

Pyaasa is arguably Guru Dutt's greatest film, and tells the story of an artist's continued thirst for love, appreciation, and above all, spiritual fulfillment.

CAST AND CREW

★ **Mala Sinha** Meena

Guru Dutt Vijay

Waheeda Rehman Gulabo

Rehman Mr. Ghosh

Johnny Walker Abdul Sattar

Leela Mishra Vijay's mother

Kumkum Juhi

Mehmood Vijay's brother

🎬 **Director** Guru Dutt

🎦 **Producer** Guru Dutt

🎵 **Music composer** S.D. Burman

🎼 **Lyricist** Sahir Ludhianvi

📖 **Scriptwriter** Abrar Alvi

🎥 **Cinematographer** V.K. Murthy

👔 **Costume designer** Bhanu Athaiya

Making the film *Pyaasa* (Thirsty) was a dream long nurtured by the actor, writer, and director Guru Dutt (see pp. 66–67). He penned his original script for the film in 1947–48, when he was barely 22 years old. Initially, it was called *Kashmakash* (Conflict). However, Dutt was told that such a serious story, coming from a novice filmmaker, might not be considered a viable investment by film producers.

Nearly a decade later, having established himself as both an actor and a director, Dutt decided to revive the project. This time he enlisted the help of writer Abrar Alvi for the screenplay, and it was he who suggested the title *Pyas* (Thirsty) to signify the central character's deep longing for emotional and creative fulfilment. Dutt eventually decided to amend this title to *Pyaasa*. According to Dutt, the inspiration came from a phrase by Greek poet Homer, which said, "Seven cities claimed Homer dead, while the living Homer begged his bread."

DISENCHANTED HERO
The film's protagonist is a struggling poet, ironically called Vijay (Victory). Ridiculed by his brothers as a good-for-nothing for his dreamy, unworldly approach to life, Vijay is also rejected by his college sweetheart, Meena, who marries someone who can offer her more material comfort. He does, however, find solace with a prostitute called Gulabo, and has his poems published "posthumously," when he is mistakenly thought to be dead.

POETRY IN MOTION
Lyricist Sahir Ludhianvi's (see pp. 147) poetry forms the backbone of the film and of Vijay's character. Dutt was partly inspired to make *Pyaasa* by Ludhianvi's poem *Chakle* (Brothels), which shows compassion for those involved in prostitution. For the film, the refrain "Jinhe Naaz Hai Hind Par Woh Kahan Hai" (Where Are Those Who Are Proud of India) was added to the poem, highlighting the left-leaning Ludhianvi's bleak view of Nehruvian socialism in post-independent India. S.D. Burman's music complements Ludhianvi's rich play of words perfectly. The two, unfortunately, fell out during the making of the film, never to work together again.

ALL-TIME CLASSIC
Pyaasa sees Dutt's finest performance as the anguished, romantic artist, lost in a materialistic and hypocritical world. The film also sees a luminous performance by actress Waheeda Rehman (see pp. 85) as Gulabo

in only her second Hindi film. *Pyaasa's* reputation has grown with time. In 2012, it was included by *TIME* magazine in its list of 100 greatest films made since 1923. A painstakingly restored version was screened in the classics section of the 72nd Venice International Film Festival in 2015.

▼ **Role playing**
Guru Dutt himself took on the role of the struggling poet Vijay in *Pyaasa* after actor Dilip Kumar failed to turn up on the appointed day of shooting.

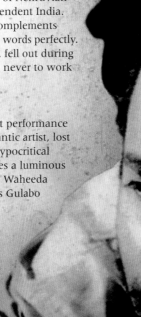

HIT SONGS

Jaane Woh Kaise Log The
(What Kind of People Were Those)
🎤 **Singer** Hemant Kumar

Yeh Duniya Agar Mil Bhi Jaye
(So What if You Get the World)
🎤 **Singer** Mohammed Rafi

Jaane Kya Tune Kahi
(I Wonder What It Is You Said)
🎤 **Singer** Geeta Dutt

NAYA DAUR

1957

Released a decade after India gained its independence, *Naya Daur* argues against the modernization of a developing nation at the cost of its poorest citizens.

▲ **Love for one's country**
The song "Ye Desh Hai Veer Jawano Ka" (This Is the Land of the Brave Young) speaks about the beauty of the land that is India.

CAST AND CREW

★ **Dilip Kumar** Shankar
  Vyjayanthimala Rajni
  Ajit Krishna
  Chand Usmani Manju
  Jeevan Kundan
  Johnny Walker Journalist
  Nazir Hussain Seth Maganlal
  Manmohan Krishna Jumman
  Leela Chitnis Shankar's mother
  Daisy Irani Chiku

📷 **Director** B.R. Chopra
🎬 **Producer** B.R. Chopra
🎵 **Music composer** O.P. Nayyar
🅰 **Lyricist** Sahir Ludhianvi
📖 **Scriptwriters** Akhtar Mirza, Kamil Rashid
🎥 **Cinematographer** M.N. Malhotra

Director B.R. Chopra had a special talent for taking socially relevant issues and weaving them into entertaining stories, utilizing Hindi cinema's popular tropes. After finalizing the story for *Naya Daur* (New Era), he approached fellow filmmaker Mehboob Khan to get his opinion. Khan cautioned him by saying that its subject had no scope for entertainment. Chopra, however, decided to press ahead with the film, provided that actor Dilip Kumar (see pp. 48–49) agreed to star in it. When Chopra initially approached the actor, he was already committed to work on another project. However, when that failed to take off, Kumar came on board for *Naya Daur*.

MAN VERSUS MACHINE
Raising critical questions about the benefits of industrialization and those it leaves behind economically, the film argues that in a developing country like India, any modernization must be carried out with awareness of its affects on both rich and poor alike. The class conflict in the film is represented by the tussle between a band of traditional tonga (horse-carriage) drivers and a bus contractor who threatens the survival of their trade. The film arrives at a rather simplistic solution through the hero's victory in a climactic race between Shankar, on the horsecart and Kundan, driving the bus.

OFF-SCREEN DRAMA
Naya Daur also made headlines due to a sensational court case during its production. Popular actress Madhubala (see pp. 72–73), who was involved with Dilip Kumar at the time, had been signed for the female lead, and had completed her first schedule of filming. But when Chopra summoned her for the next batch of filming in Bhopal, her father, Ataullah Khan, refused to let her go, citing health reasons. Madhubala was replaced with Vyjayanthimala, so Khan took Chopra to court for breach of contract. Kumar spoke in Chopra's favor, and the matter was eventually resolved with the judge ruling against Khan.

WELL-RECEIVED FILM
With its engaging and topical storyline, fine performances, and foot-tapping music, *Naya Daur* turned out to be a big draw at the box office. At the film's 100 days' celebrations, Chopra invited Mehboob Khan as the chief guest. He accepted the invitation graciously admitting as to how wrong he had been about the film's potential.

▲ **Color code**
Originally released in black and white, *Naya Daur* was digitally colorized and re-released in 2007. However, this new version failed to have a strong impact.

HIT SONGS

Saathi Haath Badhana
(Lend Me Your Hand, Friend)
🎤 **Singers** Mohammed Rafi, Asha Bhosle

Uden Jab Jab Zulfein Teri
(Whenever the Wind Sweeps Your Hair)
🎤 **Singers** Mohammed Rafi, Asha Bhosle

MOTHER INDIA

1957

The first Indian film to be nominated for an Academy Award, *Mother India* is considered to be the ultimate tribute to Indian womanhood.

CAST AND CREW

★ **Nargis** Radha
Sunil Dutt Birju
Raaj Kumar Shamu
Rajendra Kumar Ramu
Kumkum Champa
Chanchal Rupa
Sajid Khan Young Birju
Kanhaiyalal Chaturvedi Sukhilala

Director Mehboob Khan
Producer Mehboob Khan
Music composer Naushad
Lyricist Shakeel Badayuni
Scriptwriters Wajahat Mirza, S. Ali Raza
Cinematographer Faredoon A. Irani

Mother India was an ambitious project for director–producer Mehboob Khan to attempt. He had already received critical acclaim for *Aurat* (1940)—a film about a brave peasant woman who singlehandedly brings up her children after her husband abandons her. In comparison to this earlier, austere, black-and-white effort,

Mother India is a more opulent, romanticized, larger-than-life drama told in vivid Technicolor. However, in its own way, it is no less effective.

Made in the idealistic 1950s, *Mother India* indulges in ideological mythmaking, combining fierce maternalism with nationalism. The film is set against the backdrop of the exploitation of illiterate, debt-ridden farmers by unscrupulous moneylenders,

a situation that is common in India even today. The film idealizes the Indian peasant as a young bride and mother, who bears the hardships inflicted on her with stoic dignity to maintain the acceptable, moral status quo of the day.

SEARCHING FOR THE PERFECT CAST
Director Mehboob had planned to make *Mother India* in the early 1950s. While actress Nargis was his only

► **Classic shot**
This poster depicts the iconic image of an anguished Nargis pulling a plow.

NARGIS (1929–81)

One of Hindi cinema's finest dramatic actresses, Nargis gave performances that were refreshingly authentic. Born Fatima Rashid, her mother Jaddan Bai was a classical vocalist and an early pioneer of Indian films.

Nargis began her career as a child actor, and graduated to adult leading roles with Mehboob Khan's *Taqdeer* in 1943. She reached the very top with the film *Andaz* (1949), and proved to be especially successful playing women caught up in tragic love stories. She was involved in an intense relationship with actor Raj Kapoor (see pp. 44–45), before she reached the peak of her career with *Mother India*.

Nargis married her *Mother India* co-star Sunil Dutt and retired from acting, returning one last time for the film *Raat aur Din* (1967). She died of cancer the same year her son, Sanjay Dutt, made his acting debut.

choice for the central role of Radha, the casting of the other pivotal character, Birju—the wayward son who becomes an outlaw—proved to be more difficult. In his autobiography *The Substance and the Shadow* (2014), actor Dilip Kumar (see pp. 48–49) writes that he was offered the role of Birju. However, he turned it down as he felt that since he and Nargis had formed a successful on-screen romantic pair in the past, it would have been awkward casting. Mehboob had also considered Sabu Dastagir—the first Indian actor to make a name for himself in Hollywood—to play Birju, and even though Sabu was agreeable, things did not pan out. In the end, it proved to be a major breakthrough role for actor Sunil Dutt, both professionally and personally, as he and Nargis fell in love during the making of the film, and got married a few months after the film's release.

AN EXPENSIVE AFFAIR

In addition to being shot in Mehboob Studios, *Mother India* was also filmed across rural landscapes in the states of Maharashtra, Gujarat, and Uttar

◄ **An ideal cast**
While Nargis was already the reigning queen of Bollywood at the time of *Mother India*, the film proved to be a turning point in the careers of co-stars Sunil Dutt (left) and Raaj Kumar (center).

"All Hindi films come from Mother India."

JAVED AKHTAR, CITED IN T.J.S. GEORGE, *THE LIFE AND TIMES OF NARGIS*, 1994

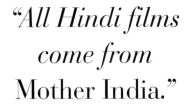

Pradesh. Cinematographer Faredoon A. Irani started filming in 1955 with some generic shots of a flood-ravaged Uttar Pradesh. Prior to the shooting of the film, actors Raaj Kumar and Nargis underwent rigorous training sessions to familiarize themselves with the techniques of various aspects of farming, from sowing to harvesting.

An epic in the truest sense of the word, *Mother India* was a costly affair that drained Mehboob of all his resources as the production went way over budget. In fact, the film's prints, which were processed at Technicolor's laboratory in London, UK, were left lying with customs because Mehboob could not pay for their release. In the end, it was Mehboob's good friend, the actress Nimmi, who had worked with him in

Aan (see pp. 46–47) and *Amar* (1954), who bailed him out by paying the customs duty, and clearing the path for the film's release.

A number of sequences from *Mother India* remain etched in public memory even today—the dramatic shots of the flood sequence; the scene showing a helpless Radha giving herself up to the moneylender Sukhilala, only to pull back in the end; and the dramatic climax involving Radha and her son.

CRITICAL ACCLAIM

No discussion of *Mother India* is complete without reference to Nargis's highly charged performance. Not only is it one of the finest seen in Indian cinema, it also earned Nargis the distinction of being the first Indian actress to win laurels abroad for her performance. In 1958, she was declared Best Actress at the Karlovy Vary Film Festival in Czechoslovakia

(now Czech Republic) and the renowned English-language periodical—*Filmindia*—exclaimed, "Nargis lives the role better than Radha could have lived it."

Mother India became the first Indian movie to be nominated in the foreign film category at the Academy Awards. Mehboob submitted a special two-hour-long version, which excluded his production company logo of a hammer and sickle. He did not want the leftist overtones of the logo to jeopardize the film's chances in the US during the Cold War. While the film did not win an Oscar, it won numerous prizes back home, including five Filmfare awards.

▼ **Resounding success**
Released ten years after Indian Independence, the nationalist theme of *Mother India* resonated with audiences. The film ran for an entire year at the Liberty Theatre in Bombay.

STORYLINE

The story is centered around the hardships faced by a peasant woman, Radha, after she is abandoned by her husband. Left to fend for herself and her family, she must tend to her land in face of flood and famine. Radha has to bring up her starving children, resist the advances of a lecherous moneylender, and, above all, ensure that she and her family live a life of dignity, even if she has to pay a high price to retain her honor and integrity.

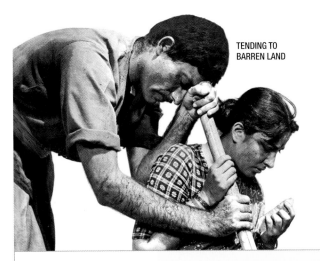

TENDING TO BARREN LAND

A WOMAN REMEMBERS	CALM BEFORE THE STORM	CHANGING FORTUNES	HITTING ROCK BOTTOM	FLOOD, FAMINE, AND VIRTUE

PLOT OVERVIEW

A WOMAN REMEMBERS

At the inauguration of an irrigation canal, Radha—a respected elderly woman in the village—is asked to do the honors. She reluctantly agrees, recalling her life and times in the village, starting with when she first arrived as a young bride ❶.

CALM BEFORE THE STORM

The newly wedded couple Radha and Shamu are very much in love. Radha helps her husband tend to their fields, while keeping the home going ❷. In due time, Radha gives birth to her first child.

CHANGING FORTUNES

The family discovers that unjust and greedy moneylender Sukhilala has tricked Shamu's mother Sundar Chachi into signing away much of their land and its produce to him. When Sukhilala demands the family honor this agreement, Radha and Shamu are forced to toil in the fields ❸.

HITTING ROCK BOTTOM

The family suffers a series of misfortunes. While working the barren land, Shamu's arms are crushed by a rock. Ashamed of his helplessness, he abandons his family ❹, leaving them to the mercy of Sukhilala. In these trying times, Radha looks after the family as best she can ❺.

FLOOD, FAMINE, AND VIRTUE

A severe storm and horrific floods ruin the harvest and famine grips the village. Unwilling to see her children go hungry, Radha almost gives in to Sukhilala's advances in the hope of providing food for her children, but in the end cannot bring herself to submit. Despite having lost a child to the famine, she encourages the villagers to persevere and not leave their land ❻. With time, the land is no longer barren. The harvest is plentiful, and Radha, her sons, and the villagers find happiness again ❼.

THE SONGS

❶
Pi Ke Ghar Aaj
(On the Way to Her Husband's Home)
Singer: Shamshad Begum
Picturized on Radha and Shamu 🎵

❷
Matwala Jiya (My Happy Heart)
Singers: Lata Mangeshkar, Mohammed Rafi
Picturized on Radha, Shamu, and the villagers 🎵

❸
Chundariya Katati Jaye
(My Clothes Are Worn Out From Hard Work)
Singer: Manna Dey
Picturized on Radha, Shamu, and their family 🎵

❹
Duniya Me Hum Aye Hain
(Into This World We Have Come)
Singers: Lata Mangeshkar, Meena Mangeshkar, Usha Mangeshkar
Picturized on Radha and her children 🎵

❺
Nagari Nagari Dware Dware
(In Every Town, At Every Door)
Singer: Lata Mangeshkar
Picturized on Radha and her children 🎵

❻
O Janewale Jao Na
(Don't Leave)
Singer: Lata Mangeshkar
Picturized on Radha and her children 🎵

❼
Dukhbhare Din Beete Re
(The Days of Sadness Have Passed)
Singer: Mohammed Rafi, Shamshad Begum, Manna Dey, Asha Bhosle
Picturized on Radha, her children, and the villagers 🎵

RADHA AS A YOUNG BRIDE

RADHA AND SHAMU IN HAPPIER TIMES

MEHBOOB KHAN (1905–64)

Often called "the DeMille of India," Mehboob Khan was one of Hindi cinema's premier filmmakers. Born in Sarar village in Gujarat, and having little formal education, he ran away from home to join the film industry. He was considered for the lead role in India's first talkie, *Alam Ara* (see p. 20), but lost out to actor Master Vithal. He graduated to directing films in the 1930s and launched his own production company, Mehboob Productions, with *Najma* (1943). While he directed films across genres, a common motif in many of his films was the clash between the simple poor and the exploitative rich.

BIRJU THREATENS SUKHILALA

THE SONS TWO

Years go by. The villagers benefit from following Radha's example. Her sons, Ramu and Birju, have grown up, and chart their own paths. Ramu is in love with Champa **8**. Birju is a rebel who resists Sukhilala's injustices, while clashing with his daughter, Rupa **9**. In time, Ramu and Champa get married and have a son **10**.

RECKLESS REVENGE

As the villagers celebrate Holi **11**— the festival of colors—Birju attacks Rupa for wearing his mother's wedding bangles, which had been pawned to Sukhilala years ago. He is beaten up and banished from the village. He returns to kill Sukhilala, but is wounded instead. When the villagers try to kill him, Birju escapes. Radha tries to stop him from leaving, but fails **12**. Blinded by hate, he becomes a bandit.

HONOR OVER FAMILY

Birju kills Sukhilala and kidnaps Rupa from her wedding. Radha attempts to reason with him, but when Birju does not listen, she tells him that she can give up a son but not the honor of the village. When Birju tries to ride away, she shoots him dead.

BIRJU TURNS TO BANDITRY

FRUIT OF SACRIFICE

Back to the present, Radha, who is regarded as the "Mother" of the village, inaugurates the canal and releases the water.

8

9 Na Main Bhagwan Hoon (I Am Not God)
Singer: Mohammed Rafi
🎵 *Picturized on Birju*

O Mere Lal Aaja (Come Back, My Son)
Singer: Lata Mangeshkar
🎵 *Picturized on Radha and Birju*

Ghunghat Nahi Kholungi (I Will Not Remove My Veil)
Singer: Lata Mangeshkar
Picturized on Ramu and Champa
🎵

10 O Gaadiwale (Slow Down, Driver)
Singer: Shamshad Begum, Mohammed Rafi
Picturized on Birju, Rupa, and the villagers 🎵

11

12 Holi Aayi Re Kanhai (The Festival of Colors is Here, O Lord Krishna)
Singer: Shamshad Begum
🎵 *Picturized on the villagers*

HOLI CELEBRATIONS IN THE VILLAGE

BIRJU, RUPA, AND THE VILLAGERS

> "[Mother India] *is a conservative, virile epic of rural life.*"
>
> **PETER BRADSHAW**, FILM CRITIC, *THE GUARDIAN*, 2002

LATA MANGESHKAR

SINGER b.1929

The dominating voice of Indian film music, Lata Mangeshkar is one of only a handful of singers to have attained adulation, fame, and total mastery of her art.

◄ India's melody queen
One of the most loved singers in Bollywood, it was said of her, "Lata catches cold, and the whole film industry sneezes."

KEY WORKS

Mahal, 1949 (see p. 332)

Barsaat, 1949

Mother India, 1957 (see pp. 56–59)

Mughal-e-Azam, 1960 (see pp. 68–71)

Bees Saal Baad, 1962 (see p. 334)

Woh Kaun Thi?, 1964

Guide, 1965 (see pp. 84–87)

Pakeezah, 1972 (see pp. 116–17)

Razia Sultan, 1983

Hum Aapke Hain Koun..!, 1994
(see pp. 220–23)

Dilwale Dulhania le Jayenge, 1995
(see pp. 230–33)

Mention Indian playback singing and there is a good chance that the first name to come up will be Lata Mangeshkar. Hers is a voice that no Indian can say they haven't heard—be it the soldier at the border, the roadside vendor, the truck driver, or a member of the country's glittering elite.

Born in Indore, Madhya Pradesh, in 1929, Lata is the eldest of five siblings—four girls and a boy. Her father, Dinanath Mangeshkar, was a well-known classical vocalist and gave Lata her earliest singing lessons when she was barely five years old. Owner of a drama company called Balwant Sangeet Natak Mandal, Dinanath initially managed to look after the family well. However, the arrival of the talkies saw most drama companies, including Dinanath's, shutting down. The Mangeshkars moved to a small trading town, Sangli, where Dinanath even dabbled in filmmaking, but the enterprise did not succeed. The family then traveled to Pune and survived on his minimal income from singing for the national public broadcaster, All India Radio.

THE BEGINNING

Dinanath's untimely death in 1942 was a shattering blow to the family. The onus of looking after them all fell on young Lata's slender shoulders. At first, she took work acting in a few Hindi and Marathi films to keep the family going. She recorded a song for the Marathi film *Kiti Hasaal* (1942), but this was later edited out of the film.

Lata's Bollywood breakthrough came in *Bari Ma* (1945), starring singer-actress Noor Jehan, in which she not only acted but also sang a couple of songs. Around this time, she trained under classical vocalist Aman Ali Khan

◀ A national treasure
Lata sang the patriotic song "Ae Mere Watan Ke Logon" in the presence of Prime Minister Nehru in New Delhi in 1963. Still recovering from the shocking defeat of India in the 1962 Sino-Indian War, Nehru was so moved by the heartfelt rendition of the song that he broke down in tears.

on her assignments in the 1980s and 1990s, concentrating on her shows abroad instead. However, whenever she sang, in films such as *Hum Aapke Hain Koun..!* (1994) and *Dilwale Dulhania le Jayenge* (1995), her songs became chart busters.

Lata has also composed music for five Marathi films, under her own name and under a pseudonym—Anandghan. The songs in these films exhibit her profound knowledge of melody and, in particular, her wonderful use of elements of Marathi folk music.

Inevitably, Lata Mangeshkar has been the recipient of every major honor, including India's highest civilian award, the Bharat Ratna, and the Dadasaheb Phalke Award for her contribution to Indian cinema. Lata Mangeshkar is that rare singer who, it has to be said, has achieved perfection in her art.

TIMELINE

● **September 28, 1929** Born in Indore to classical artist Dinanath Mangeshkar.

● **1934** Starts learning music from her father and acts in his musical plays.

● **1945** Shares screen space with Noor Jehan and sings two songs in *Bari Ma.*

● **1949** Breakthrough year as she sings for the soundtracks of a number of successful films. Becomes the top female playback singer in the country.

● **1950** Composes music for the first time for Marathi film *Ram Ram Pahune.*

● **1959** Wins her first Filmfare Award for the song "Aaja Re Pardesi" (Come Back, Foreigner) from *Madhumati* (1958).

● **1963** Immortalizes the patriotic song "Ae Mere Watan Ke Logon" (Listen, People of My Country), sung for Indian soldiers martyred in the Sino-Indian War of 1962.

● **1969** Receives the Padma Bhushan—India's third-highest civilian award—from the Government of India.

● **1970** After winning her fourth Filmfare Award, for *Jeene ki Raah* (1969), asks not to be considered for future awards, to encourage newer talent.

● **1973** Receives her first National Award for *Parichay* (1972).

● **1974** Performs live on the international stage for the very first time at the Royal Albert Hall, London.

● **1990** Receives the Dadasaheb Phalke Award at the 37th National Awards.

● **1999** Launches her eponymous perfume, Lata Eau de Parfum.

● **2001** Receives the Bharat Ratna, becoming the second vocalist to do so, after M.S. Subbulakshmi.

to expand her singing range. When Khan left for Pakistan, following the partition of India in 1947, Lata studied under other vocalists. Meanwhile the occasional singing opportunities that came her way made little impact on her fortunes.

In comparison to the more robust voices of her Punjabi contemporaries, Lata's voice was thought to be too thin. In fact, film producer Sashadhar Mukerji advised music director Ghulam Haider against using her for *Shaheed* (1948) for this reason. Haider, who warned Mukerji that one day the world would fall at Lata's feet, composed her breakthrough song, "Dil Mera Toda" (Somebody Broke My Heart) for the Bombay Talkies film *Majboor* (1948). Her first hit song "Chanda Re Ja" (Go Away, Moon) in *Ziddi* (1948) came at the same studio.

RULING THE MUSIC INDUSTRY
1949–50 saw Lata Mangeshkar explode onto the musical scene, with songs from *Andaz, Barsaat,* and *Mahal* becoming extremely popular. In particular, the haunting melody "Aayega Aanewala" (The One Who's Awaited Will Come), from *Mahal,* caught the fancy of the nation as few songs had before. Initially, Lata's singing was reminiscent of Noor Jehan, but by 1950 her unique high-pitched voice had rendered all the heavier voices of the day obsolete. Only Geeta Dutt, and to a certain extent, Shamshad Begum and Suraiya, survived the Lata onslaught. With younger sister Asha Bhosle also finding her groove in the second half of the

1950s, the sisters would rule the world of playback singing until well into the 1990s.

Lata's exceptional voice along with the superior technical training she received, enabled her to easily reach notes at both ends of the musical scale. This emboldened composers to begin creating complex musical compositions especially for her. Unsurprisingly, Lata became the first choice among female singers for all music composers. It was a golden age for Hindi cinema—a time of melody, of seeking musical perfection, of days of rehearsals, as well as countless retakes demanded by composers who were extremely hard taskmasters.

After singing thousands of songs of all types and moods in 20 different Indian languages between the 1950s and 1970s and enjoying the kind of power few have experienced in the industry, Lata began to cut down

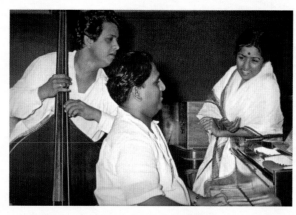

▲ A successful collaboration
Lata sharing a light, musical moment with composer duo Shankar (on the piano) and Jaikishan. One of the more successful teams in Hindi cinema, they have recorded over 400 songs together.

> *"I always say whatever skills I've imbibed are god's gift."*

LATA MANGESHKAR, *THE QUINT*, 2016

LATA MANGESHKAR BEING FELICITATED WITH THE BHARAT RATNA

DO AANKHEN BARAH HAATH

1957

Inspired by a real-life story, director V. Shantaram's idealistic melodrama is the tale of a jailer who sets out to reform six fearsome murderers in his charge.

▲ **Reformist jailer**
The jailer Adinath's eyes become the watchful eyes of heaven in a final surreal sequence, elevating him to a Gandhian figure. The Gandhian principle of non-violence as a form of resistance features prominently in the film.

CAST AND CREW

★ **V. Shantaram** Adinath
Sandhya Champa
Baburao Pendharkar Jail superintendent
Ulhas Shanker Passi
B.M. Vyas Jalia Nai
Asha Devi Mother of an inmate

🎬 **Director** V. Shantaram
⌂ **Producer** Rajkamal Kalamandir
🎵 **Music composer** Vasant Desai
🎵 **Lyricist** Bharat Vyas
📖 **Scriptwriter** G.D. Madgulkar
🎥 **Cinematographer** G. Balakrishna

After watching the screening of *Do Aankhen Barah Haath* (Two Eyes, Twelve Hands) at the Berlin Film Festival in 1958, film critic Jean Luc Godard wired a one-line review to *Cahiers du Cinema*: "Sandhya charming in story Indian jailer big heart stop." Festival juries were charmed as well—the film went on to win a Silver Bear award at Berlin and was later nominated for the Samuel Goldwyn International Award at the Golden Globes of 1959.

Do Aankhen Barah Haath was widely regarded as a return to serious cinema for director V. Shantaram, whose previous film, *Jhanak Jhanak Payal Baaje* (1955), is a Technicolor extravaganza presenting his kitschy vision of Indian classical music and dance. In stark contrast, *Do Aankhen Barah Haath* was a modestly mounted social film.

INSPIRED BY REAL LIFE
Swatantrapur, an open prison in Maharashtra's Sangli district in the 1930s, was the inspiration for writer G.D. Madgulkar's story, which deals with the rehabilitation of criminals through agricultural work. From this dry material, Madgulkar crafted a fascinating parable about trust and faith and seeking humanity in the midst of a brutal, dehumanized world.

The film follows the jailer Adinath as he chooses the six most degenerate criminals in his prison for an unusual experiment. These axe murderers and slashers are set to work on a farm, without shackles—in a macabre touch, they are given the same tools with which they committed their crimes. The jailer joins them in their labor. Cowed by his moral authority, they choose not to run away and begin to work together. By the time they grow their first crop and take it to market, each has discovered his better nature. Unfortunately, their work brings them into conflict with a local merchant whose business is threatened by their cheap produce. In a violent conclusion, the result of the jailer's experiment becomes apparent.

IN A LIGHTER VEIN
Despite its weighty theme, this is a relatively light and entertaining film. Abstaining from preachy speeches, Adinath relies instead on humor and camaraderie to get his message through. The criminals, meanwhile, resemble unibrowed silent-movie heavies and are infantilized to a man—though this brings in the laughs, it also ensures that their eventual redemption lacks a certain force. The focus remains instead on the noble jailer.

◀ **Muse on the move**
Much screen time is given to the director's muse, Sandhya, depicted here. She plays a traveling toy-seller who strides into the convicts' world with swaying hips and a clattering drum in tow.

V. SHANTARAM (1901–90)

Director V. Shantaram started out as an actor in silent cinema at Baburao Painter's Maharashtra Film Company in 1921. He set up the Prabhat Film Company in 1929, and directed a number of classics, such as *Duniya Na Mane* (see p.26), *Aadmi* (1939), and *Padosi* (1941). In 1942, he founded the production company Rajkamal Kalamandir, and shifted his focus from films with a social message to films based on music and dance. Increasingly overwrought, they were a far cry from the expressionist dramas with which he made his name.

CHALTI KA NAM GAADI

1958

Three bachelor brothers, a beautiful woman, and a rickety 1928 Chevrolet make up the ingredients of an all-time comedy classic from director Satyen Bose.

Right from its animated opening credits, *Chalti Ka Nam Gaadi* (If It Moves, Call It a Car) promises a fun ride for its audience. Thanks to the comic talents of the three Ganguly brothers—known by their screen names as Kishore Kumar (see pp.100– 01), Ashok Kumar (see p.31), and Anoop Kumar—the film more than delivers on this promise. *Chalti Ka Nam Gaadi* was reportedly produced in order to report losses to the tax authorities, but it confounded expectations by becoming a huge hit. Part romantic comedy and part knockabout farce, it remains one of the landmarks of popular Indian cinema, and a fitting showcase for the genius of singer and star Kishore Kumar.

A RIOT OF LAUGHS

Ashok Kumar plays the woman-hating Brijmohan Sharma, a boxer who runs a garage with his brothers—the bumbling Jagmohan and the amicable Manmohan. The plot sputters into motion one rainy night when the very beautiful and very drenched Renu brings in her car for repairs. When she leaves without paying, Manmohan has to track her down to collect the 5 rupees and 75 paise she owes the garage. This sweetly silly McGuffin leads the film down many amusing byways, till eventually the slapstick comedy and jalopy hijinks are discarded in favor of a more conventional mystery plot involving a couple of crooked royals who have their eyes on Renu's fortune. But that's how it goes with Kishore Kumar: as he sings in the film, sometimes you set out for Japan, but end up in China.

THE MAKING OF A CLASSIC

Chalti Ka Nam Gaadi is memorable for the effortless romantic chemistry between the lead couple—Kishore and Madhubala—which eventually led to their real-life marriage in 1960. There's much to love in this film, from Madhubala's dazzling charm to the Ganguly gang's hilarious banter. Kishore Kumar in particular brings a unique, quirky musicality to his scenes. His unconventional, oddball rhythms and mastery of verbal nonsense are seen at their best in the film's delightful song sequences.

The jazzy "Ek Ladki Bheegi Bhaagi Si" pulls off being very silly and very sensuous at the same time, while the centerpiece "Paanch Rupaiya Barah Anna," is a musical pastiche by lyricist Majrooh Sultanpuri and music director S.D. Burman, in which a creditor's plea to be paid his dues quite eccentrically incorporates everything from high-flown Urdu poetry, to folk music, to *baul* folk music, to snatches of 1930s movie songs—and even Woody Woodpecker's call.

◄ Band of brothers
The film opens with the classic title song "Babu Samjho Ishare," featuring the three Ganguly brothers driving through the streets of Mumbai in a vintage jalopy.

MADHUMATI

1958

A haunting tale of reincarnation and revenge, *Madhumati* was director Bimal Roy's biggest hit—an unexpected foray into the supernatural by the master of social realism.

The story of Madhumati's genesis is rather unusual. The story was pitched to director Bimal Roy by the Bengali filmmaker Ritwik Ghatak during his sojourn in Mumbai's commercial film industry. When Ghatak left for Kolkata to shoot his own film *Ajantrik* (1957), his draft of the screenplay was developed further by writer Rajinder Singh Bedi.

Madhumati opens with the stock elements of a Gothic suspense horror film—a dark and stormy night, an abandoned mansion, and an old caretaker holding a lantern aloft. However, Roy soon goes beyond these conventions to weave in intriguing themes of reincarnation and rebirth. These place the film in a hybrid genre that can only be described as "Indian Gothic." Launched by Kamal Amrohi's *Mahal* (1949), this genre is a uniquely Bollywood concoction of foggy moonlit nights, haunting refrains, and candle-bearing women in white. Its influence can be seen in films as recent as *Om Shanti Om* (see pp. 292–95), which borrows a pivotal plot twist from *Madhumati*.

▲ **Nature as a symbol**
Unlike most films of the period, which were shot indoors, Madhumati was filmed extensively on location.

HAUNTING TRAGEDY
The film's story takes us into the past with Anand, the lead character played by Dilip Kumar (see pp. 48–49), as he arrives at a timber plantation in the hills to work as a foreman. Drawn to the beauty of the landscape, he explores the surrounding forests where he meets the beautiful tribal girl Madhumati. Their love affair brings the two into conflict with the landowner, Raja Ugranarayan, whose dastardly actions eventually lead to Madhumati's tragic death. Anand is devastated by this turn of events. However, when he meets a girl named Madhavi who resembles his departed lover, the story takes a surprising turn. As the two lay a trap for Ugranarayan, the stage is set for Madhumati's revenge.

LYRICAL SYMBOLISM
Madhumati is frequently lyrical and sublime in the sequences where Anand follows a fugitive Madhumati into the mountain mist. The romance between the two retains its mystery throughout and holds the viewer through the story's many twists and turns. The music is memorable, particularly the haunting "Aaja Re Pardesi," rated by playback singer Lata Mangeshkar (see pp. 60–61) as one of her best songs.

Madhumati has a powerful hold that goes far beyond its status as a commercially successful film. Ghatak and Roy's involvement ensured that *Madhumati* had a layer of social realism, dealing with the oppression unleashed by feudalistic landowners. Behind the Bollywood veil, Ghatak's screenplay develops some powerful themes: ultimately, the tragic fate of Madhumati stands for the exploitation of tribal India, and the rape of nature itself.

HIT SONG

Aaja Re Pardesi
(Come to Me, Traveler)

🎤 **Singer** Lata Mangeshkar

CAST AND CREW

★ **Vyjanthimala** Madhumati
Dilip Kumar Anand
Pran Ugranarayan
Johnny Walker Charan Das

🎬 **Director** Bimal Roy
🎞 **Producer** Bimal Roy
🎵 **Music composer** Salil Choudhury
🎵 **Lyricist** Shailendra
💃 **Choreographer** B. Sohanlal
📖 **Scriptwriters** Ritwik Ghatak, Rajinder Singh Bedi
🎥 **Cinematographer** Dilip Gupta

BIMAL ROY
(1909–65)

Starting his career as a cameraman at the New Theatres in Kolkata, India, Bimal Roy broke through with his very first film *Udayer Pathe* (1944). His subsequent films established him as a sensitive filmmaker with a humanist approach and a subdued style rooted in realism. His empathy for the dispossessed and the marginalized is evident in films such as *Do Bigha Zamin* (see p. 50). His other landmark films include *Devdas* (1955), *Sujata* (1959), and *Bandini* (1963). An influential figure, Roy was a mentor for filmmakers such as Hrishikesh Mukherjee (see p. 140) and Gulzar (see pp. 142–43).

KAAGAZ KE PHOOL

1959

Tragedy under the lens: all shadows and light, Guru Dutt's brooding masterwork delves into the make-believe world of the movies.

After the commercial and artistic success of *Pyaasa* (see p. 54), actor–director Guru Dutt (see pp. 66–67) chose to collaborate with writer Abrar Alvi on another film about a romantic genius betrayed by his times. A semi-autobiographical account of the filmmaker's life, *Kaagaz ke Phool* takes a sceptical look at fame, and views failure and oblivion as the inevitable outcomes. The theme foreshadowed his own tragic fate: the film, considered a cult classic today, failed at the box office, throwing him into a state of depression which led ultimately to his suicide in 1964.

FLAWED MASTERPIECE

Kaagaz ke Phool was trashed on release for its "funeral pace" (*Filmindia*) and its "negative and pessimistic approach" (*Filmfare*). Over the years, however, its reputation has grown and the film is now widely regarded as a flawed but superbly atmospheric masterpiece. Much of the mood is built by S.D. Burman's wistful melodies and cinematographer V.K. Murthy's (see p. 51) striking chiaroscuro compositions (seen at their best in the

"… that rare film whose commercial failure is famous."

DINESH RAHEJA, WWW.REDIFF.COM

Cinemascope version). Right from the opening sequence, which is staged entirely without dialogue, the film steeps the viewer in an exquisite melancholy. As Mohammed Rafi sings in strangely tender, caressing tones about the world's betrayal, the audience is swept back in time to the glamorous world of Suresh Sinha, film director.

MELANCHOLIC JOURNEY

Married into a family of Anglicized snobs who look down on his trade, Sinha is estranged from his wife and forbidden from meeting his daughter. When he grooms a young woman named Shanti (Waheeda Rehman) for stardom, casting her as Paro in his adaptation of *Devdas*, there is much gossip about their love affair. When

it threatens to disrupt his family life, Shanti throws away her film career and becomes a teacher. Suresh's fortunes now begin to decline. His life goes into a downward spiral as he takes to drinking, losing his grip on himself. The studio forces Shanti to honor her contract and return to the movies, but by then it may be too late for Suresh Sinha.

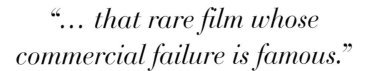

CAST AND CREW

★ **Guru Dutt** Suresh Sinha
Waheeda Rehman Shanti
Baby Naaz Pammi
Johnny Walker Rocky
Mahesh Kaul Sir B.B. Verma
Veena Bina

🎬 **Director** Guru Dutt
⬠ **Producer** Guru Dutt
🎵 **Music composer** S.D. Burman
Lyricist Kaifi Azmi
📖 **Scriptwriter** Abrar Alvi
🎥 **Cinematographer** V.K. Murthy

▶ **Bollywood's inward gaze**
Guru Dutt's intense drama about a troubled filmmaker reflects the director's cynicism about the fickle nature of fame.

GURU DUTT FILMS PRIVATE LTD'S
KAAGAZ ke PHOOL
CINEMASCOPE
Directed by GURU DUTT   Music S.D. BURMAN

GURU DUTT

ACTOR–DIRECTOR 1925–64

A master of melancholy, filmmaker Guru Dutt created some of the most haunting, lyrical images in Hindi cinema.

Guru Dutt died in 1964 at the age of 39. In his two decades in the film industry, he worked on around 20 films as an actor, director, and producer. He made his films with passion, shooting and reshooting them, perfecting them obsessively, and scrapping them entirely if he wasn't happy with the results. The images that did make it to the screen stand out for their mastery of mood, their chiaroscuro play of light and shadow, and their deep emotional intensity. Three of his films in particular—*Pyaasa, Kaagaz ke Phool,* and *Sahib Bibi aur Ghulam*—rank among the masterpieces of world cinema. They show the immense expressive possibilities of the often-derided song-and-dance genre—and the sublime heights it can reach in the hands of a great filmmaker.

EARLY INFLUENCES

Much of what is distinctive about Dutt's films comes from the musical sense he brought to cinema. Before entering the film industry, he had trained at the legendary dancer and choreographer Uday Shankar's academy in Almora, Uttarakhand. When circumstances cut his education short, Dutt took up work as a film choreographer and assistant director at the Prabhat Film Company in Pune. There, he became

▲ **Old friends**
Spanning around two decades, Guru Dutt's (right) deep friendship and professional bond with actor Dev Anand (left) began when they both were rank newcomers struggling to make their mark in Bollywood.

friends with a young actor, Dev Anand (see pp. 88–89), and the two made a pact that whoever achieved success first would help the other make his first film. That is how, in 1951, Dutt came to make *Baazi* for Navketan Films, a production company owned by Dev Anand. The film was a success,

KEY WORKS

Baazi, 1951

Jaal, 1952

Baaz, 1953

Aar Paar, 1954

Mr. & Mrs. '55, 1955 (see p. 333)

Sailaab, 1956

Pyaasa, 1957 (see p. 54)

Kaagaz ke Phool, 1959 (see p. 65)

Sahib Bibi aur Ghulam, 1962 (see pp. 90–91)

◀ **Ahead of his time**
A storytelling genius both in front of the camera and behind it, Guru Dutt challenged conventions and pushed the boundaries of popular Indian cinema.

and Dutt went on to set up his own production house, where he made Hollywood-inspired films with catchy songs that did well at the box office.

MASTER OF MELODRAMA

If Dutt had made only such breezy entertainments as *Aar Paar* and *Mr. & Mrs. '55*, he would be regarded today as an interesting but lightweight director. It was with the three films he made next—*Pyaasa*, *Kaagaz ke Phool*, and *Sahib Bibi aur Ghulam*—that Dutt really achieved greatness. These films had a few common features: they were all shot in exquisite black and white by the cinematographer V.K. Murthy (see p. 51), and starred Waheeda Rehman (see pp. 85), an actress Dutt had introduced to Hindi cinema. Their screenwriter was Abrar Alvi, a key collaborator who crafted the narratives to match the dark images in Dutt's head, and wrote the pensive lines he spoke on screen.

With *Pyaasa*, Dutt set aside his earlier Hollywood influences and made a film that was Indian to the core. The heady blend of poetry, music, drama, and evocative imagery he created was like nothing else that had come before. With this film and the ones that followed, Dutt evolved his own, personal cinematic language sometimes shaping scenes around a hummed verse or snatch of song, sometimes exploding a close, intense moment into a grandly operatic montage.

As the film scholar Arun Khopkar noted, Dutt's chosen genre was melodrama, a term that is derived from the Greek words for song and drama. The best Hindi films recognize the

complementary nature of these two elements, using song to elaborate, deepen, and resolve dramatic conflict. In Dutt's own work, the opening scenes of *Kaagaz ke Phool* and the climax of *Pyaasa*, with its soaring indictment of an inhumane world, are examples of this approach. Astonishingly, both films sustain a heightened lyricism from beginning to end.

MOVIE CLASSICS

Kaagaz ke Phool, a story about the decline and fall of a famous filmmaker, was rumored to have been inspired by Gyan Mukherjee, the director of the 1940s smash hit *Kismet* (see pp. 30–31), and Dutt's mentor in his early years. After *Pyaasa*, here was another self-destructive artist in the Devdas mould, a lost soul wandering in dark cavernous spaces illuminated by shafts of light. *Kaagaz ke Phool*'s narrative

proved to be prophetic. Dutt watched an early screening and realized from the audience's reaction that the film was "dead on arrival." The failure plunged him into a state of profound depression from which he never quite recovered.

Dutt did not direct any more films under his own name after this setback. *Sahib Bibi aur Ghulam*, adapted from another Bengali novel by Bimal Mitra, was officially an Abrar Alvi film. However, industry wisdom attributed its direction to Dutt. It is believed that, while Alvi made the film, Dutt may have supervised closely as producer and probably took over for the songs. Haunting and strongly atmospheric, the film tells the story of the collapse and ruin of a landed feudal family in Bengal, as seen through the eyes of a naive villager, played by Dutt, who is drawn to a neglected wife, played by Meena Kumari (see p. 91).

END OF AN ERA

Sahib Bibi aur Ghulam was to be Dutt's last great success. In the following years, his personal life began to fall apart. A rumored affair with Waheeda Rehman led to conflict with his wife, the singer Geeta Dutt. Their growing estrangement and the resulting separation from his children troubled him greatly. Given his dark, brooding nature, it was perhaps no surprise that, on October 10, 1964, Dutt was found dead in his apartment from an overdose of alcohol and sleeping pills. Since his untimely death, Guru Dutt's reputation has grown steadily and today, he is recognized as one of the greatest film-makers that Indian cinema has known.

► Mr. & Mrs. '55
Dutt's fifth directorial venture, this romantic comedy was entertaining even as it satirized contemporary debates on women's rights in 1950s India.

> "*Everybody is going to hurt you. You just have to find the ones worth suffering for.*"

GURU DUTT, QUOTED IN *THE ECONOMIC TIMES*, SEPTEMBER 29, 2016

TIMELINE

- **July 9, 1925** Born Vasanth Kumar Shivsankar Padukone in Bangalore, southern India.

- **1941** Studies dance and performance arts at the Uday Shankar India Culture Centre after completing his early education in Kolkata.

- **1944** Begins working in the Indian film industry as a choreographer for the Prabhat Film Company.

- **1947–49** Moves to Mumbai and works with leading directors, including Amiya Chakrabarty and Gyan Mukherjee.

- **1951** Directorial debut with the successful crime thriller *Baazi*.

- **1953** Sets up his own production house. Directs and acts in *Baaz*, considered Dutt's first major acting role in a movie.

- **26 May 1953** Marries the celebrated playback singer Geeta Dutt.

SONGSTRESS GEETA DUTT

- **1954** Achieves commercial success for Guru Dutt Films after directing and acting in *Aar Paar*.

- **1956** Produces the film *C.I.D.*, giving Raj Khosla his debut as a film director and the actress Waheeda Rehman her first major acting role.

- **1962** Produces and acts in *Sahib Bibi aur Ghulam*, which wins the Filmfare Award for Best Film the following year.

- **1962–64** Acts in productions by other companies, such as *Sautela Bhai*, *Bahurani*, *Bharosa*, and *Suhagan*.

- **1964** Dutt's last acting appearance in a feature film, as the star of *Saanj Aur Savera*.

- **October 10, 1964** Dies of a drug and alcohol overdose in Mumbai, Maharashtra, at the age of 39.

MUGHAL-E-AZAM

1960

K. Asif's magnum opus has it all: a rebellious love story set against the splendor of the Mughal court, a high-voltage clash between an emperor and his son, and a tragic ending that takes the unrequited romance to mythic heights.

CAST AND CREW

★ **Prithviraj Kapoor** Emperor Akbar
Dilip Kumar Prince Salim
Madhubala Anarkali
Durga Khote Maharani Jodha Bai
Nigar Sultana Bahar
Ajit Durjan Singh

🎬 **Director** K. Asif
⬠ **Producer** K. Asif
♫ **Music composer** Naushad
♪ **Lyricist** Shakeel Badayuni
🕴 **Choreographer** Lachhu Maharaj
▭ **Scriptwriters** K. Asif, Aman, Kamal Amrohi, Ehsan Rizvi, Wajahat Mirza
🎥 **Cinematographer** R.D. Mathur

As early as November 1945, *Filmindia* magazine displayed an advertisement for K. Asif's *Mughal-e-Azam* (The Greatest of the Mughals). The advertised film was produced by Shiraz Ali Hakim, the owner of Famous Cine Studios, and starred Veena, Chandramohan, Sapru, Nargis, and Durga Khote. It was based on Urdu dramatist Imtiaz Ali Taj's play, *Anarkali* (1922), which was itself based on a 16th-century legend. The play was a tragic tale of love between a court dancer, Anarkali, and the heir to the Mughal throne, Prince Salim, that was thwarted by Salim's father, Emperor Akbar.

Two silent film versions of the story in 1928 and a talkie in 1935 had already been made when filming for *Mughal-e-Azam* began in early 1946. However, filming was stalled due to the volatile political situation resulting from India's struggle for independence. Following the Partition, Hakim migrated to newly formed Pakistan, leaving Asif high and dry with just a quarter of the film having been shot. To add to this, actor Chandramohan passed away in 1949. With so many hurdles in the way, the completion of this much-awaited movie seemed impossible.

MAKING OF THE EPIC
It is said that before leaving for Pakistan, Hakim convinced builder Shapoorji Pallonji Mistry, whose firm had

▼ **An epic saga**
The story of a lovelorn prince who goes against his powerful father, Emperor Akbar, for the sake of his love for the beautiful courtesan, Anarkali, struck a chord with audiences across the country.

constructed Famous Cine Studio, to invest in the film. On meeting Shapoorji, Asif discovered that the builder was a huge admirer of Akbar—the project was on.

The making of *Mughal-e-Azam* finally resumed in the early 1950s, with an entirely new cast, with the exception of Durga Khote. Even then, its production continued painstakingly right through the decade at a staggering cost of about

"A benchmark film for both Indian cinema and cinema grandeur in general ..."

LAURA BUSHELL, MOVIE REVIEW FOR THE *BBC*, 2002

◄ **Immortal music**
Inspired by Indian classical and folk traditions, the award-winning music for the film by Naushad has lasting appeal.

his powers of persuasion, Asif even got the great Lachhu Maharaj, an Indian classical dancer and choreographer of Kathak, to create the dances in the film.

STAR-STUDDED PREMIERE
The premiere in Mumbai was a truly grand affair. Maratha Mandir's lobby was specially decorated for the occasion, invites were sent out in the form of royal scrolls, and the reels of the film arrived at the theater by elephant. Several dignitaries attended the premiere along with famous personalities from the film industry. However the lead pair was conspicuously absent. Furious over Asif's marriage to his sister, Dilip Kumar (see pp. 48–49) refused to attend, while Madhubala (see pp. 72–73) did not generally attend film premieres and parties. The public's response to the film was incredible—people had been waiting impatiently to watch Madhubala and Dilip Kumar light up the screen with their on-screen chemistry.

A SUPERHIT
The film proved to be a happy ending for all involved except Madhubala. During the film's shooting her congenital heart disease became worse by her having to drag heavy chains around—Asif had procured real iron chains to make the scenes more authentic. Yet she bore it all bravely, giving the performance of a lifetime as the doomed courtesan. However, the bigger tragedy was her parting ways with Dilip Kumar. The two completed *Mughal-e-Azam* under a lot of strain, not even speaking to each other during the shoot. However, none of this is visible on-screen and their love scenes are some of the most sensual and passionate to have ever been filmed in Indian cinema.

In 2004, the Shapoorji Pallonji Group undertook massive restoration and colorization, releasing the film in color and thus fulfilling Asif's dream. This made *Mughal-e-Azam* one of the first black-and-white Indian films to be made into color for a theatrical release.

▼ **A long-awaited release**
The film was released in 150 theaters across the country on August 5, 1960, almost 15 years since it had been first advertised.

₹15 million (about ₹800 million/$12,473,700 today), with its filming spread over 500 shooting days. In fact, during that time *Anarkali* (starring Pradeep Kumar and Bina Rai), a rival production by Filmistan, came out in 1953 and was hugely successful. But Asif was undeterred and carried on making *Mughal-e-Azam*.

LAVISH AFFAIR
Asif saw to it that he got the best of everything for *Mughal-e-Azam*—tailors from Delhi stitched the costumes, Hyderabadi goldsmiths made the jewelry, craftsmen from Kolhapur in Maharashtra worked on the crowns, Rajasthani ironsmiths fabricated the shields, swords, spears, daggers, and armor, specialists from Surat and Khambayat in Gujarat made the exquisite embroidery on the costumes, while the elaborate footwear came from Agra in Uttar Pradesh. Thousands of camels, horses, elephants, and soldiers—most on loan from the Indian army—were employed for the battle scenes. The major set piece, the grand Sheesh Mahal (Palace of Mirrors), took two years to make at a cost of ₹1.5 million (about ₹80 million/$1,247,400 today), using Belgian glass with intricate design work by artisans from Firozabad in Uttar Pradesh. The set attracted a flood of visitors not just from India, but also from outside the country.

LIGHTS, CAMERA, AND COLOR
With the advent of technicolor, Asif filmed the song "Pyar Kiya Toh Darna Kya" (When You Are in Love, Why Be Afraid) in color. He also shot more scenes toward the end of the movie and wanted to reshoot the entire film in color. However, spiraling costs and

impatient distributors made him release the film as it was. R.D. Mathur had to use all the ingenuity he could conjure up to capture *Mughal-e-Azam*. With Mohan Studios not having enough lights for the enormous sets, Mathur shot the film largely at night, making an arrangement with three nearby studios to borrow their lights after 6 p. m. and return them before 6 a.m. every day, so as not to hamper their work. His greatest challenge, however, was lighting the Sheesh Mahal. Renowned filmmakers David Lean and Roberto Rossellini told Asif it could not be done with all the mirrors around. But Mathur got around this challenge by bouncing light using specially made reflectors of various sizes. This process made each shot painstakingly slow.

SPECTACULAR MUSIC
Naushad's music perfectly complements the epic nature of the film, especially his evocative background score. Though about 20 songs were composed for the film, only 12 are present in the final version, of which two songs are sung by the noted classical musician Ustad Bade Ghulam Ali Khan. Having no intention of singing for the film, he asked for an astronomical ₹25,000 (about ₹1.3 million/$20,893 today) per song to put Asif off—but Asif agreed. Using

STORYLINE

In a classic tale of two star-crossed lovers, the Mughal heir to the throne of India, Salim, falls in love with a court dancer, Anarkali, much to the anger and disapproval of Salim's father, Emperor Akbar. This epic romance pits a father against a son and drives true love to challenge the protocol of royal duty.

SALIM AND ANARKALI SHARE
AN INTIMATE MOMENT

THE BIRTH OF A PRINCE	THE PRODIGAL SON RETURNS	A BEAUTIFUL DECEPTION	A LOVE STORY BEGINS	A BETRAYAL

PLOT OVERVIEW

THE BIRTH OF A PRINCE

After years of marriage, Emperor Akbar finally sees the birth of an heir. However, the young prince, Salim, grows up to be spoiled and debauched. One day, Akbar walks in to find his son drunk out of his wits; enraged, he sends Salim off to war, in the hope that a hard life will set the prince straight.

THE PRODIGAL SON RETURNS

Fearing the emperor's wrath, Salim distinguishes himself on the battlefield, having grown into a fine, regal man as befits a prince. Finally, after 14 years, the time comes for Salim to return home and his mother, Jodhabai, is overcome upon seeing her son after all these years ❶.

A BEAUTIFUL DECEPTION

To celebrate Salim's return, the sculptor Sangtarash is commissioned to create a beautiful statue. However, as the day dawns, the statue remains unfinished. The sculptor gets his model, a beautiful young woman, Nadira, to stand in place of the statue. Later, she reveals herself, to the surprise of Akbar and all assembled.

A LOVE STORY BEGINS

Struck by her beauty, Akbar names her Anarkali. Salim, too, is struck by her, seeing her perform at the Janmashthami celebrations ❷. Meeting secretly, Salim and Aanarkali fall deeply in love with each other, much to fellow courtesan, Bahar's chagrin ❸, ❹, and ❺.

A BETRAYAL

A jealous Bahar exposes their love story to Akbar, who puts Anarkali in prison ❻. But later Akbar releases her on the condition that she tell Salim that she loves him only for the throne ❼. While Salim sees Anarkali's release as a victory for love, Bahar tells him that it isn't so.

THE SONGS

A SECRET MEETING BETWEEN SALIM AND ANARKALI

Shubh Din Aayo Raj Dulara
(An Auspicious Day Has Come)
Singer: Ustad Bade Ghulam Ali Khan
Picturized on Salim and others ❶

Mohe Panghat Pe
(I Was Teased at the Riverbank)
Singer: Lata Mangeshkar
Picturized on Anarkali ❷

Teri Mehfil Mein
(In Your Gathering)
Singers: Lata Mangeshkar, Shamshad Begum
Picturized on Anarkali, Bahar, and Salim ❸

Ae Ishq Yeh Sab Duniyawale
(O Love, All These People of the World)
Singer: Lata Mangeshkar
Picturized on Suraiya and Salim ❹

Prem Jogan Ban Ke
(Losing My Sanity in Your Love)
Singer: Ustad Bade Ghulam Ali Khan
Picturized on Salim and Anarkali ❺

Mohabbat Ki Jhooti Kahani
(The False Hope of Love)
Singer: Lata Mangeshkar
Picturized on Anarkali ❻

Humen Kash Tumse Mohabbat Na Hoti
(I Wish I Was Never in Love with You)
Singer: Lata Mangeshkar
Picturized on Salim and Anarkali ❼

BAHAR, ANARKALI'S RIVAL, PERFORMS IN COURT

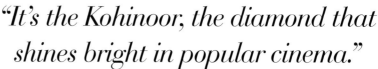

> *"It's the Kohinoor, the diamond that shines bright in popular cinema."*
>
> **NASREEN MUNNI KABIR,** FILMMAKER–AUTHOR, *THE IMMORTAL DIALOGUE OF K. ASIF'S MUGHAL-E-AZAM,* 2007

JODHA BAI UNABLE TO HAND AKBAR THE SWORD THAT MIGHT KILL HER SON

K. ASIF (1922–71)

Even though he directed just two films, K. Asif will always find his name on the list of Hindi cinema's leading and most passionate filmmakers. The nephew of the notable actor and filmmaker Nazir, Asif had an instinct for spectacle that only a few filmmakers could match. Besides his masterpiece, *Mughal-e-Azam*, his first film, *Phool* (1945), was a landmark and one of Indian cinema's earliest multi-starrers.

A REBELLIOUS DECLARATION OF LOVE	A WAR FOR LOVE	REBELLION QUASHED	A LAST ATTEMPT	QUEEN FOR A NIGHT	A FINAL PARDON

Believing Bahar's words about Anarkali's betrayal, Salim chides Anarkali for being so weak in love. However, in court, Anarkali surprises one and all, when she proclaims her love for Salim publicly ❽. Furious, Akbar orders her to be thrown back into the dungeon for openly defying his orders.

As he gets to know of Anarkali's fate, Salim is driven to furious despair and declares war on his father. Akbar takes up the challenge and gives the order for Anarkali's execution once the war begins ❾.

Meanwhile, Durjan Singh, Salim's trusted friend and advisor, gets Anarkali out of prison and brings her to Salim. However, Salim is defeated in battle and is sentenced to death, a punishment befitting a defeated warrior.

Salim is sent to his execution ❿. Anarkali agrees to accept her death sentence so he may live. But she has a last request—she be made queen before she dies so Salim's promise of making her his wife remains fulfilled.

As promised, Anarkali is made the queen of the country ⓫. However, Akbar sets his own condition to match hers—she drugs Salim in the morning so he will not interfere when Anarkali is led away to her death. As morning dawns, and Salim lies unconscious, Anarkali is taken away to be buried alive inside a brick wall ⓬.

Anarkali's mother reminds Akbar of a favor he had promised a long time ago, when she had brought the news of the Prince's birth. She now asks for her daughter's life. Akbar lets Anarkali escape through a secret tunnel away from the city, but on the condition that Salim will never know that Anarkali is alive.

❽ ❾ ❿ ⓫ ⓬

Pyar Kiya Toh Darna Kya (When You Are in Love, Why Be Afraid) *Singer: Lata Mangeshkar Picturized on Anarkali, Salim, Akbar, and others*

Bekas Pe Karam (Show Compassion to the Needy Ones) *Singer: Lata Mangeshkar Picturized on Anarkali*

Ae Mohabbat Zindabad (Long Live Love) *Singer: Mohammed Rafi Picturized on Salim and others*

Jab Raat Hai Aisi Matwali (When the Night Is So Intoxicating) *Singer: Lata Mangeshkar Picturized on Anarkali, Salim, and Bahar*

Khuda Nigehban Ho Tumhara (May God Keep an Eye Over You) *Singer: Lata Mangeshkar Picturized on Anarkali*

ANARKALI IMPRISONED AND SHACKLED

ANARKALI BOLDLY DECLARES HER LOVE FOR SALIM

MADHUBALA

ACTRESS **1933–69**

Regarded as one of Hindi cinema's most beautiful actresses, Madhubala was also blessed with a considerable gift for acting. Her legendary status has only grown with time.

She mesmerized audiences with her twinkling eyes, lopsided impish smile, and infectious laughter. But there was more to Madhubala than her looks, which almost always overshadowed her acting talent. From finely nuanced dramatic performances in *Ek Saal* (1957) and *Mughal-e-Azam* to tickling the funny bone in *Mr. & Mrs. '55* (1955), *Chalti Ka Naam Gaadi*, and *Half Ticket* (1962), Madhubala straddled both ends of the acting spectrum with ease.

▲ A star is born
The 1949 supernatural suspense thriller *Mahal*, co-starring superstar actor Ashok Kumar, finally thrust Madhubala into the spotlight.

AN EARLY START

Madhubala was born Mumtaz Jehan Begum Dehlavi in 1933. When she was a child, her father, Ataullah Khan, lost his job with the Imperial Tobacco Company at Peshawar, and the family went through rather hard times. As a result, Khan would make the rounds of film studios in Bombay (now Mumbai), looking for work for his daughter. Fortunately for them, music composer Madan Mohan's father, Rai Bahadur Chunilal of Bombay Talkies, offered her the role of Ulhas' daughter in *Basant* (1942). Not only was the film successful, but Mumtaz won the hearts of cinemagoers, leading to more film contracts.

Mumtaz became a leading lady with Kidar Sharma's *Neel Kamal* (1947) opposite Raj Kapoor at the age of 14. However, her breakthrough came with Bombay Talkies' ghost story *Mahal* (1949), where she made a major

◀ An ethereal muse
Madhubala's photoshoot with *LIFE* photographer James Burke in 1951 showed a rarely seen contemplative side to her character.

KEY WORKS

Basant, 1942

Mahal, 1949 (see p. 332)

Tarana, 1951

Mr. & Mrs. '55, 1955

Howrah Bridge, 1958

Chalti Ka Naam Gaadi, 1958 (see pp. 63)

Mughal-e-Azam, 1960 (see pp. 68–71)

impact with her haunting performance. With the success of *Mahal*, Madhubala, as she now called herself, had truly arrived.

However, by the mid-1950s, Madhubala was declared "box office poison," with most of her films, such as *Amar* (1954), flopping. The only exception was Guru Dutt's *Mr. & Mrs. '55*, which provided a vehicle for her impeccable comic timing.

REEL LIFE TO REAL-LIFE ROMANCE

In 1951, Madhubala acted opposite Dilip Kumar (see pp. 48–49) in the box office hit, *Tarana*. Subsequently, the pair co-starred in three more films,

"The Biggest Star in the World— and she's not in Beverly Hills."

DAVID CORT, *THEATRE ARTS MAGAZINE*, 1952

including *Sangdil* (1952), *Amar*, and *Mughal-e-Azam* (1960), getting closer in the process. Though Madhubala would generally keep away from film functions and parties, she attended the premiere of Kumar's *Insaniyat* (1955), escorted by him. Journalists went into a frenzy seeing them enter the Roxy cinema hand-in-hand, an acknowledgement of their relationship.

The duo then signed up for B.R. Chopra's *Naya Daur* (see p. 55), and even completed the film's first schedule. But Madhubala's father refused to let her leave Mumbai for the film's outdoor schedule—which led to actress Vyjayanthimala replacing her. Furious, Ataullah took Chopra to court for dropping her; Chopra filed a

counter suit. As the saga unfolded in court, Dilip Kumar testified against Madhubala, taking Chopra's side. Her father lost the case, and her affair with Kumar came to an end.

CAREER BEST

Madhubala turned her career around with a string of successful films in 1958, and reached the peak of her career with K. Asif's magnificent telling of the tragic Salim–Anarkali love story *Mughal-e-Azam*. Her performance as Anarkali, the doomed courtesan, is unanimously regarded as the finest performance of her career. But the film proved to be not only a physically

▶ **From screen to reality**
Madhubala made many successful films with Kishore Kumar, and the pair married in 1960.

◀ **The most successful year**
Madhubala played a singer in *Howrah Bridge* (1958) and enthralled viewers in the sensuous song "Aaiye Meherbaan" with Ashok Kumar. The year saw the release of some of her best films.

grueling shoot for Madhubala, but also emotionally taxing—she had to shoot a good part of the film after she had separated from Dilip Kumar. It is a credit to both actors that this is not apparent in their performances. Their romantic scenes in the film, especially where he is stroking her face with a feather, are highly charged.

A TRAGIC END

Madhubala's delicate looks and lively personality hid a grave condition—in 1954 she had been diagnosed with a congenital heart disorder. Dragging the heavy chains in *Mughal-e-Azam* worsened her condition, shortening her career. She was told that she did not have long to live. In 1960, she married actor-singer Kishore Kumar—some speculated to get over Dilip Kumar.

Madhubala's later releases, including *Passport* (1961) and *Sharabi* (1964), were completed by using doubles and stand-ins. Some films had to be shelved, while she was replaced in others. She tried to make a comeback, but was unable to take the strain of shooting. Madhubala would never act in a film again.

While her films with Kishore show a zany chemistry between the two, their marriage had run into problems. Nevertheless, they remained married until her death, just a few days after her 36th birthday. It was a sad and lonely end for someone labeled the "Venus of the Indian Screen," a reputation that survives.

TIMELINE

- **February 14, 1933** Born in Delhi.

- **1942** Debut as a child actor in Bombay Talkies' *Basant*.

- **1947** First appearance as a leading lady, opposite Raj Kapoor in Kidar Sharma's *Neel Kamal*. It was also the last film where she was billed as Mumtaz; thereafter she was known as Madhubala.

- **1948** Receives appreciation for her role in *Lal Dupatta*.

- **1949** Release of *Mahal*, her big breakthrough film and one of India's earliest ghost films.

- **1950** *Hanste Ansu* receives the first-ever Adults Only Certificate in independent India.

- **1954** On the set of *Bahut Din Huwe*, Madhubala is diagnosed with congenital heart disease.

MADHUBALA IN *TARANA*, HER FIRST FILM WITH DILIP KUMAR

- **1955** *Mr. & Mrs. '55* is her first big comedy hit.

- **1955** Produces her first film, *Naata*, and acts in it as well.

- **1958** Madhubala's most successful professional year, with *Chalti Ka Naam Gaadi*, *Phagun*, *Kala Pani*, and *Howrah Bridge* all becoming big successes at the box office.

- **1960** The masterpiece *Mughal-e-Azam* is released. Marries her *Chalti Ka Naam Gaadi* co-star, the actor–singer Kishore Kumar, in a civil ceremony.

- **1962** Release of her last film with Kishore, *Half Ticket*.

- **February 23, 1969** Dies in Mumbai.

- **1971** *Jwala*, her last movie—and her only film to be fully produced in color—is released posthumously.

- **2008** Commemorated on a stamp by the Postal Department of India.

ENTER THE GLAMOUR

1961–1973

Cavorting in foreign lands, bold and fashionable
heroines, and nattily dressed heroes enthralled the
audience, while a breakthrough in color technology
set new standards in cinema.

ENTER THE GLAMOUR

Cinema in the 1960s took a break from the socially conscious classics of the past. In glorious Eastman Color, the lead actors could now be seen clubbing unashamedly and traveling to exotic destinations.

Compared to the 1950s, generally considered the Golden Age of Bollywood, and the 1970s, the era of the "Angry Young Man," the decade in between is often seen as lightweight. However, it was the 1960s that began the trend of color films, lighthearted youthful romantic dramas, and a westernized, more liberal way of life for an English-speaking lead pair.

At the same time, the old kind of cinema thrived. The year 1960 produced three superhit films that were decidedly old-fashioned: *Mughal-e-Azam* (see pp. 68–71), *Barsaat ki Raat*, and *Chaudhvin ka Chand*. These "Muslim socials," set in a world of aristocrats and veiled women, resurfaced with *Mere Mehboob* in 1963. The decade also saw several tear-jerkers starring actress Meena Kumari and Rajendra Kumar. Rajendra was so successful that he was fondly labeled "Jubilee Kumar," given that his films almost always completed silver jubilees, a run of 25 weeks, at the cinema. Nevertheless, posterity remembers the 1960s for trends set by a new generation of screen idols in movies like *Junglee* (see pp. 78–79), *Waqt* (see p. 92), and *Teesri Manzil* (see p. 93).

GAY ABANDON
In the 1960s, Hindi cinema witnessed the emergence of a new kind of hero and heroine, played by actors

◄ **Glamour queen**
With her high bouffant blonde wig, winged eyeliner, and the look of a pinup, Saira Banu emerged as a 1960s fashion icon. Her retro style continues to inspire fashionistas today.

Shammi Kapoor (see p. 79), Joy Mukherjee, and Shashi Kapoor, and actresses Asha Parekh, Sharmila Tagore, and Saira Banu, among others. Portrayed as young and carefree, these upper-class characters wore fashionable clothes, drove fancy cars, and could be seen frequenting nightclubs, riding horses, skiing abroad, or sipping cocktails by the pool. Unlike the downbeat, often angst-ridden protagonists of the 1950s, these new heroes bore their troubles with a light heart, and were shown shaking a leg to peppy Western music. In *China Town* (1962), Shammi was a drummer, while in *Phir Wohi Dil Laya Hoon* (1963), Joy went around with a guitar.

Although Bollywood embraced Western popular culture, it did so with a slight self-consciousness. Scriptwriters frequently inserted phrases in English—in *Jab Pyaar Kisi se Hota hai* (1960), Asha exclaims,

▼ **Fast and furious**
Flashy sports cars became a rage in 1960s Bollywood, but these status symbols weren't just driven by the heroes and heroines—even the villains used them in high-speed chases.

▲ **Going international**
Filming in foreign locations gained popularity in the 1960s. This scene from *Sangam* (1964) was shot in Rome, with the Colosseum as a backdrop.

"Oh yes yes!" three times in one scene, and curses the comedian with the words, "You clumsy goat!"

TEMPLATE FOR ROMANCE
The romantic films of the 1960s set the template for Bollywood's portrayal of courtship for decades to come: the initial pushback by the heroine, a teasing chase by the hero, a song, an episode in which the heroine realizes the hero's intrinsic worth, followed by yet another song, and then true love. Obstacles on the path to true love were obstinate parents, class divide, villains who coveted the heroine's wealth, and the moral imperatives of family and society.

EXPLOSION OF COLOR
Technicolor had been used for hit films such as *Mother India* (see pp. 56–57) and *Ganga Jamuna* (1961), but it was an expensive technology and many filmmakers resorted to Eastman Color,

▲ Cabaret sequence
Shammi Kapoor's frenetic dancing and Helen's revealing outfits, exotic makeup, and provocative moves in this cabaret sequence from *Teesri Manzil* (1966) are abiding images from 1960s Bollywood.

in many more hit films. Another new trend was to shoot movies abroad. The likes of *An Evening in Paris* (see p. 95) and *Love in Tokyo* (1966) employed the simple strategy of attracting audiences through the films' titles.

THRILLS AND CHILLS
The 1960s were also remarkable for a number of suspense thrillers. *Bees Saal Baad* (1962) evoked an air of mystery with its haunting songs, while director Raj Khosla and actress Sadhana created three suspense sagas together: *Woh Kaun Thi?* (1964), *Mera Saaya* (1966), and *Anita* (1967). Director Vijay Anand excelled in crime thrillers such as *Teesri Manzil* (1966) and *Jewel Thief* (see p. 94). *Farz* (1967) skyrocketed actor Jeetendra (see pp. 182–83) to fame as Secret Agent 116, a character in the mold of James Bond.

▼ Rise of a superstar
The end of the 1960s saw the emergence of India's first superstar, Rajesh Khanna. He went on to dominate Bollywood in the early 1970s with major hits like *Anand* (1971).

which was more affordable. The first successful film produced in Eastman Color was *Junglee* (see pp. 78–79). It wasn't long before other filmmakers followed suit, using color to showcase scenic locales, in films such as *Professor* (1962), *Phir Wohi Dil Laya Hoon* (1963), and *Kashmir ki Kali* (1964). These were all big hits and proudly displayed the Eastman Color logo at the beginning of their credits.

After *Junglee*—shot in Kashmir—became a success, Kashmir was shown as a retreat for wealthy urban dwellers

> "The global presence of Indian movies began in the 1960s."

DAVID J. SCHAEFER, KAVITA KARAN,
BOLLYWOOD AND GLOBALIZATION: THE GLOBAL POWER OF POPULAR HINDI CINEMA, 2013

JUNGLEE

1961

The definitive hit of 1961, *Junglee* ushered in the "swinging sixties," an era of movies that spoke exuberantly to urban youth anxious to break free from the shackles of age-old traditions.

In the film *Junglee* (Wild) Shammi Kapoor unleashed his rebel-hero persona and redefined Bollywood for an entire generation of cinemagoers. The anthemic appeal of the liberating "Yahoo!" in the film, coupled with Kapoor's uninhibited dancing, was groundbreaking for Hindi film heroes. Paired opposite him in her debut role was Saira Banu, who won her only Filmfare Award nomination for Best Actress for this film.

The success of *Junglee* is also attributed to the immensely popular songs in the film, composed by the famed Shankar–Jaikishen partnership. Small wonder, then, that *Junglee* did very well at the box office. In addition to the music, another selling point was the film's setting, Kashmir, shot for

◄ **Going wild**
The hit song "Chahe Koi Mujhe Junglee Kahe" was actually shot in Kufri, Himachal Pradesh, because the snow that year in Kashmir was not thought to be adequate.

◄ **Kashmir in color**
The beauty of Kashmir was showcased for the first time in color in *Junglee*. It was the perfect setting for the romance between Raj and Shekhar.

the first time in color. Cinematographer N.V. Srinivas made impressive use of the new cost-effective but high-quality Eastmancolor film print technology from Kodak. Previously, Hindi cinema had gone back and forth between color, black-and-white, and films that were partly in color. After the success of *Junglee*, it became the norm for Hindi films to be shot entirely in color.

TAMING THE WILD
The title of the film, *Junglee*, meaning "wild," is used for the hero of the film, Shekhar—an ill-tempered workaholic who has returned to India to manage the family business. He follows in the footsteps of his mother, a stern matriarch for whom laughter is vulgar, indulged in only by the lower classes. His sister Mala is the only free spirit in this humorless aristocratic household. Unknown to her family, she is in love with Jeevan—a lowly clerk in Shekhar's office. However, when her clandestine romance is found out, Mala is forced to leave for Kashmir under the watchful eye of Shekhar. Here, Shekhar comes across the beautiful prankster, Raj, who teases him and is unafraid of his

daunting personality. Veteran writer Agha Jani Kashmiri gave witty dialogues to the young heroine, a far cry from the coy stereotypes that mainstream actresses were so often saddled with at the time.

SONG AND DANCE
In the middle of the movie, Shekhar is caught in a cabin with Raj during a snowstorm. Watching a sleeping Raj, Shekhar has a change of heart, and he falls helplessly in love with her. There is a dramatic transformation in his character, and he breaks out of the cabin with the iconic "Yahoo!,"

plunging headlong into the snow. This is the setting for the hit song "Chahe Koi Mujhe Junglee Kahe" (Let Them Call Me Wild). The classic "Yahoo!" for this song was performed by Prayag Raj, who went on to become the screenplay writer for films such as *Amar Akbar Anthony* (1977, see pp. 148–49) and *Coolie* (1983).

The party song "Suku Suku," featuring Helen and Shammi Kapoor, was yet another chart-busting song, at a time when cameo dances by Helen were fast becoming the norm for hit films. Kapoor's untamed dancing for this song was not choreographed. Other songs in *Junglee* include romantic hits like "Ehsaan Tera" (Oblige Me) and "Mere Yaar Shabba Khair" (Good Night, My Love).

HIT SONGS

Chahe Mujhe Koi Junglee Kahe
(Let Them Call Me Wild)
🎤 **Singer** Mohammed Rafi

Ehsaan Tera
(Oblige Me)
🎤 **Singer** Mohammed Rafi

CAST AND CREW

⭐ **Shammi Kapoor** Chandrashekhar "Shekhar"
Saira Banu Rajkumari "Raj"
Lalita Pawar Shekhar's mother

🎬 **Director** Subodh Mukherji
⬡ **Producer** Subodh Mukherji
🎵 **Music composers** Shankar S. Raghuvanshi, Jaikishen D. Panchal
🎵 **Lyricists** Shailendra, Hasrat Jaipuri
🎥 **Choreographer** P.L. Raj
📖 **Scriptwriter** Subodh Mukherji, Agha Jani Kashmiri
🎥 **Cinematographer** N.V. Srinivas
👕 **Costume designer** Laxman Shelke

SHAMMI KAPOOR (1931–2011)

The heartthrob of an entire generation, Shamsher Raj Kapoor broke the mold of the traditional Hindi film hero with his Elvis Presley moves and his bouffant hairstyle. However, it took 20 unsuccessful films between 1952 and 1957 before he could shed his long-haired, mustachioed look to become the Shammi Kapoor who delivered hits such as *Tumsa Nahin Dekha* (1957), *Dil Deke Dekho* (1959), *Junglee* (1961), and *Kashmir ki Kali* (1964). He won the Filmfare Award for Best Actor for *Brahmachari* (1968). He also directed two films— *Manoranjan* (1974) and *Bundal Baaz* (1976)—and did character roles all the way till *Rockstar* (2011). He married actress Geeta Bali in a secret ceremony in 1955. After her death, he married Neela Devi Gohil in 1969.

SANGAM

1964

Raj Kapoor's first venture into the realm of color movies, *Sangam* was the biggest earner of 1964, and one of the first Hindi movies that was extensively shot abroad.

▼ A hopeful heart
In the song Har Dil Jo Pyar Karega (Every Heart That Loves), three childhood friends are reunited as adults, each intent on telling the other how they feel.

With a running time of nearly four hours, *Sangam* (Confluence) is an exceptionally long film. It was the first Hindi movie to have two intermissions. Filmmaker Raj Kapoor (see pp. 44–45) took his audiences on a grand tour of Europe, shot in glorious but expensive Technicolor. *Sangam* is loosely based on the 1894 novel by English writer Hall Caines, *The Manxman*, which was also adapted into a movie by English director Alfred Hitchcock in 1929. However, the story of *Sangam* was changed considerably to suit Indian tastes.

Raj Kapoor had offered the heroine's role (Radha) to actress Vyjayanthimala (see p. 94), but had not heard back from her in a while. This prompted him to send her a tongue-in-cheek telegram that read "Bol Radha bol, sangam hoga ki nahin?" (Tell me, Radha, if *Sangam* will happen or not). Upon hearing this anecdote, the film's lyricist Shailendra worked this question into the title song.

A LOVE TRIANGLE
The film tells the story of Sundar, a poor orphan, his best friend, Gopal, and the woman they both love, Radha. Gopal refuses to act on his feelings when Sundar tells him he loves Radha. But Radha, who loves Gopal, rejects Sundar, influenced by her family's disapproval of his aimless lifestyle.

In an effort to earn Radha's respect and affection, Sundar joins the Indian Air Force and goes off to fight in a war. During a mission, he goes missing and is presumed dead. Although filled with grief at the loss of their dear friend, Gopal and Radha are finally free to acknowledge their feelings for each other. The two are set to be married

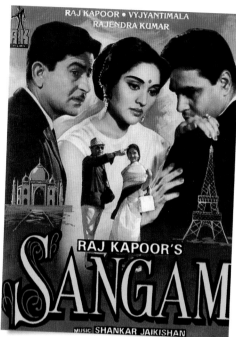

▲ **Triumphant trio**
Sangam had a winning cast. Raj Kapoor was still pulling in crowds at age 40, Vyjayanthimala was at the peak of her career, and Rajendra Kumar had so many long-running films that he was called "Jubilee Kumar."

when they learn that Sundar survived. Guilt-ridden at the thought of having been unfaithful to his friend's memory, Gopal practically pushes Radha into marrying Sundar.

Caught up in the idealization of his friendship and his love, Sundar is devastated when he finds an unsigned love letter to his wife. At times, Raj Kapoor's portrayal of the jealous husband makes him appear cruel as he suspects his blameless, distraught wife. While the situation ends in tragedy, there is some redemption for Sundar.

ABOVE AND BEYOND
Radha and Sundar's long honeymoon provided the context for some truly pioneering shots of foreign locations in Hindi films. The newly married couple visit London, Rome, Paris, and Switzerland. Radha embraces not only a marriage she had earlier resisted, but also foreign culture.

A Bharatnatyam dance expert, Vyjayanthimala traded her *ghungroos* (dancing bells) for dancing shoes to sway to the cabaret number "Mein Kya Karoon Ram." She also shed her

trademark sari to don a red swimsuit for the title track. Swimming around, assuring a highly persistent Kapoor that their "sangam" or union is not to be, Vyjayanthimala created a genuinely memorable movie moment.

Sangam featured the German–English song "Ich Leibe Dich, I Love You," during scenes of the hero and heroine's honeymoon. It was believed that the two were actually in a relationship at that point. However, the actress, has clarified in her memoirs that these rumors were encouraged by Raj Kapoor to generate interest in the movie.

CAST AWAY
When Raj Kapoor had initially conceptualized the film, under the working title *Gharonda*, he wanted to repeat the lead cast of *Andaz* (1949)—himself, Nargis (see p.57), and Dilip Kumar (see pp. 48–49). However, Dilip Kumar refused the role, and by the time work on *Sangam* eventually started, Nargis,

too, had walked out of the project. Raj Kapoor's character followed a similar arc in *Andaz* and *Sangam*. In both films he plays a flamboyant hero who is passionately in love with the heroine but becomes deeply unbalanced with jealousy, suspecting her of infidelity. Raj Kapoor won the Filmfare Awards for Best Director and Best Editing, while Vyjayanthimala took home the Best Actress title for this film.

> ## "Raj Kapoor's first foray into color ... the film was ... a visual seduction all the way."
>
> **RITU NANDA,** *RAJ KAPOOR SPEAKS,* 2002

CAST AND CREW

- ★ **Raj Kapoor** Sundar Khanna
- **Vyjayanthimala** Radha
- **Rajendra Kumar** Gopal Verma
- **Hari Shivdasani** Captain
- **Iftekhar** Indian Air Force Officer
- **Raj Mehra** Judge Mehra

- 🎬 **Director** Raj Kapoor
- 🎞 **Producer** Raj Kapoor
- 🎵 **Music composers** Shankar Singh Raghuvanshi, Jaikishan Dayabhai. Panchal
- 🎵 **Lyricists** Shailendra, Hasrat Jaipuri
- 📖 **Scriptwriter** Inder Raj Anand
- 🎥 **Cinematographer** Radhu Karmakar

▶ **Vacationing in Venice**
Seen here taking a gondola ride in Venice, Radha and Sundar travel to many European destinations, taking in activites such as a shopping spree in Paris and sledding in Switzerland.

THE BOLD
AND THE BEAUTIFUL

In the 1960s, leading ladies of the silver screen were cosmopolitan and free like never before, ushering in a new kind of heroine in Indian cinema.

The 1960s saw a slew of star heroines playing young, independent women who routinely stepped outside the bounds of strict Indian social conventions. On-screen women spent unchaperoned holidays at hill stations and went on solo overseas adventures.

This treatment, however, was a sharp departure from the standard Bollywood portrayal of women in films. In the 1949 film *Andaz*, Nargis plays a wealthy socialite who goes horseback riding and is comfortable making male friends, but has to repent her lifestyle in the end. Even as late as the 1995 hit, *Dilwale Dulhaniya Le Jayenge* (see pp. 230–233), Kajol's character Simran had to tearfully beg her father to let her go on a trip to Europe with friends.

DARING DIVAS

In 1960s' Bollywood, many of the leading ladies depicted women who enjoyed lives full of fun, choosing picnics and parties over being a homebody. Nutan, for instance, goes to watch a cabaret performance with her brother in *Tere Ghar Ke Saamne* (1963); Asha Parekh rock-and-rolls in *Teesri*

Manzil (see p.93); and Tanuja gets behind the wheel and drives through city streets with panache in *Jewel Thief* (see p.94). Equally revolutionary was Suchitra Sen's character in *Mamta* (1966), who studies law in the UK, a privilege usually reserved for men. Meena Kumari's open expression of desire for her husband in *Sahib Bibi Aur Ghulam* (see pp. 90–91), as was Waheeda Rehman's Rosie, who leaves her husband to begin a live-in relationship in *Guide* (see pp. 84–87).

This spirit of empowerment found expression in their sartorial choices. Churidars and kurtas were well-fitted, saris were tightly wound around daring blouses, while trousers appeared routinely. The taboo of women drinking was also bucked with Tanuja inviting Dev Anand on a picnic in *Jewel Thief*: "I'll get some food packed ... and we'll get some bottles of beer!" Even the famously traditional Vyjayanthimala flaunted black tights with feathers in a faux cabaret, and drank cognac in chilly Switzerland in *Sangam* (see pp. 80–81).

But, perhaps no one made waves the way Sharmila Tagore did in her role as the coquettish Deepa/Suzy in *An Evening in Paris* (see p. 95), smoking a cigarette and wearing a swimsuit. The celebration of female beauty, sex appeal, and glamour continued well into the 1970s, through stars such as Zeenat Aman and Parveen Babi.

◀ **Headturner**
Bold, unconventional, and defiant, a 22-year-old Sharmila Tagore raised eyebrows as she brazenly waterskied while wearing a racy one-piece swimsuit in the film *An Evening in Paris*.

"[Wearing a bikini] was so frowned upon during my time... it's still considered a big deal."

SHARMILA TAGORE, IN AN INTERVIEW WITH REDIFF.COM, DECEMBER 8, 2014

GUIDE

Guide broke from Bollywood conventions by portraying an adulterous heroine, a live-in relationship, and a spiritual rather than romantic resolution. It became a Hindi cinema classic.

DEV ANAND • WAHEEDA REHMAN

Nav Ketan International's

guide

EASTMAN COLOR

PROCESSED • PRINTED IN
NEW YORK

DIRECTED BY VIJAY ANAND MUSIC S.D. BURMAN

The controversial *Guide* became one of Hindi cinema's most talked about films. This was actor–producer Dev Anand's audacious venture into international markets, with the film being made in English and Hindi. In a departure from mainstream Bollywood storylines, the film's heroine, Rosie, was married, separated, and living in sin. But such a gamble was not unexpected from Navketan Films, which had a history of breaking new ground.

CAST AND CREW

★ **Dev Anand** Raju
Waheeda Rehman Rosie Marco/ Miss Nalini
Leela Chitnis Raju's mother
Kishore Sahu Marco
Gajanan Jagirdar Bhola
Anwar Hussain Gaffoor
Ulhas Raju's uncle (Mamaji)

🎬 **Director** Vijay Anand
⬡ **Producer** Dev Anand
♫ **Music** S.D. Burman
𝄞 **Lyrics** Shailendra
🕺 **Choreography** Hiralal, Sohanlal
📖 **Scriptwriter** Vijay Anand
🎥 **Cinematographer** Fali Mistry
👔 **Costume** Bhanu Athaiya, Vishwanath

GOING INTERNATIONAL
Polish-American director Tad Danielewski and Dev Anand were in talks about the possibility of collaborative projects, when Dev proposed turning R.K. Narayan's book *The Guide* (1958) into a film. The original idea was to simultaneously shoot two versions—one in English, directed by Danielewski, and another in Hindi, directed by Dev's brother Chetan Anand. The cast was to remain the same. Nobel prize-winning American author, Pearl S. Buck, was entrusted with adapting the novel into an English script. She would also be responsible for polishing the English diction of the female lead Waheeda Rehman. However, simultaneous filming of the two versions proved

problematic. Not only did it involve doing the same shot over and over again, but the two directors also had very different filming sensibilities. They disagreed on everything from the placement of the cameras to scene interpretation. Eventually, the English version was shot first. When Chetan quit the film to work on his dream project *Haqeeqat* (1964), the youngest Anand brother, Vijay, stepped in as director.

It is rumored that Vijay only agreed to come on board the project if its script was overhauled to tone down the adult content—thereby deviating from R.K. Narayan's story. His version also did away with an extraneous tiger fight scene, which had been included purely to pander to Western stereotyping of the exotic East. The English *Guide* struggled to make an impact, except for Waheeda Rehman winning a Best Actress award at the 1965 Chicago Film Festival. However, the Hindi version went on to create celluloid history.

◀ **Of love and redemption**
Guide is as much a story about love as about the flawed hero Raju, played by Dev Anand, making mistakes and finding redemption.

WRITER DISCONTENTED
Author R.K. Narayan went on record to express his unhappiness with the Hindi film adaptation of his work. He voiced his discontent in an

This classic film is also remarkable for its sensitive portrayal of a woman's need for sexual freedom."

BHAICHAND PATEL, IN *BOLLYWOOD'S TOP 20,* 2012

◄ **An actress's dilemma**
Waheeda Rehman had been told that by taking the role of the adulterous Rosie, she was committing professional suicide, but she was convinced about the film.

it the go-ahead for distribution. This brought Dev to yet another hurdle: distributors were jittery about the subject of the film. Some of the credit for the film's release goes to the hard work of the film's production controller Yash Johar, father of director Karan Johar (see pp. 248–49).

Following the film's opening, initial critical reactions were mixed and box-office takings discouraging. But as word-of-mouth publicity spread, a curious audience started coming in to the theaters and soon *Guide* became a hit. Vindication came when the movie swept the Filmfare Awards for the Best Film, Director, Dialogue, Story, Actor, Actress, and Color Cinematography. It has since become a classic.

MOVING MUSIC
Although composer S.D. Burman's music for *Guide* was passed over for awards, it is considered one of his finest scores. Burman had been in-house composer at Navketan, the Anand brothers' production house, for 15 years. He fell ill while working on the music of *Guide*, bringing the soundtrack's production to a standstill. However, Dev was adamant that he would wait for however long it took Burman to

recover, or release *Guide* with just the one song that had been recorded by that point. His wait lasted several months, but every song of the film justifies his decision.

DEMANDING DANCE ROUTINES
Under choreographer Hiralal, Waheeda Rehman delivered dance numbers that became a benchmark in the industry. A trained Bharatnatyam dancer, she was put through her paces in this depiction of a dancer. In an interview, Rehman revealed that rigorous rehearsing for the snake dance routine in the film left her in so much pain that she could barely walk for days. A lyricless piece, the dance sequence depends solely on her dancing skills and expressions to communicate a myriad of emotions—from happiness at being able to dance to the desperation of being trapped in a loveless marriage.

article written for *Life* magazine titled "How a Famous Novel Became an Infamous Film." Narayan was annoyed that the views expressed in his original work and its plot had been ignored. He was also concerned that the story's setting had been shifted from his fictional small town of Malgudi to bustling Udaipur. Finally, the ambiguous ending of his novel had been completely changed to make a hero out of the dying swami, whose selfless fast not only brings him divine enlightenment, but also produces welcome rain to the drought-struck

village. Despite all these changes, Narayan went on to win the Filmfare Best Story Award for the film.

OVERCOMING OBSTACLES
In India, naysayers had three problems with the project: that the heroine was adulterous, that the hero died at the end, and that urbane charmer Dev was playing a devout swami. The threat of offending people's sensibilities was serious enough for Dev to request the Information and Broadcasting Minister at the time, Indira Gandhi, to see the film for herself. She gave the film the necessary clearances, allowing

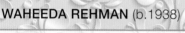

WAHEEDA REHMAN (b.1938)

Often described as Bollywood's most graceful actress, Waheeda Rehman is celebrated for her acting skills and for being a superb dancer. The Hyderabad-based actress began her career in Telugu and Tamil films. Guru Dutt introduced her as a second lead in *C.I.D.* (1956) and as his heroine in films such as *Pyaasa* (see p. 54) and *Kaagaz ke Phool* (see p. 65). She was believed to be his love interest and muse. Rehman received a National Award for Best Actress (*Reshma aur Shera*), two Filmfare Awards for Best Actress (*Guide, Neel Kamal*), and a Padma Bhushan—the third-highest civilian award in India. In later years, she played the roles of older women—such as mother and guardian—in movies like *Namak Halaal* (1982) and *Lamhe* (1991).

► **Unlikely guru**
Dev Anand played a man forced into becoming a spiritual guru by the faith of simple villagers. Anand said that he discovered his ascetic self while shooting the ending, in which his character finds enlightenment.

STORYLINE

Raju, a glib, street-smart tourist guide in Udaipur, Rajasthan, is entrusted with the task of showing around Rosie. Trapped in a loveless marriage, not allowed to follow her passion for dance, Rosie is on the brink of despair. The two grow closer and, against all odds, fall in love. Raju helps Rosie establish herself as a dancer, but with Rosie's growing success, he becomes greedy and self-centered. The two grow apart but eventually Raju redeems himself in a most unexpected way.

RAJU GUIDES TOURISTS
AROUND UDAIPUR

THE PRESENT

THE PAST

PLOT OVERVIEW

Raju is released from prison six months early. At a crossroads in his life, he feels he cannot return home as there is nothing there for him. He sets out on an aimless journey ❶ and ends up in a remote village where the locals mistake him for a holy man. He does nothing to correct their misconception, as he is revered and cared for by the village folk. When his mother and Rosie arrive at the prison six months later, he is long gone. His mother holds Rosie responsible for having alienated her son. Rosie takes this opportunity to tell his mother her side of the story.

A renowned guide in Udaipur, Rajasthan, Raju is sought out by an archaeologist, Marco, to show him and his wife, Rosie, around the city ❷. Trapped in a loveless marriage and denied her passion of dancing, Rosie makes several attempts at committing suicide. For this, she is chastized by her husband and counseled by Raju.

Rosie leaves her cheating husband and moves in with Raju ❸. This creates a rift between Raju and his family and friends as they do not support his relationship with a married woman. He throws himself into making Rosie's dreams of succeeding as a dancer come true ❹.

A talented dancer, Rosie takes the dance world by storm as Miss Nalini. She achieves fame and fortune doing what she loves most.

The relationship between Rosie and Raju deepens ❺. He works as her manager to ensure her success and their prosperity.

❶ ❷ ❸ ❹ ❺

THE SONGS

Wahan Kaun Hai Tera Musafir
(Traveler, Who Do You Know There)
Singer: S.D. Burman
Picturized on Raju

Aaj Phir Jeene ki tamanna he
(I Wish to Live Again)
Singer: Lata Mangeshkar
Picturized on Rosie and Raju

Tere Mere Sapne ab ek Rang Hain
(Our Dreams are Now the Same)
Singer: Mohammed Rafi
Picturized on Rosie and Raju

Piya Tose Naina Lage Re
(Beloved, Our Eyes Have Locked)
Singer: Lata Mangeshkar,
Picturized on Rosie

Gaata Rahe Mera Dil
(My Heart Keeps Singing)
Singer: Kishore Kumar
Picturized on Rosie and Raju

⭐ *Director Vijay Anand's innovative, low-angle tracking shots of Waheeda Rehman dancing on the wall of Chittor Fort are still shown in film studies classes.*

ROSIE AND RAJU SIGHTSEEING
IN UDAIPUR, RAJASTHAN

THE FILM'S LEADS IN
"GAATA RAHE MERA DIL"

VIJAY ANAND (1934–2004)

A long with elder brothers Dev and Chetan, Vijay Anand was a pillar of Navketan productions. An accomplished director, writer, and editor, he made his directorial debut with *Nau do Gyarah* (1957). He is most acclaimed for his stylish shot framing, especially in dance sequences. *Guide, Teesri Manzil* (1966), *Jewel Thief* (1967), and *Johny Mera Naam* (1970) were his most renowned films. His personal life attracted some controversy when he married his niece. He died of a heart attack in 2004.

RAJU AND ROSIE'S LOVE GROWS DEEPER

THE PAST

Raju falls prey to the trappings of success, gambling and drinking away Rosie's hard-earned money. She begins resenting him living off her earnings and says as much to him. The growing distance between them soon seems insurmountable ❻ . When a repentant Marco tries to re-establish contact with Rosie, Raju works to prevent it. To this end, he forges her signature on documents releasing Rosie's jewels that were in her joint account with Marco. Rosie realizes that Raju has been keeping Marco at bay, and resents him further.

Raju's crime is discovered ❼❽ and he is sentenced to three years in prison for forgery. Raju and Rosie realize that they have let misunderstanding ruin their relationship.

RETURN TO THE PRESENT

The village that reveres Raju as a holy man is wracked by drought. The villagers are divided, fighting with each other over rations. A series of misunderstandings leads the villagers to believe that Raju has volunteered to fast for 12 days to appease the gods and usher in rains ❾ .

Raju's fast attracts widespread attention and appears in the papers. His mother and Rosie travel to see him ❿ . He is momentarily tempted to end his fast, as his life seems worth living again. But a sense of responsibility to the blind faith that a community has placed in him wins over selfish concerns ⓫ . The arrival of the rains coincides with his death.

❻ ❼ ❽ ❾ ❿ ⓫

Din Dhal Jaye (When the Day Draws to a Close) *Singer: Mohammed Rafi* *Picturized on Rosie and Raju*

Saiyyan Beimaan (Dishonest Beloved) *Singer: Lata Mangeshkar* *Picturized on Rosie*

Kya Se Kya Ho Gaya (How Things Have Changed) *Singer: Mohammed Rafi* *Picturized on Raju*

Tere Mere Sapne Ab Ek Rang Hain (Our Dreams are Now the Same) *Singer: Mohammed Rafi* *Picturized on Rosie and Raju*

Allah Megh De Paani De (God, Let It Rain and Pour) *Singer: S.D. Burman* *Picturized on Raju and village folk*

This song was adapted from a Bengali song by Bangladeshi folk singer Abbasuddin Ahmed.

Hey Ram (Oh God) *Singer: Manna Dey* *Picturized on Raju, Rosie, and village-folk*

WAHEEDA REHMAN DANCING TO "SAIYYAN BEIMAAN"

"Shot in… Udaipur, Guide *was poetry on celluloid.*"

RANJAN DAS GUPTA, REVIEWER, IN *THE HINDU*, 2015

DEV ANAND

ACTOR–DIRECTOR **1923–2011**

One of Bollywood's most flamboyant stars, Dev Anand is remembered for his romantic persona and a remarkable body of work. His stylish mannerisms, his love affairs, his black suit that made women swoon, all became part of his legend.

▲ Movie poster for *Taxi Driver*
A highlight of Dev Anand's movie career, *Taxi Driver* was directed by his brother Chetan Anand. It was such a hit that the taxi used in the film—a British Hillman Minx model—became the car most used as taxis in Mumbai until the 1970s.

I n his 2007 memoir, *Romancing with Life*, the 82-year old Dev Anand wrote about looking forward to making his next movie. He had just released his film *Mr. Prime Minister* (2005) and said he was "all excited again, just like a newcomer..." Such optimism and zest for filmmaking were hallmarks of the legendary actor, director, and producer. Dev Anand led a rich and dynamic life, traveled throughout India and all over the world to shoot his films, attend festivals, and participate in goodwill delegations. He also mingled with show business icons including Charlie Chaplin, Frank Capra, and Shirley Maclaine, as well as statesmen such as India's first prime minister, Jawaharlal Nehru. He was also politically active, campaigning against the State of Emergency in 1975, and forming the National Party of India, which he later disbanded.
For most viewers, however, Dev Anand was the lovable and charismatic screen star of the 1950s–1970s. This period exists in

◀ **Sophistication incarnate**
Throughout his career, the stylish and debonair Dev Anand was the poster boy of romantic heroes, presenting to the world a carefully crafted public image of youth, glamour, and urbanity.

isolation from his later work as an actor–director, when—in the last decades of his life—he made 12 poorly received movies. Despite this, he always remained dedicated to the craft of filmmaking.

A LEGEND IS BORN
The great entertainer was born as Dharam Dev Pishorimal Anand, the son of a successful lawyer in pre-Partition Punjab. After obtaining a Bachelor of Arts degree from Government College, Lahore, Dev Anand followed his older brother, Chetan, to Mumbai in the early 1940s.

"He seems to say, how can you not love me, I am Dev Anand!"

JAVED AKHTAR, *ZEE CLASSIC LEGENDS,* 2012

KEY WORKS

Ziddi, 1948

Baazi, 1951

Taxi Driver, 1954

C.I.D., (see p. 51)

Kala Bazaar, 1960

Teen Deviyan,1965

Guide (see pp. 84–85)

Jewel Thief (see p. 94)

Johny Mera Naam, 1970

Hare Rama Hare Krishna, (see p. 108)

Des Pardes, 1978

There, he mixed with Chetan's friends and the intellectuals of the Indian Peoples' Theatre Association (IPTA), lived with the novelist Raja Rao, and worked for a short while at the military censor's office at Churchgate. His charm and good looks bagged him his first big break with *Hum Ek Hain* (1946) by Prabhat Talkies. Two years later, he shot to stardom with the hit film *Ziddi*, which also launched the careers of several other legends. This group would continue to be Dev Anand's lifetime collaborators—the playback singers Kishore Kumar (see pp. 100–101) and Lata Mangeshkar (see pp. 60–61), plus the character actor Pran (see p. 125).

STAR-CROSSED LOVERS

In 1948, Dev Anand made seven films with the actress Suraiya, the acclaimed singer–actress of Hindi cinema. However, their four-year off-screen romance faced stiff opposition from Suraiya's family. They decided to elope, but their plans were foiled and the two stars ultimately separated.

While Suraiya never recovered from the tumultuous episode and remained single for the rest of her life, the heartbroken Dev Anand eventually moved on. In 1954, he married actress Kalpana Kartik, with whom he acted in six films, including the hit *Taxi Driver*. They had two children—son Suneil and daughter Devina.

NAVKETAN AT ITS PEAK

In 1949, Dev Anand launched his film company, Navketan. The creative energy of the three Anand brothers,

▶ **Brothers collaborate**

Dev Anand (center) and brother Vijay Anand (second from right), along with the other crew members, including Hema Malini (far left) and producer Gulshan Rai, were awarded the Silver Jubilee Trophy for the film *Johny Mera Naam*.

▶ **Lauching stars**

Dev Anand's *Hare Rama Hare Krishna*, set against the 1970s hippie culture in India, launched the career of the celebrated actress Zeenat Aman, who played the role of a drug addict.

Chetan, Dev, and Vijay (see p. 87), broke new ground under this banner. They gathered together a powerhouse of talent who became big names in the film industry, including music composer S.D. Burman, lyricist Sahir Ludhianvi, director Guru Dutt (see pp. 66–67), and cinematographers Jal and Fali Mistry. With their second film, *Baazi*, Navketan found its voice in the stories of urban lives, featuring young antiheroes trying to make it in a cutthroat world. Films such as *Baazi*, *Taxi Driver*, *Kala Bazaar*, and *House No. 44* (1955) showed Dev Anand playing small-time gamblers or black marketeers. Sharp dialogue, dramatic plays of light and shadow, and an edgy, urban feel characterized these movies, while also expanding the language of Hindi cinema. When the brothers Vijay and Dev Anand partnered up—as director and actor, respectively—the success of the screen star's flamboyant romantic image reached its peak.

A HERO LIKE NO OTHER

Dev Anand's irresistible charisma made hits of movies such as *Hum Dono* (1955), *Guide*, *Jewel Thief*, and *Tere Mere Sapne* (1971). Still, he continued to act in films not made by his studio

including *Munimji* (1955), *C.I.D.*, *Asli Naqli* (1962), *Teen Deviyan*, and *Johny Mera Naam*. Along with Dilip Kumar and Raj Kapoor, he was counted among the golden trio that ruled the screen for much of the 1950s and 1960s. During this period, he became known for his lover-boy persona, fast delivery of dialogue, and rock-star swagger.

THE MAN, THE LEGACY

From 1970, Dev Anand started to direct films, too. *Hare Rama Hare Krishna* (1971) launched the career of actress Zeenat Aman (see p. 156) and *Des Pardes* (1978) introduced audiences to the screen siren Tina Munim. They were both significant movies, but such successes were few and far between.

By the time he died of a cardiac arrest in London in 2011, Dev Anand had acted in 114 films over a career spanning 65 years and—at the age of 88—was planning his next movie. Today, he is best remembered for his relentless positivity and unwavering love for the silver screen.

TIMELINE

September 26, 1923 Born Dharam Dev Pishorimal Anand in the Gurdaspur district, Punjab.

1943 Moves to Mumbai to pursue acting.

1946 Bags his first film with Prabhat Talkies, *Hum Ek Hain*.

1948 Stars in his breakthrough film, *Ziddi* after being spotted by actor Ashok Kumar. Begins his long professional association with singer Kishore Kumar.

1948–51 Gets romantically involved with actress Suraiya while filming *Vidya*.

1949 Sets up his production house, Navketan, with his older brother, Chetan.

1954 Marries actress Kalpana Kartik, his co-star from *Taxi Driver*.

1958 Wins the Filmfare Award for Best Actor for his performance in *Kala Pani*.

1962–65 Makes *Guide*, an Indian-US co-production in Hindi and English.

MOVIE POSTER FOR *PREM PUJARI*

1970 Makes his directorial debut with *Prem Pujari*, which fails at the box office.

1978 Acts in his last hit film, *Des Pardes*, in which he launches actress Tina Munim.

1980s–2011 Directs and acts in multiple films, but they fail commercially.

2001 Receives the Padma Bhushan Award for his contribution to Indian cinema.

2002 Is awarded the prestigious Dadasaheb Phalke Award.

2007 Publishes his autobiography, titled *Romancing with Life*.

December 3, 2011 Dies of a heart attack in London, UK.

SAHIB BIBI AUR GHULAM

With its haunting cinematography, unforgettable soundtrack, and mesmerizing performance by lead actress Meena Kumari, *Sahib Bibi aur Ghulam* is one of Bollywood's finest films.

CAST AND CREW

- ★ **Meena Kumari** Chhoti Bahu
  Guru Dutt Atulya Chakraborty "Bhootnath"
  Waheeda Rehman Jaba
  Rehman Chhote Sarkar
  Nasir Hussain Suvinoy Babu
  Dhumal Bansi

- 🎬 **Director** Abrar Alvi
- 🎩 **Producer** Guru Dutt
- 🎵 **Music composer** Hemant Kumar
- 🎵 **Lyricist** Shakeel Badayuni
- 🕺 **Choreographers** Sohanlal, Sudarshan Kumar
- 📖 **Scriptwriter** Abrar Alvi
- 📷 **Cinematographer** V.K. Murthy
- 👔 **Costume designer** Bhanu Athaiya

Based on the Bengali novel *Shaheb Bibi Golam* by Bimal Mitra, this film cemented Guru Dutt's reputation as one of Bollywood's great filmmakers. Dutt produced and acted in the film, and also directed the songs. Whether or not he also "ghost directed" the film has remained an unsolved mystery of Hindi cinema.

In a shift from Dutt's earlier work, *Sahib Bibi aur Ghulam* (The Master, the Wife, and the Servant) moved away from portraying the despair of a self-destructive hero and instead focused on an enigmatic heroine. The film is synonymous with the character of Chhoti Bahu, often regarded as a mirror image of lead actress Meena Kumari, who in later life, like Chhoti Bahu, also became an alcoholic.

In addition to a National Award, *Sahib Bibi aur Ghulam* won the Filmfare Awards for Best Director,

Best Cinematographer, and Best Actress. It was also nominated for the Golden Bear at the 13th Berlin International Film Festival in 1963.

MAKING A CLASSIC

Although the directorial credit for the film goes to Guru Dutt's longtime friend and confidant Abrar Alvi, the film remains inextricably entwined with Dutt's name and legend. Popular belief has it that after the failure of *Kaagaz ke Phool* (see p. 65), Dutt decided not to put his name against a film again, and the credit for direction went to Alvi, who also wrote the screenplay. Neither Alvi nor Dutt, nor any other member of the cast or crew, ever spoke about this matter.

A WALK THROUGH TIME

The film opens with the scene of a desolate mansion being torn down. At the site, Bhootnath—a suave, well-dressed man—is seen reminiscing about his past. There is then a flashback to Bhootnath arriving at the splendid mansion of the Chaudhury family, where he is staying. A simple yet

educated village lad, Bhootnath has come to the city to find work, and he is soon employed at Mohini Sindoor, a vermilion factory. Here he becomes fascinated by his employer's daughter Jaba, a spirited and flirtatious young woman who teases him. At the same time, he starts to observe the members of the aristocratic family with whom he is living, and their many eccentricities.

Chhoti Bahu is the young wife of the second son of the Chaudhury household. She pines for the love of her husband, Chhote Sarkar, who spends most of his time with a courtesan. The film is centered on the complex, yet platonic, relationship between Bhootnath and Chhoti Bahu, whom he first meets when she secretly summons him to her private chamber. Chhoti Bahu asks him to fetch her a tin of vermilion, believing the claims made in advertisements that it can inspire attraction in indifferent lovers. When the vermilion does not work, Chhoti Bahu becomes her husband's drinking companion to keep him by her side. She asks a reluctant Bhootnath, who has gradually become

Kaagaz ke Phool (see p. 65)

HIT SONGS

Na Jao Saiyan
(Don't Leave, My Love)
 Singer Geeta Dutt

Meri Jaan, O Meri Jaan
(My Love, O My Love)
 Singer Asha Bhosle

◄ **Reel and real life**
Portraying a couple whose marriage was arranged in their infancy, Guru Dutt and Waheeda Rehman were rumored to be in a relationship in real life.

" It's funny … I have become Chhoti Bahu in real life."

MEENA KUMARI, QUOTED IN *MEENA KUMARI: THE CLASSIC BIOGRAPHY*, 1972, BY VINOD MEHTA

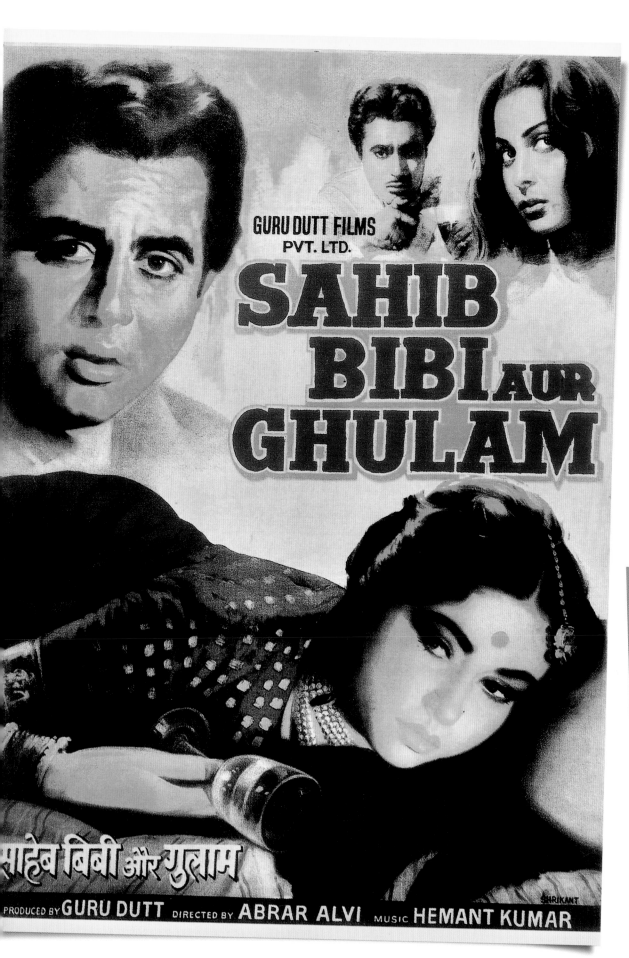

GURU DUTT FILMS
PVT. LTD.

SAHIB
BIBI AUR
GHULAM

साहेब बिबी और गुलाम

PRODUCED BY **GURU DUTT**   DIRECTED BY **ABRAR ALVI**   MUSIC **HEMANT KUMAR**

◀ **Break from the past**
The female lead of the film is shown to be an alcoholic, and openly expresses her desire for her husband who neglects her. These were radical subjects for Hindi films of the time.

her confidant, to supply her with alcohol, and he is forced to watch in despair as she sinks into alcoholism.

Bhootnath eventually grows close to Jaba, joins a construction firm, and leaves town. Some time later, the Chaudhury family are cheated of their wealth.

Many years later, when a middle-aged Bhootnath—accompanied by his wife, Jaba—comes to supervise the destruction of the mansion he had once observed so closely, the fate of Chhoti Bahu is revealed.

CASTING CHOICES
The role of Bhootnath was initially offered to Shashi Kapoor, but when he turned it down Dutt decided to play the part himself. It is said that Waheeda Rehman, who was then commonly cast in Dutt's films—and was said to be his love—wanted to play Chhoti Bahu's character. However, she looked far too young for the part, and so the role went to Meena Kumari, while Waheeda accepted the role of Jaba.

MEENA KUMARI
(1933–72)

Born Mahjabeen Bano, Meena Kumari was a child artist before she became a heroine at the age of 14. Her big break came in 1952 with *Baiju Bawra*, for which she won the Filmfare Award for Best Actress. After a series of hit films, she made history by landing three nominations for the Filmfare Award for Best Actress in 1963—she won the award for *Sahib Bibi aur Ghulam*. She was also an Urdu poet, and a collection of her poetry titled *Tanha Chand* was published posthumously. In 1952, she married film director and screenwriter Kamal Amrohi, but they separated in 1964. Meena took to drinking, and died of cirrhosis of the liver in 1972.

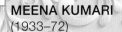

WAQT

1965

The highest-grossing movie of 1965, *Waqt* pioneered the genre of dramatic multi-star sagas involving families who are separated and reunited at the end.

Director Yash Chopra (see pp. 166–67) and his brother, producer B.R. Chopra, got together to create this story about the vagaries of time and the significance of destiny. A well-cast ensemble playing three heroes and two heroines, plus several other senior actors, all put in stellar performances. The urbane dignity of Raaj Kumar (see p. 117) balanced Sunil Dutt's flamboyance and Shashi Kapoor's quiet suffering, while the heroines, Sadhana and Sharmila Tagore (see p. 103), became fashion trendsetters with their tightly fitted churidar-kurtas and glamorously draped saris.

TWISTS AND TURNS

Waqt (Time) is the tale of how Lala Kedarnath, a prosperous businessman and father of three sons, is humbled by fate. He loses his wealth and

▲ Lost in love
One of the film's tropes is the brothers' complicated love stories. While Raja and Ravi vie for the affection of the same woman, Vijay stifles his feelings for the wealthy woman he loves.

becomes separated from his family in an earthquake. His eldest son, Raja, grows up to become a criminal in the employ of sophisticated villain Chinoy Seth. The second son, Ravi, is adopted by a rich couple and becomes a lawyer when he grows up. The third, Vijay, lives a life of poverty with his mother. Their distraught father's search for his family is put on hold when he is arrested for murder. All grown up, the three brothers find themselves thrown together by circumstance when Chinoy Seth frames Raja for murder. Ravi defends him but Vijay has been bribed to testify against him, and Raja's fate seems sealed. However, time deals the estranged brothers yet another hand.

WINNING FORMULA

Waqt's music was very popular. Singer Manna Dey's ode to vitality despite advancing years, "Ai Meri Zohrajabeen" (O My Beloved), is a song that never ages. Similarly, songstress Asha Bhosle's "Aage Bhi Jane Na Tu"

(You Don't Know What Lies Ahead) is another timeless melody that extols living in the moment. Some of *Waqt's* dialogues were equally famous.

The film won Filmfare Awards for Best Director (Yash Chopra), Best Supporting Actor (Raaj Kumar), Best Story (F.A. Mirza), and Best Dialogue (Akhtar ul Iman). This runaway hit, Chopra's third film, was just another stepping stone on the director's journey.

OPULENCE DEFINED

Waqt gave Bollywood many markers for depicting opulent urban lifestyles, including colorful sitting rooms of pink, red, and blue, and leisure time spent at swimming pools. It also featured American sports cars and convertibles, from the cute open-top that Renu drove to college to the imposing Buick Roadmaster that Vijay ferried Chinoy Seth's family and friends around in, not forgetting the yellow 1961 Austin Healey Sprite and red 1961 Fiat 1200 Spyder raced by Ravi and Raja respectively.

THE LOST AND FOUND THEME

With Nargis's debut, *Taqdeer* (1943), and Ashok Kumar's superhit *Kismet* (see pp. 30–33), movies fell in love with the idea of a child getting lost and being found in adulthood. *Waqt* discovered and *Yaadon ki Baarat* (1973) confirmed that several siblings getting lost and found would be even more exciting for audiences. Whether it was separation due to natural disasters or kidnapping, Bollywood explored it all. With *Amar Akbar Anthony* (see pp. 148–49), the formula peaked in 1977, and eventually died out in the 1980s.

▶ A popular pair
After their hit pairing in *Waqt*, Shashi Kapoor (left) and Sharmila Tagore (right) were seen in films such as *Suhana Safar* (1970) and *Aa Gale lag Jaa* (1973). The two appeared together in 10 films in three decades.

CAST AND CREW

★ **Raaj Kumar** Raja
Sunil Dutt Ravi
Balraj Sahni Lala Kedarnath
Sadhana Meena
Shashi Kapoor Vijay
Sharmila Tagore Renu
Rehman Chinoy Seth

Director Yash Chopra
Producer B.R. Chopra
Music composer Ravi
Lyricist Sahir Ludhianvi
Script writer F.A. Mirza
Cinematographer Dharam Chopra
Costume designer Bhanu Athaiya

TEESRI MANZIL

1966

With a gripping mystery at its core, *Teesri Manzil* also has fun dance numbers by Shammi Kapoor and Helen, and groundbreaking music by a young R.D. Burman.

◄ Musical thriller
This classic weaves together the elements of the lead pair's love story, the crime plot, cult hit songs, and a surprise ending.

D irector Vijay Anand's *Teesri Manzil* (The Third Floor) is a suspense thriller. Producer Nasir Hussain had initially signed actor Dev Anand (see pp. 88–89 for the film. However, when the two fell out, Hussain went with his other favorite actor, Shammi Kapoor (see p. 79). When Shammi's wife, actress Geeta Bali, passed away during filming, the grieving star stopped shooting for months. It was only after much coaxing that Shammi returned to shoot the song "Tumne Mujhe Dekha" (When You Looked at Me).

MURDER MYSTERY
The film opens with a woman (later identified as Rupa) running into a hotel and climbing up three storeys, from where she falls to her death. Reading Rupa's letters, her sister Sunita becomes convinced that Rupa committed suicide because she was being taken advantage of by Rocky, a drum player in a hotel in Mussoorie, Uttarakhand. Intent on exacting revenge, Sunita travels from New Delhi to Mussoorie. Anil, whose stage name is Rocky, overhears Sunita's plans for him and hides his real identity from her. They end up falling in love with each other. When the police disclose that Rupa was, in fact, murdered, the story takes an unexpected turn.

TRENDSETTING TUNES
From the frenetic percussion at the start of "O Haseena Zulfon Wali" to the gasping "Aaja Aaja," this film is peppered with evergreen hits. With the dramatic combination of bongo drums, trumpets, saxophones, and guitars in an entirely new flavor of orchestration, music composer R.D. Burman (see p. 109) arrived on the film scene with a considerable flourish, but not without some difficulty. Shammi usually preferred the work of Shankar–Jaikishan, but was persuaded to give R.D. Burman an audition. After he heard several of Burman's tunes, Shammi agreed to have him come on board.

While *Teesri Manzil*'s rock 'n' roll-based songs have become more popular with time, the big hit of that year was the melodious "O Mere Sona Re Sona" (Oh My Beloved), which director Anand shot with his characteristically innovative framing.

DANCE DUO
Matching the music beat for beat was the film's choreography. While P.L. Raj was Helen's regular choreographer, it is said that "Aaja Aaja" was choreographed by Harman Benjamin, who specialized in high-energy nightclub numbers.

► Shake it like Shammi
Anil (Shammi Kapoor) woos Sunita (Asha Parekh) with songs, including the catchy "O Haseena Zulfon Vaali" (O Beauty with the Beautiful Hair), until she finally falls in love with him.

> "A murder mystery with large dollops of humor and music."
>
> **ASHOK RAJ**, *HERO, VOLUME 1,* 2010

HIT SONG

Aaja Aaja
(Come to Me)
🎤 **Singers** Mohammed Rafi, Asha Bhosle

JEWEL THIEF

| 1967 |

CAST AND CREW

★ **Dev Anand** Vinay / Amar
Vyjayanthimala Shalini
Ashok Kumar Shalini's brother
Sapru Vishambhar Nath
Tanuja Anjali
Nazir Hussain Police commissioner

📷 **Director** Vijay Anand
⌂ **Producer** Dev Anand
🎵 **Music composer** S.D. Burman
♪ **Lyricist** Majrooh Sultanpuri, Shailendra
🕴 **Choreographer** Sohanlal
📖 **Scriptwriter** Vijay Anand
🎥 **Cinematographer** V. Ratna
👕 **Costume designer** Mani Rabadi

Writer-director Vijay Anand's tautly crafted suspense thriller had everything going for it—a clever script, popular stars, hit songs, and one of Bollywood's best climactic twists.

J ewel Thief was a runaway commercial success that is still studied by cinema students keen to understand its secret. The film's success is mainly attributed to writer–director Vijay Anand's mastery of his craft. Timely twists in the story, heightened by innovative camerawork, sharp editing, and evocative background music, kept the audience glued to the edge of their seats. An added appeal was the parts of the film that were shot in Sikkim, then an independent kingdom, and an exotic, international location for the Indian audience.

"Jewel Thief became a huge hit," wrote the film's star, actor Dev Anand (see pp. 88–89), in his autobiography

Romancing with Life (2007). "I flew to Delhi to attend the premier at Odeon Cinema. The crowds were jumping up and down with delirious joy."

MYSTERY LOOKALIKE

The film opens with a mysterious jewel thief whose daring heists have left the country baffled. Meanwhile, Vinay has just embarked on a career as an expert on precious stones. Confusion begins

▲ **All-singing, all-dancing finale**
The film's final song, "Hoton Mein Aisi Baat," brings the lead pair together in a colorful dance sequence starring classical dancer Vyjayanthimala.

as Vinay finds himself repeatedly mistaken for a man called Amar. The film picks up pace when Shalini and her brother arrive on the scene and assert that Vinay is actually Amar—Shalini's fiancé. Vinay decides to take advantage of being a lookalike of Amar, and goes on a mission to crack the mystery of the jewel thief. It seems that Amar may be the notorious thief. Vijay penetrates the gang and gets close to the criminal's girlfriends. The plot thickens as it is revealed that Amar is also pretending to be Vinay. The finale unfolds in the picturesque city of Gangtok, Sikkim, and the audience is left gasping at the secret of the thief.

NOIRISH GLAMOUR

Given its noir-style sequences and the number of women vying for Dev

HIT SONGS

Hoton Mein Aisi Baat
(Secret on My Lips)
🎤 **Singers** Lata Mangeshkar

Aasman Ke Neeche
(Under the Sky)
🎤 **Singers** Kishore Kumar, Lata Mangeshkar

Anand's attention, critics often describe *Jewel Thief* as a "Hitchcock-meets-James Bond" movie. The cinematography builds up the sinister ambience by revealing clues in unexpected ways, such as through eye holes in wall masks and even through a hole in the carpet. Like any James Bond movie, *Jewel Thief* has its share of glamorous women, in addition to the film's heroine. The appeal and allure of actresses Tanuja, Helen, Fariyal, and Anju Mahendru gave the film an extra edge.

VYJAYANTHIMALA (b.1936)

A successful actress of the 1950s and 1960s in Bollywood and the regional film industries of south India, Vyjayanthimala got her first big break with *Nagin* (1954). She is a trained Indian classical dancer, and nearly all her films feature popular dance numbers. In 1955, she refused a Filmfare Award for *Devdas* (1955) as she had been nominated for a Supporting Role. However, she went on to win the Filmfare Awards for Best Actress for *Sadhna* (1958) and *Gunga Jamuna* (1961). She retired from the movies after her marriage in 1968, and later in life entered politics.

AN EVENING IN PARIS

1967

Capitalizing on audiences' eagerness for on-screen glamour with its fantastic foreign locations, the film caused a stir with the appearance of its heroine Sharmila Tagore in a swimsuit.

Filmed in Paris, Switzerland, Beirut, and at Niagara Falls, *An Evening in Paris* was shot over three months on location outside India. In the 1960s, this was unusual, and it was a major selling point for the film. In fact, the movie begins with actor Shammi Kapoor looking straight into the camera and singing the immensely popular number "Dekho dekho dekho, an evening in Paris," loosely translated as "Look at this evening in Paris."

The film rode heavily on the ability of Shammi and his leading lady Sharmila Tagore to channel their glamorous, cosmopolitan, off-screen personas. Shammi was already a heartthrob, and Sharmila—with her bouffant hairstyle, knotted blouses, and the swimsuit—became a fashion icon after this film.

ROMANTIC COMEDY AND THRILLER

Sharmila's character Deepa is the daughter of a wealthy businessman. She has come to Paris to escape her failed relationships in India. Here, she meets Shyam, better known as Sam, who woos her through a series of entertaining episodes and energetic songs. Deepa's driver, Makkhan Singh, plays along with the antics of Sam, enhancing the film's comic appeal. Singing his way through Paris and Switzerland, Sam eventually makes Deepa fall in love with him.

However, this classic romantic comedy takes a darker twist when the villainous Shekhar—a gambler and drunkard—pursues Deepa for her money. The plot thickens when Shekhar and his creditor Jack realize Deepa's resemblance to Suzie, who is a dancer at Jack's nightclub. Here, Sharmila as Miss Suzie the Oriental Dancer breaks a gender stereotype when she is shown smoking on-screen. Before this film, women in Bollywood had never been shown smoking.

A kidnapping, a ransom demand, and Sharmila's double role as both Deepa and Suzie add to the mystery, leading up to a thrilling climax.

DRAMATIC HEIGHTS

The song sequences by Mohammed Rafi, the leading playback singer of the time, take the film to greater heights. While Shammi is charming as Sam in the film, the story goes that even though the actor suffered from vertigo, he had to hang from a helicopter for the shooting of the song "Aasman Se Aaya Farishta." Shammi was so nervous about the scene that he confessed to not getting any sleep the night before. He said in an interview, "Early in the morning, I went to the spot … woke up the bartender, and had two large pegs of cognac. And then I said, 'Where is the helicopter! Get me that helicopter!'"

SHAMMI KAPOOR · SHARMILA TAGORE · RAJINDER NATH & PRAN in

Shakti FILMS PRESENT

an Evening in Paris

EASTMANCOLOR

PRODUCED · DIRECTED BY·
SHAKTI SAMANTA · SHANKER JAIKISHAN

◄ Exotic locations

Posters for *An Evening in Paris* made the most of the film's foreign settings, which added glamour to the mystery played out on screen by its star-studded cast.

"I was young and felt liberated."

SHARMILA TAGORE, TALKING ABOUT *AN EVENING IN PARIS* IN AN INTERVIEW WITH NDTV, 2013

CAST AND CREW

★ **Shammi Kapoor** Sam / Shyam
Sharmila Tagore Deepa / Suzie
Pran Shekhar
Jack K.N. Singh
Rajender Nath Makkhan Singh

Director Shakti Samant
Producer Shakti Samant
Music composers Shankar S. Raghuvanshi, Jaikishen D. Panchal
Lyricist Shailendra
Scriptwriter Sachin Bhowmick
Cinematographer V. Gopi Krishna

CABARET
NIGHTS

With dancers wearing exotic clothes and makeup, swaying seductively to catchy melodies, cabaret was all about indulging the audience's guilty pleasures.

While there were several acclaimed goddesses of the cabaret sequence in Bollywood films, such as Bindu, Padma Khanna, Aruna Irani, and Jaishree T., most Indians would agree that Helen was the undisputed queen of them all.

Born Helen Richardson in 1938, of Anglo-Burmese parentage, Helen escaped to India with her family from war-torn Burma in 1943. With the help of Cuckoo, then considered to be the best Bollywood dancer, the young Helen found work as a chorus dancer. She got her big break dancing to the song "Mera Naam Chin Chin Choo" (My Name Is Chin Chin Choo) in the film *Howrah Bridge* (1958). From that point on, there was no looking back. With her exotic features, Helen made the perfect cabaret vamp and often played a foil for the chaste damsel, the cinematic heroine of the times.

Popular nightclub numbers performed by Helen, such as "Aaj Ki Raat" (Tonight) in the film *Inteqam* (1969) and "Piya Tu Ab To Aaja"

(Darling, Won't You Come Now) in *Caravan* (1971), were enormous hits at the time and also became cult favorites of future generations.

SULTRY VAMPS

Actresses who performed in the cabaret sequences of yore were never the heroines, but usually had prominent roles in the overall story.

In *Teesri Manzil* (see p.93), for example, Helen's unrequited passion for the hero and her silent observation of events as they unfold add to the atmosphere of suspense in the film. Meanwhile, in the cabaret sequence "Mera Naam Hai Shabnam" (My Name Is Shabnam) in *Kati Patang* (1970), Bindu tortures the heroine, played by Asha Parekh, with her secret knowledge of Parekh's identity. Similarly, in "Husn Ke Laakhon Rang" (Beauty's Many Colors) in *Johny Mera Naam* (1970), Padma Khanna bribes the villain Prem Nath with her stripteaselike act, in the hope that he will not kill her lover.

Cabaret died out in the 1980s when the films' heroines started performing the "bold" dance numbers themselves. Zeenat Aman's "Laila Main Laila" (Laila, I Am Laila) in *Qurbani* (1980) and Parveen Babi's "Raat Baaki" (The Night is Young) in *Namak Halal* (1982) are early examples of the shift.

◄ **Titillating performance**
Choreographers and costume designers made a huge contribution to the success of a typical Helen dance number. Her outfits were elaborate, often decorated with jewels and ostrich plumes, as in this scene from *Jewel Thief* (1967).

"Hazel-eyed - Chic - Sleek -
Gorgeously glamorous twinkle toed
Charmer of the Silver Screen."

PUBLICITY MATERIAL FOR *DIL DAULAT DUNIYA* (1972), REFERRING TO HELEN

UPKAR

1967

The top earner of 1967, *Upkar* is a patriotic, son-of-the-soil film, which swept the board at the Filmfare Awards and received a Silver Lotus at the National Awards.

The film *Upkar* (Beneficence) ushered in a new phase in popular hero Manoj Kumar's career—that of his nationalistic Mr. "Bharat" persona. It also marked his directorial debut.

THE FARMER-SOLDIER
Opening with a voice-over of the then Prime Minister Lal Bahadur Shastri's slogan *Jai Jawaan, Jai Kisan* (hail the soldier, hail the farmer), *Upkar* has Kumar playing both farmer and soldier. In the story, Bharat and Puran are stepbrothers. After their father dies, elder brother Bharat toils on the farm to put his brother through college in the city. However, while Bharat has a noble sense of his own place in the nation's development, Puran dreams of a glamorous life in the city.

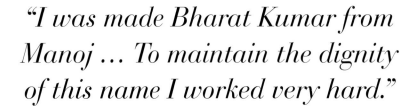

"I was made Bharat Kumar from Manoj … To maintain the dignity of this name I worked very hard."

MANOJ KUMAR, *THE TIMES OF INDIA*, AUGUST 13, 2010

The story follows the ever-diverging paths of the two brothers—Bharat enrolls in the army to fight in the Indo-Pakistan War of 1965, while Puran becomes a wartime profiteer. Eventually, an embittered and injured Bharat returns from the war to find his brother repenting for his sins by embracing the land and all its implied notions of nationhood.

FILM FIRSTS
The film boasts several firsts. Manoj Kumar's innovative camera angles—be it a view of village fields through an anklet, or the protagonist glimpsing his reflection in mirrorwork on a blouse—were original for the time, and deeply appreciated by the film fraternity.

Upkar was also the first movie in which Pran, previously typecast as a villain, could show his abilities as a character actor. Pran's Malang Chacha is a one-legged beggar who is the conscience of the village.

NATIONALISTIC AGENDA
The film depicts the realities of the India of the 1950s and 1960s. In a time when hoarders were profiting from a scarcity of food, the film promotes the nationalistic agenda of being self-reliant. It also works to instill pride in the "local" against the perceived threat of "Western" culture.

CAST AND CREW

* ★ **Manoj Kumar** Bharat
  Asha Parekh Dr. Kavita
  Prem Chopra Puran
  Pran Malang Chacha
  Kamini Kaushal Radha

* 🎬 **Director** Manoj Kumar
* **Producers** R.N. Goswami, Harkishen Mirchandani
* 🎵 **Music composers** Kalyanji Virji Shah, Anandji Virji Shah
* **Lyricists** Gulshan Bawra, Prem Dhawan, Indivar
* 🕺 **Choreographer** Surya Kumar
* 📖 **Scriptwriter** Manoj Kumar
* 🎥 **Cinematographer** V.N. Reddy
* 👔 **Costume designers** Sudha Parekh, Leena Shah

▼ **Patriotic song**
Upkar gave Hindi cinema the nationalistic anthem "Mere Desh ki Dharti" (The Soil of My Land). This award-winning song is an ode to the motherland that provides bounty for her people.

MANOJ KUMAR
(b.1937)

Born Harkishen Goswami, Manoj Kumar played standard romantic heroes throughout the 1960s in films such as *Hariyali aur Rasta* (1962). After *Shaheed* (1965), in which he portrayed the anti-colonial martyr Bhagat Singh, he made *Upkar*, *Poorab aur Paschim* (1970), *Roti Kapda aur Makaan* (1974), and *Kranti* (1981), casting himself as an idealistic hero fighting the evils that threaten his land. His work became synonymous with patriotism in Hindi cinema. In 2016, he was given the Dadasaheb Phalke Award.

PADOSAN

1968

A moderate hit on its first release, *Padosan* is now regarded as one of the most entertaining comedies in Hindi cinema, combining witty dialogue and zany situations to great effect.

CAST AND CREW

* **Sunil Dutt** Bhola
  Saira Banu Bindu
  Mehmood Master Pillai
  Kishore Kumar Vidyapati
  Om Prakash Kunwar Pratap Singh

* **Director** Jyoti Swaroop
  Producers Mehmood, N.C. Sippy
  Music composer R.D. Burman
  Lyricist Rajendra Krishan
  Choreographer Suresh Bhatt
  Scriptwriter Rajendra Krishan
  Cinematographer K.H. Kapadia
  Costume designer M.R. Bhutkar

▼ **Comic ensemble**
Vidyapati (center right) is the singing voice of tone-deaf Bhola (center left) as he tries to woo Bindu. Veteran comic actors (left to right) Keshto Mukherjee, Mukri, and Raj Kishore provide support to ensure that the illusion is complete—and the comedy spot on.

The 1952 Bengali story *Pasher Bari* (The House Next Door), by Arun Chowdhury, had already been made into a movie in Bengali, Telugu, and Tamil before Mehmood adapted it for his debut production *Padosan* (The Girl Next Door). Though Sunil Dutt was the hero of the film, actors Mehmood and Kishore Kumar (see pp. 100–101) stole the show in the comic roles of a Tamil dance teacher and a Bengali folk theater veteran, respectively.

BATTLE OF WITS
The comedy begins when Bhola, a young simpleton, falls in love with his beautiful and intelligent neighbor Bindu, who is devoted to music and dance. Bindu's tutor Master Pillai is also in love with her. This sparks a musical war for her affection that lends itself to great comedy, given that Bhola has no musical talent whatsoever.

Bhola's friend philosopher and guide Vidyapati, who runs a small theater company, helps by singing in the background as Bhola lip syncs to impress Bindu. Their strategy works, but Bindu is enraged when the ruse is revealed. She decides to take revenge, which necessitates further theatrics to make her relent.

SING-OFF
R.D. Burman (see p. 109) scored a soundtrack that was equal to the task of complementing a comedic masterpiece. The highlight of the film is a "sing-off" in the song "Ek Chatur Naar" between Mehmood and Kishore. The on-screen sing-off is said to mirror a similar duel off-screen—between classically trained Manna Dey and untrained Kishore. The song was originally sung by Kishore's elder brother Ashok in his 1941 hit *Jhoola*, and was composed by Saraswati Devi—possibly the first female composer in Hindi cinema.

SCINTILLATING STEREOTYPES
Among the many endearing aspects of the movie is its use of over-the-top stereotypes. Each character—be it the shy, simple-minded Bhola; the oily haired, paan-chewing, "arty" director Vidyapati; the bumbling troupe of actors; or even the traditional Tamil Brahmin with his sandalwood lines on the forehead, tuft of hair, and outrageous accent—works to lift the film to memorable levels of comedy.

HIT SONGS

Mere Saamne Vaali Khidki Mein
(In the Window Across from Me)
🎤 **Singer** Kishore Kumar

Ek Chatur Naar
(A Clever Woman)
🎤 **Singers** Manna Dey, Kishore Kumar

▶ **Art imitating life**
The film's poster depicts "Mere Saamne Vaali Khidki Mein," a song that critics have seen as a spoof of playback singing in Bollywood.

KISHORE KUMAR

A versatile performer, Kishore Kumar was a playback singer, actor, comedian, director, producer, and composer, who left his enduring mark on Bollywood with his many talents.

▲ **The beginning**
Kishore Kumar's comic hero persona came to the fore with some films in the mid-1950s, including *Pehli Jhalak*. Over the next decade and more, Kishore went on to act in a number of superhit comedy films such as *Half Ticket* (1962).

There are innumerable anecdotes that recount the many talents of Kishore Kumar. In 1962, Kishore and Lata Mangeshkar were to record a duet, composed by Salil Choudhury, for the film *Half Ticket*. When Lata could not make it for the recording, Kishore effortlessly sang both the male and female parts of the song "Aa Ke Seedhi Lagi" (Straight to the Heart), which remains a classic and is a timeless demonstration of Kishore's incredible versatility.

Kishore has always generated immense affection among his audiences, and is often remembered as the madcap comic of *Half Ticket*

▶ **Prolific artist**
Kishore Kumar's reputation remains untouched decades after his death, and his movies and music continue to be loved by the young and the old alike even today.

and *Padosan*; the charming hero of *Chalti ka Naam Gaadi*; the voice of Dev Anand, Rajesh Khanna, Amitabh Bachchan, Rishi Kapoor, and many others; and the first yodeler of Hindi films. He acted in more than 80 films, sang more than 1,500 songs, produced 14 films, and directed eight of them. He won eight Filmfare Awards for playback singing.

MAKING OF KISHORE KUMAR
An untrained singer, Kishore was a great admirer of K.L. Saigal, and adopted his singing style when he first came to Mumbai. It was composer

S.D. Burman who asked him to develop his own style and worked with him through the 1950s and 1960s, when Mohammed Rafi was the reigning playback singer. Kishore went on to sing for

KEY WORKS

Andolan, 1951
Naukri, 1954
Pehli Jhalak, 1955
New Delhi, 1956
Musafir, 1957
Aasha, 1957
Chalti Ka Naam Gaadi, 1958 (see p. 63)
Dilli Ka Thug, 1958
Jhumroo, 1961
Half Ticket, 1962
Mr. X in Bombay, 1964
Door Gagan Ki Chhaon Mein, 1964
Padosan, 1968 (see p. 99)
Door Ka Rahi, 1971

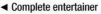

◄ **Complete entertainer**
Dilli ka Thug was representative of the Kishore genre of movies, which were usually part-comedy and part-drama, or, as in this case, crime thriller.

half his fee, causing alarm when it was time to shoot. Once he even locked up a hostile financier in a cupboard. On another occasion, he put up a sign on his door that read "Beware of Kishore." While most of his antics were said to be caused by his annoyance at not being paid, he was also known for his generosity to those in need.

A recluse, Kishore once said that his friends were some of the friendlier trees in his backyard, with names like Buddhuram and Jhatpatajhatpatpat. Nonetheless, Kishore married four times, and all his wives were actresses.

"Acting is a lie, but music comes straight from the heart."

KISHORE KUMAR

films such as *Taxi Driver* (1954), *Paying Guest* (1957), and *Guide* (see pp. 84–87).

Despite his effortless on-screen performances, Kishore's original aim was to be a playback singer rather than an actor. However, in the 1950s, he starred in Bimal Roy's *Naukri* and Hrishikesh Mukherjee's directorial debut, *Musafir*. In 1958, Kishore produced the comedy *Chalti ka Naam Gaadi* with his future wife, Madhubala, and his brothers, Ashok and Anoop. He hoped the film would fail commercially, and help him show losses for tax purposes. However, it became the second-highest earner of the year. He also produced, composed, and acted in the introspective *Door Gagan ki Chhaon Mein* and *Door ka Rahi*.

FULL THROTTLE

In 1969, he sang in the classic film *Aradhana* (see pp. 102–105). Kishore's breezy vocal in "Mere Sapnon Ki Rani" (My Dream Girl), mimed by Rajesh Khanna driving through the countryside, became an instant hit. After 22 years in the industry, he won his first Filmfare Award for the song "Roop Tera Mastana" (Your Beauty is Intoxicating) in the same film.

From then on, there was no looking back. In the 1970s, the trio of Rajesh Khanna, Kishore Kumar, and R.D. Burman were associated with films such as *Kati Patang* (1970), *Amar Prem* (see p. 113), and *Kudrat* (1981). Kishore also became the voice of the

definitive actor of the times, Amitabh Bachchan. The singer's rendition for films like *Abhimaan* (1973), *Mili* (1975), and *Aandhi* (see p. 141) are timeless.

UNCONVENTIONAL STAR

Kishore truly meant it when he said, "In this crazy world, only the truly sane man appears to be mad." He was capable of notoriously eccentric behavior. It is said that Kishore once arrived on set with only half a moustache since the producers had paid only

His second wife Madhubala was, by popular consent, Bollywood's most beautiful star.

During 1975–77, a state of emergency was declared in India by the then prime minister, Indira Gandhi. At this time, Kishore took on the establishment when he refused to sing at a rally of the ruling Congress party. This led to a complete ban of all his songs on All India Radio. Despite the ban, Kishore refused to back down.

► **Legends at work**
Left to right, actor–director Dev Anand; singer Lata Mangeshkar; Kishore Kumar, and composer R.D. Burman collaborate in a recording studio.

1929 Born Abhas Kumar Ganguly in Khandwa, Madhya Pradesh, to Kunjalal Ganguly and Gouri Devi.

1946 Appears in *Shikari*, starring his eldest brother, Ashok Kumar.

1948 Records his first song "Marne Ki Duayen" (Blessings of Death) in *Ziddi* for debutant hero, Dev Anand.

1951 Lands leading role in *Andolan*. First marriage to Ruma Guha Thakurta.

1958 Produces and acts in the hit film *Chalti ka Naam Gaadi*.

1960 Marries Madhubala.

1964 Produces, directs, and acts in *Door Gagan ki Chhaon mein*. He also composes, sings, and writes songs for the film.

1970 Wins his first Filmfare Award for the song "Roop Tera Mastana" (Your Beauty is Intoxicating) in *Aradhana*.

THAT WHICH GROWS IS A BEARD

1974 Directs *Badhti ka Naam Daadhi*. Titled to rhyme with the superhit *Chalti ka Naam Gaadi*, this film failed.

1976 Marries Yogeeta Bali.

1979 Wins Filmfare Award for the song "Khaike Paan Banaras Wala" (A Betel Leaf from Varanasi) in *Don*.

1980 Marries Leena Chandavarkar.

1981 Wins Filmfare Award for the song "Hazaar Rahein" (A Thousand Roads) in *Thodisi Bewafai*.

1984 Wins Filmfare Award for the title song of *Agar Tum na Hote*.

1985 Wins his last Filmfare Award for "Manzilein Apni Jagah Hain" (Destinations in Their Place) in *Sharabi*. With this award, he breaks the record for the most Filmfare Awards for playback singing.

1987 Dies of a heart attack at age 58.

ARADHANA

1969

Aradhana paired old-fashioned melodrama with unconventional scenarios, a steel-willed heroine with a fresh-faced hero, and soul-stirring music with a strong plotline to become the top earner of 1969.

SHARMILA TAGORE
RAJESH KHANNA
Shakti Films
aradhana
IN EASTMANCOLOR
PRODUCED & DIRECTED BY
SHAKTI SAMANTA
MUSIC
S. D. BURMAN

◀ **Vintage poster**
This poster design for the film was created by artist C. Mohan. Hand-painted posters of this type were key to a film's success.

paid off famously. *Aradhana* (Worship) became a "golden jubilee hit," running for more than 50 weeks in all major cities in India. Tagore took home the Filmfare Award for Best Actress for the movie. Based on a Hollywood hit, *To Each His Own* (1946), *Aradhana* is what is called a three-hankie weepie—a melodramatic tearjerker. In honoring the memory of her dead lover and caring for her son, the heroine suffered her way into audiences' hearts. Paired with Tagore was Rajesh Khanna, a relative newcomer with a few unsuccessful films behind him. This was the first pairing of what would go on to become the hugely popular Khanna–Tagore team.

A STAR IS BORN

Aradhana gave Tagore a strong female role, but the film was associated even more with Khanna since it was his first big hit. Sporting a Nepali-style cap, serenading the heroine on

board the famous Darjeeling toy train while driving alongside in an open-top Willys jeep, he created a frenzy with the song "Mere Sapnon Ki Rani." Female fans loved him in his Air Force uniform, both as the father, Arun, and his moustachioed, English-speaking son, Suraj. Khanna entered the movie industry after winning a talent hunt, in which the prize included a film deal. The film's director, Shakti Samanta, was on the panel of judges for this contest. Khanna's co-stars Farida Jalal and Subhash Ghai—who went on to become a respected director himself—were co-winners in this talent hunt.

Sharmila Tagore was already a star by the time she turned 25, with three Satyajit Ray films, several Bollywood hits, and a taboo-breaking bikini photoshoot behind her. She had also married India's cricketing heartthrob, the Nawab of Pataudi, Mansoor Ali Khan. At this point she took the risk of doing a film that showed her in a youth-to-old-age role, in which she would also have to play actor Rajesh Khanna's aged mother. It was an unusual decision, which

◀ **India's first superstar**
Sharmila Tagore stated in an interview that Rajesh Khanna rose to stardom after *Aradhana's* release. "I've never seen anything like that … it was phenomenal," she said.

CAST AND CREW

★ **Rajesh Khanna** Arun Verma/ Suraj Saxena
Sharmila Tagore Vandana Tripathi
Sujit Kumar Madan Verma
Abhi Bhattacharya Ram Prasad Saxena
Manmohan Shyam
Madan Puri Jailer
Farida Jalal Renu
Prakash Subhash Ghai

Director Shakti Samanta
Producer Shakti Samanta
Music composer S.D. Burman
Lyricist Anand Bakshi
Scriptwriter Sachin Bhowmick
Cinematographer Aloke Dasgupta
Costume designers Mani J. Rabadi, R. Vaidya

"What you take home is a director's movie, a man who could claim to be a feminist without needing any placards."

ZIYA US SALAM, *THE HINDU*, 2009

A MUSICAL JACKPOT

Aradhana is inextricable from the actor–playback singer phenomenon of Rajesh Khanna and Kishore Kumar, of which songs such as "Mere Sapnon Ki Rani" and "Roop Tera Mastana" (Your Beauty Is Intoxicating) were the stepping stones. Khanna maintained, "Kishore was my soul and I his body." Although Kishore had been in the business for almost 20 years, he hadn't come close to displacing top

playback singer Mohammed Rafi. But with *Aradhana*, his journey to the top gained momentum.

The soundtrack of the film captured key moments and beautiful sentiments in melody. The film's music composer S.D. Burman was ill during the making of the movie. It is said that his son R.D. Burman (see p. 109), who also went on to become a famous music composer, may have stepped in to help his father.

SHARMILA TAGORE
(b.1944)

Sharmila Tagore is one of Bollywood's most successful actresses. Beginning her film career at the age of 15, Tagore first appeared in filmmaker Satyajit Ray's critically acclaimed movie *Apur Sansar* (1959), and later worked with him in films such as *Devi* (1960) and *Nayak* (1966). Her mainstream Bollywood debut happened with *Kashmir Ki Kali* (1964). During the 1960s and 1970s, she starred in superhits such as *Aradhana*, and *Amar Prem* (see p. 113). She also appeared in critically acclaimed movies such as *Mausam* (1975) for which she received a National Award. Tagore was honored with the Filmfare Lifetime Achievement Award in 1998 and a Padma Bhushan—the third-highest civilian award in India—in 2013.

A BOLD TAKE

Aradhana dealt with premarital sex and unwed motherhood more confidently than any mainstream film before it. The lead pair's lovemaking was, for a change, not alluded to by two flowers coming together as was the norm in Bollywood movies at that time. Instead, the lead up to it was framed in a remarkably sensual song sequence ("Roop Tera Mastana"), picturized in a single wordless shot. The strong-willed heroine of *Aradhana* asserts herself when she announces to her father that she is pregnant and intends to keep her lover's child.

From the contemporary feminist viewpoint, the film can be critiqued for condemning its heroine to a lifetime of devotion to a dead man and his dreams. In the end, her reward lies in having her long-lost son publicly acknowledge her as his mother. The film may seem old-fashioned today, but for its time it was breaking relatively new ground.

◄ **An everlasting love**
Working together in more than 12 films, Sharmila Tagore and Rajesh Khanna became the hit pair of the 1970s. This shot from the song "Gun Guna Rahe Hain Bhawre" (The Bees Are Humming) captures their unparalleled chemistry.

STORYLINE

The film presents its heroine, Vandana, as the embodiment of devotion and sacrifice. When Vandana's fiancé dies, leaving her pregnant, she decides to honor his memory by bringing up their son to fulfill his father's dreams. But as an unwed mother, Vandana is scorned by society and has to face many travails throughout her life.

ARUN AND VANDANA DURING
THEIR COURTSHIP

LOVE AT FIRST SIGHT

TRAGIC DEATH

PLOT OVERVIEW

The opening scene shows Vandana being sentenced to life imprisonment for murder. Thinking of better times, she recalls her first meeting with the love of her life. Lieutenant Arun Verma falls in love with Vandana the moment he sees her ❶. She soon comes to reciprocate his feelings.

Vandana and Arun's relationship has the blessings of friends and family. Arun introduces Vandana to his colleagues and seniors as his fiancé ❷. During a function in the town, Arun plays a prank on Vandana ❸.

The two secretly tie the knot in an impromptu ceremony in a Hindu temple. A chance rain shower leaves them stranded at a remote hotel where they make love ❹. As Vandana frets about having rushed things, Arun reassures her that he will arrange their official marriage within a week. He shares with her his dream of having a son who will grow up to become an Air Force pilot just like him.

Arun's untimely death in a plane crash leaves Vandana devastated. With their marriage not yet solemnized, Vandana is left alone to face the challenging circumstances that are yet to unfold.

THE SONGS

❶

Mere Sapno ki Rani
(Oh! Woman of My Dreams)
Singer: Kishore Kumar
Picturized on Arun and Vandana

★ *Khanna and Tagore couldn't make the same dates for the shooting of the song "Mere Sapno Ki Rani." Their segments were shot separately; Khanna's in Darjeeling and Tagore's in Mumbai.*

❷

Kora Kagaz Tha Ye Mann Mera
(My Heart Was Like a Blank Paper)
*Singers: Kishore Kumar &
Lata Mangeshkar*
Picturized on Arun and Vandana

❸

Gunguna Rahe Hain Bhawre
(The Bees Are Humming)
Singers: Mohammed Rafi and Asha Bhosle
Picturized on Arun and Vandana

❹

Roop Tera Mastana
(Your Beauty Is Intoxicating)
Singer: Kishore Kumar
Picturized on Arun and Vandana

ARUN AND
VANDANA
FALL IN LOVE

A MURDER IN THE FAMILY

ANAND BAKSHI (1930–2002)

A prolific lyricist of Bollywood, Anand Bakshi provided words to more than 3,500 songs during a career spanning four decades. Working between the years 1956 and 2001, he gained popularity with films such as *Himalaya ki God Mein* (1965) and *Jab Jab Phool Khile* (1965). Bringing a new depth to compositions, he wrote for blockbusters such as *Bobby* (see pp.118–19), *Hare Rama Hare Krishna* (see p.108), *Aradhana*, *Sholay* (see pp.134–37), and *Dilwale Dulhania le Jayenge* (see pp.230–33). He was nominated for Filmfare Awards every year from 1970 to 1982.

UNWED MOTHER	IMPRISONMENT		CROSSING PATHS	REUNITED

Vandana discovers she is pregnant and chooses to keep the child to honor the promise she made to Arun ❺. However, once the baby is born, the social stigma attached to an unwed mother forces her to decide to leave the baby at an adoption center, and later adopt him. However, destiny has something else in store. Before Vandana can reach the adoption center, the child is already taken by a family.

Vandana becomes a nursemaid in the house where her child, Suraj, is being raised ❻. A member of the family—Shyam—tries to molest her. A struggle ensues and Suraj comes to her rescue, killing the attacker.

Choosing to save her son, Vandana takes the blame on herself. While she is serving her sentence, the family that had adopted Suraj leaves the town and his adoptive father dies.

Vandana is released early from jail due to her good conduct. A kind jailer, who is about to retire, offers her shelter. She accepts the offer and eventually grows fond of the jailer's daughter Renu. Meanwhile, Renu introduces Vandana to the love of her life, Suraj ❼. His striking resemblance to Arun instantly tells her that Suraj is none other than her own son.

The long-held secret is revealed during a ceremony where Suraj is rewarded for his bravery as a pilot. Prior to the function, he finds a letter from his adoptive father that reveals the truth about his parentage. On discovering this, Suraj invites Vandana to the ceremony, where he acknowledges that he is Vandana's son in front of the world. Mother and son are finally reunited.

❺   ❻   ❼

Safal Hogi Teri Aradhana
(Your Devotion Will Bear Fruit)
Singer: S.D. Burman
🎵 *Picturized on Vandana*

Chanda Hai Tu
(You Are My Moon)
Singer: Lata Mangeshkar
🎵 *Picturized on Vandana and Suraj*

Baagon Mein Bahar Hai
(Springtime in the Garden)
Singers: Lata Mangeshkar and Mohammed Rafi
🎵 *Picturized on Suraj and Renu*

★ *In the dubbed Bengali version of* Aradhana, *the playback singer Lata Mangeshkar, a Maharashtrian, sang this song in Bengali.*

SURAJ AND RENU

> "There is something known as successful music ... then there is superhit music, and finally there is Aradhana's music ..."

JAVED AKHTAR, INDIAN POET AND LYRICIST, 2016

VANDANA AND ARUN IN A MOMENT OF TENDERNESS

RAJESH KHANNA

ACTOR **1942–2012**

The early days of Indian cinema were filled with charismatic heroes, but the kind of hysteria and adulation that Rajesh Khanna generated was unprecedented—many call him Bollywood's first superstar.

T he title "superstar" was bestowed upon actor Rajesh Khanna during his heyday between 1969 and 1972. His fans put him on a pedestal, with admirers sending him letters written in blood and female devotees "marrying" his photographs. For his part, Khanna endeavored to live up to his reputation by conducting his life the way he thought a superstar should. He never arrived at shoots on time, and once organized a grand party to clash with a Filmfare Award function in which he was not being honored.

Rajesh's story eventually became as much about his his fall from superstardom as his rise to it, both equally dramatic. However, no one doubted his talent as an actor. In fact, he was nominated for the Filmfare Award for Best Actor 11 times and won three of them.

RISE TO FAME
Born Jatin Khanna and affectionately called "Kaka," Rajesh was a proficient stage actor in his college days. In 1965, his film acting career took off after he won the Filmfare–United Producers Talent Hunt. His early movies failed to make an impact, but his performance in *Aradhana* made the audience take notice. Whether he was singing romantic songs in the Himalayas, serenading the heroine from a moving jeep, or playing an Air Force officer, the dashing Khanna gave a generation of cinemagoers someone to dream about.

The year 1970–71 in particular were an outstanding ones for Khanna, appearing in a string of successful movies such as *Aan Milo Sajna* (1970), *Kati Patang,* and *Anand*. But his biggest hit that year was *Haathi Mere Saathi,* which became the highest-earning

Hindi movie at the time. Khanna's popularity contined to soar. He was followed by hysterical crowds wherever he went, girls left lipstick marks on his car, and young men emulated his style. That same year, the star also featured in a five-part story published by a popular film and entertainment magazine, *Star & Style*. So potent was the craze that *Andaz* (1971) became a hit simply because of his 10-minute role in it, and his immensely popular song "Zindagi Ek Safar Hai Suhana" (Life Is a Happy Journey) in it.

Anand was Khanna's second Filmfare Award-winning performance and the one which gave audiences the

▶ **First Indian superstar**
With his trademark tilt of the head, blink of the eyes, and disarming smile, Rajesh starred in 15 hit films from 1969 to 1971.

KEY WORKS

Aradhana, 1969 (see pp. 102–05)

Kati Patang, 1970

Haathi Mere Saathi, 1971

Anand, 1971 (see p. 112)

Amar Prem, 1972 (see p. 113)

Daag, 1973

Aap Ki Kasam, 1974

Souten, 1983

Avtaar, 1983

"I felt next to God! [H]ow mind-blowing success can be … it psyches you totally."

RAJESH KHANNA, IN AN INTERVIEW WITH *MOVIE* MAGAZINE, MAY 1990

◄ **Box office hit**
Kati Patang (1970) was one of the many successful films that actor Rajesh Khanna and director Shakti Samanta did together. Rajesh's performance in the film was praised by critics and audiences alike.

powerful image of a man dying of cancer who wants to live the few days he has left to the fullest. More success followed Khanna in 1972, with *Amar Prem* and *Bawarchi*.

FALL FROM STARDOM

In the years that followed, Khanna enjoyed intermittent success, but he never saw the same kind of adulation again. In the age of Salim–Javed's crisp scripts and Amitabh Bachchan's (see pp. 126–27) angry-man juggernaut, the romantic hero that Khanna emulated was unable to find a space. Among the hits that kept him going were *Roti* (1974), *Chhaila Babu* (1977), *Thhodi Si Bewafai* (1980), *Souten, Avtaar,* and *Agar Tum Na Hote* (1983). However, his movies dwindled in significance, and he was not able to successfully reinvent himself. Khanna also flirted briefly with politics and became a Member of Parliament (1992–96).

COURTING DEATH

Rajesh's biographer Gautam Chintamani observed: "Few actors in Indian cinema have conveyed existential angst as well as Rajesh Khanna." Indeed, Khanna made dying his speciality. He died in *Aradhana, Safar* (1970), and *Andaz* (1971), and his character's impending death was the foundation of *Anand*. Khanna

seemed to be convinced that films with his character dying was one formula that worked for him. In Hrishikesh Mukherjee's *Namak Haram* (1973), Khanna insisted on taking the role that was originally meant for actor Amitabh because that character would die and win sympathy from the audience at the end of the film.

TRAPPED IN AN IMAGE

Khanna was known to hold nightly *durbar*s (court) in which he would sit on an elevated chair, and grant an "audience" to producers to present their upcoming projects. Such behavior

led to an observation in the BBC documentary *Bombay Superstar* (1973) that Khanna had "the charisma of Rudolph Valentino, the arrogance of Napoleon." Many alleged that even his decision to get married was to attract publicity in an attempt to revive his flagging career. Swiftly following the end of a stormy relationship with actress Anju Mahendru, his decision to marry could have been taken on the rebound as well. One story goes that he deliberately made the wedding procession go past the street where Anju lived. Whatever the reason, at the age of 31, Rajesh married the 16-year-old actress Dimple Kapadia (see p. 119), who gave up a promising career to focus on her marriage. The couple separated after almost 10 years, and Dimple resumed her acting career.

It may be a tribute to Rajesh's charm, or his having made peace with his demons, that he not only became a family man over time, but his estranged wife also looked after him during his illness. Anju was present during his last days as well. His funeral was attended by millions of people, causing huge traffic jams in its wake. In death, the 1970s superstar drew the crowds he was once used to in life.

► **Crowd-puller**
During his location shoots, Rajesh Khanna was always surrounded by fans, who were waiting to get a glimpse of the superstar.

(see p. 119)

(see pp. 126–27)

MUCH-LOVED PAIR: RAJESH AND MUMTAZ

TIMELINE

December 29, 1942 Born in Amritsar; adopted and raised by his uncle and aunt, Chunni Lal and Leelawati Khanna.

1965 Wins the Filmfare–United Producers Talent Hunt. Signs movie contracts with 12 producers.

1966 First film *Aakhiri Khat* is released.

1969 Stars in his first major hit, *Aradhana*.

1971 Wins Filmfare Award for Best Actor for *Saccha Jhoota*.

1971 Acts in *Haathi Mere Saathi*. Film breaks previous records to become the top grossing of the year.

1972 Wins Filmfare Award for Best Actor for *Anand*.

March 1973 Marries 16-year-old actress Dimple Kapadia in an unexpected ceremony. The couple have two daughters, Twinkle and Rinki.

1975 Wins Filmfare Award for Best Actor for *Avishkaar*.

1980–87 Works with actress Tina Munim in 11 films, and is romantically linked with her off screen.

1991 Honored with the Filmfare Special Award for completing 25 years in the Indian film industry.

1992–96 Becomes a Member of Parliament for the Indian National Congress party.

2001 Makes TV debut with the series *Apne Paraye* and *Ittefaq*.

2005 Wins the Filmfare Lifetime Achievement Award.

July 18, 2012 Dies of cancer at his home in Mumbai.

2013 Posthumously honored with the Padma Bhushan—the third highest civilian award in India.

HARE RAMA HARE KRISHNA

1971

The novelty of *Hare Rama Hare Krishna*, set in the hippie communes of Kathmandu and featuring a hash-smoking heroine and rock music, took the country by storm.

During the flower-power era—from the late 1960s to the early 1970s—many young people from Europe and the US were traveling to Asian countries, looking for alternative ways of living. On a trip to Nepal's capital, Kathmandu, actor and filmmaker Dev Anand visited a hippie hub called The Bakery. There he met an Indian girl among the "flower children," and so the idea for *Hare Rama Hare Krishna* (Oh Rama, Oh Krishna), usually known simply as HRHK, was born.

After the box office failure of *Prem Pujari* (1970), Dev Anand's first directorial outing, HRHK would go on to revive his brand. The film was shot in Kathmandu and starred bona fide hippies as extras. The long, unkempt beards; loose tunics; flower garlands; prayer-bead necklaces; huge sunglasses; hash pipes; and kissing couples seen in the film were all the real deal. HRHK and Zeenat Aman also gave Bollywood the coolest heroine to hit the screen in India, singing a hedonistic chant that was to grip the country. The hypnotic guitar riff at the opening of the song "Dum Maro Dum" is instantly recognizable, even today.

SIBLINGS REUNITED
The film follows the brother-sister duo of Prashant and Jasbir, separated in childhood by their parents' divorce. As soon as she can, Jasbir flees her life in Canada with her father and cruel stepmother, and ends up in Kathmandu. She embraces a new identity, calling herself Janice and immersing herself in the hippie counterculture. Meanwhile, Prashant, who has grown up with his mother in India, sets out to look for his long-lost sister. Along the way, he romances local belle Shanti, falls foul of the hippies, and crosses swords with local villain Drona. When they finally meet, Janice at first assumes that Prashant's intentions are romantic, until she finally recognizes him when he sings her a song from their childhood.

HIP HIP HIPPIE
While HRHK has all the usual Bollywood trimmings—action, glamour, music, and star power—it is also a genuine attempt to explore a new way of living that was misunderstood by many Indians at the time. This hippie world was peopled by disillusioned and often troubled youth, who had escaped to the East in search of answers. The film also deals with divorce, morality, and ethics, within the limitations of prevailing social values. Perhaps that is the reason why it does not condone the sexually liberated, hash-smoking, hippie lifestyle of its heroine. That would have been unacceptable in 1970s Bollywood.

Anand initially offered the role of his sister to actress Mumtaz, but she refused it in favor of playing his love interest. As it turned out, Mumtaz's Shanti was completely overshadowed by Zeenat Aman's Jasbir/Janice. Zeenat received the Filmfare Award for Best Supporting Actress for her fine performance.

CAST AND CREW

★ **Dev Anand** Prashant Jaiswal
Zeenat Aman Jasbir Jaiswal/Janice
Mumtaz Shanti
Prem Chopra Drona

🎬 **Director** Dev Anand
🎬 **Producer** Dev Anand
🎵 **Music composer** R.D. Burman
🎼 **Lyricist** Anand Bakshi
🕺 **Choreographer** B. Sohanlal
📖 **Scriptwriter** Dev Anand
🎥 **Cinematographer** Fali Mistry

◄ Hippie chic
Dev Anand felt that the "chic, mod, and casual" Zeenat Aman fit in perfectly with the local hippie community, who served as extras in the film.

> *"It was perhaps the most modern story of the day!"*

DEV ANAND, ACTOR, DIRECTOR, AND PRODUCER

SEETA AUR GEETA

1972

Riding on the back of a boisterous, crowd-pleasing performance by Hema Malini, *Seeta aur Geeta* offered riotous entertainment, mixing high drama and comedy.

Screenwriting duo Salim–Javed (see pp. 138–39) took inspiration for *Seeta aur Geeta* (Seeta and Geeta) from Dilip Kumar's hit comedy *Ram aur Shyam* (1967), another tale of twins with radically different personalities. This time, however, the titular double role went to the heroine. The film's approach was typical of Bollywood in the 1970s: it allowed the audience to

◄ **Double trouble**
Hema Malini excels both as the submissive and demure Seeta and as the fiery, defiant Geeta, seen swinging on a celing fan in this lively poster.

leave rationality at the door of the cinema, then simply relax and enjoy the fun on screen, no matter how far-fetched.

TWIN TALE
The film tells the story of identical twins, Seeta and Geeta, who are separated at birth. The orphaned Seeta, heiress to a large fortune, suffers at the hands of her greedy relatives. Geeta, meanwhile, grows up to become a street-smart acrobat, who never backs down from fighting the good fight. When the twins run away from their respective homes, they inadvertently switch places. While Seeta finds acceptance in Geeta's home, Geeta takes it upon herself to teach her sister's tormentors a lesson.

CLASSICAL LINKS
In the naming of the twins, and in the story in general, there are allusions to the classic Hindu texts of the *Ramayana*

and the *Bhagavad Gita*. Seeta, like her namesake in the *Ramayana*, is a righteous but passive woman, whose faith in God and in the goodness of others remains firm despite the harsh treatment she receives. Geeta, on the other hand, subscribes to the *Gita*'s teachings, as told by her grandmother in the film: that every person who rises against injustice is godly, and that a lie told in the pursuit of good is equal to a hundred truths.

OFF-SCREEN ROMANCES
Seeta aur Geeta gave the team of director Ramesh Sippy and writers Salim–Javed a second hit, after *Andaaz* (1971), and Hema Malini won the only Filmfare Award for Best Actress of her career. Screenwriter Javed Akhtar (see pp.138–39) and actress Honey Irani, who played the heroine's spoiled cousin Sheela, fell in love and got married during the making of the film.

CAST AND CREW

★ **Hema Malini** Seeta/Geeta
Sanjeev Kumar Ravi
Dharmendra Raka
Manorama Kaushalya
Roopesh Kumar Ranjeet

🎬 **Director** Ramesh Sippy
🗄 **Producer** G.P. Sippy
🎵 **Music composer** R.D. Burman
🎵 **Lyricist** Anand Bakshi
🕺 **Choreographer** P.L. Raj
📖 **Scriptwriters** Salim Khan, Javed Akhtar
🎥 **Cinematographer** K. Vaikunth
👕 **Costume designers** Leena Daru, Chella Ram

▼ **Love is in the air**
A popular on-screen pair, and later a couple, Hema Malini and Dharmendra acted in more than 30 films together.

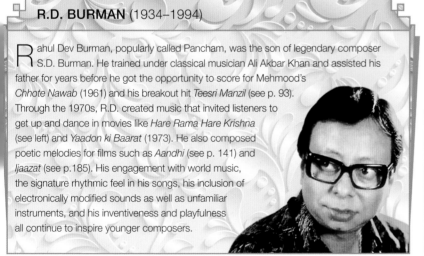

R.D. BURMAN (1934–1994)

Rahul Dev Burman, popularly called Pancham, was the son of legendary composer S.D. Burman. He trained under classical musician Ali Akbar Khan and assisted his father for years before he got the opportunity to score for Mehmood's *Chhote Nawab* (1961) and his breakout hit *Teesri Manzil* (see p. 93). Through the 1970s, R.D. created music that invited listeners to get up and dance in movies like *Hare Rama Hare Krishna* (see left) and *Yaadon ki Baarat* (1973). He also composed poetic melodies for films such as *Aandhi* (see p. 141) and *Ijaazat* (see p.185). His engagement with world music, the signature rhythmic feel in his songs, his inclusion of electronically modified sounds as well as unfamiliar instruments, and his inventiveness and playfulness all continue to inspire younger composers.

HEMA MALINI

ACTRESS b.1948

The title "Dream Girl" is inescapable when describing Hema Malini. The most beautiful actress of the 1970s was also that decade's most bankable and most controversial star.

◄ **Ethereal beauty**
Her vivacious roles, coupled with a face that captivated audiences, earned Hema Malini the nickname "Dream Girl."

Hema Malini was one of the first female stars to dictate her terms to the Bombay film industry. Producers lined up to sign her for movies, heroes were in awe of her, and the press called her an "ice maiden" as she did not mix with people easily. Her phenomenal success only added to this regal and dignified bearing. In contrast to her slightly aloof persona in real life, Hema dazzled with charm and energy on screen, carrying entire films on her shoulders. The camera and audiences simply loved her, and so did quite a number of her co-stars. Rumors of her relationships with actors such as Sanjeev Kumar (see p. 137), Jeetendra (see pp. 182–83), and Dharmendra (see pp. 152–53) gave film magazines enough fodder to discuss her personal life throughout the 1970s. In an interview, Hema was asked how many stories linking her to her co-stars were true. To which she replied, "They were all true." Her marriage, motherhood, and later political career have all been a matter of interest to her fans, too.

A STAR IS BORN
The daughter of V.S.R. Chakravarti and Jaya Chakravarti, Hema was coached by her artistic mother who had big dreams for her. Trained in the classical dance form of Bharatnatyam, Hema started getting film offers from the age of 14. Tamil director Sridhar cast her in a film but later dropped her, saying she had no star quality. A disappointed

▼ **The poster girl**
From the start of her career in the film industry, the young and beautiful Hema Malini graced the covers of many leading magazines. Her face was seen all over India.

> *"I was cast opposite multiple heroes and as luck would have it, the chemistry worked with most."*

HEMA MALINI, *MOTHER MAIDEN MISTRESS*, 2012

▲ An epic love affair

The much talked about real-life pair of Hema Malini and Dharmendra appeared in more than 30 films together, including such hits as *Sholay* and *The Burning Train*.

Hema accepted the offer to star in *Sapno ka Saudagar* (1968) to lift her mother's spirits and to make a point. Featuring Raj Kapoor (see pp. 44–45), who was 25 years older than Hema, the film did not do well but she was praised for her performance.

As Hema developed as an actress, her mother took charge and became a formidable presence in her daughter's career. Many people in the industry were also taking notice: Hema's beauty, dancing skills, and charisma invited comparisons with established actresses of the day such as Vyjayanthimala (see p. 94). Bollywood was soon to discover its true "Dream Girl."

ONE WOMAN, MANY ROLES

The young actresss continued her career with an older generation of heroes. Charming the audiences with the song "O Mere Raja" (Oh My King) in *Johny Mera Naam* (1970), Hema went on to make unconventional film choices, such as Ramesh Sippy's *Andaz* (1971), in which she played a widow and a mother. In *Lal Patthar* (1971), she took on the role of an uncouth villager opposite Raaj Kumar (see p. 117). However, it was with *Seeta aur Geeta* that she truly came into her own. Hema completely owned the double role of twin sisters, the shy Seeta and fiery Geeta, winning the Filmfare Award for Best Actress. Eventually, Sridhar—the director who had questioned her caliber some years earlier—went on to sign her as the heroine in his film *Gehri Chaal* (1973).

The year 1975 was a defining one for a new kind of Bollywood hero, due to the arrival of the "angry young man" (see p. 122–23), but it also belonged to Hema, who gave a series of hits that year such as *Sholay*, *Sanyasi*, *Dharmatma*, *Pratigya*, and *Khushboo*. Interestingly, when director Ramesh Sippy offered the blockbuster *Sholay* to Hema, she wasn't particularly impressed with the role, but could not refuse the *Andaz* director out of professional courtesy. As *Sholay*'s female lead Basanti, Hema had to deliver long, rapid-fire dialogues, something that could have been a nightmare for someone whose first language was not Hindi. Yet, she perfected the role, making it one of the most loved female characters in Hindi cinema and one of her best performances to date.

Hema was fond of her less glamorous roles in films such as *Khushboo* (1975), *Kinara* (1977), and *Meera* (1979). To prepare for the titular role in Kamal Amrohi's biopic *Razia Sultan*, she learned the Urdu language, sword fighting, and horse riding. In the 1980s, Hema was compelled to do smaller action films such as *Ram Kali* (1985) and *Aandhi-Toofan* (1985) due to tax problems.

In her career, Hema made as many as 30 films with action hero Dharmendra. She also made a successful pair with Amitabh Bachchan in films such as *Satte pe Satta* (1982) and continued to do so in later years with *Baghban* (2003) and *Baabul* (2006).

Hema also tried directing, but was not successful. The constant passion of her life remains Bharatnatyam dance.

THE DREAM GIRL

Hema spent the 1970s in a delirium of romance and heartbreak. Actors such as Sanjeev Kumar and Jeetendra were keen on marrying her, but it was Dharmendra who was the love of her life. The two tied the knot on May 2, 1980. The couple have two daughters: actress Esha Deol and Ahana Deol.

◀ The danseuse

A trained Bharatnatyam dancer, Hema Malini performs extensively with her daughters Esha and Ahana, who are also trained in the dance form.

KEY WORKS

Raja Jani, 1972

Seeta aur Geeta, 1972 (see p. 109)

Jugnu, 1973

Sanyasi, 1975

Sholay, 1975 (see pp. 134–37)

Pratigya, 1975

Dream Girl, 1977

The Burning Train, 1980

Naseeb, 1981

Satte pe Satta, 1982

Razia Sultan, 1983

TIMELINE

October 16, 1948 Born in Thanjavur district of Tami Nadu, India.

1963 Appears on the big screen for the first time in Tamil film *Ithu Sathiyam*.

1968 Debuts in Hindi cinema with *Sapno Ka Saudagar*.

1970 Release of her first Bollywood hit, *Johny Mera Naam*, opposite Dev Anand.

1973 Receives the Filmfare Best Actress Award for the superhit movie *Seeta aur Geeta*.

1975 Stars in blockbuster hit *Sholay*.

1976–1980 Becomes the highest-paid Bollywood actress along with actress Zeenat Aman.

1979 Appears in the critically acclaimed film *Meera*.

1980 Marries actor Dharmendra in a private ceremony.

1981 Gives birth to daughter Esha Deol.

1985 Gives birth to daughter Ahana Deol.

1992 Directs her first film, *Dil Aashna Hai*, chooses future superstar Shah Rukh Khan for his first role.

2000 Becomes first woman chairperson of the National Film Development Corporation (NFDC).

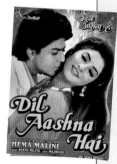

HEMA'S FIRST DIRECTORIAL VENTURE, IN 1992

2000 Receives the Padma Shri Award and the Filmfare Lifetime Achievement Award.

2003 Makes a comeback with *Baghban*, opposite Amitabh Bachchan.

2004 Joins the Bharatiya Janata Party (BJP), a political party.

2003–09 Serves as member of parliament in the Rajya Sabha—upper house of Parliament.

2011 Directs *Tell Me Oh Khuda*.

2014 Gets elected to the Lok Sabha—lower house of Parliament—from Mathura.

ANAND

1971

Shot in just over 20 days, *Anand* tells the moving story of a man's *joie de vivre* in the face of incurable cancer, and his ability to inspire those around him.

Coming at the peak of actor Rajesh Khanna's (see pp. 106–07) career, *Anand* (Bliss) boasts memorable dialogues by Gulzar (see pp. 142–43) and melodious music by Salil Chowdhury. Khanna upped his charm quotient to great effect as the terminally ill Anand, who wishes to live life to the fullest in the little time he has left. Amitabh Bachchan (see pp. 126–27)—gangly, almost awkward in this early stage of his career—was just right for the role of the intense Dr. Bhaskar Banerjee, who is so disillusioned by the plight of his patients that he becomes abrupt and short-tempered.

A GRAND LIFE
Diagnosed with an incurable cancer, Anand reaches out to doctors Prakash Kulkarni and Bhaskar Bannerjee in Mumbai. His irrepressible charm and zest for life leave a lasting impression on the two doctors and others he comes into contact with, including the concerned Matron D'Sa, Bhaskar's beloved Renu, his domestic help Ramu Kaka, Kulkarni's wife, and stage performer Issa Bhai. He inspires the brooding Bhaskar to embrace life.

"Life should be grand, not long," he says, laughing, singing, hitting it off with strangers, and playing pranks. His ready smile, positive outlook, and philosophy of getting the most out of life inspire his friends to follow in his footsteps. But as Anand's condition worsens, his well-wishers become

desperate, trying whatever remedies they can in a futile attempt to cure their friend.

A LASTING FRIENDSHIP
Believed to be modeled on the friendship between Hrishikesh Mukherjee (see p. 140) and actor–director Raj Kapoor (see pp. 44–45), the film's mainstay is the friendship between Anand and Bhaskar. Mukherjee initially offered the role of Anand to Kishore Kumar (see pp.100–101), with Mehmood playing Bhaskar, but finally cast Khanna and Bachchan. The two went on to win Filmfare Awards for Best Actor and Best Supporting Actor, respectively, for their performances in the film. The movie also won the National Award for Best Hindi Film and the Filmfare Best Film Award.

◄ **Life record**
Anand chronicles observations and life lessons on a tape recorder, which suddenly starts playing at the exact moment when Bhaskar implores his dead friend to resume his banter.

▼ **A winning combination**
The on-screen chemistry between the young Amitabh Bachchan (left) and Rajesh Khanna (right) in *Anand* prompted Mukherjee to repeat this casting in *Namak Haraam* (1973).

HIT SONGS

Kahin Door Jab Din Dhal Jaye
(When the Sun Sets at the Horizon)
🎤 **Singer** Mukesh

Zindagi Kaisi Hai Paheli Haye
(What Sort of a Mystery Is Life)
🎤 **Singer** Manna Dey

CAST AND CREW

★ **Rajesh Khanna** Anand
Amitabh Bachchan Dr. Bhaskar Bannerjee
Ramesh Deo Dr. Prakash Kulkarni
Sumita Sanyal Renu
Seema Mrs. Suman Kulkarni
Lalita Pawar Matron D'Sa
Johnny Walker Issa Bhai

🎬 **Director** Hrishikesh Mukherjee
🎦 **Producers** Hrishikesh Mukherjee, N.C. Sippy
🎵 **Music composer** Salil Chowdhury
🎼 **Lyricists** Gulzar, Yogesh
📖 **Scriptwriters** Hrishikesh Mukherjee, Gulzar, D.N. Mukherjee, Bimal Dutta
🎥 **Cinematographer** Jaywant Pathare
👔 **Costume designers** M.R. Bhutkar, Mohan Pardesi

AMAR PREM

1972

Sharmila Tagore and Rajesh Khanna delivered yet another hit together with *Amar Prem*, the touching tale of a love that withstood the test of time and the hypocrisies of society.

Among the string of hits that Shakti Samanta directed, *Amar Prem* (Immortal Love) was his favorite. An adaptation of noted Bengali writer Bibhuti Bhushan Bandopadhyay's story *Hinger Kochuri* (Savory Snack), this film marked Sharmila Tagore's (see p. 103) comeback after the birth of her son. While the book dwelled on a motherless child who finds a mother figure in a kind prostitute, in the film the focus shifts to the prostitute and her lover.

A MAKESHIFT FAMILY

The film tells the story of Pushpa, who is abandoned by her husband and scorned by her village because she is unable to bear a child. She is

sold to a brothel in Kolkata. There, the cynical, lonely, alcoholic Anand Babu, who is deeply unhappy in his marriage, becomes her regular and only customer. Pushpa befriends a neighbor's young son, Nandu, who is mistreated by his stepmother. For a while, Anand Babu, Pushpa, and Nandu fill a void in each others' lives. But their happiness is cut short by a society that would rather they suffer apart than be happy together, outside acceptable definitions of family. The three drift apart, perhaps never to meet again. However, fate has something else in store for the trio.

ALL ABOUT A SONG

Amar Prem is considered to be the finest hour of the lyricist–music director duo Anand Bakshi (see p. 105) and R.D. Burman (see p. 109). Renowned for his peppy, Western-inspired tunes, Burman surprised everyone with semi-classical melodies, such as "Raina Beeti Jaye" and the devotional-music-inspired "Bada Natkhat Hai Yeh Krishan Kanhaiya" (The Mischievous Rogue That Is Young Krishna), which suited Bakshi's thoughtful lyrics.

The song "Chingari Koi Bhadke," romantically shot in what appears to be a boat near Kolkata's Howrah Bridge, was actually shot at Natraj studios in Mumbai. The crew could not shoot at Howrah Bridge because the authorities feared crowd control becoming an issue. It is said that the smell of the stagnant water became so fetid that Sharmila used to keep chewing gum in her mouth to prevent herself from feeling sick.

GREAT WRITING

The sensitive dialogue penned by Ramesh Pant struck a chord with the audiences. At once quirky and memorable, the line "Pushpa, I hate tears"—delivered to great effect in the film in Rajesh Khanna's (see pp.106–

107) trademark drawl—remains to this day a significant marker in pop culture. Pant and Aravinda Mukherji won the Filmfare Award for Best Dialogue and Best Screenplay, respectively.

▲ **Of love and sacrifice**
Sharmila Tagore has a powerful central role in *Amar Prem* portraying the selfless Pushpa, who manages to find enduring love—romantic and maternal—in a world that hurts her at every turn.

"*Amar Prem … portray[s] … three strangers … who unexpectedly find each other and love.*"

PRADEEP SEBASTIAN, WRITER, *DECCAN HERALD*, 2012

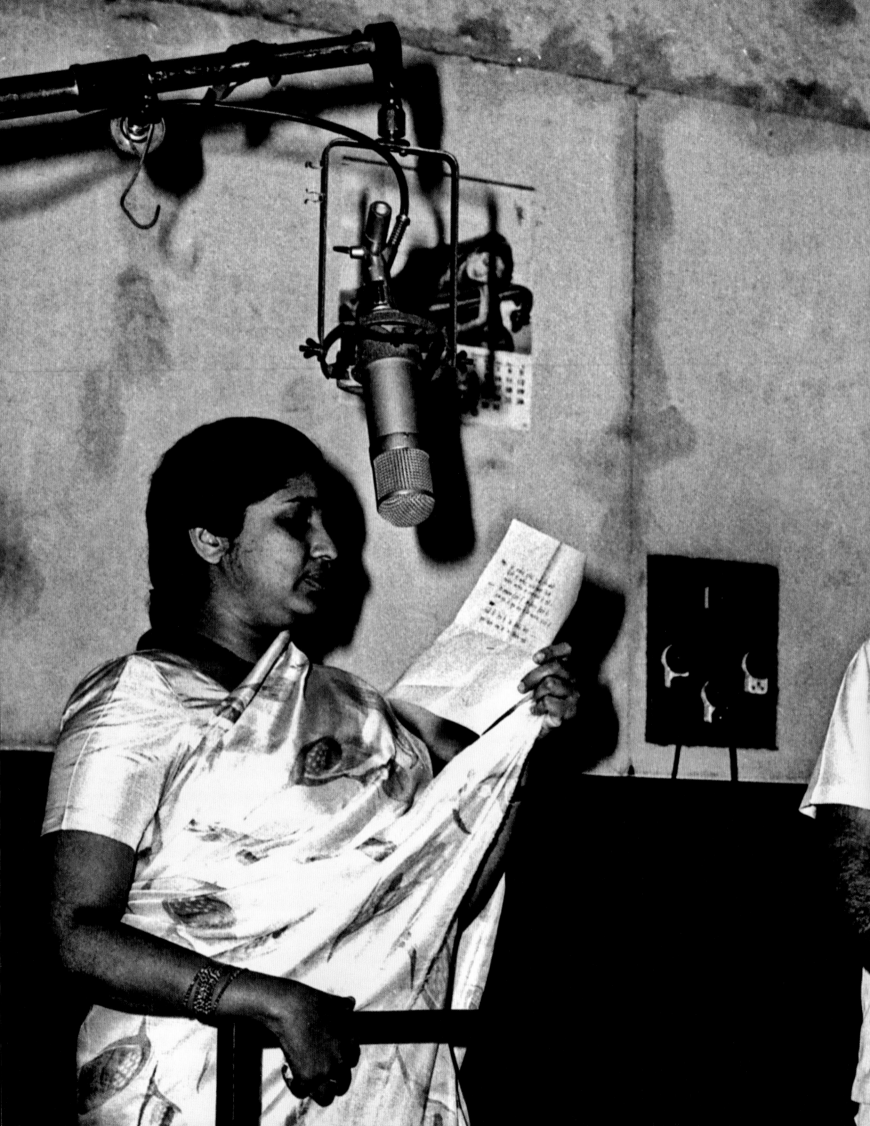

PLAYBACK SINGING

In Indian films, songs are pre-recorded by professional singers—who are stars in their own right—and actors lip-sync to them while filming.

The earliest actor–singers in films were mostly theater performers, and sometimes musically trained courtesans, who sang and were recorded as they acted. The accompanying musicians played out of the frame. In the 1930s, playback technology revolutionized this scenario, allowing singers to record in a studio and the actors to later lip-sync to these recordings.

The systematic use of playback singing began in 1935 with New Theatres' Bengali movie *Bhagya Chakra*, also made in Hindi as *Dhoop Chhaon* in the same year. It led to the emergence of professionals who exclusively sang, and didn't need to look the part or act. However, the singers did have to perform in keeping with the emotions that the actors would portray on screen. The relationship between actors and their "singing voices" became like a close friendship. "I have lost my voice," said filmmaker Raj Kapoor on hearing of singer Mukesh's death. "Kishore Kumar was my soul, I was his body," said the actor Rajesh Khanna.

In the 1930s and 1940s, K.L. Saigal was the nation's favorite singer. In the 1940s, a time dominated by singing star Suraiya, and the weighty, low-pitched voices of Noorjehan and Shamshad Begum, entered Lata Mangeshkar (see pp. 60–61), who set a new standard with her light, sweet voice. So successful was the diva that she withdrew from the Filmfare Awards (see pp. 282–83) in 1969 to give other singers a chance. Mohammed Rafi was another legend who ruled the sound waves from the 1950s to 1970s. His contemporaries included Mukesh, who was associated with melancholy numbers, and Talat Mahmood who sang ghazals (Urdu songs). The versatile Kishore Kumar (see pp. 100–101) and Asha Bhosle were the voices of romantic Bollywood in the 1970s and 1980s. Bhosle appears in the *Guinness Book of World Records* for having recorded more than 11,000 singles.

VERSATILE VOICES
Earlier, most playback singers would perform everything from ghazals to disco songs, with romantic duets, devotional numbers, semi-classical songs, and qawwali numbers in between. Later, composers started choosing different voices for specific numbers, such as Usha Uthup for club songs. Even in the 1990s, one could identify Kumar Sanu, Alka Yagnik, and Udit Narayan as the leading singers. But in the 2000s, composers began to use a larger variety of voices for each film.

◀ **Legendary singers**
In the 1950s, when Mohammed Rafi (right) was a singing star, Asha Bhosle (left) was just embarking on what would become a glittering career.

"The sovereignty of the song sequence might account for the rise of the playback star."

SANGITA GOPAL AND SUJATA MOORTI, *GLOBAL BOLLYWOOD,* 2008

PAKEEZAH

1972

For the director, Kamal Amrohi, *Pakeezah* was more than just a film, it was an all-consuming passion. It also created the role of a lifetime for his wife and lead actress, Meena Kumari.

HIT SONGS

Chalte Chalte
(On the Road of Life)

🎤 **Singer** Lata Mangeshkar

Thade Rahiyo, O Baanke Yaar
(Do Keep Waiting, My Flirtatious Lover)

🎤 **Singer** Lata Mangeshkar

Inhi Logon Ne
(These People)

🎤 **Singer** Lata Mangeshkar

The story of the making of *Pakeezah* (Pure) is every bit as epic and dramatic as the film itself. Actress Meena Kumari (see p. 91) and filmmaker Kamal Amrohi married in 1952, and started planning *Pakeezah* in 1956. Through the story of a reluctant courtesan haunted by her quest for true love, Amrohi wanted to showcase his beautiful and gifted wife at her best. However, the film was delayed by his perfectionism and then because the couple separated in 1964. Shooting for the film recommenced, on a token payment of a gold guinea for Meena Kumari, when they came together to finish the film in 1969. *Pakeezah* was finally released in 1972, at a time when the Indian social fabric was rapidly changing. Indian cinema had become bolder with films such as *Hare Rama Hare Krishna* (see p. 108), which was based on the decadence of the

CAST AND CREW

★ **Meena Kumari** Sahibjaan / Nargis
Raaj Kumar Salim Ahmed Khan
Veena Nawabjaan
Ashok Kumar Shahabuddin
Nadira Gauharjaan

🎬 **Director** Kamal Amrohi
◔ **Producer** Kamal Amrohi
🎵 **Music** Ghulam Mohammed, Naushad
♪ **Lyricists** Kaifi Bhopali, Kaifi Azmi,
Majrooh Sultanpuri, Kamal Amrohi
🕺 **Choreography** Gauri Shankar,
Lachhu Maharaj
📖 **Script writer** Kamal Amrohi
🎥 **Cinematographer** Josef Wirsching
👕 **Costume designer** Meena Kumari

and dance, and the precious honor of aristocrats, all came from Amrohi's memories of the UP of his youth. Yet, despite his nostalgia, he made this film as a critique of such a society, in which women like Sahibjaan are denied a life of love and respect.

In the film, Sahibjaan's mother Nargis is also a courtesan, who dies in isolation after being rejected by the aristocratic father of her husband, Shahabuddin. The infant Sahibjaan is brought up and trained as a courtesan by her aunt Nawabjaan, and kept away from her father. The beautiful and talented Sahibjaan becomes a desired courtesan, but she is infatuated with a mysterious stranger, who secretly leaves her a note praising the beauty of her feet. This is Salim, a forest ranger, who is also Shahabuddin's nephew. Salim wants to marry Sahibjaan, and gives her the name "Pakeezah." They elope, but Sahibjaan, traumatized by the humiliation Salim faces on her account, flees from the wedding ceremony. Later, she is invited to dance at Salim's wedding. A distraught Sahibjaan does so, cutting her feet by

▼ **Tender love**
The palpable on-screen chemistry between Meena Kumari and Raaj Kumar produced some of the most memorable scenes in *Pakeezah*. This lovely image is a part of a publicity shoot for the film.

hippie culture in India then. *Pakeezah*, with its old-world charm, had come almost a decade too late, and opened to a tepid response. Meena Kumari's untimely death shortly after the film's release was the final twist in the saga, catapulting the movie to cult status.

ROMANCE AND TRAGEDY
This film is the tale of Sahibjaan, a courtesan in the decadent feudal set-up of Uttar Pradesh (UP), north India. *Pakeezah*'s world of elaborately executed salutations, Urdu poetry, courtly gatherings of song

◀ **Eye for detail**
Among other aspects of the film, it was equally famous for its carefully constructed, detailed sets, which evoked the grandeur and life of a bygone age.

▲ **Grand premiere**
After 16 years in the making, *Pakeezah* was released at the iconic Maratha Mandir in Mumbai, Maharashtra, on January 3, 1972. It is said that prints of the film were carried in a palanquin.

dancing on broken glass. Unable to bear her suffering, Nawabjaan berates Shahabuddin for the hypocrisy of his class, informing him of Sahibjaan's parentage. Chaos marrs a long-awaited reconciliation and tragedy ensues.

PERFECTIONIST AT WORK
Writer–director Kamal Amrohi only made four films, including *Mahal* (1949) and *Razia Sultan* (1983). Obsessed with *Pakeezah*, he made sketches for the *havelis*, or mansions, himself, modeling them on his family home in Amroha, UP. A perfectionist, he agonized for days over a shot because he was dissatisfied with a sunset, and even had an entire set demolished when he noticed a slight angle to it. On seeing the colored reels of *Mughal-e-Azam* (1960), for which he was a writer, Amrohi abandoned his black-and-white version of *Pakeezah*, and restarted it in color. Later, he switched to a Cinemascope lens, which

had just come into fashion, further contributing to the movie's excessively slow rate of progress.

SWAN SONG
The making of *Pakeezah* was marked by the deaths of several key contributors to the film. Cinematographer Josef Wirsching created some iconic scenes, but his work had to be completed by R.D. Mathur after his death in 1967. Ghulam Mohammed provided exquisite semi-classical music for his magnum opus, but died in 1968. The background music was then composed by music director, Naushad. However, the death that defined *Pakeezah* was that of its leading lady, Meena Kumari. By the time shooting for the film resumed in 1969, she was already an alcoholic suffering from liver cirrhosis. Padma Khanna, who was then a newcomer, doubled for her when dramatic dancing was required, such as for the climactic song, "Aaj Hum Apni" (Today, I Shall). The great Bollywood tragic actress died on March 31, 1972, at age 39, and never saw the success of her swan song.

RAAJ KUMAR (1926–96)

Born Kulbhushan Pandit, Raaj Kumar got his first break with *Rangili* (1952) while working as a sub-inspector with the Bombay Police in the late 1940s. His portrayal of Nargis's husband in the 1957 film *Mother India* (see pp. 56–59) also brought him attention, but he became a sensation with *Dil Ek Mandir* (1963) and *Waqt* (see p. 92), and won the Filmfare Award for Best Supporting Actor for both. Later in life, he starred in the hits *Saudagar* (1991) and *Tiranga* (1993). The stylish, pipe-smoking actor was outspoken and eccentric, with a theatrical style of delivering dialogue—especially of patronizingly calling his opponents "jaani"—which is the subject of affectionate humor even today.

"I have lived with Pakeezah *almost as long as I lived with its creator."*

MEENA KUMARI, 1972

BOBBY

1973

A superhit film made with a fresh lead pair, *Bobby* became the template for a host of Bollywood teen romances that followed over the next two decades.

◄ Tripping on typography
More than conveying the subject of the film, the poster's use of psychedelic colors and flower power motifs alludes to the movie's youthful energy.

A surprise offering from R.K. Films, *Bobby* was different from most movies that Raj Kapoor (see pp. 44–45) had directed before. It was a teenage love story, did not star Kapoor as the hero, its music was not scored by Kapoor's regular composers Shankar-Jaikishan, and it did not have an underlying political philosophy. Reeling from the financial losses due to the box office failure of his labor of love *Mera Naam Joker* (1970), Raj Kapoor had decided that the next movie he produced would be a low-budget teenage love story. In an industry that tends to pass off established middle-aged actors in roles as young adults, 20-year-old Rishi Kapoor and 16-year-old Dimple Kapadia acting their age provided a welcome change. While Rishi won a fan following among college students, Dimple became a national sweetheart.

Bobby pioneered the genre of teenage romance in Bollywood films. Its storyline of thwarted young lovers, feuding families, rebellion, and death (or at least a close shave with it) became the hallmarks of successful films such as *Ek Duje ke Liye* (1981), *Love Story* (1981), *Qayamat se Qayamat Tak* (see pp. 194–97), and *Maine Pyar Kiya* (see p. 206).

PUPPY LOVE
The film tells the story of Raja, the neglected son of wealthy socialite parents, who falls in love with Bobby, the granddaughter of his former governess. Their relationship is frowned upon by Raja's father Mr. Nath, who considers the differences in the two families' social standing unacceptable. Raja convinces his father to meet with Bobby's family to discuss their marriage. However, this meeting only serves to alienate the two families further as insults are traded.

When Mr. Nath engineers Raja's engagement to a mentally challenged woman in a bid to broker a business partnership with her father, the

▲ Goan flavor
In addition to setting contemporary fashion trends, *Bobby* showcased vibrant Goan attire, specifically that of the region's colorful fishing community.

lovestruck couple is forced to elope. Mr. Nath posts a reward for their return, placing their lives in jeopardy at the hands of a bounty hunter, Prem Chopra. As the two fathers rescue their children from this peril, and each saves the other's child from drowning, they realize the error of their ways.

RECREATING ROMANCE
It is said that Raj Kapoor recreated his first meeting with actress Nargis in Raja's first meeting with Bobby on

◄ Rustic dance number
The orchestration of the folksy "Jhoot Bole Kauwa Kaate" includes traditional wind instruments such as shehnais, and daflis for percussion.

"Class rivalry was only spice for a recipe that stressed breathless, obsessive, juvenile love."

ASHIS NANDY, *THE SECRET POLITICS OF OUR DESIRES,* 1998

HIT SONGS

Hum Tum Ik Kamre Mein Bund Ho
(If You and I Were Locked in a Room)
🎤 **Singers** Lata Mangeshkar,
Shailendra Singh

Mein Shayar To Nahin
(I May Not Be a Poet)
🎤 **Singer** Shailendra Singh

celluloid. The story goes that Raj Kapoor arrived unannounced at actress and filmmaker Jaddanbai's apartment to enquire after a studio for his upcoming production *Aag*. The door was answered by Jaddanbai's daughter Nargis, who had come from the kitchen with flour still on her hands. While conversing with him, she swept aside a strand of hair, leaving a streak of flour on her face. This moment of love at first sight was immortalized in *Bobby*, long after Raj Kapoor and Nargis had gone their separate ways.

DARLING DEBUTANTE

While shooting for *Bobby*, Dimple met superstar Rajesh Khanna and had a whirlwind wedding with Khanna, who was 15 years her senior. They were married during the film's production, so some scenes had to be strategically shot to keep Dimple's hands—still covered in bridal henna—out of sight of the camera.

When the film released six months later, it was a roaring success and its married heroine, then pregnant with her first child, was embraced by the

nation. This flew in the face of a belief long held in Bollywood that being married reduced the marketability of an actress. At the time Dimple observed, "I don't think my success was as much of a high as getting married to this superstar. I used to be a big fan of his, it was a dream come true." She bowed out of Bollywood in deference to her marriage and family, but returned to the screen after a 10-year hiatus.

TREND-SETTING

Like the lead pair, the film's fashion was fresh and young, too. Dimple's bold outfits, including everything from bikinis to maxis, and all hemlines in between, broadened the definition of youth style to include the daring and defiant. Rishi Kapoor sported bellbottomed trousers, fitted pullovers, and tailored blazers—all suitably accessorized with scarves and ties. The prints were loud and the colors, vibrant. Soon, *Bobby*-inspired outfits began to make their way onto the fashion market.

The film's soundtrack was equally influential. *Bobby* managed the remarkable feat of having each of its eight songs hit the bull's-eye. It is said that Raj Kapoor had a bank of tunes from his favorite composer duo Shankar–Jaikishan (Jaikishan having passed away in 1970), and simply gave new composers Laxmikant–Pyarelal these tunes to

DIMPLE KAPADIA (b.1957)

As a 16-year-old, Dimple Kapadia had a dream launch in Raj Kapoor's super-hit film *Bobby*. The same year she made headlines by unexpectedly getting married to superstar Rajesh Khanna. She quit films to set up home and raise their daughters Twinkle and Rinke. After separating from her husband, she returned to films with *Saagar* in 1985. She gained acclaim for films like *Kaash*, *Drishti*, and *Lekin* and won the National Award for Best Actress for *Rudali* (1993). She continues to play strong character roles. Outside of her film career she creates designer candles, sold under the label The Faraway Tree.

arrange for *Bobby*. New playback singer Shailendra Singh sang for Rishi, and Lata Mangeshkar lent her dulcet tones to the young heroine. The lilting Goan refrain in "Na Mangu Sona Chandi" (I Don't Want Gold or Silver) and the folksy lyrics of "Jhoot Bole Kauwa Kaate" (If You Lie, a Crow Will Bite You) added extra color to an already brilliant movie soundtrack.

▶ **Rising stars**
Both Rishi Kapoor and Dimple Kapadia bagged the Filmfare Awards for Best Actor and Best Actress, respectively, for their debut movie; Kapadia shared hers with Jaya Bachchan for the film *Abhimaan*.

CAST AND CREW

★ **Rishi Kapoor** Raja (Raj Nath)
Dimple Kapadia Bobby Braganza
Pran Mr. Nath
Prem Nath Jack Braganza
Durga Khote Mrs. Braganza
Prem Chopra Prem

🎬 **Director** Raj Kapoor
⬠ **Producer** Raj Kapoor
🎵 **Music composers** Laxmikant S. Kudalkar, Pyarelal R. Sharma
🎵 **Lyricists** Anand Bakshi, Vitthalbhai Patel
🕺 **Choreographer** Sohanlal
▭ **Scriptwriters** K.A. Abbas, V.P. Sathe
🎥 **Cinematographer** Radhu Karmakar
👔 **Costume designer** Mani Rabadi

ANGRY YOUNG MEN
1973–1981

At a time of sociopolitical turmoil, the angry young man arrived on the scene to challenge the status quo, raising a powerful voice against injustice and corruption.

ANGRY
YOUNG MEN

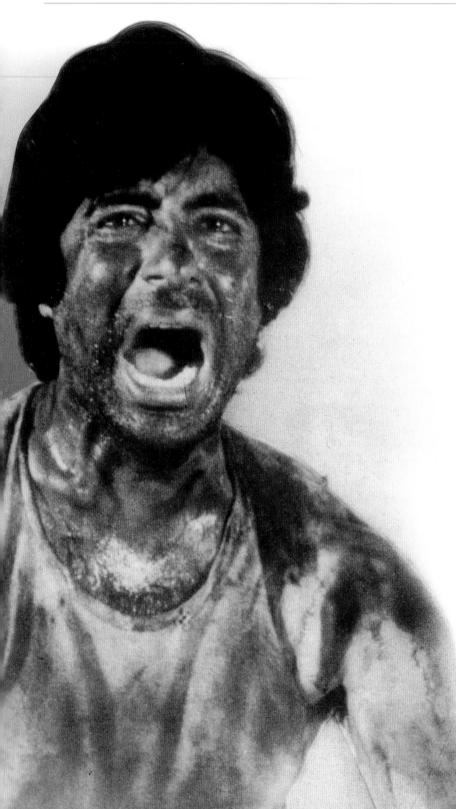

Tapping into the vast political and social discontent of the 1970s, Bollywood projected fury and vengeance onto the cinema screens—a sharp turn from the glamour years of the previous decade.

At a time of labor strikes, crippling unemployment, and student unrest, the "angry young man" was the answer to society's search for a different, more relevant kind of hero.

The label "angry young man" was first used in the UK during the promotion of John Osborne's play *Look Back in Anger* (1956). It became a popular media catchphrase to describe disillusioned young writers critical of the establishment. Years later in India, the lanky Amitabh Bachchan (see pp. 126–27)—with his smouldering eyes—and a script from the talented screenwriter-duo Salim Khan and Javed Akhtar (see pp. 138–39) conveyed an intense on-screen rage so successfully in *Zanjeer* (see pp. 124–25) that the Indian press picked up the term to describe his performance.

At 31, Amitabh wasn't exactly young. Before *Zanjeer* hit the screens in 1973, he had been a struggling actor for nearly five years. It took the genius of Salim–Javed to appreciate the intensity that the actor brought

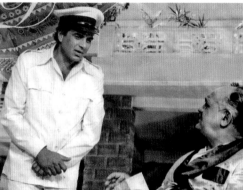

▲ Comic relief
Deviating from 1970s anti-establishment trends, *Chupke Chupke* (1975) gave audiences a sidesplitting storyline and a rare chance to see action hero Dharmendra in a comic role.

to his roles, and it was they who recommended him for the parts of furious Vijay in *Zanjeer*, the laconic Jai in *Sholay* (see pp. 134–37), and the despondant Vijay in *Deewar* (see p. 130).

ALL ABOUT ANGER
The angry hero archetype created by Salim–Javed is a complex character. Traumatized, he is as tragic as he is angry, searching for retribution but often in a self-destructive way that results in death. As Javed Akhtar said, "Amitabh's anger was mixed with hurt and tears." Several of Amitabh's characters harbor these layers of emotion: in *Zanjeer,* he wakes up in

◄ The archetype of anger
Amitabh won the Filmfare Award for Best Actor in 1980 for his powerful portrayal of an oppressed coal miner, who battles his inner demons and rises up to fight injustice in the film *Kala Patthar*.

a sweat from nightmares about the murder of his parents; in *Deewar*, he carries the words "My father is a thief" tattooed on his arm and longs for the mother who repudiated him; in *Trishul* (1978), he is raised by his mother to wreak vengeance upon his father, who deserted them; in *Shakti* (1982), he again grows up feeling resentful and abandoned by his father.

Remarkably for Hindi cinema, the "angry young man" was the first hero not to sing songs: Amitabh as Vijay (his favorite screen name) in *Zanjeer*, *Deewar*, and *Kala Patthar* (1979) does not sing at all, while in *Trishul* he performs only one cynical song about love. Interestingly, in the all-time-superhit *Sholay*, Amitabh's strong and silent character is without any parent-induced trauma or simmering rage and he even sings a song of undying loyalty for his best friend.

AN UNJUST WORLD

The anger of Amitabh's persona stemmed from social problems at large: the plight of the poor, the humiliation faced by social outcasts, the unfair privilege of the powerful few, and the injustice shown to women—especially single mothers, such as those portrayed by Nirupa Roy in *Deewar*, Waheeda Rehman (see p. 85) in *Trishul*, and Rakhee (see p. 145) in *Laawaris* (1981).

Even outside of Salim–Javed's scripts, Amitabh's characters suffer indignities. In *Muqaddar ka Sikandar* (see p. 154), he is falsely labeled a thief as a child and haunted by his beloved's rejection. In *Laawaris*, he plays the ultimate social outcast—an illegitimate child. It is interesting to note that Amitabh himself maintains that "the first powerful depiction, or in a sense the birth, of the so-called 'angry

young man' was designed by Mehboob Khan in *Mother India* (see pp.56–59), where the character Birju, played so brilliantly by Sunil Dutt, was depicted."

ALTERNATIVE ANGER

The "young men" of 1970s arthouse cinema voiced the fury of the oppressed even more effectively, albeit without any song-and-dance routines. In 1976, Naseeruddin Shah (see p. 185) presented a hard-hitting depiction of Dalit (the lowest caste) angst as Bhola, who rages against upper-caste dominance in *Manthan*. He also played the anti-colonial rebel Sarfaraz in *Junoon* (1978) and was cast in *Albert Pinto ko Gussa Kyun Aata hai* (1980), which analyzes an exploitative capitalist system. In 1980, Govind Nihalani chose actor Om Puri to star in *Aakrosh* as a tribesman who is so oppressed that he retreats into total silence, only to break it at the end of the film with lacerating screams. The pair collaborated again in *Ardh Satya* (1983), with Puri playing a police inspector, who buckles under the

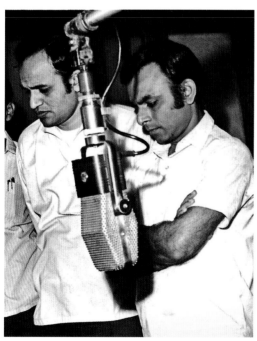

◀ **The sound of fury**
The versatile and edgy soundtracks created by composer-brothers Kalyanji–Anandji perfectly complemented the high drama of the "angry young man" films of 1970s Bollywood.

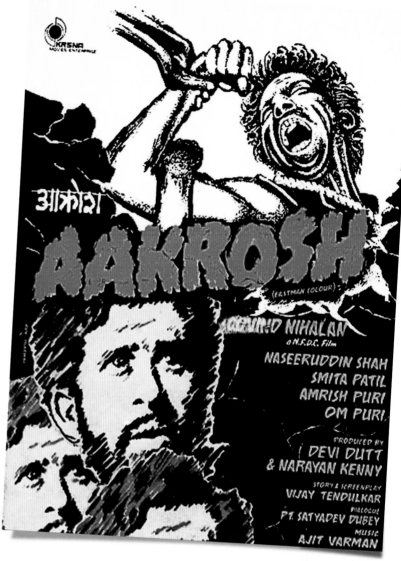

▲ **Heart of darkness**
Govind Nihalani's debut film *Aakrosh* takes an uncompromising look at the violence and wrath resulting from an unending cycle of social inequity.

machinations of his political masters.

By the 1980s, anger personified by Amitabh turned into machismo and vigilantism in films such as *Mard* (1985) and *Shahenshah* (1988). The last of the 1970s "alternative" anger came in comic bursts of rage from Naseeruddin Shah and Ravi Baswani as "everyman" heroes in *Jaane Bhi do Yaaron* (see p. 178).

OTHER MAINSTREAM OFFERINGS

Although the 1970s came to be defined as the era of the "angry young man," Bollywood did not abandon more traditional themes, and in 1975, it released Vijay Sharma's mythological film *Jai Santoshi Ma*, a rival blockbuster to *Deewaar*. As for the "angry young man" himself, Amitabh appeared in the charming romance *Mili* (1975), the musical drama *Abhimaan*, (1973), and the comedy *Chupke Chupke* (see p.

140), directed by Hrishikesh Mukherjee (see p. 140), known for painting quaint middle-class portraits. Amitabh also starred in director Manmohan Desai's crazy entertainers, showing off his comedic talent—the song "My Name Is Anthony Gonsalves" from *Amar Akbar Anthony* (see pp. 148–49) is as far from an "angry young man" as it could get.

But Amitabh wasn't the only mover and shaker at the time. Rajesh Khanna (see pp. 106–107) had a short, glorious reign; the Hema Malini–Dharmendra (see pp. 110–11 and pp. 152–53) pairing had a loyal following; Rishi Kapoor (see p. 202) entertained with his dance moves; and Zeenat Aman (see p. 156) won many hearts. Punchy dialogue and action were the forte of Dharmendra, Shatrughan Sinha, and Vinod Khanna (see p. 128). The decade also saw some masala musicals such as Nasir Hussain's *Yaadon ki Baarat* (1973).

ZANJEER

A trendsetting blockbuster, *Zanjeer* marked the beginning of the "angry young man" era and shot actor Amitabh Bachchan to fame with the help of its fantastic script.

CAST AND CREW

★ **Amitabh Bachchan** Vijay Khanna
Jaya Bhaduri Mala
Ajit Khan Teja
Pran Sher Khan
Om Prakash D'Silva
Bindu Mona
Keshto Mukherjee Gangu
Iftekhar Police Commissioner

🎬 **Director** Prakash Mehra
🎬 **Producer** Prakash Mehra
🎵 **Music composers** Kalyanji Virji Shah, Anandji Virji Shah
🎵 **Lyricist** Gulshan Bawra
🕺 **Choreographer** Satya Narayan
📖 **Scriptwriters** Salim Khan, Javed Akhtar
🎥 **Cinematographer** N. Satyen
👔 **Costume designer** Vasant Mahajan

The film *Zanjeer* (The Chain) gave Indian cinema a new kind of hero—one who was not so much angry as a seething volcano of fury waiting to erupt. After nearly five years of acting in forgettable films such as Prakash Verma's *Bansi Birju* (1972), and in other hero's hits, such the Rajesh Khanna-led *Anand* (see pp. 112); Amitabh Bachchan (see pp. 126–27) finally found his own unique persona. The brooding silences and psychological complexity of *Zanjeer*'s Inspector Vijay made the audience sit up and take notice. Writer–lyricist Javed Akhtar remembers that while watching the film, the audience did not clap and whistle as was the norm in movie halls; instead they sat in awed silence.

For *Zanjeer*, writers Salim–Javed (see pp. 138–39) drew inspiration from

◄ **Breakthrough hit**
Writers Salim–Javed paid for an advertisement of *Zanjeer* to appear in the local trade magazine *Screen* on the day of the movie's release. It featured on the inside back cover and gave the writers as much prominence as the lead star.

Giulio Petroni's Western *Death Rides a Horse* (1967), in which a child sees his family being murdered by the villains and commits some of their characteristics to memory in order to identify and take revenge on them when he grows up.

CHAINED TO A MEMORY

The film revolves around Vijay, who witnesses his parents' brutal murder as a young child. He is haunted by the memory of their masked killer's bracelet, which has a single white horse charm on it. This quiet, reserved child named Vijay grows up to become a police inspector who still has nightmares about a white horse and becomes unbalanced in his fury against criminals. He befriends strongman Sher Khan and falls in love with the roadside knife-sharpener Mala.

While pursuing illicit liquor smugglers, Vijay runs afoul of arch villain Seth Dharam Dayal Teja and his moll Mona. When his persistence

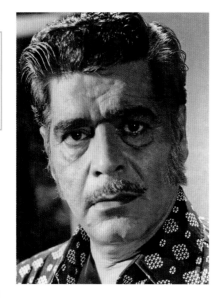

▲ **The unflappable Ajit**
The role of Teja was the root of the Ajit legend, as he played the epitome of the cool-headed kingpin, psychoanalyzing his opponents and drawling out suave witticisms.

becomes a thorn in Teja's side, he has the inspector implicated in a false bribery case, and later tries to have him killed. Vijay has to promise a terrified Mala that he would give up his quest for revenge. But his anonymous informer exhorts him to keep fighting the good fight. Bound by his promise and unable to act on any leads, Vijay goes into such depression that Mala relents, releasing him from his oath. When Vijay finally discovers the identity of the masked killer of his nightmares, vengeance is his for the taking.

A NATION'S PSYCHE

Most analysts agree that *Zanjeer* and Amitabh's persona in it tapped into the collective sentiment of the nation at the time. The conditions prevalent in the 1970s made audiences warm to characters like Vijay, who would have seemed out of place in a more hopeful, post-independence era. The realities that *Zanjeer* reveals are of smugglers flourishing as businessmen with impunity, spurious medicines in the

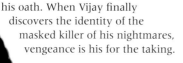

◀ **Victorious Vijay**
Zanjeer was the first time Amitabh took the on-screen name Vijay. The actor went on to use this on-screen moniker in more than 20 films, including hits, such as *Deewaar* and *Don*, and considers it lucky.

markets, urban crime becoming a normalized phenomenon, and rampant corruption in the police force. When assassins offer the character of Sher Khan a large sum of money for killing a policeman, he observes cynically: "He must be a very honest policeman." The growing frustration and bottled-up anger of a country found expression in the enraged outbursts of Amitabh's character.

ANYONE BUT AMITABH

Zanjeer was offered to a number of heroes before it came to Amitabh. However, they all imposed conditions which could not be met. Dharmendra (see pp. 152–53) and Mumtaz had initially been announced as the lead pair, but Dharmendra wasn't available for shooting on the required dates. According to producer–director Prakash Mehra, Raaj Kumar (see pp. 117) agreed to take the role but needed the filmmaker to come to the south where he was shooting another movie, while Dev Anand (see pp. 88–89) wanted more songs in the film.
Salim–Javed were convinced about Amitabh, despite his slew of flops, after seeing him in S. Ramanathan's adventure comedy *Bombay to Goa* and Mukul Dutt's drama *Raaste ka Pathhar* (both 1972). They felt the role would suit him better than it would their friend, the then-reigning heartthrob Rajesh Khanna (see pp.106–107). Pran

"*I selected Amitabh because of the emotions his eyes could generate.*"

PRAKASH MEHRA, DIRECTOR, IN AN INTERVIEW WITH SYED FIRDAUS ASHRAF FOR REDIFF

seconded their choice and soon Mehra was convinced. The distributors were jittery but Mehra refused to change his hero after committing to him. The far more successful Jaya Bhaduri came on board, possibly because she was in a relationship with Amitabh at the time. Mehra and Amitabh went on to make a formidable team that gave hits, such as *Muqaddar ka Sikandar* (see pp. 154), *Lawaaris* (1981), *Namak Halaal* (1982), and *Sharaabi* (1984).

WRITTEN BY SALIM–JAVED

Fed up of the relative anonymity of writers in the film industry, Salim–Javed started demanding more recognition and credit for their work. When the early posters of *Zanjeer* did not feature their names, the two went and hired a painter to stencil "Written by Salim–Javed" on all the posters they could find.
Later, to convince the producers of *Sholay* that Amitabh would be suitable for the hero's role, the writer duo organized a special screening of *Zanjeer* for filmmakers G.P. Sippy and Ramesh Sippy. When Amitabh was signed for their film, the market became much more confident about the possibilities of the actor and *Zanjeer* got a smoother release. Salim–Javed went on to write several scripts that reinforced Amitabh's quiet "angry young man" persona, including Yash Chopra's *Trishul* (1978) and *Kaala Patthar* (1979).

PRAN (1920–2013)

As a villain, Pran Krishan Sikand was so convincingly evil that no Indian parent wanted to name their child "Pran". Having played lead roles in Lahore, Pakistan, Pran came to Mumbai after India's partition. He soon became a leading villain in films with established actors such as Raj Kapoor (see pp. 44–45) and Dilip Kumar (see pp. 48–49). By the mid-1970s, Pran did more serious and comic roles. He won his first Filmfare Award for *Upkar* (see p. 98). In his career spanning 60 years, he appeared in as many as 350 films. He received the Padma Bhushan—the third-highest civilian award—in 2001 and the Dadasaheb Phalke Award in 2013.

AMITABH BACHCHAN

ACTOR b.1942

Voted the millennium's greatest actor in a BBC poll, Amitabh Bachchan is more than just an extraordinary actor. He is also a national icon and one of the most popular Indians on social media.

Son of well-known Hindi poet Harivansh Rai Bachchan, Amitabh Bachchan was not new to the world of the performing arts—in college, he starred in theater productions as well as in the boxing ring. Although he went on to work as a sales executive in Kolkata, it was always his dream to act.

In 1969, director Khwaja Ahmad Abbas (see p. 41) launched Amitabh's film career in *Saat Hindustani*. A black-and-white film in the age of color, it failed to woo the masses, but it did earn Amitabh the National Award for Best Newcomer.

▲ **Reel-life couple**
In Hrishikesh Mukherjee's *Abhimaan*, Amitabh plays a singer whose pride gets the better of him when his wife becomes the more popular singer.

THE ACTOR
Amitabh evolved as an actor through his work in a dozen films, including *Anand* (see p. 112) and *Parwana* (1971). However, it was with Prakash Mehra's *Zanjeer* that he established himself as a bankable solo hero. Labeled the "angry young man" for his role in the film, he attained megastar status. He married his co-star Jaya Bhaduri the same year.

A series of hits cemented Amitabh's position in the industry. He was fortunate to have creative scriptwriters and to work with some great directors, who sustained his success through the 1980s. With screenwriters Salim–Javed (see pp. 138–39) at the helm, Amitabh worked his "angry young man" image in movies with acclaimed directors such as Ravi Tandon, Yash Chopra (see pp. 166–67), Ramesh Sippy, and Chandra Bhanot. He diversified into comedy with Prakash Mehra's *Hera Pheri* (1976) and *Namak Halaal* (1982), Manmohan Desai's *Amar Akbar Anthony*, Raj Sippy's *Satte pe Satta* (1982), and Hrishikesh Mukherjee's *Chupke Chupke* (see p. 140).

◀ **A champion**
In Manmohan Desai's action comedy *Naseeb* (1981) Amitabh plays a full-time waiter who also boxes part-time in order to earn extra money to fund his younger brother's education.

> " *An actor's career should not and cannot end, the stream should run ceaselessly.* "

AMITABH BACHCHAN, *INDIA TODAY*, JANUARY 12, 2013

KEY WORKS

Saat Hindustani, 1969

Zanjeer, 1973 (see pp. 124–25)

Abhimaan, 1973

Deewaar, 1975 (see p. 130)

Sholay, 1975 (see pp. 134–37)

Kabhi Kabhie, 1976 (see pp. 144–47)

Amar Akbar Anthony, 1977 (see pp. 148–49)

Silsila, 1981 (see p. 165)

Lawaaris, 1981

Coolie, 1983

Sharaabi, 1984

Shahenshah, 1988

Paa, 2009

Piku, 2015 (see p. 327)

Pink, 2016

▲ A happy ending
The film *Coolie* was supposed to end in the death of Amitabh's character, Iqbal, but Manmohan Desai changed the ending to a happy one after the actor's close shave with death during filming.

A NATION'S HERO

In 1982, while performing a stunt in *Coolie*, Amitabh suffered a serious accident. India united in prayer as he fought for his life for the two months he was in Mumbai's Breach Candy Hospital. The daily health bulletins were reminiscent of the "mass hysteria" witnessed during former Prime Minister Jawaharlal Nehru's days in hospital.

Amitabh made his foray into the political arena in 1984. He was urged by the family friend and then Prime Minister Rajiv Gandhi to contest the parliamentary elections for the Allahabad constituency. Although up against Hemvati N. Bahuguna, a formidable leader who had never lost an election, Amitabh won with a landslide 188,000 votes—a record margin in the constituency.

EBB AND FLOW

Amitabh's success story took a dip in the late 1980s. Following political allegations during his parliamentary tenure, the star had to fight a bitter battle to clear his name under the V.P. Singh regime in 1987. At the same time, he battled Myasthenia gravis, a rare disease that slowed his reflexes. After the superhit *Shahenshah*, a string of films, including *Toofan* (1989) and *Jaadugar* (1989), failed at the box office, but he bounced back in the 1990s with *Hum* (1991) and *Khuda Gawah* (1992).

He then took a break from films to float his own media enterprise: ABCL (Amitabh Bachchan Corporation Limited), but it proved an unfortunate venture. His return to the silver screen with ABCL's *Mrityudaata* (1997) was disastrous, while the Miss World pageant organized by ABCL the same year in Bangalore faced resistance from various groups due to a perceived culture clash.

RISING FROM THE ASHES

After a string of flop films, the tide turned with David Dhawan's *Bade Miyan Chhote Miyan* (1998)—a big hit at the box office. The new millennium resurrected Amitabh's career with Aditya Chopra's *Mohabbatein* (2000) and Karan Johar's *Kabhi Khushi Kabhi Gham* (see pp. 270–71). Amitabh's choice of roles became more diverse and discerning, from slick thrillers such as *Aankhen* (2002) and *Kaante* (2002) to the family drama *Baghban* (2003). He appeared in a cameo in Yash Chopra's last film *Veer-Zaara* (see p. 339).

The year 2005 was the best of Amitabh's career since 1978. At the age of 63, he delivered four hits: *Bunty aur Babli*, *Sarkar*, *Waqt*, and *Black*. With his tremendous performance in *Paa* (2009), he scooped up every possible award. He made his Hollywood debut with a cameo in *The Great Gatsby* (2013). Back home, he delivered hits such as *Piku* and *Pink*.

On Twitter, Amitabh remains among the top Indians with an awe-inspiring following across generations. Having a Padma Vibhushan, India's second-highest civilian award, and several national and international awards, he occupies an exalted position in both Indian culture and the world of film.

◄ All in the family
Amitabh Bachchan shared screen time with son, Abhishek Bachchan, and daughter-in-law, Aishwarya Rai Bachchan, for the first time in the hit song "Kajra Re" (Your Kohl-Lined Eyes) from *Bunty aur Babli* (2005).

TIMELINE

October 11, 1942 Born to renowned poet Harivansh Rai Bachchan and social activist Teji Bachchan.

1969 Moves to Mumbai from Kolkata after quitting his job with a shipping company. Gets a voice-over job in Mrinal Sen's *Bhuvan Shome*.

1969 Cast by K.A. Abbas for black-and-white film *Saat Hindustani*.

1973 Screenwriters Salim–Javed recommend him for the lead in Prakash Mehra's *Zanjeer*.

1973 Marries co-star Jaya Bhaduri after a brief romance that started on the film set of *Ek Nazar* (1972).

1974 Birth of daughter Shweta.

1975 Release of blockbuster *Sholay*.

1976 Birth of son Abhishek, who also becomes a Bollywood actor.

1979 Debut in playback singing with the song "Mere Paas Aao" (Come to Me) in *Mr. Natwarlal* (1979).

1984 Accepts Padma Shri, the fourth-highest civilian award in India.

1991 Wins a National Award for his role in *Agneepath* (1990).

2000 *Kaun Banega Crorepati* is his first appearance on television.

2000 First Bollywood star to have his wax statue at Madame Tussauds, London.

2001 Accepts the Padma Bhushan, the third-highest civilian award in India.

2004 Becomes UNICEF's international goodwill ambassador.

2015 Accepts the Padma Vibhushan, the second-highest civilian award in India.

2016 Wins National Award for his stellar performance in *Piku*.

AMITABH PLAYS A GRUMPY, AGING FATHER IN THE COMEDY DRAMA *PIKU*

ANKUR

| 1973 |

Winner of three national and 45 international awards, *Ankur* is a classic of realistic cinema in India. It is among the pioneers of the new wave of such films in Bollywood.

Shot in Yellareddiguda, near Hyderabad in southern India, *Ankur* (The Seedling) depicts life in a traditional village, where the landlord's word is law. Based on newspaper reports of actual incidents, *Ankur* heralded a tradition of realistic cinema, which focused on social issues. Such cinema refused to gloss over the hard facts, and studied the inner lives of characters regardless of entertainment value. *Ankur* featured authentic accents and natural sounds, unheroic heroes, and psychological realism—and no song and dance.

Director Shyam Benegal had written the story for *Ankur* while he was still in college. He sought financing for

years before Blaze Film Enterprises—the largest distributor of advertising films in India—agreed to back him. The investment paid off as the film made money for its producers.

FEUDAL FORCE

Set in feudal India, *Ankur* tells the story of landowner Surya and his relationship with the landless Kishtaya, a deaf-mute, alcoholic potter, and his wife, Lakshmi. When Surya humiliates Kishtaya, he runs away, abandoning his wife. Surya, who is betrothed to child bride Saroj, gets involved in an intimate relationship with the "untouchable" Lakshmi. However, he abandons Lakshmi when she becomes pregnant with his child, with the suggestion that she have an abortion. Lakshmi refuses to comply, having always yearned for a child but been unable to have one

with her husband. When Kishtaya returns to the village, Surya's excessive reaction sows the seeds of rebellion and change.

MAKING OF A CLASSIC

Shyam Benegal had originally wanted to cast actress Waheeda Rehman (see p. 85) as Lakshmi, but when she turned the part down, he gave it to a relative newcomer, Shabana Azmi (see p. 177). Shabana had graduated from the Film and Television Institute of India (FTII), where she studied acting.

Azmi brought a new level of authenticity to her character by studying and adopting the regional Dakkhani accent. She went so far as to learn to pound red chiles as it was done in the village where the film was set. With this, her first big film, she set new standards in method acting. In turns sweet, suffering, and fierce, her portrayal of Lakshmi is impressive.

▲ **Stark reality**
Ankur portrayed the sexual exploitation of vulnerable women, revealing it as a routine aspect of feudal relations in rural India.

Ankur received critical acclaim, winning the Swarna Kamal at the National Awards, while Shabana Azmi and Sadhu Meher received the Best Actress and Best Actor awards. It was also nominated for a Golden Bear—the top prize for best film—at the Berlin International Film Festival.

CAST AND CREW

★ **Anant Nag** Surya
  Shabana Azmi Lakshmi
  Sadhu Meher Kishtaya
  Priya Tendulkar Saroj

🎬 **Director** Shyam Benegal
⌂ **Producers** Lalit M. Bijlani, Mohan J. Bijlani, Freni Variava
♫ **Music composer** Vanraj Bhatia
▢ **Scriptwriter** Shyam Benegal
📷 **Cinematographer** Govind Nihalani
👕 **Costume designer** Swadesh Pal

► **Expressing outrage**
Lakshmi bursts out in rage against the violence of Surya, who abuses the traditional power structure to torture her helpless husband Kishtaya.

SHYAM BENEGAL
(b.1934)

One of the pioneers of Indian "new wave" cinema, Shyam Benegal was a copywriter and advertising filmmaker before turning to cinema. His films *Ankur*, *Nishant* (1975), *Manthan* (1976), and *Bhumika* (1977) laid the foundation of a genre of realistic films that studied social inequalities in the country. He introduced actors Naseeruddin Shah, Shabana Azmi, and Smita Patil to Indian cinema. Benegal received the National Award for Best Hindi Film six times, the Padma Bhushan in 1991, and the Dadasaheb Phalke Award in 2005.

GARM HAVA

1973

A key film of Indian "parallel cinema", *Garm Hava* is a sensitive portrayal of a Muslim family who remain in India after the traumatic events of India's partition.

The directorial debut of M.S. Sathyu, *Garm Hava* (Scorching Winds) is based on an unpublished story written by Urdu writer Ismat Chughtai. Made by stalwarts of the Leftist Indian People's Theatre Association (IPTA), the film was a key work of the socially conscious parallel cinema movement. It was nominated for a Palme d'Or at the Cannes Film Festival, won a National Award for the Best Feature Film on National Integration in 1974, and received Filmfare Awards for Best Story, Best Dialogue, and Best Screenplay. *Garm Hava* is most associated with the towering lead performance by Balraj Sahni (see p. 50), who capped his distinguished career with this film.

WINDS OF CHANGE
The film documents the experiences of Salim Mirza—a Muslim shoe manufacturer—in post-partition India. While his extended family moves to Pakistan, Mirza chooses to stay in India, believing that the social turmoil and differences between Hindus and Muslims will normalize gradually.

> "It took me 15 years to repay the loan."
>
> **M.S. SATHYU** ON THE FINANCES OF THE FILM, CITED BY ANUJ KUMAR, REVIEWER, *THE HINDU*, 2013

However, this does not happen. He suffers one setback after another—from being refused loans to losing his family home. His family is worse for his decision to stay as well, with his daughter losing two fiancés to Pakistan and committing suicide, and his son being refused employment. Mirza is on the verge of giving up and and migrating to Pakistan when he finds an unexpected, ideological solution.

THORNY ROAD TO SUCCESS
For all the acclaim *Garm Hava* received after its release, Sathya faced an uphill battle in getting the film made. He found it hard to find producers who were willing to back the venture, because of fears it could contribute to communal tension between Hindus and Muslims. Protests took place in Agra over the controversial content of the film and the production team had to deploy dummy crews in the city to divert attention, while they filmed discreetly in other locations. The Indian film censor board took eight months to certify the film.

► **A full circle**
When Mirza's ailing mother is on her deathbed, he takes her to visit their family home one last time. The house holds a lifetime of memories for the old woman, which come flooding back in bittersweet voiceovers.

FILMS ON THE PARTITION OF INDIA

The Partition of India is one of the most traumatic events in the history of the Indian subcontinent. Only a few films have dealt with this subject, each taking a different point of view: communal bigotry (*Dharmputra*, 1961); relationships (*Earth*, 1998); the travails of a Pakistani-Muslim and Indian-Sikh couple (*Gadar: Ek Prem Katha*, 2001); and women-centric (*Pinjar*, 2003). The award-winning TV film, *Tamas* (1988), takes a close look at the riots during Partition and the politics behind them.

DEEWAAR

| 1975 |

An iconic antihero blazes his way to critical acclaim and box office success—rewriting the rules along the way—in this exceptional screenplay by the talented writer duo Salim–Javed.

CAST AND CREW

★ **Amitabh Bachchan** Vijay Verma
Shashi Kapoor Ravi Verma
Neetu Singh Leena Narang
Parveen Babi Anita
Nirupa Roy Sumitra Devi

🎬 **Director** Yash Chopra
🎭 **Producer** Gulshan Rai
🎵 **Music composer** R.D. Burman
🎼 **Lyricist** Sahir Ludhianvi
📖 **Scriptwriters** Salim Khan, Javed Akhtar
🎥 **Cinematographer** Kay Gee

Trade pundits give many reasons for the extraordinary success of *Deewaar* (Wall), which is said to be loosely based on the life of the gangster Haji Mastan. However, it is commonly agreed that it was the film's theme of disillusionment with the establishment, especially capitalism, that helped it connect with the masses. Actor Amitabh Bachchan (see pp. 126–27) plays the protagonist of the film, the brave, yet selfish antihero who has no faith in the law of the land. As Vijay, in *Deewaar*, Amitabh cemented his position as the "angry young man" of Bollywood, and emerged as a cult hero for the masses.

◀ **Working the docks**
The Mumbai docks play a large role in Vijay's life. It is here that he works as a porter, takes a stand against a local goon, and channels goods through as a smuggler.

Despite a relatively weak soundtrack, *Deewaar* had many iconic dialogues, such as "Main aaj bhi pheke hue paise nahi uthaata" (I still don't pick up money that is thrown at me)—Vijay's line as he demands respect from a capitalist throwing a wad of notes at him as a reward for his work. This, and many such lines, were quickly added to the music LP record and re-released in the market to boost sales.

ON TWO SIDES OF THE LAW
Considered by Amitabh to have been the "perfect script," this film tells the now familiar story of two brothers on different sides of the law—both vying for the love of their mother, Sumitra.

◀ **Surrender to god**
Vijay holds a tenuous relationship with God, whom he holds responsible for his lot in life. Compelled to pray for his dying mother's life, his anger and anguish burst out in a combative address to the idol in the lines, "Aaj khush toh bahut hoge tum" (You must be very happy today).

Framed as a flashback, the film focuses on Vijay, who is embittered when his father abandons the family. His childhood is spent facing humiliations as he struggles to survive in Mumbai. He goes from dock worker to dockyard smuggler, gradually acquiring the material possessions he aspired to as a child. As he moves up in the nefarious world of smuggling, his brother, Ravi who joins the police force, is entrusted with the job of bringing him to justice.

RESOUNDING SUCCESS
Deewaar remains among the top five films of Amitabh's illustrious career, and perhaps one of the 10 best Bollywood films of all time. It went on to win seven Filmfare Awards, including one for Best Film. It was an incredible commercial success, and ran for more than 100 weeks at cinemas.

Poster designer Diwakar Karkare created marvelous designs for this Yash Chopra classic; the original first prints of the film are fetching upward of ₹1,90,000 ($3,000) at film memorabilia auctions, four decades after its release.

PARVEEN BABI (1949–2005)

Born into a royal dynasty in Junagarh, Gujarat, Parveen Babi began her career as a successful model, before debuting as an actress in director B.R. Ishara's *Charitra* (1973). She shot to the big league with two successive hits—*Majboor* (1974) and *Deewar* (1975). Along with Zeenat Aman (see p. 156), she was one of the two glamour girls of the 1970s and 1980s, delivering a string of hit films with actor Amitabh Bachchan. The 1977 film *Amar Akbar Anthony* (see pp. 148–49), *Kaala Patthar* (1979), *The Burning Train* (1980), *Shaan* (1980), and *Khud-Daar* (1982) are some of her many noteworthy performances.

JULIE

1975

An honest reflection of the time in which it was created, *Julie* depicts families facing an all-too-real situation. The genuine appeal of its lead actress and its hit songs made it a success.

Bollywood is known for lavish spectacles and pure entertainment, but in the 1970s several popular films broke the mold of escapism to show a more realistic slice of life. One such film is *Julie*, which effortlessly tackled the sensitive social taboos of unmarried motherhood and inter-religious marriage—subjects that resonate with audiences even today. Through the film, director K.S. Sethumadhavan was able to convey a simple story that could happen to any family.

DEALING WITH A TABOO
Many critics agree that *Julie* owes its success to Lakshmi's convincing performance of an appealing but ordinary girl in an Anglo-Indian family. Julie's family is far away from Britain, yet her mother, Maggie, takes huge pride in her British roots, and talks endlessly about returning "home." Her father, Morris, is a kind man, but likes his liquor, and Maggie enjoys fighting with him after he has had one too many. Julie develops a forbidden crush on her friend's brother Shashi, and they have a brief fling. He leaves for college, but Julie is pregnant. She is forced to confide her secret to her mother, who, for fear of shaming the family, decides to send Julie away to have the baby in secret, and give it up for adoption.

Julie returns home to help support the family after her father dies. She bumps into Shashi and her secret spills out. However, the couple's plan to marry is opposed by their mothers as Julie is a Christian and Shashi a Hindu.

TALENTED CAST AND CREW
Lakshmi's Julie is a carefree girl whose life is turned upside down, and her acting expresses all the anguish of a young girl suddenly forced to grow up quickly. As her mother, actress Nadira (see p. 47) nearly steals the movie. After years of playing a vamp, or temptress, she dominates each scene as the not-very-likable but charismatic

mother, actress Nadira (see p. 47)

mother. The is also the first Hindi film role for actress Sridevi (see pp. 204–05), who plays Julie's 12-year-old sister. Hindi film stalwarts Utpal Dutt and Om Prakash also give fine supporting performances as Shashi's and Julie's fathers.

Music composer Rajesh Roshan was just getting started when he penned the score for *Julie*, winning the Filmfare Best Music Director Award. Its hit song "My Heart Is Beating," is one of the first Indian movie songs with English lyrics, which helped escalate its popularity among young people. The outstanding music, great acting, and a story that people could connect to, made *Julie* a winner.

> ## "When it hit the screens, [Julie] swept the youth with its bold theme."
> **VIJAY LOKAPALLY,** JOURNALIST, *THE HINDU*, 2015

HIT SONGS

My Heart Is Beating
🎤 **Singer** Preeti Sagar

▼ A winning debut performance
Actress Lakshmi began her career in Bollywood in the title role for *Julie*. She won a Filmfare Award for Best Actress for her performance in the film.

CAST AND CREW

★ **Lakshmi** Julie
Vikram Shashi Bhattacharya
Nadira Margaret "Maggie"
Rita Bhaduri Usha Bhattacharya
Utpal Dutt Mr. Bhattacharya
Om Prakash Morris
Achala Sachdev Devki Bhattacharya
Sridevi Irene

🎬 **Director** K.S. Sethumadhavan
⬠ **Producers** B. Nagi Reddy, Chakrapani
🎵 **Music composer** Rajesh Roshan
𝄞 **Lyricists** Harindranath Chattopadhyay, Anand Bakshi
📖 **Scriptwriter** Chakrapani
🎥 **Cinematographer** Roy P.L.

B. NAGI REDDI PRESENTS

a bold daring true to life story of young love

Vijaya Productions (P) Ltd.'s

JULIE

DIRECTION
K.S. SETHUMADHAVAN
EXECUTIVE PRODUCER
RAM CHHABRA
MUSIC
RAJESH ROSHAN

THE MOTHER

From moral compass to support system, matriarch to friend, the mother in Hindi films has evolved over time, leading to some iconic performances.

Deserted, widowed, or separated by acts of fate or nature, the Bollywood "Maa," or mother, is often a single parent who toils through adversity and humiliation to raise her children. In earlier movies, this makes her son the man in her life, the focus of her love, hopes, and sacrifice. Her existence revolves entirely around her son, whom she nurtures well into adulthood, hoping to leave him in the capable hands of a good "bahu," or daughter-in-law. Actress Leela Chitnis made a career of such roles, in movies such as *Awaara* (see pp. 40–43) and *Guide* (see pp. 84–87). Another "career mother," Nirupa Roy is the iconic "Maa" of *Deewaar* (see p. 130). Her sons—played by Amitabh Bachchan (see pp. 126–27) and Shashi Kapoor—fight for "possession" over her in a moral battle leading to the iconic victory dialogue "Mere paas Maa hai" (I have mother by my side).

MOTHER REDEFINED

Bollywood mothers bear the cross of doing the right thing, even if that is at the expense of their beloved sons. In *Mother India* (see pp. 56–59), Nargis plays a mother figure, not just to her two sons, but to an entire village who look to her for guidance. So when she has to choose between her errant son and what is right, she shoots her son down. In *Vaastav* (1999),

actress Reema Lagoo is a mother who kills her near-insane criminal son to liberate him from a life of suffering.

The mother figure has become more well-rounded recently. Contemporary mainstream mothers are no longer expected to be the upholders of stock values and traditions. In *Dostana* (2008), Kirron Kher comically adjusts to the possibility of her son being gay. In *Jaane Tu ya Jaane Na* (2008), working mother Ratna Pathak Shah is more concerned about social activism than her son's meals. Dolly Ahluwalia of *Vicky Donor* (see p. 343) runs a beauty parlor by day, and she unabashedly shares a drink with her mother-in-law in the evenings.

The affluence of on-screen families today has taken the edge off the mother's suffering. With audiences craving newer stories and fresher characters, the Bollywood mother has gained a new lease on life. In a radical departure from his "Maa" of *Deewaar*, Amitabh—now in his sixties—has since had screen mothers including 94-year-old Zohra Sehgal, who watches wrestling matches on TV in *Cheeni Kum* (2007), and the 30-year-old Vidya Balan (see p. 312) in *Paa* (2009).

▶ **Rebirth saga**
In Rakesh Roshan's *Karan Arjun*, a mother uses the power of prayer to ensure that her dead sons are reborn to avenge their family's suffering.

"The maternal figure is put on a pedestal, you don't see her as someone with … an interior life."

JAI ARJUN SINGH, *MOTHERS AND OTHERS*, 2013

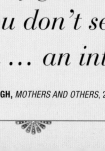

SHOLAY

A constant re-release favorite, *Sholay* has long passed from movie to myth, with its immortalized characters and dialogues that are still invoked in daily life.

The gold standard for Bollywood films, *Sholay* (Embers) was not only successful at the time of its release, but enjoys unprecedented longevity. The film's iconic characters, heartwarming songs, and dramatic storyline captivated audiences of all ages. Even the dialogues in the movie proved to be so famous that the producers released a record containing only the lines from the film—a first for any Bollywood movie. Such was *Sholay*'s popularity, that it ran at Mumbai's Minerva Theatre, which had a capacity of some 1,500 people, for five straight years, from 1975 to 1980. In fact, the terminus near the theater was called the "*Sholay* bus stop." The enormous success of *Sholay* can be attributed to a large extent to the pioneering enthusiasm of the filmmakers,

◄ The golden-hearted thug
Strong and silent Jai falls for Radha, the reclusive widowed daughter-in-law of Thakur, and she reciprocates quietly.

whose fresh perspective and unconventional choices resulted in a movie like no other. At that time, for instance, it was unthinkable to feature a dacoit (bandit) who did not worship the goddess Bhavani or wear long, red *tilaks* on his forehead. Even the decision to shoot the film in Ramanagara, Karnataka, instead of Rajasthan—the industry's favorite location for dacoit movies—was deemed to be unusual.

EAST AND WEST
Director Ramesh Sippy and writers Salim Khan and Javed Akhtar (see pp. 138–39) were strongly influenced by Hollywood Westerns such as *The Magnificent Seven* and *Butch Cassidy and the Sundance Kid*, and by Akira Kurosawa's *Seven Samurai*. Rugged outlaws and valiant heroes in vast

desolate landscapes, horses, bounties, an epic battle between good and evil ... *Sholay* ticked all the boxes for a classic "curry Western." *Sholay*'s larger-than-life villain Gabbar Singh, played by Amjad Khan, became an enormous phenomenon and was, perhaps, the first baddie to appear in commercials for a product aimed at children.

CASTING CONUNDRUM
By the 1970s, Sanjeev Kumar, Dharmendra (see pp. 152–53), and Hema Malini (see pp. 110–11) were already established stars and seemed appropriate for the roles of the village leader, or Thakur, the macho yet lovable Veeru, and the vivacious Basanti, respectively.

◄ Best friends
A motorcycle with a sidecar felt just right to represent the legendary Jai–Veeru friendship. Special camera rigs were fixed on to a 1942 BSA WA 500cc motorbike to shoot the song "Ye Dosti" (This Friendship).

CAST AND CREW

★ **Dharmendra** Veeru
Amitabh Bachchan Jai
Sanjeev Kumar Thakur
Hema Malini Basanti
Jaya Bhaduri Radha
Amjad Khan Gabbar Singh
Asrani Jailer

🎬 **Director** Ramesh Sippy
◠ **Producer** G.P. Sippy
♫ **Music composer** R.D. Burman
A♪ **Lyricist** Anand Bakshi
🕺 **Choreographer** P.L. Raj
▭ **Scriptwriters** Salim Khan, Javed Akhtar
📽 **Cinematographer** Dwarka Divecha
👕 **Costume designer** Stephen Desouza

> ## "An extraordinary and utterly seamless blend of adventure, comedy, music, and dance."
>
> **FILM SOCIETY OF LINCOLN CENTER,** 2006

However, there was a lot of anxiety about who to cast as the introverted Jai, and the villainous Gabbar.

Scriptwriters Salim–Javed were convinced that Amitabh Bachchan (see pp. 126–27) was the right fit for Jai and persuaded the producers by showing them Amitabh's film *Zanjeer* (see pp. 124–25). Danny Denzongpa, who exuded suitable menace in *Dhund* (1973), was chosen for the pivotal role of Gabbar. However, a scheduling conflict with Feroze Khan's *Dharmatma* (1975) forced him to refuse the part. In their vexed search for a suitable replacement, Salim–Javed remembered the relatively unknown Amjad Khan

from his work in the theater world. While the screen test worked well, Amjad was extremely nervous; his voice was considered too "weak" for such a powerful villain. Anxiety about his ability to succeed in the role continued until the end, but the choice ultimately proved wildly successful.

LOVE IN THE AIR
Both on and off screen, romance surrounded the making of this epic film. The already-married Dharmendra fell in love with Hema, who had recently been proposed to by Sanjeev Kumar. Dharmendra originally wanted to play the role of Thakur, but was so besotted with Hema that he agreed to play Veeru, who pairs up with Hema's character, Basanti. The actor would even bribe the lighting boys to make mistakes during the shots of romantic scenes, so he could get to embrace her repeatedly. The other offscreen couple, Jaya and Amitabh, got married and went to London for their honeymoon. Meanwhile, Javed fell for actress and scriptwriter Honey Irani and wanted his writing partner, Salim, to intervene with her mother. Salim's cheeky

◀ **Intrepid village belle**
The spirited, brave, and beautiful Basanti is kidnapped and tortured by the sadistic Gabbar. Even in the face of his brutal treatment, she refuses to bow down.

description of Javed ("... he's a fine boy, only he drinks a bit ...") inspired the scene in *Sholay* where Jai goes to Basanti's family to propose marriage on behalf of Veeru and, as a prank, misrepresents him in the same way.

PATH TO PERFECTION
Made for ₹30 million (about ₹615 million/$9.5 million today), it is estimated that *Sholay* earned approximately ₹150 million (about ₹2 billion/$31 million today) in revenues. This was a "big budget" film in every sense. Roads, telephone lines, and utilities were installed on location, stunt directors and special effects experts were flown in, and a number of scenes, such as the train robbery and the family massacre sequence, took several weeks to shoot.

As a result, the project went three times over the original budget and took twice as long to finish than had originally been

▲ **The dreaded Gabbar Singh**
Veeru, enraged by Gabbar's attacks on the people he loves, manages to overpower the bandit in this action-packed scene.

scheduled. Ramesh Sippy's perfectionism meant that no effort was spared to achieve the ideal shot—for example, making Hema dance in the scorching heat of May, to get the right expression of anguish. He even ensured that the movie was released in grand 70 mm and with stereophonic sound.

The initial reaction to the movie was disastrous. The young, popular actress, Jaya as a widow? The charismatic Sanjeev Kumar a disabled old man? A lead character dying? And so much violence! Critics and industry experts mercilessly panned the film and its director. But once word of mouth from the first wave of audiences spread, the crowds started flowing in.

AMJAD KHAN (1942–90)

Having started his career as a child actor, Amjad Khan went on to work as a theater artist. Huge audiences flocked to cinemas to see his portrayal of Gabbar Singh in *Sholay*—his first significant role in films—and this character came to be considered one of the "best" Hindi film villains, along with Mogambo from *Mr. India* (see pp. 188–91). In the 1970s and 1980s, Khan played both villains and character roles in hits such as *Muqaddar ka Sikandar* (p. 154), *Kaalia* (1981), *Yaarana* (1981), *Laawaris* (1981), and *Satte pe Satta* (1982). He played Wajid Ali Shah in Satyajit Ray's *Shatranj ke Khiladi* (1977), and showed his comedic skills in *Qurbani* (1980) and *Love Story* (1981). He suffered health complications following an accident, and died at the age of 51.

STORYLINE

An epic story of friendship and vengeance, *Sholay* is set in the village of Ramgarh, which is being terrorized by the notorious dacoit (bandit) Gabbar Singh. Baldev Singh, the village Thakur (local landowner) hires Jai and Veeru—loyal friends and petty outlaws—to capture the dacoit alive and save the village from their oppressor.

A COMIC SCENE FEATURING
THE JAILER, JAI, AND VEERU

THAKUR LOOKS FOR JAI AND VEERU	PARTNERS-IN-CRIME	GABBAR AND GANG	CHARMING THUGS	THAKUR'S STORY
Thakur Baldev Singh, a retired police officer, asks a jailer to find two criminals, Jai and Veeru, whom he remembers as brave and compassionate from an earlier encounter. He needs them for a special job.	**The criminals** and best friends, Jai and Veeru, are joyriding on a motorbike they have just stolen ❶. They are caught and sent to prison, where they are located by Thakur's goon. Thakur offers them a deal—capture the dreaded dacoit Gabbar alive and be paid handsomely. Initially reluctant, Jai and Veeru soon agree.	**Gabbar's men enter Ramgarh** and intimidate the villagers, demanding sacks of grain. Jai and Veeru confront the bandits and manage to get rid of them. Gabbar is angered by the failure of his men and they are made to pay dearly for it.	**The introverted Jai** falls in love with Thakur's soft-spoken, widowed daughter-in-law, Radha. Beginning a new relationship is taboo for a widow, so they share an unspoken bond. Meanwhile, the garrulous Veeru romances Basanti, the chatty and cheerful village horse-cart driver.	**During the festival** of Holi ❷, the dacoits launch a surprise attack. Jai and Veeru wonder why Thakur does not pick up a gun to help them. Thakur reveals that as a police officer many years ago, he had arrested Gabbar, who escaped and murdered his entire family. To cause further humiliation, Gabbar cut off Thakur's arms.

THE SONGS

Ye Dosti (This Friendship)
Singers: Kishore Kumar, Manna Dey
Picturized on Jai and Veeru

★ The first sequence for "Ye Dosti" beautifully complements the sad version of the song, which is used for the emotional finale of the film.

Holi Ke Din (On the Day of Holi)
Singers: Kishore Kumar, Lata Mangeshkar
Picturized on Veeru and Basanti

A DETERMINED THAKUR

VEERU AND BASANTI CELEBRATE HOLI

"Indian film history can be divided into Sholay BC and Sholay AD."

SHEKHAR KAPUR, CITED BY ANUPAMA CHOPRA IN *SHOLAY, THE MAKING OF A CLASSIC*, 2000

SANJEEV KUMAR (1938–85)

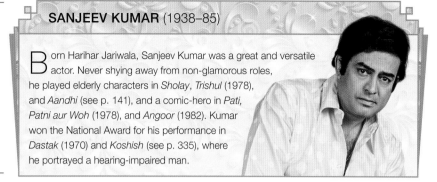

Born Harihar Jariwala, Sanjeev Kumar was a great and versatile actor. Never shying away from non-glamorous roles, he played elderly characters in *Sholay*, *Trishul* (1978), and *Aandhi* (see p. 141), and a comic-hero in *Pati, Patni aur Woh* (1978), and *Angoor* (1982). Kumar won the National Award for his performance in *Dastak* (1970) and *Koshish* (see p. 335), where he portrayed a hearing-impaired man.

AN ATTACK ON GABBAR'S DEN	VEERU WOOS BASANTI	GABBAR STRIKES BACK	REVENGE AT LAST
Jai and Veeru are stunned by Thakur's story. They promise to capture Gabbar for free to help him take revenge. On receiving information that Gabbar has gone to buy arms from a gypsy camp, they sneak in during the dacoits' revelries ❸ and blow up the ammunition, but Gabbar manages to escape.	**Veeru has been pursuing Basanti** ardently. He sends Jai to plead his case with Basanti's aunt. Jai manages to give a poor impression of his friend while seeming to do the exact opposite. Drunk and despondent, Veeru climbs a water tank threatening suicide. A romantic song later ❹, Basanti melts.	**To counter Jai and Veeru** as defenders of the village, Gabbar kills the young son of the village Imam (Islamic leader). The frightened villagers want to send the duo away to avoid further troubles, but the Imam himself convinces them to fight Gabbar's tyranny. The dacoits then kidnap Basanti. Enraged, Veeru rushes to Gabbar's camp but is captured by the dacoits. The evil Gabbar makes Basanti dance to keep Veeru alive ❺.	**Jai attacks Gabbar's den** and frees Veeru and Basanti. He convinces Veeru to escape with Basanti and return with help, while he holds the dacoits at bay. Veeru returns too late and Jai dies in his arms ❻. Thakur fights Gabbar using his head and feet. He prevails and almost kills Gabbar but the police arrive to arrest the villain. A distraught Veeru is consoled by Basanti.

A GYPSY CAMP DANCER, PLAYED BY
HELEN, ENTERTAINS GABBAR'S MEN

Koi Haseena
(A Beautiful Woman)
*Singers: Kishore Kumar,
Hema Malini*
☺ *Picturized on Veeru and Basanti*

Jab Tak Hai Jaan
(Until I Live)
*Singer: Lata Mangeshkar
Picturized on Basanti,
Veeru, and Gabbar* ☺

Mehbooba Mehbooba
(Beloved, Beloved)
Singer: R.D. Burman
☺ *Picturized on Jalal Agha and Helen*

Ye Dosti
(Sad version)
*Singer: Kishore Kumar
Picturized on Jai and Veeru* ☺

JAI AND VEERU
IN A GUN BATTLE

✪ *R.D. Burman's "Mehbooba Mehbooba" was inspired by the song "Say You Love Me" by Greek singer Demis Roussos.*

SALIM–JAVED

SCREENWRITERS b.1935 and b.1945

For more than a decade, "Written by Salim–Javed" was a badge that Bollywood movies wore with pride. The powerful writer duo gave Bollywood some of its most enduring hits, boosting the status of screenwriters in Hindi cinema.

▶ A legendary partnership
The first writers for film in Bollywood to achieve star status, Salim–Javed have been described as the "most successful screenwriters of all time."

KEY WORKS

Seeta Aur Geeta, 1972 (see p. 109)

Zanjeer, 1973 (see pp. 124–25)

Deewaar, 1975 (see p. 130)

Sholay, 1975 (see pp. 134–37)

Don, 1978 (see p. 156)

Shakti, 1982

Mr. India, 1987 (see pp. 188–91)

Back in the 1960s, when the young Salim Khan used to assist senior writer Abrar Alvi, he asked his boss if one day writers would be paid as much as stars. Alvi laughed at the proposition because writers then were underpaid and treated like backroom clerks. In 1980, when *Dostana* (1980) was released, the celebrated writer duo Salim Khan and Javed Akhtar were paid more than the top star of the time, Amitabh Bachchan (see pp. 126–27), received for his role in the film.

Credited with this unimaginable shift in the status of Bollywood scriptwriters, by the end of the 1970s the pair towered over actors and directors. It was a long way from their early careers, when posters for even a successful film such as *Zanjeer* did not carry credits for the writers, they said to have hired a painter to stencil "Written by Salim–Javed" over posters across Mumbai. Five years later, publicity material for hits such as *Don* featured their names at the top.

The duo's trademarks included preparing detailed screenplays, giving a contemporary spin to old formulas, creating intense moments and memorable characters, and writing some of the sharpest dialogue in Bollywood history. They belonged to the rare breed of writers who offered filmmakers the complete package: story, screenplay, and dialogue.

STAR-MAKERS
Salim Khan and Javed Akhtar's contributions to Bollywood history go beyond their craft. They gave stars Amitabh Bachchan and Amjad Khan their big breaks. Amitabh had been around for a while and had made several unsuccessful films, when Salim–Javed persuaded Prakash Mehra to cast him in the blockbuster *Zanjeer*. Dismissed as merely a "Lambu" (tall guy) by most filmmakers, Amitabh reached a turning point in his career thanks to the "angry young man" persona penned by Salim–Javed. Raising Amitabh's stature with each film, the two went on to write as many as 10 films for Amitabh out of the total of 21 that they wrote together.

When Danny Denzongpa was unable to play the villain's role for the hit film *Sholay*, it was Salim–Javed who introduced Amjad Khan to director Ramesh Sippy as an alternative. Javed had seen the young actor perform in a play. Going far beyond their role as screenwriters, the pair also involved themselves in tasks such as teaching Hema Malini (see p. 110–11) to

deliver her dialogues at breakneck speed for the film *Sholay*. Being hugely invested in their films, as part of the publicity material for *Sholay* the two claimed, "This is a prediction by Salim–Javed… *Sholay* will gross ₹10 million (about ₹130 million / $2 million today) in each major territory… "

WRITTEN BY SALIM–JAVED
Starting from runaway hits such as *Andaz* (1971) and *Haathi Mere Saathi* (1971), Salim–Javed were on a roll throughout the 1970s. *Seeta Aur Geeta*, *Zanjeer*, *Yaadon ki Baaraat* (1973), *Deewaar*,

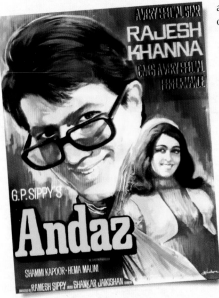

◀ A journey begins
Andaz (1971) was the first significant film for which Salim–Javed wrote the screenplay; though they were credited only for "Additional Script Work" as part of the Sippy Films Story Department.

▶ **The unceremonious split**
Ego issues and misunderstandings at the time of writing *Mr. India* caused the duo to part ways in 1981, but the story was made into a film later. Salim and Javed eventually became friends again.

Sholay, Don, Trishul (1978), *Kala Patthar* (1979), and—ending the decade—*Dostana* all bore testimony to their talent. These movies used dramatic formulas such as lost-and-found families and father-son conflict to great effect, with larger-than-life villains and heroes, realistic dialogue, biting wit, and a quotient of cool. *Sholay* is recognized as their greatest work and also Hindi cinema's all-time hit, but it is the story of *Deewaar* that is credited with being the best Bollywood script ever. The popularity the film's dialogue was reflected when the celebrated music composer A.R. Rahman (see pp. 244–45)

quoted a line from *Deewaar* during his acceptance speech at the 2009 Academy Awards. Receiving the award for Best Original Score for the song "Jai Ho!" (Victory to Thee) from Danny Boyle's *Slumdog Millionaire* (2008), Rahman quoted the line "Mere Paas Ma Hai" (I Have Mother On My Side).

By the 1980s, however, the magic seemed to be missing from their scripts. Even though *Kranti* (1981) was a hit and their last film together, *Shakti*, was widely appreciated, the two writers agree that the intensity of their work had lessened. This was likely due to a lack of experimentation or the pressure of surpassing their earlier successes.

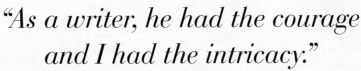

"As a writer, he had the courage and I had the intricacy."

JAVED AKHTAR, POET–LYRICIST, ABOUT SALIM KHAN

LIFE AFTER THE SPLIT
A mix of ego issues, misleading sycophants, and misunderstandings led the two writers to part ways in 1981. They are very cordial now and speak about the split gracefully. "Once they separated, I couldn't get that kind of intensity again," said star Amitabh Bachchan, whose own career took a dip at this time. Post-split, Salim Khan wrote a few films, of which *Naam* (1986) was most successful, while Javed Akhtar wrote hits such as *Betaab* (1983) and *Saagar* (1985). Akhtar turned to writing song lyrics, winning a Padma Bhushan and five National Awards. He is the father of Bollywood directors Farhan (see p. 265) and Zoya Akhtar. Khan is the father of superstar Salman Khan (see pp. 224–25).

TIMELINE

● **November 24, 1935** Salim Khan born in Indore, India.

● **January 17, 1945** Son of poet–writer Jan Nisar Akhtar, Javed Akhtar born in Gwalior, India.

● **1964** Salim Khan marries Sushila Charak.

● **1966** Salim Khan appears in *Teesri Manzil*, his best-known role. Assists writer Abrar Alvi.

● **1964–70** Javed Akhtar gets minor writing assignments. Assists poet Kaifi Azmi.

● **1971** The duo develops stories for *Adhikar* and *Andaz* together, but not as a team.

● **1972** The duo writes story and dialogue for *Seeta Aur Geeta* as a team.

● **1972** Javed Akhtar marries actress and screenwriter Honey Irani.

● **1974** The duo gets Filmfare Awards for Best Story and Best Screenplay for 1973 film *Zanjeer*.

● **1975** Release of their biggest blockbuster movies, *Deewaar* and *Sholay*.

● **1975–80** *Sholay* runs for five years at the Minerva cinema hall in Mumbai.

● **1976** The two receive Filmfare Awards for Best Story, Best Screenplay, and Best Dialogue for *Deewaar*.

● **1981** Salim Khan and Javed Akhtar split. Salim Khan marries actress Helen (while still married to Sushila Charak).

● **1981–2017** Javed Akhtar writes song lyrics for 105 films.

● **1983** Release of *Shakti*, Salim–Javed's last film together, and the only one to feature both Amitabh Bachchan and Dilip Kumar.

● **1984** Javed Akhtar marries Shabana Azmi (after divorce from Honey Irani).

● **1986–96** Salim Khan writes for 11 films.

● **1987** Release of *Mr. India*, the last script they worked on together before splitting up. The script was picked up by director Shekhar Kapoor six years after the split.

● **2015** Release of Diptakirti Chaudhuri's book *Written By Salim–Javed*.

CHUPKE CHUPKE

1975

This classic comedy—featuring the most successful action heroes of the 1970s speaking in convoluted and academic Hindi—continues to be a barrel of laughs.

Hrishikesh Mukherjee's *Chupke Chupke* (Hush Hush) was released in the same year as *Deewaar* (see p. 130) and the mother of all Indian blockbusters, *Sholay* (see pp. 134–37). With such action-packed competition, the quietly hilarious *Chupke Chupke* not only made its mark but has endured, just like the other two classics. Though it starred two of *Sholay*'s lead actors—Amitabh Bachchan (see pp. 126–27) and Dharmendra (see pp. 152–53)—*Chupke Chupke* was a rib-tickling farce.

BESTING THE BROTHER-IN-LAW

The games begin when newly married botany professor Parimal becomes exasperated with his wife Sulekha's hero-worship of her brother-in-law, Raghav. Since Raghav hasn't seen him yet, prankster Parimal pretends to be his new chauffeur. Raghav is high-minded about the use of pure, almost archaic, Hindi, uncorrupted by English or street lingo. The new "driver" takes this—and other eccentricities—comically far as the story unfolds. Parimal's friend Sukumar, an English professor, is bullied into acting as Parimal. A bespectacled, tortured Sukumar teaching faux botany when he'd rather be discussing *Julius Caesar* a favorite of Bachchan's fans.

LAUGH RIOT

Based on Bengali writer Upendranath Ganguly's story *Chhadobeshi*, the film was a remake of the Bengali film *Chhadmabeshi* (1971). Thanks to Gulzar's witty dialogue, the film was packed with unusual Hindi and excellent puns. The comic timing of Amitabh, Dharmendra, and Om Prakash did complete justice to the writing. Cinema critic Jai Arjun Singh has described the film as Wodehousian, given its plot involving impersonation and the resulting misunderstandings.

▲ **Reel life**
Amitabh and Jaya Bachchan had been married for two years when they were paired up in *Chupke Chupke*. The film ends with their characters' marriage ceremony.

N.C. SIPPY PRESENTS
HRISHIKESH MUKHERJEE'S

CHUPKE CHUPKE

Eastmancolor

DIRECTED BY
HRISHIKESH MUKHERJEE · S.D. BURMAN · ANAND BAKSHI · GULZAR · JAYWANT PATHARE
MUSIC   LYRICS   DIALOGUE   PHOTOGRAPHY

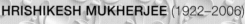

◄ **The right mix**
The cast of *Chupke Chupke* presented a rare mix of actors who were appreciated not only for their star value but also for their comic timing.

CAST AND CREW

★ **Dharmendra** Parimal Tripathi
Om Prakash Raghavendra (Raghav) Sharma
Sharmila Tagore Sulekha Chaturvedi
Amitabh Bachchan Sukumar Sinha
Jaya Bachchan Vasudha

🎬 **Director** Hrishikesh Mukherjee
🏠 **Producers** Hrishikesh Mukherjee, N.C. Sippy
🎵 **Music composer** S.D. Burman
𝄞 **Lyricist** Anand Bakshi
📖 **Scriptwriters** Gulzar, D.N. Mukherjee
🎥 **Cinematographer** Jaywant Pathare
👔 **Costume designers** M.R. Bhutkar, Meena Sippy

HRISHIKESH MUKHERJEE (1922–2006)

Fondly called Hrishi Da, Mukherjee directed his first hit, *Anari*, in 1959. Many of his films, such as *Anupama* (1966) and *Satyakam* (1969), had a core of intense emotions and lofty ideals. In the 1970s, he delivered classics such as *Abhimaan* (1973) and *Mili* (1975), and the immortal comedies *Chupke Chupke* and *Gol Maal* (see p.157). Removed from the drama of big-budget potboilers and the stark minimalism of arthouse cinema, his work was often termed "middle of the road." Mukherjee observed, "Middle class is the class I know and I always wove stories around it."

AANDHI

1975

Set against a political backdrop, *Aandhi* took the nation by storm as parallels were drawn between the female protagonist and the then prime minister of India, Indira Gandhi.

▲ **An unconventional hero**
Despite a script that focused on its female lead, actor Sanjeev Kumar shone in his understated portrayal of J.K., a soft-spoken underachiever.

CAST AND CREW

★ **Suchitra Sen** Aarti Devi
  Sanjeev Kumar J.K.
  Om Shivpuri Chandrasen
  Om Prakash Lallu Lal

🎬 **Director** Gulzar
◔ **Producer** J. Om Prakash
♫ **Music composer** R.D. Burman
♪ **Lyricist** Gulzar
📖 **Scriptwriters** Gulzar, Bhushan Banmali
📷 **Cinematographer** K. Vaikunth
👕 **Costume designer** Padma Rani

▼ **A powerful performance**
As Aarti, actress Suchitra Sen portrays a strong woman carving a niche for herself in the murky, male-dominated world of Indian politics.

The year 1975 was a fruitful one for writer–director Gulzar; three of his best-known films—*Aandhi*, *Mausam*, and *Khushboo*—were released. But it was *Aandhi* (The Storm) that embroiled him in political controversy. Based on Hindi writer Kamleshwar's story, the film features a strong-willed, successful female politician. This sari-clad character's streak of gray hair, dominant personality, and separation from her husband left *Aandhi* open to the charge that it was a comment on the then Prime Minister Indira Gandhi.

A WOMAN OF SUBSTANCE
The film begins with politician Aarti Devi running into her estranged husband, hotel manager J.K., while campaigning for an election. Many years ago, much to the displeasure of her wealthy and ambitious father, Aarti had fallen in love with and married J.K., who was then an unambitious hotel employee. But

she was also drawn to the political career that her father wanted for her and which repelled her husband. Unable to reconcile these aspects of her personal and professional life, Aarti parted ways with her husband. On meeting after so many years, the couple realize that they had never stopped loving each other. However, living in the public eye makes Aarti vulnerable to slander, and this continues to place a strain on the relationship.

Aarti Devi's role had initially been offered to Vyjayanthimala, who did not feel comfortable taking it on. It was then performed to great acclaim by Bengali star Suchitra Sen. Sanjeev Kumar won the Filmfare Award for Best Actor and the film won the Filmfare Critics Award for Best Movie.

POLITICAL CONTROVERSY
Gulzar maintained that "Mrs Gandhi was one of the best models of a politician for an actress to play, but the film had nothing to do with her life."

However, the publicity material for the film emphasized the resemblance, to the extent that a billboard explicitly stated: "See the story of Indira Gandhi." It was for this reason that *Aandhi* was banned 23 weeks after its release, during the suspension of constitutional rights known as the Emergency that was declared by Indira Gandhi. It was only when the opposition party came to power that *Aandhi* was cleared and released on television. In his defense, Gulzar maintained that he was simply trying to respond to the political maneuvering he saw around him, while making an emotional story about a public figure's personal life.

HIT SONGS

Tere Bina Zindagi Se Koi Shikwa To Nahi
(I Have No Complaints from a Life Without You)
🎤 **Singers** Lata Mangeshkar, Kishore Kumar

Iss Modh Se Jaate Hain
(Walking Along This Bend in the Road)
🎤 **Singers** Lata Mangeshkar, Kishore Kumar

Tum Aa Gaye Ho, Noor Aa Gaya Hai
(You Have Brought the Light with You)
🎤 **Singers** Lata Mangeshkar, Kishore Kumar

GULZAR

WRITER b.1934

One of India's most respected poet-lyricists, Gulzar has contributed to Bollywood in many ways, from penning movie scripts and songs to directing films. After an Oscar, Grammy, and five National Awards, he is still going strong.

As a young man in the 1950s, an idealistic Gulzar left his family business to become a poet and joined veteran director Bimal Roy (see p. 64) as an assistant. He rose to become a colossus of Bollywood, shaping six decades of Hindi films and their songs.

Gulzar embodies multiculturalism as a way of life: here was a Punjabi boy, educated in Urdu and English, speaking Hindustani, who made himself proficient in Bengali. He can write a TV series on the Urdu poet Mirza Ghalib, invoke a simile from rural Uttar Pradesh or Punjab, and translate the Bengali poetry of Rabindranath Tagore, even as he makes witty use of English phrases in Hindi songs and dialogues. This

allows Gulzar the vast cultural and emotional range that makes his body of work unique.

POETRY ON CELLULOID
Gulzar was born as Sampooran Singh Kalra in a village called Dina in Jhelum district (now in Pakistan). Although his family migrated to India before the India–Pakistan partition, he witnessed the horrors of this period and his work often carries the grief of people being violently divided. Unwilling to join the family business and unable to make his kin appreciate his poetry, he walked out to find his calling in Mumbai, earning his keep by working in a garage. His poetry helped him to make friends with the likes of music composer Salil Choudhury and lyricist Shailendra. He went on to write the lyrics of "Ganga Aaye Kahan se" (Where Does Ganga Come From?) from the film *Kabuliwala* (1961), "Mora Gora Ang Layi Le" (Take Away My Fair Color) from *Bandini* (1963), and became an assistant to the director

Bimal Roy. His creative collaboration with director Hrishikesh Mukherjee (see p. 140) started with *Aashirwad* (1968) and led to classics such as *Anand* and *Guddi* (1971).

DIRECTORIAL VENTURE
Gulzar's directorial debut was *Mere Apne* (1971), a film about the angst of unemployed youth. Over the next decade, he worked on a wide range of themes: *Koshish* is about a hearing-and-speech-impaired couple; *Mausum* (1975) is based on a prostitute's relationship with her mother's lover; and *Kinara* (1977) is a sensitive tale about a dancer and the man responsible for her blindness. Strong yet atypical stories, moving performances, and enduring music are hallmarks of all these critically acclaimed films. In this period, he formed creative partnerships with music composer R.D. Burman (see p. 109) and actor Sanjeev Kumar (see p. 137), whom he went on to cast in the hilarious comedy *Angoor* (1982).

Later, Gulzar directed the thoughtful *Ijaazat* and *Lekin...*, among others. In the 1990s, he made two explicitly political films, *Maachis* about the disaffected youth of Punjab and *Hu Tu Tu* (1999), his last directorial effort, based on the corrupt soul of the contemporary political system.

THE WORDSMITH
Throughout these years, Gulzar pushed the envelope in writing. In 1969, his song "Hamne Dekhi Hai Un Aankhon Ki Mahakti Khushboo" (I Have Seen the Fragrance of Those Eyes), bemused contemporary poets—how can eyes be fragrant? But this was the beginning of a new kind of poetry

in Bollywood, consisting of abstract imagery, and new metaphors and idioms. His title song for the famous early 1990s Hindi tele-serial *Jungle Book* declared the forests are abuzz with the news that a "flower in knickers" has bloomed. The use of the word "chaddi" (knickers)

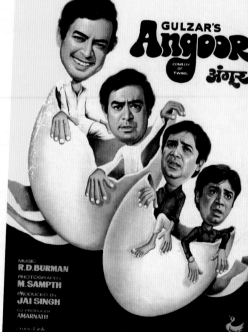

▲ **Two-twin comedy**
Angoor, a rib-tickler based on Shakespeare's *A Comedy of Errors*, is recognized as one of the finest comedies in Bollywood's history.

▼ **Gulzar's *Guddi***
The 1971 drama *Guddi*, created by the director–scriptwriter duo of Hrishikesh Mukherjee and Gulzar, provides a rare behind-the-scenes look at the film industry.

KEY WORKS

Anand, 1971 (see p. 112)

Mere Apne, 1971

Koshish, 1972

Aandhi, 1975 (see p. 141)

Mausam, 1975

Ijaazat, 1987 (see p. 185)

Lekin..., 1991

Maachis, 1996

Slumdog Millionaire, 2008

"I believe words should amaze or amuse."

GULZAR, IN AN INTERVIEW WITH PRODUCER–DIRECTOR NASREEN MUNNI KABIR, *IN THE COMPANY OF A POET,* 2012

did not sit well with critics, but the song came to be considered a most lovable description of childhood.

More recently, Gulzar has still managed to raise eyebrows with his lyrics, often incorporating English phrases, street lingo, or swear words. "Beedi Jalaile" (Light Up) from *Omkara* (see p. 289) and "Kajrare Kajrare" (Your Kohl-lined Eyes) from *Bunty Aur Babli* (2005) are some examples of these. Even today, some people are surprised that this somber, kurta-clad poet has written the outrageously titled song "Bloody Hell" from *Rangoon* (see p. 345). However, the folk idioms, creative metaphors, and witty conversational flavors that he brings to this song and so many others more than redeem them—and make them hits to boot.

Gulzar employs the same techniques when writing dialogue, which has also contributed immensely to some of the great comedies of Bollywood—*Chupke Chupke* (see p. 140), *Angoor* (1982), and *Chachi 420* (1997).

THE LEGEND CONTINUES
In the last two decades, Gulzar has written for the biggest Bollywood

directors. He has received numerous accolades, including the Academy Award and a Grammy for the song "Jai Ho" (*Slumdog Millionaire*). He has also received the Padma Bhushan— the third-highest civilian award in India—and in 2013, he was awarded the prestigious Dadasaheb Phalke Award. Away from the film world, he also continues to publish poetry and short stories.

Gulzar married actress Rakhee (see p. 145) in 1973. Though the couple separated, they remain good friends and brought up their daughter Meghna together. Gulzar affectionately calls this relationship the "longest short story of my life."

► **The storyteller**
Despite being one of the most celebrated lyricists and writers, Gulzar leads a life away from the limelight.

(see p. 289) ... (2005) ... (see p. 345) ... (see p. 140) ... (see p. 145)

KABHI KABHIE

1976

Kabhi Kabhie reveals actor Amitabh Bachchan in a romantic mood during his "angry young man" days, elevating the character of the tragic poet-hero to epic proportions.

CAST AND CREW

★ **Amitabh Bachchan** Amitabh "Amit" Malhotra

Shashi Kapoor Vijay Khanna

Rakhee Pooja Khanna

Waheeda Rehman Anjali Malhotra

Rishi Kapoor Vikram "Vicky" Khanna

Neetu Singh Pinky Kapoor

Naseem Sweety Malhotra

📽 **Director** Yash Chopra

🎬 **Producer** Yash Chopra

🎵 **Music composer** Khayyam

🎼 **Lyricist** Sahir Ludhianvi

📖 **Scriptwriters** Pamela Chopra, Sagar Sarhadi

🎥 **Cinematographers** Romesh Bhalla, Kay Gee

👔 **Costume designers** Jennifer Kendal, Rajee Singh

It was brave of director Yash Chopra (see pp. 166–67) to produce a romantic feature in an era of action films. *Kabhi Kabhie* (Sometimes), with its publicity tag of "Love is Life," is a love triangle that broke the myth that Amitabh Bachchan (see pp. 126–27) was only suited to action roles.

Kabhi Kabhie was shot in Kashmir, and became a classic because of its songs and riveting performances. The film was not well received in the trade journals as it broke several stereotypes.

However, its successful performance at the box office, turned the tide of criticism in the film's favor.

ROMANCE ACROSS GENERATIONS
In *Kabhi Kabhie*, Pooja, a young college student, is in love with a poet, Amit. Destiny moves them apart as Pooja is married off to an architect, Vijay, against her wishes. Amit is heartbroken, but eventually marries Anjali, who has a past. Vijay is a carefree man with a zest for life, oblivious of Pooja's affair, and an admirer of Amit's poetry.

Moving two decades ahead, the film introduces Vicky, son of Vijay and Pooja, who is in love with Pinky, the daughter of Shobha and Dr. R.P. Kapoor, played by Simi Garewal and Parikshit Sahni, respectively. Amit and Anjali have a spoiled daughter, Sweety, who also falls in love with Vicky. The film then weaves a complicated and emotionally stirring

▼ **A romantic moment**
Pooja and Amit, played by Rakhee (right) and Amitabh (left), meet in college and fall madly in love with each other. Here they visualize a perfect future together.

◄ **An emotional family saga**
A complex story of unrequited love, sacrifice, and marriage, the film featured a star-studded cast with big industry male leads such as Amitabh Bachchan (top), Shashi Kapoor (right), and Rishi Kapoor (bottom).

RAKHEE (b.1947)

Rakhee worked in several Bengali films, but it was in Hindi cinema that she received popular acclaim. She debuted with Rajshri productions' *Jeevan Mrityu* (1970) opposite Dharmendra (see pp. 152–53). Through the 1970s, she worked with a string of leading men, including Rajesh Khanna (see pp. 106–107) and Shashi Kapoor. She considers her performances in *Blackmail* (1973) and *Tapasya* (1976) her best. From the late 1980s, Rakhee played the role of the mother in films such as *Ram Lakhan* (1989) and *Karan Arjun* (see p. 236). The winner of a National Award, Rakhee has been nominated for a total of 16 Filmfare awards of which she has won three. She married lyricist Gulzar (see pp. 142–43) in 1973, but the couple separated soon after.

a duet by Mukesh and Lata Mangeshkar (see pp. 60–61), topped the charts. So did the song "Main Pal Do Pal Ka Shayar Hoon" (I'm But a Poet for a Moment or Two), also sung by Mukesh, which had an alternative version "Main Har Ik Pal Ka Shayar Hoon" (I'm a Poet in Every Moment of Life) in the film. The songs complemented the characters and displayed the great range of the celebrated poet Sahir. If the romantic poetry of the title track suited Amitabh, the energetic duets of Lata and Kishore Kumar (see pp. 100–101) brought to life the youthful romance of Rishi Kapoor (see p. 202) and Neetu Singh. The album became an all-time top seller.

story around the three couples whose destinies intertwine as life moves on, leading to an unexpected climax.

CATCHY SOUNDTRACK
Yash Chopra initially considered music composers Laxmikant S. Kudalkar and Pyarelal R. Sharma to create the score

BREAKING NEW GROUND
Kabhi Kabhie was Yash Chopra's second film with Amitabh and Shashi Kapoor after *Deewaar* (see p. 130), and

role in which he is neither young nor angry. However, he went on to prove them wrong by delivering a virtuoso performance as the brooding romantic poet, who is expressively passionate in the first half, and bitter and negative in the second.

Yash Chopra also gambled on his scriptwriter, Sagar Sarhadi, who was not well-known at the time. Yet, Sagar wrote the poignant tale of love and longing with the intensity and skill of a veteran.

Another problem was that Rishi was reluctant to join the film's multi-star cast as he wanted to work in projects

with a single lead. With Amitabh and Shashi taking pivotal roles, he did not see much scope for himself. It was only after persuasion from chief assistant director Ramesh Talwar that he gave in.

WELL-DESERVED RECOGNITION
Kabhi Kabhie made its mark at the Filmfare Awards the following year. Running for over 50 weeks at the box office, this golden jubilee cemented *Kabhi Kabhie*'s nine nominations at the award ceremony. Amitabh and Rakhee were nominated in the Best Actor and Best Actress categories, and Shashi and Waheeda Rehman (see p. 85) were nominated for Best Supporting Actor and Actress, respectively. Mukesh received a nomination for the title track, and another for the song "Main Pal Do Pal Ka Shayar Hoon." The film eventually won four awards—Best Music (Khayyam), Best Lyricist (Sahir), Best Screenplay (Sagar), and Best Playback (Male), which went to Mukesh for the title song. Both the "risks" shouldered by Yash Chopra for this project—Khayyam and Sagar—ultimately proved successful.

> "*Kabhi Kabhie ... changed the way people romanced. It changed the way people dreamed of love. It changed love itself.*"
>
> THE HINDU, 2015

of the film. However, the duo did not react favorably to the romantic title track "Kabhi Kabhie Mere Dil Mein" (Sometimes in My Heart). The film's lyricist, Sahir Ludhianvi, then made a suggestion that music composer Khayyam steer the project.

For Yash Chopra it was a tough call because although Khayyam was a famous music director of 1950s and 1960s, he had not seen much success in his last few ventures. Yash Chopra decided to bring him in on instinct, and the rest is history. The film delivered a soundtrack consisting entirely of hit songs. The title track, a version of which was sung solo by Mukesh (see p. 43), and another in

compared with the previous film, Shashi had a more prominent role, a fact that was not forgotten during the film's shooting. After each of Shashi's impressive scenes Amitabh would joke, "Yeh *Deewaar* ka badla le rahe ho kya?" (Is this payback for *Deewaar*?).

Prior to the film's release, trade people questioned the judgement of Amitabh, celebrated for his "angry young man" roles, for taking up a

▶ **Exotic setting**
Kabhi Kabhie was shot in Kashmir, and the film's stunning cinematography beautifully reflected the passage of time. As the seasons changed, so did the landscape of Kashmir.

STORYLINE

Amit's poetry wins Pooja's heart in college. They fall in love, but are not destined to be together. Pooja marries Vijay, a kindhearted soul who genuinely loves her. Amit marries Anjali, but he still lives in the past and longs for Pooja. As time passes, their paths cross again when their children get to know each other. This sets in motion a chain of events leading to a surprising climax.

SHASHI KAPOOR AS THE
ARCHITECT VIJAY KHANNA

PLOT OVERVIEW

FALLING IN LOVE	AN ARRANGED MARRIAGE	PAST MEETS PRESENT	NEXT GENERATION
❶ **A college student**, Pooja, is entranced by Amit's poetry. They meet on campus and fall in love ❷. However, Pooja's parents want her to marry an architect, Vijay Khanna.	**Pooja asks Amit** never to stop writing. Unable to defy her parents' wishes, she marries Vijay ❸. Vijay is madly in love with his beautiful wife. He is a fan of Amit's poetry and requests Pooja to sing a poem from his book *Kabhi Kabhie* ❹. Meanwhile, a dejected Amit quits poetry and starts working at his father's construction company.	**20 years later**, Pooja and Vijay's son, Vicky, falls in love with Pinky, a fellow student in college ❺. Pooja is now a TV anchor who interviews Amit and learns that he has stopped writing poetry. Vijay goes to the studio to meet the celebrity poet and invites Amit to come home for a drink. Pooja and Amit are nostalgic about their past.	**Vicky and Pinky** spend time together in the hills, and their love blossoms ❻. Pinky's parents dote on her and go out of their way to indulge her wishes. Vicky tells his father about Pinky. Vijay is ecstatic that Vicky has fallen for the daughter of his friends, Shobha and Dr. Kapoor, and approves their relationship.

THE SONGS

❶

**Main Pal Do Pal Ka Shayar Hoon
(I'm But a Poet for a Moment or Two)**
Singer: Mukesh
🎧 *Picturized on Amit*

❷

**Surkh Jode Ki Yeh Jagmagahat
(The Shine of This Red Bridal Dress)**
Singers: Lata Mangeshkar, Pamela Chopra
Picturized on Pooja 🎧

❸

**Kabhi Kabhie Mere Dil Mein
(Sometimes In My Heart)**
Singers: Lata Mangeshkar, Mukesh
🎧 *Picturized on Pooja and Amit*

....

⭐ *Amitabh Bachchan's parents, Teji and Harivansh Rai Bachchan, make an appearance in the film as Pooja's parents during the scene in which she gets married to Vijay.*

....

❺

**Pyar Kar Liya To Kya
(So What If We're In Love)**
Singer: Kishore Kumar
🎧 *Picturized on Vicky*

❻

**Tere Chehre Se
(I Can't Take My Eyes Off Your Face)**
Singers: Kishore Kumar, Lata Mangeshkar
🎧 *Picturized on Vicky and Pink*

**Kabhi Kabhie Mere Dil Mein
(Sometimes In My Heart)**
Singer: Mukesh
Picturized on Amit 🎧

POOJA IS
IMPRESSED BY
AMIT'S POETRY

VICKY AND PINKY
FALL IN LOVE

"Chopra's grand theme was love, and it was seldom a simple affair."

THE TIMES OF INDIA, 2012

VICKY AND PINKY

SAHIR LUDHIANVI (1921–80)

Sahir Ludhianvi was born as Abdul Hayee to a family of land owners residing in the Karimpura locality of Ludhiana, Punjab. He moved to Mumbai and made his debut as a lyricist in Bollywood with the film *Azadi ki Raah Par* in 1948. Sahir had a long and successful career as a lyricist and worked with noted music directors of the 1950s and 1960s, including Roshan, Madan Mohan, Khayyam, and S.D. Burman. He won his first Filmfare Award for Best Lyricist for the film *Taj Mahal* (1963), followed by another in 1976 for *Kabhi Kabhie*. He was awarded the Padma Shri, the fourth-highest civilian award of India, in 1971.

A SECRET UNVEILED	LOVE TRIANGLE	FACE-OFF	PAST MISTAKES FORGIVEN
Dr. Kapoor reveals that Pinky is an adopted child. On learning the truth, Pinky leaves for Shyamnagar, in search of her biological mother. There she meets her birth mother, Anjali, who is married to Amit. The couple have a daughter, Sweety. Anjali showers a lot of attention on Pinky, upsetting Sweety, and making Amit suspicious **7**. Pinky is saddened to know that Anjali wants to keep their relationship a secret.	**Vicky follows Pinky** and reaches Shyamnagar. There he bumps into Sweety and starts working at her father's construction site. Vicky pretends to be attracted to Sweety, who soon falls in love with him **8**. Sweety's parents want her to marry Vicky. Pinky begs Vicky not to fool Sweety and her parents anymore. Anjali learns the truth about Pinky and Vicky's affair.	**A suspicious Amit pushes Anjali** to tell the truth about Pinky's identity. Anjali reveals that Pinky is her child from before her marriage to him. Amit is angry and unforgiving. Vijay comes to Shyamnagar for work and is invited by Amit to dinner. Amit meets Pooja and they reminisce about the past. Vijay overhears their conversation and confronts Amit, who tells him the truth about his affair with Pooja. Vijay dismisses this information and forgives his wife. Anjali requests Amit to forgive her, but he is unwilling to do so. She decides to leave the house forever.	**Sweety discovers** Pinky and Vicky's affair. In anger, she runs away from home and gets caught in the middle of a demolition at the construction site. Vicky, Pinky, Amit, and Vijay chase after her. Amit and Vijay rescue their children from the fire. Sweety learns the truth about Vicky and Pinky's relationship. A distraught Amit sees the error in his ways and makes up with Anjali. Pinky and Vicky get married **9**.

7 ⬤ ──────────────────────── **8** ⬤ ──────────────── **9** ⬤

Main Har Ek Pal Ka Shayar Hoon
(I'm a Poet in Every Moment of Life)
Singer: Mukesh
Picturized on Amit 🎭

Chahe Chale Churiya
(Even If Knives Get Used)
Singers: Kishore Kumar,
Lata Mangeshkar
Picturized on Vicky,
Sweety, and Pinky 🎭

AMIT QUESTIONS ANJALI ABOUT
HER RELATIONSHIP WITH PINKY

Mere Ghar Aayi Ek Nanhi Pari
(A Little Angel Has Come to My House)
Singer: Lata Mangeshkar
🎭 *Picturized on Anjali*

⭐ *Rishi Kapoor and Neetu Singh met and fell in love during the filming of* Kabhi Kabhie.

AMAR AKBAR ANTHONY

1977

A wacky but immensely endearing film about three "lost and found" brothers, Manmohan Desai's *Amar Akbar Anthony* celebrates India's intrinsic pluralism in all its glory.

Constantly being badgered by critics who favored the "new wave" art films over his more commercial endeavors, Manmohan Desai (see p. xx) once famously said, "the word logic is itself illogical." Known to entertain the masses in his own particular style, Desai liked to pack his films with plenty of crowd-pleasing sequences. The director was on top form in *Amar Akbar Anthony*. Its hit sequences include a visually challenged mother being cured by spiritual leader Sai Baba, Mother Mary hinting a clue to a murderer, and a mother receiving a blood transfusion from her three lost children. There are many firsts to *Amar Akbar Anthony*, one of which is that it was Manmohan Desai's first film as a producer with the launch of his famous MKD production company. Desai created a record with *Amar Akbar Anthony* as it was his fourth hit within a span of six months; the other three films were *Chacha Bhatija, Parvarish,* and *Dharam Veer* (see p. 150).

THE THREE MUSKETEERS
The film tells the story of Kishanlal, his wife, and their three young children, who are separated from each other while trying to escape the henchmen of a villainous mob boss, Robert. The film fast-forwards 22 years, introducing the audience to the boys, now grown up—

CAST AND CREW

- ★ **Amitabh Bachchan** Anthony Gonsalves
- **Vinod Khanna** Amar Khanna
- **Rishi Kapoor** Akbar Allahabadi
- **Shabana Azmi** Lakshmi
- **Neetu Singh** Dr. Salma Ali
- **Parveen Babi** Jenny
- **Pran** Kishanlal
- **Jeevan** Robert
- **Nirupa Roy** Bharati

- **Director** Manmohan Desai
- **Producers** Manmohan Desai, Subhash Ghai
- **Music composers** Laxmikant S. Kudalkar, Pyarelal R. Sharma
- **Lyricist** Anand Bakshi
- **Scriptwriters** Prayag Raj, K.K. Shukla, Kader Khan
- **Cinematographer** Peter Pereira
- **Costume designer** Leena Daru

Amar, a policeman raised as a Hindu; Akbar, a Muslim singer; and Anthony, a lighthearted scamp raised by a Catholic priest. The three brothers reunite and decide to teach Robert a lesson.

EPIC PERFORMANCES
Widely praised for his portrayal of Anthony, Amitabh Bachchan (see pp. 126–27) deservedly picked up the Filmfare Award (see pp. 282–83) for Best Actor. He delivers some of the film's best-loved lines, including, "Aise toh life mein aadmi do-eech time bhagta hai; Olympic ka race ho ya police ka case ho!" (A man runs this way on only two occasions, Olympic race or a police case!). Iconic scenes such as the one where a drunken and injured Anthony talks and tends to his wounds in his reflection in a mirror are

◄ **Comic character**
Amitabh's amusing role—Anthony Gonsalves—was named after a famous music arranger, who was music composer Pyarelal Sharma's senior.

◄ **Iconic brawl**
This famous fight sequence between Vinod Khanna, a cop, and Amitabh Bachchan, the goon, would be re-enacted in Rohit Shetty's *Singham* (2011) several decades later.

Amar Akbar Anthony is one of the first mainstream Hindi films with three hit qawwali-inspired numbers—"Pardah Hai Pardah," "Tayyab Ali Pyar Ka Dushman," and "Shirdi Waale Sai Baba" (Sai Baba from Shirdi). Within the first six months of its release, the record sales had exceeded one million.

A RECORD-BREAKER
Amar Akbar Anthony created a storm at the box office, with its advance bookings running for months. It also became the first film to celebrate a silver jubilee (running for 25 weeks) in 11 theaters in Mumbai, a record equaled only by *Hum Aapke Hain Koun..!* (see pp. 220–23), 17 years later. It also holds the record of registering 87 percent collections in its silver jubilee week for Mumbai territory. It ran past a glorious 75 weeks (a platinum jubilee) at the Opera House, Mumbai. The merchandise of the film, such as T-shirts and erasers, were hugely popular. Corporate entities such as Amul Butter and Indian Bank joined the craze; the bank's hoardings proclaimed "Amar Akbar Adi (Amar, Akbar *et al*) bank with Indian Bank!" The first Hindi film to be aired on Channel 4 in the UK, the film was also a smash hit in Trinidad, breaking records set by *Sholay* (see pp. 134–37) and *Kabhi Kabhie* (see pp. 144–47).

examples of his versatility and great comic timing. Praising the actor, the *Trade Guide* magazine mentioned in its review, "Amitabh is the life and soul of the film. The Catholic youth's portrayal is near perfect." Rishi Kapoor (see p. 202) as the betel-chewing Akbar lives the role, infusing it with the required youthful exuberance. Vinod Khanna (see p. 154), portraying the eldest brother, is the straight man to Amitabh and Rishi's comic characters, while Nirupa Roy also delivers the goods in the role of a clichéd Bollywood mother (see pp. 132–33).

BLOCKBUSTER MUSIC
Sung by Kishore Kumar (see pp. 100–101), the song "My Name Is Anthony Gonsalves" is interspersed with Amitabh humorously stringing together a lot of English words in nonsensical sentences. The music of the film has many firsts to its credit. The song "Humko Tumse Ho Gaya Hai Pyaar" (I Have Fallen in Love With You) is the only number in the history of Hindi cinema that brings together the four playback legends—Lata Mangeshkar (see pp. 60–61), Mukesh (see p. 43), Mohammed Rafi, and Kishore Kumar .

► **Religious pluralism**
Amar Akbar Anthony celebrates India's model of unity in diversity through its three iconic characters from different faiths.

MULTI-STARRERS
Hindi cinema has seen several multi-starrers but only a few have succeeded or become classics. Mehboob Khan's *Andaz* (1949), starring Dilip Kumar (see pp. 48–49), Nargis, and Raj Kapoor (see pp. 44–45), can be called the first trendsetting multi-starrer. This was followed by *Baadbaan* (1954), the last film of Bombay Talkies. In 1965, Yash Chopra's *Waqt* (see p. 92) fared exceptionally well at the box office. Manoj Kumar's *Roti Kapda aur Makaan* was the biggest hit of 1974, preceding *Sholay*. However, some multi-starrers have received a merely lukewarm reaction, such as *The Burning Train* (1980) and *Shaan* (1980).

> ## "[Amar Akbar Anthony] *is now a byword in religious plurality.*"
>
> **RACHEL DWYER**, PROFESSOR, CITED IN *AMAR AKBAR ANTHONY: BOLLYWOOD, BROTHERHOOD, AND THE NATION*, 2016

DHARAM VEER

1977

Set in a mythical kingdom, Manmohan Desai's spectacularly colorful film is a crowd-pleasing story, packed full of brave princesses, bold heroes, and meddling villains.

CAST AND CREW

★ **Dharmendra** Dharam Singh
Jeetendra Veer Singh
Zeenat Aman Rajkumari Pallavi
Neetu Singh Roopa
Pran Jwala Singh
Jeevan Prince Satpal Singh
Indrani Mukherjee Princess Meenakshi

🎬 **Director** Manmohan Desai
⬡ **Producer** Subhash Desai
🎵 **Music composers** Laxmikant S. Kudalkar, Pyarelal R. Sharma
🎼 **Lyricists** Anand Bakshi, Vithal Bhai Patel
🕺 **Choreographer** Kamal
📖 **Scriptwriter** Prayag Raj
🎥 **Cinematographer** N.V. Srinivas

◀ **Multi-starrer hit**
Desai's signature style featuring a star-studded cast was evident on *Dharam Veer*'s eye-catching film poster, showing all four leading actors.

A romantic comedy, action-adventure, period piece, costume drama, murder-mystery, and musical extravaganza—the movie *Dharam Veer* (Righteous Warrior) has something for everyone. A high-production spectacle, the film's thrills and spills stop at nothing to entertain the audience.

MYTHICAL DRAMA
The story centers on Prince Satpal Singh's desperate attempt to prevent the prophecy that his death is writ at the hands of his yet unborn eldest nephew. When he tries to kill his sister, Princess Meenakshi, to prevent the prophecy coming true, he is foiled by huntsman Jwala Singh. Jwala marries the princess, but soon after is thought to be dead after an encounter with a tigress. The mourning princess is married off to somebody in a nearby kingdom, where she gives birth to Jwala's twin sons. Meanwhile,

Prince Satpal continues his quest for self-preservation. He tries to kill his sister's older twin son and swaps the younger twin with his own child. However, unbeknown to him, Jwala's loyal falcon, Sheroo, saves the older twin, while Satpal's wife swaps the two babies back again.

The older twin, Dharam, is raised by a humble blacksmith, while the younger twin, Veer, grows up as the crown prince. Unaware they are related, they become best friends. But once Prince Satpal learns that the crown prince Veer is not his own son, he conspires against him, orchestrating a series of events that pit Veer against Dharam.

FANTASTICAL FILM
While a story about brothers separated at birth might be a frequently used plotline in Bollywood films, everything else about the film is spectacularly unusual for Bollywood. Set in

two neighboring kingdoms during some unspecified historical time period, the film borrows from the traditions of Ancient Rome, medieval Europe, and the Arabian Nights, and combines them to create its own fantastical, albeit unashamedly anachronistic, mythical world.

There are plenty of special effects and theatrical set pieces that keep the film rattling along, including swashbuckling sword fights at sea, horses that leap over castle walls, and warriors who perform gravity-defying acrobatics. A real crowd-pleaser of its time, *Dharam Veer* was the year's second-highest box office earner.

MANMOHAN DESAI (1937–94)

With a career spanning more than three decades, director Manmohan Desai was known for making films for the masses. During the 1970s and 1980s, he helped to create a new genre, combining all the elements audiences loved to see on the screen—romance, action, lavish costumes, great stunts, fabulous locations, and song and dance. Alongside the celebrated scriptwriting duo Salim–Javed (see pp. 138–39), Desai is credited with establishing masala movies in Hindi cinema.

SHALIMAR

1978

A thrilling film about a dangerous challenge to win a rare gem, *Shalimar* was among the first big-budget collaborations between Bollywood and Hollywood.

This big-budget jewel heist caper marked a bold attempt to mix elements of Hollywood and Bollywood. Featuring English and American stars, the film was released in English as *Raiders of the Sacred Stone*. Although it did not exactly sparkle at the box office, *Shalimar* (Rare Gem) has now found its niche as a cult classic.

DO OR DIE

At the start of the film, the thief S.S. Kumar finds a mysterious invitation in a stolen wallet. This invitation to visit the private island of British recluse Sir John Locksley is addressed to a Raja Bahadur Singh. Kumar disguises himself as the son of the intended guest and travels to the island.

When he arrives on the tiny island, Kumar finds himself in a den of deadly thieves and notorious criminal masterminds. The British host—a retired arch-criminal—explains to the guests why he has invited them all.

"*Shalimar is a caper film to end all caper films.*"

KRISHNA SHAH, *INDIA TODAY,* OCTOBER 13, 2014

Dying of cancer, Locksley has a last wish: he wants to find a successor to take over his criminal empire. In order to choose a worthy successor, he sets a challenge—the winner will be whoever can steal the spectacular Shalimar from him. But any thief who bungles the burglary must pay with his, or her, life.

The island is crawling with heavily armed guards willing to lay down their lives to protect the gem. In addition, the other guests discover the truth that Kumar is a common street criminal. With the stakes so high, the chances of Kumar finding the gem and winning the challenge seem next to impossible.

INDO–US PARTNERSHIP

Having studied film at institutes such as UCLA and Yale University, the film's director Krishna Shah tried to establish an American audience for Hindi cinema long before other filmmakers broke that barrier. To help achieve his goal, Shah imposed a strict, three-month shooting schedule. Each scene was shot in English first and then in Hindi. When the actors were not filming, they were improving their English language skills.

Dharmendra (see pp. 152–53) is said to have worked hard on his English accent until the early hours, but always showed up first thing in the morning. Rex Harrison's Hindi dialogue, on the other hand, had to be dubbed.

Despite the fact that *Shalimar* did not do so well at the box office, the film opened up new opportunities for joint partnerships and paved the way for later Bollywood actors and filmmakers to make it in the US.

▼ **A blazing chemistry**
Zeenat Aman plays the role of Dharmendra's ex-flame as well as the villain's mole in the film.

CAST AND CREW

- ★ **Dharmendra** S.S. Kumar
- **Zeenat Aman** Sheila Enders
- **Rex Harrison** Sir John Locksley
- **Sylvia Miles** Countess Rasmussen
- **John Saxon** Col. Columbus
- **Shammi Kapoor** Dr. Bukhari
- **Prem Nath** Raja Bahadur Singh

- 🎬 **Director** Krishna Shah
- ⬭ **Producer** Suresh Shah
- 🎵 **Music composer** R.D. Burman
- **Lyricist** Anand Bakshi
- 🏃 **Choreographer** Hiralal B.
- ▭ **Scriptwriter** Krishna Shah
- 📷 **Cinematographer** Harvey Genkins
- 👕 **Costume designer** Bhanu Athaiya

DHARMENDRA

ACTOR b.1935

Bollywood's original action hero, he has been a darling of the masses for more than 50 years. Whether giving a kiss or packing a punch, Dharmendra always delivers.

◀ **Versatile veteran**
In recognition of his vast and varied body of work, Dharmendra has been honored with Lifetime Achievement Awards from several high-profile platforms such as the IIFA (International Indian Film Academy), Zee Cine Awards, and MAMI (the Mumbai International Film Festival).

Born Dharmendra Singh Deol, Dharmendra has many achievements to his credit, including being the recipient of India's third-highest civilian honor the Padma Bhushan in 2012 and Filmfare's Lifetime Achievement Award in 1997. He was even voted among the top 10 most handsome men in the world in a 1970s poll. Yet possibly the most enduring achievement of this star is that his posters still decorate the dhabas (local eateries) of North India, and fans still line up to watch his films in his native Punjab.

Born in Punjab's Ludhiana district, Dharmendra was obsessed with movies from a very young age. He would walk for miles to get to the nearest cinema hall, and such was his devotion to contemporary heartthrob Suraiya that he made that journey to see her in *Dillagi* (1949) some 40 times. He entered a talent-spotting contest sponsored by *Filmfare*, where his good looks drew plenty of attention. In 1958, Dharmendra caught the train to Mumbai to become a star.

AN ACTOR'S JOURNEY
As a young struggler in the film industry, Dharmendra's beginnings were auspicious. The first film he signed was Bimal Roy's *Bandini* (1963),

---

KEY WORKS

Anupama, 1966

Phool aur Patthar, 1966

Satyakam, 1969

Yaadon ki Baraat, 1973

Dost, 1974

Sholay, 1975 (see pp. 134–37)

Chupke Chupke, 1975 (see p. 140)

▲ Honesty pays
In Hrishikesh Mukherjee's *Satyakam*, Dharmendra plays a conflicted man whose honest principles are tested time and again.

where the newcomer held his own against veteran actors Nutan and Ashok Kumar (see p. 31). However, *Bandini* was released two years after his next film Arjun Hingorani's *Dil Bhi Tera, Hum Bhi Tere* (1960). While he made his mark in Chetan Anand's war drama *Haqeeqat* (1964), O.P. Ralhan's *Phool aur Patthar* (1966) skyrocketed him to stardom. As Shaka, the macho criminal who falls in love with a widow, he won over the hearts of many a woman in the audience.

Dharmendra was never part of any competition, making his mark as an actor who lives only to entertain. His run of films with director Hrishikesh Mukherjee (see p. 140) became a distinguished chapter in his career. He played a sensitive novelist in *Anupama* (1966), and, in the classic *Satyakam* (1969), he shone as an idealist who sticks to his rigid notions of honesty even as his life—and his dream of a new India—is shattered. He gave a loveable comic performance in *Chupke Chupke*.

THE KING OF HEARTS
The 1970s saw Dharmendra ride a wave of successful action films. The bankable star gave huge hits such as *Mera Gaon Mera Desh* (1971) and *Charas* (1976). *Sholay* (see pp. 134–37) topped this list, playing at Bombay's Minerva Theatre for five years. The audience loved

"Veeru" performing his drunken suicide scene and indulging in comic banter with Hema Malini (see pp. 110–11). Dharmendra and Hema were the most successful on-screen pairing of the 1970s, their timing perfectly matched in films such as *Seeta aur Geeta* (see p. 109) and *Dream Girl* (1977). The pair did more than 30 films together.

In the 1980s, Dharmendra was part of several multi-star movies, most notably with directors J.P. Dutta, Raj Kumar Kohli, and Shibu Mitra. This included hits such as *Aag Hi Aag* (1987) and *Hukumat* (1987).

A MAN OF MANY ROLES
Dharmendra also produced movies under his banner Vijayta Films. He launched

► King of action
Dharmendra rose to fame as an action hero starring in a series of blockbusters including *Sholay*, seen here, in which he also flexed some comedy muscle.

his sons, Sunny Deol in *Betaab* (1983) and Bobby Deol in *Barsaat* (1995). He also produced *Ghayal* (1990) with Sunny, sweeping the Filmfare Awards and winning a National Award for Best Popular Film. Dharmendra also acted in Punjabi movies from the 1990s.

In 2007, he put in an appearance in Sriram Raghavan's noir thriller *Johnny Gaddaar* and *Apne* in which he co-starred with sons Sunny and Bobby Deol. In 2011 and 2013 he appeared in *Yamla Pagla Deewana*, parts 1 and 2, with both his sons. In 2004, Dharmendra was elected a Member of Parliament from Bikaner, Rajasthan, representing the Bharatiya Janata Party.

BEYOND FAME
In addition to his numerous Lifetime Achievement Awards, Dharmendra has also received the Living Legend Award from FICCI (Federation of Indian Chambers of Commerce and Industry).

Few know that the man famous as the original "He-Man" of Bollywood is a prolific writer of poetry. This son of the soil is happiest when tending his farm in Lonavla, near Pune, Maharashtra. The diffident actor is absent from social media and avoids publicity. As he himself admits, he would like to be remembered as a man who lived by his heart and in the hearts of the people.

"*If the audience can take you up ... they [can] bring you down.*"

DHARMENDRA, CITED BY PIYA HINGORANI IN *DAILY O*, DECEMBER 10, 2016

December 8, 1935 Born the son of a school headmaster.

1958 Moves to Mumbai to embark on a film career after entering a competition in *Filmfare* magazine.

1960 *Dil bhi Tera, Hum bhi Tere* marks his film debut.

1966 Becomes a major star, and a heartthrob, with a macho-romantic role in *Phool aur Patthar*.

1971 The dacoit (bandit) drama *Mera Gaon Mera Desh* is a big hit.

1975 Stars in the Bollywood blockbuster *Sholay*. In his role as a prankster in *Chupke Chupke*, he excels at comedy.

1977 Swashbuckler *Dharam Veer* becomes one of the highest earning movies of the decade.

1983 Sets up his production company, Vijayta Films.

1983 With the film *Betaab*, Dharmendra launches his son Sunny's career.

1995 Dharmendra's son Bobby makes his debut in *Barsaat*, a romantic hit.

1997 Receives the Filmfare Lifetime Achievement Award.

2012 The government of India awards Dharmendra the Padma Bhushan—the third-highest civilian award.

2013 Produces *Yamla Pagla Deewana 2*, in which he stars alongside his two sons.

POSTER FOR *YAMLA PAGLA DEEWANA 2*

MUQADDAR KA SIKANDAR

1978

An iconic Amitabh Bachchan film, and one of the actor's most popular performances, *Muqaddar ka Sikandar* ran successfully for more than 75 weeks all over India.

CAST AND CREW

★ **Amitabh Bachchan** Sikandar
Vinod Khanna Vishal
Rakhee Kaamna
Rekha Zohra
Amjad Khan Dilawar

Director Prakash Mehra
Producer Prakash Mehra
Music composers Kalyanji V. Shah, Anandji V. Shah
Lyricists Anjaan, Prakash Mehra
Scriptwriters Laxmikant Sharma, Vijay Kaul, Kader Khan
Cinematographer N. Satyen

▼ **Kings of melody**
Music composers Anandji (left) and Kalyanji (right) hold the platinum discs they were awarded for this film, as lead actor Amitabh Bachchan looks on.

A tragic tale, *Muqaddar ka Sikandar* (Conqueror of Destiny) tells the story of a selfless hero who, as he moves through life, loses nearly everything that he desires or cares about. Although playing such a character went against actor Amitabh Bachchan's larger-than-life hero image, he felt it connected him more closely with his audience, claiming that viewers could identify with the deep losses that Sikandar suffers.

Sikandar's tragic path begins with his unrequited love for Kaamna, which leads him to seek solace in the arms of Zohra, a kind-hearted courtesan. He becomes friends with Vishal, a struggling lawyer who risks his life to save Sikandar from his enemies. Vishal moves in with Sikandar, through whom he meets Kaamna and they fall in love. Shortly after, Sikandar's step-sister's wedding is arranged, but her in-laws threaten to stop the marriage when they learn of his connection with Zohra. To save Sikandar from further disrepute, Zohra ends her life. When Dilawar, an admirer of Zohra, tries to avenge her death, this action-packed movie reaches its dramatic conclusion.

A HEROIC PERFORMANCE
Amitabh gives a fine performance as Sikandar in the film. His character is compared to Karna, the selfless hero of the classic Hindu epic *Mahabharata*, as well as to Devdas, the romantic hero of Sarat Chandra Chattopadhyay's cult novel.

A COURTESAN'S SONG
Musical highlights include the title track picturized on a dashing Amitabh riding on a motorbike on the roads of Mumbai, India. The song "Salaam-e-Ishq Meri Jaan" (Salutations, my love), is an iconic Bollywood *mujra*—courtesan's song—which is filmed on Rekha and Amitabh. The two share a sizzling chemistry in the film, admittedly even overshadowing Amitabh's romantic track with the film's main heroine, Rakhee.

VINOD KHANNA
(1946–2017)

Actor–producer Vinod Khanna started his career in Bollywood with negative roles, before moving on to play the lead. By the late 1970s, he was only second in popularity to Amitabh Bachchan. Despite this success, Vinod decided to take a break from films, seeking spiritual solace from Indian Godman "Osho." He successfully revived his career in 1987, delivering hits such as *Insaaf* (1987) and *Satyamev Jayate* (1987). The late 1990s saw him shift into character roles.

SATYAM SHIVAM SUNDARAM

1978

CAST AND CREW

★ **Zeenat Aman** Rupa
Shashi Kapoor Rajeev
A.K. Hangal Bansi
Padmini Kolhapure Young Rupa

🎬 **Director** Raj Kapoor
🎩 **Producer** Raj Kapoor
🎵 **Music composers** Laxmikant S. Kudalkar, Pyarelal R. Sharma
🎼 **Lyricists** Pandit Narendra Sharma, Anand Bakshi, Vitthalbhai Patel
🕴 **Choreographer** Sohanlal
📖 **Scriptwriter** Jainendra Jain
🎥 **Cinematographer** Radhu Karmakar

Showman Raj Kapoor explored the notion of beauty in *Satyam Shivam Sundaram*. This allegorical film made a mark, not least for the erotic presentation of lead actress Zeenat Aman.

Director Raj Kapoor's most controversial film, *Satyam Shivam Sundaram* (Truth, God, and Beauty) was an attempt to drive home the idea that true beauty lies in the spirit. Yet the film portrayed its heroine, played by Zeenat Aman (see p.156), in an extremely erotic fashion, laying itself open to charges of exploitation and voyeurism. Raj Kapoor (see pp.44–45) maintained, however, that even if the audience came for Aman's sex appeal, they would leave thinking more about the film's core theme.

A string of melodies by singer Lata Mangeshkar (see pp.60–61) won the Filmfare Award for Best Music Direction for the Laxmikant–Pyarelal duo (see box below).

IN THE EYES OF THE BEHOLDER
The film tells the story of Rupa, a village girl with a golden voice and a huge scar on her face from a childhood accident. Rajeev, an engineer supervising the building of a dam in her village, falls in love with Rupa, who manages to keep her scar hidden from him. But when he sees it on their wedding night, he is repelled and refuses to believe that Rupa is the same woman he fell in love with. To help Rajeev see beyond Rupa's scar and embrace her reality, she must indulge his fantasy by continuing to romance him with her face partly hidden.

BEHIND THE SCENES
Raj Kapoor had initially considered Hema Malini (see pp. 110–11) for the lead, but she was not open to wearing the revealing clothes required for the role. The story of how Zeenat convinced the director to cast her instead has become the stuff of film legend. Dressed in village attire, her face made up to look burned, she turned up at Raj Kapoor's house and landed the part.

Satyam Shivam Sundaram was planned as a small-budget film, but it did not remain so. It was shot in Loni, Maharashtra, and large amounts of water had to be transported to the location for the film's flood scenes.

◀ **Breaking taboos**
Zeenat Aman shed her Western image for that of a rural Indian girl for this film, but her outfits were, in fact, bolder than ever.

HIT SONG

Satyam Shivam Sundaram
(Truth God Beauty)
🎤 **Singer** Lata Mangeshkar

"The film that hopes to create more than an erotic myth."

VIR SANGHVI, *INDIA TODAY*, 2015

LAXMIKANT (1937–98) PYARELAL (b.1940)

This popular team, comprising Laxmikant S. Kudalkar and Pyarelal R. Sharma created music for more than 600 Hindi films, spanning almost four decades. Laxmikant started out as a mandolin player, while Pyarelal played the violin. After the success of their first film, *Parasmani* (1963), there was no looking back. The duo, which gave hits like *Dosti* (1964), *Bobby* (see pp.118–19), and *Ek Duje ke Liye* (1981), produced a chartbusting "Choli ke Peechhe" (*Khalnayak*, 1993) even toward the end of their careers. They won seven Filmfare awards.

DON

1978

Don was a slick action film and a monster hit. It is one of six blockbusters that superstar Amitabh Bachchan delivered in his most successful year ever.

Produced by cinematographer Nariman A. Irani, *Don* paired Amitabh Bachchan (see pp. 126–27) with Zeenat Aman for the first time. A compelling script by Salim–Javed (see pp. 138–39), Amitabh's powerful performance, and great music by Kalyanji Anandji, made the film a golden jubilee hit, running for more than 50 weeks at cinemas. Dialogues such as "Don ko pakadna mushkil hi nahi, namumkin hai" (Catching Don isn't just difficult, it is impossible) have attained cult status. With its riveting screenplay and well-crafted characters, *Don* has enjoyed great popularity, leading to a number of remakes in various languages as well as a reboot in 2006, with superstar Shah Rukh Khan (see pp. 214–15) as Don.

▲ **Gold mafia**
In the 1970s, prohibitive laws in India led to the rampant smuggling of gold. Many films of the era, such as *Don*, included this theme to depict a dark, dangerous, and glamorous world.

THE MOST-WANTED CRIMINAL

Don revolves around an international smuggler, Don, who is one of Interpol's most-wanted criminals. When police commissioner D'Silva kills Don in an encounter, he decides to have a look-alike, Vijay, impersonate the gangster, in a bid to round up the rest of his crime ring. Things fall apart when D'Silva dies, taking the truth about the impersonator's true identity with him. This leaves Vijay vulnerable to attacks from the cops and rival gangsters.

Don presented Amitabh in three diverse shades—as a sophisticated, stylish gangster in the initial reels, a country bumpkin speaking the Awadhi dialect, and finally as a man who has transformed into Don—a role he is supposed to assume for the cops. The part earned him the Filmfare Award for Best Actor.

LAST-MINUTE HIT

Integral to Don's success is its music. While all the songs were huge hits, it was "Khaike Paan Banaraswala," sung by Kishore Kumar (see pp. 100–101) that proved to be most successful, winning him the Filmfare Award for the Best Male Playback Singer. It was added at the last moment at the suggestion of actor-director Manoj Kumar (see p. 98), Chandra Barot's mentor. The song was penned by lyricist Anjaan, who hailed from Benares (now Varanasi). The third Filmfare Award went to Asha Bhosle for the song "Yeh Mera Dil."

◀ **Style quotient**
In the film, one of Amitabh's avatars is that of the stylish Don, who carries off his formal attire with menacing poise.

ZEENAT AMAN (b.1951)

Born in Mumbai, Zeenat Aman studied in the US and returned to India as a journalist. After becoming the first South Asian to win the Miss Asia Pacific crown, she had a brief modeling career, and then turned to films. Her sense of style and Western sensibilities helped her win roles in films such as *Hare Rama Hare Krishna* (see p. 108), where she played a hippie. At the time, Westernized characters were shown in an unflattering light, but Zeenat changed public perception with her hip roles in films such as *Heera Panna* (1973) and *Yaadon ki Baaraat* (1973).

GOL MAAL

1979

This timeless comedy by Hrishikesh Mukherjee poked fun at the autocratic tendencies of old patriarchs. The film's cast was lauded for its comic timing and iconic performances.

◀ **Complementary characters**
Amol Palekar (left), soft spoken and good humored as Ram, was a perfect contrast to Utpal Dutt (right) who played Bhawani with blistering bravado. The comic pairing would appear together again in *Naram Garam* (1981).

Depressed after the failure of his intense film *Alaap* (1977), director Hrishikesh Mukherjee decided to try his hand at comedy. Talking about the comedies he made, Mukherjee said, "I had thought corruption would end once we became independent. But this was not so. Then I thought there was nothing left to do but laugh." Apart from *Gol Maal* (Chaos), the filmmaker went on to deliver comedies such as *Naram Garam* (1981) and *Chupke Chupke* (see p. 140). Shot in Mukherjee's bungalow in Mumbai in just 40 days, *Gol Maal* has become a timeless classic that never ceases to impress audiences.

A COMEDY OF DELIBERATE ERRORS
The film introduces us to Ram—a good humored young man who loves sports and music. In order to get and keep a coveted job, he has to stay in the good books of the old-fashioned boss

Bhawani Shankar. The old disciplinarian abhors frivolity, feeling that people should only focus on work, and has some seriously eccentric notions about the younger generation. He thinks that men who shorten their names or do not keep mustaches are not to be trusted.
   Thus Ram becomes "Ram Prasad Dasarath Prasad Sharma," who speaks impeccable Hindi, shows no interest in sports or films, and wears utterly unfashionable kurtas borrowed from his friend Deven Verma, who appears in a cameo playing himself. His boss falls for the act. However, when Bhawani sees him skipping work to watch a football match in modern attire, Ram has to create a twin brother Lakshman. Deven comes up with the kurta and a fake mustache and Lakshman becomes "Lucky," Ram's clean-shaven twin who is delightfully insolent towards Bhawani. While Bhawani tries to foist the boring Ram on his daughter Urmi, she loses her heart to "Lucky." The ensuing chaos leaves a hapless Bhawani even more paranoid.

CLASS ACTS
In the double role of two brothers with opposite personalities, Amol Palekar alternated between sunglasses and stylishly twirling key

▶ **A lucky choice**
Bindiya Goswami as Urmi falls for the mustache-less "Lucky" played by Amol Palekar. Her character is as opinionated as Lucky, in contrast to Lucky's boring "brother" Ram.

rings, and oiled hair and short kurtas. He was presented with the Filmfare Award for Best Actor for the role. Deena Pathak, who plays an actress and requested to pitch in as Ram's fake mother, brilliantly transforms herself into the stereotype of a pious widow. A respected name in Bengali theater and cinema, Utpal Dutt is remembered by Hindi film audiences as the funny old man of *Gol Maal* and received a Filmfare Award for Best Performance in a Comic Role for the film.

KARZ

1980

Musical spectacular, supernatural thriller, and romantic murder mystery—*Karz* is all these things and more. It is also remembered as a classic example of 1980s masala.

▼ **The perfect choice**
Rishi Kapoor was the obvious choice for the lead role due to his heartthrob status and excellent dancing skills—essential for the film's success.

B efore making his name with *Karz* (Debt), director Subhash Ghai had already established his filmmaking credentials with the crime thrillers *Kalicharan* (1976) and *Vishwanath* (1978). Although both films had been successful, Ghai wanted to stretch his artistic vision and try something different. He decided to make a musical thriller. While looking for inspiration, he came across an American film, *The Reincarnation of Peter Proud* (1975), in which a bereaved mother recognizes the soul of her dead son in another man. Ghai took this seed of an idea and used it to construct his plot, embracing several genres: romance, crime, and the supernatural. Most importantly, *Karz* was set to a pulsating disco soundtrack. When the final production blasted onto cinema screens in 1980, Ghai had proved that he could deftly combine these familiar cinematic ingredients into a spicy mix to produce the vibrant Bollywood style known as "masala."

REINCARNATION THEME
The story centers on aristocratic businessman Ravi Verma, who is killed

▶ **Villainous role**
Simi Garewal played the seductress audiences love to hate. She ages 20 years, transforming from the young Kamini into the elegant Rani Saheba.

▶ **Reliving the past**
The reincarnated Monty has a flashback to the crucial moment when, as Ravi Verma, he set off on his fateful honeymoon car journey.

by his wife, the gold-digging Kamini, on their honeymoon. In order to gain full control of Ravi's wealth, Kamini ejects his mother and sister from the family mansion. Ravi is reincarnated as Monty, who is raised as an orphan. By the time he is 21, Monty has a successful career as a disco pop star, but his life is often interrupted by visions. While on holiday near Ravi's home, he realizes that these visions are of a past life and decides to investigate further. It is only a matter of time before Monty discovers that he is the reincarnation of Ravi, and when he runs into Ravi's mother and sister, Ravi's mother also recognizes her son's spirit in Monty. Meanwhile, he has fallen in love with Tina, a young woman who has been raised by Ravi's evil wife Kamini. The film builds to its climactic end, in which karma determines the fate of the key players.

Reincarnation had been used as a theme in earlier Bollywood movies, but Ghai's unusual take on the classic Hindi film theme had a completely

DISCO SOUNDTRACK
The disco tracks that capture the spirit of the era helped the film become the highest grosser of the year. In 1980, when disco was losing its popularity on the dancefloors of the US and the UK, it was flourishing in the nightclubs of India and was alive and well in Bollywood. Reflecting its time, *Karz* featured a singing-dancing hero with an infectious disco soundtrack. Some of the most memorable moments in the film are Monty's dance numbers,

their work in *Karz*, Laxmikant–Pyarelal took home their seventh Filmfare Award for Best Music Director.

A SLOW-BURNING CLASSIC
While the film is considered a classic today, *Karz* received a lukewarm reception from critics on its release. It has increased in popularity over time, attracting a cult following for its disco vibe. Several of its songs have stood the test of time, with "Om Shanti Om" and "Dard-E-Dil" (Aching Heart) becoming firm favorites with all age groups. Over the past couple of decades, *Karz* has enjoyed its own reincarnation, with a number of films taking inspiration from it, including *Karzzz* (2008), an unabashed remake, and Farah Khan's *Om Shanti Om* (2007), which paid homage to the film's disco soundtrack, as well as featuring a cameo performance by Rishi Kapoor.

> ## "Everywhere I went people played or hummed the guitar theme."
>
> **SIMI GAREWAL**

original treatment, one that has been emulated by other filmmakers in the years since. What made *Karz* different was that instead of having the same actor play both parts, before and after reincarnation, the film cast different actors. The other key piece of casting was of the elegant actress Simi Garewal in the part of the fiendish Kamini. Garewal was initially not keen to play such a negative role but a persuasive Ghai managed to convince her. Ghai's assurance was proved right when Garewal was nominated for the 1981 Filmfare Award for Best Supporting Actress.

set to music provided by duo Laxmikant–Pyarelal. Known for combining Indian classical and folk music with pop and disco beats, the pair also sampled popular disco tunes for the soundtrack. Strains of George Benson's "We As Love" can be heard in "Ek Hasina Thi" (Once There Was a Beauty). When Monty performs the song, we hear the same riff that Ravi played just before his death, reinforcing the reincarnation theme. The big hit from *Karz*, "Om Shanti Om" (Om Peace Om), borrowed its calypso rhythm from Trinidadian calypso and soca musician Lord Shorty. This now classic song accompanies one of the film's most famous scenes, in which Monty descends from a giant stylus and dances on a revolving dance floor that resembles a record player. For

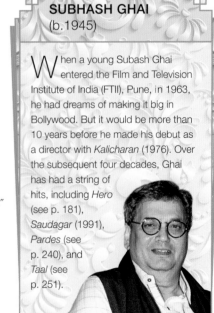

THE VILLAIN

Bollywood has a wide array of villainous characters, from the rural landlord and moneylender to smugglers, businessmen, corrupt politicians, and even rich brats.

Veteran poet–lyricist Javed Akhtar (see pp. 138–39) once pointed out, "You can analyze the nature of a society by seeing who its villains are." This statement rings true for the characterization of the villain in Hindi cinema.

MANY FACES OF THE VILLAIN

In the 1950s, films evoked India's rural realities and often made the landlord or moneylender a villain. In *Mother India* (see pp. 56–57), actor Kanhaiyalal Chaturvedi memorably plays Sukhilala, the village moneylender, who tries to sexually exploit a helpless woman in exchange for food for her starving children. Meanwhile, Pran acted in *Madhumati* (see p. 64) and *Ram aur Shyam* (1967), playing the well-dressed villain, wielding a whip or gun. During this time, women were also seen in villainous roles, although they were more domesticated, usually playing the cruel stepmother or mother-in-law.

In the 1960s and 1970s, as a socialist ethic was being propagated by the Indian state, having a private bar or sitting by the pool signified evil and corruption. In stories of urban India, crooked businessmen and smugglers became the favored villains, played by seasoned actors such as Ajit or Madan Puri. Ajit played this villain so well that countless "Ajit jokes" are still a part of Indian popular culture. The younger actors, Prem Chopra and later Ranjit, played rich, entitled, lascivious sons. Prem's leering dialogue delivery in *Bobby* (see pp. 118–19): "Prem naam hai mera, Prem Chopra" (My name is Prem, Prem Chopra) is classic. Vamps such as Helen, Bindu, and Padma Khanna provided the erotica that heroines were not supposed to. However, as heroines became bolder through the 1970s and 1980s, the vamp faded away.

CULT VILLAINS

As far as villains go, two will remain etched forever in the memory of film aficionados. In 1975 came Gabbar Singh, the sadistic gangster in *Sholay* (see pp. 134–35), played by actor Amjad Khan (see p. 135). His famous dialogues from the film entered public consciousness. Gabbar's popularity was later matched by Mogambo in *Mr. India* (see pp. 188–91) and his line, "Mogambo khush hua!" (Mogambo is pleased!). Actor Amrish Puri was a staple villain in the 1980s and 1990s. With time, as film plots became more realistic, the super-villain paled into a more subtle and ambiguous antagonist.

▶ **Crime lord, Mogambo**
With his blond wig and an army of followers who robotically shouted "Hail Mogambo," Amrish Puri played the role of the super-villain to perfection.

"The stronger the villain, the more charismatic becomes the image of the hero."

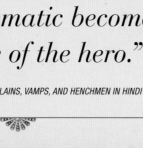

TAPAN K. GHOSH, *BOLLYWOOD BADDIES: VILLAINS, VAMPS, AND HENCHMEN IN HINDI CINEMA*, 2013

KHUBSOORAT

1980

This classic light-hearted comedy by director Hrishikesh Mukherjee reminds its audience that in life it is important to strike a balance between fun and discipline.

(see p. 140)

(see p. 169)

Director Hrishikesh Mukherjee (see p. 140) conceived *Khubsoorat* (Beautiful) specially for lead actress Rekha (see p. 169). The film came to her at a time when she had begun to gain recognition as an accomplished actress thanks to her fine performances in *Do Anjaane* (1976), and especially *Ghar* (1978). Here, Rekha gives what is easily the most likeable performance of her career.

RULING THE ROOST

Rekha plays the exuberant Manju, whose elder sister Anju is married into a household run by the strict matriarch Nirmala, who keeps the

► **Young love**
The romance between the boisterous Manju and the young doctor, Inder, in *Khubsoorat* has many tender and heartwarming moments such as this.

family together on an extremely short leash. The fun begins when Manju visits her sister for a few days, and turns the Gupta household on its head. Much to Nirmala's disapproval, Manju encourages the family members to loosen up, have some fun, and if need be, even revolt against house rules and regulations. Amidst all the madness, a romance develops between Manju and Nirmala's third son, Inder.

Rekha's Manju is the heart and soul of the film. Her infectious sense of fun in her first full-fledged comic role spills over not just to members of the Gupta household, but also to the audience. Her banter with the stern-faced matron, in particular, is a delight to watch.

ORDINARY LIVES

Mukherjee's films have always been full of empathy for

his very real and identifiable characters, who come mostly from the middle class. His films provide a rare insight into an ordinary person's life, and are often full of deft humorous strokes that touch the heart. In this sense, *Khubsoorat* is no exception. The simple, light-hearted story is brought to life through memorable performances by its talented cast, aided by dialogue that is at once charming, witty, and thought-provokingly perceptive.

One of Mukherjee's last successful films, *Khubsoorat* won Filmfare Awards in 1981 for Best Film, Best Actress, and Actor in a Comic Role, awarded to Keshto Mukherjee.

In addition to being remade in two regional languages—Tamil and Malayalam—in the 1980s, *Khubsoorat* was revisited in 2014, with actress Sonam Kapoor taking on Rekha's role and Ratna Pathak Shah reprising her mother Dina Pathak's iconic role as the strict authoritarian. While the remake got its share of decent reviews, it pales in comparison to the original.

CAST AND CREW

★ **Ashok Kumar** Dwarka Prasad Gupta
Rekha Manju Dayal
Rakesh Roshan Inder Gupta
Dina Pathak Nirmala Gupta
Aradhana Anju Dayal
Keshto Mukherjee Ashrafi Lal

🎬 **Director** Hrishikesh Mukherjee
🎬 **Producers** N.C. Sippy, Hrishikesh Mukherjee
🎵 **Music composer** R.D. Burman
🎵 **Lyricist** Gulzar
📖 **Scriptwriters** Shanu Banerjee, D.N. Mukherjee, Gulzar
🎥 **Cinematographer** Jaywant Pathare
👔 **Costume designers** New Stylo, Leena Daru, Maksud Bhai

◄ **Taking on the matriarch**
As the film nears its climax. Nirmala's husband Dwarka Prasad is called on to mediate between his irate wife and the repentant Manju.

SPARSH

SPARSH

1980

Moving away from a stereotypical portrayal of the visually impaired, *Sparsh* depicts a blind man's sensibilities with an emotional maturity that struck a chord with audiences.

S ai Paranjpye was a producer for Doordarshan, the national television channel, when she was asked to do a 10-minute documentary on a blind school for the International Day of Disabled Persons. This experience was to become the basis for her feature film *Sparsh* (Touch).

LOVE AND OTHER HANDICAPS
Sparsh centers on the relationship between Anirudh Parmar, the blind principal of a school for the blind, and widow Kavita Prasad. On the surface, the film appears to be about the challenges suffered by blind people, but as the story unfolds the audience begins to realize that blindness can mean much more than a lack of sight.
  Before beginning work on her documentary, Paranjpye had been worried that seeing the blind children would upset her. However, when she arrived and found the children engaged in a game of tug of war, her fears melted away. The principal of the school, Mr. Mittal, warned her against idealizing the blind: "For God's sake don't make us out to be saints." And so the kind, intelligent, funny, and self-sufficient character, Anirudh, is also extremely touchy. His sense of dignity is so easily

"A timeless gem … that address[es] the normal–abnormal binary."

ANUJ KUMAR, *THE HINDU*, 2017

offended that he flies into a rage if a waiter gives a bill to his sighted companion, or a guest offers to make tea. Thus, when Kavita, who has been clinging to memories of her husband, falls in love with Anirudh, he feels that she is "sacrificing" herself out of a sense of duty and nobility. He fails

to see that spending time with him and the schoolchildren has given her fulfilment, allowing her to overcome her grief. His ego creates barriers they both have to overcome.

WINNING PERFORMANCES
Sighted actor Naseeruddin Shah won the National Award for Best Actor for the film. Shah had studied Mittal in detail, learning to turn his ears instead of his eyes toward the speaker, creating the correct body

language for his part. Paranjpye recalls, "A distraught Mr. Mittal met me: 'Please take your hero off my back,' he begged, 'I'm getting paranoid … I can't go to the loo because I feel Naseer may be watching.'"
  Sparsh also won the National Award and the Filmfare Award for Best Film in 1985 (after a four-year delay in the release date). Paranjpye won the National Award for Best Screenplay, and the Filmfare Award for Best Director and Best Dialogue.

CAST AND CREW

★ **Naseeruddin Shah** Anirudh Parmar
   Shabana Azmi Kavita Prasad
   Sudha Chopra Manjul
   Mohan Gokhale Jagdish
   Om Puri Dubey

📽 **Director** Sai Paranjpye
⌂ **Producer** Basu Bhattacharya
♫ **Music composer** Kanu Roy
♪ **Lyricist** Indu Jain
📖 **Scriptwriter** Sai Paranjpye
🎬 **Cinematographer** Virendra Saini

◄ **A troubled couple**
Sai Paranjpye described *Sparsh* as the love story of a physically handicapped man and an emotionally handicapped woman. The actors are seen here in a tender moment.

SAI PARANJPYE
(b.1938)

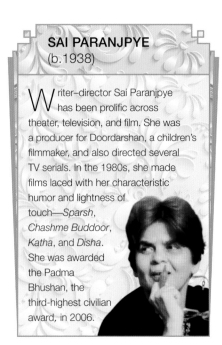

W riter–director Sai Paranjpye has been prolific across theater, television, and film. She was a producer for Doordarshan, a children's filmmaker, and also directed several TV serials. In the 1980s, she made films laced with her characteristic humor and lightness of touch—*Sparsh*, *Chashme Buddoor*, *Katha*, and *Disha*. She was awarded the Padma Bhushan, the third-highest civilian award, in 2006.

CHASHME BUDDOOR

1981

Sai Paranjpye's gently witty, observant film is a delightfully comic look at youth, friendship, bachelor life, and first love in the Delhi of the 1980s.

CAST AND CREW

★ **Farooq Shaikh** Siddharth Parashar
Deepti Naval Neha
Omi Rakesh Bedi
Jomo Ravi Baswani
Saeed Jaffrey Lallan Miyan

🎬 **Director** Sai Paranjpye
🎬 **Producer** Gul Anand
🎵 **Music composer** Raj Kamal
🎼 **Lyricist** Indu Jain
🎥 **Cinematographer** Virendra Saini
📖 **Scriptwriter** Sai Paranjpye
👕 **Costume designer** Maqsood Bhai

An overflowing, makeshift ashtray, three friends wordlessly sharing a cigarette, a ghazal playing in the background—this opening scene of *Chashme Buddoor* (May You be Saved from the Evil Eye) sets the stage for an intelligent, timeless comedy.

THREE MUSKETEERS
The film revolves around the friendship of three roommates—Omi, Jomo, and Siddharth—and the object of their affection, Neha.

While the self-confessed smooth operators Omi and Jomo strike out with their pretty neighbor, it is the bumbling bookworm Siddharth who manages to catch her eye when she comes around to their bachelor pad selling detergent. As the couple's relationship blossoms, Omi and Jomo, unable to stomach their friend's "success," convince Siddharth that Neha is a flirt who romanced them as well. The consequent misunderstandings are resolved in a madcap climax.

YOUNG LOVE
The film's plot was a framework for writer–director Sai Paranjpye's (see p. 163) slice-of-life take on young lives and loves in the Delhi of the 1980s. It showcases everything from dates in Lodhi Garden to bonding over coffee and tutti-frutti ice cream at Talkatora Stadium. It's an affectionate take on the well-intentioned, perpetually broke youth who indulge in cigarettes and are on the lookout for love—in all the wrong places. Weaving its way down the laid-back roads of a simpler time, this film finds its way into the hearts of audiences even today.

BEING BOLLYWOOD
Chashme Buddoor takes a whimsical, self aware look at Bollywood, warts and all. Flashback sequences are introduced by characters announcing "flashback!" and staring back into the camera. Many a key moment in the film is accentuated with a relevant Bollywood song playing on the record or the radio. The lead pair laughingly discuss the improbability of romantic song scenarios

◄ **"Miss Chamko"**
Deepti Naval shines as Neha, the feisty Delhi girl who takes on a job selling Chamko detergent to fund her singing lessons.

▲ **Budding bromance**
Three men with very different personalities and an endearing friendship traipse around India's capital city—seen here at the India Gate—in this hit comedy.

just as they burst into song themselves. And of the three friends, only Siddharth can get the motorbike to start, because, as Jomo observes, "hero hai" (He's the hero).

COLORFUL PERFORMANCES
Deepti Naval and Farooq Shaikh made one of the most appreciated non-star pairs of the 1980s and went on to act in films such as *Saath Saath* (1982) and *Rang Birangi* (1983). The role of the lovable Lallan Miyan is played by actor Saeed Jaffrey with great elan. This acerbic, soft-hearted cigarette stall owner forever pursues the three friends for his due money, but melts the moment their love lives, or Urdu couplets, are invoked.

FAROOQ SHAIKH
(1948–2013)

Farooq Shaikh belonged to the league of actors whose roles were authentic, not heroic. Essaying the role of a helpless, gentle lover in *Bazaar* (1982), a migrant taxi driver dreaming of home in *Gaman* (1978), and a nobleman's son in *Umrao Jaan* (see p.168–69), Shaikh won the hearts of audiences. His much-appreciated play *Tumhari Amrita* (1992) ran for 12 years. He won the National Award for his role in *Lahore* (2010).

SILSILA

1981

Silsila relied more on its star cast to resonate with audiences than its story. While it was not a box office success, it did set the tone for subsequent Yash Raj films.

CAST AND CREW

★ **Amitabh Bachchan** Amit Malhotra
Rekha Chandni
Jaya Bachchan Shobha Malhotra
Sanjeev Kumar Dr. V.K. Anand
Shashi Kapoor Shekhar Malhotra
Kulbhushan Kharbanda Inspector
Kulbhushan

🎬 **Director** Yash Chopra
🎬 **Producer** Yash Chopra
🎵 **Music composers** Hariprasad
Chaurasia, Shiv Kumar Sharma
🎵 **Lyricists** Javed Akhtar, Harivansh
Rai Bachchan, Rajinder Krishan, Nida
Fazli, Hasan Kamal
🎥 **Cinematographer** Kay Gee
📖 **Scriptwriters** Yash Chopra,
Sagar Sarhadi

▼ **Poetic beauty**
Shot in Amsterdam, the song "Ye Kahan Aa Gaye Hum" (Where Have We Arrived) features couplets recited in Amitabh Bachchan's rich baritone. This is in keeping with his character of a poet.

Silsila (A Chain of Events) was based around the extra-marital relationship between Amit played by Amitabh Bachchan (see pp. 126–27) and Chandni essayed by Rekha (see pp. 169), former lovers, now married to other people. While neither the subject nor the treatment were particularly novel, it was the casting of *Silsila* that was expected to create the buzz necessary to fill theaters.

Director Yash Chopra (see pp. 166–67), by his own admission, had dithered with the casting, first considering actress Padmini Kolhapure as the "other woman" and Poonam Dhillon as the wife, soon replacing them with Parveen Babi and Smita Patil, respectively. Eventually, he engineered a casting coup by prevailing upon Jaya Bachchan, Amitabh's wife, to come out of retirement to play his on-screen wife and Rekha, the "other woman." In Chopra's own words: "It was one of the most interesting, one of the biggest, one of the most challenging cast in a film ever done in the history of Indian cinema."

A STORMY AFFAIR

The film revolves around lovebirds Amit and Chandni's tumultuous romance. When Amit's brother Shekhar is killed in combat, he leaves behind his pregnant girlfriend Shobha. Amit marries Shobha to protect her honor, and a crestfallen Chandni ends up marrying Dr. Anand. Injured in a car accident, Shobha is saved by none other than Dr. Anand. As the lives of the two couples intersect, Amit and Chandni rekindle their romance, much to the despair of their significant others, and call into question the sanctity of the institution of marriage.

SIGNATURE STYLE

Silsila did not garner the success that Chopra had expected, running for about 16 weeks in the theaters. While the film did not do well at the box office, it has gone on to become a cult classic. It has elements that eventually came to be associated with Yash Raj films—heavy reliance on romance and emotional content, depiction of the lifestyle of the elite, famous heroines wrapped in chiffon yardage, and extensive use of foreign locales (see pp. 234–35). The film also marked a dip in Chopra's career, which was revived by *Chandni* (see p. 202).

CLASSIC TUNES

The music of *Silsila* is as fresh today as it was when it was released. The folk song "Rang Barse" (Colors Galore), penned by famous poet and Amitabh's father Harivansh Rai Bachchan, can still be heard playing on the Indian festival of colors, Holi. With *Silsila*, Javed Akhtar, half of the famed screenwriting duo Salim–Javed (see pp. 138–39), embarked upon a highly successful solo career as a lyricist. He penned four songs for the film, including the title track and "Neela Aasmaan So Gaya" (The Blue Sky Is Asleep). Amitabh's haunting rendition of the song, initially rejected by audiences, went on to become a classic.

The film was the first Bollywood collaboration of composers Pandit Shiv Kumar Sharma and Pandit Hari Prasad Chaurasia. Both maestros of Hindustani classical music, Sharma and Chaurasia were masters of the santoor—a stringed instrument—and the flute, respectively, which feature in the soundtrack.

YASH CHOPRA

DIRECTOR–PRODUCER **1932–2012**

A trailblazer in the world of Hindi cinema, Yash Chopra made some of the most stylish romances—narrating stories of love and tragedy with great sensitivity.

▼ King of romance
The acknowledged master of the romantic genre, Yash Chopra was a prolific director and producer, making more than 50 films in his lifetime and winning six National Film Awards and 11 Filmfare Awards.

With a career spanning more than five decades, Yash Chopra outlasted many other directors by changing with the times and adapting his style to the tastes of the audience. He established himself as a master director, especially romances, with an ear for music, and an eye for future stars. Some of his films were simple love stories, while others tackled social issues. His directorial debut, *Dhool ka Phool* (1959) was a touching study of illegitimacy, while later in his career *Lamhe* divided cinemagoers by broaching the topic of quasi-incest. He could also handle the action genre with equal aplomb—*Deewar* is a prime example.

MAN BEHIND THE CAMERA
The key to Yash Chopra's success in making films that audiences connect with lies in the formative years of his

▲ Behind-the-scenes
Yash Chopra and actor Amitabh Bachchan on the sets of the 1979 film *Kaala Patthar*. The duo worked together on several blockbuster films, including *Deewar* and *Silsila*.

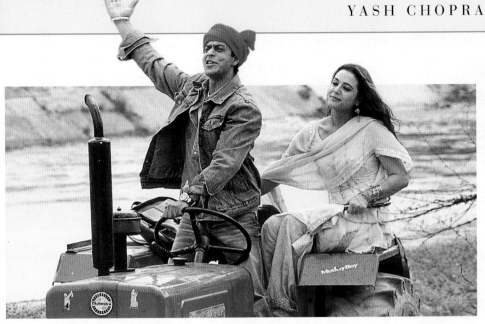

◀ **Cross-border romance**
Yash Chopra directed *Veer-Zaara*, an epic romance of lovers separated from one another for two decades.

● **September 27, 1932** Born in pre-partition Lahore. Spends most of his childhood at the home of his elder brother, B.R. Chopra, who is 18 years older.

● **1947** India's partition forces the Chopra family to move to Delhi, and then to Mumbai. B.R. Chopra becomes a film producer and takes Yash Chopra under his wing as an assistant director.

● **1959** Debuts as director with *Dhool ka Phool*, a drama about social prejudice surrounding illegitimacy. The film is one of several he will make for his brother's production company.

● **1970** Marries Pamela Singh.

● **1971** Establishes his own production company, Yash Raj Films, in collaboration with Rajesh Khanna.

● **1973** Releases *Daag: A Poem of Love*, his first as both director and producer.

● **1981** Releases the blockbuster film *Chandni*, which is influential in restoring the popularity of the romantic musical in Bollywood. The film wins the National Film Award for Best Popular Film Providing Wholesome Entertainment.

● **1991** Directs and produces *Lahme*. The film does not perform well at the box office, but wins the Filmfare Award for Best Film.

POSTER OF THE CRITICALLY ACCLAIMED FILM *LAMHE*

● **1993** Directs newcomer Shah Rukh Khan in musical thriller *Darr: A Violent Love Story*.

● **2012** Returns to directing eight years after his last film, *Veer-Zaara*, with *Jab tak hai Jaan*. The film would be his last directorial venture.

● **October 21, 2012** Dies of dengue fever in Mumbai, less than a month after his 80th birthday. He does not live to see the release of his last film.

childhood. He was born in Lahore in 1932, before India was partitioned. As a teenager, he experienced the disruption and drama of the country being divided into India and Pakistan. His family moved to Delhi, and then to Mumbai—an event that profoundly affected his outlook on life and his creative vision.

Nostalgia for his birthplace is often apparent in Yash Chopra's films, from 1995's *Dilwale Dulhania le Jayenge* (see pp. 230–33), featuring the fertile fields of Punjab, to *Veer-Zaara*, in which an Indian pilot falls in love with a Pakistani woman. In both films, the filmmaker romanticizes the rural landscape and presents an idea of shared similarities between India and Pakistan. Yash Chopra not only excelled at portraying romantic relationships, but also at depicting an idealized national identity.

Another theme that has permeated Yash Chopra's films from early on in his career is that of people being lost and found. *Dhool ka Phool* challenged viewers with the tale of an illegitimate Hindu child separated from his birth parents and raised by a Muslim family. Several years later, *Waqt* unraveled the story of three brothers who are separated by a disaster, and struggle to reunite. Released just after the 1965 India–Pakistan War, *Waqt* struck a chord with cinemagoers and inspired countless other films with similar themes of loss and recovery.

DIRECTION TO PRODUCTION

Yash Chopra learned the craft of filmmaking while working as an assistant director under his elder brother, Baldev Raj Chopra. The pair also made several movies together with Yash as director. *Waqt*'s success gave him the confidence to set up his own production company, Yash Raj Films, in 1971. His first independent film was *Daag: A Poem of Love* (1973). Starring superstar Rajesh Khanna (see pp. 106–107) as a man accused of having two wives, the film was a critical and box office triumph.

Yash Chopra went on to make more than 50 films. Many of these were blockbusters, especially those that stayed true to the director's romantic vision, with beautiful costumes, lush scenery, melodious songs, and happy endings.

ROMANCE IN BEAUTIFUL LOCATIONS

Although his films mine deep personal emotions, and are not afraid to tackle subjects such as poverty and inequality, Yash Chopra maintains a sensory opulence with heroes and heroines in stylish clothes, elegant houses, luxury cars, and picturesque surroundings.

In *Chandni*, Yash Chopra used the scenic Swiss Alps as the backdrop for the lead pair's romance, with the heroine taking center stage rather than the hero. He made several films set in Switzerland—as the fairy tale scenery complemented his utopian tales of love—for example producing *Dilwale Dulhaniya le Jayenge*, *Mujhse Dosti Karoge!* (2002) and *Mere Yaar ki Shaadi hai* (2002). Even the psychological thriller *Darr: A Violent Love Story* (see p. 213) makes the theme of obsessive love compelling to watch, partly because of its sumptuous visuals of the Alps. Shot in neighboring Germany, the love story *Dil to Pagal hai* is considered one of the director's best films, combining all his trademark elements: picturesque locations, a dreamy soundtrack, and the most romantic of endings.

> *"I wanted to be honest to the script and the characters, but I also wanted to portray my artists as best as I could visually."*

YASH CHOPRA IN AN INTERVIEW WITH FILM CRITIC RAJEEV MASAND

KEY WORKS

Waqt, 1965 (see p. 92)

Deewaar, 1975 (see p. 130)

Kabhi Kabhie, 1976 (see pp. 144–47)

Silsila, 1981 (see p. 165)

Chandni, 1989 (see p. 202)

Lamhe, 1991

Dil to Pagal hai, 1997

Veer-Zaara, 2004 (see p. 339)

UMRAO JAAN

1981

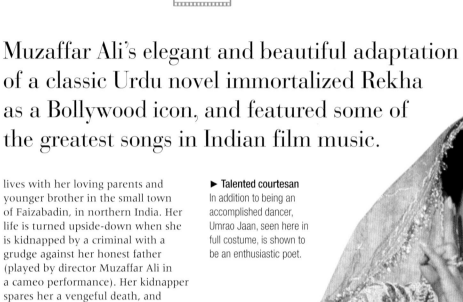

Muzaffar Ali's elegant and beautiful adaptation of a classic Urdu novel immortalized Rekha as a Bollywood icon, and featured some of the greatest songs in Indian film music.

CAST AND CREW

★ **Rekha** Amiran
Farooq Shaikh Nawab Sultan
Naseeruddin Shah Gohar Mirza
Raj Babbar Faiz Ali

🎬 **Director** Muzaffar Ali
⬤ **Producer** Muzaffar Ali
🎵 **Music composers** Mohammed Zahur "Khayyam," Akhlaq Mohammed Khan
🎵 **Lyricist** Akhlaq Mohammad Khan "Shahryar"
🕴 **Choreographer** Kumudini Lakhia
📖 **Scriptwriters** Shama Zaidi, Javed Siddiqui, Muzaffar Ali
🎥 **Cinematographer** Pravin Bhatt
👔 **Costume designer** Subhashini Ali

A much-adored Bollywood classic, *Umrao Jaan* is a tragic period drama about a beautiful and sophisticated woman left heartbroken by a decadent world. Inspired by the 1899 Urdu novel *Umrao Jaan Ada* written by Mirza Hadi Ruswa, director Muzaffar Ali created a cinematic portrayal of 1840s Lucknow that was rich in detail, lavish costumes, and classical poetry and song.

A QUEEN IS BORN

Set in the first half of the 19th century, the film opens with the engagement ceremony of 12-year-old Amiran, who lives with her loving parents and younger brother in the small town of Faizabadin, in northern India. Her life is turned upside-down when she is kidnapped by a criminal with a grudge against her honest father (played by director Muzaffar Ali in a cameo performance). Her kidnapper spares her a vengeful death, and instead spirits her away to Lucknow, where he sells her off to the madam of a brothel. Here, in a city famed for its riches and refinement, she is given a new name, Umrao, and raised to become a courtesan. Trained in the graceful arts of poetry, song, and dance, she becomes cultured enough to seduce wealthy and powerful men.

One night, while singing "In Aankhon Ki Masti Ke," she catches the eye of Nawab Sultan, a rich and handsome nobleman. The two are introduced, and fall in love over poetry and song. But Nawab is soon forced to make a choice between his love for Umrao and the demands made by his family for a socially appropriate marriage.

Too cowardly to fight social conventions for the woman he loves, Nawab leaves Umrao for a more

► **Talented courtesan**
In addition to being an accomplished dancer, Umrao Jaan, seen here in full costume, is shown to be an enthusiastic poet.

HIT SONGS

Dil Cheez Kya Hai
(What Is a Heart Worth?)
🔑 **Singer** Asha Bhosle

Yeh Kya Jagah Hain Doston
(What Place Is This, My Friend?)
🔑 **Singer** Talat Aziz

In Aankhon Ki Masti Ke
(The Intoxicating Beauty of These Eyes)
🔑 **Singer** Asha Bhosle

▲ In a man's world
Brothel intermediary Gohar Mirza (left) negotiates Umrao's meeting with Nawab Sultan (right), just as he does all her interactions with the outside world.

suitable match. Heartbroken, she rebounds into the arms of bandit chieftain Faiz Ali, who at least is honest in his wooing. Rejecting her life as a courtesan, she elopes with him into the hills. But when Ali, a wanted man, is killed by the police, Umrao finds herself back in Lucknow, trapped in a life she cannot seem to escape. Against the backdrop of the Siege of Lucknow during the Indian Rebellion of 1857, Umrao is forced to flee the city. Despite ending up in her home village and being reunited with her family, Umrao once again encounters prejudice and

has to return to Lucknow and an uncertain future.

INTOXICATING EYES

"There are thousands intoxicated by these eyes," Umrao sings early in the film. But for Rekha, it would be millions. *Umrao Jaan* cemented Rekha's place in the pantheon of Indian movie icons. She won the coveted National Award for Best Actress for her performance. Considered one of her greatest roles, Rekha mesmerized audiences as Umrao, with her dark, expressive eyes that conveyed an impressive depth and range of emotion, from lovestruck hope to desolate loneliness.

In an interview, director Muzaffar Ali explained why he cast Rekha for the role: "I saw Rekha's picture, a close-up, and I saw her eyes. She is someone who has been hurt a lot, but stands up stronger." Although she was not a trained dancer, Rekha rehearsed extensively for the classic *mujra* dance form under the guidance of legendary Kathak dance guru Gopi Krishna, so as to correctly execute Kumudini Lakhia's stellar choreography. Ali rejected the noisy commercial style of most Indian films of the late 1970s and early 1980s for his more cultured vision of a well-known South Asian literary novel. To adapt it for film, Ali

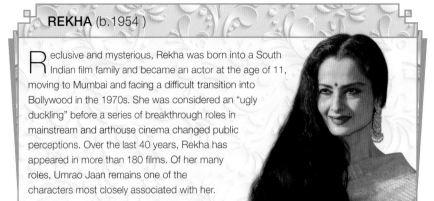

REKHA (b.1954)

Reclusive and mysterious, Rekha was born into a South Indian film family and became an actor at the age of 11, moving to Mumbai and facing a difficult transition into Bollywood in the 1970s. She was considered an "ugly duckling" before a series of breakthrough roles in mainstream and arthouse cinema changed public perceptions. Over the last 40 years, Rekha has appeared in more than 180 films. Of her many roles, Umrao Jaan remains one of the characters most closely associated with her.

changed some elements of the original book, but much of the narrative and its underlying themes—the moral hypocrisy of traditional patriarchal society and its unjust treatment of women—were left intact. Ali paid particular attention to period detail, recreating the rich upper-class decadence of 19th-century Lucknow through luxurious costumes, authentic props, and even the actors' manners and speech. Cinematographer Pravin Bhatt helped Ali create a rich visual style, emulating the art of the period.

CULT CLASSIC

A classical elegance infuses the film's soulful soundtrack through the use of traditional instruments and moving compositions by the celebrated music director Khayyam. The lyrics were written by the Urdu poet Shahryar, who only rarely wrote lyrics for Bollywood films. Playback singer Asha

Bhosle deliberately sang in a low register to lend a husky sensuality to Umrao's voice. The collaborations resulted in songs that are considered the finest examples of Bollywood film music, and pinnacles of Asha Bhosle's career, including "Dil Cheez Kya Hai," "Justuju Jiski Thi," "In Aankhon ki Masti ke," and "Yeh Kya Jagah Hai Doston."

The film achieved only average box office returns upon release, but won enormous critical acclaim and swifly became a cult classic after winning several National Film Awards, including Best Music Direction, Best Art Direction, and Best Actress, as well as the Filmfare Award for Best Director, in 1982. Asha Bhosle also won a National Award for Best Female Playback Singer.

"If there were 100 people watching the shoot, 99 were there to watch Rekha."

FAROOQ SHAIKH IN AN INTERVIEW WITH REDIFF.COM, NOVEMBER 2006

▶ Forbidden couple
When Nawab Sultan refuses to frequent the brothel any more, Umrao visits him at his friend's house (seen here), where she is insulted and judged by the household staff.

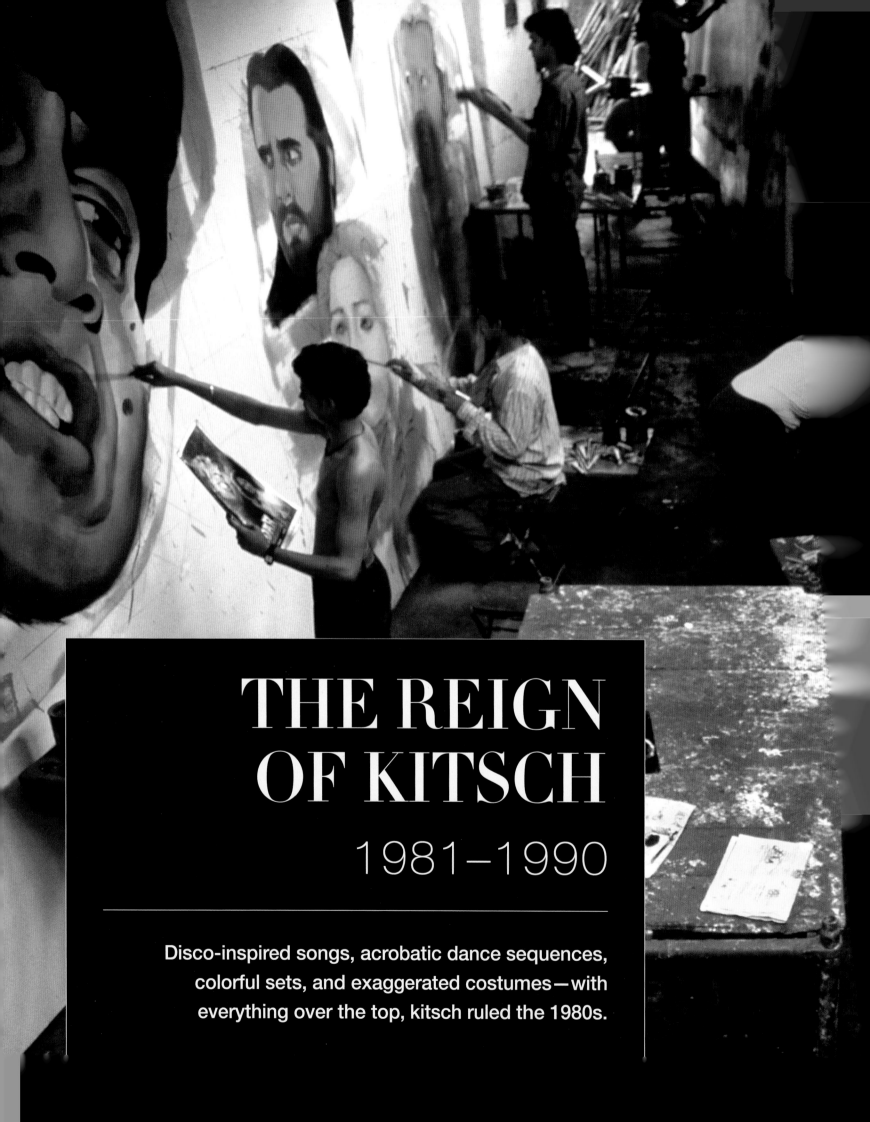

THE REIGN OF KITSCH

1981–1990

Disco-inspired songs, acrobatic dance sequences, colorful sets, and exaggerated costumes—with everything over the top, kitsch ruled the 1980s.

THE REIGN OF KITSCH

The 1980s was a mixed bag in Bollywood, where poignant storytelling from new, sensitive filmmakers jostled for space against over-the-top, unabashedly kitschy, escapist offerings.

Barring some exceptions, the 1980s saw unprecedented levels of shoddy aesthetics, crude violence, and heavy melodrama in Bollywood. However, this period did introduce some interesting elements into Hindi cinema, including the "politician as villain" character, which grew out of the nation's political climate. The State of Emergency of 1975–77—when the government suspended constitutional procedures—brought people face to face with the brute force wielded by the state. In 1984, following this tumultuous period, Prime Minister Indira Gandhi was assassinated by her own bodyguards. High levels of political-bureaucratic corruption remained, and the Bofors scandal of the mid-1980s—involving a deal between the Indian government and the Swedish arms manufacturer AB Bofors—was the first big scam in which political leaders stood accused.

These real-life examples led to the creation of a different type of on-screen nemesis. Until then, the traditional villain had been the rural landowner, money lender, dacoit, smuggler, or the urban businessman, but this decade saw a demonization of politicians, bureaucrats, and the police.

The 1980s also saw a major change in viewing habits. The attendance of family audiences in cinemas dropped sharply with the arrival of the Video Home System, or VHS. Financially hit by this technology, producers began making films for "front-benchers"—males who wanted cheap tickets—that led to films aimed at titillation and simplistic themes.

VIOLENT VIGILANTES

With this background, Bollywood birthed the idea of gruesome justice in the face of political power, with unprecedented levels of gratuitous violence. The decade began with *Meri Awaz Suno* (1981) in which Jeetendra (see pp. 182–83) killed his corrupt foes after facing grisly torture.

In *Inquilab* (1984), Amitabh Bachchan (see pp. 126–27) walked into parliament to shoot corrupt ministers dead. Films such as *Andha Kanoon* (1983), *Akhree Raasta* (1986), and *Pratighaat* (1987) kept the revenge

◀ **The hit formula**
Marked by foot-thumping music, acrobatic gyrations, and larger-than-life sets, filmmakers made money on the hit pair of Jeetendra–Sridevi in remakes of South Indian films such as *Himmatwala* (left), *Tohfa* (1984), and *Maqsad* (1984).

"We saw a lot of pure masala films during that time."

TARAN ADARSH, CRITIC, *HINDUSTAN TIMES,* 2013

---

going. Actor Sunny Deol in *Arjun* (1985) appealed to the audience, as he meted out punishment to politicians who manipulated honest youth. Nana Patekar's *Ankush* (1986) also played on a similarly violent theme. Anil Kapoor found his niche with *Mr. India* (see pp. 188–89), and became a hero in the hit film *Tezaab* (see p.198), described as a "violent love story."

A rare, sensitive offering in this category—and a fine example of angst in the 1980s—was actor Om Puri's role in *Ardha Satya* (1983). Puri played the honest but frustrated policeman Anant Velankar, who strangles a politically connected goon played by Sadashiv Amrapurkar, before giving himself up.

DOWNFALL OF THE GREATS

This era saw Bollywood stars taking up mediocre roles. Amitabh mutated from a strong and silent hero into an aging avenger who sported the word *Mard* (a "real" man) carved on his chest in *Mard* (1985), and fought an obviously fake crocodile in *Ganga Jamuna Saraswati* (1988).

◀ **Disco king**
Bappi Lahiri composed the music for some of the biggest chartbusters of the disco era.

▶ **Style over substance**
Khoon Bhari Maang (1988) saw Rekha glam up the screen with costumes and hairdos typical of the 1980s.

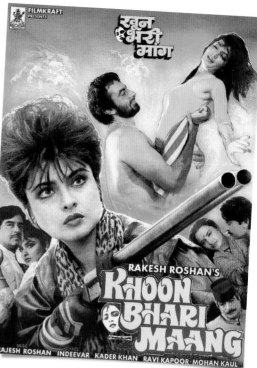

Dharmendra (see pp. 152–53) starred in a spate of films by Raj Kumar Kohli, with names such as 1982's *Badle ki Aag* (Fire of Vengeance) and 1984's *Jeene Nahin Doonga* (Won't Let You Live). Hema Malini (see pp. 110–11) was reduced to playing a rape victim in a B-grade film called *Durgaa* (1985), while Dimple Kapadia was seen castrating her rapists in *Zakhmi Aurat* (1988).

THE "SOUTH MOVIE"

Kitschy Hindi films made by producers and directors of Telugu and Tamil cinema were also a definitive feature of the 1980s. Plots from successful South Indian movies were shot relatively cheaply in Hindi. Filmmaker T. Rama Rao made the family dramas *Judaai* (1980) and *Maang Bharo Sajana* (1980) with Jeetendra, and the highly violent *Andha Kaanoon* (1983) and *Inquilaab* (1984) with Rajnikanth and Amitabh Bachchan, respectively. Hyderabad's Padmalaya Studios churned out monster hits such as *Himmatwala* (see p. 180), *Mawaali* (1983), and *Tohfa* (1984). Even today, the lurid sets, crass lyrics, and dances remain humorous reference points in popular culture. Sridevi (see pp. 204–205), a glamorous diva in South Indian films, played a snake-woman with panache in *Nagina* (see p.184).

Several movies depicted exploitative sexual violence, and double entendre and vulgar gestures entered the Hindi film industry. The low-point was Marathi actor Dada Kondke's sex-comedies, such as *Andheri Raat mein Diya Tere Haath mein* (1986) and *Khol de Meri Zubaan* (1989).

SO BAD IT'S GOOD

Mithun Chakraborty began the decade by appearing in *Wardat* (1980), reprising his role as Gunmaster G-9, a disco-dancing spy—seen

earlier in *Suraksha* (1979). He then shot to stardom with *Disco Dancer* (see p. 175), playing electric guitars that were noticeably not plugged in. His rise paralleled that of composer-singer Bappi Lahiri. A fine musician in the 1970s, his music in the 1980s was often tainted with charges of plagiarism. Filmmakers Ramsay Brothers, and their horror-gore-and-sleaze factory, churned out the likes of *Purana Mandir* (1984) and *Purani Haveli* (1989). Using cheap props and effects, they wrapped up films quickly and recovered their costs at the box office.

Some films from this era are fondly remembered for taking things a little too far. Mithun Chakraborty reprised Michael Jackson's *Thriller* with hilarious fake zombies in *Kasam Paida Karne wale ki* (1984), while *Teri Meherbaniyan* (1985) featured the dog Moti on a mission to avenge his master Jackie Shroff's death, killing three villains and weeping at Jackie's grave to the theme song. And in a scene from the 1989 film *Clerk*, the 52-year old college student Manoj Kumar healed his father's heart attack by playing a patriotic song. The decade also saw the emergence of many comic-book villains—Black Cobra, Sir Judah, and Dr. Dang, to name a few.

HIDDEN GEMS

Thankfully, the era was redeeemed by arthouse classics such as *Ardha Satya* (1983), *Jaane bhi do Yaaro* (see p. 178), *Umrao Jaan* (see pp. 168–69), *Masoom* (see p. 177), and *Saaransh* (see p. 179). By the time Amitabh Bachchan tried to reinvent himself as a vigilante superman in *Shahenshah* (1988), the next generation of young, romantic heroes was knocking at the door.

ROCKY

1981

A Bollywood teen romance, *Rocky* was the launchpad for a young Sanjay Dutt. A family enterprise of sorts, the film was directed and produced by his famous father, Sunil Dutt, who also made a cameo appearance in the movie.

◀ The "bad boy" of Bollywood
Dubbed one of the more controversial stars in Bollywood, Sanjay Dutt's popularity has only increased since *Rocky*, with strong performances in gangster movies, crime thrillers, and comedies.

The film *Rocky* opens with a scene showing Shankar, a high-minded union leader on a construction crew, struggling to keep the workplace safe by lobbying their money-hungry boss, Ratanlal. When Shankar dies in a suspicious work-related accident, his young son Rakesh is traumatized by the event and cannot cope with the tragedy. He is sent to live with another family, who name him Rocky. The boy grows up to be a regular, fun-loving, disco-dancing young man, with a crush on Renuka, daughter of the now-deceased Ratanlal, and has no memory of his real family. When he discovers his real identity as Shankar's son and the fact that his father's death was not an accident, Rocky's world collapses and he vows revenge. Will he finish his father's fight?

TROUBLED BEGINNINGS

Sanjay Dutt is the son of Bollywood power couple Sunil and Nargis Dutt. His father hoped to make Sanjay a megastar, and launched his career with *Rocky*, following the trend of other Bollywood stars who helped initiate their children's film careers. The film was a typical 1980s Hindi revenge drama, but a much more dramatic tale was happening off-screen. Shortly after shooting began, Nargis fell ill and her husband had to take her to the US for treatment. Diagnosed with terminal cancer, Nargis returned to India and Sunil, desperate to be near his wife in her final days, handed over the task of finishing the film to his colleagues. Just a few days before *Rocky* finally premiered, Nargis died. At the first screening of the movie, one seat in the front of the auditorium was left empty in Nargis' memory.

SHINING THROUGH THE STRUGGLE

The film achieved only moderate success at the box office. Although Sanjay's emotional scenes were impressive, and his resemblance to his mother made an impact, critics found his performance unprofessional and unpolished.

In shock after his mother's death, Sanjay could not find solace in his career, and soon entered rehab for drug addiction. On his return to India after two years of therapy, the actor revealed to an interviewer that his father had told him he was now on his own. Despite the rockiest of starts, Sanjay has gone on to build a notable career, fighting his personal demons along the way. His story will soon be the subject of a biopic made by celebrated director Rajkumar Hirani.

> ## "I keep the bad-boy image just to make my fans happy."
>
> SANJAY DUTT, IN AN INTERVIEW WITH *BBC*, 2005

CAST AND CREW

★ **Sanjay Dutt** Rakesh / Rocky D'Souza
Tina Munim Renuka Seth
Shanker Sunil Dutt
Shakti Kapoor R.D.
Amjad Khan Robert
Anwar Hussain Ratanlal
Aruna Irani Kathy

Director Sunil Dutt
Producer Amarjeet
Music composer R.D. Burman
Choreographer Suresh Bhatt
Scriptwriter Bharat B. Bhalla
Cinematographer S. Ramachandra
Costume designer Bhanu Athaiya

HIT SONGS

**Aa Dekhen Zara
(Come On and See)**
🎤 **Singers** Kishore Kumar,
Asha Bhosle

**Kya Yehi Pyar Hai
(Is This Love?)**
🎤 **Singers** Kishore Kumar,
Lata Mangeshkar

**Doston Ko Salam
(Greetings, My Friends)**
🎤 **Singer** Kishore Kumar

DISCO DANCER

1982

With his glittery costumes and pelvic thrusts, *Disco Dancer*'s hero Jimmy earned himself statues in Russia, a shrine in Tokyo, fans across Asia, and theme parties in Europe.

HIT SONG

I Am a Disco Dancer
🎤 **Singer** Vijay Benedict

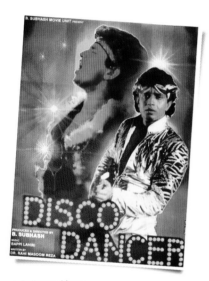

▲ **Bollywood icon**
With his glitzy costumes and kitschy style, Mithun Chakraborty achieved iconic status as Jimmy in *Disco Dancer*. The film is still revered on cult fan sites and Facebook groups.

Exemplifying the phrase "cult classic," *Disco Dancer* enjoys its fair share of fans, who fondly indulge the film's eccentricities. The movie's highlights include a villain trying to kill a musician by electrocuting him with his guitar, a singer going through "guitar phobia," shining disco balls as a near-constant backdrop, one of Bollywood's most comic death scenes, and—to top it all off—some sensational Indian disco songs.

Composer Bappi Lahiri was catapulted to success with *Disco Dancer*. His music for the film gave disco a fresh lease of life in India after the fad had died out in the West. The songs are still reprised (pop star M.I.A. made a version of "Jimmy" in 2007) and Michael Jackson reportedly told the hit composer that he had enjoyed the songs. Director Babbar Subhash was another winner, continuing on to further success with small-budget 1980s potboilers such as *Adventures of Tarzan* (1985) and *Dance Dance* (1987).

DEATH BY GUITAR
Mithun Chakraborty's portrayal of Jimmy in *Disco Dancer* is a far cry from the actor's serious dramatic role in the award-winning period film *Mrigayaa* (1976). Jimmy is an ambitious street performer who lives for his self-sacrificing mother, and his mission in life is to avenge her humiliation by the evil businessman P.N. Oberoi. He achieves his revenge by unseating Oberoi's son as India's disco darling, winning over his daughter, and ruining his business. When Jimmy's mother is accidentally killed by a guitar rigged by the villains to electrocute him, he is left with a deathly fear of guitars. But Jimmy's disco-dancing days are far from over.

INDIA'S ANSWER TO ELVIS
A film that is best described as "so bad it's good," *Disco Dancer* was the 1980s idea of aspirational India, filled with all things shiny and colorful. A poor boy fighting a rich man, Mithun was no less of an "Angry Young Man" than other characters of the 1970s and 1980s—only in spangled costumes.

But how did the actor learn to dance like he did? "I was a huge fan of Elvis Presley … I tried to copy his steps … but I developed my own style of dancing as I couldn't replicate all his moves. It's nothing but the Elvis Presley style of dancing gone wrong!" says Mithun.

▼ **Disco fever**
Mithun Chakraborty's signature moves and Bappi Lahiri's songs gave India its disco anthems for decades to come.

CAST AND CREW

★ **Mithun Chakraborty** Jimmy / Anil
Kim Rita Oberoi
Om Shivpuri P.N. Oberoi
Om Puri David Brown
Karan Razdan Sam Oberoi
Geeta Siddharth Radha
Kalpana Iyer Nikki Brown
Yusuf Khan Vasco

🎬 **Director** B. Subhash
💿 **Producer** B. Subhash
🎵 **Music composer** Bappi Lahiri
🎼 **Lyricist** Anjaan
🕺 **Choreographer** Suresh Bhatt
📖 **Scriptwriter** Rahi Masoom Raza
🎥 **Cinematographer** Nadeem Khan
👕 **Costume designers** Kishore Bajaj, Allen Gill, Shahjahan

ARTH

RITA PAL PRESENTS
ANU ARTS
ARTH
अर्थ

DIRECTION
MAHESH BHATT · MUSIC CHITRA & JAGJIT SINGH · PRODUCED BY KULJIT PAL

1982

Groundbreaking in its depiction of true autonomy for a woman outside of marriage, *Arth* was radical for its time and remains relevant even today.

◀ **Art wars**
In *Arth*, two leading ladies of art house cinema shared screen space to great effect. From Shabana's quiet resolve to Smita's haunting insecurity, it was a clash of the titans.

Mahesh Bhatt's *Arth* (Meaning) is the story of a woman's journey toward independence and emotional fulfilment. The sixth film that Bhatt directed and the first one he wrote himself, *Arth* is the story of an extramarital affair, but focuses more on the plight of the abandoned wife.

The story revolves around Pooja, who, having grown up an orphan, longs for the ideal of domesticity, complete with the "security" of a loving marriage. Her world falls apart when her husband, Inder, leaves her to move in with Kavita, the actress with whom he's having an affair. Pooja, however, soon decides that she must try to move on with her life and learn to fend for herself. Meanwhile, battling her own demons, Kavita also comes to realize that she does not need the insecurity of a relationship with a married man, so rejects Inder and also starts out on the path toward personal independence.

RADICAL REFUSAL
As a demonstration of her growing confidence during the course of the film, Pooja turns down a marriage proposal from her confidante and friend Raj, a departure from all the norms of fictional romance. Instead, she seeks fulfilment by adopting and caring for the daughter of her domestic helper, a woman who has been imprisoned for killing her abusive, alcoholic spouse.

The film's storyline was deemed so bold at the time that the film's distributors asked for it to be changed. But *Arth* stood its ground. As a result, the film's release was delayed for many months. Only after the lead actress Shabana Azmi won the National Award for her performance as Pooja, did Rajshri Productions agree to distribute the film.

STAR RIVALRY
As leading ladies of the Parallel Cinema movement, Shabana Azmi and Smita Patil could not escape comparison. The media hyped their rivalry to fever pitch after *Arth*, in which both delivered powerhouse performances. With Shabana bagging awards for her portrayal of Pooja, it is said that Smita felt "shortchanged" and began to resent Bhatt for it.

GLITTERING GHAZALS
In keeping with the tone and elegance of the film, it is only fitting that its soundtrack was made up of a collection of evocative ghazals—Urdu poetry set to music. Ghazals such as Kaifi Azmi's popular "Tum Itna Jo Muskura Rahe ho" (What Sadness Hides Behind Your Smile) and "Jhuki Jhuki Si Nazar" (Your Lowered Eyes) are considered to be timeless classics.

CAST AND CREW

★ **Shabana Azmi** Pooja Malhotra
Kulbhushan Kharbanda Inder Malhotra
Smita Patil Kavita Sanyal
Raj Kiran Raj

🎬 **Director** Mahesh Bhatt
⬡ **Producer** Kuljit Pal
♫ **Music composers** Jagjit Singh, Chitra Singh
A♪ **Lyricist** Kaifi Azmi
📖 **Scriptwriters** Mahesh Bhatt, Sujit Sen
🎞 **Cinematographer** Pravin Bhatt
👕 **Costume designer** Manya Patil Seth

> *"The film that changed my life is Mahesh Bhatt's Arth."*
>
> **SHABANA AZMI** CNN IBN

MAHESH BHATT (b. 1948)

One of Bollywood's most unconventional personalities, producer–director Mahesh Bhatt has always been open about his personal life—such as being a drug user who was born out of wedlock—and its influence on his work. His early masterpieces include *Arth* and *Saraansh* (see p. 179). *Daddy* (1989), *Sir* (1993), and *Zakhm* (1998) also attracted great critical acclaim, as well as being commercially successful. Later films like *Aashiqui* (1990) and *Dil Hai Ki Manta Nahin* (1991) were out-and-out box office hits. In 1999, Bhatt retired from directing to become a writer, producer, and mentor. His company, Vishesh Films, still turns out regular hits, such as *Aashiqui* (1991), *Raaz* (2002), and *Murder* (2004).

MASOOM

1983

Masoom tugs at the heartstrings with its exceptional performances, moving storyline, soul-stirring music, and upbeat message.

Director Shekhar Kapur's debut film, *Masoom* (Innocent), is among veteran actor Naseeruddin Shah's favorites. Lead actress Shabana Azmi recalls that while she and Shah had played every kind of couple on screen—rural and urban, rich and poor—"In *Masoom*, the love affair was between Shekhar Kapur and Naseer. Shekhar won Naseer's trust." That trust led to a performance that saw Shah take home a Filmfare Best Actor trophy. The film also won the Critics' Award for Best Film and the Best Music award.

INNOCENT VICTIM

Masoom tells the story of D.K. Malhotra, who lives happily with his wife, Indu, and their daughters, Rinky and Mini, in Delhi. But suburban bliss is turned upside-down when D.K. has to take responsibility for a son he did not know he had from a brief affair with a woman named Bhavana who has recently died. Indu is devastated by the revelation and cannot forgive her husband or tolerate the child, Rahul, whom she considers a constant reminder of her husband's infidelity.

As the adults fester under the weight of blame and guilt, Rinky and Mini are more gracious and compassionate, welcoming Rahul into the family. Rahul becomes closer to D.K., whom he has been told is his uncle, and also tries to establish a relationship with Indu, but she rebuffs him. Her cold behavior becomes so untenable that D.K. plans to send Rahul off to boarding school, much to the dismay of the three children. It takes almost losing Rahul for Indu to realize how much he has come to mean to her.

NOVICE TALENT

Previously a chartered accountant and model, Kapur had no movie-making experience when he started work on the film. Not only did he learn on the job, he also demonstrated with *Masoom*, and later *Mr. India* (see pp. 188–91), a special ability for directing children. Gulzar (see pp. 142–43), a veteran in writing for and about kids, penned the screenplay. Based on the 1980 novel *Man, Woman and Child* by American author Erich Segal, he carefully adapted the storyline to match the cultural sensibilities of an Indian audience.

HIT SONGS

Tujhse Naraaz Nahin Zindagi (I am Not Angry with You, Life)
🎙 **Singers** Anup Ghoshal, Lata Mangeshkar

Lakdi Ki Kathee (A Wooden Rocking Horse)
🎙 **Singers** Vanita Mishra, Gauri Bapat, Gurpreet Kaur

CAST AND CREW

* ★ **Naseeruddin Shah** D.K. Malhotra
* **Shabana Azmi** Indu Malhotra
* **Saeed Jaffrey** Suri
* **Jugal Hansraj** Rahul
* **Urmila Matondkar** Rinky

* 🎬 **Director** Shekhar Kapur
* **Producer** Chanda Dutt, Devi Dutt
* 🎵 **Music composer** R.D. Burman
* **Lyricist** Gulzar
* **Scriptwriter** Gulzar
* 🎥 **Cinematographer** Pravin Bhatt
* 👔 **Costume designers** Mani Rabadi, Bhawna Somaya

▲ **Innocent face**
Several posters for *Masoom* positioned child actor Jugal Hansraj's angelic face prominently, his expression of innocence clearly matching the title of the film.

SHABANA AZMI (b.1950)

A regular in art-house cinema, Shabana Azmi also found success in mainstream movies like *Amar, Akbar, Anthony* (see pp. 148–49) and *Parvarish* (1977). She won the National Award for Best Actress five times—for *Ankur* (see p. 128), *Arth* (see across), *Khandhar* (1984), *Paar* (1984), and *Godmother* (1999). She also won the Filmfare Best Actress Award for *Swami* (1977), *Arth*, and *Bhavna* (1984). A feminist and social activist, she has been involved in politics and was awarded the third-highest civilian honor, the Padma Bhushan, in 2012.

◄ **Believable stars**
Masoom stood out for its understated, nuanced performances. The three child actors especially won over audiences with their realistic and intuitive acting.

JAANE BHI DO YAARO

1983

The inspired lunacy of this satirical black comedy and cult classic is a scathing commentary on the depressing truths of a decaying social order.

During the era when formula films such as *Himmatwala* (see p. 180) and *Tohfa* (1984) were becoming the norm in Bollywood, along came a film that critic Jai Arjun Singh called "almost a genre unto itself." This film gave Hindi cinema a new depth.

POLITICAL SATIRE

Jaane bhi do Yaaro (Let It Go, Friends) follows two idealistic but naive photographers, Vinod and Sudhir, who are commissioned by newspaper editor Shobha to document the nefarious activities of builders Tarneja and Ahuja. The two investigators gather evidence against the builders, and discover that they are in cahoots with D'Mello, a corrupt municipal commissioner who gives them contracts for government projects. However, Vinod and Sudhir soon figure out that Shobha is also a blackmailing opportunist. When

> *"You create humor out of something painful."*
>
> KUNDAN SHAH, DIRECTOR, QUOTED IN *JAANE BHI DO YAARO: SERIOUSLY FUNNY SINCE 1983*, 2010

D'Mello is murdered, everybody wants to get control of the corpse to serve their own ends, leading to a series of darkly comic events. The laughathon ends up with a corpse on skates, and finally on stage dressed as Draupadi about to

▶ **Dark satire**
The film satirizes the rampant corruption of the powerful in India's news media, as well as in its politics, business, and bureaucracy.

be disrobed. The film's 15-minute *Mahabharata* climax gained a cult following in its own right.

CREATIVE PARTNERSHIP

The film's production was a mix of equally zany episodes and almost overwhelming troubles. It was made by a bunch of young, talented people, many of whom, such as Kundan Shah, Naseeruddin Shah, Om Puri, Satish Shah, production controller Vidhu Vinod Chopra, and the film's editor Renu Saluja, were from the Film and Television Institute of India (FTII), Pune. The film relied on goodwill: for example, Naseeruddin

Shah did not agree with many scenes, but performed with gusto anyway. Whenever there was a money problem while filming, he said, "take it out of my salary." Shah and director Kundan Shah were paid a nominal fee for the film.

Despite its cult status today, the film lay in cans for a year after its completion. Director Kundan Shah eventually won the National Award for Best First Film; Baswani received the Filmfare Award for Best Comedian.

▼ **Gullible duo**
Ravi Baswani (left) and Naseeruddin Shah (center), play the roles of photographers who are tricked into doing the bidding of the newspaper editor Bhakti Barve (right).

CAST AND CREW

- ★ **Naseeruddin Shah** Vinod Chopra
- **Ravi Baswani** Sudhir Mishra
- **Bhakti Barve** Shobha Sen
- **Pankaj Kapoor** Tarneja
- **Satish Shah** Commissioner D'Mello
- **Om Puri** Ahuja
- **Satish Kaushik** Tarneja's secretary
- **Neena Gupta** Priya

- 🎬 **Director** Kundan Shah
- 🏠 **Producer** National Film Development Corporation (NFDC)
- 🎵 **Music composer** Vanraj Bhatia
- 📖 **Scriptwriters** Kundan Shah, Sudhir Mishra
- 🎥 **Cinematographer** Binod Pradhan
- 👔 **Costume designer** Sujata Desai

SAARANSH

1984

CAST AND CREW

★ **Anupam Kher** B.V. Pradhan
Rohini Hattangadi Parvati Pradhan
Soni Razdan Sujata Suman
Madan Jain Vilas Chitre
Nilu Phule Gajanan Chitre
Alok Nath Pandit
Suresh Chatwal Police inspector

🎬 **Director** Mahesh Bhatt
🎬 **Producer** Rajshri Productions
♪ **Music composer** Ajit Varman
A♪ **Lyricist** Vasant Dev
📖 **Scriptwriter** Mahesh Bhatt
🎥 **Cinematographer** Adeep Tandon
👕 **Costume designer** Amal Allana

The story of a grieving elderly couple, this rare gem deals with issues of life and death, and also of rampant corruption and injustice in society.

A young man of 28 playing a distraught 65-year-old who has lost his son—Hindi cinema could not have come up with a more challenging and impressive debut than the one Anupam Kher made in *Saaransh* (The Gist). A struggling theater actor, Kher had prepared for the role for months. However, a few days before shooting began he was told that the producers would prefer established actor Sanjeev Kumar for the part. "I went to director

Mahesh Bhatt's house and called him a cheat for doing this to me," Anupam recalled later. The incident led to Bhatt calling up the producers to say that he would only make the film with Kher—and they agreed. The actor-director duo went on to work on significant films such as *Janam* (1985), *Daddy* (1989), and *Dil hai ki Manta Nahin* (1991).

THE GIST OF LIFE

Saaransh tells the story of B.V. Pradhan and his wife Parvati, an elderly couple living in Mumbai, who lose their U.S.-based son and cannot come to terms with their loss. Faced with an indifferent, ill-behaved bureaucracy when he tries to collect his son's ashes, a depressed Pradhan has suicidal thoughts. The couple rent out their room to a struggling actress, Sujata, who is in a relationship with the son of a politician. Sujata gets pregnant but her boyfriend offers no support and his father threatens her. The old couple help Sujata in the face of mounting intimidation by the politician's goons.

Meanwhile, Parvati starts believing that Sujata's unborn baby is a reincarnation of her dead son. Struggling with his own grief, Pradhan has the difficult task of supporting his grieving wife and convincing her otherwise.

A SENSITIVE STORY

When Mahesh Bhatt wrote the story of *Saaransh*, he had recently experienced the death of a friend—the son of his spiritual mentor U.G. Krishnamurti. But this was not a new

subject for Bhatt. The director has talked about being drawn toward issues such as death, rebirth, and the idea of god. "These are things that would weigh me down as a young boy. I had also seen an elderly teacher and his wife grapple with the death of their son," he said in an interview. The director channeled his sensitivity and compassion into the story of *Saaransh*. The film was India's entry to the 1985

▲ **Grief and rage**
The film touches on themes such as bureaucratic red tape and corruption through Pradhan's interactions with police and custom officials.

Academy Awards for Best Foreign Film. *Saaransh* also won several Filmfare Awards: Kher for Best Actor, Bhatt for Best Story, and Madhukar Shinde for Best Art Direction.

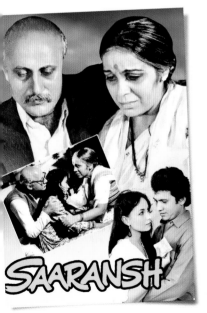

◀ **Profound loss**
Young actors Anupam Kher, 28, and Rohini Hattangadi, 32, convincingly portray the grief of an old couple mourning the loss of their son.

ANUPAM KHER (b.1955)

Anupam Kher caught India's imagination in 1984 while playing the role of a grieving father in *Saaransh*. Surprisingly, he has come to be better known for his comic and villainous roles. He won the Filmfare Award for Best Comedian for films such as *Ram Lakhan* (1989), *Lamhe* (1991), *Khel* (1992), *Darr* (see p. 209), and *Dilwale Dulhania le Jayenge* (see pp. 230–33). He also won the National Special Jury Award for *Daddy* and *Maine Gandhi Ko Nahin Mara* (2005). Kher is always the first choice for significant character roles. In 2016, he was awarded the Padma Bhushan—India's third-highest civilian award.

HIMMATWALA

1983

Credited with making actress Sridevi a pan-Indian star, *Himmatwala* also inspired other Telugu film producers to remake their hit films in Hindi.

CAST AND CREW

★ **Waheeda Rehman** Savitri
Jeetendra Ravi
Sridevi Rekha
Amjad Khan Sher Singh
Bandookwala
Kader Khan Narayandas Gopaldas

🎬 **Director** K. Raghavendra Rao
⬡ **Producer** G.A. Seshagiri Rao
🎵 **Music composer** Bappi Lahiri
𝄞 **Lyricist** Indeevar
🏃 **Choreographer** Saleem
📖 **Scriptwriters** K. Raghavendra Rao, Kader Khan
🎥 **Cinematographer** K.S. Prakash Rao

With its trite plot, garish set, gaudy costumes, and senseless dance numbers, *Himmatwala* is typical of much of Bollywood's output in the 1980s, and is another reason why critics regard the era as Hindi cinema's lowest point. But, audiences have never cared much for critics' opinions so long as a film entertains, and in that respect *Himmatwala* delivers. It was made in the early days of video cassette recorders, which allowed the more affluent classes to begin watching films at home. This led filmmakers to target the masses—who made up the bulk of cinemagoers—with a wave of loud masala flicks. *Himmatwala* is one such film that became a trendsetter for Hindi cinema.

THE BRAVE MAN

Himmatwala is a remake of the Telugu film *Ooriki Monagadu* (1981). The film introduces Ravi, who, on his return to the village as a newly qualified engineer, learns from his mother the truth about how his father was driven out of the village 20 years ago after Sher Singh brought a false charge against him. Ravi vows to clear his father's name and get revenge on Sher Singh, while also straightening out the latter's haughty daughter.

CAREER LAUNCHER

The film resurrected lead actor Jeetendra's career, which had been reeling from the disastrous run of his own production, *Deedar-e-Yaar* (1982). In fact, after

◀ **Fashion statement**
In keeping with Hindi cinema's dress codes, Sridevi's character appears in Western attire as the shrew, and switches to "decent" Indian clothes once she learns the error of her ways.

Himmatwala's success, he starred in several Hindi remakes of Telugu hit films and became the genre's poster boy. The film also proved to be the big break for actress Sridevi (see pp. 204–205) in Bollywood. Following lukewarm reactions to a supporting role in *Julie* (see p. 131) and a lead part in *Solva Sawan* (1979), she was an instant hit in *Himmatwala*, as audiences flocked to see her voluptuous figure, especially those "thunder thighs," on screen.

The song "Nainon Mein Sapna," in which the lead pair is seen doing dance steps reminiscent of phys-ed exercises around hundreds of painted clay pots and multicolored feather dusters, is a major spectacle. The song became a standard-bearer for similar sequences in future films, and even popularized meaningless lyrics such as "Oui Amma" and "Mamma Mia Pom Pom." *Himmatwala* was revisited in 2013, in a film of the same name starring Ajay Devgn, but was a miserable flop.

▲ **Kitsch factor**
Wearing kitsch costumes, the lead pair in *Himmatwala*, Jeetendra and Sridevi, dance in elaborate sets—typical of the South Indian style of filmmaking that was popular during the 1980s.

HIT SONGS

Taki Oh Taki
(Staring at Each Other)
🎤 **Singers** Kishore Kumar, Asha Bhosle

Nainon Mein Sapna
(Dreams in My Eyes)
🎤 **Singers** Lata Mangeshkar, Kishore Kumar

HERO

Hero introduced future stars Jackie Shroff and Meenakshi Seshadri to Bollywood, and saw a new generation of fans flocking to the theaters to feast their eyes on a new idol.

CAST AND CREW

★ **Jackie Shroff** Jackie
  Meenakshi Seshadri Radha Mathur
  Sanjeev Kumar Damodar Mathur
  Amrish Puri Pasha
  Shammi Kapoor Shrikanth Mathur
  Shakti Kapoor Jimmy Thapa

🎬 **Director** Subhash Ghai
◠ **Producer** Subhash Ghai
🎵 **Music composers** Laxmikant S. Kudalkar, Pyarelal R. Sharma
♪ **Lyricist** Anand Bakshi
🏃 **Choreographer** Saroj Khan
🎞 **Scriptwriter** Subhash Ghai
🎥 **Cinematographer** Kamlakar Rao

Jackie Shroff and Meenakshi Seshadri had begun their careers with roles in *Swami Dada* (1982) and *Painter Babu* (1983), respectively, both of which had fairly modest box office returns. It was director Subhash Ghai who turned both actors into overnight sensations by casting them as the romantic leads in *Hero*—a love story that blends the brash elements typical of 1980s Bollywood cinema with some tantalizing musical numbers.

CHARMING RUFFIAN

The film introduces its lead character (also called Jackie), as an orphan who is brought up by the crime lord Pasha and immersed in a life of crime. When Pasha is arrested, Jackie kidnaps police chief Shrikant's daughter, Radha, to force his release. Holed up together, Jackie and Radha end up falling in love. Radha's love makes Jackie see the error of his ways and he surrenders himself to the law. Nevertheless, Shrikant is unwilling to accept his daughter's choice of life partner. The real trouble begins when the lecherous drug addict Jimmy—who

is aligned with Pasha—enters the scene and threatens to drive a permanent wedge into their relationship. It is up to Jackie to rescue his love and save the day.

START OF A LEGACY

Hero gave lead actor Jaikishen Kakubhai Shroff his screen name. Such was the film's success that Jackie teamed up with director Subhash Ghai to make eight more films. The film also proved to be the vehicle for actress Meenakshi Seshadri's future success too. Born Shashikala Seshadri, the young Tamil actress had won the Miss India beauty pageant in 1981. After her role in *Hero*, she starred in several hit films including the critically acclaimed *Damini* (1993).

Subhash Ghai initially struggled to find financial backing for *Hero*, as it followed *Karz* (see pp. 198–99), which had flopped at the box office. It helped *Hero's* finances that Ghai offered product placement in the film for the Rajdoot 350 motorbike model, which was ridden by the hero in a racing scene. The director himself makes a

fleeting appearance in the film as an irate car driver during the song and dance number "Ding Dong Baby."

MEMORABLE MUSIC

Hero is also memorable for the sad song "Lambi Judai" (A Long Separation) accompanied by a haunting flute piece. The song was recorded by Pakistani folk singer Reshma, who was visiting Mumbai at the time. The song "Tu Mera Jaanu Hai" (You Are My Beloved) proved to be singer Anuradha Paudwal's big break in Bollywood.

◀ **A hero figure**
A director-financed movie full of daredevilry, romance, and intensity, *Hero* shot Jackie Shroff to overnight stardom in Bollywood.

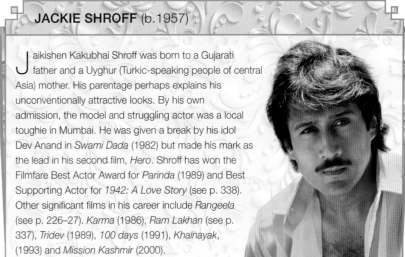

JACKIE SHROFF (b.1957)

Jaikishen Kakubhai Shroff was born to a Gujarati father and a Uyghur (Turkic-speaking people of central Asia) mother. His parentage perhaps explains his unconventionally attractive looks. By his own admission, the model and struggling actor was a local toughie in Mumbai. He was given a break by his idol Dev Anand in *Swami Dada* (1982) but made his mark as the lead in his second film, *Hero*. Shroff has won the Filmfare Best Actor Award for *Parinda* (1989) and Best Supporting Actor for *1942: A Love Story* (see p. 338). Other significant films in his career include *Rangeela* (see p. 226–27). *Karma* (1986), *Ram Lakhan* (see p. 337), *Tridev* (1989), *100 days* (1991), *Khalnayak*, (1993) and *Mission Kashmir* (2000).

JEETENDRA

ACTOR b.1942

From the mid-1960s until the late-1980s, Jeetendra was one of the busiest men in show business, starring in nearly 200 films—an achievement few actors could boast of.

Jeetendra enjoyed a long film career, lasting nearly four decades. Yet, despite being a box office draw, he never won an acting award during this time. Jeetendra made no secret of the fact that the lack of awards and critical reception did not bother him, as his only interest was to please his audience. It was a sensible strategy, because in Bollywood, drawing in the crowds is the key to guaranteeing work in the industry.

During the 1980s, it seemed like everything Jeetendra touched turned to gold. Hits such as *Tohfa* (1984), *Kaamyab* (1984), *Swarag se Sunder* (1986), and *Dharam Adhikari* (1986) ensured that he was continuously in demand. In fact, Jeetendra was consistently ranked as the nation's most popular actor alongside Amitabh Bachchan (see pp. 126–27).

EARLY LIFE

Born in 1942 as Ravi Kapoor, the young Jeetendra had no intention of starting a career in films. His father, Amarnath Kapoor, supplied costume jewelry to Bollywood, and Jeetendra stumbled into the profession by chance. He worked as a delivery boy for his father after school, and during one of his visits, he had the opportunity to interact with renowned producer V. Shantaram (see p. 62). When Ravi asked if he could watch the shooting of *Navrang!* (1959), the producer suggested that he play a small part in the film instead. Another film part followed, this time a small role in *Sehra* (1963), and although the scene required 30 retakes, Shantaram took a shine to the budding actor. He cast Ravi opposite his daughter Rajshree in *Geet Gaya Patharon ne*, and renamed him Jeetendra. The film became a hit, and Jeetendra's path as an actor was set.

SETTING NEW TRENDS

After several attempts to land a big role, Jeetendra finally played the lead in Ravikant Nagaich's *Farz*, a film that would establish him as a household name. *Farz* introduced Jeetendra as a dancer, and launced his trademark look in a white shirt, white trousers, and white shoes. The all-white ensemble was an attempt to set himself apart from other romantic heroes of the day, who often wore black clothes to impart a slimline look. Blessed with a naturally thin body, Jeetendra figured that an all-white attire would enhance his presence on the silver screen.

Subsequently, the actor launched another trend with his signature dance moves. His next few films showcased his dancing talents, including *Humjoli* and *Caravan*, earning him the epithet

▼ Serious side
Jeetendra is seen here working with renowned wordsmith Gulzar (left) in *Parichay* (1972), where he was given the opportunity to perform in a more sensitive and serious role.

KEY WORKS

Geet Gaya Patharon ne, 1964
Farz, 1967
Humjoli, 1970
Caravan, 1971
Khushboo, 1975
Kinara, 1977
Himmatwala, 1983 (see p. 180)

▼ Multi-faceted artist
A versatile actor with seemingly boundless energy, Jeetendra could play the action hero, romantic lead, or a family man with equal aplomb in any film.

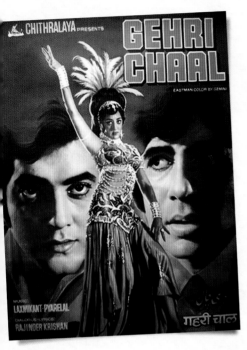

▲ Poster boy
In the action-thriller *Gehri Chaal* (1973), Jeetendra starred with Amitabh Bachchan and Hema Malini. He paired up with Malini again for hit films such as *Khushboo* and *Kinara*.

"Can you imagine, from 1976 onward I did 60 films in the South [India] in 11 years!"

JEETENDRA

Kewal P. Kashyap's *Parivaar* (1967), Dulal Guha's *Dharti Kahe Pukar ke* (1969) and Narindra Suri's *Badi Didi* (1969). He appeared opposite Babita in *Farz*, and this pairing was repeated in *Aulad* (1968), *Banphool* (1971), and *Ek Hasina Do Diwane* (1972). He conquered hearts with Reena Roy in *Jaise ko Taisa* (1973), *Apnapan* (1978), *Asha* (1980), and *Pyaasa Sawan* (1981). The popular actress Rekha (see p. 169) partnered with him in the 1970s and 1980s in hits such as *Jaal* (1986). His other leading ladies included Hema Malini (see pp. 110–11) and Neetu Singh, as well as Sridevi (see pp. 204–205) and Jaya Prada, with whom he starred in more than 20

films. The 1970s and 1980s were a phenomenally productive time for Jeetendra, with films such as comedy-drama *Himmatwala* (see p. 180), a box office hit. Roles continued to come his way in the 1990s, but began to dry up into the new millennium. However, Jeetendra still appeared in a few films and television shows, and his contribution to the industry was acknowledged with a series of Lifetime Achievement Awards. Yet, for the veteran actor, the adoration of the audience and the consistent commercial success of his films provided the ultimate gratification.

"Jumping Jack." What he lacked in formal training, Jeetendra made up for with enthusiasm: he made it look quite easy on screen, but he found dancing a challenge, practicing for four or five days before shooting a film.

LADIES' MAN
Whenever Jeetendra hit a rough patch, his fanbase in southern India helped him sustain his career: for example, in 1974 he acted in *Bidaai*, a movie by famed South Indian producer–director L.V. Prasad, which was a major success. In a roundabout way, this film also led to Jeetendra's marriage. Despite acting with some of Bollywood's most beautiful women, his heart belonged to his longtime sweetheart Shobha, a former air hostess who is now a successful television producer. He promised Shobha that they would get married if *Bidaai* was a hit: it was, and the pair duly got married.

However, Jeetendra's devotion to his wife did not dampen the on-screen chemistry he had with his numerous female stars, including Leena Chandavarkar, Jeetendra's love interest in *Bidaai*. Another attractive actress who was wooed on-screen by Jeetendra to the delight of audiences nationwide, Nanda was one of the highest paid actresses in the 1960s and was known to propel her leading men to stardom—Jeetendra was no exception. The pair made three hit films together—

▶ Disco inferno
Wearing his trademark white trousers and white shoes, the "Jumping Jack" of Bollywood gyrates with his leading lady Poonam Dhillon, in the 1980 film *Nishana*.

see p. 180; see p. 169; see pp. 110–11; see pp. 204–205

TIMELINE

- **April 7, 1942** Born as Ravi Kapoor in Amritsar, Punjab.

- **1959** Makes an appearance in V. Shantaram's *Navrang*.

- **1964** Plays the lead role in *Geet Gaya Patharon ne* opposite V. Shantaram's daughter Rajshree.

- **1967** Stars in *Farz*, establishing himself as a leading man of Bollywood.

POSTER OF THE FILM *FARZ*

- **1971** Appears in three successful films—*Ek Nari Ek Brahmachari*, *Caravan*, and *Banphool*.

- **1974** Marries Shobha—the couple have two children Ekta (b.1975) and Tusshar (b.1976).

- **1983** Stars opposite Sridevi in *Himmatwala*.

- **1983** Appears in *Arpan* with Reena Roy.

- **1986** Plays a village leader in the blockbuster *Swarag se Sunder*.

- **1987** Stars in Rakesh Roshan's family drama *Khudgarz*, based on the Biblical rivalry between Cain and Abel.

- **1990** Appears in 11 big-screen releases, including *Haatim Tai*, *Zahreelay*, *Nyay Anyay*, and *Thanedaar*.

- **1993** Plays the lead role in 10 films, including *Geetanjali*, *Rang*, and *Aasoo Bane Angaarey*.

- **2003** Appears in a cameo role opposite his son Tusshar in *Kuchh to Hai*.

- **2003** Wins the Filmfare Lifetime Achievement Award.

- **2005** Wins the Screen Lifetime Achievement Award.

- **2012** Wins the Zee Cine Award for Lifetime Achievement.

NAGINA

1986

A flagship fantasy movie, this blockbuster with a strong female lead was among the top earners of the year, and is still remembered for Sridevi's iconic snake dance.

After years of angry young men on the Bollywood screen, *Nagina* was a fascinating representation of an angry young woman—in the form of a shapeshifting snake. Creatures who can transform their physical form, such as werewolves and vampires, are found in folklore worldwide. The *ichchadhaari naag* or *naagin*—the shapeshifting snake-man or snake-woman—is India's version of this mythical creature, and has inspired many films.

Bollywood snake films often feature a snakewoman taking revenge against the hunter or snake charmer who has killed her mate, and *Nagina* is no exception. As is usual in these films, the snake-woman is not the villain—rather, it is the scheming, greedy humans who are the bad guys. This film also includes another recurring theme of snake movies: the snake

> *"Sridevi carried the film on her back. It was her all the way"*
>
> **RISHI KAPOOR,** CITED IN *INDIA TODAY,* JUNE 30, 1987

charmer's obsession with possessing the almighty *mani*, a magical gem said to be found on the heads of cobras.

SERPENTINE STORY
Powerful snake charmer Bhairon Nath transfers a king cobra's life-force into its dead victim, a child called Rajiv, to revive him. However, in doing so he inadvertently sets the cobra's stricken mate on the quest to be reunited with her beloved. A grown-up Rajiv returns to his ancestral home after spending 15 years overseas. He finds himself drawn to a mysterious woman, Rajni, who alludes to a relationship much longer than the few days they have spent together. Rajiv is besotted and, after Rajni wins over his disapproving mother with her beauty, the two eventually marry. However, when Bhairon identifies Rajni as an *ichchadhaari naagin*—a shapeshifting snake-woman—she has to overcome her mother-in-law's fears, Rajiv's suspicions,

and Bhairon's machinations to acquire her dead *naag*'s *mani*, of which only she knows the whereabouts.

ONE-WOMAN SHOW
Actress Jaya Prada was the original choice to play Rajni but declined the role, citing a fear of snakes. However, Sridevi (see pp. 204–205) made the role her own, not just with her famous snake dance, but also with a career-defining performance that brought to life the full range of her character's emotions, from love to fury. With the film's success, Sridevi became the most sought-after actress in Bollywood. This was also the first Hindi film in which the actress, a non-native speaker, dubbed her own lines. Filmfare awards were not given out in the year of the film's release as the film industry was on strike, but Sridevi was presented with a special retrospective Filmfare Award in 2013 for her stunning performance as Rajni.

◀ **Hypnotic snake dance**
The Bharatnatyam dance *mudra* (posture) *Sarpashirsha* (snake's hood) is used to dramatic effect in the film by Sridevi, guided by choreographer Saroj Khan.

HIT SONG

**Main Teri Dushman, Dushman Tu Mera
(I Am Your Enemy, You Are My Enemy)**

🎤 **Singer** Lata Mangeshkar

CAST AND CREW

★ **Sridevi** Rajni
Rishi Kapoor Rajiv
Sushma Seth Rajiv's mother
Amrish Puri Bhairon Nath

🎬 **Director** Harmesh Malhotra
◔ **Producer** Harmesh Malhotra
🎵 **Music composers** Laxmikant Shantaram Kudalkar, Pyarelal Ramprasad Sharma
🎵 **Lyricist** Anand Bakshi
🕺 **Choreographer** Saroj Khan
📖 **Scriptwriters** Jagmohan Kapoor, Ravi Kapoor
🎥 **Cinematographer** V. Durga Prasad
👕 **Costume designers** Shantaram Sawant, Kachins

IJAAZAT

1987

A sensitive story of complicated interpersonal relationships, *Ijaazat* is also remembered for its nuanced acting and a much-loved hit song.

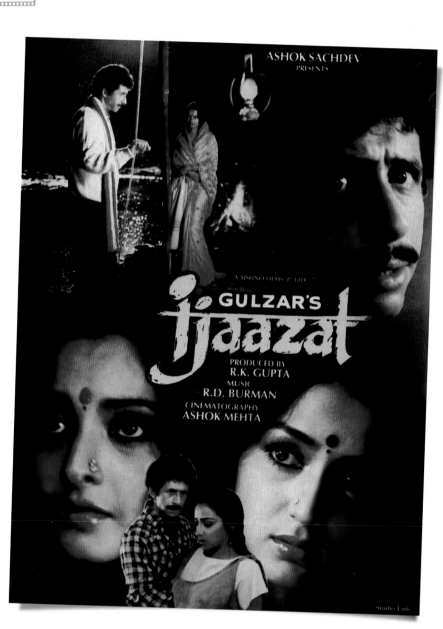

▶ The ties that bind
The film's moody poster emphasizes the tragic love triangle that plays out between Mahender, Maya (bottom right), and Sudha (bottom left).

CAST AND CREW

★ **Naseeruddin Shah** Mahender
Rekha Sudha
Anuradha Patel Maya
Shammi Kapoor Mahender's grandfather
Shashi Kapoor Sudha's husband

🎬 **Director** Gulzar
🎞 **Producer** R.K. Gupta
🎵 **Music composer** R.D. Burman
📝 **Lyricist** Gulzar
📖 **Scriptwriter** Gulzar
🎥 **Cinematographer** Ashok Mehta
👔 **Costume designer** Leena Daru

Written and directed by Gulzar (see pp. 142–43), this film is based on the Bengali story *Jatugriho* (House of Lac) by Subodh Ghosh. Sanjeev Kumar (see p. 137) was Gulzar's first choice to play the male lead, but could not come on board because of health issues. The director felt the only other actor who could do justice to the role was Naseeruddin Shah—a choice that paid dividends.

LEAVING LOVE

Ijaazat (Permission) opens in the waiting room of a train station where a divorced couple, Mahender and Sudha, meet after years apart. The film unfolds in a series of flashbacks as they recount their life together.

Mahender and another woman, Maya, love each other and live together. However, the free-spirited Maya refuses to be tied down. When she disappears, leaving just a poem by way of a goodbye, Mahender decides to marry Sudha, according to his grandfather's wishes. Mahender and Sudha grow to love each other, but memories of Maya persist. So, when Maya reappears in Mahender's life, Sudha silently bows out of it, leaving him just as Maya had done before. Mahender suffers a heart attack when he realizes Sudha has left him. While Maya takes care of the ailing Mahender, she realizes that he loves Sudha. Intent on reuniting the two, Maya drives off, leaving Mahender one final time.

STRONG WOMEN

Gulzar generally wrote strong, often unconventional, female characters, and the quirky, impetuous poet Maya has her own take on society and relationships. She rejects the institution of marriage and forms a bond with Mahender, and through him, with Sudha, whom she refers to as "Didi" (elder sister). Sudha, too, feels a degree of empathy for the troubled Maya. However, she refuses to stay in a marriage in which her husband's attentions are so divided. Even as Mahender tries to do "what is true and right" by both women, Sudha decides to follow her own path.

SIGNATURE SONG

Ijaazat is also notable for the hit song "Mera Kuch Saaman" (Some of My Possessions). When Gulzar gave composer R.D. Burman (see p. 109) the unusual, blank verse lyrics, the latter exclaimed: "Next you'll ask me to compose music for the headline of *The Times of India!*" The song went on to win the National Award for Best Lyricist and Singer.

NASEERUDDIN SHAH (b. 1949)

The angry young man of Indian parallel cinema, Naseeruddin Shah is known for his scathing critique of Bollywood. Starting his career in the theater, Shah made his debut with the critically acclaimed *Nishant* (1975). A stellar name in Hindi art movies as well as commercial cinema, Shah has taken serious roles in films as varied as *Sparsh* (see p. 163), *Aakrosh* (1981), *Mohra* (1995), and *The Dirty Picture* (2012). He has won three National Awards and 18 Filmfare Awards.

MASALA BECOMES
THE NORM

It is generally agreed that Bollywood films made in the 1980s were the worst in the industry's history. The overall look of the films tends to support this view.

The 1980s were the decade when the VHS (video home system) revolution erupted in India, and audiences were happy to watch films in the comfort of their homes. In an attempt to woo viewers back to the cinema, Bollywood started to produce films that embraced all things shiny, colorful, and showy.

A significant number of Bollywood movies made at this time veered toward melodramatic storylines, histrionic performances, and higher decibel levels. Meanwhile, smaller budgets resulted in low production values, which meant that the sets, costumes, props, and color schemes were often very garish. Screen fashions, as excessive as the storylines and sets, favored glittering makeup, heavily sequined dresses, chunky costume jewelery, and fussy accessories such as hats, veils, and headbands. An excellent example of this is the styling of heroine Rekha in *Khoon Bhari Maang* (1988).

SONG AND DANCE EXTRAVAGANZAS
No mention of Bollywood during this period is complete without a nod to the over-the-top dance sequences featured in films from Padmalaya Studio. Of particular note is the song "Nainon Mein Sapna" (In My Dreams) from *Himmatwala* (see p. 180), picturized on a heavily bejeweled Sridevi (see pp. 204–05) and Jeetendra (see pp. 182–83) as they dance on a

beach decorated with thousands of brightly colored pots and giant wagon wheels. Similarly, in the hit film *Tohfa* (1984), the two actors are once again filmed on a beach, cavorting around hundreds of brass pots. The cult song "Pyar Ka Tofa" (Gift of Love), picturized this time on the actress Jaya Prada and Jeetendra, is performed with hundreds of multicolored saris hanging or draped around the set.

DISCO DIVAS
Bollywood of the 1980s was also influenced by the worldwide disco phenomenon. *Disco Dancer* (see p. 175) with Mithun Chakraborty, the song "Om Shanti Om" (Peace) in *Karz* (see pp. 158–59) with Rishi Kapoor, and the song "Saara Zamaana" (The Entire World) in *Yaarana* (1981) with Amitabh Bachchan (see pp. 126–27) are testimony to a passion for flashing colored lights and shiny metallic clothes, which were so representative of the era. The low-budget films made by director Babbar Subhash also added pink smoke and psychedelic backdrops to the heady mix in movies such as *Kasam Paida karne Wale ki* (1984).

▶ **The art of melodrama**
This poster from *Sheshnaag* (1990) echoes the aesthetic excesses of the film it advertises, which is about mythical shape-shifting snakes.

" … everyone was dancing on pots, pans and suddenly hundreds of dancers are behind the main pair."

KARAN JOHAR, DIRECTOR–PRODUCER, CITED BY TEJASWANI GANTE IN *PRODUCING BOLLYWOOD: INSIDE THE CONTEMPORARY FILM INDUSTRY*, 2012

MR. INDIA

1987

The biggest superhero film of the 1980s, *Mr. India* was a roaring success, and its dialogues remain etched in the minds of generations of Indian cinemagoers.

CAST AND CREW

★ **Anil Kapoor** Arun Verma / Mr. India
Sridevi Seema Soni
Amrish Puri Mogambo
Satish Kaushik Calendar
Annu Kapoor Mr. Gaitonde
Ajit Vachani Teja
Sharat Saxena Daaga
Ashok Kumar Prof. Sinha
Aftab Shivdasani Jugal

📽 **Director** Shekhar Kapur
⬠ **Producer** Boney Kapoor
🎵 **Music composers** Laxmikant S. Kudalkar, Pyarelal R. Sharma
🅰 **Lyricist** Javed Akhtar
🏃 **Choreographer** Saroj Khan
📖 **Scriptwriters** Salim Javed, Javed Akhtar
🎥 **Cinematographer** Baba Azmi

Long before *Mr. India* was filmed, writer Javed Akhtar had worked on the idea of a film featuring an invisible superhero. He wanted to cast Amitabh Bachchan in the role because of the immense popularity of the actor's voice. When the star refused, as he was unsure about a film in which he would not actually be "seen" for long on-screen, a young Anil Kapoor was recruited to do the job. Similarly, before producer Boney Kapoor stepped in, other producers were unsure if the available technology was equipped to handle the special effects required to depict an invisible character.

However, the hard work invested in the special effects, the outstanding performances, and the emotional depth of the film have enabled *Mr. India* to endure the test of time.

UNFORGETTABLE CHARACTERS
At the time of making *Mr. India*, Anil was a relative newcomer with only *Woh Saat Din* (1983) and *Mashaal* (1984) behind him. He was very keen to work with actress Sridevi, who was then a big star.

Sridevi's portrayal of Seema is both sweet and sensual, and the song "Kaate Nahin Kat Te Yeh Din" (Can't Pass These Days) is one of Bollywood's most passionate

▲ **Crime lord**
Mogambo, played by Amrish Puri, became a memorable Bollywood archvillain with his blond wig, a bubbling pink acid pool in his den, and an army that robotically shouted "Hail Mogambo!"

songs. It took several days to film this number, and Sridevi was said to be suffering from a high fever during the shoot. In another scene in the film, she did a hilarious imitation of Charlie Chaplin, which was widely praised.

However, it is the villain Mogambo who has become the film's most iconic character. Dialogues for Mogambo were still being written when much of the shooting was completed because Akhtar was still working out the details to his satisfaction. The famous dialogue "Mogambo khush hua" (Mogambo is pleased) became a national catchphrase, but not without a tussle. When director Shekhar Kapur felt the line was being repeated too often and suggested editing out several instances, Akhtar convinced him to keep them, saying "Even when [cricketer] Kapil Dev hits a six, people will say, 'Mogambo khush hua!'"

SHOOTING AN INVISIBLE MAN
In 1987, *Mr. India* was a risky and technically challenging film to make. The core team of Boney Kapoor, Shekhar Kapur, and Javed Akhtar had decided that the special effects for the film should not be added

◀ **Little terrors**
The children were the emotional anchor of *Mr. India* and their natural performances were a key element of the film's success.

"Iconic films are made not just by one person. It is a team work."

BONEY KAPOOR, *THE INDIAN EXPRESS*, 2015

post-production because the technology available at that time would have made the shots look tacky. This meant that everything had to be shot on camera. Later, in a moment of nostalgia, Kapur reminisced how the team had to spend hours on the sets just to hide the wire that held a bottle of Coca Cola in mid air. Hiding the wire that held the flying statue of the monkey god Hanuman also proved challenging. However, it was achieved thanks to the innovative special effects team with Peter Pereira and Arun Patil, as well as action director, Veeru Devgan.

▶ **Visible action**
Anil Kapoor is rumored to have spent a lot of time cajoling the producer, his elder brother Boney, to give him more scenes in which his character would not be invisible.

SHEKHAR KAPUR
(b.1945–)

The reputation of director Shekhar Kapur rests on three critically acclaimed, but vastly different, Hindi films. *Masoom* (see p. 177) is a sensitive drama about a child born of an extramarital affair; *Mr. India* (1987) is a sci-fi comic caper; while *Bandit Queen* (1994) is a gut-wrenching portrayal of dacoit Phoolan Devi, which also won the National Award for Best Feature Film in 1996. Kapur also directed *Elizabeth* (1998)—winner of the BAFTA Award for Best British Film— and its sequel, *Elizabeth: The Golden Age* (2007). He lives and works in London now.

STORYLINE

This film follows the life of an impoverished but generous young man Arun Verma, who looks after several orphaned children. When he finds a secret device that makes its wearer invisible, he turns into the invisible superhero Mr. India. Crime reporter Seema falls in love with Mr. India and, together, they try to fight the evil Mogambo, who dreams of world domination. Will they succeed?

SEEMA AND JUGAL IN A
CHAPLIN DISGUISE

ARUN: AN ORDINARY MAN

PLOT OVERVIEW

An international syndicate, headed by the villainous Mogambo, is hatching a plan to destroy India. They are already smuggling arms and are responsible for food contamination. Mogambo wants to further his plans by getting hold of a gadget, invented by an Indian scientist, that makes its wearer invisible. Meanwhile, in Mumbai, Arun and his charges—a group of orphaned children—live together in a rented house. Even though money is tight, they are all happy ❶.

Mogambo needs access to a place close to the sea to run his nefarious business. Arun's house would be perfect for this. Arun's landlord—who is a part of Mogambo's gang—threatens Arun and the children to make them leave the house. He uses the excuse that they have not paid rent. To save themselves, Arun decides to sublet a room to Seema, a headstrong journalist he has recently met. But there is just one problem—Seema hates children ❷. However, soon she befriends them.

Arun meets his father's friend, Professor Sinha, who tells him about a gadget that his father had invented. This gadget can make its wearer invisible. Arun tries on the device and becomes invisible. Meanwhile at work, Seema mistakenly overhears a suspicious telephone conversation involving Mogambo's men. She decides to disguise herself as a Hawaiian singer to solve the mystery ❸, but she is captured by Mogambo's men. Arun uses the gadget to become invisible and saves Seema. He introduces himself as Mr. India.

Seema is infatuated with the mysterious Mr. India ❹, and is unaware that he is actually Arun. She finds herself in close proximity to Mr. India time and again, as they fight criminals together.

❶ • • ❷ • ❸ • ❹

THE SONGS

Zindagi Ki Yahi Reet Hai (happy version) (This Is The Way Life Is)
Singer: Kishore Kumar
Picturized on Arun and the orphans
☺

ARUN'S TRADEMARK
BUCKET HAT

★ *Two of Arun's young "orphans" grew up to be actor Aftab Shivdasani and choreographer Ahmed Khan.*

A medley of parody songs from different films
Singer: Shabbir Kumar and Anuradha Paudwal
Picturized on Seema, Arun, and the orphans ☺

Karte Hain Hum Pyar (We Love)
Singer: Kishore Kumar and Kavita Krishnamurthy
Picturized on Seema and Arun
☺

Hawa Hawai (Airy Fairy)
Singer: Kavita Krishnamurthy
Picturized on Seema
☺

ARUN AND THE CHILDREN
PLEAD TO GET BACK THEIR
FOOTBALL BACK FROM SEEMA

HAWA HAWAI
DANCE SEQUENCE

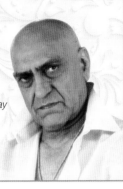

AMRISH PURI (1932–2005)

Remembered for his portrayal of villains on-screen, Amrish Puri was a theater actor until the 1970s. His performances in Shyam Benegal's films *Nishant* (1975), *Manthan* (1976), and *Bhumika* (1977) were noted, but he gained popularity with *Hum Paanch* (1980), *Shakti* (1982), and *Hero* (see p. 181). As Mogambo in *Mr. India*, he became the only villain to challenge the supremacy of Gabbar Singh in *Sholay* (see pp. 134–37). He was also seen in a supporting role in the superhit *Dilwale Dulhaniya le Jayenge* (see pp. 230–33). He won the Filmfare Best Supporting Actor Award for *Meri Jung* (1985), *Ghatak* (1996), and *Virasat* (1997).

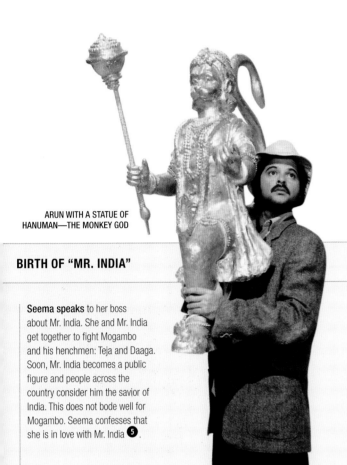

ARUN WITH A STATUE OF HANUMAN—THE MONKEY GOD

BIRTH OF "MR. INDIA"

Seema speaks to her boss about Mr. India. She and Mr. India get together to fight Mogambo and his henchmen: Teja and Daaga. Soon, Mr. India becomes a public figure and people across the country consider him the savior of India. This does not bode well for Mogambo. Seema confesses that she is in love with Mr. India ❺.

Mogambo is infuriated. He continues to spread terror, killing thousands, including one little girl under Arun's care ❻. Bombs have been planted all over the country, and soon Mogambo will succeed in his plan of destroying India. He also kidnaps the children, Seema, and Arun, and hopes to trap Mr. India when he comes to save them.

In the confusion that ensues, Arun misplaces the gadget. However, somehow he escapes, and manages to deactivate the missiles that Mogambo is ready to launch. The missiles explode, killing Mogambo and all his men. Arun, Seema, and the children are free and escape in the nick of time.

❺

Kaate Nahi Kat Te Yeh Din (Can't Pass These Days)
Singer: Kishore Kumar and Alisha Chinai
Picturized on Mr. India and Seema

A STILL FROM THE SONG "KAATE NAHI KAT TE YEH DIN"

❻

Zindagi Ki Yahi Reet Hai (sad version)
(This Is The Way Life Is)
Singer: Kishore Kumar
Picturized on Arun and the orphans

★ *Huzaan Khodaiji, who was playing little Tina, had to be given medicine by her mother so she would sleep and not burst into giggles during her death scene.*

AT TINA'S FUNERAL

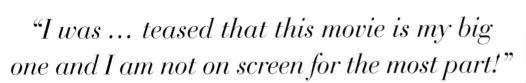

"I was … teased that this movie is my big one and I am not on screen for the most part!"

ANIL KAPOOR, *THE HINDU*, 2015

ANIL KAPOOR

ACTOR b.1956

With sheer determination, Anil Kapoor emerged as the superstar of the 1980s. He has acted in more than 100 films, and is considered Bollywood royalty.

Actor Anil Kapoor made his global breakthrough with *Slumdog Millionaire* (2008), the rags-to-riches story of a poor boy made wealthy beyond his dreams after winning a television quiz show. The movie's plot was a work of fiction, but Anil's own life story was not so different from that of the hero, played by Dev Patel. Born in a poor suburb of Mumbai, India, Anil was one of seven family members who lived together in a single room. However, the Kapoor family shared something bigger—a passion for the movies. In time, his father and elder brother would go on to become film producers, and his younger brother an actor.

FINDING HIS OWN SPACE

Anil once said in an interview that he sneaked out of school whenever he could to watch movies. When he was just seven years old, he landed a movie role for himself, playing a child actor. The film was never released, but once Anil had experienced life on a set, he knew there was no other future for him. He signed up for every acting, singing, and dancing class he could, even as his school lessons fell by the wayside.

In 1979, Anil scored his first role in *Hamare Tumhare*, playing a young man living in a cramped apartment with his family—a role for which he was well prepared. In 1983, he landed his first role as a lead actor in *Woh Saat Din*, playing the part of a charismatic musician.

MAKING OF A SEASONED ACTOR

Anil got his first big Bollywood break in *Mashaal* (1984), directed by the legendary director Yash Chopra (see pp. 166–67). It was a challenging role for the young actor, especially

▶ **The ageless star**
Anil Kapoor rocks the mustache in *Taal* (1999). In a career spanning four decades in the film industry, he has shaved off his mustache for just three films.

◀ **In character**
Anil Kapoor nailed the look of the "tapori," a vagabond and ruffian, in the hit film *Ram Lakhan* (1989). The colorful clothes and street-style dancing of his tapori movies continue to entertain.

KEY WORKS

....

Karma, 1986

Mr. India, 1987 (see pp. 188–91)

Tezaab, 1988 (see p. 198)

Parinda, 1989 (see p. 199)

Lamhe, 1991

1942: A Love Story, 1994 (see p. 338)

Nayak, 2001

Dil Dhadakne Do, 2015

> *"If I commit to something, I will give it my 100 percent. I am just a boy from Chembur."*

ANIL KAPOOR, *HINDUSTAN TIMES*, 2016

the intense scenes he shared on-screen with veteran actor Dilip Kumar (see pp. 48–49). Although he had not been the first choice for the part, and was recruited only after two other actors turned it down, he delivered a realistic and gritty performance.

During the 1980s, Anil mostly took on comic roles—some successful, others disappointing. In 1987, he signed up for *Mr. India*, the first Indian superhero film. The promotional blurb of the epic claimed it was "a decidedly delicious mix of patriotism, comedy, science fiction, romance, and adventure." As unlikely a hit as it may seem from that description, the film went on to

attain a cult status and made Anil a superstar. After his success as the invisible hero of *Mr. India*, it seemed that there was no way that Anil could disappear from the silver screen.

▶ On the hot seat
Seen here opposite actor Dev Patel, Anil Kapoor plays the part of a game-show host in *Slumdog Millionaire* (2008). Anil was nervous about acting in an English film, but so determined was he to do a good job that he took the host's chair home from the movie set, to practice sitting on it.

▶ Bold attempt
1942: A Love Story (1994) was the first Hindi film that was not given an adult rating, despite having a scene with the actors kissing, previously considered inappropriate for a young audience.

With the onset of the 1990s, he took on a number of challenging films that went on to win awards, such as *Virasat* (1997) and *Taal* (1999). The political thriller *Pukar* (2000) also earned him accolades for his portrayal of a national hero facing sabotage.

HEADING WEST
Anil made his foray into the international scene with *Slumdog Millionaire* (2008), directed by British director Danny Boyle. The film was nominated for 10 Academy Awards, of which it won eight. He extended his global reach with the popular US television show *24* (2010), also purchasing the rights to produce and act in the Indian version of the show. He later acted in the blockbuster film *Mission Impossible: Ghost Protocol* (2011) as an Indian tycoon who falls victim to a secret agent. While some critics found the role one-dimensional, others have praised Anil for helping raise the profile of Indian actors globally.

Four decades after his first brush with Bollywood, Anil Kapoor remains a vibrant

on-screen presence. A critic has aptly described his recent performances in films such as *Shootout at Wadala* (2013) as a treat, and a powerful reminder of just why he became a superstar in Bollywood and beyond.

It was certainly a long way from his childhood as a "slumdog" to *Slumdog Millionaire*, but Anil Kapoor has earned his place in the spotlight through his rich and varied acting career. Today, his family is following in his footsteps, and his children are also players in the film industry.

TIMELINE

December 24, 1956 Born on Christmas Eve, in a Mumbai suburb.

1979 Debuts in Bollywood in *Hamare Tumhare*. Meets his future wife, Sunita Bhambhani.

1983 Lands the lead role in *Woh Saat Din*, a film produced by his father.

1984 Marries Sunita Bhambhani. Receives first Filmfare Award as Best Supporting Actor for *Mashaal*.

1991 Shaves off his trademark mustache for his character in *Lamhe*, which is hailed as a modern classic.

1993 Wins second Filmfare Award for Best Actor for *Beta* (1992), co-starring actress Madhuri Dixit. The pair become a leading screen couple.

1999 Plays the character of a degenerate music superstar in *Taal*.

2001 Wins his first National Film Award for *Pukar*. A string of powerful performances will follow in this decade.

2001 Stars in *Nayak: The Real Hero*. An expensive film, it does not do well at the box office, but later becomes a cult classic.

PUKAR'S DRAMATIC POSTER

2002 Produces his first film, *Badhaai Ho Badhaai*, and also stars in it.

2008 Produces *Gandhi, My Father* (2007) and wins the National Film Award: Special Jury Award, jointly with the film's director, Feroz Abbas Khan.

2014 Launches his film production company, Antila Ventures.

2015 Wins his third Filmfare Award for Best Actor for *Dil Dhadakne Do* (2015).

2016 Kickstarts a campaign run by the charity Plan India to highlight the plight of Indian children who are forced into child labor.

QAYAMAT SE QAYAMAT TAK

1988

Young cinegoers were thrilled to see a film with lead characters close to their own age, and a touching story of love conquering all in this tale of teenage romance.

▲ **Family feud**
Raghuveer Singh (seated, center) refuses Jaswant (right) and Dhanraj Singh's (extreme left) request to marry their sister to his son Ratan Singh (extreme right), pitting the families against each other for generations.

The summer of 1988 saw the release of a timeless love story that enchanted Bollywood fans who became devoted to its two young lead actors, Aamir Khan (see pp. 228–29) and Juhi Chawla. Mansoor Khan's *Qayamat se Qayamat tak* (Till Death Do Us Part) is a retelling of William Shakespeare's *Romeo and Juliet*. The film is not the first love story to resonate with teenage audiences, but *QSQT*, as the film is popularly known, became iconic for its fresh approach, its true-to-life representation of first love, the on-screen chemistry between the lead characters, and its music.

QSQT was a bolt from the blue. In the late 1980s, filmmakers mostly depended on seasoned actors to play lead characters in their films, and made violent features that did not capture the interest of viewers anymore. Moreover, the VHS (Video Home System) revolution and piracy kept people from going to the cinemas. *QSQT*, with an unfamiliar cast of new actors and a first-time director, changed the way people perceived cinema, and helped Bollywood find its way again.

DAWN OF LOVE
The film's smitten teenagers, Raj and Rashmi, hail from two families that hate each other. The enmity is so great that Raj's father, Dhanraj Singh, murders the son of his rival, Raghuveer Singh, and is sent to prison.

Raj has followed his dreams to study music at college. He returns home to help with a family matter. There he meets Rashmi and falls in love with her. Rashmi has no idea that the boy she has fallen for is the son of her father's sworn enemy.

Rashmi's father, Randhir Singh, who is the son of Raghuveer Singh, soon finds out the truth about Raj, and plans her marriage to another man. The young couple decide to defy their families and run away to be together. Will their love overcome years of bitter hatred and revenge?

Can feuding families put aside their differences for the sake of their children's happiness?

SCREEN VIRGINS
Nearly all the actors had little on-screen experience prior to their performance in *QSQT*. Aamir had played a small role of a college student in Ketan Mehta's *Holi* (1984). He also had a notable part in the revenge drama *Raakh* (1989), which was not released until after *QSQT*. Juhi Chawla had a small role to her name in Karan Kapoor's *Sultanat* (1986), after which she signed up for *QSQT*.

Yet, perhaps it was their relative inexperience that helped make the pair so convincing. Aamir confessed to a journalist that he was incredibly nervous during the shooting of *QSQT*. This bashful shyness made his character even more appealing and believable. As a young man still finding his way in life and in love, his performance was magnetic to adolescents, and he became a heartthrob overnight.

Juhi likened her performance in the movie to acting in a college play, with plenty of playful jokes and

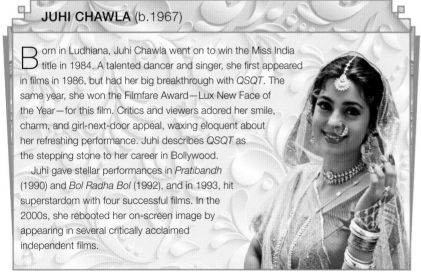

JUHI CHAWLA (b.1967)

Born in Ludhiana, Juhi Chawla went on to win the Miss India title in 1984. A talented dancer and singer, she first appeared in films in 1986, but had her big breakthrough with *QSQT*. The same year, she won the Filmfare Award—Lux New Face of the Year—for this film. Critics and viewers adored her smile, charm, and girl-next-door appeal, waxing eloquent about her refreshing performance. Juhi describes *QSQT* as the stepping stone to her career in Bollywood.

Juhi gave stellar performances in *Pratibandh* (1990) and *Bol Radha Bol* (1992), and in 1993, hit superstardom with four successful films. In the 2000s, she rebooted her on-screen image by appearing in several critically acclaimed independent films.

CAST AND CREW

★ **Aamir Khan** Raj
Juhi Chawla Rashmi
Dalip Tahil Dhanraj Singh
Arun Mathur Raghuveer Singh
Alok Nath Jaswant Singh
Arjun Ratan Singh
Goga Kapoor Randhir Singh

🎬 **Director** Mansoor Khan
🎥 **Producer** Nasir Hussain
🎵 **Music composers** Anand Shrivastav, Milind Shrivastav
🕺 **Choreographer** Suresh Bhatt
📃 **Scriptwriter** Nasir Hussain
🎞 **Cinematographer** Kiran Deohans
👔 **Costume designers** Bilquis Khan, Nikhat Khan, Nuzhat Khan, Sonia

"Mansoor creates an endearing equation around the shy, aloof Raj and spirited, jabbering Rashmi."

REDIFF.COM, 2013

laughs. She said there were no egos, no frayed nerves, and no stress during the film's shooting. Her sense of positivity and delight worked to her advantage on screen. Juhi was told by her director to simply be herself, advice that would lead her to a successful film career.

Juhi recalls doing three scenes for her screen test with Aamir. Although she felt she had more acting experience than he did, Aamir was the nephew of the

producer Nasir Hussain, and had worked as his assistant before. So, he had no problem showing Juhi how she should do her scenes.

DEDICATED DIRECTOR

Two different endings were filmed for QSQT, but for everyone involved with the film, the actual ending was a

► **Dramatic scene**
In a quintessential filmy fight sequence, Aamir Khan as Raj (right) fights a goon sent to kill him by Rashmi's father, Randhir Singh, toward the end of the film.

happy one. QSQT went on to win an astounding seven Filmfare Awards out of 11 nominations, including an award for Best Film and Best Director.

The first-time director, Mansoor Khan, was not keen on making the film in the beginning, but his father convinced him to take on the challenge. He was not the kind to simply follow in his father's footsteps, and wasn't impressed by the glitz and glamour of Bollywood. However, once he decided to get involved, Mansoor

completely immersed himself in the making of QSQT, hoping to win over a younger audience.

Mansoor actively participated in creating the film's soundtrack with music composers Anand and Milind Shrivastav, who were relatively new in the industry. Some critics speculate that Mansoor, a musician himself, was more interested in creating the music than making the film. Together the trio tried all kinds of fresh, new ideas while returning once again to the traditional strength of the melody.

SETTING A STANDARD

During the filming of QSQT, the cast had no idea what a phenomenon the film would become. They were new to the silver screen and were determined to prove themselves. The steady, slow success of QSQT had a great impact on subsequent films in Bollywood. Musical romance had found a place in Hindi cinema again. Giving romantic lead roles to two young people marked a welcome shift away from the violent and angry older heroes, typical of Bollywood in that era. There have been several rumors about remaking QSQT. However, the film's cast believes that just like first true love, QSQT can never be repeated.

◄ **Young love**
Raj and Rashmi, played by Aamir Khan and Juhi Chawla, shown here, fall in love against the wishes of their fathers in this Bollywood version of *Romeo and Juliet*, set in contemporary India.

STORYLINE

Raj and Rashmi fall in love with each other, blissfully unaware that their parents are sworn enemies. When they discover the truth about their families, the lovebirds flee to the countryside in order to begin a new life. They are soon discovered by their angry parents, who are determined to put a stop to this illicit relationship, leading to dire consequences.

PLOT OVERVIEW

FAMILIES AT WAR

Madhumati is pregnant with Ratan's child. Jaswant and Dhanraj, Madhumati's brothers, go to Ratan's house and request his father, Raghuveer, to allow Ratan to marry their sister. Raghuveer turns down their request. Ratan abandons Madhumati and agrees to marry someone of his father's choice. Madhumati is heartbroken and commits suicide.

Dhanraj shoots Ratan at his wedding and goes to jail. Their families are now sworn enemies. Jaswant raises Dhanraj's son, Raj. Dhanraj is released from prison, in time to see his son sing at his college farewell function **❶**. The two are reunited.

RASHMI PHOTOGRAPHS RAJ WHILE HE'S OUT FOR AN EVENING JOG

FORBIDDEN LOVE

Raj goes back to his village, Dhanakpur, for a family errand. He sees Rashmi, Ratan's niece, and is smitten. He sneaks into her birthday party, pretending to be someone else. Raj is spotted by Randhir, Rashmi's father, and the family rivalry is stirred again. Raj and Rashmi bump into one another at a holiday camp in Mount Abu. Infatuated, they take every chance to be together.

Rashmi leaves Mount Abu for Sitanagar, to meet her friends. On the way, she is accosted by a bunch of thugs and runs into the jungle to save her life. There she bumps into Raj again, who is separated from his friends **❷**. They spend time together, and Rashmi falls in love with Raj **❸**. Raj is wary, as he knows Rashmi is from the family of his father's enemy. However, she is oblivious to this truth.

THE SONGS

Papa Kehte Hain
(My Father Tells Me)
Singer: Udit Narayan
😊 *Picturized on Raj*

Kahe Sataye
(Why Do You Trouble Me So)
Singer: Alka Yagnik
😊 *Picturized on Raj and Rashmi*

Gazab Ka Hai Din
(Such a Brilliant Day)
Singers: Udit Narayan, Alka Yagnik
😊 *Picturized on Raj and Rashmi*

★ *A "teaser" ad campaign for the film featured the words, "Who is Aamir Khan?" without any images. By the time the film's posters appeared, people were curious about this young star.*

RAJ SINGS AT HIS COLLEGE FAREWELL PARTY

RASHMI EXPRESSES HER LOVE FOR RAJ

RAJ AND RASHMI START A
NEW LIFE IN THE WILDERNESS

MANSOOR KHAN (b.1958)

A reluctant filmmaker, Mansoor Khan is the son of Nasir Hussain, a director–producer–writer. An engineering graduate, Mansoor was coaxed into making *QSQT* by his father. Mansoor gave a modern twist to the familiar story and made it his own. His hero was conflicted but unwavering, and his heroine did whatever it took to get what she wanted. *QSQT* was a game-changer for Bollywood. Today, Mansoor is more interested in organic farming, but he made history with *QSQT*.

OLD WOUNDS	RUNAWAY LOVERS	NEW LIFE	TRAGEDY STRIKES
Rashmi meets Dhanraj and learns the truth about her family's rivalry. The couple know that their families want to tear them apart. Randhir soon learns about Raj, who is asked to stay away. Under threat from his family, he promises never to see her again ❹. Rashmi's family vows to marry her off immediately. When the couple try to meet, Randhir tries to run Raj off the road.	**Raj and Rashmi** decide to elope. Raj hides outside Rashmi's house, hoping to escape with her on his motorbike. He is discovered and is beaten up by Rashmi's father. Rashmi's grandmother stops Randhir from killing Raj. Eventually, Rashmi's best friend manages to sneak her out, and the lovers manage to run away.	**Raj and Rashmi** find an abandoned old temple and decide to make it their new home ❺. Raj fetches utilities for the "house," while Rashmi takes care of cooking. On a shopping trip, Raj stumbles upon a "wanted notice" in a newspaper and starts preparing for impending danger.	**Raj and Rashmi are soon** discovered. Their families gradually close in. Rashmi's father hires goons to kill Raj and instructs them to leave no witnesses behind. Randhir reaches the temple on pretext of meeting Rashmi. He lies to her that he is willing to accept Raj in his family. Meanwhile, Raj gets into a scuffle with the goons and kills one of them. Dhanraj is alerted about Randhir's treachery and he, too, reaches the temple. Rashmi learns the truth and runs out to alert Raj. Randhir's man is about to shoot Raj, but he spots Rashmi and shoots her. Raj overpowers the goon and kills him. Rashmi breathes her last. Raj is devastated and kills himself with a dagger that Rashmi gave him. The lovers are together, never to be separated.

Ae Mere Humsafar
(Oh, My Companion)
Singers: Udit Narayan, Alka Yagnik
Picturized on Raj and Rashmi

Many of the gorgeous outdoor scenes were filmed in Udagamandalam (Ooty), a popular summer resort in southern India famed for its beautiful blue hills and eucalyptus and pine forests.

Akele Hain To Kya Gum Hai
(So What If We're Alone,
There's No Reason to Be Sad)
Singers: Udit Narayan, Alka Yagnik
Picturized on Raj and Rashmi

DHANRAJ TRIES TO SAVE HIS SON,
RAJ, BUT IS STOPPED BY RANDHIR

"*The film practically redefined the way the hero operated in popular Hindi cinema.*"

THE HINDU, 2016

TEZAAB

| 1988 |

Pitched as a "violent love story," this film made actress Madhuri Dixit an overnight sensation and dazzled audiences with the hit song "Ek Do Teen."

The best-performing movie of 1988, *Tezaab* (Acid) took Bollywood by storm. It ran in theaters for more than 50 weeks, received four Filmfare Awards, including Best Actor for Anil Kapoor (see pp. 192–93), and landed Madhuri Dixit her first nomination for Best Actress. *Tezaab* was also the first of many films that Madhuri and Anil made together throughout the 1990s, and its success was said to have been partly due to the red-hot on-screen chemistry between the lead pair.

ACID TEST
Tezaab is the story of two young lovers, Mahesh Deshmukh and Mohini, whose lives take a dark turn. Mahesh is an idealist who aspires to join the Indian armed forces. While at college, he makes a bet with his friends that he can make his beautiful fellow student Mohini fall in love with him. Before long, he is in love with her too. However, her violent and alcoholic father Shyamlal owes money to ruthless gangster Lotiya Pathan. The only way he can repay his debt is to make money using Mohini. He plans to force her into dancing and prostitution, as he did to her mother, who died after he threw acid on her while she was resisting him.

When Mahesh tries to intervene, Shyamlal enlists the gangster's help to stop him. A flurry of violence ensues, culminating in Mahesh being thrown in prison. When he is released, Mahesh returns to Mumbai, transformed from an idealist into a gangster. He goes by the name Munna, and is ready to take revenge and rescue Mohini.

STAR POWER
Tezaab was Madhuri's breakthrough role, making her a star overnight and starting her on the path to becoming a Bollywood icon. Coming on the heels of Anil's highly successful film *Mr. India* (see pp. 188–91), the film also confirmed his star status. Not only did *Tezaab* do wonders for their individual careers, it established the two as a hit pair. Looking back at what the film did for her career, Madhuri said in an interview in 2012 in the *Mumbai Mirror*, "I had never done anything like this before. There had been a lot of anguish, hysteria, and over-the-top scenes. Till then, I had been playing 'sweet' girl roles." In *Tezaab*, Madhuri grew up.

Her chartbusting song "Ek Do Teen" also played a big part in the film's success, and its popularity led to producers wanting similar dance numbers with Madhuri in their films.

▲ **Action-packed blockbuster**
Tezaab's poster grabbed audiences with the promise of action and romance. In fact, the film's plot was loosely based on the Hollywood movie *Streets of Fire* (1984).

CAST AND CREW

- ★ **Anil Kapoor** Mahesh Deshmukh
- **Madhuri Dixit** Mohini
- **Anupam Kher** Shyamlal
- **Chunky Pandey** Baban
- **Kiran Kumar** Lotiya Pathan
- **Suresh Oberoi** Inspector Gagan Singh
- **Annu Kapoor** Abbas Ali

- 🎬 **Director** N. Chandra
- 🎥 **Producer** Dinesh Gandhi
- 🎵 **Music composers** Laxmikant S. Kudalkar, Pyarelal R. Sharma
- 🎵 **Lyricist** Javed Akhtar
- 💃 **Choreographer** Saroj Khan
- 📖 **Scriptwriters** N. Chandra, Kamlesh Pandey
- 🎞 **Cinematographer** Baba Azmi
- 👔 **Costume designer** Tubhi Pawar

◄ **Mohini's memorable dance**
The song "Ek Do Teen," performed by Madhuri Dixit, was a major element of the film's success. Dixit rehearsed the seven-minute dance sequence for 16 days with choreographer Saroj Khan, and its filming took a week.

HIT SONGS

Ek Do Teen
(One Two Three)
🎤 **Singer** Alka Yagnik

So Gaya Yeh Jahan
(The World Is Asleep)
🎤 **Singers** Nitin Mukesh, Alka Yagnik, Shabbir Kumar

Jeena Nahin Mujhe Hain Marna
(Let Me Die)
🎤 **Singers** Amit Kumar, Anuradha Paudwal

PARINDA

1989

Perhaps the most influential Indian gangster movie of all time, *Parinda*'s gritty, stylish realism and superb cinematography brought the Mumbai underworld to life.

CAST AND CREW

★ **Jackie Shroff** Kishen
Nana Patekar Anna Seth
Anil Kapoor Karan
Madhuri Dixit Paro
Anupam Kher Inspector Prakash

Director Vidhu Vinod Chopra
Producer Vidhu Vinod Chopra
Music composer R.D. Burman
Lyricist Khurshid Hallauri
Choreographer Bhushan Lakandri
Scriptwriters Imtiaz Hussain, Shiv Kumar Subramaniam
Cinematographer Binod Pradhan

◀ **Taking flight**
Although *Parinda* was remade as the Hollywood thriller *Broken Horses* in 2015, the original still packs a powerful punch.

O ften listed as one of the 100 greatest Indian films, *Parinda* (Bird) was India's entry in the Academy Awards Best Foreign Language Film category in 1990. Two key actors made their mark with *Parinda*: Nana Patekar *(see box)* won the coveted National Film Award for Best Supporting Actor for his nuanced portrayal of a psychopath; Jackie Shroff, meanwhile, won the Filmfare Award for Best Actor for bringing great depth to the inner conflict of a loving brother and loyal friend.

SAVAGE UNDERBELLY
In the film, brothers Kishen and Karan grow up on the streets of Mumbai. To give his younger brother a better life, Kishen joins a gang led by Anna Seth—a cool, ruthless mobster.

When Karan returns home from the US, he is unaware that Kishen has become a gangster. He makes this discovery only after the murder of Inspector Prakash, who was his best friend and his girlfriend Paro's brother. Devastated, he confronts his brother.

Kishen tries to prevent Karan from being dragged into the underworld, but Karan is determined to get his revenge. He learns about the mafia from his friend Iqbal, who has inside information about various gangs. Karan wants to join Anna, but to do this he must first show solidarity to the gang by killing Iqbal. Anna locks the two in a room with a gun, knowing Karan will not do it. In order to help his friend, Iqbal shoots himself.

Karan, now a gangster, gets drawn deeper into the deadly underworld, pitting one gang against another in his quest for vengeance, until a final and bloody confrontation.

NEW REALISM IN BOLLYWOOD
From its opening shot of the Mumbai skyline at sunset, city lights rising to the sound of American composer Aaron Copeland's *Fanfare for the Common Man* (1942), *Parinda* set new standards for Indian cinema. Grounded in a realistic urban landscape, *Parinda* influenced many successors in this genre. Favoring real locations over studio sets, director Vidhu Vinod Chopra (see p. 287), his cinematographer Binod Pradhan, and editor Renu Saluja raised the bar in visual storytelling, using dynamic tracking shots, tight close-ups, and sharp edits. The end result was a gripping narrative with emotional intensity and dynamic pace.

▼ **Brothers in arms**
Actors Anil Kapoor (right) and Jackie Shroff acted together in many films, and played brothers again in *Ram Lakhan* (1989) and *Roop ki Rani Choron ka Raja* (1993).

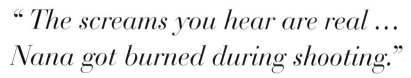
" *The screams you hear are real ... Nana got burned during shooting.*"
VIDHU VINOD CHOPRA, DIRECTOR, *PARINDA*

NANA PATEKAR
(b.1951)

V ishwanath "Nana" Patekar is an Indian actor and filmmaker who has worked extensively in Bollywood and in the Marathi film industry. His award for *Parinda* was the first of many, including Filmfare Awards in the categories of Best Actor, Best Supporting Actor, and Best Villain. In 2013, he was honored with a Padma Shri—one of the highest civilian awards. He spent two months in a hospital after being seriously injured in a fire during the filming of *Parinda*.

MADHURI DIXIT

ACTRESS b.1967

Madhuri Dixit was Hindi cinema's number one female star for most of the 1990s. She had it all: gorgeous looks, a dazzling smile, phenomenal acting talent, and extraordinary dancing ability.

D espite her incredible success in Bollywood, Madhuri Dixit could be considered as one of its unluckiest actresses. She reached her peak at a time when Hindi cinema was not producing its best work, so it speaks volumes that although she gave several flawless performances, people still tend to think of her dancing talent first. In this regard, she was more fortunate because she featured in some of the most well-known dance-oriented songs that came out of Bollywood from the late 1980s onward.

DIFFICULT START

Born to a middle-class Maharashtrian family, Madhuri was studying to be a microbiologist when she was offered her first role in the film *Abodh* (1984). An adequate performance from her did not, unfortunately, stop the film from sinking at the box office. The same year, she also acted in the pilot of a TV serial, *Bombay Meri Hai*, only to have Doordarshan—India's national television channel—reject it.

Following supporting roles in *Awaara Baap* (1985) and *Swati* (1986), Madhuri was signed on by director Subhash Ghai to perform a dance number in *Karma* (1986). Ghai noticed her talent and decided to "relaunch" her. Dropping her scene in *Karma*, he advised her to stop accepting supporting roles and promised her something better. He then put out huge

▲ **An early start**
In her first film, *Abodh*, Madhuri Dixit played a naïve young bride, who, through the course of the film, comes to realize the true worth of marriage.

▼ **Versatile performer**
In her role as courtesan Chandramukhi in Sanjay Leela Bhansali's 2002 film *Devdas*, Madhuri delivers a sensitive, nuanced performance, besides dancing beautifully.

"Madhuri is the most complete woman … the greatest star."

M.F. HUSSAIN, INDIAN ARTIST, DIRECTOR OF *GAJA GAMINI*

advertisements in trade magazines, declaring the birth of a new star. He himself would direct Madhuri in two extremely successful films: *Ram Lakhan* (1989) and *Khal Nayak* (1993).

QUEEN OF THE NINETIES
Madhuri's big breakthrough finally came with filmmaker N. Chandra's *Tezaab*, which made her a star. In addition to her fine portrayal of the daughter of an alcoholic, her nimble-footed dance to the film's chart-buster "Ek Do Teen" (One Two Three) took the country by storm. This was the first in a series of big hits with choreographer Saroj Khan. In an interview, Khan recalled that Madhuri, a trained Kathak dancer, rehearsed for the song for 17 days.

Madhuri won her first Filmfare Award for Best Actress for *Dil* (1990), which she followed with highly effective performances in *Saajan* (1991), *100 Days* (1991), and the directorial debut of actor Nana Patekar (see p. 199), *Prahaar* (1991). It is alleged she became involved with *Saajan* co-star Sanjay Dutt but the relationship ended with his arrest in 1993 for the illegal possession of firearms during the time of the Mumbai bombings.

Beta, her second film with Indra Kumar after *Dil*, made Madhuri the top heroine of the Hindi film industry. She also won her second Filmfare Award for Best Actress. In a fiery performance, she plays an illiterate man's wife, who exposes her scheming mother-in-law. A major highlight of the film is the song "Dhak Dhak Karne Laga" (My Heart Is Beating), easily her most popular.

Madhuri reached the peak of her career with the family drama *Hum Aapke Hain Koun..!* for which she won her third Filmfare Award for Best Actress. Her on-screen histrionics and

KEY WORKS
Tezaab, 1988 (see pp. 198–99)
Dil, 1990
Saajan, 1991
Beta, 1992
Hum Aapke Hain Koun..! 1994 (see pp. 222–25)
Mrityudand, 1997
Dil to Pagal Hai, 1997
Gaja Gamini, 2000
Devdas, 2002 (see pp. 276–79)
Dedh Ishqiya, 2014

dancing charmed no less an artist than M.F. Hussain, who made her his muse. He would not only produce a series of paintings of her but also direct her in the film *Gaja Gamini*.

Although Madhuri has done some truly high-caliber work as an actress, it has been mostly in some unremarkable films. A noted exception was filmmaker Prakash Jha's stinging tale of gender inequality, *Mrityudand* (1997), in which she gives a career-best performance. The same year, she also bounced back from a prolonged slump at the box office with Yash Chopra's love triangle *Dil to Pagal Hai*, winning a fourth Filmfare Award for Best Actress. Madhuri married US-based cardiovascular surgeon Dr. Shriram Nene in 1999.

MAKING A COMEBACK
After her marriage, Madhuri went on to have a major impact in films such as *Pukar* (2000), in which, despite playing a character with negative shades, she managed to gain the audience's empathy. She also starred in director Sanjay Leela Bhansali's *Devdas*, where she vividly brought courtesan Chandramukhi's character to life, winning a Filmfare Award for Best Supporting Actress.

After a sabbatical in the US, Madhuri returned to films with Yash Raj Films' *Aaja Nachle* (2007), fittingly cast as a choreographer. The film is a showcase for Madhuri's dancing talent. Although she was as radiant as ever, and her

▶ **Fighting injustice**
Mrityudand sees Madhuri give a blazing performance as an educated woman entering a conservative, feudal family and confronting the injustices she witnesses.

▲ **Contentious words**
A legal case was brought against Madhuri's song "Choli Ke Peeche Kya Hai" (What Is Under the Bodice?) from *Khal Nayak*, with claims that the lyrics were suggestive and degraded Indian culture.

acting cannot be faulted, the film proved to be a disappointment, both critically and commercially.

Madhuri returned to India with her family in 2011, and has worked on three films since—performing a dance number in the 2013 film *Yeh Jawaani hai Deewani* (see p. 315), and fully fledged roles in *Dedh Ishqiya* (2014) and *Gulaab Gang* (2014). While her performances are good, the films themselves lack spark. Madhuri is now more often seen on television, as a celebrity judge on dance-based reality shows, than she is on the big screen.

TIMELINE
● **May 15, 1967** Born in Mumbai to Shankar and Snehlata Dixit.

● **1984** Makes her debut as leading lady in *Abodh*. The film is a box-office failure.

● **1988** Attains star status with *Tezaab*. Her dance sequence "Ek Do Teen" is a highlight of the film.

● **1989** Stars in the hit film *Ram Lakhan*, opposite Anil Kapoor.

● **1991** Wins her first Filmfare Award for Best Actress in *Dil*.

WITH ACTOR ANIL KAPOOR IN *RAM LAKHAN*

● **1992** Is given the nickname "Dhak Dhak girl" after her hit song from *Beta*.

● **1993** Wins her second Filmfare Award for Best Actress in *Beta*.

● **1994** Makes the most successful film of her career: *Hum Aapke Hain Koun..!*

● **1995** Receives the third Filmfare Award of her career for Best Actress in *Hum Aapke Hain Koun..!*

● **1998** Wins her fourth Filmfare Award for Best Actress in *Dil to Pagal Hai*.

● **17 October 1999** Marries US-based cardiovascular surgeon Dr. Shriram Nene.

● **2002** Gives her last performance, in *Devdas*, before taking a sabbatical to start a family.

● **March 18, 2003** Madhuri becomes a mother when her son Arin is born.

● **March 8, 2005** Becomes a mother for the second time when her son Ryan is born.

● **2007** Returns to Bollywood with the dance drama *Aaja Nachle*.

● **2008** Awarded the Padma Shri—the fourth-highest civilian award—for her contribution to Indian cinema.

● **2011** Moves back to India from the US with her husband and two sons.

● **2014** Returns to films once again with *Dedh Ishqiya*.

CHANDNI

1989

After a decade in which most movies were over-the-top action pictures, *Chandni* turned back time, winning audiences back to the classic romantic love triangle once again.

CAST AND CREW

★ **Rishi Kapoor** Rohit Gupta
Sridevi Chandni Mathur
Vinod Khanna Lalit Khanna
Waheeda Rehman Mrs. Khanna

🎬 **Director** Yash Chopra
🎬 **Producers** Yash Chopra, T. Subbarami Reddy
🎵 **Music composers** Shiv Kumar Sharma, Hariprasad Chaurasia
𝄞 **Lyricist** Anand Bakshi
🕺 **Choreographer** Saroj Khan
📖 **Scriptwriters** Kamna Chandra, Umesh Kalbagh, Arun Kaul, Sagar Sarhadi
🎥 **Cinematographer** Manmohan Singh

Opening in cinemas so packed with enthusiastic crowds that the studio had to scramble to find more screens, *Chandni* struck a chord with film and music fans. Yet, the film was not merely a crowd-pleaser; it was also a game-changer, marking the end of a string of lukewarm productions from director Yash Chopra (see pp.166–67). *Chandni* indicated a return to the glorious all-singing, all-dancing Bollywood spectacle after years of action films. Playing the lead character Chandni, Sridevi (see pp. 204–05) gave a fabulous performance that entranced audiences, inspired young actresses, and influenced popular fashion. She portrayed a woman who enjoyed and experienced life at its fullest despite all its ups and downs and difficult choices.

The film tells the story of Chandni, who catches the eye of handsome, well-to-do Rohit at a wedding. His posh, urbane family objects to Rohit's alliance with the small-town Chandni. However, he is completely smitten, and a date is set for their wedding.

Then, an unfortunate accident leaves him paralyzed and their relationship starts to break down under the pressure of the awful circumstances and his interfering family.

Brokenhearted, Chandni must make her own way in the world, and she takes up a job in another city. Her boss Lalit romances her, to the delight of his mother, but Chandni has not forgotten her first love. Just as she begins to resign herself to her fate, events take an unexpected turn and Chandni has to make a choice.

RETURN OF ROMANCE

Yash Chopra's mission in making *Chandni* was to display the huge emotional range of love, from delight to doubt, from bliss to bitterness. In an interview, he recalled driving through the streets of Mumbai plastered with movie posters, all showing men holding guns. That was the moment when he decided to make his next movie all about love. The audiences, in response, adored the film.

The film's rich musical score by Shiv Kumar Sharma and Hariprasad Chaurasia broke all records, and the lyrics, by Anand Bakshi, were praised for their down-to-earth realism. After years of shallow music, *Chandni* helped to remind directors just how much meaning music could bring to the movies. Sridevi's portrayal of Chandni became the benchmark for young actresses aspiring to play such a role themselves.

Chandni proved to be a step in the right direction for Bollywood—a return to escapist, romantic films that were hugely popular with the public.

RISHI KAPOOR
(b.1952)

A member of the ubiquitous Kapoor clan, Rishi Kapoor had his first brush with the big screen as a teenager in his father Raj Kapoor's 1970 film *Mera Naam Joker* (see p. 335). His breakthrough came in 1973 with the teen-sensation *Bobby* (see pp. 118–19), which earned him a Filmfare Award for Best Actor. A string of romantic roles followed, although he acted in many multi-starrers, too. In 1980, he married his teenage sweetheart Neetu Singh. Since the 2000s he has moved on to playing supporting roles.

▶ **Dancing diva**
"Mere Haathon Mein" gained instant popularity, and remains a classic. It is still played often at Indian weddings.

HIT SONGS

Mere Haathon Mein
(The Bangles on My Hand)
🎤 **Singer** Lata Mangeshkar

Chandni O Meri Chandni
(Chandni, O My Chandni)
🎤 **Singers** Sridevi, Jolly Mukherjee

Tere Mere Hothon Pe
(Sweet Nothings on Our Lips)
🎤 **Singers** Lata Mangeshkar, Babla Mehta

CHAALBAAZ

Sridevi's superb comic timing, dancing skills, and on-screen charisma made her the perfect choice for the dual roles of the polar opposite twins in *Chaalbaaz*.

▲ **Leading lady**
Sridevi's powerful performance in the role of the twins reduced the cinema giants Rajinikanth and Sunny Deol to the rank of supporting artists.

As well as being a classic comedy, the 1989 film *Chaalbaaz* (Trickster) is also counted as one of Sridevi's finest performances. A blockbuster hit of the year, the film garnered both commercial and critical acclaim.

ONE WOMAN, TWO ROLES
The story revolves around Anju and Manju, identical twins (both played by Sridevi) who are born into a wealthy family, but separated by a twist of fate. Manju grows up in the slums, in poverty. Streetwise and self-reliant, she dreams of becoming a dancer. Anju, on the other hand, is brought up in a wealthy household but is unhappy. She finds herself constantly under the threat of physical and mental harm from her cruel uncle, who is trying to get his hands on the family fortune, following the mysterious death of her parents. In an only-in-the-movies plot

twist, Anju falls in love with Jaggu (Rajinikanth), a taxi driver, while Manju wins the affection of a rakish rich boy, Suraj (Sunny Deol). Neither sister knows about the other, and neither suitor knows they have fallen for a twin. Somehow their paths collide, leading to a comedy of errors.

While the film's plot may be a little hard to believe, Sridevi is wonderfully believable in both of her roles. As Manju, she shines with confidence and life—she is a young woman able to take care of herself. As Anju, she is quite different, quivering with fear and anxiety. Her dancing is especially wonderful, particularly the stunning *tandava* (divine dance of Shiva) sequence, which empowers Anju so that she is no longer afraid or weak.

A FRESH SPIN
The theme of identical twins separated at birth is not a new one. *Chaalbaaz* is itself a remake of *Seeta aur Geeta* (see p. 109). However, director Pankaj Parashar, who is better known for his work on television, brought a deft commercial eye to this version, with a more quirky spin on the familiar story.

Chaalbaaz is generally regarded as one of Sridevi's standout

performances. The actress won the Filmfare Award for Best Actress for the film—in recognition of her comic timing, her compelling presence on the screen, and her twin triumphs in playing both the roles so effectively. Choreographer Saroj Khan also won a Filmfare award for her fantastic dance sequences, especially for "Na Jaane Kahan Se Aayi Hai" (Who Knows Where She Has Come From?), also known as "the rain song." Ever the professional, Sridevi performed this sequence when she was suffering from a high fever. The popular song also won playback singer Kavita Krishnamurthy a Filmfare nomination.

▼ **Dancing in the rain**
The hugely popular song "Na Jaane Kahan se Aayi Hai" (Who Knows Where She Has Come From?), featuring Sridevi (left) and Sunny Deol (right) won awards for its delightful choreography.

CAST AND CREW

★ **Sridevi** Anju Das/Manju Das
Sunny Deol Suraj
Rajinikanth Jaggu
Anupam Kher Tribhuvan Das

🎬 **Director** Pankaj Parashar
🎞 **Producer** A. Poorna Chandra Rao
🎵 **Music composers** Laxmikant S. Kudalkar, Pyarelal R. Sharma
🎵 **Lyricist** Anand Bakshi
🕺 **Choreographer** Saroj Khan
📖 **Scriptwriters** Rajesh Mazumdar, Kamlesh Pandey
🎥 **Cinematographer** Manmohan Singh
👔 **Costume designer** Narayana B. Rao

"Sridevi's performance rocked the box office."

THE TIMES OF INDIA, 2012

SRIDEVI

ACTRESS b.1963

One of the few Bollywood actresses with the charisma and talent to outshine the heroes in her films, Sridevi ruled the silver screen in the 1980s and 1990s.

Prodigiously talented, Sridevi was a child star in Tamil films and then a top actress in Malayalam, Telugu, and Kannada films before making her Bollywood debut.

She followed in the footsteps of Tamil heroines Hema Malini (see pp. 110–11) and Rekha (see p. 169), stars of numerous hits who could command almost any fee they asked for.

BEGINNING WITH A BANG

After a small role in *Julie* (see p. 131), Sridevi's first lead in a Hindi film was in *Solva Saawan* (1978). While this made little impact, her next outing was the 1983 blockbuster *Himmatwala*, which put her firmly on the map. Her athletic dances and an appearance in a swimsuit helped to get her noticed. The same year also saw her in the breakthrough film, *Sadma*, in which she played a woman suffering from amnesia. The following year, she acted in another big earner, *Tohfa*, with Jeetendra (see pp. 182–83), and in 1986 she rocked the box office again in a rather unconventional role—as a shape-shifting snake-woman in *Nagina* (see p. 184).

THE SRIDEVI ERA

After proving herself to be a box office draw, Sridevi concentrated on films where she was the lead, which gave her plenty of scope to experiment with her craft. In 1987, she starred in the action-sci-fi hit, *Mr. India*. Her sequence impersonating veteran Hollywood comedian Charlie Chaplin in the movie was memorable for her impeccable comic timing, and her songs "Hawa Hawaii" and "Kaate Nahin Katate" (These Days Don't Pass Even When I Wish So) became all the rage. Sridevi carried the 1989 film *Chaalbaaz*, for which she won her first Filmfare Award, more or less reducing veterans Sunny Deol and Rajnikanth to supporting actors. Her

◀ **Dazzling diva**
The versatile actress has many iconic dance numbers to her credit, such as "Hawa Hawaii" (see left), "Mere Haathon Mein" (In My Hands), and "Naino Mein Sapna" (Dreams in My Eyes).

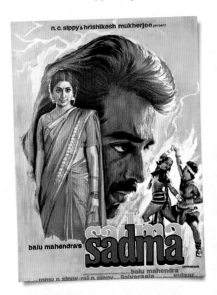

▲ **A star is born**
Sridevi showed her intense dramatic flair to great effect in *Sadma*. She made a bold move by taking on an unconventional role in the film, which helped propel her to Bollywood stardom.

KEY WORKS

Himmatwala, 1983 (see p. 180)

Sadma, 1983

Mr. India, 1987 (see pp. 188–91)

Chandni, 1989 (see p. 202)

Chaalbaaz, 1989 (see p. 203)

English Vinglish, 2012

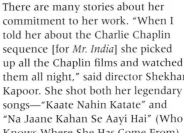

◀ **Hit duo**
Sridevi acted in more than 10 films with Anil Kapoor. The pair delivered many massive box office hits, ranging from the sci-fi film *Mr. India* to intense dramas like *Lamhe.*

unwavering self-confidence shined through in the film, and seemed like a celebration of her strong independent screen persona.

The same year also saw Sridevi act in *Chandni*, gaining the caché of being a heroine in a film directed by Yash Chopra (see pp. 166–67); the two were lauded for bringing romance back to the screen after a decade of predominantly violent movies. Sridevi's chiffon saris came to be known as the "Chandni look" and set a huge fashion trend. She also sang the title song of the film. Yash Chopra cast her again in *Lamhe* (1991), which saw Sridevi take on a double role. Although the film did not score highly at the box office, it brought Sridevi a second Filmfare Award.

In the 1990s, Sridevi was an established name in the industry and she acted in the much-hyped, mega-budget film *Roop Ki Rani Choron Ka Raja* (1993). She also tried her hand at roles with negative overtones: *Laadla* (1994) saw her as an industrialist who mistreats her husband and his family, while *Judaai* (1997) showed her selling her husband for the riches she desired.

A BREAK AND A COMEBACK

There was a break in Sridevi's acting career following her marriage to producer Boney Kapoor in 1997, when she took time off to be with her family, mainly raising her daughters. After resuming her career, Sridevi tried her hand at a television series called *Malini Iyer* in 2004, and won acclaim for her goofy role as a Tamil housewife married into a Punjabi family.

A new phase began when she returned to the big screen, wowing critics and audiences alike in *English Vinglish* (2012). Sridevi played a wife and mother who learns English to gain the respect of her family—finding independence and renewed confidence in herself in the process.

THE CONSUMMATE PROFESSIONAL

When she first arrived in Bollywood, Sridevi could barely speak Hindi and in some movies her voice had to be dubbed. Rekha dubbed for Sridevi in the 1986 film *Akhree Raasta*.

Her work ethic and professionalism are well-recognized in the film industry. After her father's death, she took a brief break, returning to shoot *Lamhe* after the 15 days of ritual mourning. "That girl is something else," director Yash Chopra said of her. He recalled, "she went ahead and did the comedy scene full throttle. After shooting, she'd go to her room, put the pictures of her parents on her dressing table and cry her heart out."

There are many stories about her commitment to her work. "When I told her about the Charlie Chaplin sequence [for *Mr. India*] she picked up all the Chaplin films and watched them all night," said director Shekhar Kapoor. She shot both her legendary songs—"Kaate Nahin Katate" and "Na Jaane Kahan Se Aayi Hai" (Who Knows Where She Has Come From) when she was unwell.

In her prime, Sridevi worked three shifts a day, commanding a large fee and becoming the highest paid actress of her day. She worked with veteran stars such as Dharmendra (see pp. 152–53), Rajesh Khanna (see pp. 106–107), and Amitabh Bachchan (see pp. 126–27), as well as younger actors, such as Sunny Deol, Jackie Shroff (see p. 181), and Sanjay Dutt. In two distinct phases of her career, she was paired with Jeetendra, and then with Anil Kapoor (see pp. 192–93).

PRIVATE STAR

Sridevi was not one to pour her heart out to the media. This reluctance to talk about her private life gave her an aura of mystery. In 2013, Filmfare felt it had been remiss in recognizing her talent, so retrospectively gave her a Filmfare Special Award for *Nagina* and *Mr. India*. The same year, she was also awarded the Padma Shri, the fourth-highest civilian award in India.

▼ **The comeback**
Sridevi returned to the silver screen with the 2012 comedy-drama *English Vinglish*. She was appreciated by critics and audiences alike, and earned a Filmfare nomination.

> *"In a male dominated industry she can make a film run on her own."*
>
> JEETENDRA, VETERAN ACTOR, *INDIA TODAY*, 1987

TIMELINE

● **August 13, 1963** Born in Tamil Nadu, India.

● **1969** Debuts at the age of four in Tamil film *Thunaivan.*

● **1976** First role as leading lady in Tamil film *Moondru Mudichu.*

● **1979** Debuts in Bollywood as a leading lady in *Solva Sawan.*

● **1983** Filmfare declares her as "Unquestionably No. 1" with the success of *Himmatwala.*

● **1983** Receives critical acclaim for portraying the role of a woman suffering from amnesia in *Sadma.*

● **1990** First Filmfare for double role in *Chaalbaaz.*

● **1992** Acts with superstar and veteran actor Amitabh Bachchan in *Khuda Gawah.*

● **1997** Release of *Judaai*—last film before a career break. Receives a Filmfare nomination for the film.

● **1997** Marries producer Boney Kapoor.

● **2004** Appears in television series *Malini Iyer.*

● **2012** Makes a comeback to the big screen with *English Vinglish*, receiving her ninth Filmfare nomination.

● **2013** Receives Padma Shri for her contribution to cinema.

● **2015** Acts in Tamil film *Puli.*

● **2017** Release of *Mom*, which is credited as her 300th film on the big screen.

CASSETTE COVER OF *JUDAAI*—THE FILM'S MUSIC TOPPED THE CHARTS.

POSTER FOR SRIDEVI'S 2017 FILM, *MOM*

MAINE PYAR KIYA

1989

A tale of innocent love, *Maine Pyar Kiya* marked a turning point for the 1980s Bollywood industry with its music, quotable dialogue, and compelling debut performances.

The late 1980s was not a particularly exciting time for Bollywood filmmakers. The audiences were fed up with over-the-top disco dances and action-hero antics that were so typical of that decade. Around this time, writer and director Sooraj Barjatya came up with a simple boy-meets-girl romance and filled the void. A story of love and friendship, *Maine Pyar Kiya* (I Have Loved) drew families back to the movie theaters. The film and its soundtrack were instant hits—no young cinemagoer could resist their appeal. Featuring a fresh new pair of lead actors, the film is credited with providing its leading man, Salman Khan, with his first big break.

INNOCENT LOVE
The film introduces us to an innocent girl named Suman, who lives a modest life with her father in the countryside. She is sent off to stay with well-to-do family friends of her father's as he has to travel abroad on business for a few months. The small-town girl is surprised to find that she is sharing the house with a big-city boy, Prem, who is the son of her hosts. As the two become friends, Prem assures Suman that it will remain a platonic relationship—that is, until they fall in love. However, Prem's father does not approve as he has already found a suitable partner for his son—a city

> *"The film redefined friendship and romance in Bollywood ..."*
>
> **TIMES OF INDIA**, 2015

girl named Seema. When Suman's father returns, the two friends argue and Prem's father scorns Suman, accusing her of being a gold digger. An insulted Suman returns home. But Prem decides to fight for his love.

THE CHOCOLATE BOY
Salman Khan was not the first choice of the lead for director Sooraj Barjatya. However, Khan played the role of Prem to perfection. Launching his career as a superstar, the role provided him with his first Filmfare Award for Best Male Debut, and also a fan base that made his later movies box office hits.

Maine Pyar Kiya is also remembered for its wardrobe. Khan's cool demeanor was complemented by carefully designed leather bomber jackets covered in patches. The wardobe for Bhagyashree—who played Suman—also became popular for its freshness, including a cap that read "friend," copies of which went on sale as merchandise. Appreciated for portraying the

many moods of young love with skill, Bhagyashree also won the Filmfare Award for Best Female Debut. The music—around a third of the running time—was also a big part of its success and was a hit with young audiences.

HIT SONGS

Kabootar Ja Ja Ja
(Pigeon, Fly Away)

🎤 **Singers** Lata Mangeshkar, Balu

Dil Deewana Bin Sajna Ke
(Crazy Heart Without My Beloved)

🎤 **Singer** Lata Mangeshkar

▶ **A musical romance**
The story of two friends who fall in love against the wishes of their fathers, this musical romance holds a special place in the hearts of all those who grew up in India in the 1980s.

GHAYAL

1990

This hit film from 1990 is known for its action sequences and a power-packed, macho performance by award-winning actor Sunny Deol.

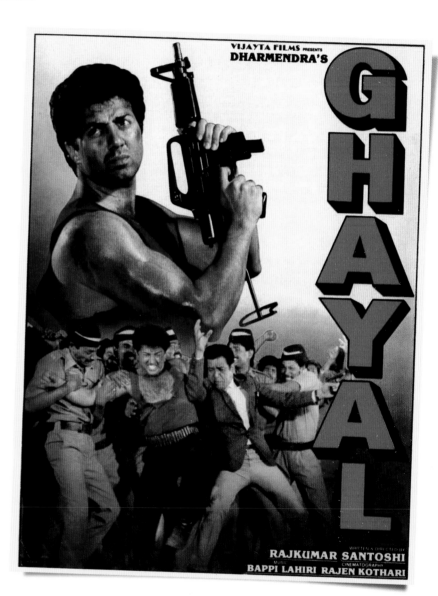

VIJAYTA FILMS PRESENTS
DHARMENDRA'S

GHAYAL

RAJKUMAR SANTOSHI
BAPPI LAHIRI RAJEN KOTHARI

CAST AND CREW

- ★ **Sunny Deol** Ajay Mehra
- **Meenakshi Seshadri** Varsha Bharti
- **Raj Babbar** Ashok Mehra
- **Moushumi Chatterjee** Indu Mehra
- **Amrish Puri** Balwant Rai
- **Om Puri** ACP Joe D'Souza
- **Kulbhushan Kharbanda** Ashok Pradhan

- **Director** Rajkumar Santoshi
- **Producer** Dharmendra
- **Music composer** Bappi Lahri
- **Lyricist** Indeevar
- **Scriptwriter** Rajkumar Santoshi
- **Cinematographer** Rajan Kothari

► **Challenging role**
This vivid poster left audiences in no doubt that *Ghayal* was an action-packed thriller. Deol rose to the challenge with a gripping and physically demanding performance.

While many lackluster action movies of the 1980s were generic "shoot-'em-ups," *Ghayal* (Injured) took the conventional formula and gave it a compelling revenge story, strong dramatic performances, and a truly memorable heroic turn from Sunny Deol; the role brought him a National Award winner.

AN ACTION DRAMA

Ajay is a talented amateur boxer who lives with his businessman brother Ashok and his wife. While away at a training camp, Ajay gets a strange phone call from his brother. Ashok tries to tell him something important, but the call is cut off abruptly. Ajay returns home to find his brother missing. Ajay's investigation leads him to Ashok's business partner Balwant Rai, who is a respectable man with friends in law enforcement. However, Ajay finds out that Rai has secrets that

run deep. He discovers that his brother has been murdered. With no help from police, Ajay decides to take matters into his own hands, but is framed for the murder and is also accused of having an illicit relationship with his sister-in-law. Unable to bear the trauma, the sister-in-law commits suicide. Ajay is determined to expose the culprits and bring them to justice. However, he has to keep himself out of their clutches. With his faith in the law of the land crushed, Ajay decides to take down Balwant Rai on his own.

POWER-PACKED PERFORMANCE

Director and writer Rajkumar Santoshi created an explosion at the box office with *Ghayal*, his debut film, which became the top earner of the year. However, Santoshi had had to wait for more than two years to get the film off the ground as he struggled to find a producer and to secure a star in the lead. Santoshi was keen to cast Deol but was worried that the actor would not agree to work with a new director. Eventually, Santoshi not only succeeded in persuading Deol to act in the film, but also convinced Deol's father, Dharmendra, to produce it. Deol gave a larger-than-life performance in the film. His powerful portrayal of a man raging against an army of evil connected well with the audiences, who felt his anger with each bellowing scream. With some moments of comedy and romance to lighten the mood, the film is driven by Deol's knockout performance.

RAJKUMAR SANTOSHI (b.1958)

Son of director and producer P.L. Santoshi, Rajkumar Santoshi is an award-winning Indian director and producer who is known for his hard-hitting films such as *Lajja* (2001) as well as the comedy *Andaz Apna Apna* (see p. 217). After assisting director Govind Nihalani in critically acclaimed films such as *Ardh Satya* (1982), he went on to direct films such as *Ghayal* and *Damini* (1993), both of which won him the Filmfare Award for Best Director. A versatile director, Santoshi is known for making films in a variety of genres including action, comedy, and romance.

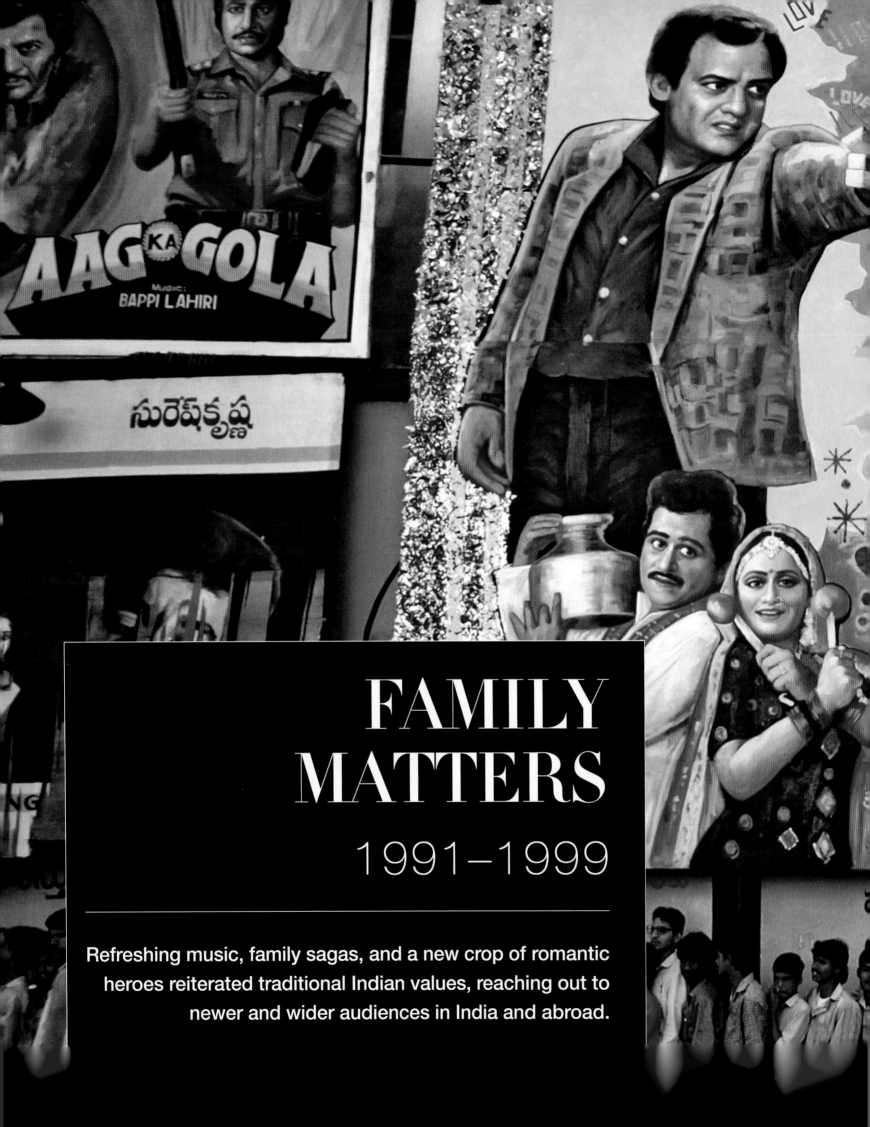

FAMILY MATTERS

1991–1999

Refreshing music, family sagas, and a new crop of romantic heroes reiterated traditional Indian values, reaching out to newer and wider audiences in India and abroad.

FAMILY MATTERS

The 1990s saw a return to melody, a rediscovery of family values and the big fat Indian wedding, an acknowledgement of the diaspora as a viable audience, and the early production of "indie" films.

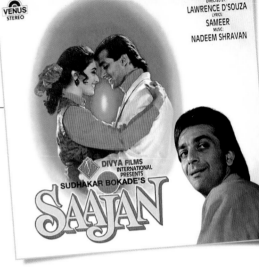

▲ **The frontman**
In the 1990s, Govinda (left) established himself as an actor-comedian who displayed an earthy sense of humor, connecting with his audience in films such as *Dulhe Raja* (1998).

After the aesthetic lows of the 1980s, the only direction for Hindi cinema to go was up. With films offering male-oriented action fare such as *Aag hi Aag* (1987) or *Paap ko Jalaakar Raakh kar Doonga* (1988), the biggest casualties in the industry had been romantic and musical features. The 1980s were perhaps the weakest years not just for filmmaking, but also for the deteriorating Hindi film music industry. This decline, especially of the musical content, meant that the hip and trendy audience stopped watching Hindi films.

MAGNETIC MUSIC

It would take the son of a fruit juice seller from Delhi to bring the much-needed melody back into Hindi films. Gulshan Kumar left his father's business and acquired a shop in Delhi to sell LP records and audiocassettes. Eventually, he began manufacturing his own audiocassettes, selling cheaply priced cover versions of popular songs from Hindi films. His business grew and he shifted to Mumbai, where he branched out into film production. He broke through with features such as *Lal Dupatta Mal Mal ka* (1989) and *Aashiqui* (1990), which were huge successes because of their music. Not all his films were successful, but their music almost always was. Gulshan's brutal murder in 1997 shocked the entire country and raised questions regarding the connection between Mumbai's underworld and the film industry.

Following Gulshan, several other music companies such as TIPS and Venus entered film production.

▲ **Musical marvel**
Saajan (1991) was a superhit film of this decade with extremely popular music. All its singers were nominated for Filmfare Awards.

While the first half of the 1990s was dominated by the rich music of the composer duo Nadeem Saifi and Shravan Rathod, the latter part of the decade brought into the spotlight a young man from Chennai, India— A.R. Rahman (see pp. 244–45)—who turned Hindi film music on its head in films such as *Rangeela* (see pp. 226–27) and *Taal* (see p. 251).

▲ **King of audiocassettes**
Gulshan Kumar was the founder of Super Cassettes Industries Private Limited, an Indian music company that launched the label "T-Series."

▲ All about family
In the 1990s, Bollywood preferred to make features that extolled traditional Indian values, which is on display in films such as *Hum Aapke Hain Koun..!*

ROOTED IN TRADITION

With music back on track, a film like *Hum Aapke Hain Koun..!* (see pp. 220–23) brought the big affluent Indian family and the glorious Indian wedding into focus, becoming one of the highest grossing features in Bollywood history. The film was followed by *Dilwale Dulhania le Jayenge* (see pp. 230–33), another family saga that would reiterate the importance of Indian values, including respect for elders and marrying with parental consent. Almost every romantic Hindi film at this time had to keep Indian traditions in mind and include a wedding or engagement song, or maybe even both.

The 1990s was an era of globalization in which films such as *Dilwale Dulhania le Jayenge* helped open up viable markets for Bollywood outside India, reaching out to the Indian diaspora settled abroad. These movies also established the trend of shooting a good part of the story, including the songs, in foreign locales. In *Aur Pyaar ho Gaya* (1997) the heroine went to Switzerland in search of her supposed husband-to-be, while the husband in an arranged marriage took his wife to Rome in *Hum Dil de Chuke Sanam* (see pp. 256–57) to reunite her with her true love.

REFORMED HERO

The decade also saw prominent directors of mainstream Bollywood—Sooraj R. Barjatya (see p. 223), Aditya Chopra (see p. 231), Karan Johar (see pp. 248–49), and Sanjay Leela Bhansali

(see p. 257)—come to the forefront. The phenomenal success of *Jo Jeeta Wohi Sikandar* (see p. 212), *Hum Aapke Hain Koun..!*, and *Dilwale Dulhania le Jayenge*, for Aamir Khan (see pp. 228–29), Salman Khan (see pp. 224–25), and Shah Rukh Khan (see pp. 214–15) respectively, saw the three Khans consolidate their position through the decade as superstars of Hindi cinema. Their fan following included an elite audience, and they made it fashionable for the "classes" to watch Hindi films in theaters once again. In particular, Shah Rukh's rise in Bollywood was quite striking. Unlike the other two Khans, he started with a brief stint in television but had no connections in the film industry, and is an entirely self-made star.

However, the actor who really connected with the masses was Govinda (see p. 238). His partnership with director David Dhawan was most successful, and the two delivered a series of rip-roaring comedies throughout the decade. Their journey began with *Swarg* (1990), but really took off with the twin successes of *Shola aur Shabnam* (1992) and *Aankhen* (1993). Some of their prominent hits include *Coolie No.1* (1995), *Deewana Mastana* (1997), and *Hero No.1* (see p. 238).

EDGY CINEMA

The end of the decade saw not just the construction of new modern multiplexes, such as PVR

Anupam in Delhi in 1997, and the advent of a mall culture, but also the rise of a fresh strain of independent cinema. A major trendsetter on this front was Nagesh Kukunoor's *Hyderabad Blues* (1998). An engineer from Hyderabad working in the US, Kukunoor made the film on a shoestring budget from his earnings.

The film took a fresh, humorous, and realistic look at a Non-Resident Indian (NRI), played by Nagesh himself, who comes back to Hyderabad after 12 years and struggles to adjust, while his parents try to arrange his marriage. Other gritty independent films of the late 1990s included *Bhopal Express* (1999) and *Split Wide Open* (1999).

▶ Rise of the Khans
A major hit in Bollywood, Aamir (left) and Salman (right)—two of the three super-Khans—regaled viewers with their comic timing in the 1994 superhit *Andaz Apna Apna*.

JO JEETA WOHI SIKANDAR

1992

Set against a sporting background, *Jo Jeeta Wohi Sikandar* is one of the most effective coming-of-age films of Bollywood.

CAST AND CREW

★ **Aamir Khan** Sanjaylal "Sanju" Sharma

Ayesha Jhulka Anjali

Mamik Ratanlal Sharma

Pooja Bedi Devika

Deepak Tijori Shekhar Malhotra

🎬 **Director** Mansoor Khan

🎥 **Producer** Nasir Hussain

🎵 **Music composers** Jatin Pandit, Lalit Pandit

🎼 **Lyricist** Majrooh Sultanpuri

🕺 **Choreographers** Farah Khan, Suresh Bhatt, Madhav Kishen

📖 **Scriptwriters** Mansoor Khan, Nasir Hussain

🎞 **Cinematographer** Najeeb Khan

👔 **Costume designer** Ashley Rebello

Any film that celebrates the triumph of human spirit in a sporting field is usually a surefire winner with audiences. After all, who doesn't like the feel-good factor of watching the underdog prevail against the odds? *Jo Jeeta Wohi Sikandar* (He Who Wins Is King), certainly triumphs in that regard.

▲ **Varied themes**
Despite being a sports drama, the film touches on the concept of friendship, one of the many themes depicted in *JJWS*.

▶ **Changing gear**
Aamir Khan plays the part of Sanju, who transforms from a wayward teenager into a confident adult while competing in a grueling, climactic cycling race.

Inspired by British director Peter Yates' film *Breaking Away* (1979), *JJWS* serves up a rich, multilayered story that covers an array of subjects, notably the class divide, strained familial relationships, the joys and tribulations of love, and above all, personal growth.

In *JJWS*, Sanju is introduced as a happy-go-lucky youngster, content to stay in the shadow of his more stoic and responsible older brother, Ratanlal. Things change, however, when Sanju has to take his brother's place in the annual inter-collegiate cycling race after the latter is indisposed. The film charts Sanju's coming of age as he faces up to the challenge.

PERFECT CASTING

Aamir Khan (see pp. 228–29) gives a stellar performance as Sanju—who starts as a college prankster and eventually matures into a responsible adult—proving why he is considered one of Bollywood's finest actors. Although cast as a character who is about 10 years younger than him, Aamir plays the part with great ebullience, while Aamir's nephew, Imran Khan, puts in an assured performace as the lead character's childhood avatar.

For the role of the female lead, Anjali, Mansoor had initially cast Girija, who had made a major impact with Mani Ratnam's Telugu film, *Gitanjali* (1989). However, the actress left the project part way, paving the way for Ayesha Jhulka to take on the role. Bollywood superstar Akshay Kumar (see p. 279) unsuccessfully auditioned for the role

of Shekhar—Sanju's rival in the cycle race—and actor Milind Soman even shot some scenes, before Deepak Tijori bagged the role.

MUSICAL DELIGHT

Among *JJWS*'s highlights is its music. The soundtrack of "Pehla Nasha" (First Elation) was particularly popular with audiences. Filmed in slow motion with lip-sync, the sequence is one of the

finest Bollywood representations of the euphoria that comes with falling in love for the first time, and marked the brilliant debut of the song's choreographer Farah Khan (see p. 293).

JJWS won Filmfare Awards for Best Film and Best Editing. Despite his riveting performance, Aamir Khan lost out on the Best Actor award to Anil Kapoor (see pp. 192–93), for the latter's performance in *Beta* (1992).

> "JJWS *weaves a compelling human story around multiple themes.*"

SUKANYA VERMA, FILM CRITIC, 2014

DARR: A VIOLENT LOVE STORY

1993

A film that explores love in its obsessional form, *Darr: A Violent Love Story* is one of the many films that saw the rise of the "antihero" and helped make Shah Rukh Khan a star.

In *Darr* (Fear), director Yash Chopra (see pp. 166–67) breathes cinematic life into a subject previously unseen on the Bollywood big screen—obsessive love. The story's heroine, Kiran, is betrothed (and later married off) to a naval commando officer, Sunil Malhotra. But that doesn't stop her from falling prey to the machinatations of a creepy stalker. Kiran is unaware that the obsessive lover is her old college mate,

Rahul Mehra, who has been besotted with her ever since their college years and longs to be with her.

STAR ANTAGONIST

Arguably, what is most intriguing about the film is how actor Shah Rukh Khan (see pp. 214–15), playing the role of the stalker, manages to steal every scene that he stars in. He gives a performance that captures the character's vulnerable state, which is reflected in the stammer he affects everytime his character utters the heroine's name. *Darr* released soon after Shah Rukh's breakthrough film *Baazigar* (see p. 216) and is among the trio of movies, also including *Anjaam* (1994), that would establish the role of

the antihero in Bollywood. Initially, Aamir Khan (see pp. 228–29) was offered the part of Rahul, but he turned it down. This paved the way for Shah Rukh to put his unique stamp on the role.

The public's empathetic reaction to Shah Rukh's characterization, and the resulting attention he received, irked the film's lead protagonist, Sunny Deol, to such a degree that he never worked with director Yash Chopra again.

IMPROBABLE SUCCESS

Darr's sumptuous cinematography and catchy soundtrack are among its major

highlights. The songs "Jaadoo Teri Nazar" and "Tu Mere Saamne", picturized on Shah Rukh in the film, became popular hits.

Darr was a runaway success at the box office and went on to win the National Award for Best Popular Film Providing Wholesome Entertainment. It also received a Filmfare Award for Best Cinematography. Anupam Kher (see p. 179), who plays the role of Kiran's brother in the film, won a Filmfare Award for Best Actor in a Comic Role. The film was also remade in Kannada as *Preethse* (2000), and proved extremely popular with viewers in southern India.

CAST AND CREW

★ **Sunny Deol** Sunil Malhotra
Juhi Chawla Kiran Malhotra
Shah Rukh Khan Rahul Mehra
Anupam Kher Vijay Awasti

🎬 **Director** Yash Chopra
🎞 **Producer** Yash Chopra
🎵 **Music composers** Shivkumar Sharma, Hariprasad Chaurasia
🎼 **Lyricist** Anand Bakshi
💃 **Choreographers** Saroj Khan, B.H. Tharun Kumar
📖 **Scriptwriters** Honey Irani, Javed Siddiqui
🎥 **Cinematographer** Manmohan Singh
👕 **Costume designers** Simple Kapadia, Gauri Khan, Neeta Lulla, Anja San

HIT SONGS

Jaadoo Teri Nazar
(Your Glance Is Magical)
🎤 **Singer** Udit Narayan

Tu Mere Saamne
(You Are There in Front of Me)
🎤 **Singers** Lata Mangeshkar, Udit Narayan

Likha Hai Yeh
(This Has Been Written)
🎤 **Singers** Lata Mangeshkar, Hariharan

▼ **Irresistible beauty**
The leading lady, Juhi Chawla (see p. 194), is presented beautifully and tastefully on-screen like all Yashraj heroines. Shah Rukh fantasizes about the character she plays, as shown in this movie still.

SHAH RUKH KHAN

ACTOR b.1965

An outsider when he stepped into the Hindi film industry, Shah Rukh Khan went on to conquer Bollywood, becoming one of its biggest stars both in India and around the world.

▶ "King Khan"
Shah Rukh has maintained his rank as Bollywood's top actor throughout his career. Along with Dilip Kumar (see pp. 48–49), he holds the record for the highest number of Filmfare Awards.

Before he became "King Khan"—the mega-box-office draw with legions of female fans swooning over his famous stretched-arms pose—Shah Rukh Khan was a student at a Delhi University college. Unlike most Bollywood stars, he did not have any family connections to the industry, nor an influential patron to turn to for help. Shah Rukh entered the film industry as an outsider who had to make his own path to Bollywood stardom.

STARTING OUT

Shah Rukh began his acting career in the 1989 television drama *Fauji*. He soon became a regular fixture on the small screen, appearing in many critically acclaimed shows such as *Wagle Ki Duniya* (1988–90), *Circus* (1989–90), and a TV film *Idiot* (1991).

When his mother passed away in 1991, Shah Rukh moved to Mumbai to overcome his grief and also to try his luck in films. The industry, however, was as crowded as ever: the children of former actors, directors, and producers tended to be given the most coveted roles, making stardom more of an inheritance than a reward for acting skill.

With nothing to lose, Shah Rukh was happy to take roles that were rejected by other lead

▲ Poster boy of the 1990s
Shah Rukh created a niche for himself as the quintessential lover. In *Pardes* (see p. 240), he plays the romantic hero who travels all the way to America to rescue the heroine.

KEY WORKS

Deewana, 1992

Baazigar, 1993 (see p. 216)

Dilwale Dulhania le Jayenge, 1995 (see pp. 230–33)

Devdas, 2002 (see pp. 274–77)

Swades, 2004

Chak De! India, 2007 (see p. 298)

My Name Is Khan, 2010

◄ **Bollywood's favorite on-screen couple**
Shah Rukh and Kajol have acted together in seven films. Their crackling on-screen chemistry made them tremendously popular with the audiences.

Kaun Banega Crorepati—the Indian version of the hit television gameshow *Who Wants to be a Millionaire*.

In a career spanning nearly three decades, Shah Rukh has received numerous national and international accolades. In 2005, the government of India awarded him the Padma Shri—the fourth highest civilian honor—for his contribution to cinema. In 2007, his wax statue was installed in London's Madame Tussauds museum. And in the following year, his name appeared in *Newsweek*'s list of the world's 50 most powerful people. Now that Shah Rukh is in his fifties, he is leaving the romantic lead roles to the

the world, helping to turn the Bollywood product into a global phenomenon. In the mid 2000s, he starred in the films *Swades* and *Chak De! India*, in which he steps out of the mold of a romantic hero. These two performances earned him huge critical acclaim, and many consider them highlights of his career.

actors—roles that were either seen as too risky or too offbeat. When Salman Khan (see pp. 224–25) turned down *Baazigar*, and Aamir Khan (see pp. 228–29) passed on *Darr* (see p. 213)—both wary of playing the part of an antihero—Shah Rukh saw these as golden opportunities, and put in sensational performances that helped the films become box office hits.

GAME CHANGER

By the mid 1990s, Shah Rukh had cemented his place in the industry, starring in a string of commercial hits and winning multiple awards. But this was just the beginning. On October 19, 1995, director Aditya Chopra's debut, *Dilwale Dulhaniya le Jayenge*, opened at the theaters, starring Shah Rukh in the lead role, and became an instant blockbuster. Not only did the film propel the actor to superstar status; it also crystallized his on-screen image—that of a young cosmopolitan Indian who isn't afraid to express love and reveal his vulnerable side. It was a star persona that straddled the traditional and the modern, captivating much of the female Indian audience.

During the following decade, Shah Rukh delivered one blockbuster after another, including *Kuch Kuch Hota Hai* (see pp. 246–47), *Kabhi Khushi Kabhie Gham* (see pp. 270–71), *Devdas*, and *Kal Ho naa Ho* (2003). Most tellingly, his films began drawing the Indian diaspora to theaters around

> ## "I'm happy ... that people know me ... I love being a star."
>
> **SHAH RUKH KHAN,** *THE GUARDIAN*, 2006

BRANCHING OUT

In 2002, Shah Rukh and his wife, Gauri, floated their production house, Red Chilies Entertainment, on the public stock market. The company has since produced nearly a dozen films and successfully branched out into several other sectors including visual effects, merchandising, film distribution, and film marketing.

Besides acting and producing, Shah Rukh has also presented awards ceremonies, performed at stage shows around the world, and hosted

brigade of younger actors following in his footsteps. Instead, he is carving out different types of roles for himself, as seen in the recent films *Dear Zindagi* (2016) and *Raees* (2017). Whatever lies in store for Shah Rukh, one thing is certain: his star is far too bright to burn out overnight, and if he takes on the right roles, it might become even brighter with age.

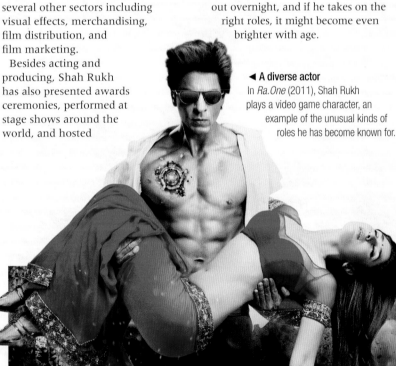

◄ **A diverse actor**
In *Ra.One* (2011), Shah Rukh plays a video game character, an example of the unusual kinds of roles he has become known for.

TIMELINE

● **November 2, 1965** Born in Delhi.

● **1989** Makes television debut in *Fauji*.

● **1991** Marries Gauri Chibber after a six-year courtship.

● **1991** Moves to Mumbai to enter the Bollywood film industry.

● **1992** Wins the Filmfare Award for Best Male Debut for his role in *Deewana*. The film also sees the Shah Rukh–Kajol romantic pairing together for the first time.

● **1993** Stars in *Baazigar*—his first film as an antihero—and begins carving a niche for himself in villain roles.

● **1995** Stars in the highest and second-highest grossing films of the year, *Karan Arjun* and *Dilwale Dulhania le Jayenge*. The latter cements his place as a Bollywood star.

● **1998** Stars in *Kuch Kuch Hota hai*, directed by Karan Johar, ushering in one of the most notable actor–director collaborations in Bollywood history.

● **2002** Floats Red Chillies Entertainment on the stock market, and enters the filmmaking business to produce big budget hits.

● **2005** Stars in *Paheli*, India's entry for the Academy Awards for the Best Foreign Language Film.

● **2007** French government confers on him the Officier dans Ordre des Arts et des Lettres (Officer of the Order of Arts and Letters).

● **2008** Acquires ownership rights of the Indian Premier League T-20 cricket team, Kolkata Knight Riders.

● **2016** Plays the role of a therapist in *Dear Zindagi*, which also stars actress Alia Bhatt.

● **2017** Stars in the action crime thriller, *Raees*, produced by Red Chillies Entertainment.

A RED CHILLIES FILM, *RAEES* WAS SHAH RUKH'S POPULAR RELEASE IN 2017

BAAZIGAR

1993

Introducing Shah Rukh Khan in his first role as an antihero, *Baazigar* shows the young Bollywood lead in a darker light, garnering both box office success and critical acclaim.

Abbas and Mustan's *Baazigar* (Gambler) is a riveting crime thriller that came at a time when Shah Rukh Khan (see pp. 214–15) was still a newcomer in the industry. *Baazigar* offered the actor the chance to stand out from the crowd by casting him in a new kind of lead—that of the antihero.

Playing a character who is both vicious and charming, Shah Rukh took on a role quite unlike the honorable, romantic heroes usually played by a Bollywood leading male. But the risk paid off. *Baazigar* scored a huge hit at the box office, earning Shah Rukh rave reviews and his first Filmfare Award. The film also paired Shah Rukh and Kajol for the first time, in an on-screen romance that would become a favorite among Bollywood audiences. Most notably, Shah Rukh's

character in *Baazigar* formed the template for the antihero persona that he would return to in subsequent films *Darr* (see p. 213) and *Anjaam* (1994).

A REVENGE DRAMA

Inspired by *A Kiss Before Dying* (1991), a British-American noir film, *Baazigar* is about a young man's obsession with bringing down business mogul Madan Chopra. Assuming a false identity, antihero Ajay sets about destroying everything dear to wealthy Chopra. He is prepared to go to any lengths

to achieve his ends. He cunningly defrauds Chopra and woos Chopra's daughter, Seema, and it is when he faces a choice between love and following through with his vendetta that his darker side emerges. This sets the film's tone as Ajay wreaks more havoc, breaking every moral code in the process so he can fulfill his ultimate aim. *Baazigar* isn't a typical "whodunit" thriller; the intrigue lies in what drives Ajay to carry out his brutal acts—the film keeps the audience guessing about his motives.

AN UNUSUAL FILM

If Ajay is an unusual hero, then *Baazigar* is an unusual film, which doesn't smooth over its lead's seamy side: his duplicitous nature, his simplistic world view, his murderous instinct. Ajay isn't just a cardboard cutout villain; he's a complex character—a dutiful son, a sensitive partner, and a ruthless rival.

With an unsympathetic lead, there was a high chance that the film might have bombed at the box office. However, *Baazigar* rewrote the rule book. Besides being the fourth-highest grossing film of that year, it garnered four Filmfare Awards. Like many Bollywood films, *Baazigar* straddles various genres—thriller, romantic drama, and a tearjerker—yet manages to emerge as an impressive, entertaining whole.

> ### HIT SONGS
>
> **Baazigar O Baazigar**
> (Gambler O Gambler)
>
> 🎤 **Singers** Kumar Sanu, Alka Yagnik
>
> **Yeh Kaali Kaali Aankhein**
> (Your Beautiful Dark Eyes)
>
> 🎤 **Singers** Kumar Sanu, Alka Yagnik

> "*Baazigar was a bold move for directors Abbas–Mustan.*"
>
> FIRSTPOST.COM, 2013

▼ **A tale of revenge**
Shah Rukh is an antihero who seeks revenge on a businessman by seducing his two daughters, played by Kajol (left) and Shilpa Shetty (right).

> ### CAST AND CREW
>
> ★ **Shah Rukh Khan** Ajay Sharma
> **Kajol** Priya
> **Shilpa Shetty** Seema
> **Raakhee** Ajay's mother
> **Dalip Tahil** Madan Chopra
>
> 🎬 **Directors** Abbas Burmawalla, Mustan Burmawalla
> 🎥 **Producer** Ganesh Jain
> 🎵 **Music composer** Anu Malik
> ✍ **Lyricists** Nawab Arzoo, Dev Kohli
> 💃 **Choreographer** Saroj Khan
> 📖 **Scriptwriters** Robin Bhatt, Akash Khurana, Javed Siddiqui
> 🎥 **Cinematographer** Thomas A. Xavier

ANDAZ APNA APNA

1994

A failure at the box office at the time of its release, *Andaz Apna Apna* has since grown to become a cult comedy classic, consistently impressing and amusing its audiences.

CAST AND CREW

★ **Aamir Khan** Amar
Salman Khan Prem
Raveena Tandon Karishma
Karisma Kapoor Raveena
Paresh Rawal Teja/Ram Gopal Bajaj
Shakti Kapoor Crime Master Gogo

▥ **Director** Rajkumar Santoshi
◠ **Producer** Vinay Kumar Sinha
♫ **Music composer** Tushar Bhatiah
♪ **Lyricist** Majrooh Sultanpuri
🏃 **Choreographer** Saroj Khan
▭ **Scriptwriters** Rajkumar Santoshi, Dilip Shukla
🎥 **Cinematographer** Ishwar Bidri
👕 **Costume designers** Ashley Rebello, Shagun, Anna Singh

When *Andaz Apna Apna* (Everyone Has Their Own Style) opened, it failed to attract audiences to the theater. This was possibly due to a lack of publicity; in some territories, the film was marketed via posters for only three days. And yet, more than two decades on, the film is regarded fondly, and has even attained cult status for its comic ingenuity.

SLACKER COMEDY

Andaz Apna Apna is about two slackers, Amar and Prem, who both have an ambition to get rich quick. Opportunity knocks when they learn that the rich heiress Raveen Bajaj is looking for a suitable husband. This sets off a comic chain of events as the pair compete against each other in a bid to woo her, both hoping to marry her and stake a claim in her fortune.

While many films of the 1980s and 1990s feature a subplot that adds comic relief to the main storyline, *Andaz Apna*

▲ **Heroes to the rescue**
When Karishma and Raveena are kidnapped by Gogo, the dimwitted heroes try to take charge of the situation, resulting in a comic standoff.

Apna is the exact opposite—the weighty subplot keeps the comic mayhem in check. Among the film's charms are its cast of well-drawn characters—the lazy buffoons Amar and Prem, the confused and harried female leads Raveena and Karishma, and the two inane henchmen Robert and Bhalla. All these characters are played to great effect by an eclectic cast of actors, and each of them makes an impression that stays with the audience long after the end credits.

A TRIBUTE TO BOLLYWOOD

Andaz Apna Apna is also an endearing tribute to the classics of Indian cinema and television. Many scenes make references to famous Hindi films, film characters, and hit TV series. Among

others, the film pays homage to Ramanand Sagar's *Ramayan* (1986), the character Mogambo from the film *Mr. India* (see pp. 188–91), the Spaghetti Western classic *Sholay* (see pp. 134–37), and the song "Papa Kehte Hain" (My Father Used to Say) from the hit movie *Qayamat Se Qayamat Tak* (see pp. 194–97). In addtion to the nonstop high jinks, *Andaz Apna Apna* offers Bollywood aficionados a delightful spot-the-reference game, which is perhaps another reason for the film's enduring appeal.

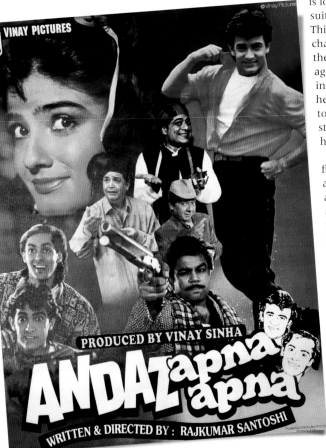

VINAY PICTURES
PRODUCED BY VINAY SINHA
ANDAZ apna apna
WRITTEN & DIRECTED BY : RAJKUMAR SANTOSHI

◀ **Ensemble cast**
The film's ensemble cast not only had Aamir and Salman sharing screen space for the first time, but also included comedy giants Deven Verma, Jagdeep, and Javed Khan.

PARESH RAWAL (b.1950)

Paresh Rawal made his Bollywood debut as a villain in the film *Arjun* (1985). For the next decade and a half, he played the villain in numerous films. In 2000, he was cast in a comic role in the hit comedy *Hera Pheri*, after which he began to be recognized as a comic actor. A recipient of the National Film Award, three Filmfare Awards, and a Padma Shri (the fourth highest civilian honor in India), Rawal is regarded as one of the most versatile actors in Hindi cinema today.

THE GREAT INDIAN
WEDDING

Bollywood moviegoers love a lavish, larger-than-life wedding scenario. It's the stuff of happy endings, a cause for celebration, and a backdrop for drama.

The vast majority of Hindi films reflect the conservative Indian obsession with getting youngsters married off, but the event of the wedding itself only became a major part of Bollywood screenplays during the 1990s. While films in the 1970s and 1980s reflected the anger in society, films in the 1990s increasingly targetted the aspirational, urban demographic as well as a successful Indian diaspora. These films celebrated nostalgia, identity, and tradition. The screen wedding gave plenty of opportunities for colorful costumes, lavish sets, song and dance, dramatic tension, and feel-good moments.

EXTRAVAGANT AFFAIRS

The game-changer was Rajshri Productions' hit *Hum Aapke Hain Koun..!* (*HAHK*, see pp. 220–21). The film followed the wedding of the lead pairs' siblings, with a song for every ceremony, be it the engagement or the bride's sisters hiding the groom's shoes, making regional rituals popular across the country. While critics called *HAHK* an extended wedding video, it became the first Hindi film to gross more than

◄ **Best-laid plans**
Yash Raj's *Band Baaja Baaraat* is the story of two wedding planners who innovate by offering this service to middle-class families of Delhi.

₹1 billion ($15.6 million dollars). It set a trend for traditional wedding extravaganzas that could be profitably distributed worldwide.

Rajshri Productions followed this up with *Hum Saath Saath hain* (1999) and *Vivah* (2006)—both with weddings as the focal point. Yash Raj Films' *Dilwale Dulhania le Jayenge* (see pp. 230–33) became one of Bollywood's top earners, and featured a love story set against the backdrop of the heroine's arranged marriage with the villain. An updated version of this trope was seen in the successful *Humpty Sharma ki Dulhania* (2014). Yash Raj also presented *Band Baja Baraat* (2010) and *Mere Brother ki Dulhan* (2011). Recently, half of *Ye Jawani hai Diwani* (see p.315), shot in a palatial hotel in Udaipur, and all of *Shaandaar*, (2015), shot in Yorkshire in the UK, were centered around the elite dream of destination weddings.

Many families now plan their weddings in imitation of the Bollywood ideal, regardless of whether their local customs include all those rituals or not. Smaller ceremonies traditionally held at home, like the sangeet (music) and mehendi (henna), have now become events, complete with DJs and designer dresses, thanks to Bollywood. Some films, like *Tanu Weds Manu* (see p. 305) and *Queen* (see pp. 320–21), have used the wedding to focus on the hidden rifts in family life, patriarchal traditions, and small-town aspirations.

"The big fat Bollywood wedding has become a trademark attraction of all that is Bollywood."

JYOTSNA KAPUR, *THE POLITICS OF TIME AND YOUTH IN BRAND INDIA,* 2013

HUM AAPKE HAIN KOUN..!

1994

A family favorite, the song-and-dance extravaganza *Hum Aapke Hain Koun..!* made the "big fat Indian wedding" and its related rituals fashionable all over again.

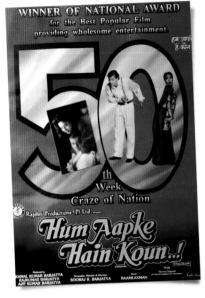

▲ **Breaking box office records**
This poster celebrates the phenomenal success of the film, marking its 50th week on the big screen.

There were many who doubted the prospects of success for *Hum Aapke Hain Koun..!* (Who Am I to You) before its release. The three-hour-plus film, popularly known as *HAHK*, contained little drama, no villains, and much family revelry. Jokingly described as "14 songs, two weddings, and a funeral," this idealized family film, promoting traditional Indian values, nevertheless confounded its critics as it struck an emotional chord with the audience. Although lacking a conventional plot or dramatic structure, it went on to become one of the most successful Hindi films ever made.

Hum Aapke Hain Koun..! is an opulent remake of Rajshri Production's earlier hit, *Nadiya ke Paar* (1982). The film traces the blossoming love story of Prem and Nisha, whose elder siblings, Rajesh and Pooja, get married amid much celebration by the two families. But then tragedy strikes and the young lovers must face a difficult decision.

It took director Sooraj Barjatya close to two years to write the script. He had the pressure of high expectations after the success of *Maine Pyar Kiya* (see p. 206). He initially began with a story on similar lines, but gave up after a few months, as it made little sense to repeat himself. It was his father and one of the film's producers, Rajkumar Barjatya, who suggested that he rework *Nadiya Ke Paar*. Initially hesitant about the lack of a villain and scarcity of drama, the director eventually came around, and was enthused by the time shooting began. He based every character and situation on what he had observed in his own family.

HAHK was the second of Barjatya's four projects with Salman Khan (see pp. 224–25), whose character was called Prem in all four films. Barjatya recalled in an interview that when he narrated the story of *HAHK* to Salman, the actor laughed and said that there was no specific hero or heroine. Everyone was the hero of the film. In fact, one of the strengths of the film is the depth of every character. The film also conveys a strong feeling of family bonds, and the romance of its younger couple provides the film with some of its most tender and heartwarming moments.

DRIVEN BY MUSIC
Like most Bollywood films, the music is crucial to *HAHK*. The songs work on multiple levels, moving the story forward, as well as exploring the various inter-character dynamics. It is said that Barjatya had more than 50 sittings with the composer,

◀ **The big Indian family**
The film revolves around a big, happy family—and the loose plot plays on the family members' relationships with each other.

CAST AND CREW

- ★ **Madhuri Dixit** Nisha
- **Salman Khan** Prem
- **Mohnish Bahl** Rajesh
- **Renuka Shahane** Pooja
- **Anupam Kher** Professor Choudhury
- **Reema Lagoo** Mrs. Choudhury
- **Alok Nath** Kailash Nath

- 🎬 **Director** Sooraj R. Barjatya
- 💧 **Producers** Kamal K. Barjatya, Rajkumar Barjatya, Ajit K. Barjatya
- 🎵 **Music composer** Raamlaxman
- 🎼 **Lyricists** Ravinder Rawal, Dev Kohli
- 🕺 **Choreographer** Jay Borade
- 📖 **Scriptwriters** Sooraj R. Barjatya, Keshav Prasad Mishra, S.M. Ahale
- 🎥 **Cinematographer** Rajan Kinagi

▶ A touch of romance
The pair of Salman Khan and Madhuri Dixit were praised for their on-screen chemistry as Prem and Nisha.

Raamlaxman, while writing the script, and it took the latter a good three months to record the songs. Barjatya narrated the script to his artists, including the songs. The soundtrack not only complements the film but also became the top-selling album of 1994. Even today, the film's songs continue to be an integral part of North Indian weddings. Actor–screenwriter Salim Khan (see pp. 138–39) suggested dropping two songs from the film. Barjatya agreed to do this, but later reinstated them after seeing audiences' positive response to the soundtrack.

A GRAND CELEBRATION
Barjatya recalls that at the premiere, while some industry insiders loved the film, many consoled him for having made a flop. The film was initially released with a limited number of prints, but its popularity grew and the film soon achieved a much wider distribution.

HAHK had great influence on mainstream Hindi cinema, and wedding songs and marriage rituals became a necessary element in succeeding films. In fact, people began recreating the film's wedding games and ceremonies at their own wedding. Some women also started to copy the outfits worn by Madhuri Dixit (see pp. 200–01).

The film won two National Awards—the Best Popular Film Providing Wholesome Entertainment, and Best Choreography. It also won five Filmfare Awards—Best Film, Best Director, Best Actress, Best Screenplay, and a Special Jury Award for singer Lata Mangeshkar (see pp. 60–61).

MADHURI'S ADMIRER
After the film, Madhuri found an admirer in celebrated painter, M.F. Hussain. He watched the film many times, and painted portraits of the actress in various moods and poses. He eventually went on to direct her in a film, *Gaja Gamini* (2000).

"A Hum Aapke Hain Koun..! comes once in a lifetime; every film cannot be a hit."

SOORAJ BARJATYA, 2012

STORYLINE

As two families come together with the wedding of their elder children, another love story develops between the younger siblings during the wedding rituals and ceremonies. However, in a tragic turn of events, the younger couple's marriage plans are put in jeopardy.

THE WEDDING CEREMONY

PLOT OVERVIEW

A MATCH FOR THE ELDER SON

❶ **Brothers Rajesh and Prem** live with their uncle Kailash Nath after their parents' death. Kailash Nath's friend's daughter, Pooja, is suggested as a match for the elder brother, Rajesh. Pooja and Rajesh like each other and get engaged ❷.

THE BIG FAT INDIAN WEDDING

Soon after, preparations begin for Rajesh and Pooja's wedding, which is conducted amid much fun and festivities. ❸ The younger siblings of the two, Prem and Nisha, keep coming across each other, and strike up a rapport. ❹ After the grand wedding, Pooja goes to Kailash Nath's household ❺.

TUFFY, THE FAMILY DOG

NEWS OF A GRANDCHILD

Pooja fits in beautifully at Kailash Nath's house, warming to the family. Soon after, Rajesh and Pooja announce they are expecting a baby ❻. Nisha represents her parents at Pooja's baby shower. Attracted to Nisha, Prem is thrilled at the prospect of her visiting.

YOUNG LOVE

❼ **Prem escorts Nisha** to the baby shower. They begin to experience the first flushes of love following their repeated encounters ❽. Like her sister, Nisha endears herself to Kailash Nath's family, bringing much liveliness into the proceedings. The baby shower is celebrated with much merriment ❾.

---

① · · ② · · · ③ · ④ · · · ⑤ · · ⑥ · · · ⑦ ⑧ · · · · ⑨

Hum Aapke Hain Koun (Title Song)
Singers: Lata Mangeshkar, S. P. Balasubrahmanyam
Picturized on Prem and Nisha

Wah Wah Ram Ji (All Praise the Lord)
Singers: Lata Mangeshkar, S. P. Balasubrahmanyam
Picturized on Pooja, Nisha, Rajesh, and Prem

Samdhi Samdhan (In-Laws)
Singers: Lata Mangeshkar, Kumar Sanu
Picturized on Kailash Nath and Mrs. Choudhury

Joote De Do, Paise Le Lo (Give Back the Shoes and Take the Money)
Singers: Lata Mangeshkar, S. P. Balasubrahmanyam
Picturized on Prem and Nisha

Baabul (Father)
Singers: Sharda Sinha
Picturized on Pooja, Nisha, Professor Choudhury, and Mrs. Choudhury

Dhiktana Dhiktana
Singer: S. P. Balasubrahmanyam
Picturized on Prem, Pooja, Rajesh, and the entire family

Yeh Mausam Ka Jadoo (Love Is in the Air)
Singers: Lata Mangeshkar, S. P. Balasubrahmanyam
Picturized on Prem and Nisha

Didi Tera Devar Deewana (Sister, Your Brother-In-Law Is Crazy)
Singer: Lata Mangeshkar, S. P. Balasubrahmanyam
Picturized on Nisha, Prem, and the family

Chocolate, Lime Juice
Singers: Lata Mangeshkar
Picturized on Nisha

THE TWO SISTERS

★ *The family makes a pilgrimage to Ram Tekri, where Nisha and Pooja meet the two brothers Prem and Rajesh.*

THE FAMILY SINGS AND CELEBRATES AT A PRE-WEDDING CEREMONY

> *"I just want to say that I'm a filmmaker because I witnessed Hum Aapke Hain Kaun."*

KARAN JOHAR, FILM DIRECTOR–PRODUCER

SOORAJ BARJATYA (b.1964)

Despite having made just six films in three decades, Sooraj R. Barjatya is widely regarded as one of the best filmmakers in Bollywood. Most of his films have been big box office successes and reflect a strong sense of Indian traditions, celebrating family values. All his heroes are called Prem (love). He produces his films under the Rajshri banner founded in 1947 by his grandfather, Tarachand Barjatya.

A GRANDSON AND HAPPY TIMES	BITTERSWEET PARTING	TWIST OF FATE	WEDDING BELLS
With Rajesh out of the country and Pooja's baby due any day, Nisha helps look after the household, particularly Prem. They declare their love for each other ❿. Pooja gives birth to a son. Her family, the Choudhurys, join in to celebrate the birth of their grandson ⓫ and Rajesh also returns from abroad.	⓬ **After all the celebrations**, the Choudhurys have to go back home ⓭.	**Accompanying Pooja to her parental home**, Prem confesses his love for Nisha. On reaching home, Pooja is pleasantly surprised to find that Nisha loves Prem, too ⓮. However, before things can move any further, Pooja has a terrible fall and dies.	**The families decide** that Nisha should marry Rajesh to take care of his baby. Both Prem and Nisha agree to sacrifice their love. On the day of the wedding, Rajesh learns about Prem and Nisha's love for each other and steps aside. Prem and Nisha get married.

Pehla Pehla Pyar Hai (First Love)
Singer: S. P. Balasubrahmanyam
Picturized on Nisha and Prem

Dhiktana Dhiktana
Singers: S. P. Balasubrahmanyam, Lata Mangeshkar, Udit Narayan, Shailendra Singh
Picturized on Prem, Nisha and the family

Mujhse Juda Hokar
Singers: Lata Mangeshkar, S. P. Balasubrahmanyam
Picturized on Nisha and Prem

Maye Ni Maye (O Mother)
Singer: Lata Mangeshkar
Picturized on Nisha and the family

Lo Chali Main (Here I Go)
Singer: Lata Mangeshkar
Picturized on Pooja

MADHURI IN HER PURPLE SARI

LOVE WINS IN THE END

PREM AND NISHA CONFESS THEIR LOVE FOR EACH OTHER

SALMAN KHAN

ACTOR b.1965

Bollywood's very own *enfant terrible*, Salman Khan is the quintessential hero with his handsome looks, muscular physique, and charismatic attitude.

◄ **The superstar**
Salman Khan's portrayal of the crooked yet affable police inspector in *Dabangg* was a hit with the masses.

One of India's biggest superstars, Salman Khan has appeared in more than 80 films in a career that spans more than three decades. A huge presence in India, as well as among the Indian diaspora worldwide, Salman presents many different faces to the world—actor, dancer, singer, TV show host, and painter.

Born Abdul Rashid Salim Salman Khan in 1965 in the small town of Indore, Madhya Pradesh, Salman is the eldest son of reputed screenwriter Salim Khan (see pp. 138–39) and his first wife Salma. He went to high school in Bandra, an upscale suburb of Mumbai, but dropped out of his tertiary studies at St. Xavier's College.

BELOVED HERO

Coming from an illustrious film family, Salman always had good prospects in the movie business, but it was his film-star persona—a potent combination of bad-boy antics on-screen and stories of his benevolent nature in real life—that has made him a true superstar in the industry. Whether he is playing a romantic hero, as he does in *Saajan*, an action man as in the 1995 film *Karan Arjun* (see p. 236), or the warm-hearted simpleton of *Bajrangi Bhaijaan* (see p.326), Khan continues to be an object of hysteria

for his die-hard fans. With his body-builder physique, eye-popping dance style, and instant audience appeal, he is omnipresent in cinema blockbusters, pop videos, and at award ceremonies. His looks are often in the news, too: in 2004, *People* magazine voted him the seventh-best-looking man in the world.

A FLYING START

Salman made his debut in a supporting role in *Biwi Ho To Aisi* (1988). Within a year, director Sooraj Barjatya chose him to play the lead role in *Maine Pyar Kiya*. The story, about two friends who fall in love, not only brought him his first Filmfare nomination for Best Actor, but also created his most famous and loved on-screen character—Prem. In time Prem would become Salman's alter ego, the endearing boy next door.

More success followed in the early 1990s with a major role in *Hum Aapke Hain Koun..!* The film, a romance story set against the backdrop of a big Indian family, was rooted in traditional values and broke all box office records. Films such as the 1994 comedy *Andaz Apna Apna* (see p. 217), romantic drama *Saajan*, and action thriller *Karan Arjun* were commercial hits, but otherwise the decade was a washout. A poor selection of scripts, and films that just didn't spark at the box office, saw

> *"The kind of control he has today on his emotions, his projection, he literally flirts with the camera."*

DIRECTOR SOORAJ BARJATYA ON SALMAN KHAN, THE TIMES OF INDIA, 2015

▲ **Grooving along**
Salman's song and dance routines are always a hit with audiences, as in this scene from *Karan Arjun* where he can be seen on the right.

Salman's standing in the film industry drop; out of the 29 films he acted in during this time, only 11 received any critical or popular recognition.

By the late 1990s, Salman was moving back to center stage. In 1996, he played a musician in *Khamoshi*, directed by Sanjay Leela Bhansali. Although it was critically acclaimed, the film was not a commercial success. However, in 1999 Salman made another film with Bhansali, which was a big hit and cemented the actor's romance hero image—*Hum Dil de Chuke Sanam* (see pp. 256–57). Around this time, Salman embarked on a relationship with actress Aishwarya Rai, his co-star in *Hum Dil De Chuke Sanam*. Their high-profile relationship was subject to a frenzy of media speculation as the pair's sensual chemistry sizzled on-screen.

In 2003, Salman gave a tour-de-force performance in the multiple-award-winning film *Tere Naam*, directed by Satish Kaushik. Salman played the role of Radhe Mohan, an obsessed lover prone to violence who loses his

KEY WORKS

Maine Pyar Kiya, 1989 (see p. 206)
Saajan, 1991
Hum Aapke Hain Koun..!, 1994 (see pp. 220–23)
Tere Naam, 2003
Dabangg, 2010 (see p. 304)
Bajrangi Bhaijaan, 2015 (see p. 326)

mind and ends up in a mental asylum. Kaushik was impressed with Salman, too. In an interview with Indian newspaper *The Times of India*, he said, "As an actor he had real guts to take up the challenge of such an unconventional role." Salman himself took an uncomplicated view of his

▲ **The tough guy**
Later in his career, Salman went on to acting in action dramas like *Ek Tha Tiger* and *Wanted*—playing the good guy who beats up villians.

acting: "On-screen, I am like I am in real life … For me, acting comes straight from the heart … I think that to feel the character's pain I have to be myself. Somewhere audiences see that."

During this time, Salman also got back into the comedy-hero mold. His roles in films such as *Mujhse Shaadi Karogi* (2004), *No Entry* (2005), and *Partner*

▶ **Double the romance**
Starring as both Prince Vijay and his lookalike, actor Prem Dilwale, Salman woos Princess Maithili (Sonam Kapoor) in *Prem Ratan Dhan Payo* (2015), a romance of mixed-up identities.

(2007) tickled audiences with their borderline slapstick humor, proving that he is one of the few actors who can straddle the genres of comedy and action with equal panache.

ACTION-HERO AVATAR
The film *Dabangg* (see p.304) marked a shift in Salman's on-screen persona. A comic-book mix of romance, comedy, and action-hero antics, the film displayed his complete catalogue of skills. The character of Chulbul Pandey, the khaki-clad, black-aviator-toting, corrupt cop with a heart of gold, has been etched in the public imagination.

Perhaps surprisingly, the character of a rustic simpleton has become one of Salman's trademarks in his films since *Dabangg*: *Bodyguard*, *Dabangg 2*, *Kick*, and *Sultan* (2016) were all blockbusters.

A man of many talents, Salman's popularity with audiences of all ages led him, perhaps inevitably, to try his hand at television. He hosted a popular game show in 2008, and went on to host the *Big Boss* India in 2010.

HERO IN REAL LIFE
Many stories abound of Salman's philanthropy. In 2007, he founded the Being Human foundation, which runs multiple projects working with the poor and underprivileged in India. It helps supply healthcare and surgery programs for children, provides training and opportunities for the less abled, and supports the education of street and slum children in Mumbai. Salman uses his immense pull as a superstar to further the charitable causes of his foundation.

TIMELINE

December 27, 1965 Born as Abdul Rashid Salim Salman Khan.

1988 Makes his debut in the film *Biwi Ho To Aisi*.

1989 Has his first hit as the romantic hero Prem in *Maine Pyar Kiya*.

1994 His second film with Sooraj Barjatya, *Hum Aapke Hain Koun..!* breaks box office records.

1998 First appearance of the trademark shirtless Salman Khan in the hit song "O O Jaane Jaana" (Oh Darling) in *Pyaar Kiya To Darna Kya*.

THE 1998 *HUM SAATH-SAATH HAIN* WAS A FAMILY ENTERTAINER.

1998 Has a brush with the law, which results in a rocky period in his career and leads to intense media scrutiny of his personal life.

2003 *Tere Naam* is a hit, revives Salman's career, and restores the confidence of his producers and distributors.

2007 Launches Being Human—A Salman Khan Foundation charity to help the underprivileged children of India.

2008 Makes his television debut by playing host in two seasons of the game show *10 Ka Dum* (The Power of 10).

2010 Cast as the host for four seasons of the television show *Big Boss* India.

2011 Launches his own production company Salman Khan Being Human (SKBH) Productions.

2011 Children's film *Chillar Party* from SKBH Productions wins the National Film Award for Best Children's Film.

2012 Paired with actress Katrina Kaif in the action-packed, espionage adventure *Ek Tha Tiger*.

2015 *Bajrangi Bhaijaan* wins the National Film Award for Best Popular Film Providing Wholesome Family Entertainment.

2016 Plays a middle-aged, ex-wrestling champion in *Sultan*, another blockbuster action drama hit.

RANGEELA

1995

Set in the glitzy world of Mumbai's film industry, *Rangeela*
is a box office blockbuster that worked its magic to rocket
its director and leading lady to stardom.

This easy-on-the-eye romantic comedy was something of a departure for Telugu film director Ram Gopal Varma, who began his career with a string of adventure and action movies. *Rangeela* (Colorful), along with its original score and soundtrack, turned out to be his first major success in Bollywood.

DIRECTOR AND HIS MUSE

Varma wrote the script for *Rangeela* himself, and the film's storyline reflects his fascination with a particular star of Bollywood. He created the character of Mili Joshi, a chorus-line dancer trying to achieve stardom in the film industry, echoing his infatuation with the beauty of the leading lady, Urmila Matondkar. Life mirrored art, and Urmila became an overnight superstar thanks in part to a director who paid homage to her incredible good looks in every shot. Right from the opening dance sequence in the film, Mili dazzles, showing off her moves in front of a variety of dancers dressed as judo students, schoolchildren, and even soldiers with AK-47 rifles.
In the film, Mili lives with her parents and younger brother in the suburbs of Mumbai and spends her days as an extra on film sets, watching and waiting for a chance to slip into a leading role. An opportunity presents itself when Gulbadan, a leading lady from a movie

being filmed, runs off to marry her chauffeur. Mili, dancing like a siren on the beach, is spotted by the film's lead actor, Raj Kamal, who arranges for her to be auditioned for the role of the heroine. Overcoming a disastrous audition with the help of her friend Munna, Mili is soon on her way to stardom. However, dazzled by the glitz and glamour of the film industry, she fails to notice that both men, Raj and Munna, have fallen in love with her.

FROM REAL TO REEL

A love triangle and a rags-to-riches storyline may not win prizes for originality in Bollywood, but *Rangeela*'s great cinematography lifts it above the ordinary. Just as the Hollywood blockbuster *La La Land* (2016) drew on the magic of Tinseltown, *Rangeela* springs to life against the backdrop of Mumbai's film industry.
The title "Rangeela" serves the real film and the fictional film that catapults Mili to stardom, and much of the film's humor springs from this duality, through parodies and vignettes. Film buffs have spotted that the leading lady Gulbadan, played by

▲ **Striking the right note**
Kitschy and brightly colored to reflect the title of the film—"rangeela" means "colorful"—this poster features the film's lead actors.

Shefali Shetty, and her dominating mother, are an echo of real-life actress Sridevi (see pp. 204–205), who was often accompanied on set by her business-manager mother in the 1980s. The aspirational but tortured director, Steven Kapoor, appears to

◀ **The siren**
Stylish and stunningly beautiful, Urmila Matondkar combines sensuous dance moves with a touch of innocence in her role as Mili, the ingénue who rises to stardom.

RAM GOPAL VARMA (b.1962)

Born in Hyderabad, Ram Gopal Varma became the first filmmaker from southern India to carve a path in Hindi films. A film buff who studied engineering, Varma rose from being a video store owner to a leading film director, starting out in the Telugu film industry. *Shiva* (1990), his debut action thriller, was followed by a string of adventure films and crime dramas, which included *Gaayam* (1993), a violent political drama, and *Satya* (see p. 241), a crime epic based on Mumbai's underworld. The first installment of a trilogy, *Satya* is regarded as Varma's masterwork. Subsequent films such as *Company* (2002) and *Sarkar* (2005) established him as the inventor of "Mumbai noir"—a genre of gritty, realistic films with psychological depth.

CAST AND CREW

★ **Jackie Shroff** Raj Kamal
Aamir Khan Munna
Urmila Matondkar Mili Joshi
Shefali Shetty Gulbadan
Avtar Gill P.C.
Gulshan Grover Steven Kapoor

🎬 **Director** Ram Gopal Varma
🗄 **Producer** Ram Gopal Varma
🎵 **Music composer** A.R. Rahman
🖊 **Lyricist** Mehboob
🕺 **Choreographers** Ahmed Khan,
Saroj Khan
📖 **Scriptwriter** Ram Gopal Varma
🎥 **Cinematographer** W.B. Rao
🧵 **Costume designers** Manish
Malhotra, Shaahid Amir

"One of my primary motives in Rangeela *was to capture Urmila's beauty eternally on camera.*"

RAM GOPAL VARMA, DIRECTOR, *DECCAN CHRONICLE*, 2017

Unshaven and wearing a leather cap and black string vest, Aamir dressed himself to play the orphan, picking up ideas from kids on the street. Raised in Mumbai, delivering the film's dialogue came naturally to him.

Munna's comic performance in a five-star hotel as he tries to keep pace with Mili's success is one of the high points of the film. His struggle to confess his true feelings for Mili adds poignancy to the plot. Munna acts as a counterpoint to the suave, well-dressed Kamal, who takes center stage in Mili's cinematic love scenes.

CROWNING ACHIEVEMENT

The film's soundtrack of seven songs, including an instrumental theme song, won the Filmfare Best Music Award in 1995. It was the first original Hindi film score by A.R. Rahman (see pp. 244–45), and he went on to compose some of Hindi cinema's greatest music, as well as picking up two Oscars for the 2008 British film *Slumdog Millionaire*. Lyricist Mehboob and the legendary playback

demand Spielbergian levels of respect in the film. Penny-pinching producer P.C. trades on comic pessimism, while cinematographer W.B. Rao gives a Hitchcock-like cameo appearance.

BIRTH OF A STAR

Rangeela worked its magic for many of those involved in the production. Aamir Khan (see pp. 228–29) plays the character of Munna, an orphan close to Mili's family who grows up to become a hot-headed ticket scalper. The role was a career-changer for Aamir, who had become typecast as a romantic hero in earlier productions.

▼ **Playing the part**
Aamir Khan grooves with a troupe of junior artists, posing as Mumbai's gangsters, in the dance sequence "Mangta Hai Kya" (What Do You Want?).

▶ **Sizzling chemistry**
Aamir Khan romances Urmila's character, working hard to profess his love for her. Sensual and graceful, their dance sequences set the screen on fire.

singer Asha Bhosle also received Filmfare Awards for "Tanha Tanha Yahan Pe Jeena," which along with "Rangeela Re" became mainstream hits. Ahmed Khan was awarded a Filmfare Award for Best Choreography.

Fashion designer Manish Malhotra, another of *Rangeela*'s award winners, became successful in the fashion industry despite receiving criticism for Urmila's revealing outfits. An early critic even suggested that "this movie will survive on the lack of Urmila's clothes." The image of Mili dancing on the beach in a succession of tantalizing costumes endures, yet Urmila went on to prove that she is far more than a babe on a beach; starring in a string of award-winning films that included psychological dramas and crime thrillers.

HIT SONGS

Rangeela Re
(Let's Be Colorful Together)
🎤 **Singers** Asha Bhosle,
Aditya Narayan

Hai Rama
(Oh, Lord)
🎤 **Singers** Hariharan, Swarnalatha

Tanha Tanha Yahan Pe Jeena
(Living Here in Utter Solitude)
🎤 **Singer** Asha Bhosle

AAMIR KHAN

ACTOR–PRODUCER b.1965

A versatile actor, courageous producer, innovative director, and social activist, Aamir Khan has been pushing the boundaries of Bollywood in a career spanning 30 years.

Aamir Khan was born into the world of Indian cinema—interviewed in 2016, he said, "I grew up with films being made around me." His father was the film producer Tahir Hussain, who, despite some successes, struggled financially and discouraged his son from following in his footsteps. But Khan developed his own passion for theater and film—he first appeared on screen at the age of eight, in the 1973 film *Yaadon ki Baaraat*, directed by his uncle Nasir Hussain. While a student, Khan worked as a stagehand at the National Center for the Performing Arts in Mumbai, watching and learning from actors during rehearsals. After small theater roles in the city, the 19-year-old Khan had his first screen performance in *Holi* (1984), a coming-of-age-drama.

▲ **Heartthrob role**
Initially typecast as a handsome "chocolate hero," Khan excelled in his portrayal of an aimless college cruiser turned responsible sportsperson in *Jo Jeeta Wohi Sikander*.

Nasir, keen to launch his son, Mansoor, as a film director and his nephew as an actor, came up with a vehicle to accomplish this in one go: a romance called *Qayamat se Qayamat tak,* inspired by William Shakespeare's play *Romeo and Juliet*. "I was doubtful and worried about how Aamir would face the camera especially for the song sequence and other flamboyant scenes," recalled Mansoor on the film's 25th anniversary. "I always knew him as this very shy and quiet cousin of mine." But the film's fresh, young appeal and hit soundtrack made it the biggest film of 1988, establishing Khan as a "chocolate boy" heartthrob with a Filmfare Best Debut Award.

By the turn of the century, Khan was an established leading man with a string of commercial hits behind him, such as the romance drama *Dil* (1990), *Raja Hindustani* (see p. 237), and *Sarfarosh* (see p. 250). He also wrote the screenplay for his own comedy-drama, *Hum Hain Rahi Pyar ke* (1993).

KEY WORKS

Qayamat se Qayamat tak, 1988 (see pp. 194–97)

Jo Jeeta Wohi Sikandar, 1992 (see p. 212)

Lagaan, 2001 (see pp. 266–69)

Dil Chahta hai, 2001 (see pp. 264–65)

Rang de Basanti, 2006 (see p. 288)

Taare Zameen par, 2007 (see p. 296)

Ghajini, 2008

3 Idiots, 2009 (see pp. 302–303)

Dhobi Ghat, 2011

PK, 2014 (see pp. 324–25)

Dangal, 2016 (see p. 331)

BOWLING A GOOGLY

In the late 1990s, Khan came up with an unconventional film project: a period drama about cricket. Producers weren't prepared to fund it without major changes, so Khan set up his own production company, Aamir Khan Productions. "When I did *Lagaan*, everyone said sports films wouldn't work in India, period films wouldn't work in India … I was saying, 'It may be a disaster, but I just love it and I want to do it'," he later commented.

Lagaan established Khan as an innovative force in Bollywood. One of the biggest hits of 2001, the film won a National Award, an Oscar nomination for Best Foreign Film, and international acclaim as the first serious bid to bridge the gap between Bollywood and Western films. *Time* magazine ranked *Lagaan* as one of its 25 All-Time Best Sports Movies. Khan's image as an innovator was bolstered still further by his role in *Dil Chahta hai* (2001), a sleek and stylish film directed by

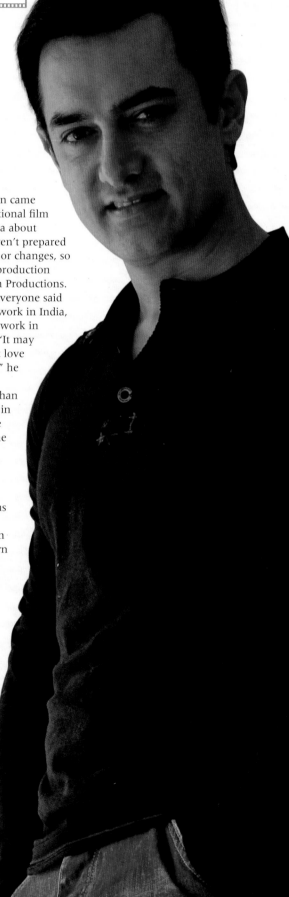

▶ **Style and substance**
A talented and intelligent actor, Khan has starred in many popular films across the genres, from comedies to social dramas.

◄ Motivation
Drawn to a film's message, rather than its box office viability, Khan took on *Rang de Basanti*, despite the number of films already made about the freedom fighter Bhagat Singh.

par. The film, about a boy with dyslexia, helped to raise awareness of the condition in India.

BREAKING RECORDS
Khan has received eight Filmfare Awards but remains sceptical about the value of Indian film awards, refusing to attend acceptance ceremonies. With a reputation as a "perfectionist," he makes just one film a year or every two years, in a variety of roles and genres. The result has been box office records for some of the highest-grossing Bollywood films: the action-packed *Ghajini*; the hilarious *3 Idiots*; the fast-paced *Dhoom 3* (2013); the satire *PK*, and the sports biopic *Dangal*. However, Khan maintains, "I do not believe that I am a perfectionist … perfection is something no one can achieve."

Farhan Akhtar (see p. 264) and aimed specifically at young urban audiences.

In 2001, despite professional highs, Khan's life was beset with personal problems. In October, he and his wife of 16 years, Reena, separated and filed for divorce, with Reena taking custody of their two children. "I didn't even work for almost two years as I was coping with it," said Khan.

At the end of 2005, he married Kiran Rao, an assistant director. In the same year, he rebooted his career with *Mangal Pandey* (2005), based on the true story of the Indian soldier who started the Indian rebellion of 1857.

FIGHTING FOR A CAUSE
In 2006, Khan had a big hit with *Rang de Basanti*, a film with an anti-corruption message that spurred public debate about how young Indians should challenge social injustice. Khan himself became more engaged in social activism, joining the protest against the displacement of local people caused by the Gujarat government's Narmada Dam project. The Gujarat government condemned Khan's comments, demanding an apology from him, but he refused to give it. His 2006 film *Fanaa* met with protests and an unofficial statewide ban

as a result. India's prime minister at the time, Manmohan Singh, spoke in Khan's defense, saying: "Everyone has the freedom of expression. If someone says something … that doesn't mean you should start protesting."

Khan later produced *Peepli Live* (2010), a satirical film about the media's coverage of suicides among farmers. He also hosted an acclaimed TV series, *Satyameva Jayate* (Truth Alone Triumphs), which began in 2012, drawing attention to social issues, such as female feticide. Khan's directorial debut came in 2007 with the award-winning *Taare Zameen*

► Hit men
Khan attributes much of his success as an actor to his vision as a director. He is shown here on the *PK* set with Raj Kumar Hirani, who also directed him in *3 Idiots*—both hit films.

> *"I give my failures as much importance as my success."*
>
> **AAMIR KHAN**

- **March 14, 1965** Born in Mumbai to parents Tahir and Zeenat Hussain.

- **1973** First appearance on screen at age eight in *Yaadon ki Baaraat*.

KHAN'S FIRST FILM ROLE LASTED A LITTLE LONGER THAN THE DURATION OF A SONG

- **1984** Debuts playing a rebel student in Ketan Metan's experimental film *Holi*.

- **1986** Marries his childhood sweetheart, Reena Dutta, against her parents' wishes.

- **1988** Launches full-time acting career with *Qayamat se Qayamat tak*.

- **2001** *Lagaan* premieres in Bhuj, Gujarat, where it was filmed, before its worldwide release.

- **2002** Khan and Reena Dutta file for divorce by mutual consent; she takes custody of their children.

- **2003** Awarded the Padma Shri—the fourth-highest civilian award—for services to Indian cinema.

- **2005** Marries 32-year-old Kiran Rao, assistant director on *Lagaan*.

- **2006** Begins a career resurgence with hit film *Rang de Basanti*.

- **2007** Makes his award-winning directorial debut with *Taare Zameen par*.

- **2008** Action drama *Ghajini* breaks box-office records for highest-grossing film.

- **February 2, 2010** Father, Tahir Hussain, passes away after a heart attack.

- **2012** Hosts first season of reality TV show *Satyameva Jayate* about social problems in India.

- **2016** Aamir Khan Productions' *Dangal* sets a new box-office record for highest-grossing film.

DILWALE DULHANIA LE JAYENGE

1995

A quintessentially romantic film that perfectly blends the values of East and West, *Dilwale Dulhania le Jayenge* became the longest-running Indian film of all time.

CAST AND CREW

★ **Shah Rukh Khan** Raj Malhotra
Kajol Simran Singh
Amrish Puri Baldev Singh
Farida Jalal Lajwanti "Lajjo" Singh
Anupam Kher Dharamvir Malhotra
Satish Shah Ajit Singh
Parmeet Sethi Kuljeet Singh

🎬 **Director** Aditya Chopra
◻ **Producer** Yash Chopra
🎵 **Music** Jatin-Lalit
🎼 **Lyrics** Anand Bakshi
🕺 **Choreography** Saroj Khan
📖 **Scriptwriters** Aditya Chopra, Javed Siddiqui
📷 **Cinematographer** Manmohan Singh
👗 **Costume** Anaita Shroff Adajania

Dilwale Dulhania le Jayenge, (The Brave-Hearted Will Whisk Away the Bride), known as *DDLJ*, marks the spectacular directorial debut of Aditya Chopra. The film is about a romance between a fun-loving boy, Raj, and a traditional Punjabi girl, Simran, both living in London, who meet on a train trip through Europe with their friends. When Simran's loving but stern father finds out about her affair, he is furious and decides to immediately move back to Punjab, India, where he promised Simran to his best friend's son, Kuljeet, almost 20 years ago.

CASTING THE LEAD PAIR
A romantic film needs perfect on-screen chemistry between the hero and heroine. In this regard, *DDLJ* has the ideal lead pair playing Raj and Simran. Kajol was always Chopra's first choice for Simran, and even though she initially had doubts about portraying a character far more submissive than herself, it was Shah Rukh Khan (see pp. 214–15) who dillydallied and took his time to sign on the dotted line. Having made offbeat choices early in his career, when he played an obsessive lover and antihero in a series of successful films,

▼ **Classic Bollywood**
Raj and Simran dramatically declare their love in a beautiful mustard field in Punjab. The scene is one of the most memorable moments in Hindi cinema.

> ## "It's a flawed, contradictory movie—aggressive and tender, stiff and graceful, clichéd and fresh … It's also, I think, a classic."

CHARLES TAYLOR, REVIEWER, SALON, 2004

he was uncertain about taking on the role of a lovable, romantic hero. Fortunately, for him and the film, he ultimately agreed. *DDLJ* proved to be a career-defining role for Shah Rukh, playing the perfect son and ideal lover, and it gained him a legion of female fans of all ages.

MODERN YET TRADITIONAL
The film has all elements of a typical Bollywood film, especially its expounding of Indian values, so much so it is considered very "Indian." It is therefore ironic that the film has Non-Resident Indians (NRIs) living in the UK as its major characters.

▲ A touch of simplicity
Shah Rukh Khan's black hat with a simple feather was loved by the youngsters for its freshness.

DDLJ takes a rather sanitized look at Indians abroad; for while these people might be modern on the outside, their values are intrinsically traditional. The film gives the Indian diaspora a perfectly romanticized vision of their own lives, at the same time reflecting their nostalgia for a country and culture they have left behind.

The film gave its audiences new hope and new tropes. In Chopra's tale, unlike most regular love stories of the time where rebellious young lovers elope, Raj follows Simran all the way to Punjab to seek her father's consent to marry her. Raj is the sort of man who might flirt with Simran, but would never take sexual advantage of her, even when they are stranded together alone in the middle of nowhere. Through Raj's character, Chopra reinforces his message by portraying him as someone who, despite being modern, is entrenched in Indian values.

The contemporary look and feel notwithstanding, for many, the film was steeped in traditional stereotypes that surround women. For instance, despite

living in London, Simran's father has already promised her hand in marriage to a man of his choice, just like many traditional arranged marriage setups in India. Even Simran's mother and her confidante, reminds Simran of the perils of dreaming of a free life. But while such issues are raised in the film, Chopra ultimately plays safe by adhering to the status quo of mainstream Hindi cinema's conventional treatment of women, and ensures that he ends up with a rose-tinted love story.

TRENDSETTER
DDLJ has now become a part of Hindi cinema lore because of its memorable scenes, hit songs, clever script, and stylish costumes. The famous scene where Simran runs to catch up with Raj on a moving train or the "Bade bade deshon mein aisi chhoti chhoti baatein hoti rehti hain" (In large countries, such small incidents keep happening) sequence impressed the audiences immensely. Chopra's skill in balancing the film's first half, set in modern Europe, and the second half set in rustic Punjab is also noteworthy.

Along with *Hum Aapke Hain Koun..!* (see pp. 220–23), *DDLJ* shaped the language of mainstream Hindi cinema through the 1990s, especially when it came to romance and family. The film's influence can be seen in many later films, which have tried in vain to recapture its magic.

SUCCESS ABROAD AND AT HOME
Most importantly, *DDLJ* opened up a huge, viable overseas market for Bollywood films among the Indian diaspora the world over. In India,

it had a historic run at the box office and the film continues to be screened for well over 1,000 weeks at the Maratha Mandir cinema in Mumbai. The film had an unforgettable tagline "Come … Fall in Love," which made audiences, especially the young, flock to the cinemas in huge numbers.

Besides winning the National Award for Best Film Providing Wholesome Entertainment, *DDLJ* also bagged an astonishing 10 Filmfare Awards— setting a record at that time for the most Filmfare trophies won by a single film. *Dilwale Dulhania le Jayenge* is one

▲ A romance to remember
The love story of Raj and Simran not only conquered the hearts of millions of people but also took romance to new heights.

of the biggest Bollywood hits ever. It has been referenced in many other productions over the decades since its release, including the films *Bachna Ae Haseeno* (2008) and *Humpty Sharma ki Dulhania* (2014)— largely because of its epic success, youthful freshness, as well as its international appeal.

KAJOL (b.1974)

Kajol follows in the footsteps of her grandmother Shobana Samarth, her great aunt Nalini Jaywant, her aunt Nutan, and mother Tanuja—all fine performers in their own right. Born in Mumbai, she made her acting debut in 1992, breaking through the following year with *Baazigar* (see p. 216). Kajol established herself as a leading actress in Hindi cinema with her brilliant performances in films such as *Gupt: The Hidden Truth* (1997), *Pyaar Kiya Toh Darna Kya* (1998), *Kuch Kuch Hota Hai* (see pp. 246–47), *Fanaa* (2006), and *My Name is Khan* (2010). In 2011, she was awarded the Padma Shri, the fourth-highest civilian award in India.

STORYLINE

This boy-meets-girl story features a rich, party-going young man and a simple, middle-class girl who fall in love. Set against picturesque European locations, the two embark on a train trip. Gradually Raj and Simran discover a deep love, only for it to be torn apart by an overbearing father who is steeped in tradition.

RAJ AND SIMRAN
ON THEIR EUROPEAN TRIP

PLOT OVERVIEW

A HOME AWAY FROM HOME

To give his family a better life, Baldev Singh moved from Punjab to England, making his home in London **1**. However, he still yearns for his homeland and feels very much an outsider in England. Baldev and his wife, Lajwanti, have brought up their two daughters, Simran and Rajeshwari, with strong, traditional Indian values. But the eldest daughter Simran dreams of breaking free **2**.

A CLASH OF CULTURES

In the meantime, a spoiled, rich Indian boy shoplifts beer from Baldev's store. Furious at this misdemeanor, the encounter reinforces Baldev's dislike for Indians who forget their roots and culture, especially the young ones who fail to respect their elders.

A LAST HOLIDAY

Unknown to Simran, her father fixed her marriage almost 20 years ago to his best friend's son, Kuljeet, back in Punjab. Simran dejectedly accepts her fate, but wants to go on one last trip to Europe with her friends to enjoy what remains of her single life. Reluctantly, Baldev lets her go.

FALLING IN LOVE

Simran nearly misses her train, and Raj gives her a helping hand onto the moving car. Right from their first meeting, Raj flirts continually with Simran, though she finds him overbearing and self-centered **3**. Fate pushes them together when they miss their train to Zurich and are separated from their friends **4**. While they are trying to catch up with their group, Raj and Simran find they are drawn to each other. By the time the trip is over and they have to part ways in London, they realize they are head over heels in love **5**.

THE SONGS

Ghar Aaja Pardesi
(Come Home, O Foreigner)
*Singer: Manpreet Kaur,
Pamela Chopra*
Picturized on Baldev Singh

Mere Khwaabon Mein Jo Aaye
(The One Who Comes Into
My Dreams)
Singer: Lata Mangeshkar
Picturized on Simran and Raj

Ruk Ja Oh Dil Diwane
(Stop, O Mad Heart)
*Singer: Udit Narayan,
Asha Bhosle*
*Picturized on Raj
and Simran*

Ho Gaya Hai Tujhko Toh Pyar
(You Have Fallen in Love)
Singer: Udit Narayan
Picturized on Raj and Simran

Zara Sa Jhoom Lun Main
(Shall I Dance a Little Bit More?)
Singer: Asha Bhosle, Abhijeet Bhattacharya
Picturized on Raj and Simran

SIMRAN DANCES FOR
RAJ IN THE SNOW

"A bunch of young people came together to make a special film."

SHAH RUKH KHAN, FILMFARE, 2015

ADITYA CHOPRA (b.1971)

Few filmmakers have had the kind of directorial debut that Aditya Chopra had. Filmmaker Yash Chopra's son, Aditya Chopra began his cinematic journey by assisting his father and went on to direct *DDLJ* (1995), *Mohabbatein* (2000), *Rab Ne Bana Di Jodi* (2008), and *Befikre* (2016). He has transformed his father's company, Yashraj Films, into the premier filmmaking and distribution company in India today. Yashraj Films has been involved with some of the biggest Bollywood films of recent years.

THE CHARMING RAJ MALHOTRA

BACK TO INDIA

On her return, Simran's head is full of Raj and her memories of the trip. Baldev overhears Simran confessing her love for Raj to her mother and is furious. He decides to take the entire family back to India immediately and get Simran married off to Kuljeet. Raj, too, realizes his deep love, and comes to Simran's house only to find that the family has left. He decides to follow Simran to India. ❻

THE MARRIAGE IS ARRANGED

A happy Baldev is reunited with his friend and relatives in India, though Simran is miserable, upset by her parents' order that she forget Raj. To her surprise, Raj turns up at her house ❼. Simran asks Raj to elope with her, but Raj insists he will only marry her with her father's consent, which looks unlikely. Without explaining who he is, Raj endears himself to everyone, including Kuljeet. Simran gets engaged to Kuljeet ❽, but she tries various ways to avoid her fiancé, and spends time with Raj in secret.

SIMRAN PARTICIPATES IN THE HINDU RITUALS OF SEEING THROUGH A SIEVE AT KARVA CHAUTH

LOVE TRIUMPHS

As the secret of Raj's true identity is revealed, he makes a last-ditch effort and confesses his love for Simran. Baldev, however, remains adamant and tells Raj to leave. A fuming Kuljeet follows Raj to the station with his friends and beats up Raj. Baldev reaches the station and stops the fight. Simran arrives with her mother and is in tears as she sees her beloved leaving. As the train with Raj aboard starts moving, Simran begs her father to let her go with him. Realizing that no one could love his daughter more than Raj, he relents and lets her go.

❻   ❼   ❽

Tujhe Dekha Toh Ye Jaana Sanam
(The Moment I Saw You, I Knew Love)
Singers: Lata Mangeshkar, Kumar Sanu
Picturized on Raj and Simran

Mehndi Laga Ke Rakhna
(Keep Your Hands
Decorated with Henna)
Singers: Udit Narayan,
Lata Mangeshkar
Picturized on Raj, Simran,
and others

Ghar Aaja Pardesi
(Come Home, O Foreigner)
Singers: Manpreet Kaur, Pamela Chopra
Picturized on Baldev and family

⭐ *The song was shot in mustard fields in Gurgaon (now Gurugram) on the outskirts of India's capital, New Delhi.*

THE MANDOLIN
PLAYED BY RAJ
TO WOO SIMRAN

SIMRAN RUNS TO
RAJ AS THE TRAIN
IS ABOUT TO LEAVE

92377

FOREIGN
LOCALES

Bollywood filmmakers have often shot in foreign locations to entice audiences, but by the 1990s, these had become part of the stories themselves.

I n 1965, Raj Kapoor's *Sangam* (see pp. 80–81) started the trend of filming in exotic locales. An ordinary story was boosted by showing the lead pair vacationing all over Europe—Venice, Paris, and in particular, Switzerland. The incongruity of cholis, kurtas, and Indian song-and-dance routines in a landscape of Alpine huts, verdant pastures, and snowy peaks struck a chord with audiences. Later, films such as *An Evening in Paris* (see p. 95) and *Purab aur Paschim* (1970) showed the hero and heroine cavorting through various far-flung destinations.

By the 1990s, the Indian film industry was riding high, fueled by success at home and trading on the nostalgia of the millions of people of Indian origin living abroad. Directors knew that films held extra appeal for the diaspora when transplanted to locales familiar to them—Europe, the US, and Australia. There was also a growing appetite in urban India for travel, everyone wanted to see beautiful, faraway places on the silver screen.

AROUND THE WORLD
Director–producer Yash Chopra (see pp. 166–67) prompted a flurry of location shoots in Switzerland, following the runaway success of films such as *Chandni* (see p. 202) and *Dilwale Dulhania le Jayenge* (see pp. 230–33). The latter featured a whirlwind rail tour of Europe, showcasing many tourist attractions. In fact, Yash Chopra filmed in Switzerland so often in the 1980s and 1990s that, after his death, a statue was erected in the Swiss town of Interlaken in his memory.

Novelty such as this soon became the norm. *Kuch Kuch Hota hai* (see pp. 246–47) was mostly filmed in Mauritius, and its title song was shot in picturesque locations that included Loch Lomond in Scotland. From St Mark's Square in Venice to the streets of Prague and a recreation of La Tomatina festival in Spain, filmmakers spared no effort in creating a visual treat for audiences.

Locations in the West also helped filmmakers tackle subjects that were taboo on home soil. The 2008 comedy *Dostana*, one of the rare Bollywood films to deal with homosexuality, is set in Miami. Similarly, *Salaam Namaste* (2005), which focused on the topic of live-in relationships and pregnancy out of wedlock, is based in Australia.

Today, foreign locations serve as more than pretty backdrops: the place has come to be a part of the story. The 2010 film *My Name is Khan* is set in the US post-9/11, and deals with the prejudice that the Muslim community faced at the time, while the coming-of-age comedy *Queen* (see pp.320–21) shows the lead traveling to Amsterdam and Paris—a journey that changes her life.

▶ **A European affair**
The picturesque setting of Switzerland serves as the perfect backdrop for the lead pair's romance in *Dilwale Dulhania le Jayenge*.

> *"Whenever I enter Switzerland, I feel it is so peaceful, so romantic."*

YASH CHOPRA IN AN INTERVIEW WITH *THE HINDU*, 2011

KARAN ARJUN

1995

Riding on the popularity of two Bollywood stars, Salman Khan and Shah Rukh Khan, *Karan Arjun* is a gripping revenge saga that struck gold at the box office.

CAST AND CREW

★ **Salman Khan** Karan Singh/Ajay
Shah Rukh Khan Arjun Singh/Vijay
Kajol Sonia Singh
Rakhee Durga Singh
Amrish Puri Thakur Durjan Singh
Mamta Kulkarni Bindiya Singh
Johnny Lever Linghaiyya

🎬 **Director** Rakesh Roshan
🎞 **Producer** Rakesh Roshan
🎵 **Music composer** Rajesh Roshan
🎶 **Lyricist** Indeevar
🕺 **Choreographer** Chinni Prakash
📷 **Scriptwriters** Sachin Bhaumik, Ravi Kapoor
🎥 **Cinematographer** Kaka Thakur
👕 **Costume designers** Pramila Roshan, Gauri Khan, Sunetra

Bollywood films are usually a one-person show, driven by a star who appeals to a specific audience base. However, sometimes a film is made starring two leading actors, with roles that do justice to both of their acting talents. *Karan Arjun* is one such rare film, featuring Salman Khan (see pp. 224–25) and Shah Rukh Khan (see pp. 214–15) together.

TALE OF REINCARNATION
Karan Arjun follows the story of the two brothers of its title—Karan and Arjun—who are murdered by their uncle Thakur Durjan Singh, intent on taking the estate belonging to the brothers' late father. In grief, the boys' mother Durga Singh refuses to accept that her sons are dead, and believes that they will return. Karan and Arjun are reborn as Ajay and Vijay respectively. Although they are initially hostile toward each other, when they find out their past identities, they unite to seek revenge.

A RECIPE FOR SUCCESS
With romance, action, and memorable music, *Karan Arjun* had all the elements of a mainstream blockbuster. While director Rakesh Roshan had worked with Shah Rukh before in *King Uncle* (1993), it was his first time with Salman. The film saw other important collaborations, too. It featured Bollywood's sweetheart couple— Shah Rukh and Kajol, who first appeared together in the 1993 thriller *Baazigar* (see p. 216). The sizzling chemistry between the two was much talked about, most notably due to the song "Jaati Hoon Main" (I Am Leaving). Salman was cast opposite the actress Mamta Kulkarni—a pair that Hindi audiences had not seen before. Actor Hrithik Roshan (see p. 263), who went on to become a star in the 2000s, worked as the assistant director, helping his father put together the film.

A BLOCKBUSTER
The right mix of star power and a great story made *Karan Arjun* a hit. In fact, it became the second highest grossing Indian film of the year, after *Dilwale Dulhania le Jayenge* (see pp. 230–233).

▼ **Brothers on a mission**
A shared painful past makes the brothers Karan and Arjun embark on the path of vengeance.

▲ **A mother's pain**
Rakhee's character and her prophetic words, "Mere Karan Arjun Aayenge" (My Karan Arjun will come back), gained an iconic status over the years.

It was also nominated for 10 Filmfare Awards—winning two—Best Action (Bhiku Varma) and Best Editing (Sanjay Varma).

Karan Arjun's success was a reminder that Indian audiences still had a soft spot for mainstream cinema with big stars and dollops of melodrama.

HIT SONGS

Jaati Hoon Main
(I Am Leaving)
🎤 **Singers** Kumar Sanu, Alka Yagnik

Yeh Bandhan Toh
(This Special Bond of Love)
🎤 **Singers** Kumar Sanu, Udit Narayan, Alka Yagnik

Jai Maa Kali
(Hail, Mother Kali)
🎤 **Singers** Kumar Sanu, Alka Yagnik

RAJA HINDUSTANI

1996

A love story between a rich girl and a poor boy, *Raja Hindustani* proved that romantic dramas with a social conscience can also be hugely successful films.

CAST AND CREW

★ **Aamir Khan** Raja Hindustani
Karisma Kapoor Aarti Sehgal
Suresh Oberoi Mr. Sehgal
Archana Puran Singh Shalini Sehgal
Johnny Lever Balvant Singh

🎬 **Director** Dharmesh Darshan
🎬 **Producers** Ali Morani, Karim Morani, Bunty Soorma
🎵 **Music composer** Nadeem–Shravan
💃 **Lyricist** Sameer
🕺 **Choreographer** Raju Khan
📖 **Scriptwriter** Robin Bhatt
📽 **Cinematographer** W.B. Rao
👔 **Costume designer** Manish Malhotra

▼ **Blazing romance**
The first film to feature Aamir and Karisma as a romantic couple, *Raja Hindustani* became known for the intense on-screen chemistry between its stars.

A remake of the 1965 film *Jab Jab Phool Khile* starring Shashi Kapoor, Dharmesh Darshan's *Raja Hindustani* (Indian King) reprises an age-old theme in popular Hindi cinema— the fight between the rich and the poor. Such films are a sub-genre of romantic dramas and follow a template: a boy and a girl belonging to different classes fall in love. The parents of the richer protagonist oppose the match, leading the lovebirds to rebel. Chaos and tussle follow, but in the end, love triumphs: *Raja Hindustani* was no different.

TEXTBOOK PLOT
The film tells the story of Raja Hindustani, a taxi driver who doubles as a tour guide. A country bumpkin, Raja's life changes when he meets Aarti Sehgal, a rich girl from Mumbai. The two fall in love, but Aarti's father, Mr. Sehgal, is against the alliance. Further complicating matters is Aarti's vicious stepmother, Shalini, who along with her brother plan to swindle Mr. Sehgal out of his assets. Can young love triumph over class conflict?

WHAT WORKED
A simple love story, *Raja Hindustani* primarily worked because of its lead actors, Aamir Khan (see pp. 228–29) and Karisma Kapoor, who brought their characters to life. The film also featured the longest screen kiss in Hindi cinema to date— a notable fact for a conservative film culture. The music by Nadeem–Shravan also became very popular. In fact, several songs such as "Kitna Pyaara Tujhe Rab Ne" (God Made You So Pretty) and "Aaye Ho Meri Zindagi Mein" (You've Come Into My Life Like Spring) had already become chartbusters by the time the film was released. However, nothing matched the popularity of the song "Pardesi Pardesi" (Don't Leave Me, You Stranger), which pulled huge crowds into theaters. It was also

▲ **Dramatic pairing**
The poster played on the lead pair's love story, which became the selling point of the film.

nominated for three Filmfare Awards, and won the Best Male Playback Singer (Udit Narayan). Overall, *Raja Hindustani*'s soundtrack sold more than 11 million copies, becoming the third best-selling album of the 1990s, after *Aashiqui* (1990) and *Dil To Pagal Hai* (1997).
Raja Hindustani stormed the box office, earning more than 15 times its budget. It was nominated for 11 Filmfare Awards, winning five. The movie was that rare Bollywood success: bagging awards and winning over audiences in India and abroad.

KARISMA KAPOOR
(b.1974)

Karisma Kapoor made her Bollywood debut in the 1991 musical drama *Prem Qaidi*, and acted in several other box office hits, including *Jigar* (1992), *Raja Babu* (1994), and *Coolie No. 1* (1995). However, *Raja Hindustani*—for which she won her first Filmfare Award—is considered her breakout role. She also won the National Film Award for Best Supporting Actress in *Dil To Paagal Hai* (1997). In the early 2000s, she worked in critically acclaimed films such as *Fiza* (2000) and *Zubeidaa* (2001). She got married in 2003, and with the exception of one film in 2012, *Dangerous Ishhq*, has quit acting.

"Raja Hindustani *was a pure entertainer.*"

AAMIR KHAN, *I'LL DO IT MY WAY: THE INCREDIBLE JOURNEY OF AAMIR KHAN*, 2012

HERO NO.1

1997

A funny family drama, *Hero No.1* saw a famous Bollywood collaboration—between a filmmaker and an actor—on familiar territory: making audiences laugh.

CAST AND CREW

★ **Govinda** Rajesh Malhotra/Raju
Karisma Kapoor Meena Nath
Paresh Rawal Dinanath
Kader Khan Dhanraj Malhotra
Satish Shah Pappi

🎬 **Director** David Dhawan
⬡ **Producer** Vashu Bhagnani
🎵 **Music composers** Anand Shrivastav, Milind Shrivastav
🎼 **Lyricist** Sameer
🕺 **Choreographer** B.H. Tharun Kumar
📖 **Script writer** Rumi Jaffrey
🎥 **Cinematographer** K.S. Prakash Rao
👔 **Costume designer** Neeta Lulla

The pairing of actor Govinda and filmmaker David Dhawan produced 17 films, from the late 1980s to the late 2000s. Most of these movies—around a dozen made in the 1990s alone—belonged to a certain sub-genre of comedy: light-hearted escapist fare that was low on realism and high on laughs. Marked by simple, lowbrow humor and a hero dressed in garish clothes, these films were primarily popular among, in Bollywood's language, the "masses:" India's tier-two towns. *Hero No.1* was one of the most popular films of the lot. The film is also a part of the "No.1" franchise of comedy films, starring Govinda as the lead, including box office hits, such as *Coolie No.1* (1995) and *Jodi No.1* (2001).

Many believe *Hero No.1* to be inspired by

▶ **The comedy masters**
The director–actor duo, Govinda and David Dhawan, are seen sharing a candid moment here.

◀ **Inspired by a classic**
Hero No.1 is believed to be inspired by *Bawarchi*. Like Rajesh Khanna's character, Govinda, too, dons the cook's hat in a squabbling family.

Bawarchi (1972), a film by Hrishikesh Mukherjee (see p. 140). *Hero No.1* is the story of Rajesh Malhotra, the son of a wealthy businessman, who becomes a domestic servant in his girlfriend Meena's house to impress her grandfather, Dinanath, who is opposed to their alliance. Nearly every member of Meena's family is undergoing a crisis of some sort—either personal or professional. Slowly, Raju (Rajesh's assumed moniker as a domestic help) gets acquainted with them and starts solving their problems, endearing himself to Dinanath and winning his trust, thus paving the way for his own marriage with Meena. The comedy caper was accompanied by fun, catchy songs such as "Sona Kitna Sona hai" (You Are Gold) and "Maine Paidal se Jaa Raha tha" (I Was Walking By).

BREAKING THE CLASS DIVIDE
The Govinda–Dhawan collaboration is an important chapter in the history of Bollywood, especially the 1990s, because it helped break the class divide in mainstream Hindi cinema. Unlike many popular films of the decade, Dhawan's films had a stripped-down quality to them. They were often set in

small towns and villages. The heroes in these films weren't larger than life, had no special abilities, and led regular lives: as porters, wastrels, and country bumpkins. More importantly, the success of these films proved Indian audiences' broad taste and their willingness to engage with different kinds of stories. *Hero No.1* was a notable box office success. With a modest budget, the film was a hit, earning more than double what it cost to make.

GOVINDA
(b.1963)

Born in 1963 as Arun Kumar Ahuja, Govinda is known for his comic timing and dancing skills. In a career spanning more than three decades, Govinda's filmography ranges from family, drama, and romance to action and comedy, but he has attained the status of a cult comic actor over the years. His list of hit comedies in the 1990s include *Raja Babu* (1994), *Coolie No.1* (1995), and *Haseena Maan Jaayegi* (1999). After a series of flops in the early 2000s, the actor made a comeback of sorts with *Bhagam Bhag* (2006) and *Partner* (2007), movies that were fairly successful at the box office.

BORDER

1997

An epic war drama about real events during the India–Pakistan War of 1971, *Border* was an ambitious film that tried to tell a personal as well as an historic story.

◀ **Band of brothers**
The film shows the development of the characters as individuals and their friendships, lending the war story a touch of humanity.

Army and Air Force contributed vehicles and weaponry to it, including Hawker Hunter planes.

AN UNEVEN BATTLE
Set during the war, the film tells the story of a small battalion of 120 Indian soldiers led by Major Kuldip Singh Chandpuri, who are tasked with holding the Indian border post of Longewala against the 2,500-strong Pakistani strike force. The battalion must keep its position for a night until the Air Force can reinforce them at dawn.

Leading up to this pivotal defense, the men have a long wait in the desolate Thar Desert along the northwestern border of India. During this time, they get to know each other, telling each other about their backgrounds and families. They also develop as characters, such as Dharamvir, the lieutenant who is initially unable to shoot an insurgent, but must learn to kill. Once the enemy

tanks start to roll over the border, the men are given a choice either to retreat on foot or hold their post. They choose to remain and a desperate battle ensues.

PARTRIOTIC APPEAL
Border was the highest grossing Bollywood movie of 1997, and won numerous awards, including four Filmfare Awards and two National Awards.

The soundtrack became very popular, particularly "Sandese Aate hain," a song about a soldier's suffering, which became a national hit. Although the lyrics of some songs contained an anti-war message, there was no denying the patriotic appeal of *Border*. The film was screened at the 2016 Independence Day Film Festival to commemorate 70 years of Indian independence. A planned sequel to the movie failed to materialize.

▼ **Attention to detail**
Border was filmed on location in the Thar Desert, Rajasthan, using loaned military equipment and sparing no expense on impressive special effects to recreate the destruction at the end of the battle.

CAST AND CREW

★ **Sunny Deol** Kuldip Singh Chandpuri
Sunil Shetty Bhairon Singh
Akshaye Khanna Dharamvir Singh
Jackie Shroff Andy Bajwa
Rakhee Dharamvir's mother
Tabu Kuldip Singh's wife
Pooja Bhatt Kamla
Kulbhushan Kharbanda Havildar Bhagheeram

🎬 **Director** J.P. Dutta
💰 **Producer** J.P. Dutta
🎵 **Music composer** Anu Malik
✍ **Lyricist** Javed Akhtar
📖 **Scriptwriter** J.P. Dutta
🎥 **Cinematographers** Ishwar R. Bidri, Nirmal Jani
👕 **Costume designer** Bindiya Goswami

Directed by J.P. Dutta, *Border* is a three-hour war film based on the Battle of Longewala, an engagement during the 1971 India–Pakistan War. Dutta's brother saw action during the War, so this film had a great personal resonance for him. In this big-budget blockbuster, Dutta portrays action based on events from the actual battle and also explores the backstory of the men who fought alongside each other. Such was the scale of the award-winning production that the Indian

> *"Dutta … recreates the palpable tension of the coming battle."*
>
> **ANUPAMA CHOPRA,** *INDIA TODAY,* 1997

PARDES

1997

A hit love story, *Pardes* is also a celebration of traditional Indian culture and an insightful commentary on the adoption of Western values by Indian expatriates.

◄ The moment of truth
Ganga is consoled by Arjun, who shares her traditional Indian values and respect for the motherland, after a painful altercation with her Westernized fiancé, Rajiv.

Rajiv. While Ganga's father agrees to the match, the prospective groom, Rajiv, is resistant to the idea of an Indian bride. Kishorilal decides to send his foster son Arjun ahead of Rajiv—who has never visited India—to pave the way for Rajiv's visit. Arjun and Ganga become friends.

The trouble begins when Ganga goes to L.A. to live with Kishorilal's family prior to the marriage. There she finds a world very alien to her—culturally, socially, and economically. To top it all, Rajiv behaves offensively the entire time she is there. The only one Ganga feels she can turn to is her friend and confidant, Arjun.

WESTERN VICES

The film offers an insightful criticism of the Indian tendency to place Western culture on a pedestal at the expense of homegrown traditions, particularly in the non-resident Indian (NRI) community. The story models the good Indian immigrant—Arjun—who retains the Indian values of the motherland, and his polar opposite—Rajiv—the fallen immigrant, who has been corrupted by Western influences. Each of these characters offers the audience a glimpse into aspects of the hidden expectations many Indians have of "going abroad" to fulfil their aspirations, contrasting the dream with the reality. Ganga, on the other hand, epitomizes the best of Indian culture and values.

Although some critics found the story a bit heavy-handed in its portrayal of expatriate life, *Pardes* was a huge commercial hit and one of the first major Bollywood pictures

to enjoy success in the US. Mahima Chaudhary won the Filmfare Award for Best Newcomer for her performance as Ganga. The soundtrack, created by the composer duo Nadeem–Shravan, was awarded the Star Screen Award for Best Music Director. The film was later remade in the Telugu language of southern India as *Pelli Kanuka*.

▲ From India, with love
An Indian musical with a Western backdrop, *Pardes* is a story of love, not only between a man and a woman, but also between Indians, especially those living away from home and their motherland.

Subhash Ghai's *Pardes* (Foreign Country) is an early attempt by Bollywood to portray the lives and experiences of Indian expatriates. A blockbuster hit in India, the film was also released internationally. Its soundtrack enjoyed particular success, with several hits enduring today.

CLASH OF CULTURES

The film's story centers on Ganga, an Indian woman living with her extended family in a rural village. Her idyllic life changes when Kishorilal, a close friend of her father's, stays with them while visiting India. A wealthy expatriate living in Los Angeles, Kishorilal still has strong ties with India and its culture. He is so impressed with Ganga and her devotion to Indian values and traditions, that he proposes she marry his very Westernized son,

SATYA

1998

With its raw and unflinchingly realistic look at the Mumbai underworld, Ram Gopal Varma's *Satya* changed the face of Indian gangster films forever.

CAST AND CREW

★ **J.D. Chakravarthy** Satya
Urmila Matondkar Vidya
Paresh Rawal Amod Shukla
Manoj Bajpayee Bhiku Mhatre

🎬 **Director** Ram Gopal Varma
🎬 **Producer** Ram Gopal Varma
🎵 **Music composers** Vishal Bhardwaj, Sandeep Chowta
🎤 **Lyricist** Gulzar
🕺 **Choreographer** Ahmed Khan
📖 **Scriptwriters** Saurabh Shukla, Anurag Kashyap
🎥 **Cinematographers** Gerard Hooper, Mazhar Kamran

▼ **The face of Mumbai**
The climax of the film depicts a religious procession making its way down the streets of Chowpatty, showcasing Mumbai in all its glory, complete with thronging masses and color.

Considered one of the finest gangster movies to emerge from Bollywood, *Satya* (Truth) stands out among such hallmark crime films as *Parinda* (see p. 199) and Ram Gopal Varma's own *Company* (2002). Starkly filmed on location in Mumbai's grimy underbelly, *Satya* offers a dark and unwavering look into a brutal world.

CAUGHT UP IN CRIME
The focal point of the story is Satya, a young man who moves to Mumbai to earn a living. However, he inadvertently becomes entangled in the Mumbai underworld and starts working for a gangster named Bhiku Mhatre. He also falls in love with his neighbor, Vidya, an aspiring singer, from whom he hides his gang affiliations. As Satya spirals deeper and deeper into an unforgiving and violent gangland, he discovers, much too late, that in a crime-filled world there is little redemption and certainly no way out. What immediately singles *Satya* out from mainstream Hindi cinema of the

period is its gutsy, realistic treatment of life in the darker corners of the city. The film brought an authenticity to the screen, which was rarely seen in Bollywood at that time.

INSPIRED BY TRUE EVENTS
Varma researched extensively for *Satya* by interacting with various people from Mumbai's underworld. According to him, every character in the film is based on a real person he met or had heard about. Among the many well-defined and layered characters in the film, Manoj Bajpayee's Bhiku Mhatre is the most dark and powerful. Described by Varma as a "wild cat," Mhatre's character was a breakthrough role for Bajpayee, who won several awards for his performance.

The strength of the acting was perhaps a result of Varma's freewheeling style of filmmaking, which allowed the actors to improvise as they saw fit. With Varma's implicit trust in the actors and excellent writing, the final film comes together coherently. If there is a weaker side to the film, it is the characterization of

MANOJ BAJPAYEE
(b. 1969)

One of the country's finest actors, Manoj Bajpayee hails from the village of Belwa in Bihar. An aspiring actor since childhood, he became involved in theater while at college in Delhi. After minor roles in *Droh Kaal* (1994) and *Bandit Queen* (1994), he finally got his big break in films with his explosive performance as Bhiku Mhatre in *Satya*. Despite ups and downs in his career, Bajpayee has consistently proved himself as a performer across a wide genre of films.

Satya. Varma admitted later that inconsistencies in the character may have disconnected Satya from viewers.

SUCCESSFUL CINEMA
A commercially successful and critically acclaimed film, *Satya* ushered in the "Mumbai noir" genre of filmmaking, which shed light on the darker aspects of the city. Despite naysayers who felt the film glorified violence by creating empathy for its criminal characters, *Satya*'s cinematic power and influence on almost every Bollywood gangster film that followed it cannot be in doubt.

HIT SONGS

Goli Maar Bheje Main
(Put A Bullet In The Brain)
🎤 **Singer** Mano

Badalon Se
(From The Clouds)
🎤 **Singer** Bhupinder Singh

DIL SE..

1998

A romantic drama set against a political backdrop, *Dil Se..* saw masterful filmmaker Mani Ratnam melding the personal with the political to great effect.

▼ **The chart topper**
The hit song "Chaiyya Chaiyya" was shot on top of a moving train with Shah Rukh Khan and Malaika Arora dancing to choreographer Farah Khan's moves. She later jokingly thanked Shah Rukh for not falling off the train.

Every once in a while, a mainstream Hindi film throws the rulebook out of the window. Such a film draws the audiences using familiar tropes—famous actors, a romantic story, foot-tapping songs—yet, it doesn't kowtow to our expectations. In fact, it creates some of its own. The 1998 romantic thriller *Dil Se..* (From the Heart) by director Mani Ratnam (see p. 278) is one such film.

A POLITICAL FILM

There's much about *Dil Se..* that confounds expectations. On the surface, the film is a love story, and yet its leads—Amar, a program executive at All India Radio and Meghna, an Assamese insurgent—don't get together until the end of the film. In fact, for most of the film's duration, the audience isn't even sure if Meghna even likes Amar. She is an inscrutable figure—reticent about her feelings, and evasive about who she is and what she wants. Amar, on the other hand, is her polar opposite—a man who has fallen in love at first sight, he doesn't know when and how to back off, and doesn't understand the meaning of no.

But it turns out, Amar and Meghna aren't that different from each other. Both of them are, in their own ways, obsessed. If Amar is fixated on winning Meghna's love—so much so that he follows her, erroneously believing that one day he will be able to win her over—then she's after something more elusive: an independent state, set up through violence, killing tens of hundreds in the process, including India's President.

▲ **The look of the film**
The cover of the film's audio cassette shows how some of the popular songs in the film are picturized on lead pair Shah Rukh Khan and Manisha Koirala.

Dil Se.. is a rare political film, that pits the civilians against the State. But it does so with intelligence—by not taking sides and by showing both sides of the story. More often than not Bollywood films water down complexities in a bid to be crowd pleasers, casting actors known for playing villainous parts to portray anti-establishment characters—so that the audience doesn't have to strain to pick a side. But *Dil Se..* is different. It shows Manisha Koirala, a popular actress, playing an insurgent; similarly, her leader is a famous Bengali actor, Sabyasachi Chakrabarty. Ratnam, however, doesn't go out of his way to make them likeable, either. He simply tells their story, and leaves the audience to make up its own mind.

A MUSICAL TREAT

Amid the rebellion, the violence, and the fiery unrequited love—are heart-thumping songs, with poetic lyrics by Gulzar (see pp. 142–43) and music by composer A.R. Rahman (see pp. 244–45). Winner of two Academy Awards for film soundtracks, Rahman has composed countless bestselling hits in his career, but the music for *Dil Se..* still ranks among one of his finest film works. Cinematographer Santosh Sivan shot the songs so evocatively that their picturization alone makes the film.

A COLLABORATIVE EFFORT

An impressive list of producers added heft to the film. The executive producers, alongside Ratnam, were noted Indian directors Shekhar Kapur (see p. 189) and Ram Gopal Varma (see p. 226). Ratnam also showed an instinct for spotting talent in his selection of cast and crew members. Many of them were previously untested, but later went on to make their mark in Indian cinema. *Dil Se..* was the first major role for actor Piyush Mishra, the noted music director, singer, and lyricist. The film also saw the debut of actress Preity Zinta, who went on to become a Bollywood star in the following decade. Other notable crew members included dialogue writer Tigmanshu Dhulia, who later became an established filmmaker in his own right with successful films such as *Paan Singh Tomar,* and assistant director Shaad Ali.

Although *Dil Se..* wasn't a box office success, it did receive its fair share of accolades, winning six Filmfare Awards and two National Film Awards. Moreover, unlike many of its contemporaries, the film has aged well, with a story that remains as relevant as ever to India's political landscape. Above all, *Dil Se..*'s longevity proves a heartening truth—that art, at its finest, can trump commerce.

▶ **The explosive climax**
Seen here at the film's climax, Meghna and Aman must follow the troubled path of their love.

CAST AND CREW

★ **Shah Rukh Khan** Amar Varma
Manisha Koirala Moina/Meghna
Preity Zinta Preeti Nair
Sabyasachi Chakrabarty A terrorist
Piyush Mishra CBI Officer

🎬 **Director** Mani Ratnam
🏠 **Producers** Mani Ratnam, Ram Gopal Varma, Shekhar Kapur
🎵 **Music composer** A.R. Rahman
🅰 **Lyricist** Gulzar
🕺 **Choreographer** Farah Khan
📖 **Scriptwriter** Mani Ratnam
📷 **Cinematographer** Santosh Sivan
🧵 **Costume designers** Pia Benegal, Manish Malhotra

HIT SONGS

Chaiyya Chaiyya
(Come, Let's Walk in the Shade)
🎤 **Singers** Sukhwinder Singh, Sapna Awasthi

Dil se Re
(Title Song)
🎤 **Singers** A.R. Rahman, Anuradha Sriram, Anupama, Febi Mani

Jiya Jale
(My Heart's on Fire)
🎤 **Singers** Lata Mangeshkar, M.G. Sreekumar, and Chorus

"Mani Ratnam masterfully weaves an unforgettable tale of love in the backdrop of terrorism."

MURTAZA ALI KHAN, CRITIC, *HUFFINGTON POST,* 2016

A.R. RAHMAN

MUSIC COMPOSER b.1966

Nicknamed "the Mozart of Madras," A.R. Rahman is one of India's most celebrated musicians. He is a powerful force in world music and has produced a phenomenal body of work for film and stage.

Few musicians around the world have won as many plaudits or sold as many albums as A.R. Rahman; estimates put his sales of cassettes, CDs, and downloads at more than 200 million since 1992. In a career that spans more than 25 years, Rahman has donned many hats—composer, instrumentalist, singer-songwriter, music producer, philanthropist—and has become a tour de force in world music. Renowned for his ability to mix traditional Indian sounds with electronic beats, combining ancient and contemporary instruments, Rahman has integrated his distinctive sound into mainstream musical traditions. Rahman's talents have been recognized globally for his work with collaborators including Michael Jackson, Dido, and will.i.am, and his soundtracks for popular films such as *Elizabeth: The Golden Age* (2007), *Slumdog Millionaire* (2008), and *Couples Retreat* (2009), among many others. A familiar face at international awards ceremonies, he has won two Academy Awards, two Grammys, and a Golden Globe.

PRODIGIOUS TALENT

Music was always in Rahman's blood. He grew up under the musical wing of his father, R.K. Shekhar, a composer for Tamil and Malayalam films, and began learning to play the piano at age four. Spending hours in his father's studio in Chennai, he mastered several instruments including the keyboard, piano, synthesizer, harmonium, and guitar—all while he was still a boy. At age 9, Rahman lost his father, but his love for music lived on. By age 11, he was playing in the Malayalam orchestra of composer M.K. Arjunan, who gave the boy his first big break playing keyboards for a movie soundtrack. He continued to work with other famous composers, such as Ilaiyaraaja, who was the first Asian to create a symphony for the London Philharmonic Orchestra. Word of the talented youngster's ability spread and

▲ **Perfect score**
Rahman's soundtrack, which combined orchestral melodies with traditional Tamil sounds, beautifully complemented the emotional drama of *Roja*—a moving story of love and patriotism in a time of political turmoil.

KEY WORKS

Roja, 1992 (see p. 337)

Rangeela, 1995 (see pp. 226–27)

Bombay, 1995

Dil se.., 1998 (see pp. 242–43)

Taal, 1999 (see p. 251)

Slumdog Millionaire, 2008

127 Hours, 2010

► **Cinematic symphony**
Rahman rehearses with the Birmingham City Orchestra in March 2004 for two concert performances featuring music from his film soundtracks, demonstrating the crossover appeal of his compositions.

it was not long before he was working and touring with more celebrated musicians, including violinist and composer L. Shankar and tabla maestro Zakir Hussain. Rahman won a scholarship to study at the Trinity College of Music in London, where he "started practicing piano." In 1989, he converted to Islam, changing his name from A.S. Dileep Kumar to Allah Rakha Rahman.

MUSIC FOR THE STARS
After a stint composing popular ad jingles, he landed his first movie soundtrack in 1992 for Mani Ratnam's *Roja*. Its theme song "Tamizha Tamizha" (People of the Land) was a huge hit and established Rahman as a household name in Tamil Nadu, where he built his own recording and mixing

"If music wakes you up, makes you think, heals you … then the music is working."

A.R. RAHMAN

studio with state-of-the-art equipment and a team of sound engineers. From this creative base, he began a new phase in his career, establishing himself as a masterful composer for the Tamil, Hindi, and international film industry.

After the success of *Roja*, a stream of producers and directors from Bollywood and Hollywood came knocking on Rahman's door. He composed and produced a string of impressive Bollywood soundtracks through the 1990s, including the music for *Rangeela*, *Dil Se*, and *Taal*. His original composition for the Tamil film *Muthu* (1995) was a sensation in Japan and earned Rahman a devoted

◄ **Art meets technology**
Although he has mastered many instruments, the synthesizer remains Rahman's first love because it combines melodic sound and technology.

following there. The highlight of the decade was his soundtrack for *Bombay*, which became the best-selling Indian album, notching up sales of more than 12 million copies worldwide. Of particular note in this album are the songs "Hamma Hamma," for which Rahman himself sang the vocals; the hugely popular "Uyire/Tu Hi Re" (It's Only You) sung by Hariharan; and the instrumental "Bombay Theme"—a global hit that appeared on numerous compilations and was later reused in several films and commercials.

THE LEGEND LIVES ON
In the new millennium, Rahman was busier than ever. Aside from three world tours, he performed for charity fundraisers, collaborated with artists such as Michael Bolton and Mick Jagger, and composed a Punjabi song for the opening ceremony of the 2012 London Olympics with Danny Boyle. Rahman had previously worked with Boyle on films such as *Slumdog Millionaire* (2008) and *127 Hours* (2010).

Music is not Rahman's only passion. Over time, he has emerged as a noted philanthropist. He funds a number of charitable projects through the A.R. Rahman Trust, such as the Sunshine Orchestra, which gives world-class training in Indian and Western classical music to underprivileged children.

◄ **Oscar triumph**
An operatic combination of old and new India, the soundtrack for *Slumdog Millionaire* (2008) won Rahman the Academy Award for Best Soundtrack. The song "Jai Ho" (Be Victorious) also won an Oscar for Best Song.

A.R. RAHMAN'S *BOMBAY DREAMS* AT THE APOLLO VICTORIA THEATRE IN LONDON, UK

- **Januay 6, 1966** Born A.S. Dileep Kumar in Chennai, Tamil Nadu.

- **1987** Composes the advertising jingle for Allwyn watches.

- **1989** Converts to Islam, changing his name to Allah Rakha Rahman.

- **1992** Scores his first soundtrack, for *Roja*, a Tamil film directed by Mani Ratnam.

- **1993** Wins the Rajat Kamal (Silver Lotus) award for Best Music Director at the National Film Awards for *Roja*.

- **1995** Wins the Filmfare Award for Best Music Director (Tamil), the first of several such awards.

- **2002** Commissioned by English composer Andrew Lloyd Webber to write the music for *Bombay Dreams*.

- **2006** Launches his own recording label, KM Music.

- **2007** Collaborates with Shekhar Kapur on the score for *Elizabeth: The Golden Age*.

- **2008** Writes the score for his first Hollywood film, *Couples Retreat*, and wins the BMI London Award for Best Score.

- **2008** Establishes the KM Music Conservatory, a college for classical Indian and Western music in Chennai.

- **2009** Appears in *Time* magazine's list of World's 100 Most Influential People.

- **2009** Performs at the White House for former US President Barack Obama and Prime Minister of India Manmohan Singh.

- **2010** Awarded an Honorary Fellowship by Trinity College London.

- **2010** Receives the Padma Bhushan, India's third highest civilian award.

- **2015** Wins 15th consecutive Filmfare Award for Best Music Director.

KUCH KUCH HOTA HAI

1998

Directed by a debutant, the romantic drama *Kuch Kuch Hota Hai* was a colossal box office success, ushering in the fresh directorial style of Karan Johar.

CAST AND CREW

★ **Shah Rukh Khan** Rahul Khanna
   Kajol Anjali Sharma
   Rani Mukherji Tina Malhotra
   Salman Khan Aman Mehra
   Anupam Kher Principal Malhotra

🎬 **Director** Karan Johar
⬠ **Producers** Yash Johar, Hiroo Johar
🎵 **Music composers** Jatin Pandit, Lalit Pandit
♪ **Lyricist** Sameer
🕺 **Choreography** Farah Khan
📖 **Scriptwriter** Karan Johar
🎥 **Cinematographer** Santosh Thundiyil
👔 **Costume** Manish Malhotra

Karan Johar first worked with actor Shah Rukh Khan (see pp. 214–15) as an assistant director, on the blockbuster *Dilwale Dulhania le Jayenge* (see pp. 230–31). Shah Rukh was impressed with Johar's work and encouraged him to direct his own film, promising that he and Kajol, his *DDLJ* co-star, would act in it. In less than three years, Johar had the script ready, and Shah Rukh and Kajol, as promised, were on board.

The rest of the casting, however, proved far more troublesome. The film was a love triangle of sorts, and Johar needed a second actress to play the third role in the triangle. He approached more than half a dozen stars for the part, but they all turned him—an unknown—down. Eventually, he reached out to a newcomer, Rani Mukherji, who had acted in only one Hindi film before.

Another role that proved tricky to cast was that of Aman Mehra who had an extended cameo in the film. After a long hunt, the part finally went to Salman Khan (see pp. 224–25). Until then, he had shared the screen with Shah Rukh only once before, in *Karan Arjun* (see p.236). At long last, with three major stars and an almost untried newcomer, filming could finally begin on Johar's debut movie, *Kuch Kuch Hota Hai* (Something Happens).

THREE'S COMPANY

Kuch Kuch Hota Hai tells the story of the outgoing and popular Rahul, and his best friend, the fun-loving, tomboyish Anjali, both students at

▼ **College romance**
Rahul's charming and loveable character, coupled with Anjali's open and ingenuous personality, endeared this winning pair to audiences of all ages.

▲ **Forever young**
Kuch Kuch Hota Hai's young characters were brought to life by the vivacious trio—Kajol (left), Shah Rukh, and Rani (right)—in a blend of drama, romance, and entertainment in a college setting.

St Xavier's College, Mumbai. Anjali realizes that she's in love with Rahul, but he has instead fallen for Tina, the principal's daughter. Heartbroken, Anjali leaves the college. The film then jumps to more than a decade later, when we find out that after college Rahul marries Tina, who dies giving birth to a daughter, also named Anjali. Father and daughter find eight letters written by Tina to her daughter, with instructions that each letter is to be read, one at a time, on Anjali's first eight birthdays. As the content of each letter is revealed, the young Anjali realizes her mother has given her a mission that could change everything.

EAST MEETS WEST
Johar's characters were carefully crafted to represent a globalized, aspirational way of life. They spoke a mixture of Hindi and English, the

HIT SONGS

Kuch Kuch Hota Hai
(Something Happens)
🎤 **Singers** Udit Narayan, Alka Yagnik

Ladki Badi Anjaani Hai
(That Mysterious Girl)
🎤 **Singers** Kumar Sanu, Alka Yagnik

professors were cool, lenient, even sexy, and the taboo of remarriage after the death of a spouse was not frowned upon. And yet, the film beat with an Indian heart, its storytelling following the much-loved Bollywood tropes: family always comes first, romantic love is almost completely devoid of carnal desire, and songs carry the story forward. *Kuch Kuch Hota hai* reflected an India after economic liberalization (initiated seven years earlier, in 1991)—a nation flitting between the local and the global, tradition and modernity, a state available to few, but aspired to by many.

A costume designer himself, Johar had a distinct look in mind for the characters in the film—hip, youthful, and with international appeal. He brought noted fashion designer and friend Manish Malhotra on board and worked closely with him to pick the right outfits for the actors. *Kuch Kuch Hota Hai* was style-conscious, with characters wearing costumes from international brands such as DKNY and Polo Ralph Lauren. Even the film's most prominent setting—Rahul and Anjali's college—seemed inspired by the American television series, *Beverly Hills, 90210*.

BREAKTHROUGH SUCCESS
The movie's soundtrack, which comprised eight songs composed by brothers Jatin and Lalit Pandit, was lighthearted, peppy, and filled with emotions that appealed to youth. It was the most popular Bollywood album of the year, selling about eight million copies. In fact, nearly a decade later, the film's title track "Kuch Kuch Hota Hai" was voted best song of the last decade, in a poll conducted by Indian news channel, NDTV. And in a similar BBC poll on the top Bollywood soundtracks of all time the title track ranked third; that list was topped by *DDLJ*. Johar's

first two films, *Kuch Kuch Hota Hai* (see pp. 246–47) and *Kabhi Khushi Kabhie Gham* (see pp. 270–71), share a number of similarities, most important of which is how they both tapped into and opened up the overseas market for Bollywood films, creating a new influx of revenue, reaching out to a huge diaspora audience, and setting the trend for future Bollywood movies.

As the highest-grossing film in India that year, *Kuch Kuch Hota hai* enjoyed major box office success at home. On the international front, it became the first film to collect $5 million outside India. It was also a massive critical success, winning

◀ **New-age parents**
The friendly camaraderie between Rahul and young Anjali reflected a changing India, in which the close bond between father and child was a far cry from the stern, deferential relationship seen in films from the 1990s.

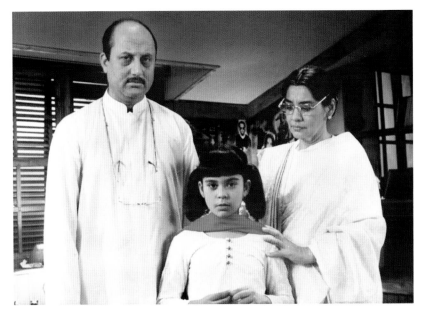

▲ **Agent of change**
Young Anjali joins forces with her grandparents, played by Anupam Kher (left) and Farida Jalal (right) to give her father another chance at happiness.

eight Filmfare Awards and a National Film Award for Best Film Providing Wholesome Entertainment. It was, till then, only the third film, after *Guide* (see pp. 84–87) and *DDLJ*, to win four major awards (Best Film, Best Director, Best Actor, and Best Actress) at Filmfare. A dream debut for a 26-year-old director, *Kuch Kuch Hota hai* paved the way for Johar's massive success in Bollywood as a leading filmmaker and, later, producer of several superhit films.

RANI MUKERJI
(b.1978)

Making her Bollywood debut with *Raja Ki Ayegi Baraat* (1997), Rani Mukerji quickly became a Bollywood star, acting in several hit films opposite prominent actors. Winner of seven Filmfare Awards, Rani has played her most memorable roles in such films as *Saathiya* (2002), *Hum Tum* (2004), *Yuva* (see p. 282), *Black* (2005), and *Bunty Aur Babli* (see p. 341). In October 2014, she married filmmaker Aditya Chopra. After a three-year sabbatical from films, Rani returned to the screen in *Hitchki* (2017).

> "Kuch Kuch Hota Hai *had an organic innocence ...*"
>
> **KARAN JOHAR**, 7TH JAGRAN FILM FESTIVAL, 2016

KARAN JOHAR

DIRECTOR–PRODUCER b.1972

The director-producer of several acclaimed blockbusters, Karan Johar is known for his versatility, and has emerged as one of the most powerful figures in Bollywood today.

When Karan Johar made his directorial debut with the 1998 romantic drama *Kuch Kuch Hota Hai*, he was just 26 years old. A massive hit, the film became the highest-grosser in India that year, and the highest-grossing Hindi film worldwide. The film swept the board for all the major Indian film awards, including eight Filmfares—Johar won for Best Director and Best Screenplay—and a National Film Award for the Best Film Providing Wholesome Entertainment. The son of veteran film producer Yash Johar, Karan had arrived on the stage early and with a bang—and he was just getting started.

Three years after his debut, Johar hit the theaters with another blockbuster. *Kabhi Khushi Kabhie Gham*—an opulent family drama featuring the biggest Bollywood stars—had mixed reviews, but became the highest-grossing Indian film of 2001 in the overseas market.

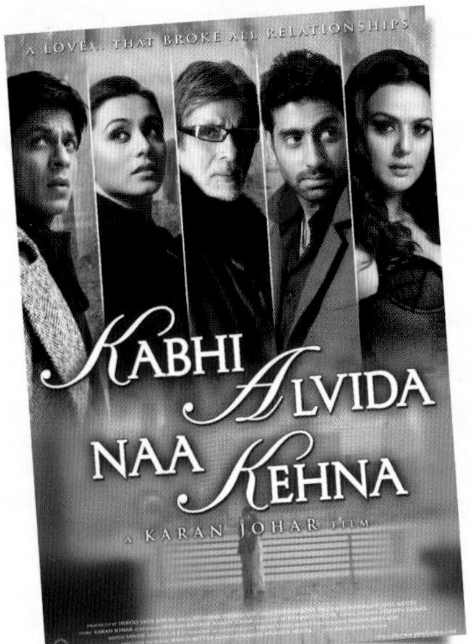

AN UNSUITABLE BOY

In a span of three years, Johar had become one of the biggest names among Bollywood directors, and he had not even turned 30. Yet, his career aspirations were not always clear-cut.

In his memoir, *An Unsuitable Boy* (2017), Johar writes about his troubled childhood, saying he felt "alone" and "different." His classmates often teased him, calling him "fatty" and "pansy." He didn't have many friends in school either, and had only a vague idea of what he wanted to become.

Things changed when he began assisting filmmaker Aditya Chopra on the latter's directorial debut, *Dilwale Dulhania Le Jayenge* (see pp. 230–33). After a confused adolescence, Johar had finally found his calling, and the abiding feeling that came with it— that he "finally belonged somewhere."

The success of *Kabhi Khushi Kabhie Gham* was followed by *Kal Ho Naa Ho* (2003), a Nikkhil Advani film that Johar wrote and produced. The latter film's massive success led to Johar's next directorial effort, *Kabhi Alvida Naa Kehna* (2006), which bravely tackled the theme of marital infidelity— a tricky subject that gave most Bollywood filmmakers cold feet.

THE DHARMA BRAND

Johar, however, has not just been a successful filmmaker. In his long career, he's proved his business acumen, too. After the death of his father in 2004, he took control of the family production company, Dharma Productions, and took it to astounding

▲ **Infidelity in the limelight**
From left to right, Shah Rukh Khan, Rani Mukerji, Amitabh Bachchan, Abhishek Bachchan, and Preity Zinta starred in *Kabhi Alvida Naa Kehna*.

KEY WORKS

Kuch Kuch Hota Hai, 1998
(see pp. 246–47)

Kabhi Khushi Kabhie Gham, 2001
(see pp. 270–71)

Kabhi Alvida Naa Kehna, 2006

My Name is Khan, 2010

Student of the Year, 2012
(see p. 311)

Bombay Talkies, 2013

Ae Dil Hai Mushkil, 2016

▶ **Brand Johar**
With his strong public persona, Johar has grown into a brand name himself.

heights. In the next decade, Dharma Productions produced more than two dozen films, many of which became blockbusters. As producer, Johar gave an opportunity to many first-time directors with these films.

Johar's films—whether as director or producer—have established him as a maker of big-budget Bollywood films that put charged, emotional dramas front and center, and which are marked by plush sets, foreign locales, big stars, glossy costumes, and intricately choreographed dance numbers. As a result, his films appeal to a certain Indian demographic, which has strong familial ties, is upwardly mobile, and aspires to be global.

In his later career, Johar has diversified his oeuvre—tackling race and religion in post-9/11 America in *My Name is Khan*; a teenage romantic drama in *Student of the Year*; and a partly autobiographical film, based on his brush with unrequited love in *Ae Dil Hai Mushkil*. He also directed a short film in the anthology film *Bombay Talkies*, commemorating 100 years of Indian cinema. (The film also had segments shot by other leading

◀ **A memorable partnership**
Karan Johar has worked with actor Shah Rukh Khan (right) on several blockbusters. *My Name is Khan* was one of their many successful collaborations.

Bollywood directors Dibakar Banerjee, Zoya Akhtar, and Anurag Kashyap.)

Johar's most noted and long-standing collaboration has been with Bollywood star and good friend Shah Rukh Khan (see pp. 214–15). He has directed Shah Rukh in four films, and has also designed his costumes for more than half a dozen films, including blockbusters such as *Dilwale Dulhania Le Jayenge*, *Veer-Zaara* (2004), and *Om Shanti Om* (see pp. 292–95).

DONNING MANY HATS
Johar has a strong public persona and, unlike some other Bollywood directors, appears on many platforms. He frequently hosts award ceremonies, serves as a judge on reality TV shows,

and has also acted in a few films. He played the antagonist in the 2015 period crime-drama film, *Bombay Velvet*, and his critically acclaimed performance was a highlight of the film.

Beyond his role as a director and a producer, Johar's most notable stint has been as the host of a popular talk show, *Koffee with Karan*. The show sees Johar interview Bollywood celebrities, who share candid truths from their personal and professional lives. A witty show, with a fair share of gossip, *Koffee with Karan* was first aired in 2004, and has since then completed five seasons, all of them generating impressive Television Rating Points (TRPs).

In the two decades of his career so far, Johar has shown his versatility by donning several hats—director, producer, distributor, and actor, as well as TV show host, judge, and awards presenter—and he shows no sign of slowing down. Indeed, any history of Bollywood would be incomplete without him.

▼ **The ace producer**
Johar took over his father's Dharma Productions. Under his leadership, the studio has produced high-grossing films such as *Badrinath ki Dulhania* (2017), a classic Bollywood romantic comedy.

TIMELINE

● **October 1995** Bollywood debut as an assistant director in the blockbuster *Dilwale Dulhania Le Jayenge*.

● **October 1998** His first film as director, the romantic drama *Kuch Kuch Hota Hai*, breaks box-office records, and wins numerous awards.

● **December 2001** Directs a big-budget multi-star family drama, *Kabhi Khushi Kabhie Gham*, a box office success in both India and abroad.

● **November 2003** Writes and produces *Kal Ho Naa Ho*, which is both a critical and a box office success.

● **November 2004** Hosts the first season of a Bollywood talk show, *Koffee with Karan*, making his TV debut.

● **August 2006** Based on the bold subject of marital infidelity, his third film as director is *Kabhi Alvida Naa Kehna*.

● **September 2006** Becomes the first Indian filmmaker to be on the jury for the Miss World competition.

● **February 2010** His next directorial effort, *My Name is Khan*—much of which is set in post-9/11 America— releases to remarkable critical acclaim and impressive box office success.

● **October 2012** Introduces three newcomers—Alia Bhatt, Varun Dhawan, and Sidharth Malhotra— to the industry with the romantic drama *Student of the Year*. All have become established actors.

● **May 2013** Directs a short movie in the anthology film *Bombay Talkies*.

● **October 2016** Release of his directorial effort *Ae Dil Hai Mushkil*.

● **January 2017** Publishes his memoir, *An Unsuitable Boy*.

● **February 2017** Becomes single parent to twins, a boy and a girl, through surrogacy.

THE OMNIBUS FILM CELEBRATES 100 YEARS OF HINDI CINEMA

"*Few writers have such solid control over their screenplay as Karan Johar does.*"

RAJEEV MASAND, FILM CRITIC

SARFAROSH

1999

CAST AND CREW

★ **Naseeruddin Shah** Gulfam Hassan
Aamir Khan Ajay Singh Rathod
Sonali Bendre Seema
Inspector Salim Mukesh Rishi
Sultan Pradeep Rawat

🎬 **Director** John Matthew Matthan
⬡ **Producer** John Matthew Matthan
🎵 **Music composers** Jatin Pandit,
Lalit Pandit
♪ **Lyricists** Indeevar, Israr Ansari,
Nida Fazli, Sameer
📖 **Scriptwriter** John Matthew Matthan
🎥 **Cinematographer** Vikas Sivaraman
👔 **Costume designer** Lovleen Bains

Sarfarosh is a riveting crime thriller that delicately touches on the subject of patriotism and skillfully tackles a storyline about cross-border terrorism.

> *"When I read the script ... I realized the social implications of what the film is trying to say."*
>
> **AAMIR KHAN**, *THE TIMES OF INDIA*, 1999

John Matthew Matthan's *Sarfarosh* (Fervor) revolves around an intense, tough-as-nails cop, Ajay Singh Rathod. An Assistant Commissioner of Police, Ajay is a no-nonsense man who is determined to track down a gang involved in the trafficking of arms into India. His mission is complicated by his relationship with Gulfam Hassan, a ghazal singer who emigrated to Pakistan as a child, during the partition of India in 1947.

The portrayal of Ajay is the embodiment of sheer aggression—a type of performance Indian audiences had not seen from Aamir Khan (see pp. 228–29) before. He had debuted in 1988 with a romantic drama, *Qayamat se Qayamat tak* (see pp. 194–97), and had played the role of a cop just once before, in *Baazi* (1995). With the exception of a few films, he wasn't known for playing characters with a violent streak to them. *Sarfarosh* changed that.

GREAT NARRATIVE

Like most good films, *Sarfarosh* features well-written, complex characters. While Ajay is an intense and sincere hero, his nemesis Gulfam is charming and sly. Then there is Inspector Salim, who is unfairly treated by his own department because he is a Muslim.

Sarfarosh, through its characters, highlights a number of social issues. For example, it touches on the concept of Islamophobia, while insisting on the need for Hindu–Muslim unity. It shows how terrorism can affect everyday lives, and how art can bring Pakistanis and Indians together.

Sarfarosh also stands out from regular Bollywood thrillers and films about terrorism in the way it was written and filmed. For instance, the film's storyline is nuanced, it doesn't use jingoism as a crutch, and it does not exaggerate its villain. In fact, the character of Gulfam, a fresh departure from stereotypical Bollywood villains, is the film's high point—a man caught between his love for art and a desire for vengeance.

CROWD PLEASER

Despite its serious storyline, the film is still a mainstream entertainer, especially noteworthy for its engaging music. A ghazal sung by Jagjit Singh, "Hoshwalon Ko Khabar Kya" (How Would the Sensible Know What It Means to Be Clueless?), is still popular. In addition to the music, *Sarfarosh* has other elements that make it a crowd pleaser: characters providing

▲ **Typically "Bollywood"**
Sonali Bendre and Aamir Khan shared a fiery chemistry on screen. They both looked stunning performing a racy number, "Jo Haal Dil Ka" (State of My Heart), shown here on the film poster.

comic relief, an engaging plot, and a satisfying climax. So it is not surprising that *Sarfarosh* received wide critical acclaim and won four Filmfare Awards: the Critics Award for Best Movie, Best Editing, Best Screenplay, and Best Dialogue. It also won the National Film Award for Best Popular Film Providing Wholesome Entertainment. Seven years in the making, *Sarfarosh* was worth the wait.

◀ **Suspense thriller**
Ajay (left) attends a concert by Gulfam and becomes friends with him. Their bond is tested in a surprising turn of events toward the end of the film.

TAAL

With a masterful soundtrack by A.R. Rahman, *Taal* reaffirmed the importance of music in Bollywood—and the role it could play in turning a film into a hit.

CAST AND CREW

★ **Anil Kapoor** Vikrant Kapoor
Akshaye Khanna Manav Mehta
Aishwarya Rai Mansi
Alok Nath Tara Babu
Amrish Puri Jagmohan Mehta
Mita Vasisht Prabha Shankar
Saurabh Shukla Bannerjee

🎬 **Director** Subhash Ghai
💠 **Producer** Raju Farooqui
🎵 **Music composer** A.R. Rahman
✍ **Lyricist** Anand Bakshi
🕺 **Choreographers** Shiamak Davar, Ahmed Khan, Saroj Khan
📖 **Scriptwriter** Sachin Bhowmick
🎥 **Cinematographer** Kabir Lal
👔 **Costume designer** Shaahid Amir

▶ **Singing sensation**
Mansi, played by Aishwarya Rai, becomes an international MTV sensation because of her extraordinary voice. Here she performs on stage to "Kahin Aag Lage" (If a Fire Sparks, Let it Burn!).

Some songs are eternal. It doesn't matter whether they are part of a film, an album, or are stand-alone numbers: they are destined to last, to be replayed, and to be remembered. Composing one such song is tough, but creating an entire soundtrack in which nearly every song stakes a claim to immortality is an incredible achievement. This is precisely what A.R. Rahman (see pp. 244–45) managed with *Taal* (Rhythm). Nearly two decades later, the film's soundtrack is still fresh and captivating.

LOVE TRIANGLE
Taal is the story of Manav and Mansi, who fall in love. However, their parents, especially Manav's, are opposed to their marriage because of class differences. Manav is the son of a wealthy industrialist and lives in Mumbai, whereas Mansi is the daughter of a poor folk singer and lives in Chamba, Himachal Pradesh. A misunderstanding between the two drives them apart. Later, Mansi meets Vikrant Kapoor, a famous music director, and begins performing in his productions, which remix some of her father's songs. He eventually falls in love with Mansi. The film then follows each of the three characters as they try to understand what is right for them, and what they want from life.

MUSICAL MASTERPIECE
Taal's music was wildly popular, selling more than 1.8 million copies within a month of its release. The film's soundtrack also received

▲ **Together in Chamba**
Manav is bewitched by Mansi's beauty, as shown here. He falls in love with her irrespective of her low social status.

several Filmfare Awards. Rahman won an award for Best Music, Anand Bakshi for Best Lyrics, and Alka Yagnik won for Best Female Playback Singer. Rahman and director Subhash Ghai collaborated on two more films in subsequent years: *Kisna: The Warrior Poet* (2005) and *Yuvvraaj* (2008).

The film was a box office hit—the third-highest-grossing film of the year—and was nominated for 11 Filmfare Awards. It also performed well internationally, featuring in *Variety*'s top 20 box office list. It so impressed American film critic Roger Ebert that in 2005 he included it in his Overlooked Film Festival.

The enthusiastic reception to *Taal*, both in India and abroad, reaffirmed something valuable—that a film based on good music can cross borders.

HIT SONGS

Taal Se Taal Mila
(Match Your Rhythm to Mine)
🎤 **Singers** Alka Yagnik, Udit Narayan

Ishq Bina Kya Jina Yaaron
(There's No Life Without Love)
🎤 **Singers** Sonu Nigam, Anuradha Sriram, Sujatha Mohan

Ramta Jogi
(Wandering Yogi)
🎤 **Singers** Alka Yagnik, Sukhwinder Singh

GLAMOUR QUEENS

From the 1990s onwards, many Indian models sought a career in films after winning renowned beauty pageants. Some went on to become big film stars.

Models in India have often shot to stardom through beauty pageants. For instance, Zeenat Aman (see p. 156) won the title of Miss Asia Pacific in 1970, and landed her first major role in *Hare Rama Hare Krishna* (see p. 108) a year later. Meenakshi Sheshadri won the Miss India title in 1981, and soon appeared in *Hero* (see p. 181), opposite Jackie Shroff (see p. 181), in 1983. Another film star, Juhi Chawla, (see p. 194) became Miss India in 1984, and then debuted in the multi-starrer *Sultanat* in 1986. However, it was only in the 1990s that Indian models started winning international beauty pageants on a regular basis. This all-important recognition helped them rise to stardom, making pageants a foolproof platform for entering Bollywood.

REIGNING STARS

In 1994, Sushmita Sen won the Miss World pageant and Aishwarya Rai (see pp. 256–57) won Miss Universe. Both soon became prominent names in Bollywood. Aishwarya, in particular, has had a successful acting career, appearing in films such as the 2002 version of *Devdas* (see pp. 276–79) and *Dhoom 2* (2006), helmed by leading Bollywood directors. Sushmita, an outsider in the industry, has enjoyed a successful run in Bollywood, too, with films such as *Main Hoon na* (2004) and *Maine Pyaar Kyun Kiya* (2005).

The late 1990s saw three more beauty pageant winners—Diana Hayden (Miss World, 1997), Gul Panag (Miss India, 1999), and Yukta Mookhey (Miss World, 1999)—making their debuts in films. However, they found limited success in the industry.

As in 1994, the year 2000 saw beauty queens Lara Dutta and Priyanka Chopra (see pp. 280–81), winning the Miss Universe and Miss World titles, respectively. Continuing the trend, Priyanka entered Bollywood and eventually became a superstar. She has regularly acted in big budget films, several of them featuring her in diverse roles, such as *Aitraaz* (see p. 279) and *Barfi!* (2012). Priyanka has arguably been the most successful beauty-pageant winner in Bollywood, becoming an international star with her performance in a popular American TV series *Quantico* (2015).

Beauty pageants continue to offer a springboard for aspiring models who use them to ease their way into the glamorous world of Bollywood. And so, with every Indian model who wins a pageant, Bollywood now looks for a star beneath the crown.

▶ Role model
Sushmita Sen (center) became the first Indian woman to win the prestigious Miss Universe title in 1994, inspiring other talented models to participate in global beauty pageants.

"Many beauty queens sought careers in the movies, setting new standards for beauty in Bollywood."

MANISH TELIKICHERLA CHARY, *INDIA: NATION ON THE MOVE*, 2009

AISHWARYA RAI

ACTOR **b.1973**

Natural beauty Aishwarya Rai's fairy-tale rise to stardom has taken her from model and Miss World winner to a successful crossover career in the movies.

On November 19,1994, in Sun City Entertainment Center, South Africa, a voice boomed in a crowded stadium: "… and Miss World 1994 is Miss India." From the moment those words were uttered, Aishwarya Rai's flight to fame took off. She took the world by storm with her dazzling beauty and charm, and passed milestone after milestone to emerge as a global celebrity and style icon for millions around the world.

BEFORE BOLLYWOOD

Born on November 1, 1973 in Mangalore, Karnataka, Aishwarya was four years old when her family moved to Mumbai. Apart from academic pursuits, she also trained in Indian classical music and dance. Her blue-green eyes and radiant beauty were spotted when she was in the ninth grade, and she was cast in her first commercial, for the stationery company Camelin Pencils. She moved on to modeling, winning an international supermodel contest organized by Ford Models in 1991. A feature in *Vogue* magazine by ace American fashion photographer Steven Meisel led to a Pepsi commercial, directed by adman Prahalad Kakkar. which put her on Tinseltown's radar.

After appearing in several more advertisements, Aishwarya decided to enter the 1994 Femina Miss India contest. Although she won several sub-contests and was a popular choice in the race, Aishwarya lost the crown to Sushmita Sen and was placed first runner-up. Later that year, she won the Miss World crown, serving the pageant motto "Beauty with a purpose" with earnest dedication. She continued modeling, and won top endorsement deals from numerous global brands, including diamond company De Beers, the

▲ **Miss World 1994**
Oozing confidence, elegance, and charisma, Aishwarya impressed both judges and audiences alike with her effortless glamour and insightful answers in the Miss World pageant.

Swiss watch company Longines, and the beauty giant L'Oréal, while also launching her career in films.

ON-SCREEN BEAUTY

Aishwarya began her work in Indian cinema with Mani Ratnam's critically acclaimed *Iruvar* (1997), a Tamil

▶ **Grace personified**
Often called "the most beautiful woman in the world," Aishwarya is also a trained Indian classical dancer. Her graceful and expressive performance in *Taal* proved that she was more than just a "pretty face."

political saga for which her dancing abilities received high praise. The same year saw the release of her first Hindi film, *Aur Pyaar ho Gaya*, for which she won the Screen Award for Best Female Debut. In 1999, she gave a brilliant performance opposite Salman Khan in Sanjay Leela Bhansali's *Hum Dil De Chuke Sanam* (see pp. 256–57), showing great emotional range as Nandini Durbar. Her talent as an actress and dancer was further asserted in Subhash Ghai's hugely successful film *Taal* (1999).

Aishwarya continued to wow critics and audiences with Bhansali's epic drama *Devdas*, which proved to be a hallmark of her career. In this big-budget adaptation of Sharat Chandra Chattopadhyay's Bengali novel by the same name, Aishwarya

> *"For me, it's not about breaking big in Hollywood, but having interesting experiences."*

AISHWARYA RAI, IN AN INTERVIEW WITH *TIME* MAGAZINE, OCTOBER 27, 2003

KEY WORKS

Taal, 1999 (see p. 251)

Hum Dil De Chuke Sanam,1999 (see pp. 256–57)

Devdas, 2002 (see pp. 274–77)

Chokher Baali, 2003

Bride & Prejudice, 2004

Jodhaa Akbar, 2008 (see pp. 300–01)

The Pink Panther 2, 2009

▲ **Cameo role**
Aishwarya grooves with Shah Rukh Khan to the tunes of the hit item song "Ishq Kamina" (Wretched Love) in *Shakti: The Power*. In this movie, she makes a special appearance as Shah Rukh's gorgeous and sultry "fantasy girl."

starred alongside Bollywood legends Madhuri Dixit and Shah Rukh Khan, and won her second Filmfare Award for Best Actress for her performance as Paro. Always one to push boundaries, Aishwarya also explored Bengali cinema with Rituparno Ghosh's *Chokher Bali,* in which she portrays the plight of a young widow. The film was a sleeper hit and won her the Best Actress trophy at the Anandalok Awards show, one of the biggest events in the Bengali film industry.

In 2006, she appeared in Sanjay Gadhvi's *Dhoom 2* and, in 2007, in Mani Ratnam's *Guru.* The films were significant projects not only due to their commercial success but also because they were the stage on which she met her future partner, Abhishek Bachchan. After a courtship of three months, the star couple were engaged on January 14, 2007, and tied the knot in a low-key ceremony.

CROSSOVER STAR

Aishwarya made her Hollywood debut in 2004 with Gurinder Chadhha's *Bride & Prejudice*—an adaptation of Jane Austen's novel, *Pride and Prejudice.* Aishwarya played the female lead,

which was an Indian take on the intelligent and independent heroine, Elizabeth Bennet. She poured herself effortlessly into the mold of the character and won worldwide recognition as an actress with the talent and international appeal to take on a wide range of roles. Over the next few years, her choice of films reflected the scope of her talents. In Paul Mayeda Berges' *Mistress of Spices* (2005) she played the mysterious spice seller with otherworldy powers. In Jag Mundhra's *Provoked* (2006), she depicted Kiranjit Ahluwalia, a real-life victim of domestic abuse. In 2007, she starred in Doug Lefler's action flick *The Last Legion,* playing an Indian warrior, Mira. Recently, she starred in Harald Zwart's *The Pink Panther 2,* with Hollywood veterans Andy Garcia,

Steve Martin, and Jean Reno. Respected for more than her acting skills, Aishwarya was the first Indian actress to be invited to be a jury member at the Cannes Film Festival, in 2003. She has been a regular participant at the prestigious event ever since. Today, she has achieved an enviable status of being one of the first few successful crossover movie stars from Bollywood.

GIVING BACK

Aishwarya's humanitarian efforts led to her appointment as International Goodwill Ambassador for UNAIDS (combatting HIV/AIDS) in 2012. She has also established the Aishwarya Rai Foundation for the underprivileged, sponsored cleft-palate surgery for 100 children through the Smile Train Charity, and appeared in multiple health awareness campaigns.

After a five-year hiatus during which she focussed on her family, Aishwarya returned to the big screen with three films—*Jazbaa* (2015), *Sarbjit* (2016), and Karan Johar's *Ae Dil Hai Mushkil* (2016).

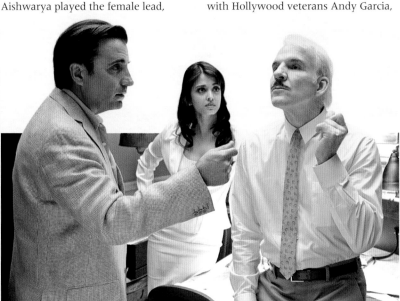

◀ **The Pink Panther 2**
In this reprise of the Pink Panther comedies, Aishwarya (center) plays Sonia, a seductive criminology expert, alongside Andy Garcia (left) and Steve Martin (right) as Inspector Clouseau.

TIMELINE

● **November 1, 1973** Born in Mangalore, Karnataka.

● **1991** Wins the international supermodel contest organized by Ford Models.

● **1993** Gains recognition as a model and actress after appearing in a Pepsi commercial with celebrities Aamir Khan and Mahima Chaudhary.

● **1994** Places second in the Miss India contest, losing out to Sushmita Sen. Moves on to win the Miss World crown.

● **1997** Wins Star Screen Award for Most Promising Newcomer for her first Bollywood film, *Aur Pyar Ho Gaya.*

● **2001** Joins several Bollywood stars, including Aamir Khan and Anil Kapoor, for the Craze 2001 concert tour of North America.

● **2002** Receives critical acclaim for her role in *Devdas,* which was featured by *Time* magazine in a list of "Ten best films of the millennium."

AISHWARYA FEATURES ON A POSTER FOR *BRIDE & PREJUDICE*

● **2003** Becomes the first Indian actress to be a jury member at the Cannes Film Festival.

● **2004** Stars in the commercial hit *Bride & Prejudice,* her first role in an English-speaking film.

● **2005** Appointed brand ambassador for Pulse Polio, a Government of India initiative to eradicate polio in the country.

● **2006** Stars in the box office hit *Dhoom 2,* India's highest-grossing film that year.

● **2007** Marries actor Abhishek Bachchan.

● **2008** Wins the Filmfare Award for Best Actress for her performance in the period drama *Jodhaa Akbar* opposite Hrithik Roshan.

● **2009** Recieves the Padma Shri, the fourth-highest Indian civilian award for her contributions to the Arts.

● **2012** Awarded the *Ordre des Arts et des Lettres,* a French national award.

HUM DIL DE CHUKE SANAM

1999

A colorful and vibrant musical, *Hum Dil de Chuke Sanam* was Sanjay Leela Bhansali's first commercial success and brought Aishwarya Rai much-needed credibility as an actress in Hindi films.

JHAMU SUGHAND presents

Hum Dil De Chuke Sanam

A SANJAY LEELA BHANSALI FILM

MUSIC ISMAIL DARBAR   LYRICS MEHBOOB   CINEMATOGRAPHY ANIL MEHTA

www.humdildechukesanam.com

An opulent film filled with vivid colors, palatial sets, gorgeous costumes, melodious music, heady romance, and above all, heightened melodrama, *Hum Dil de Chuke Sanam* (I Have Given My Heart Away Darling) is regarded as the blueprint of a typical Sanjay Leela Bhansali film. It established him as one of mainstream Hindi cinema's premier filmmakers.

FORTUNATE FIND

Hum Dil de Chuke Sanam, abbreviated as *HDDCS*, begins with Sameer Rossellini traveling to India from Italy to learn classical music from reputed singer Pundit Durbar. A romantic relationship develops between him and Durbar's daughter, Nandini, during his stay at Durbar's house. Durbar is furious when he finds out about the clandestine affair, as he had already planned for Nandini to marry a lawyer, Vanraj. Sameer is asked to leave, and a reluctant Nandini is married off to Vanraj. When Vanraj finds out about her true love, he decides to take her to Italy to reunite her with Sameer. The film is a tribute to selfless love and the sacrifices it entails.

Writer Pratap Karvat was determined to work with Bhansali after watching his directorial debut *Khamoshi: The Musical* (1996). He tried to contact Bhansali repeatedly to set up a meeting with him, but when that didn't work out, Karvat narrated the story to Bhansali over a phone call. The ploy

worked: Bhansali was hooked on the idea and asked Karvat to meet him the same day. Looking for a story for the audience that had rejected *Khamoshi: The Musical*, Bhansali saw strong potential in Karvat's story with a Gujarati backdrop.

Even before *HDDCS*, filmmaker Bapu's *Woh 7 Din* (1983) saw actor Naseeruddin Shah (see p. 185) trying to unite his on-screen wife, Padmini

◄ **Love triangle**
Based on a classic love triangle—as reflected in this poster—the film was director Sanjay Leela Bhansali's first commercial hit.

CAST AND CREW

★ **Salman Khan** Sameer Rossellini
Aishwarya Rai Nandini
Ajay Devgn Vanraj
Vikram Gokhale Pundit Durbar

Director Sanjay Leela Bhansali
Producer Sanjay Leela Bhansali
Music composers Ismail Darbar, Anjan Biswas
Lyricist Mehboob
Scriptwriters Sanjay Leela Bhansali, Amrik Gill, Kenneth Phillips, Pratap Karvat
Cinematographer Anil Mehta
Costume designer Neeta Lulla, Shabina Khan

HIT SONGS

Aankhon Ki Gustakhiyan
(The Games Eyes Play)
Singers Kavita Krishnamurthy, Kumar Sanu

Nimbooda
(Small Lemon)
Singers Kavita Krishnamurthy, Karsan Sagathia

Dholi Taro Dhol Baje
(Drumbeater, Your Drum Is Beating)
Singers Kavita Krishnamurthy, Vinod Rathod, Karsan Sagathia

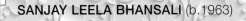

Kolhapure, with the man she loved before her marriage. *Woh 7 Din* was a more intimate drama, but with *HDDCS*, Bhansali dazzled audiences with his larger than life yet sensitive treatment with a strong emotional core.

AISHWARYA'S BREAKTHROUGH
Despite her fine acting debut in director Mani Ratnam's Tamil political drama, *Iruvar* (1997), the Hindi film world had yet to see Aishwarya Rai's (see pp. 254–55) magic; her work in earlier films such as *Aur Pyaar Ho Gaya* (1997) and *Aa Ab Laut Chalen* (1999) had not made an impact.

Many people advised Bhansali not to choose Aishwarya for the role of Nandini. Apart from doubting her acting ability, they also felt that her look was too sophisticated and western for the character. Bhansali, however, was determined she should play the part, and stood by his decision. He had her hair styled in a long plait and ensured her character wore traditional Indian outfits. Aishwarya responded with a fine performance that captured every shade of Nandini.

FROM REEL LIFE TO REAL LIFE
The screen romance of the lead pair, Salman Khan (see pp. 224–25) and Aishwarya, merged with their real-life love affair during the making of the film, resulting in scintillating chemistry on screen. It is alleged that Salman even wanted a different ending in which Aishwarya and his character would end up together, and sought help from Sooraj Barjatya to persuade Bhansali. But once again, Bhansali stood firm.

A MUSICAL TREAT
With music so integral to the story, it was surprising that Bhansali entrusted it to a newcomer, Ismail Darbar, a violinist who had played for various composers, including A.R. Rahman (see pp. 244–45). Bhansali was clear that he wanted someone who would give a lot of time to the project. It is said that the duo worked for a full two years on the film's music. All the planning and hard work resulted in a meticulously composed and beautifully filmed soundtrack. The song, "Dholi Taro Dhol Baje," picturized with Gujarati folk dance, garba, was shot by Bhansali on a floor made of acrylic. The cinematographer, Anil Mehta, had a pit built under the floor and had it painted white, so lights could be placed and bounced off to give the floor a glow—the song became a major hit.

THE FOREIGN LOCALE
The Italian scenes in the film were shot in Hungary, with the landmark Széchenyi Chain Bridge used as the location for the film's poignant finale. According to Bhansali, the locations in Hungary were perfect, especially the bridge which served as an important backdrop. However, he also felt that audiences would be unfamiliar with Hungary, and decided it was best to the story in Italy.

Hum Dil De Chuke Sanam proved to be a huge success. It went on to win four National Awards—Best Cinematography, Art Direction, Music, and Choreography—as well as the Filmfare Awards for Best Film, Director, and Actress, among others.

SANJAY LEELA BHANSALI (b.1963)
Few filmmakers in Bollywood today can match producer–director Sanjay Leela Bhansali's opulent, larger-than-life cinema and visualization of songs. Bhansali's films often transport the viewer back to a more classical era of Indian cinema. Having studied Film Editing at the Film & Television Institute of India (FTII), Pune, he began as an assistant director to director Vidhu Vinod Chopra before turning director himself. His breakthrough came with his second film, *Hum Dil de Chuke Sanam*. Bhansali has become known for including particularly strong female characters in all of his films.

> *"Every moment of Hum Dil De Chuke Sanam was memorable."*
>
> AISHWARYA RAI, *FILMFARE*, 2000

▼ **Intense chemistry**
The chemistry of the lead pair, Salman Khan and Aishwarya Rai, is often attributed to their then off-screen love affair.

THE AGE OF BIG MONEY

2000–PRESENT

The 2000s set new benchmarks for Bollywood, with huge
box office receipts, larger-than-life films, strong women
leads, big studios, and even bigger budgets.

THE AGE OF BIG MONEY

The turn of the millenium ushered in a new era of epic movies, big studios, and burgeoning budgets; however, it was also a time when experimental filmmaking made a comeback.

▲ **Expensive comedy caper**
Largely shot in the United Arab Emirates and with a cast of luxury cars, Anees Bazmee's *Welcome Back* is a typical Bollywood film of this era.

Bollywood has always tapped into the nation's mood, and mainstream films that offer feel-good escapism not only distract and entertain audiences—they also reflect people's joys, struggles, frustrations, and aspirations. The story of Bollywood in the 21st century reflects India's rising influence and economic growth in the new millennium.

THE BIG MONEY CLUB

The big-budget, cotton candy romances of the 1990s were such sure-fire commercial successes that production houses such as Yash Raj Films, Dharma Productions, churned out a large quantity of such films. But the audiences were changing, as were their tastes. By the 2000s the Bollywood dream machine had grown, and to sustain the appeal and magic that kept audiences hooked, the films needed to be even bigger, bolder, and shinier. And so, the measure of success

▲ Multiplex cinema halls
Multiscreen cinema halls, such as the PVR theater chain, have sprouted up all over Indian cities, enabling a wider reach for movies.

changed; big budgets meant huge box office receipts. In 2008, Aamir Khan's film *Ghajini* broke box office records, creating the ₹100-crore ($15 million) club in Bollywood. In the next five years, around 25 films hit the ₹100-crore mark, and later in 2014, the ₹300-crore ($46 million) club was established by *PK* (see pp. 324–25). Film budgets became bigger; *Dhoom 3* (2013) from the Yash Raj stable had a budget of ₹1.75 billion ($27 million), and the Salman Khan-starrer *Prem*

◄ *Bajirao Mastani*'s grand sets
No expense was spared for Bajirao's court: 50 ft (15 m) pillars were built, along with with lavish chandeliers, streams of water, and gold lotuses.

Ratan Dhan Payo (2015) was made for ₹1.8 billion ($28 million). Big films meant bigger returns, and production houses splurged like never before. In *Veer: An Epic Love Story of a Warrior* (2010), Salman Khan's six outfits cost ₹2 million ($31,000) each, while Shah Rukh Khan's costumes in the superhero film *Ra.One* (2011) cost ₹45 million ($700,000) each. As the film industry grew bigger, Bollywood also went global, and international production houses such as Walt Disney Pictures and Fox Star Studios also entered the scene. Soon, Bollywood was going places, quite literally. Increased budgets were not the only development, and locations became more glamorous to cater to new global audiences. While earlier films such as *Kabhi Khushi Kabhie Gham* (see pp. 270–71) and *Diwale Dulhaniya le Jaayenge* (see pp. 230–33) were shot in familiar locales such as London and Switzerland, in the late 2000s Bollywood found other exotic locations. In *Rockstar* (2011) the hero wooes his lady through the streets of Prague, and in the spy romance *Ek tha Tiger* (2012) Salman Khan runs through Havana, Dublin, and Hong Kong. In *Tamasha* (2015) the lead pair dances on the beaches of Corsica.

A NEW LANGUAGE OF CINEMA

The 2000s also saw an unusual shift in the movie business. Not all the big-budget blockbusters were successful, and as a result some studios turned their attention to small-budget, script-driven films with affordable actors. For example, Karan Johar (see pp. 248–49) produced *The Lunchbox* (2013), a modest movie made for ₹90 million ($1.4 million); the film ended up making more than ₹1 billion

($15 million). Similarly, Yash Raj Studios invested in *Dum Laga ke Haisha* (2015), a film about a middle-class, small-town couple in Haridwar, Uttarakhand—a far cry from the extravagant productions of the mainstream.

As well as proving popular with domestic audiences, many of these gritty, realistic films became the toast of international film festivals. *The Lunchbox* won the Critics Week Viewers Choice Award at the Cannes Film Festival and was India's official entry for the British Academy of Films and Television Awards (BAFTA). The drama *Titli* (2014) won the Best First Foreign Film Award from the French Syndicate of Cinema Critics 2016, while indie film *Masaan* (2015) won the Avenir Prize in the Un Certain Regard at the Cannes Film Festival 2015. The British Film Institute (BFI) dedicated 2017 to celebrating Indian cinema that pushed the boundaries of

► Recreating history
Filmmakers of period films such as *Jodhaa Akbar* (pictured here) and *Devdas* spent a lot of time and money replicating opulent jewelry worn in these times.

◄ Bollywood goes international
Beautiful locations are typical of recent films; for example, *Dil Dhadakne Do* (2015) is about a dysfunctional family on a Mediterranean cruise.

typical Bollywood-style filmmaking by delving into issues such as caste, gender, and sexuality.

THE NEW-AGE HEROINE

Around this time, a series of scripts reinvented Bollywood's heroines. With the huge success of *The Dirty Picture* (2011), *Kahaani* (see p. 312) and *English Vinglish* (2012), Bollywood started taking its actresses seriously. Smaller, well-written films that reimagines the heroine were suddenly in demand. It wasn't a coincidence that heroines now had stronger roles; no longer happy to play second fiddle, Bollywood's leading ladies realized the potential of the market and worked harder than ever for these roles. Vidya Balan (see p. 312), who played the role inspired by the controversial actress Silk Smitha in *Dirty Picture* (2011), gained weight, drank, and smoked to get into the skin of her character. Priyanka Chopra (see pp. 280–81), meanwhile, visited centers for autistic people to research her role of an autistic girl in *Barfi!* (2012).

All this translated into commercial success; made on a budget of ₹170 million ($2.6 million), *Queen* (see pp. 320–21), generated more than ₹1.08 billion ($16.8 million), while *Piku* (see p. 327) and *Pink* (2016), both of which have women in central roles, saw immense box office success.

The following section tells the story of a Bollywood that's growing and changing. It also chronicles, one hit at a time, what goes into making the Bollywood dream bigger, bolder, and shinier.

KAHO NAA... PYAAR HAI

2000

A tale of love across an unbridgeable social divide, *Kaho naa... Pyaar hai* is a delightful dose of charm and humor, with a subplot involving a murder and mistaken identity.

CAST AND CREW

★ **Hrithik Roshan** Rohit and Raj
Ameesha Patel Sonia Saxena
Anupam Kher Mr. Saxena
Dalip Tahil Shakti Malik
Tanaz Currim Neeta
Mohnish Behl Inspector Kadam
Ashish Vidyarthi Inspector Shinde

🎬 **Director** Rakesh Roshan
🏠 **Producers** Rakesh Roshan, Filmkraft Productions (I) Pvt. Ltd
🎵 **Music composer** Rajesh Roshan
♪ **Lyricists** Saawan Kumar Tak, Vijay Akela, Ibrahim Ashq
🕺 **Choreographer** Farah Khan
📖 **Scriptwriters** Ravi Kapoor, Honey Irani
🎥 **Cinematographer** Kabir Lal

▼ **Stars in the making**
The film rocketed Hrithik Roshan and Ameesha Patel to stardom. Hrithik is one of a handful of actors to have successfully taken on dual roles. In each scene, he was careful to disguise his right hand, which has six fingers.

The familiar rich-girl-meets-poor-boy formula is given a makeover in director Rakesh Roshan's romantic thriller *Kaho naa... Pyaar hai* (Say... You Love Me), or *KNPH*. The film marked the debut of Rakesh's son, Hrithik Roshan, as lead actor, and of Ameesha Patel as lead actress. Both debut actors shone in the film, Hrithik playing the dual roles of Rohit and lookalike Raj with panache, and Ameesha portraying the young and naive Sonia.

Even though the critics were not overly impressed with the film, they were unanimous in declaring it highly entertaining, attributing its appeal largely to the charisma of its leading man.

Hrithik plays Rohit, an aspiring singer who works as a car salesman to earn money on the side. When the wealthy Mr. Saxena comes to the showroom to buy a car for his daughter Sonia's birthday, Rohit delivers the car and ends up performing at her party.

◀ **Forces of darkness**
Unbeknown to Rohit, his boss, Malik (second from left), is plotting against him and Sonia, in cahoots with her scheming father Mr. Saxena (right).

THE COURSE OF TRUE LOVE
The attraction between Rohit and Sonia is undeniable and, as Cupid intervenes, they end up on a cruise ship together. As the evening progresses, the couple fall drunkenly into a lifeboat, which gets detached from the ship and drifts off to an island, which is the setting for their love story.

After a frantic search, the two are rescued. But the return to civilization is not pleasant, as Mr. Saxena disapproves of the relationship and is determined to separate the lovers. Rohit is determined to prove himself worthy of Sonia, but events take an unexpected turn: a murder, a drug cartel, and a handsome stranger (Raj) in New Zealand disrupt the love story.

BEGINNER'S LUCK
Box office numbers were not the only positive outcome for *Kaho naa... Pyaar hai*. It was

as if the film, and those involved in it, had been sprinkled with gold dust. Both debut actors became popular, with Bollywood finding its new superstar in Hrithik. The immense success of the film was a surprise even for Rakesh Roshan. Although he thought it was "a well-made film with very good music and an interesting storyline," nothing prepared him for its overwhelming popularity: it became the highest-grossing film of 2000, and the sixth-highest grosser of the entire decade.

CASTING ISSUES
Hrithik had worked as an assistant director before, but never been in front of the camera. Rakesh Roshan had initially wanted superstar Shah Rukh

HIT SONGS

Kaho Na Pyaar Hai
(Say You Love Me)
🎤 **Singers** Udit Narayan, Alka Yagnik

Na Tum Jaano Na Hum
(Neither You Nor Me Know)
🎤 **Singers** Lucky Ali, Ramya

Ek Pal Ka Jeena
(We Live for Just a Moment)
🎤 **Singer** Lucky Ali

Khan (see p. 215–16) for the lead role; the two had worked before on *Koyla* (1995). However, Hrithik persuaded his father to try someone new and different, little knowing that would be him. The role of Sonia was originally destined for Kareena Kapoor, but the actress walked off the set a week into the shoot, citing creative differences. In walked a fresh face—Ameesha.

OVERNIGHT SENSATIONS

Hrithik took his preparation for the role seriously: he weight-trained to bulk up and sculpt his physique for the role of the urban, Non-Resident Indian (NRI) Raj, with advice from superstar Salman Khan (see pp. 224–25). Hrithik's handsome face, fit body, and charming demeanor made him India's new pin-up, attracting a legion of female fans: he received a reported 30,000 marriage proposals. The nation's cultlike devotion to the actor was such that a new word emerged in popular culture to describe the buzz: "Hrithikmania." Ameesha, too, was a hit as she made the role of the frivolous, rich girl Sonia her own. Hrithik went on to become the first actor in the history of Bollywood to win the Filmfare Award for both the Best Debut and Best Actor.

His father, producer and director Rakesh Roshan, also enjoyed victory at the annual film industry ceremonies, winning Best Film and Best Director at all the major awards events including, the Filmfare and International Indian Film Academy (IIFA) awards.

A MUSICAL TREAT

The music of the film was another coup for Rakesh Roshan, who wrote the score. The soundtrack, supported by Farah Khan's ace choreography, became Bollywood's best-selling album of the year. Playback singer Lucky Ali, whose voice is heard on tracks such as "Na Tum Jano Na Hum" and "Ek Pal Ka Jeena," was propelled into the limelight, although he had been working in the industry for decades. That year, Lucky Ali won Best Playback Singer at the Filmfare Awards, as well as Best Male Playback Singer at the IIFA, Star Screen, and Zee Cine Awards.

All in all, *Kaho naa... Pyaar hai* won an incredible 102 awards, prompting the Limca Book of Records to feature the achievement.

> *"I thought ... the film would become a moderate success, but not in my wildest imagination did I expect it to become such a huge hit."*

RAKESH ROSHAN, *THE QUINT*, 2016

HRITHIK ROSHAN
(b.1974)

Growing up in the shadow of his father, film director Rakesh Roshan, Hrithik set his heart on a career in Bollywood when he was still a boy. He was first cast in *Bhagwaan Dada* (1986), with father Rakesh playing the lead. Following his sensational debut in *Kaho naa... Pyaar hai*, he acted in films such as the science fiction movie *Koi... Mil Gaya* (2003), bike thriller *Dhoom 2* (2006) and historical biopic *Jodhaa Akbar* (2008), cementing his position in the industry as one of India's highest paid, and much-loved actors.

▼ Signature move
Although Hrithik was nervous when it came to the dance numbers, his fist-pumping in "Ek Pal Ka Jeena," seen here, became a signature move.

DIL CHAHTA HAI

2001

A landmark film of the 21st century, *Dil Chahta hai* launched several careers, sealed reputations, and created a new idiom for characters, stories, and relationships in Bollywood.

JAVED AKHTAR & CHANDAN SIDHWANI PRESENT

DIL CHAHTA HAI

AN EXCEL ENTERTAINMENT PRODUCTION

दिल चाहता है

MUSIC SHANKAR EHSAAN LOY · LYRICS JAVED AKHTAR · CO-PRODUCER PRAVIN TALREJA · PRODUCED BY RITESH SIDHWANI · STORY, SCREENPLAY, DIALOGUE & DIRECTION FARHAN AKHTAR

www.dilchahtahai.com

CAST AND CREW

* ★ **Aamir Khan** Akash Malhotra
  Saif Ali Khan Sameer Mulchandani
  Akshaye Khanna Siddharth Sinha
  Preity Zinta Shalini
  Sonali Kulkarni Pooja
  Dimple Kapadia Tara Jaiswal
  Ayub Khan Rohit

* **Director** Farhan Akhtar
* **Producer** Ritesh Sidhwani
* **Music composers** Shankar Mahadevan, Loy Mendonsa, Ehsaan Noorani
* **Lyricist** Javed Akhtar
* **Choreographer** Farah Khan
* **Scriptwriter** Farhan Akhtar
* **Cinematographer** Ravi K. Chandran
* **Costume designer** Arjun Bhasin

When first time writer–director Farhan Akhtar's *Dil Chahta hai*, starring Aamir Khan (see pp. 228–29), was released in August 2001, it had to contend with *Lagaan* (see pp. 266–69)—a period drama also starring the same lead actor that had been playing to full houses for almost two months by then.

Dil Chahta hai (The Heart Yearns) only did middling business at the box office. However, its realistic portrayal of the lives of rich, urban boys in Mumbai struck a chord with the Indian public. *Dil Chahta hai* acquired a special status as the film that tipped its hat to old Bollywood, but also changed the film idiom, giving Hindi films a distinct style not seen before. It spawned several films that tried to look and sound like it, but none could match its inherent, unique freshness.

UNUSUAL ROMANTICS

The film is about friendship, love, and the coming of age of three college-going friends. It concerns the characters Akash Malhotra, Siddharth Sinha, and Sameer Mulchandani, three individuals who share a strong bond but very different takes on love.

Akash does not indulge in long-term relationships and is averse to the idea of true love. However, he struggles to stick to his "principles" when he meets Shalini. Sameer, on the other hand, is a hopeless romantic who falls in love very easily. He meets Pooja through a meeting arranged by his parents, but is heartbroken to find that she is in love with someone else. In contrast, Siddharth is a mature and sensitive person who does not believe in petty romances. He falls for an older divorcée, Tara Jaiswal, much to the chagrin of his family and friends.

A DIRECTOR INSPIRED

Farhan wrote *Dil Chahta hai* when his mother, Honey Irani, a well-established scriptwriter herself, threatened to throw him out of the house if he didn't do something with his life. He was around 25 years old at the time and was trying his hand as a writer for advertisements and television. *Dil Chahta hai*'s story,

◀ **It's a hit!**
The fun, quirky poster for *Dil Chahta hai* was designed to appeal to a young, chic, and urbane audience. The film itself was winner of the National Film Award for Best Feature Film in Hindi, 2001.

◀ **Star-crossed lovers**
Aamir Khan's character, Akash Malhotra, is a cad who falls for Shalini in the typical style of Bollywood romance.

About Nothing. Eventually, however, it was Farhan's own creative instinct, and his training as a writer in advertising, that helped him to add layers to the story, making it more than just a romance.

FARHAN AKHTAR (b.1974)

Born into a talented and influential family of actors and writers, Farhan worked as an apprentice with director Yash Chopra (see pp. 166–67) on the set of *Lamhe* (1991) at the age of 17. He came back to Bollywood 10 years later, and when he did, he did so as a writer, director, actor, producer, singer, and lyricist.

While his *Dil Chahta hai* changed the way Bollywood films were written, planned, and shot, his adaptation of the 1978 cult film *Don* (2006) set off a trend of remaking classics in Bollywood. Two years later, with his acting debut in *Rock On* (2008), he also launched his singing career. With two National Awards, Farhan remains critically and commercially successful.

> ## "Dil Chahta hai *is a rare film on male camaraderie.*"
>
> **ZIYA US SALAM,** EDITOR, *THE HINDU*, 2001

which plays out mostly in flashback, came from several sources—memories recorded in Farhan's diaries about his trips to Goa, a visit to New York in 1996, a story narrated by a childhood friend, and scenes from the Shakespeare play *Much Ado*

COVERING ALL BASES
Initially, Farhan decided to focus on Akash and Shalini's love story, but he felt it made the script sound too conventional. He had grown up as a Bollywood insider, hailing from a family of big industry names, and had binge-watched all kinds of films with his family members. His curiosity led him to wonder about the fate of "the hero's best friends," as their stories always appeared to fade after reel three. For this reason, his own script went in deliberate, inspired tangents, chasing the stories of Sameer and Pooja, and Siddharth and Tara.

Although the film's casting took a long time to finalize, with the role of Akash being offered to stars such as Hrithik Roshan (see p. 263), Abhishek Bachchan, and Akshaye Khanna, before being given to Aamir Khan,

Farhan had clarity about how his film would look and sound. Farhan wrote the film's dialogue first in English and then took two months to translate it into Hindi, making sure that the characters not just spoke in regular, everyday language, but that they also sounded like the actors playing them.

TREND-SETTER
Farhan had the detailed look of the set and each character in mind, and in order to execute his idea he appointed Suzanne Caplan Merwanji as the film's production designer. Working closely with the art director, costume designer, makeup and hair stylists' team, and even the cinematographer, Suzanne streamlined the look of the film. *Dil Chahta hai* set off several fashion trends, including

spiffy, close-cropped hairstyles, vibrant shirts with side slits, loose-fitting linen pants, and Aamir's soul patch (a small goatee).

The film brought a new kind of discipline in filmmaking to Bollywood. After 15 months of extensive pre-production, the film was shot over a four-month period in Mumbai, Goa, and Sydney. No mobile phones were allowed on the sets and the schedules finished on time.

Dil Chahta hai also pushed the musical trio of Shankar Mahadevan, Ehsaan Noorani, and Loy Mendonsa, into the big league. The soundtrack, a mix of high-energy dance numbers and moody melodies, used instruments not heard in India before, such as the didgeridoo (an indigenous Australian wind instrument), and remains immensely popular today.

▶ **Pals for life**
The film's protagonists, Akash (left), Sameer (center), and Siddharth (right), are three best friends who laugh at each other's mistakes.

HIT SONGS

Dil Chahta Hai
(The Heart Yearns)
🎤 **Singers** Shankar Mahadevan, Clinton Cerejo

Koi Kahe Kehta Rahe
(People Can Keep Talking)
🎤 **Singers** Shankar Mahadevan, Shaan, KK

Jaane Kyon
(Don't Know Why)
🖊 **Singers** Udit Narayan, Alka Yagnik, Caralisa Monteiro

Tanhayee
(Loneliness)
🖊 **Singer** Sonu Nigam

LAGAAN: ONCE UPON A TIME IN INDIA

2001

Using the cricket pitch as a battlefield, *Lagaan* tells the story of a group of villagers living under the British Raj, who are challenged by their colonial rulers to a high-stakes match.

Drawing on India's British colonial past, *Lagaan: Once Upon a Time in India* is a clever, courageous, and ultimately moving film with a classic theme—the triumph of the human spirit over adversity.

In *Lagaan*, this adversity is faced by the peasants of a small farming village. The region's king has been reduced to a ruler in name only, and the people are under the thumb of a British garrison, run by Captain Andrew Russell. Despite being stricken by drought and paltry harvests, the downtrodden villagers are compelled by the sadistic commander to pay the annual *"lagaan"* or tax.

This particular year, the farmers can only pay half the usual tribute, but the Captain decides to double the tax. Desperate for reprieve, the villagers first petition their king for help, but the monarch is powerless. In a final attempt, the villagers get together to protest directly to the Captain, who challenges them to a cricket match—a game the farmers have no knowledge of—to decide the matter.

CINEMATIC MASTERPIECE

Deftly combining whimsy and drama, writer and director Ashutosh Gowariker (see pp. 301) tells his story with equal measures of pathos and gentle humor. Just like the motley band in Japanese filmmaker Akira Kurosawa's *Seven Samurai* (1954), the village cricket team—hastily put together by the main protagonist Bhuvan, played by Aamir Khan—makes up in grit what it lacks in polish. Each character is well-defined,

◀ **Dressing the part**
Costume designer Bhanu Athaiya, an Oscar winner for *Gandhi* (1982), researched the period in detail to achieve an authentic look for British soldiers from the 1800s.

and immediately involves the audience in their personal problems as well as their wider, collective struggles. In essence a serious tale, it is *Lagaan*'s poignancy and playfulness, combined with an engrossing narrative, that made the film so watchable.

MONEY MATTERS

Ironically, the film almost didn't get made because director Gowariker couldn't find a producer for it. He had first approached Aamir Khan as an actor and producer, who promptly rejected him, wanting nothing to do with the project. Khan even tried to talk the director out of the project. The period drama set in a rural context lacked everything that typical mainstream Bollywood films have—glamour, edge, and spectacle. The limited success of Gowariker's two previous movies did not help matters either. However, the director persisted, presenting Khan with a detailed script and narrating it to him scene by scene until the actor was finally persuaded to star in the film.

The matter of his lead man resolved, Gowariker still had to find a producer. Of those producers he approached some weren't interested; others were keen, but wanted significant changes to the plot, such as ending the cricket match with the murder of the Captain. At a loss, the director went back to Khan, who agreed to be producer. Financier Jhamu Sughand was soon on board, and his talents were essential in raising funds for what would be one of the most expensive Indian films ever made. Impressed by the quality of the script and the patriotic storyline, Sughand had faith in the project, and the money was eventually in place— the movie was ready to be filmed.

THE PERFECT LOCATION

With art director Nitin Chandrakant Desai, Gowariker set out to find the ideal location for the fictional village

CAST AND CREW

★ **Aamir Khan** Bhuvan
Gracy Singh Gauri
Rachel Shelley Elizabeth Russell
Paul Blackthorne Captain Andrew Russell
Suhasini Mulay Yashodamai
Yashpal Sharma Lakha
Aditya Lakhia Kachra
Narrator Amitabh Bachchan

Director Ashutosh Gowariker
Producers Aamir Khan, Mansoor Khan
Music composer A.R. Rahman
Lyricist Javed Akhtar
Choreographers Terence Lewis, Raju Khan, Saroj Khan, Vaibhavi Merchant
Scriptwriters Ashutosh Gowariker, Kumar Dave, Sanjay Dayma
Cinematographer Anil Mehta
Costume designer Bhanu Athaiya

◀ **Royal setting**
The magnificent and awe-inspiring Vijay Vilas Palace, built in 1929, was the perfect choice as the location for the headquarters of the intimidating Captain Russell.

of Champaner. It needed to be extremely dry so that the drought in the storyline would seem plausible, and have no electricity or other visible signs of 20th-century civilization. They eventually settled on Kunariya, an ancient village near Bhuj in the Kutch region of Gujarat. With their location chosen, Desai commissioned the locals to build an authentic-looking Kutch settlement a few months before cast and crew were due to arrive. Finally, after five years of preparation, Gowariker's inspirational story was ready to spring into life.

INTERNATIONAL ACCLAIM

All this effort eventually produced a film that was a great success. Winning eight National Film Awards and nine Filmfare Awards in India, *Lagaan* also struck gold internationally. Despite the film's running time of almost four hours—overly long by Hollywood standards—audiences were not deterred. People were reportedly lining up around the block for tickets in London's Piccadilly Circus.

Meanwhile, movie reviewers in the UK and US were united in their praise, heralding *Lagaan* as the first crossover

▲ National pastime
Once considered a sport meant only for upper-class "gentlemen," cricket today is one of the most popular sports in India, played by people of all classes.

Bollywood hit. It broke ground around the world, making its way onto the UK's list of top ten films of the year. It also became the first Indian movie to secure a nationwide release in China and enjoyed an unprecedented nine weeks of screening in Paris. *Lagaan* was also nominated for the Academy Award for Best Foreign Language Film.

INDIA AT THE OSCARS

Occasionally, a Bollywood film infiltrates the global mainstream and attracts a wide audience. *Lagaan* was one such film, taking the world of cinema by storm, and attracting the attention of the Academy of Motion Picture Arts and Sciences, who award the Oscars. *Lagaan* became the third Indian film in the history of the Academy Awards to be nominated for Best Foreign Language Film. Since 1957 India has sent more than 40 films to the Oscars, and three of these have been nominated. India's first submission was *Mother India* (see pp. 56–59) and in 1988, director Mira Nair's *Salaam Bombay* was nominated. Although this epic tale of Bombay's street children did not win the Oscar, it picked up a host of other international awards.

"*Lagaan is a well-crafted, hugely entertaining epic that has the spice of a foreign culture.*"

ROGER EBERT, *ROGER EBERT'S MOVIE YEARBOOK 2005,* 2004

STORYLINE

Set in 1893, when India was under British colonial rule, *Lagaan: Once Upon a Time in India* opens on the drought-stricken villagers of Champaner in central India. The simple farmers must face insurmountable odds and win a dire challenge on which their very survival depends.

SUHASINI MULAY (b.1950)

Suhasini Mulay is equally at home in front of the camera as she is behind it. Her first job, at the age of 15, was to be the face of Pears soap. Director Mrinal Sen saw promise in her and cast her in *Bhuvan Shome* (1969). However, the young actress had her sights set on filmmaking. In her long career, she has made over 60 documentaries, winning National awards for four of them. She was tempted back to acting to play Bhuvan's mother, Yashodomai, in *Lagaan*.

	UNJUST TAXES	THE DARE	THE DILEMMA	A HELPING HAND	PRACTICE BEGINS
PLOT OVERVIEW	**Champaner is** a small village in the drylands of central India ❶. The village is run by the British commander, Captain Russell, who demands an annual tax despite meager harvests caused by the severe drought.	**One of the farmers**, the rebellious and spirited Bhuvan, leads a delegation of villagers to their king to protest the steep tax. Later, during a cricket match, Captain Russell hears Bhuvan calling cricket a silly game and challenges him to beat the British team in a match. If they win, the villagers will pay no tax for three years, but if they lose, they will have to pay triple the amount.	**Having accepted** the challenge, the villagers now face the stark reality that they have never played cricket before. Bhuvan inspires them to rise to the challenge ❷ and they begin selecting the 11-man team based on the skills each villager has developed in their daily farming life.	**Despite protests by** the villagers, Bhuvan recruits an "untouchable" (a person of low class) named Kachra for the team. Kachra has a shriveled hand that is practically useless, except for one thing—it is perfect for spin-bowling a cricket ball. Bhuvan persuades the disgruntled villagers into accepting Kachra as a teammate.	**Once Bhuvan has united** the team, which includes people from different religions and castes, practice begins in earnest. Captain Russell's sympathetic sister Elizabeth secretly coaches the team, which only has three months to prepare for the critical match. Bhuvan's love interest Gauri is jealous of the time Bhuvan spends with Elizabeth ❸.
THE SONGS	**Ghanan Ghanan (Dark Clouds of Thunder)** *Singers: Udit Narayan, Sukhwinder Singh, Alka Yagnik, Shankar Mahadevan, Shaan* *Picturized on all the villagers* ⭐ *A burst of rain broke out when the song "Ghanan Ghanan" began to play during the first public screening of* Lagaan *at a theater in Bhuj, Gujarat, where the film was shot.*		**Mitwa (Companion)** *Singers: Udit Narayan, Srinivas, Sukhwinder Singh, Alka Yagnik* *Picturized on Bhuvan and Gauri*		**Radha Kaise Na Jale (How Could Radha Not Be Jealous?)** *Singers: Asha Bhosle, Udit Narayan, Vaishali Samant* *Picturized on Bhuvan, Gauri, and Elizabeth*

THE GOD KRISHNA AND HIS BELOVED RADHA ARE ENACTED BY BHUVAN AND GAURI AT A FESTIVAL DANCE

ENGLISH ACTRESS RACHEL SHELLEY, WHO PLAYS ELIZABETH

VILLAGE WOMEN FROM GUJARAT, INDIA

THE DOUBLE-CROSS

Bhuvan and Gauri confess their love for each other while Elizabeth realizes that she loves Bhuvan as well **4**. One of the team, the woodcutter Lakha, makes a clandestine deal with Captain Russell to throw the match in exchange for a bribe. Lakha is motivated by jealousy, as he is also in love with Gauri.

THE FINAL ELEVEN

Each member of the final team begins intense training and practice for the critical match **5**. The batsmen include Lakha, the blacksmith Arjan, the potter Ismail, and the mute drummer Bagha. The rest of the 11 include the village doctor, Ishwar, as wicketkeeper, Kachra, the disabled spinner, all-rounder Deva, fortune-teller Guran, chicken farmer Bhura, and land-owner Goli as the seamer.

THE MATCH

Russell and his officers win the toss and choose to bat, scoring almost 300 runs. Meanwhile, Lakha keeps dropping catches and Kachra struggles to spin because the ball is new and he is used to practicing with old balls. Lakha's treachery is revealed and he promises to make amends.

A SECOND INNING

After Kachra bowls a hat-trick with the now worn ball, the villagers go in to bat. The innings start promisingly with Deva notching up a decent cache of runs. But by the end of the day, four batsmen are injured and they only have a third of the runs needed to win **6**.

THE VICTORY

The last innings begin with Bhuvan scoring a century, followed by a half-century from Ismail. Bhuvan faces the last over. He tries to hit a six, and Russell catches the ball, but discovers his foot is beyond the boundary. The catch is actually six runs. The villagers win the match.

THE REPRIEVE

After losing the match, Captain Russell must pay taxes on behalf of the villagers. The garrison shuts down and Russell is transferred to Africa. The drought eventually passes and the experience has united the villagers, who learn to put aside class and caste differences.

4

O Rey Chhori
(Hey Girl)
*Singers: Udit Narayan,
Alka Yagnik,
Vasundhara Das
Picturized on Bhuvan,
Gauri, and Elizabeth*

5

Chale Chalo
(Keep Going)
*Singer: A.R. Rahman
Picturized on Bhuvan
and his cricket team*

⭐ *A behind-the-scenes film about the making of* Lagaan, *titled* Chale Chalo: The Lunacy of Filmmaking, *was released in 2003.*

6

O Paalanhaare
(Oh Nurturing Lord)
*Singers: Lata
Mangeshkar,
Sadhana Sargam,
Udit Narayan
Picturized on Gauri
and Yashodamai*

"It is a film that you instinctively take to because it is one of the most brilliant films ever made."

AMITABH BACHCHAN, *THE TIMES OF INDIA,* 2002

KABHI KHUSHI KABHIE GHAM...

2001

A grand and lavish melodrama with a warm, pulsating heart, *Kabhi Khushi Kabhie Gham...* established the brand of films that its director Karan Johar is now famous for.

Few films in Bollywood have received so much love and scorn at the same time as *Kabhi Khushi Kabhie Gham...* (Sometimes There's Happiness, Sometimes Sorrow...), Karan Johar's second film as a director. *K3G*, as the film is popularly known, has come to define the larger-than-life, glamorous Bollywood productions of the 2000s that show good-looking and rich Indian families, along with their middlebrow sensibilities and middle-class melodrama. The film has also come to embody and illustrate what Bollywood does best—visually sumptuous familial sagas that make you weep, laugh, and want to break into a song and dance. *K3G* is the kind of film that Indians, at home and abroad, go to watch with their families.

A SPLENDID IDEA

Karan (see pp. 248–49) was just 26 years old and still glowing from the critical and commercial success of his first film *Kuch Kuch Hota hai* (see pp. 246–47), when he conceived the idea of *K3G*—an epic *Ramayana* set in modern times. The storyline was simple—the elder, adopted son is banished by his rich businessman father, and is eventually brought back home, many years later, by his younger brother.

Karan discussed the film's concept with his parents, who liked the idea. He soon started writing the script with a friend, Sheena Parikh, who had a different take on things. However, Karan was very clear that he wanted to direct a "mammoth family saga," such as *Kabhi Kabhie* (see pp. 144–47), spanning three generations. He was also obsessed with the idea of having six superstars on the poster of his film.

CASTING THE BEST

Karan and his father, Yash Johar, first approached Amitabh Bachchan (see pp. 126–27) to offer him a role in *K3G*. A veteran Bollywood producer, Yash nonetheless became quite emotional when the veteran actor Amitabh agreed to accept the role. *K3G* also marked Amitabh's return to Dharma Productions after 10 years: his previous venture with them had been *Agneepath* (1990).

Karan signed the remaining cast—Shah Rukh Khan (see pp. 214–15), Kajol (see p. 231), Jaya Bachchan, Kareena Kapoor, and Hrithik Roshan (see p. 263)—on the same day. He only had one expectation from all his actors—to "look good and do their job." Karan decided not to organize any rehearsals for the cast, except for the scene involving a climactic encounter between Amitabh and Hrithik.

TRICKY DIRECTION

The film's shooting began in Mumbai in October 2000, with the song "Bole Chudiyan" (Tinkling Bangles), which involved the six heavyweights. The pressure was immense and Karan fainted on the sets. However, he continued to direct the song while lying in bed. The film encountered a variety of other issues as well. For example, Hrithik's debut film, *Kaho naa... Pyaar hai* (see pp. 262–63), had been a huge hit, while several of Shah Rukh's recent films had not done well. People started comparing the two actors, calling

Kabhi Khushi Kabhie Gham...
"It's all about loving your parents"
- KARAN JOHAR

Music: Jatin-Lalit, Sandesh Shandilya · Lyrics: Sameer
Director of Photography: Kiran Deohans · Director of Choreography: Farah Khan
Production Design / Art : Sharmishta Roy

कभी खुशी कभी गम

◀ **A traditional family**
Amitabh Bachchan (center) plays the role of Yash Raichand, a conventional man who banishes his son, Rahul, for breaking a family custom and marrying a girl below their class.

CAST AND CREW

★ **Amitabh Bachchan** Yashvardhan "Yash" Raichand
Jaya Bachchan Nandini Raichand
Shah Rukh Khan Rahul Raichand
Kajol Anjali Sharma
Hrithik Roshan Rohan Raichand
Kareena Kapoor Pooja Sharma

🎬 **Director** Karan Johar
🏠 **Producer** Dharma Productions
🎵 **Music composers** Babloo Chakravorty, Jatin Pandit, Lalit Pandit, Sandesh Shandilya
🕺 **Choreographer** Farah Khan
📖 **Scriptwriters** Karan Johar, Sheena Parikh
🎥 **Cinematographer** Kiran Deohans
👔 **Costume designers** Manish Malhotra, Shabina Khan, Rocky S.

◀ Magnificient sets
Waddesdon Manor in Buckinghamshire, UK, was featured as Yash Raichand's house in *K3G*. Its interiors, however, were recreated in a Mumbai studio.

The movie had to be a commercial success, too. With so much at stake, Karan spared no expense. It was shot in three countries across multiple sets. For filming the song, "Yeh Ladka Hai Allah," the busy Chandni Chowk market in Delhi was recreated in a studio across several sets. The song "Suraj Hua Maddham" was shot at the Great Pyramids of Giza, Egypt; "Deewana Hai Dekho" (He's Crazy) was shot at the British Museum, UK; and about 100 dancers were flown in from the UK to Mumbai for eight days to shoot the song, "You Are My Soniya."

RISING LIKE A PHOENIX
A big-budget film of about ₹500 million ($7.8 million), *K3G* was released on

Hrithik the next superstar, which created some tension on the sets. In order to avoid a rift between them, the screenplay not only had to tell the story in an engaging manner, but also had to appease the vanity of the star cast. To acheive this, songs were neatly distributed between all six superstars, and all of them were given their own big scene in order to leave a personal mark on the film.

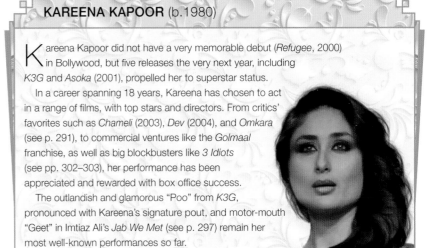

KAREENA KAPOOR (b.1980)

Kareena Kapoor did not have a very memorable debut (*Refugee*, 2000) in Bollywood, but five releases the very next year, including *K3G* and *Asoka* (2001), propelled her to superstar status.

In a career spanning 18 years, Kareena has chosen to act in a range of films, with top stars and directors. From critics' favorites such as *Chameli* (2003), *Dev* (2004), and *Omkara* (see p. 291), to commercial ventures like the *Golmaal* franchise, as well as big blockbusters like *3 Idiots* (see pp. 302–303), her performance has been appreciated and rewarded with box office success.

The outlandish and glamorous "Poo" from *K3G*, pronounced with Kareena's signature pout, and motor-mouth "Geet" in Imtiaz Ali's *Jab We Met* (see p. 297) remain her most well-known performances so far.

December 14, 2001, to a lukewarm response from critics. This upset Karan as a lot was riding on the film. Three days later, while traveling to the Liberty Cinema in Mumbai's Marine Lines, Karan found himself stuck in a terrible traffic jam. He asked a cop about the holdup and was told, "It's a line for advance booking, for this

new film, *Kabhi Khushi Kabhie Gham....* We have been called for crowd control." Stunned, Karan got out of his car and ran to see the phenomenon for himself. What he saw before him was like a scene from his own film.

K3G was a blockbuster, and it remains Karan's most successful film to date. The film's soundtrack sold 2.5 million units within 30 days. Even now, every two years, new rights are negotiated and *K3G* rakes in more money.

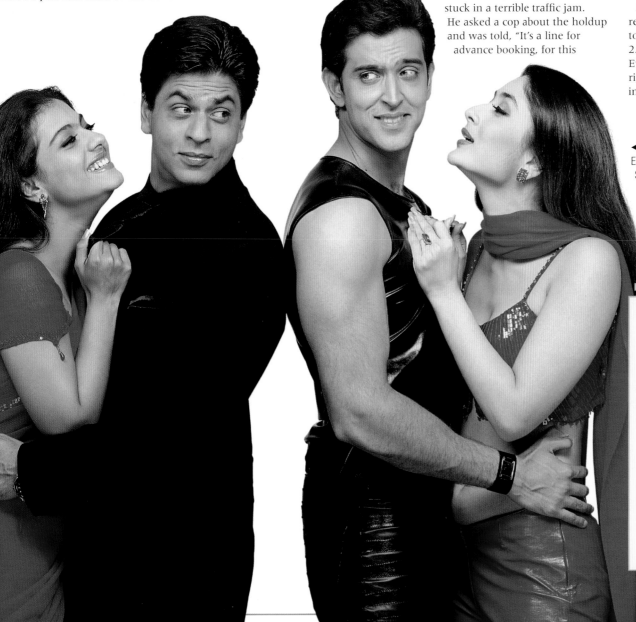

◀ Perfect costumes
Each actor in the film—Kajol (far left), Shah Rukh Khan (left), Hrithik Roshan (right), and Kareena Kapoor (far right)—was styled differently. Karan, along with the costume designers of the film, shopped in the US, London, Milan, and New Delhi to get the right look for each character.

HIT SONGS

Kabhi Khushi Kabhie Gham
(Sometimes There's Happiness, Sometimes Sorrow)
🎤 **Singer** Lata Mangeshkar

Suraj Hua Maddham
(The Setting Sun)
🎤 **Singers** Alka Yagnik, Sonu Nigam

You Are My Soniya
(You are My Darling)
🎤 **Singers** Alka Yagnik, Sonu Nigam

Yeh Ladka Hai Allah
(This Boy, Oh Lord)
🎤 **Singers** Alka Yagnik, Udit Narayan

SONG AND DANCE

In Bollywood, almost every film is a musical. Song and dance are key ingredients of the traditional and successful Hindi film.

The Indian tradition of blending theater, music, and dance goes all the way back to the *Natya Shastra*, an ancient Hindu text on the performing arts from around the 2nd century BCE. From its very beginnings, Indian cinema tapped into this rich tradition. The first full-length Indian film, *Raja Harishchandra*, featured a dance sequence, while the first Indian talkie, *Alam Ara* (see p. 20), contained seven songs. Then, after a series of films that were almost nonstop songs, around six to ten song-and-dance sequences in each film was established as the norm. Until recently, most films made in the Western style—without music and dance—have been considered outside the mainstream, with limited appeal and a lack of commercial success.

TOE-TAPPING TUNES

Songs can play many roles in a film, from pure entertainment to furthering the plot. Lyrics and dialogue are often written by different writers, and the sequences can be semi-realistic or dreamlike, dramatically changing locations and costumes. A film's soundtrack can drive its success just as a hit song can hook audiences. Producers often release the soundtrack before the film to draw in audiences.

Although actors appear to sing, they are usually miming lines sung by professional singers, often celebrated in their own right, like the sisters Lata Mangeshkar (see pp. 60–61) and Asha Bhosle. Kishore Kumar (see pp. 100–101) was one of the few actors also famed for his singing.

Today, dancing is a crucial skill for any aspiring Bollywood star. In the early days of Bollywood, dancing styles took their lead from folk and classical Indian dance traditions, particularly Kathak and Bharatnatyam. But dance styles have evolved, along with the music, reflecting international influences such as belly dancing, disco, and hip hop. Choreographers have always played key roles in setting the tone of a movie, be it Chiman Seth's rustic dances in *Mother India* (see pp. 56–59) or Farah Khan's club moves in *Dil Chahta Hai* (see pp. 264–65).

In a 2016 interview, Bollywood star Shah Rukh Khan (see pp. 214–15) signaled a change in Indian tastes saying, "the younger filmmakers… know that we don't need to just shove in a song any more," although he admitted, "It'll take a lot of time to take the songs out of us."

◀ **Dancing diva**
Actress Deepika Padukone's graceful and high-energy dancing in director Sanjay Leela Bhansali's *Goliyon Ki Raasleela Ram-Leela* (2013) brought the folk song "Nagade Sang Dhol" to life.

"[Hollywood] should imbibe our song and dance culture. [They] could do wonders with it."

IRRFAN KHAN, ACTOR, IN *THE TRIBUNE*, JUNE 1, 2015

DEVDAS

2002

Devdas set the gold standard for period films in Bollywood with breathtaking sets, stunning costumes, spectacular song-and-dance sequences, and extravagant melodrama.

CAST AND CREW

★ **Shah Rukh Khan** Devdas
Aishwarya Rai Paro
Madhuri Dixit Chandramukhi
Jackie Shroff Chunnibabu
Kirron Kher Sumitra Chakraborty

🎬 **Director** Sanjay Leela Bhansali
🎭 **Producer** Bharat Shah
🎵 **Music composer** Ismail Darbar
🎼 **Lyricist** Nusrat Badr
🕺 **Choreographers** Pandit Birju Maharaj, Saroj Khan, Vaibhavi Merchant, Pappu Malu
📖 **Scriptwriters** Prakash Kapadia, Sanjay Leela Bhansali
🎥 **Cinematographer** Binod Pradhan
👔 **Costume designers** Abu Jani, Sandeep Khosla, Neeta Lulla, Reza Shariffi

The year 2002 was all set to be Bollywood's worst year ever. Of the 120 films released by June, 119 had lost money; in July, *Devdas*, an expensive project, with a reported budget of ₹500 million ($7.8 million), was to be released. Sanjay Leela Bhansali's film, which released in approximately 325 theaters across India, wasn't just a hit: it went on to win five National Awards, and was nominated for both a BAFTA and an Oscar in the Best Foreign Language Film category.

BHANSALI'S VISION

The story of *Devdas*, complete with three of Indian cinema's favorite themes and characters—the love triangle, a man unable to fight the system (in this case his landed, feudal father), and the prostitute with a heart of gold—remains not just the most filmed non-epic story in India, but also provides a template for love stories in Hindi cinema. Versions of the story had already been made in several Indian languages. Bhansali, whose *Hum Dil de Chuke Sanam* (see pp. 256–57) was a massive hit, was fixated on remaking *Devdas*. In his words, he aimed to make his version "bigger, better, and more spectacular than any classical movie made in Indian cinema." However, bringing this grand and ambitious vision to life on screen required extreme commitment and numerous sacrifices. On-screen, *Devdas* was breathtaking in its beauty and scale, but behind the scenes it had been

◀ **Period costumes**
The vintage suits, cravats, handkerchiefs, and shoes worn by Devdas in the initial reels of the film were sourced from old clothing stores in London.

▶ **Superb casting**
The film boasts a strong cast of big industry names, including Aishwarya Rai (see pp. 254–55), winner of the 1994 Miss World pageant.

merciless in extracting the very best from the entire cast and production team.

LARGER THAN LIFE

Devdas was mostly shot in Film City, Mumbai, where 20th-century Kolkata and Benares were recreated on six sets. It took art director Nitin Desai about nine months to research the sets, and even longer to create them. The set for Chandramukhi's brothel, which was to be on the banks of the river Ganges in Benares, was constructed around an artificial lake. Gallons of water had to be brought in regularly to refill the lake. The hall in which Chandramukhi danced had 60 carved domes along with a 6 ft-(1.8 m-) tall chandelier. Cinematographer Binod Pradhan used energy supplied by 42 generators to light the huge set. In all, 5,000 bulbs lit up the brothel at night with the help of 700 lightmen. Paro's glass room, designed to reflect her beauty, was decorated with 122,000 pieces of stained glass.

UNFORTUNATE EVENTS

Devdas was a challenge not just because of the large size of its sets, but also because of the problems that arose during filming. Two crew members died in accidents on set, and the film's producer, Bharat Shah, was jailed for several months for his alleged criminal links. There were even rumors that *Devdas* had been financed by Dubai-

based crime syndicates, a charge that was never proven. However, Shah's arrest led to cash shortages, and Bhansali had to borrow money from friends to keep the project afloat. There were also times when production stalled as the technicians refused to work until they had been paid. Despite these problems, Bhansali was resolute and no expense was spared in the filming of *Devdas*. For example, Chandramukhi's elaborate costumes cost nearly ₹1.5 million ($24,000) each. The cheapest set cost ₹30 million ($500,000) and the most expensive, the brothel, cost ₹120 million ($2 million).

RESOLUTE CAST

During the "Dola Re Dola" (Swaying) duet dance sequence with Madhuri Dixit (see pp. 200–201), Aishwarya Rai's ears started to bleed because of the heavy earrings that she was wearing. However, Aishwarya continued to perform, not telling anyone until after the shoot. Madhuri performed "Kaahe Chhed Mohe" (Why Do You Tease Me So) in a *ghaghra* (skirt) that weighed 66 lbs (30 kg). "Even when I stopped dancing, my *ghaghra* wouldn't stop swirling. It was almost impossible to do the shot," she later said.

The stars knew that *Devdas* was a film on which reputations would rest for posterity, so despite heavy costumes and gruelling night shifts, they were dedicated until the end. Shah Rukh Khan (see pp. 214–15) even asked Dilip Kumar (see pp. 48–49) for tips on how he had prepared for the role of the tragic hero in Bimal Roy's 1955 adaptation of the story.

Despite all the hardships and setbacks during its production, *Devdas* was a dazzling testament to Bhansali's determination to mount an emotionally intense and visually seductive celebration of this tragic Indian love story on-screen.

▶ **Ultimate love story**
Devdas (2002) was the third Hindi version of Sarat Chandra Chattopadhyay's 1917 novel, proving that this tragic story of undying love continues to inspire filmmakers.

KIND-HEARTED COURTESAN

Since its birth, Bollywood has been fascinated by the fantasy figure of the gorgeous and glamorous courtesan with a heart of gold, such as Meena Kumari in *Pakeezah* (see pp. 116–17) or Madhuri Dixit in *Devdas*.

Barring a few exceptions, the courtesan is an archetype concocted out of Bollywood's simultaneous obsession with, and contempt for, the figure of a sexually liberated, financially independent woman. In most films the courtesan begins by flaunting her beauty and body through captivating song and dance. She must then either be saved by the virtuous hero via marriage or redeem herself through suffering and sacrifice. This moral arc is based on one trait that all courtesans must possess and exhibit—a heart that's pure and immaculate. This is her golden ticket to domestic and box office success.

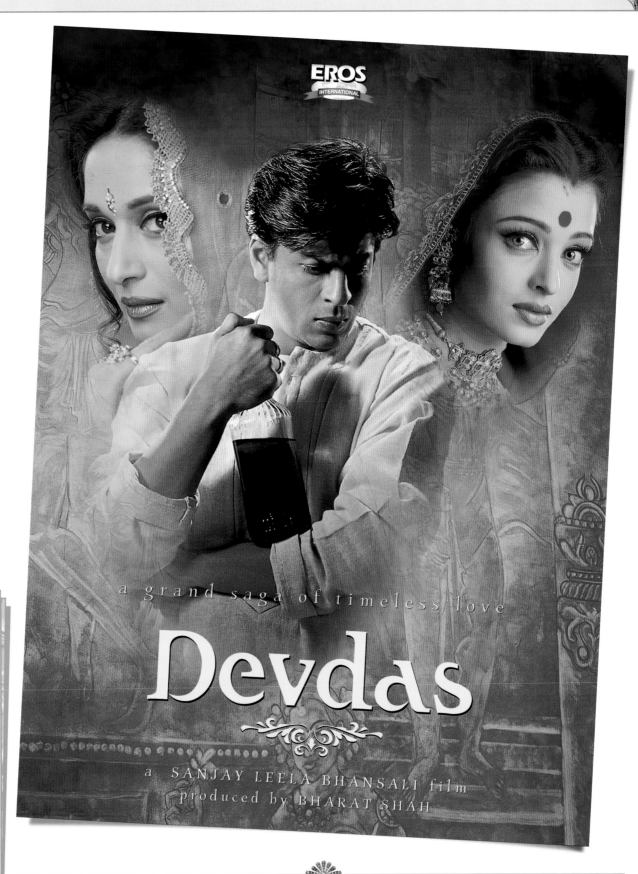

a grand saga of timeless love

Devdas

a SANJAY LEELA BHANSALI film
produced by BHARAT SHAH

"The film's … elaborate sets … compete with the story and characters for the audience's attention."

COREY K. CREEKMUR, HEAD OF FILM STUDIES AND DIRECTOR OF GRADUATE STUDIES, THE UNIVERSITY OF IOWA

STORYLINE

Childhood sweethearts Devdas and Paro have fallen in love. This causes a rift between their families, who refuse to let them get married. Paro gets married off to a rich, older man at the behest of her mother. A tormented Devdas turns to alcohol for comfort and moves into a brothel. He continues to pine for Paro, even refusing the advances of a beautiful courtesan, Chandramukhi.

SHAH RUKH KHAN AS DEVDAS

| FRIENDS REUNITED | ROMANCE UNFOLDS | THINGS FALL APART | |

PLOT OVERVIEW

Kaushalya Mukherjee receives news that her son Devdas is about to return home to Kolkata from London. She is ecstatic and tells Sumitra, her neighbor. Sumitra rushes to give this news to Paro, her daughter, who has kept an oil lamp lit for Devdas for 10 years **1**.

Devdas returns home and goes straight to his childhood friend, Paro, which upsets his mother. Paro is shy and refuses to show her face to Devdas. He looks upon her beauty while she sleeps, under the moonlight **2**. Everyone believes that Devdas and Paro are destined to be together, except Devdas's parents who are against this union. Paro and Devdas continue to meet and their friendship turns to love **3**.

Sumitra takes the proposal for Paro's marriage with Devdas to the Mukherjees **4**. Kaushalya humiliates her and rejects the proposal. Sumitra is devastated, and promises to arrange a marriage for Paro to a man richer than Devdas. Unable to convince his father to agree to his marriage, Devdas leaves his parents' house. He writes a letter to Paro, begging her to forget their love. Paro agrees to marry Thakur Bhuvan Chaudhry, a widower with three grown children.

Devdas meets his friend Chunnibabu, who takes him to a brothel. There he meets a courtesan, Chandramukhi, who falls in love with him **5**. Devdas realizes his mistake in abandoning Paro. He returns to her while her wedding is underway and asks her to elope. Paro refuses, reminding him of the way he and his family had humiliated hers. Devdas watches as Paro gets married to another man **6**.

THE SONGS

1

Silsila Ye Chahat Ka
(This Story of Love)
Singer: Shreya Ghoshal
🎵 *Picturized on Paro*

2
Woh Chand Jaisi Ladki
(That Girl Like The Moon)
Singer: Udit Narayan
🎵 *Picturized on Devdas and Paro*

Bairi Piya
(Vengeful Lover)
Singers: Shreya Ghoshal, Udit Narayan
🎵 *Picturized on Devdas and Paro*

3

4
Morey Piya
(My Lover)
Singers: Shreya Ghoshal, Jaspinder Narula
🎵 *Picturized on Devdas, Paro, and Sumitra*

5
Hamesha Tumko Chaha
(I Have Always Loved You)
Singers: Kavita Krishnamurthy, Udit Narayan
🎵 *Picturized on Devdas and Paro*

Kaahe Chhed
(Why Do You Tease Me So)
Singers: Kavita Krishnamurthy, Madhuri Dixit, Birju Maharaj
🎵 *Picturized on Chandramukhi and Devdas*

6

DEVDAS AND PARO MEET SECRETLY

★ *Bhansali and Ismail Darbar, the composer, had serious creative differences. Five months before the film's completion, Darbar walked out for the fifth time. Bhansali let him go and asked a rookie, Monty, to complete the film's score.*

SAROJ KHAN (b.1948)

Saroj Khan joined Bollywood as a child artist aged three. By the age of 13 she became an assistant to the dance director B. Sohanlal. Saroj became an independent choreographer with *Geeta Mera Naam* (1974), but only found fame when she worked with actress Sridevi (see pp. 204–205) 12 years later. She also choreographed another dancing diva, Madhuri Dixit (see pp. 200–201). Saroj was the first artist to receive a Filmfare Best Choreography Award for "Ek Do Teen" (One Two Three) from *Tezaab* (see p. 198).

REFUGE IN A BROTHEL	THE PROMISE	EXILED	KALIBABU'S REVENGE	KEEPING HIS PROMISE

Paro learns her husband is still in love with his deceased first wife. She accepts her loveless marriage and dutifully fulfils her responsibilities. Devdas moves to Chandramukhi's brothel and becomes an alcoholic **7**. He is unable to forget Paro and thinks about her constantly.

Devdas's father is on his deathbed and asks to see him. Devdas fails to do this, and arrives late and drunk at his funeral. Paro urges Devdas to stop drinking, but he is stubborn. However, he promises Paro that before he dies, he will come and see her one last time.

Devdas discovers his greedy sister-in-law Kumud has stolen the keys to the family safe. He confronts her but Kumud lies and blames Devdas for the theft. Kaushalya believes her and slaps Devdas. He leaves home forever. Paro arrives at the brothel looking for Devdas and meets Chandramukhi.

Paro invites Chandramukhi to *Durga Puja* (Hindu festival) celebrations at her husband's home **8**. Bhuvan's son-in-law Kalibabu, a frequent visitor to the brothel, reveals Chandramukhi's background. He also tells Bhuvan of Paro's relationship with Devdas. Bhuvan forbids Paro from leaving the *haveli* (mansion).

Devdas returns to the brothel 9. His health has deteriorated due to his alcoholism. He tells Chandramukhi he needs to leave, and decides to travel around the country. On the train he meets Chunnibabu, who urges him to drink. Devdas drinks, knowing it will be fatal. On the verge of death, Devdas travels to Paro's house to keep his promise. Paro learns the man dying at her doorstep is Devdas and rushes to meet him. Bhuvan orders the servants to close the gates. Devdas sees a blurry image of Paro running toward him just before the gate shuts. He whispers Paro's name with his last breath, and inside the *haveli*, Paro's lamp flickers out.

7 · · **8** · **9**

Maar Daala
(He Gave Me Grief)
Singer: Kavita Krishnamurthy
Picturized on Chandramukhi *and Devdas*

Dola Re Dola
(Swaying)
Singers: Shreya Ghoshal,
Kavita Krishnamurthy, K.K.
Picturized on
Chandramukhi and Paro

PARO AND CHANDRAMUKHI
DANCE TO THE TUNES OF
"DOLA RE DOLA"

Chalak Chalak
(Wine Splashing)
Singers: Shreya Ghoshal,
Udit Narayan, Vinod Rathod
Picturized on Chandramukhi,
Chunnibabu, and Devdas

DEVDAS AND CHUNNIBABU IN
CHANDRAMUKHI'S BROTHEL

"… an exploration of passion, lost love, and social restrictions."

LAURA BUSHELL, MOVIE REVIEW FOR BBC, 2002

YUVA

A socio-political drama, Mani Ratnam's *Yuva* weaves together the lives of three men from different backgrounds after their worlds collide in a terrible incident in Kolkata.

A film about India's corrupt political system, *Yuva* (Youth) impressed audiences with its socio-political theme, detailed camera work, rapid-fire editing techniques, and slow-motion action sequences that brilliantly captured the energy of the city of Kolkata. The film was shot twice, back-to-back, first in Hindi with the Bollywood cast, and then in Tamil with a different set of actors.

RESTLESS YOUTH

Yuva begins, unusually, at its climax when Arjun, a young college student, hitches a ride with Michael Mukherjee, a student activist, to follow his girlfriend. Meanwhile, Lallan Singh—a gangster—takes aim from the window of a truck and fires three bullets at Michael. Who these three characters is revealed in a series of flashbacks that begin with Lallan, who is hired by a corrupt politician, Prosonjit, Bhatacharya, to kill his rivals. Lallan is a notorious and flamboyant character who shows his vulnerability only to his wife, Shashi, whom he abuses as well as adores. The second flashback introduces Michael, the student activist, who is fighting the government's corrupt ways. Bhatacharya tries to bribe him with an admission to a US university, but Michael refuses.

The third pillar of the story is Arjun Balachandran, a college student from a wealthy family who wants to migrate to the US. However, his life takes an unexpected turn when he falls in love with Mira, who is engaged to an industrialist. Arjun is pursuing Mira to declare his love when the gunshots change his life forever.

GREAT RECEPTION

Yuva won the Filmfare Award for Best Screenplay and Fimfare Critics Award for Best Film. Much appreciated for their work, Abhishek Bachchan and Rani Mukerji (see p. 247) won the Filmfare Awards for best supporting actors. The film suffered a few mishaps. Vivek Oberoi broke his leg during an action scene, and Mani Ratnam suffered a heart attack while the shoot was on.

◀ **Multi-starrer drama**
Yuva was Mani Ratnam's production banner, Madras Talkies' biggest multi-starrer, and his second venture in Hindi cinema after *Dil Se...*

a MANI RATNAM film
Yuva

CAST AND CREW

★ **Ajay Devgn** Michael Mukherjee
Abhishek Bachchan Lallan Singh
Rani Mukerji Shashi Biswas
Vivek Oberoi Arjun Balachandran
Kareena Kapoor Mira
Esha Deol Radhika
Om Puri Prosonjit Bhatacharya

🎬 **Director** Mani Ratnam
◯ **Producer** Mani Ratnam
♫ **Music composer** A.R. Rahman
𝄞 **Lyricist** Mehboob
🕺 **Choreographer** Brinda
▭ **Scriptwriter** Mani Ratnam
📷 **Cinematographer** Ravi K. Chandran

MANI RATNAM (b.1956)

One of India's most influential directors (of mainly Tamil films), Mani Ratnam is celebrated for his realistic narratives. His films are noted for their technical expertise in areas such as editing, art direction, and background score. A former management consultant, Ratnam was a late starter in films. After a string of failures in the 1980s, his turning point was the Tamil film *Mouna Ragam* (1986). He won national recognition with a trilogy of political films—*Roja* (see p. 337), *Bombay* (see p. 338), and *Dil Se..* (see pp. 242–43). Ratnam's strength lies in his handling of screenplays and casting. He allows his actors to be spontaneous on-screen. The wiinner of three Filmfare Awards, he was honored with the Padma Shri, India's fourth-highest civilian award, in 2002.

AITRAAZ

2004

Romance meets subversive drama head on in *Aitraaz*—a morality tale about sexual harassment that turns traditional notions of male and female sexuality upside down.

A bbas–Mustan's *Aitraaz* (Objection) borrows significantly from Barry Levinson's Hollywood film *Disclosure* (1994), starring Michael Douglas and Demi Moore. It deals with the themes of revenge and rape, albeit packaged in the Bollywood wrapper of hit songs and dances.

FEMME FATALE

Aitraaz introduces the audiences to a happily married Raj Malhotra, who is anticipating a promotion to the position of CEO in the company he works for. However, things get complicated when Raj's ex-flame Sonia Roy suddenly walks back into his life, as the wife of his 70-year-old boss, Ranjit Roy. Raj first met Sonia many years ago while working in Cape

Town, South Africa. The two fell in love, but had a falling out when she chose her career over their unborn child. When they meet again, Sonia wants to pick up where they left off, but Raj rejects her advances. Incensed, she accuses him of attempted rape. A courtroom drama unfolds as Raj is called on to defend his character, with only his wife, Priya, in his corner.

GOING AGAINST THE GRAIN

The film's lead pair is cast in roles that are in complete contrast to their previous screen appearances and their public personas. Action hero Akshay Kumar displays an unusual vulnerability and quiet dignity as a loyal husband. Priyanka Chopra (see pp. 280–81), still in the early years of

▲ **Close encounters**
Raj is introduced to his ex-flame Sonia—who has returned as the wife of his boss—during an office function at which she helps him get a promotion.

her career, draws on untapped reserves of menace to play the bold seductress. Widely appreciated for her performance in the film, Priyanka won a Filmfare Award for Best Performance in a Negative Role, making her only the second actress to win this award.

Although the film raises interesting questions about the battle of the sexes, patriarchy triumphs in the end. Priya the good wife, stands for everything that is considered precious in traditional relationships and society, and Sonia epitomizes corrupt "Western" ways.

▲ **Trademark thriller**
Aitraaz has all the elements of a typical Abbas–Mustan potboiler. It is a fast-paced thriller complete with intrigue, romance, glamour, and an unexpected climax.

"*Aitraaz ... was a turning point in my career.*"

PRIYANKA CHOPRA, IN AN INTERVIEW WITH FILM CRITIC RAJEEV MASAND

CAST AND CREW

★ **Akshay Kumar** Raj Malhotra
Kareena Kapoor Priya Saxena
Priyanka Chopra Sonia Roy
Amrish Puri Ranjit Roy
Annu Kapoor Ram Choitrani

🎬 **Directors** Abbas A. Burmawalla, Mustan A. Burmawalla
🎞 **Producer** Subhash Ghai
🎵 **Music composer** Himesh Reshammiya
🎼 **Lyricist** Sameer
🕺 **Choreographers** Ganesh Acharya, Raju Khan, Ashley Lobo
📖 **Scriptwriters** Shyam Goel, Shiraz Ahmed
🎥 **Cinematographer** Ravi Yadav
👔 **Costume designer** Manish Malhotra

AKSHAY KUMAR
(b.1967)

H aving worked on more than 100 films, Akshay Kumar is one of Hindi cinema's highest-paid actors. A former martial arts teacher, he started his career in action thrillers in the 1990s, earning the nickname the "Indian Jackie Chan." Broadening his range to include comedy, romance, and drama, he received Filmfare Awards for his work in *Ajnabee* (2002) and *Garam Masala* (2006). His recent box office hits includes *Rustom* (2016), for which he received the National Award in 2017. He was awarded the Padma Shri in 2009 and the Asian Award for Outstanding Achievement in Cinema in 2011.

PRIYANKA CHOPRA

ACTRESS b.1982

A glamorous style icon, award-winning actress, and a sharp businesswoman, Priyanka Chopra has made waves in India and globally because of her talent and committment to her brand.

Celebrated for her beauty, dancing and singing skills, and professionalism, the talented actress Priyanka Chopra has appeared in nearly 50 films in her short career, and won a large number of awards for her performances.

Priyanka grew up in various parts of India and Canada, because of her father's assignments in the Indian army. She attributes her adaptibility and international outlook to this mobile childhood. When she was 13, she moved to the US to live with an aunt and she attended high school there. Hard as it is to believe, the girl who went on to be crowned Miss World was taunted for her dark skin when she was a schoolgirl in the US.

At the age of 17, Priyanka participated in the 2000 Miss India pageant, where she finished second. She went on to win the much-coveted Miss World crown the same year. Now an established beauty queen, Priyanka started receiving film offers, and her career in the film industry began to gain momentum. Although Priyanka claims to have hated the life of an actress after her first two films were shot down, she stuck at it. A very hard worker, she appeared as the lead in up to six films in 2004, including the hit movie *Mujhse Shaadi Karogi* and the award-winning *Aitraaz*.

While her beauty may have won her lead roles, it was her robust self-belief and dogged determination to prove herself that drove her to experiment with character roles early on.

◄ **Off the beaten path**
With her bold portrayal of an ambitious sexual predator in *Aitraaz*, Priyanka Chopra was able to prove her willingness to take on unconventional roles to her audience.

► **Accomplished performer**
In addition to Priyanka's talents as an actress, she is also a trained Kathak dancer and has studied Western classical music.

> *"After I won Miss India I realized I do not like failing. I just like being the best."*
>
> **PRIYANKA CHOPRA**

She accepted a difficult role in *Aitraaz*, which was a story about sexual harassment in the workplace, but with a twist—here, it was a woman who was in the position of power. The film was a leap of faith for Priyanka, and went on to score the first Filmfare Award of her career.

THE PERFECTIONIST

Priyanka's professionalism and dedication towards her work has earned her a special place in an industry that is known for its difficult divas. For her character in the film *Don*, a remake of a 1978 cult film with the same title (see p. 156), Priyanka underwent martial arts training and performed her own stunts.

Fashion was yet another highpoint of her career. Directed by Madhur Bhandarkar, the film explored the troubled lives of models on and off the catwalk. To play her character Meghna, Priyanka first gained 13 lb (6 kg), only to lose it later on as a part of a transformation from small-town girl to top model. A breakaway from the stereotypical Bollywood film, *Fashion* was a female-dominated story with no male leads, and for her role, Priyanka won a Filmfare Award for Best Actress, as well as a National Film Award.

In the film *What's Your Raashee?*, Priyanka played 12 different characters, working hard on her body language and her voice to make each of her on-screen characters distinct.

In Anurag Basu's *Barfi!*, Priyanka moved away from glamorous and sultry roles to play an autistic young woman. She visited psychiatric treatment centers, and spent time with people affected by autism to get her character right. Her hard work paid off, and *Barfi!* was a big success. She showed similar rigor in her preparation for *Mary Kom* (2014), spending four months in intense training, and going on a strict diet to give a convincing performance as a female boxing champion. That year, it was the

▲ **Adding substance**
Priyanka Chopra was cast in *Krrish* after director Rakesh Roshan had seen her performance in *Aitraaz*. Despite the fact that *Krrish* is about the male lead, Priyanka packs a powerful punch.

first Hindi film to premiere on the opening night of the Toronto International Film Festival, and it gave Priyanka global recognition.

ADDING FEATHERS TO HER CAP

After conquering Bollywood, Priyanka turned her eyes to the West. She scored the lead part in the prime-time drama *Quantico*—a TV series about a team of FBI cadets whose training class is infiltrated by a terrorist. In 2016, she received the American People's Choice Award for Favorite Actress in a New TV Series for her role in *Quantico*,

becoming the first South Asian actress ever to be honored with this award. Priyanka has also reversed the roles, presenting awards at the Emmy and the Academy Award ceremonies.

Priyanka took her musical career to new heights when she signed with an international record label, and has worked with singer will.i.am on her debut album *In My City*, and with US rapper Pitbull on a single, "Exotic."

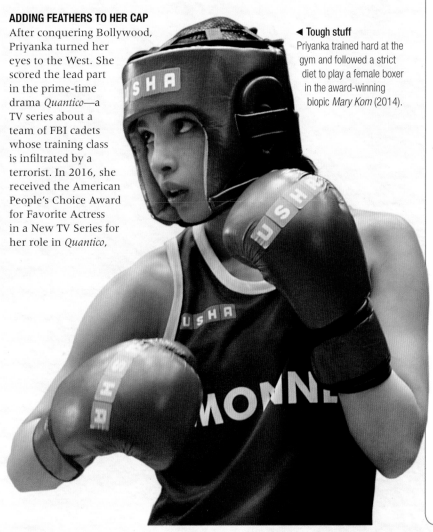

◀ **Tough stuff**
Priyanka trained hard at the gym and followed a strict diet to play a female boxer in the award-winning biopic *Mary Kom* (2014).

KEY WORKS

Aitraaz, 2004 (see p. 279)
Don, 2006
Fashion, 2008 (see p. 299)
Kaminey, 2009
What's Your Raashee, 2009
7 Khoon Maaf, 2011
Barfi!, 2012
Bajirao Mastani, 2015 (see p. 330)

TIMELINE

1982 Born in Jamshedpur, Jharkhand, to parents who were physicians in the army.

2000 Becomes the fifth Indian woman to be crowned Miss World.

2002 Makes her debut in the Tamil film *Thamizhan*. It is dubbed in Hindi and released as *Jeet: Born to Win*.

CROWNED MISS WORLD IN 2000

2002 Debuts in Bollywood with *The Hero: Love Story of a Spy*. The film is a box office hit, and Priyanka wins the Stardust Best Supporting Actress Award.

2005 Wins her first Filmfare Award for Best Performance in a Negative Role in *Aitraaz*.

2006 *Krrish* (see p. 285) and *Don* are released. Both films are successful.

2008 Stars in the hit film *Fashion*.

2010 Appointed national UNICEF Goodwill Ambassador for Child Rights for her work in promoting children's rights and girls' education.

2015 Lands breakthrough role in *Quantico*, an American television espionage drama series.

2015 Founds her production company, Purple Pebbles Pictures.

2016 *Time* magazine includes her on its list of the 100 most influential people in the world.

2016 Appointed global UNICEF Goodwill Ambassador.

2016 Honored with the Padma Shri, the fourth highest civilian award in India.

2017 Films a new action comedy in Florida based on the American TV series *Baywatch*.

FILMFARE
AWARDS

The Filmfare Awards celebrate excellence in Indian cinema. Originally a Bollywood phenomenon, the awards have spread to regional film industries as well.

Initially known as the Clare Awards, the Filmfare Awards were launched by the Times of India Group in 1954 and were named after the late film critic, Clare Mendonca. The first edition of the ceremony, held on March 21, 1954, was a modest affair with only five awards—Best Film, Director, Actor, Actress, and Music Director. More than 20,000 readers of the English-language film glossy *Filmfare* voted for their favorites to decide the winners. Bimal Roy (see p. 64) took home "The Black Lady"—as the statuette showing a dancing woman is called—for both Best Film and Best Director with *Do Bigha Zamin* (see p. 50). Dilip Kumar (see pp. 48–49) and Meena Kumari (see p. 91) took the acting honors for *Daag* (1952) and *Baiju Bawra* (1952), respectively. *Baiju Bawra* also won Naushad the award for Best Music Director.

GAINING POPULARITY
From the second edition, more categories were added—Supporting Actors, Story, Cinematography, and Sound. As the awards gained popularity, more technical prizes were included, and a nomination system was introduced, with three selections in each category. The voting system also underwent a change, combining public opinion with that of a jury.

Meena Kumari created history in 1963 when she garnered all three of the nominations for Best Actress. In 1984, Shabana Azmi (see p. 177) overtook Meena, by gaining four of the five nominations in the same category. Gulzar (see pp. 142–43) stands tall in the list of winners with 20 awards to his name, while actors Dilip Kumar and Shah Rukh Khan (see pp. 214–15) have each won an incredible eight Best Actor gongs. Nutan and her neice Kajol (see p. 231) lead the Best Actress tally with five awards apiece.

Among the films, *Black* (2005) picked up 11 Filmfare Awards in 2006, including those for Best Film, Director, Actor, and Actress. Coincidentally, this was the second time a Sanjay Leela Bhansali (see p. 257) film had achieved this incredible feat, following his earlier *Devdas* (see pp. 274–77), which had also won all the four major awards.

Once the exclusive awards of Bollywood, the Filmfares today are one of many film awards in India. They may no longer be unique, but their historical significance and solid reputation still make them one of the most prestigious film awards to win.

◀ **The proud winners**
In 2004, Preity Zinta and Hrithik Roshan won the best acting trophies for *Kal Ho Naa Ho* (2003) and *Koi… Mil Gaya* (2003), respectively.

> "*The Filmfare Awards have truly become an institution. It salutes an industry that has its own style …*"

RENU SARAN, *HISTORY OF INDIAN CINEMA,* 2012

DHOOM

2004

A high-octane thriller, *Dhoom* kickstarted one of Bollywood's most successful movie franchises.

▼ Super bikes
Each motorbike was uniquely styled for the character who rode it, and as the cinematographer Nirav Shah said, "the bikes dictated the look of the film."

CAST AND CREW

★ **Abhishek Bachchan** Jai Dixit
John Abraham Kabir
Uday Chopra Ali Akbar Fateh Khan
Esha Deol Sheena
Rimi Sen Sweety Dixit

🎬 **Director** Sanjay Gadhvi
🎞 **Producers** Shahnaab Alam, Aditya Chopra, Yash Chopra
🎵 **Music composers** Pritam Chakraborty, Salim Merchant, Sulaiman Merchant
🎼 **Lyricist** Sameer
💃 **Choreographers** Vaibhavi Merchant, Remo D'Souza, Ashley Lobo
📖 **Scriptwriter** Vijay Krishna Acharya
🎥 **Cinematographer** Nirav Shah
👔 **Costume designer** Anaita Adajania

The action thriller *Dhoom* (Bang), by Yash Raj Films, is best summed up by actor Uday Chopra, as "Bikes, chicks, speed, fun!"

ACTION-PACKED PLOT
The film centers on Mumbai police officer Jai Dixit, who is assigned to track down the turbo-charged biker gang running rings around the cops with a wave of daring robberies. Led by the cunning Kabir, the gang eludes the police with stunts and tricks, including riding up a ramp to hide in the back of a moving truck and posing as pizza delivery boys.

Dixit enlists the aid of fun-loving bike mechanic and racer Ali, and sets a trap for the bikers. However, the plan fails dismally as Dixit is outwitted by Kabir. Meanwhile, Ali is tempted to join Kabir's side, while the action shifts to Goa, where Kabir plans to pull

off one last heist, at India's biggest casino, on New Year's Eve. Ali agrees to take part in it, but for Dixit the chase is still on.

BOX OFFICE BLAST
Although the film received mixed reviews from critics, its adrenaline-fuelled thrills drove it to the top of the box office. The title song, "Dhoom Machale" (Have a Blast!) also became an international hit. The sequels, *Dhoom 2* (2006) and *Dhoom 3* (2013) follow the template with stars Hrithik Roshan (see p. 263) and Aamir Khan (see pp. 228–29) respectively playing antagonists. To date, *Dhoom* and its hit sequels have become the biggest Bollywood franchise, earning well over ₹8.4 billion ($130 million).

"When you put Uday, John, Esha, Rimi, and me on the same sets, there is bound to be a lot of dhoom!"

ABHISHEK BACHCHAN, REDIFF.COM, 2004

KRRISH

2006

Director Rakesh Roshan's ambitious project *Krrish* inspired a new generation of Indian superhero films, and raised the bar for special effects in Bollywood.

Sequel to the 2003 sci-fi flick *Koi… Mil Gaya* (see p. 339), *Krrish* is credited with building an original superhero film franchise in Bollywood.

This is the story of Krishna Mehra, a young man who has inherited remarkable superpowers from his father, including a high IQ and superhuman abilities that allow him to outrun horses and leap huge distances.

Krishna grows up with his grandmother in a remote part of northern India. She teaches him to hide his powers from the world, but he eventually uses his gifts to save a young woman called Priya in a hang-gliding accident in the forest. Smitten, he follows Priya to her home in Singapore. He keeps his powers hidden until a circus fire forces him to act. Donning a broken mask—and thereby creating his alter ego, Krrish—the superhero saves a group of children.

> "*Krrish is an attempt to lay the foundations of a superhero in our cinema.*"
>
> **HRITHIK ROSHAN,** *THE HINDU,* 2006

Later, Krishna learns that his father Rohit had been hired by corporate titan Dr. Siddhant Arya to build a machine that sees into the future, but his father was killed when he tried to stop Arya's evil plans. Krishna puts on his mask for a final showdown with Arya on his island base.

SUPER AMBITIONS

"I want to make a film that will take the industry to the next level," said director Rakesh Roshan of *Krrish* shortly before its release. He went on to say, "I think it will be remembered as the first film in our industry that proved we are no less than any Hollywood film." Rakesh brought in the best talent from around the world, including special effects experts from Hollywood. He also hired acclaimed Hong Kong martial-arts choreographer Tony Ching, who trained Hrithik in wushu—a form of Chinese martial art—and wirework, which is displayed in the film's numerous flying scenes.

Hrithik explained, "this genre was non-existent here" till *Krrish*. It clicked at the box office and won many fans, despite mixed reviews from critics. It also inspired other Bollywood superhero films such as *Ra.One* (2011) and *A Flying Jatt* (2016).

CAST AND CREW

★ **Hrithik Roshan** Krishna Mehra/ Krrish/Rohit Mehra

Priyanka Chopra Priya

Rekha Sonia Mehra

Naseeruddin Shah Dr. Siddhant Arya

🎬 **Director** Rakesh Roshan

🎞 **Producer** Rakesh Roshan

🎵 **Music composer** Rajesh Roshan

🎼 **Lyricists** Ibraheem Ashk, Nasir Faraaz, Vijay Akela

💃 **Choreographers** Farah Khan, Raju Khan, Vaibhavi Merchant

📖 **Scriptwriter** Sachin Bhowmick

🎥 **Cinematographer** Santosh Thundiyil

👔 **Costume designer** Manish Malhotra

▶ **A new kind of hero**
Krrish was a one-of-a-kind Indian superhero—opening up a new genre for the Hindi film industry.

LAGE RAHO MUNNA BHAI

2006

Independence leader Mahatma Gandhi was a fading figure from the past, until the comic-gangster film *Lage Raho Munna Bhai* helped India rediscover his peace-loving ideas.

Early on in its production, one of director Rajkumar Hirani's bright and breezy romantic comedies took on a serious agenda. When a tea boy asked the crew who Mahatma Gandhi was, Hirani was astounded, and the film became a mission. "If I stop you and say something about Mahatma Gandhi, you'll brush me off saying 'boring …'," explained Hirani in an interview. "But if it's entertainment, then this changes. If you explain something to a kid through an interesting story, he'll be hooked."

THEY'RE BACK!
Sanjay Dutt's Munna Bhai, the crook with a heart of gold, and his loyal sidekick Circuit, played by Arshad Warsi, were already popular with cinemagoers. In their first film, *Munna Bhai MBBS* (2003), Munna pretended to be a medical student to woo a girl. In the second one, the gangster fakes the title of professor to win his girl, but comes to believe in Gandhian philosophy by the end of the film.

At the outset, the pair of goons are on the payroll of corrupt building magnate Lucky Singh, who evicts homeowners through bribery or violence, in order to seize their property. Off duty, Munna is infatuated with Jhanvi, a beautiful radio jockey played by Vidya Balan

CAST AND CREW

- ★ **Sanjay Dutt** Murliprasad "Munna Bhai" Sharma
- **Vidya Balan** Jhanvi
- **Arshad Warsi** Circuit
- **Boman Irani** Lakhbir "Lucky" Singh
- **Dilip Prabhavalkar** Mahatma Gandhi
- **Dia Mirza** Simran L. Singh
- **Jimmy Shergill** Victor D'Souza

- **Director** Rajkumar Hirani
- **Producer** Vidhu Vinod Chopra
- **Music composers** Shantanu Moitra, Sanjay Wandrekar
- **Lyricist** Swanand Kirkire
- **Scriptwriters** Rajkumar Hirani, Vidhu Vinod Chopra, Dr. Abhijat Joshi
- **Cinematographer** C. K. Muraleedharan
- **Costume designers** Subarna Ray, Chaudari, Sheena Parikh

▲ **Riding high**
Entertaining as well as enlightening, *Lage Raho Munna Bhai* was the first Hindi film to be shown in the United Nations auditorium in New York, and was a highlight in the world cinema section of the 2007 Cannes Film Festival.

> *"I call those two divine fools. They're goons … but in these films they're helping people constantly."*

RAJKUMAR HIRANI, REDIFF.COM, SEPTEMBER 4, 2006

► **Let's dance**
Despite the film's serious social message, typical Bollywood elements were not left out. In this scene, Munna imagines his wedding to Jhanvi in a dream sequence, as they dance through the streets of Mumbai.

(see p. 312). Captivated by her "Good Morning, Mumbai" voice on local radio, he enters a phone-in quiz about Mahatma Gandhi to win the chance to meet her. But Munna does not know enough about Gandhi, and his trusted friend Circuit takes it upon himself to ensure his boss and best friend wins the quiz. He uses any means possible, even bullying and violence, to line up experts so Munna can learn everything there is to know about Gandhi.

MY FRIEND GANDHI

In a bid to make a good impression, Munna tells Jhanvi he is a professor of history. She invites him to give a speech about Gandhi at the seaside home she shares with her elderly father and his five pensioner friends. Again, Munna needs to find a quick solution to keep up the charade. At this point, Hirani brings a hilarious twist to the story. After three days and nights spent studying at the Gandhi Museum, Munna looks up to find Gandhi's ghost come to tutor him in person. With Gandhi now close at hand, Munna enchants his

audience with words of wisdom on forgiveness and "turning the other cheek." However, it's not long before the consequences of Munna's thug life return to haunt him, especially when his boss Lucky tries to make Munna an accomplice in his cunning schemes. Unfortunately, Lucky's plan involves evicting Jhanvi and her housemates from the property they have been living in for years.

THE BEGINNING OF A MOVEMENT

Throughout this part of the film, Gandhi's ghost suggests various peaceful strategies to help get the house back. These methods are dubbed *Gandhigiri* (meaning following the teachings of Gandhi) by Munna. Using his lessons from Gandhi, Munna helps the old folks get their home back. Jhanvi's radio station gives Munna his own show, offering *Gandhigiri* advice to troubled callers. Many listeners, such as a suicidal son who lost a huge sum of his father's money and an old man who protests against a corrupt official who is withholding his pension, find the non-violent practices surprisingly effective. Soon, Munna becomes a true believer in the philosophy and no longer needs Gandhi's spirit to guide him. He has actually taken Gandhian philosophy to heart and the masses, and changed lives for the better.

► **Gandhi's way**
Dilip Prabhavalkar's understated performance as Gandhi was the perfect counterfoil to Dutt's rough-and-ready Munna. Prabhavalkar's transformation to Gandhi was so realistic that Dutt failed to recognize him out of costume!

Lage Raho Munna Bhai was a box-office blockbuster, celebrated internationally for the message about alternative, peaceful protest. Ironically, the celebrations had to be cut short because Dutt was arrested shortly after the film's release. He was acquitted of some of the charges, but had to serve three years in Yerwada Central Jail from 2013 to 2016.

With the first two installments of the franchise proving to be such a success, a third Munna Bhai film was on the cards immediately after Dutt was released from prison, due to roll out in 2018.

REAL-WORLD IMPACT

Dr. Abhijat Joshi, a professor and expert on Mahatma Gandhi, who helped write the screenplay for

VIDHU VINOD CHOPRA (b.1952)

Director, screenwriter, and producer Vidhu Vinod Chopra has achieved both critical and popular acclaim since his first mainstream Hindi movie, *Sazaaye Maut* (1981). He agreed to produce the first Munna Bhai film after others rejected it and was rewarded with a series of two runaway successes. When writing screenplays, Chopra is said to stick closely to three commandments: you will entertain, you will not sell your soul when you entertain, and you will treat each film as if it is your last film.

Lage Raho Munna Bhai, was amazed by the response to the film. It had such a deep impact on people, especially the youth, that an epidemic of real-world *Gandhigiri* followed. The word he invented entered everyday vocabulary and inspired a rash of non-violent protests across India. "Gandhian philosophy was valid when conditions were much more tough," commented Hirani. "I'm sure it is valid today. We just have to believe in it."

RANG DE BASANTI

2006

Rang de Basanti is a 21st-century social commentary that honors the spirit of 20th-century Indian freedom fighters, invoking their memory in a battle against modern injustice.

The movie begins with Sue (Alice Patten), a British filmmaker, chancing upon the diary of her grandfather, a British officer in India during colonial rule. Inspired to make a documentary about the lives of the revolutionaries the diary describes, she travels to Delhi. There she meets five young men and casts them to play the roles of freedom fighters Bhagat Singh (Siddharth), Chandrashekhar Azad (Aamir Khan), Ram Prasad Bismil (Atul Kulkarni), S. Rajguru (Sharman Joshi), and Ashfaqullah Khan (Kunal Kapoor).

Rang de Basanti (Color It Saffron) draws a link between British India and the India of today by splitting events into past and present. While enacting the lives of revolutionaries in the documentary, the boys come to understand the value of sacrifice and commitment to a noble cause, and even feel the contrast with their own, more hedonistic lifestyles.

One theme of the film is government corruption. In a crucial scene, the film cuts between the image of a British colonial officer and a modern Indian politician. And when a young pilot, Ajay Rathod (Madhavan), is killed in a jet fighter crash that could have been prevented the boys protest, but fail to make an impact on the unjust system. They all soon decide that they must become the revolutionaries they have been enacting in order to get justice.

AWARDS AND ACCLAIM

Just before the film's release, the Indian censor board ordered it to be cleared by the Indian Defense Ministry because of its references to the MiG-21 fighter jet. Air Marshal Padamjit Singh Ahluwalia said he found the film "very inspiring" for youngsters.

Rang de Basanti was released on January 26, 2006, India's Republic Day, and enjoyed a record-breaking opening week. It was chosen as India's official entry to the Golden Globe Awards, the Academy Awards, and was nominated for a BAFTA. A.R. Rahman (see pp. 244–45) won the Filmfare Best Music Director Award. The song "Rang De Basanti" was even used by a flash mob at Chhatrapati Shivaji Terminus, Mumbai, on November 27, 2011, in honor of those who had died in the 11/26 attack.

THE RDB EFFECT

The film struck a chord with its audience, tapping into the public's anger and frustration with India's corrupt political system. It sparked an upsurge in public activism against corruption and perceived injustice, with candlelit vigils and protests over long-running court cases. It even led to a wider debate about patriotism and citizenship. Actor Kunal Kapoor said he thought the film portrayed "patriotism in a package that the youngsters understood and empathized with." In an interview on the film's 10-year anniversary, Rakeysh Omprakash Mehra said, "What I'm trying to say is, we got independence from the *goras* [the British]. But we got enslaved by our own. Now we're killing each other."

▼ **Emotive graffiti**
"Inquilab Zindabad," meaning "Long Live the Revolution," was first used by Bhagat Singh in 1929. Here, the phrase emphasizes the sense of patriotism felt by the protagonists in the film.

HIT SONGS

Khalbali
(Commotion)
🎤 **Singers** A.R. Rahman, Mohammed Aslam, Nacim

Rang De Basanti
(Color It Saffron)
🎤 **Singers** Daler Mehndi, K.S. Chitra

Khoon Chala
(Raging Blood)
🎤 **Singer** Mohit Chauhan

CAST AND CREW

★ **Aamir Khan** Daljeet "DJ"
Siddharth Karan R. Singhania
Sharman Joshi Sukhi
Kunal Kapoor Aslam
Atul Kulkarni Laxman Pandey
Soha Ali Khan Sonia/Durga Vohra

Director Rakeysh Omprakash Mehra
Producers R.O. Mehra, Ronnie Screwvala, P.S. Bharathi
Music composer A.R. Rahman
Lyricist Prasoon Joshi
Choreographers Ganesh Acharya, Vaibhavi Merchant, Raju Sundaram
Scriptwriters P. Joshi, Rensil D'Silva
Cinematographer Binod Pradhan
Costume designers Lovleen Bains, Arjun Bhasin

OMKARA

2006

Bridging the gap between arthouse and mainstream cinema, Vishal Bhardwaj's *Omkara* is a hard-hitting, rustic rendering of Shakespeare's *Othello* that pulls no punches.

A gripping tale of betrayal, deception, and revenge set in contemporary India, *Omkara* is considered to be a display of career-defining performances by its star-studded cast.

Ajay Devgn plays Omkara, a political enforcer for a corrupt local politician Tiwari Bhaisaab (Naseeruddin Shah) in Meerut, in western Uttar Pradesh. He abducts the object of his affections, Dolly Mishra, just before her wedding to another man. However, she is persuaded by Omkara to pretend to her father that she eloped with him.

An ashamed and angry father warns, "Any daughter who can dupe her own father will never be anyone's to claim," the only dialogue that closely follows the original text of *Othello*—"Look to her, Moor, if thou hast eyes to see. She has deceived her father and may thee."

▶ **What's in a name?**
The film's title was decided by a popular vote. The public was given a choice between "Omkara," "Issak" (Love), and "O Saathi Re"(Oh Companion), all of which also appear as song titles in the film.

The line returns to haunt Omkara after he promotes his young comrade Kesu Upadhyaya instead of his loyal lieutenant Langda Tyagi. Seething with anger, Langda plots his revenge. Under the pretense of being a loyal friend, he subtly poisons the relationship between Omkara, Kesu, and Dolly with suspicions of infidelity, a deception that ultimately leads to anguish and bloodshed.

THE BARD IN INDIA
Vishal Bhardwaj was first inspired to adapt Shakespearean drama for the Indian screen after watching *Throne of Blood* (1957), Japanese director Akira Kurosawa's take on *Macbeth*. Bhardwaj then adapted *Macbeth* into the dark and moody *Maqbool* (2003) before moving on to *Othello* with *Omkara*. In a slight departure from the source material, he used the issue of caste, instead of race, to give the eponymous antihero the status of an outsider. Bhardwaj would return to Shakespeare again in 2014 with *Haider*, a Hindi version of *Hamlet*.

A stickler for perfection, Bhardwaj insisted on acting workshops for the entire cast of *Omkara* so that they could relate to the characters better. "I tried to make them [the actors] as non-filmy as possible," he said.

Bhardwaj not only co-wrote and directed the film, but composed the music as well. He ensured that the dialogue was authentically hard-edged, using several swear words across the narrative, earning the film an "A" (restricted for adults) certification. Bhardwaj knew this would limit his audience, but said in an interview:

"I just want the film to make enough money to let me make another film the way I want to." The film failed to become a box-office hit, but was acclaimed by critics both in India and abroad, winning over audiences in the UK and US. *Omkara* was showcased on the international film festival circuit in 2006. It won numerous accolades, including three National Film Awards.

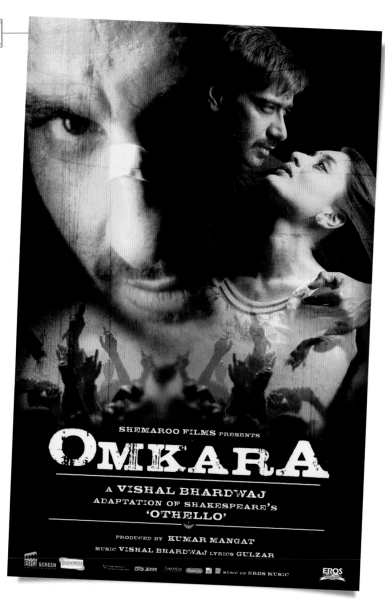

SHEMAROO FILMS PRESENTS
OMKARA
A VISHAL BHARDWAJ
ADAPTATION OF SHAKESPEARE'S
'OTHELLO'
PRODUCED BY KUMAR MANGAT
MUSIC VISHAL BHARDWAJ LYRICS GULZAR

CAST AND CREW

- ★ **Ajay Devgn** Omi "Omkara" Shukla
- **Kareena Kapoor** Dolly Mishra
- **Saif Ali Khan** Langda Tyagi
- **Vivek Oberoi** Kesu Upadhyaya

- 🎬 **Director** Vishal Bhardwaj
- 🏠 **Producer** Kumar Mangat Pathak
- 🎵 **Music composer** Vishal Bhardwaj
- **Lyricist** Gulzar
- 🎭 **Choreographers** Ganesh Acharya, Bhushan Lakandri
- 📝 **Scriptwriters** Vishal Bhardwaj, Robin Bhatt, Abhishek Chaubey
- 🎥 **Cinematographer** Tassaduq Hussain
- 👔 **Costume designers** Dolly Ahluwalia, Shaahid Amir

VISHAL BHARDWAJ (b.1965)

Vishal Bhardwaj started his career in the film industry as a music composer. He wrote his first song at the age of 17 for *Yaar Kasam* (1985), and won the Filmfare R.D. Burman Award for New Music Talent for *Maachis* (1996). Bhardwaj resolved to become a director after watching Quentin Tarantino's *Pulp Fiction* (1994)—"It messed up my head … it showed me the power of storytelling … and that violence can be so entertaining." *Makdee* (2002) was his directorial debut. He still composes the music for his films, often working with the lyricist Gulzar (see pp. 142–43).

ITEM NUMBER

With a seductive "item girl," a catchy melody, and raunchy lyrics, Bollywood's steamy item songs get feet tapping and audiences singing along.

The feel-good factor in almost every Bollywood movie is the "item number." This is an infectious song-and-dance routine and is usually independent of the main plot. These sequences appear as a fantasy-come-true and feature visually delightful performances by highly paid dancers or celebrities who make a special appearance in the movie.

The role of these guest stars is to use their dance moves to inject a musical highlight into the storyline and give any film instant mass appeal. The best item numbers generate huge revenue from downloads and continue to be lasting YouTube hits. They set the trend on dance floors at weddings and parties all over the country long after the film has faded from memory, as was the case with the song "Sheila Ki Jawani" (Sheila's Youth) in *Tees Maar Khan*.

The forerunners of item girls appeared in the 1930s as immodest cabaret "vamps," or gangster's molls. Actresses such as Cuckoo and Helen gave memorable performances up to the 1970s (see pp. 96–97). The next wave of item numbers saw Madhuri Dixit in *Tezaab* (see p. 198) jiving to

"Ek, Do, Teen" (One Two Three), Urmila Matondkar in *China Gate* (1998) grooving to "Chamma Chamma," and Malaika Arora shimmying across the carriage roofs of a moving train to "Chaiyya Chaiyya" in an iconic segment from *Dil Se..* (see pp. 242–43).

THE ITEM GIRL

Critics began to use the term "item number" after Shilpa Shetty made a one-off appearance in *Shool* (1999), driving men to distraction as she danced to "Main Aai Hoon UP Bihar Lootne" (I've Come to Take Over UP and Bihar). Directors exploited the potential of these sexually charged, drop-in performances, and hired specialist music directors, costume designers, and choreographers to create these spectacular scenes. The money poured into the production of item numbers is well worth it, as the popularity of the songs can impact the film's box office success.

Despite their popularity, however, item numbers have also attracted criticism. Many feel that the routines objectify women while censors have rated them as adult content and banned them from television. But item numbers remain the money-spinning bedrock of Bollywood movies, giving aspiring actresses a shot at instant stardom, while offering established stars the chance to stay in the spotlight.

◀ Sultry fillers
Item girl Malaika Arora Khan raises temperatures with her dance to the hit song "Munni Badnaam" (Notorious Munni) in *Dabangg* (2010).

"People have made it sound, like, crude and crass, so I would just call it as (sic) a special song …"

MALAIKA ARORA KHAN, *DAILY PIONEER*, APRIL 19, 2015

OM SHANTI OM

A big-budget homage to Bollywood films of a bygone era, *Om Shanti Om* is an entertaining take on the quirky fantasies created by popular Indian cinema.

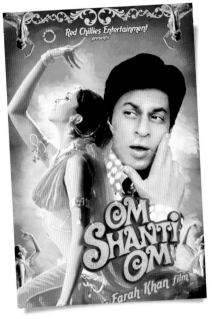

▲ **Talented twosome**
Although cast opposite one of the biggest names in Bollywood, debutante Deepika Padukone more than held her own against veteran superstar Shah Rukh Khan.

In 2004, director Farah Khan got together with Shah Rukh Khan's production house Red Chillies Entertainment to make her first movie *Main Hoon Na* (see p. 339), a hit spy thriller with entertaining songs, beautiful choreography, celebrities such as Shah Rukh Khan (see pp. 214–15), and Sushmita Sen (see pp. 252–53), and newcomers Amrita Rao and Zayed Khan. To make *Om Shanti Om* (Peace Be Upon You), which was a much more ambitious project in terms of scale and scope, Farah once again teamed up with Red Chillies and Shah Rukh Khan. However, this time Farah wanted to pay an entertaining tribute to the recurring themes of Hindi cinema of the 1960s and 1970s. In collaboration with Shah Rukh's writer friend, Mushtaq Sheikh, she wrote a screenplay that celebrated classic Bollywood motifs, such as rebirth, class differences, double roles, dark villains, suffering old mothers, and musical numbers in which characters break into song simply to provide audiences a lighthearted interlude.

PAST MEETS PRESENT
Shah Rukh was a huge star by the time *Om Shanti Om* was made, while his co-star—model Deepika Padukone

CAST AND CREW

★ **Shah Rukh Khan** Om Prakash Makhija/Om Kapoor
Deepika Padukone Shantipriya/Sandy
Arjun Rampal Mukesh "Mike" Mehra
Kirron Kher Bela Makhija
Shreyas Talpade Pappu Master

🎬 **Director** Farah Khan
⌂ **Producers** Shah Rukh Khan, Gauri Khan
♫ **Music composers** Vishal Dadlani, Shekhar Ravjiani
♪ **Lyricist** Javed Akhtar
🕺 **Choreographer** Farah Khan
📖 **Scriptwriters** Mushtaq Sheikh, Farah Khan
🎥 **Cinematographer** V. Manikandan
👔 **Costume designers** Karan Johar, Manish Malhotra, Sanjeev Mulchandani

(see pp. 328–29), the daughter of badminton legend Prakash Padukone—was a newcomer. At the casting stage, Farah took playful liberties with reality and cast Deepika as Shantipriya, a celebrated Bollywood star while Shah Rukh portrays Om Prakash Makhija (Omi), a struggling, junior artist madly in love with the leading lady.

Om Shanti Om is a modern take on the 1980 hit Bollywood film *Karz* (see pp. 158–59) and its title comes from the song of the same name. In fact, Farah's film opens with the original song from *Karz* being shot; actor Rishi Kapoor dances on stage, director Subhash Ghai (see p. 159) is behind the camera, and Omi is an extra.

In order to place Deepika and Shah Rukh's characters among the pantheon of old-time Bollywood actors, Farah digitally superimposed present-day actors onto old footage of classic Hindi movies. The same trick is used in the song "Dhoom Tana" in which Deepika seems to stand next to actors from the past such as Sunil Dutt and Rajesh Khanna (see pp. 106–107). The song sequence opens on a set with dark

clouds painted in the background and percussionists with large drums—a throwback to classic, large-scale Bollywood musical superhits.

CELEBRITY BASH
Other songs in the film are equally enjoyable and original. In the very entertaining song sequence, "Dard-e-Disco" (Pain of Disco), Shah Rukh struts around showing off his six-pack abs, lip-syncing to Sukhwinder Singh's voice and Javed Akhtar's lyrics. The most popular song in the film, "Deewangi Deewangi" (Craziness) features more than 30 Bollywood actors of all ages making cameo appearances. Some of the stars in the song include veteran actors Dharmendra (see pp. 152–53), and Jeetendra (see pp. 182–83) and younger celebrities such as Priyanka Chopra (see pp. 280–81) and Rani Mukerji (see p. 247). The multi-star coterie grooving to an infectious melody made for an epic musical number and another popular hit. The presence of these stars was a clear indication of the respect Shah Rukh and Farah command in Bollywood.

One person who was not pleased with the film was veteran Hindi film actor Manoj Kumar. In the beginning of the film, Omi sneaks into the premiere of Shanti's film *Dreamy Girl*, by pretending to be Manoj Kumar. Unhappy at the comical portrayal, Kumar threatened to sue and the

◄ Retro razzmatazz
With its retro styling and high drama, the film takes audiences on a nostalgic trip to Bollywood's past. The main characters' first meeting at a red carpet event captures Bollywood's typically over-the-top treatment of the first stirrings of love.

◄ Star power
Shah Rukh Khan's undeniable charm, unabashed star power, and knockout physique became the highlight of his performance in the superhit song "Dard-e-Disco."

filmmakers apologized. Although Kumar accepted the apology, he went to court and succeeded in getting the film's producers to edit out the scenes that lampooned him.

Om Shanti Om was very well-received in India—a huge box office success that also garnered high praise from critics for its fun-loving tone. The film was also released all over the world and was particularly successful in Japan. In 2016, Farah announced that there were plans to make a Japanese musical stage production based on the film.

FARAH KHAN
(b.1965)

Farah Khan got her big break when Saroj Khan, senior choreographer of *Jo Jeeta Wohi Sikandar* (see p.212) left the project. Since then, Farah has choreographed a range of films, including *Dil To Pagal Hai* (1997), the famous "Chaiyya Chaiyya" (In the Shade) song from *Dil Se* (see pp.242–43), *Monsoon Wedding* (2001), and the West End/Broadway production, *Bombay Dreams*. She transitioned to film direction with the spy thriller *Main Hoon Na* (see p.339). She also directed *Tees Maar Khan* (2010) and *Happy New Year* (2014), with Shah Rukh Khan.

"Om Shanti Om *is smart enough to take a handful of self-directed jibes.*"

RAJEEV MASAND, FILM JOURNALIST, RAJEEVMASAND.COM

STORYLINE

Om Prakash Makhija (Omi) is an ambitious young actor in the Hindi film industry of the 1970s. His dream is to become a Bollywood superstar and win the love of celebrity actress Shantipriya. However, Omi's hopes come crashing down when he learns that Shanti is in a relationship with a famous movie producer, Mukesh Mehra, who murders her to protect his career. Omi dies in a futile effort to save Shanti but meets his nemesis once again when he is reborn 30 years later as Om Kapoor.

OMI AND SHANTIPRIYA DRESSED IN THE BRIGHT, GLITTERY COSTUMES OF 1970S BOLLYWOOD

1970s

PLOT OVERVIEW

Om Prakash Makhija is in love with film star Shantipriya. He attends the premier of Shanti's film, *Dreamy Girl*, and has a chance encounter with the star. ❶ He then sneaks in to watch the movie and dreams about acting in a movie with her. ❷

OMI WITH HIS MOTHER, BELA

When a fire gets out of control during a shoot, Omi, who has a minor role in the film, comes to the rescue and saves Shanti. Shanti and Omi grow close and become friends. ❸

Omi follows Shanti and overhears her conversation with producer Mukesh Mehra. He discovers that Mukesh and Shanti have married in secret, and Shanti is pregnant with his child. Omi is heartbroken. ❹

Mukesh pretends to be happy and invites Shanti to the set of their soon-to-be-launched film, *Om Shanti Om*. He promises to cancel the film, reveal their relationship to the public, and have a grand wedding on the set. Instead, he lures Shanti to the set and uses his lighter to start a fire.

Omi, who happens to be at the same location, tries to rescue Shanti but is stopped by Mukesh's guards who throw him out. Omi is then hit by a car owned by Rajesh Kapoor, a well-known movie actor; Omi dies in the accident.

THE SONGS

❶
Ajab Si (Something Strange)
Singer: KK
Picturized on Omi and Shantipriya

❷
Dhoom Tana
Singers: Abhijeet Bhattacharya, Shreya Ghoshal
Picturized on Shantipriya, Omi, and others

★ *"Dhoom Tana" was the first Indian film song where actors were digitally juxtaposed with images of stars from older films.*

❸
Main Agar Kahoon (If I Said)
Singers: Sonu Nigam, Shreya Ghoshal
Picturized on Omi and Shantipriya

❹
Jag Soona Soona Lage (The World Feels Empty)
Singers: Rahat Fateh Ali Khan, Richa Sharma
Picturized on Omi

MUKESH'S LIGHTER

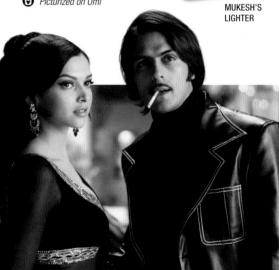

CHARMING MUKESH GUIDES THE UNSUSPECTING SHANTIPRIYA INTO A TRAP

SHANTIPRIYA PERFORMS A SONG SEQUENCE IN THE STYLE OF CLASSIC BOLLYWOOD CINEMA

ARJUN RAMPAL (b.1972)

A former model, Arjun Rampal began his film career in 2001 with *Pyaar Ishq Aur Mohabbat*. A respected actor, Rampal has starred in more than 40 films, including *Don—The Chase Begins Again* (2006), *Ra.One* (2011), *Om Shanti Om,* and smaller art-house films, such as *The Last Lear* (2007). His stellar performance in *Rock On!!* (2008) won him a Filmfare Award and a National Award for Best Supporting Actor.

> *"Farah Khan's re-birth saga … paints the seventies pop culture in Andy Warhol-ish strokes."*
>
> THE TIMES OF INDIA, MOVIE REVIEW, NOVEMBER 10, 2007

2000s

Omi is reborn as Rajesh and Lovely's son, Om Kapoor, who grows up to be a famous actor. Nicknamed "OK," he lives the luxurious life Omi once dreamt of. While shooting a song sequence for a film ❺, OK suffers a panic attack because of his crippling fear of fire.

At an award show after-party ❻, an introduction to Mukesh triggers past-life memories. Later OK is reunited with Omi's mother, Bela, and friend, Pappu, and conspires with them to avenge Shanti's death by making Mukesh confess to his crime.

OK convinces Mukesh to revive the *Om Shanti Om* project. OK finds Sandhya, also known as Sandy, a Shantipriya lookalike, and hires her to torment Mukesh by making him believe Shanti is still around. Throughout the film's shooting, OK and his friends continue to stage incidents to remind Mukesh of his heinous crime.

During the music launch of the film, OK lets Mukesh know through a song that he is aware of the truth behind Shanti's death ❼. Mukesh runs after Sandy, who is present at the launch, believing her to be Shanti's spirit. After she accidentally cuts her arm and bleeds, Mukesh realizes that she is not a ghost at all. Enraged, he goes to confront OK about the deception but is hit by a chandelier and loses consciousness.

OK has a confrontation with Mukesh. While they are arguing, "Sandy" shows up and reveals that the fire had failed to kill Shanti. Instead, she was buried alive under the floor below the chandelier. During the fight, another fire breaks out. Just as OK is about to kill Mukesh, "Sandy" drops the chandelier on Mukesh, killing him instantly. As the real Sandy rushes to the scene, OK realizes that "Sandy" was, in fact, Shantipriya's ghost all along.

❺ ❻ ❼

**Dard-e-Disco
(Pain of Disco)**
Singers: Sukhwinder Singh, Caralisa Monteiro, Nisha, Marianne
☻ *Picturized on OK*

Deewangi Deewangi (Craziness)
Singers: Shaan, Udit Narayan, Shreya Ghoshal, Sunidhi Chauhan, Rahul Saxena
Picturized on OK and other
☻ *Bollywood stars*

**Dastaan-E-Om Shanti Om
(The Story of Om Shanti Om)**
Singer: Shaan
☻ *Picturized on OK, Mukesh, and Sandy*

"Dastan-E-Om Shanti Om" and its staging was inspired by the stage musical, Phantom of the Opera, *including the chandelier that plays a key role in the final moments of the film.* ✪

OM KAPOOR STAGES A DRAMATIC MUSICAL SHOWDOWN

THREE KHANS—SAIF, SALMAN, AND SHAH RUKH—IN "DEEWANGI DEEWANGI"

TAARE ZAMEEN PAR

| 2007 |

Taare Zameen par is a heart-tugging film about a misunderstood young boy who is struggling in school, until his art teacher recognizes that the child has dyslexia.

CAST AND CREW

★ **Darsheel Safary** Ishaan Awasthi
Aamir Khan Ram Shankar Nikumbh
Tisca Chopra Maya Awasthi
Vipin Sharma Nandkishore Awasthi
Tanay Chheda Rajan Damodran
Sachet Engineer Yohaan Awasthi

🎬 **Director** Aamir Khan
⬡ **Producer** Aamir Khan
🎵 **Music composers** Shankar Mahadevan, Ehsaan Noorani, Loy Mendonsa.
🎼 **Lyricist** Prasoon Joshi
🕺 **Choreographer** Shiamak Davar
📖 **Scriptwriter** Amole Gupte
📷 **Cinematographer** Setu (Satyajit)
👔 **Costume designer** Priyanjali Lahiri

For the film *Taare Zameen par* (Like Stars on Earth) actor–producer Aamir Khan took on the role of director as well. He created a touching story about a young boy suffering from dyslexia. The boy's problems are misunderstood both by his parents and a society focused on pushing children to succeed. Aamir joined the project, which had been initiated by actor-director Amole Gupte and his wife, Deepa Bhatia, who felt that people in India did not fully understand the symptoms of dyslexia. Gupte was later credited as writer and creative director of the film.

A TOUCHING STORY

The star of *Taare Zameen par*, Darsheel Safary, was 11 years old at the time of the

► Everyone's choice

Several young boys auditioned for the role of Ishaan. However, Amole Gupte recalls that "Darsheel had the mischief in his eyes to be Ishaan."

film's release. He plays Ishaan Awasthi, a dreamer and young artist who has great difficulty with reading, understanding the alphabet and numbers, and following instructions. Aamir, one of Bollywood's most astute actors, plays the role of Ram Shankar Nikumbh, an art teacher who recognizes Ishaan's challenges, but also appreciates his other skills, including his talent for art.

MOVIE WITH A MESSAGE

In a rare move for a Bollywood film, the opening credits of *Taare Zameen par* give the child actor Safary the top billing. Despite being a Bollywood superstar, Aamir's name appears only after Safary's. Unusually, too, Aamir does not appear on screen until about halfway through the film.

The film's sensitive handling of a subject that few people are aware of in India, reassured sufferers that there is no shame in dyslexia. The film also called for parents and educators to look out for early signs of learning difficulties in children. Just as Aamir's character Nikumbh showed in the film, extra support and love can go a long way to resolving children's problems. The film generated a great deal of conversation about dyslexia and helped many parents understand how to treat their children more sensitively.

However, *Taare Zameen par* is also an entertaining film—with beautiful songs, some touching moments, and natural performances. The film won

▲ Ishaan's boarding school
Misunderstood by his parents, Ishaan is sent away to a boarding school. More than half of the film was shot at the New Era High School (above), located in Panchgani, Maharashtra.

many awards, including the prestigious National Award for Best Film on Family Welfare. It was also India's official entry for the best foreign language film at the Oscars in 2007, making it the second of three films produced by Aamir Khan to be sent to the Oscars—the other two being *Lagaan* (see pp. 268–69) and *Peepli Live* (2010).

Young actor Darsheel Safary was also picked out for his convincing performance, winning the Filmfare Critics Award for Best Actor.

JAB WE MET

2007

A popular romantic film with a fresh treatment for an old story, *Jab We Met* continues to play well with audiences, long after its release.

(see p. 271)

For his second film *Jab We Met* (When We Met), director Imtiaz Ali cast real-life couple, Kareena Kapoor (see p. 271) and Shahid Kapoor, in the leading roles. It was their fourth film together and would turn out to be their biggest hit.

A ROMANTIC TALE

Imtiaz was a young filmmaker when he came up with the idea of *Jab We Met*. It tells the tale of a man and a woman who meet by accident and take a long time to realize that they love each other while circumstances, or other lovers, pull them in different directions. Meanwhile, the couple take a journey along some very scenic routes accompanied by several beautiful songs, which contribute to the film's romantic atmosphere. As is often the case in these romantic tales, it takes the pair a while to finally acknowledge that they are in love, but, fortunately, it is not too late.

Imtiaz's lead characters are often flawed, as they are in this case, and perhaps that is one of the reasons why audiences make such a strong emotional connection with them—because they are like us.

LASTING SUCCESS

The film was shot in Mumbai, Chandigarh, Shimla, Manali, and the Rohtang Pass in the Himalayas. This is where the hit song "Yeh Ishq Haye" was filmed, with masses of choreographed Indian and Tibetan dancers.

The film was an instant hit at the box office and has remained popular, especially with the younger, teenage audience who watch it over and over.

The enduring popularity of the film's soundtrack has helped. The song "Mauja Hi Mauja" still plays a lot at dance and wedding parties.

ALL RIGHT IN THE END

Unfortunately, the couple split up around the time of the film's promotion. Some even speculated that the split was a publicity stunt, however, it turned out to be real.

The film faced other casting issues, too. In an interview, actor Bobby Deol revealed that he was originally supposed to be in the film (which at an early stage was titled "Geet," the name of Kareena Kapoor's character). However, there were delays in the production, and at some point Bobby realized that Shahid had been signed for the role instead.

Today, *Jab We Met* is recognized as one of Kareena's finest performances and the film was nominated for several awards. Most of Imtiaz's later films have been box office successes, too, though harsher critics have noted that they tend to reuse *Jab We Met*'s winning formula.

CAST AND CREW

- ★ **Kareena Kapoor** Geet Dhillon
- **Shahid Kapoor** Aditya Kashyap
- **Tarun Arora** Anshuman
- **Pavan Malhotra** Geet's uncle
- **Dara Singh** Geet's grandfather

- 🎬 **Director** Imtiaz Ali
- 🎞 **Producer** Dhillin Mehta
- 🎵 **Music composers** Pritam Chakraborty, Sandesh Shandilya
- 🎵 **Lyricist** Irshad Kamil
- 🕺 **Choreographers** Saroj Khan, Bosco Martis, Caesar Gonsalves
- 📖 **Scriptwriter** Imtiaz Ali
- 🎥 **Cinematographer** Natarajan Subramaniam
- 👔 **Costume designer** Manish Malhotra

▼ **Multiple award winner**
Kareena Kapoor received wide acclaim for her portrayal of Geet, winning several awards, including the Filmfare Awards for Best Actress as well as International Indian Film Academy Awards.

▲ **The train**
The film's most pivotal moments take place on a train, which is where the two lead actors meet for the first time.

HIT SONGS

Mauja Hi Mauja
(Oodles of Fun)
🎤 **Singer** Mika Singh

Yeh Ishq Haye
(This Love)
🎤 **Singer** Shreya Ghoshal

Nagada Nagada
(Beat the Drum)
🎤 **Singers** Sonu Nigam, Javed Ali

IMTIAZ ALI (b.1971)

Imtiaz Ali developed an early interest in the arts while taking part in college plays. His career began with TV shows and he made his first film *Socha na tha* in 2005. Imtiaz's films are packed with romance, heartache, and popular songs. One of the most highly regarded filmmakers in Bollywood, he has also directed box office hits such as *Love Aaj Kal* (2009), *Rockstar* (2011), *Cocktail* (2015) , and *Highway* (2014).

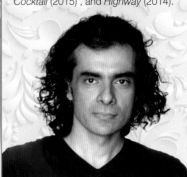

CHAK DE! INDIA

2007

An inspiring story about the Indian women's national hockey team, this fictionalized film also explores the sexism and religious prejudice that prevail in India's sporting fraternity.

HIT SONG

Chak De! India
(Go For It, India!)

🎤 **Singers** Sukhwinder Singh, Salim–Sulaiman, Marianne D'Cruz

CAST AND CREW

★ **Shah Rukh Khan** Kabir Khan
Vidya Malvade Vidya Sharma
Sagarika Ghatge Preety Sabharwal
Shilpa Shukla Bindia Naik
Arya Menon Gul Iqbal
Seema Azmi Rani Dispotta
Chitrashi Rawat Komal Chautala
Nisha Nair Soimoi Kerketa

🎬 **Director** Shimit Amin
🎞 **Producers** Aditya Chopra, Yash Chopra
🎵 **Music composers** Salim Merchant, Sulaiman Merchant
🎼 **Lyricist** Jaideep Sahni
📝 **Scriptwriter** Jaideep Sahni
🎥 **Cinematographer** Sudeep Chatterjee
👔 **Costume designer** Mandira Shukla

The Indian women's national hockey team that won a gold medal at the Commonwealth Games in 2002 inspired scriptwriter Jaideep Sahni to pen *Chak De! India* (Go For It, India!). Once the script was written, Jaideep learned that by coincidence his lead character, Kabir Khan, resembled a Muslim Indian player, Mir Ranjan Negi, who had faced false accusations of fixing a match against Pakistan in the 1982 Asian Games.

In itself, *Chak De! India* is a wonderful and spirited story of a defamed field hockey player who redeems himself by leading a ragtag team of women who come together from different parts of India. These women face sexism from officials and even their family members. Yet, with steely determination, they

▼ **Girl power**
The all-girl team of hockey players look up to their coach, Kabir Khan, who takes the team to victory against all odds.

practice hard and grow confident, finally proving everyone wrong by winning the World Hockey Championship.

PATRIOTIC MASTERPIECE
The highlight of *Chak De! India* is the film's lead character, played by Shah Rukh Khan (see pp. 214–15) who, despite his superstar persona, steps back to keep the limelight on the young women. The script was originally offered to Salman Khan (see pp. 224–25), but he left the project due to creative differences. However, Shah Rukh, who had starred in a number of romantic films, felt comfortable enough to share the screen with several young actresses, most of them unknown to the audience.

Set in contemporary India, the film also has a patriotic undertone. In fact, the song "Chak De! India" gripped the nation and became a rousing anthem, playing at several sporting and patriotic events. *Chak De! India* is a very entertaining film that makes audiences fall in love with every player in the team,

rooting for the underdogs. In spite of the film's predictable outcome, director Shimit Amin brings a healthy dose of suspense to the screen through an engaging narrative. Jaideep's sharp script includes the often-quoted pep talk, "Sattar Minute" (Seventy Minutes), that Shah Rukh delivers to his team on the spirit of sportsmanship.

Critics loved *Chak De! India* and the film was a box office success. It was the third-highest-grossing Indian movie of 2007, and won four Filmfare Awards including Best Actor for Shah Rukh. The film also received a National Award in the category of Best Popular Film Providing Wholesome Entertainment. Critics often say that Shah Rukh gave the best performance of his career in *Chak De! India*.

SULAIMAN (b.1970) AND SALIM (b.1974)

Sulaiman and Salim Merchant are the sons of Bollywood musician Sadruddin Merchant. They shot to fame with Ram Gopal Varma's *Bhoot* (2003) and since then have composed music for films such as *Rab ne Bana di Jodi* (2008) and *Krrish* (see p. 285), for which they won a Filmfare Award for Best Background Score. Their hit songs include "Mar Jawan" (I Could Die), "Haule Haule" (Slowly), and the popular dancehall number "Ainvayi Ainvayi" (Just Like That).

FASHION

Fashion is Bollywood's realistic exploration of the Indian fashion industry's underbelly, which is not all glitz and glamour.

CAST AND CREW

★ **Priyanka Chopra** Meghna Mathur
Kangana Ranaut Shonali Gujral
Mugdha Godse Janet Sequeira
Arbaaz Khan Abhijeet Sarin
Arjan Bajwa Manav Bhasin

🎬 **Director** Madhur Bhandarkar
🎩 **Producers** Ronnie Screwvala,
Siddharth Roy Kapur, Deven Khote,
Zarina Mehta, Madhur Bhandarkar
🎵 **Music composers** Salim Merchant,
Sulaiman Merchant
🎵 **Lyricist** Irfan Siddiqui
📖 **Scriptwriters** Madhur Bhandarkar,
Anuradha Tiwari
🎥 **Cinematographer** Mahesh Limaye
👔 **Costume designers** Narendra
Kumar Ahmed, Rita Dhody

► **Supermodels**
Fashion probes the flipside of the glitzy lives of models through three main characters—(from left to right) Janet, Meghna, and Shonali.

rise and fall as she works her way through the exciting, seductive, and messy world of the fashion industry. Apart from being a classic Bollywood entertainer, the film also explores a range of social issues such as drug abuse, prejudice against homosexuality, and the exploitation of women.

Bhandarkar met many people in the fashion industry, including models, as part of his extensive research on the film. He wanted to understand the struggles that models face at different levels of their career. However, he was careful enough to fictionalize all his characters.

RAVE RECEPTION
The film's lively soundtrack was extremely well received. Some of the popular songs include "Mar Jawan" (I Could Die) by Shruti Pathak and Salim Merchant, "Kuch Khaas" (Something Special) by Mohit Chauhan and Neha Bhasin, and "Fashion Ka Jalwa" (Display of Fashion), sung by Sukhwinder Singh.

But most of all, *Fashion* is remembered for Priyanka's nuanced performance. The supermodel showed her acting prowess in a difficult role, which required her to portray the various stages in a young model's life. With this film, Bollywood finally seemed to take Priyanka seriously as an actress. She received numerous awards including a National Award for her performance in *Fashion*.

From the condition of women bar dancers in Mumbai (*Chandini Bar*, 2001), to the existence of pedophilia in India's upper-class society (*Page 3*, 2005), Madhur Bhandarkar has explored a range of social issues in India through his films. In *Fashion*, he went one step further by exploring the dark secrets of the Indian fashion industry. In a masterstroke, he cast former Miss World Priyanka Chopra (see pp. 280–81) as the lead character, along with many supporting actors who included real-life models.

BHANDARKAR'S AMBITION
Fashion is the story of a naïve young girl, Meghna, who moves from Chandigarh to Mumbai to become a supermodel. The film traces her

"The film ... travels through the dark recesses of the lead characters."

THE TIMES OF INDIA, 2016

JODHAA AKBAR

2008

A landmark epic, *Jodhaa Akbar* is a lavish interpretation of the story of a 16th-century Mughal emperor and his Rajput bride, complete with spectacular sets, rich costumes, and great songs.

CAST AND CREW

★ **Hrithik Roshan** Jalaluddin Akbar
Aishwarya Rai Jodhaa Bai
Ila Arun Maham Anga
Suhasini Mulay Rani Padmavati

Director Ashutosh Gowariker
Producers Ronnie Screwvala, Ashutosh Gowariker
♫ **Music composer** A.R. Rahman
Lyricist Javed Akhtar
Scriptwriters Haider Ali, Ashutosh Gowariker
Cinematographer Kiran Deohans
Costume designer Neeta Lulla

After the success of *Lagaan* (see pp. 266–69), director Ashutosh Gowariker was approached by writer and actor Haider Ali, an old friend, to make a film based on *Mughal-e-Azam* (see pp. 68–71). However Ali did not want Gowariker to simply remake the 1960 Bollywood classic. Instead, he suggested a prequel to *Mughal-e-Azam* based on the love story of the Mughal emperor Akbar the Great and his Rajput bride Jodhaa Bai. In an interview, Ali said, "Ashutosh is the only director who could do justice to a film of such a level." He added that he was inspired by how well Gowariker had handled difficult subjects, such as nationalism and the Hindu caste system, in *Lagaan*.

DELAYS AND CONTROVERSIES

Gowariker and Ali encountered a number of challenges while researching the story of Akbar and Jodhaa Bai, as history is not very clear about the details. So while many events shown in the film may be true, some of the plot is historically debatable. For example, several scholars maintain that Jodhaa was not married to Akbar but to his son Jahangir instead, while others claim that Akbar's wife was never known as Jodhaa Bai. Whether or not it is historically accurate, the film has a clear message that promotes peace, as well as Hindu-Muslim unity.

However, when it opened, the film was met with protests, mostly from members of the Rajput community, who felt it downplayed their importance in Indian history. At one point, the film was banned in the states of Uttar Pradesh, Rajasthan, Haryana, and Uttarakhand. This ban was only lifted when the film's producers approached the Supreme Court of India.

2002 film *Devdas* (see pp. 274–77). Neeta Lulla spent a long time studying 16th-century Muslim and Rajput court dress to give her stunning costumes an authentic feel. The fabulous jewels worn by lead actress Aishwarya Rai (see pp. 254–55) were commissioned from top Indian jewelry brand Tanishq.

Art director Nitin Desai's team also carried out extensive research, including taking numerous detailed photographs of the forts in Amer (near Jaipur) and Agra, to help him construct the sets in his studio in Karjat, near Mumbai, where a substantial part of the film was shot.

Jodhaa Akbar won numerous awards, including a National Award for best costume, and another for the choreography of "Azeem-O-Shan Shehenshah." It also won the Filmfare Award of 2009 for best film, while Hrithik Roshan won the Filmfare Award for Best Actor, A.R. Rahman for Best Background Score, and Ashutosh Gowariker for Best Director.

"Jodhaa Akbar *draws you into its drama just moments into the film.*"

RAJEEV MASAND, FILM CRITIC, 2008

◄ Haute couture

The film's striking costumes were a source of inspiration for India's fashion industry. Copies of the *lehengas* (skirts) worn by Aishwarya Rai were sold by high-fashion retailer Samsaara.

GRAND VISION

Controversies aside, *Jodhaa Akbar* is without a doubt highly entertaining. It was a huge success, both at the box office and as a magnificent realization of the director's grand creative vision. Gowariker made good use of the talents of his costume designer, Neeta Lulla, and his art director, Nitin Chandrakant Desai, both of whom had worked on the lavish

MUSICAL TRIUMPH

The grandeur of *Jodhaa Akbar* is matched by the film's dramatic lyrical music, composed by A.R. Rahman (see pp. 244–45). Previously Rahman's best work included the music for *Lagaan* and *Swades* (2004). But with *Jodhaa Akbar*, he excelled himself. His rich score includes the melodious Hindu prayer "Mann Mohana" (Lord Krishna), a Sufi qawwali "Khwaja Mere Khwaja" (O Benefactor of the Poor), and a romantic song "Jashn-E-Bahaaraa." But the crowning glory is "Azeem-O-Shan Shehenshah," which was accompanied by hundreds of dancers in rich, colorful costumes.

▲ Symbolic meaning

A sword, shield, and flower highlight the film's themes of war and love in this stylish poster.

ASHUTOSH GOWARIKER (b. 1964)

This Oscar-nominated filmmaker has directed eight films, including *Lagaan* (2001), *Swades* (2004), and *Mohenjo Daro* (2016). Gowariker started his career as an actor in Ketan Mehta's *Holi* (1984), where he met another young actor, Aamir Khan, who later became the producer and star of the epic drama *Lagaan*. Gowariker often makes lengthy films, with running times of more than three hours and featuring major stars, grand sets, and striking costumes.

▼ Extravagant undertaking

The scene featuring the song "Azeem-O-Shan Shehenshah" took 15 days to shoot, and involved around 400 dancers and 2,000 extras, acting as citizens of Agra.

3 IDIOTS

2009

Rajkumar Hirani's *3 Idiots*, with its social commentary, witty dialogue, and upbeat songs, made an instant connection with audiences in India and many other countries across the world.

▼ **The jaunty three**
Many young students in India could easily identify with the irreverent attitude and goofy antics of the film's three main protagonists.

CAST AND CREW

- ★ **Aamir Khan** Ranchoddas "Rancho" Shamaldas Chanchad
- **Kareena Kapoor** Pia Sahastrabuddhe
- **R. Madhavan** Farhan Qureshi
- **Sharman Joshi** Raju Rastogi
- **Boman Irani** Viru Sahastrabuddhe

- 🎬 **Director** Rajkumar Hirani
- 🎞 **Producer** Vidhu Vinod Chopra
- 🎵 **Music** Shantanu Moitra
- ♪ **Lyrics** Swanand Kirkire
- 📖 **Scriptwriters** Rajkumar Hirani, Abhijat Joshi
- 🎥 **Cinematographer** C.K. Muraleedharan

The film was Rajkumar Hirani's third collaboration as a director with producer Vidhu Vinod Chopra. Previously, the two of them had worked together on the Munna Bhai film series (*Munna Bhai M.B.B.S.* and *Lage Raho Munna Bhai*), which was a huge success at the box office and won over critics and audiences alike.

For *3 Idiots,* Hirani and Chopra chose the popular actor Aamir Khan as the lead, and turned to Chetan Bhagat's bestselling book, *Five Point Someone* (2004), for their story. However, this choice became mired in controversy when Bhagat claimed that he was paid very little for the book's rights, and that the film's opening credits failed to mention either his name or his book. The controversy eventually died down, but the episode did help to bring about a positive change in the way that Bollywood studios now treat writers whose books are adapted for films.

A TALE OF OLD FRIENDS

With its funny, tongue-in-cheek dialogue and high energy levels, *3 Idiots* is narrated by former engineering student Farhan Qureshi, now an acclaimed wildlife photographer. He recounts his time as an undergraduate at a prominent college in India. His recollections are mostly about his close friendship with his roommates, Raju Rastogi and Ranchoddas "Rancho" Shamaldas Chanchad—the pivotal figure of the group, and of the film.

The story opens 10 years after the three friends have graduated. We are told that Rancho's whereabouts have been a mystery since that time. However, when Qureshi and Rastogi manage to discover where Rancho is living, they decide to embark on a road trip to visit their old friend. As they travel to Shimla and then on to Ladakh, they learn about a secret Rancho had kept from them.

COLLEGE DAYS

While the hunt for Rancho goes on, Qureshi continues to narrate the highs, lows, and pressures of his student days, and of Rancho's fierce determination to change the system.

The trio's main adversary during these years is the dean of their college, Dr. Viru Sahastrabudhhe. A firm believer in tradition, his old-fashioned way of running the institution and his sadistic use of corporal punishment for students who dare to challenge him makes him greatly feared—by everyone apart from Rancho. Most of his wrath is therefore directed at Rancho and his two friends, Rastogi

▲ **The stern professor**
Boman Irani's character, a strict, uptight dean of an engineering college, forms a stark contrast to his irreverent, fun-loving students.

and Qureshi. But the iron-handed dean also has a soft spot for his two daughters—especially his youngest, Pia, a medical student who goes on to become Rancho's love interest.

HIT SONGS

The film's tuneful and highly energetic songs, composed by Shantanu Moitra, were extremely well-received. "All Izz Well" (All Is Well), with its funky beat and fun lyrics, became an instant hit. It accompanies the unusual sight of the three friends and their mates in the college washroom, showering and playing pranks. Equally enjoyable and imaginative is the bright and colorful "Zoobi Doobi," sung by Shreya Ghoshal and Sonu Nigam.

However, the most striking song in the film comes as the opening credits start to roll, showing Rastogi and Qureshi traveling through the Himalayas in a red car with another college friend, as they anticipate finally being reunited with Rancho. It is the beautiful song "Behti Hawa Sa Tha Woh" (He Is Like the Wind), performed by Shaan. Its haunting melody stays with viewers long after they have finished watching the film.

A BIG SUCCESS

With its catchy tunes, views on India's education system, excellent writing, and fine comic timing, *3 Idiots* was hugely popular with audiences, especially with college students. Even their parents seemed to connect with the film's message. *3 Idiots* broke box office records in India in its opening week and ultimately helped to establish the "₹2 billion club"—films with gross receipts of ₹2 billion ($30 million) or more at the box office.

The film was also a critical success. *3 Idiots* bagged the big three Filmfare awards: Best Film, Best Director, and Best Supporting Actor (for Boman Irani). But the film also did well overseas, not only in the usual markets of the US and UK, where many Indians reside, but also in many East Asian countries. The theme of the pressures that Indian students face seemed to resonate with Chinese, Japanese, and Korean students, whose education systems are similar to India's. *3 Idiots* opened up these new markets for other Bollywood movies.

▲ **Young romance**
The playful chemistry between Pia and Rancho, especially in the dream sequence song "Zoobi Doobi," reminded audiences of frothy college romances.

RAJKUMAR HIRANI (b.1962)

One of India's most successful filmmakers, Rajkumar Hirani started his career in advertising and as a film editor. His four films, *Munna Bhai M.B.B.S.* (2003), *Lage Raho Munna Bhai* (2006), *3 Idiots* (2009), and *PK* (2014), all produced by Chopra, have been huge box office hits. The latest, *PK*, grossed ₹3.4 billion ($53 million) and was the most profitable Bollywood film on record, until it was beaten by *Chennai Express* (2013) and the recent *Dangal* (see p. 331).

> *"It's a breezy entertainer and it's got its heart in the right place."*
>
> **RAJEEV MASAND,** FILM CRITIC, 2009

DABANGG

2010

Dabangg is a superhit Bollywood film set in a small town in the heart of India that tells the story of a corrupt, violent policeman with a heart of gold.

CAST AND CREW

★ **Salman Khan** Chulbul Pandey
Sonakshi Sinha Rajjo
Arbaaz Khan Makhanchan Pandey
Vinod Khanna Prajapati Pandey
Dimple Kapadia Naina Pandey
Sonu Sood Chedi Singh

🎬 **Director** Abhinav Kashyap
💰 **Producers** Arbaaz Khan, Malaika Arora Khan, Dhilin Mehta
🎵 **Music composers** Sajid Ali, Wajid Ali, Lalit Pandit
🎵 **Lyricists** Faiz Anwar, Lalit Pandit, Jalees Sherwani
🕺 **Choreographer** Farah Khan
📖 **Scriptwriters** Dilip Shukla, Abhinav Kashyap
🎥 **Cinematographer** Mahesh Limaye
👔 **Costume designers** Alvira Khan, Ashley Rebello

Debut director Abhinav Kashyap decided on an action-packed, light-hearted, larger-than-life film with *Dabangg*, a complete contrast to his brother Anurag Kashyap's (see p. 310) indie style of gritty, realistic filmmaking.

Abhinav considered several actors for the lead role of Chulbul Pandey, but finally settled with one of Bollywood's biggest stars—Salman Khan (see pp. 224–25). And for Salman's stepbrother, Makhanchan, he chose Salman Khan's real-life brother, Arbaaz, who also came on board as the film's producer.

GOOD COP, BAD COP

In Abhinav's film, set in the small town of Laalgunj, in the north Indian state of Uttar Pradesh, he creates a vast cast of characters around the corrupt but good-hearted cop Pandey. The well-meaning policeman, who calls himself "Robin Hood Pandey," faces challenges from a local politician and goon named Chedi Singh (Sonu Sood). His problems worsen when his archenemy tries to pit him against his stepbrother Makhanchan (Makkhi). His

mother, played by the lovely Dimple Kapadia (from Raj Kapoor's 1973 hit *Bobby*) has remarried and his stepfather has no love for Pandey.

Despite all this, he falls in love with Rajjo, the village belle, played by Sonakshi Sinha, who sells clay pots to support her family.

CHARM OFFENSIVE

The film primarily rests on Salman's charm, his talent for action sequences, and his dancing skills. In the film, Pandey has an easy-going and optimistic approach to life, even when his personal life is undergoing immense turmoil.

Dabangg also introduced Sonakshi Sinha, the daughter of one of India's prominent actors-turned-politicians, Shatrughan Sinha, and his one-time actress wife Poonam Sinha, to the viewers. Since her debut in *Dabangg*, Sinha has gone on to become a leading star in Hindi cinema with several hits to her credit.

MISSION ACCOMPLISHED

Dabangg was a massive hit at the box office in India as well as in several international markets. The success of the film was attributed to Salman's star power and the film's breezy approach to an otherwise violent plot. The soundtrack of the film was a huge hit with the public as well. This was particularly true for the song "Munni Badnam Hui," an item number (see pp. 290–91) performed by Malaika Arora Khan, who is also one of the film's producers. The song's sexually suggestive lyrics led to some controversy, but it became an instant hit with the audience. Malaika's fiery and racy dance performance received acclaim as well.

◀ **Played too well**
Dabangg showcased Sonakshi Sinha's acting skills, but also led to her being typecast in earthy roles for some time to come.

▲ **Looking the part**
To ensure the character of Chulbul Pandey looked as much as possible like a real-life policeman, Salman Khan tried out nearly 50 styles of mustache to get it right for the film.

HIT SONGS

**Tere Mast Mast Do Nain
(Your Beautiful Eyes)**
🎤 **Singer** Rahat Fateh Ali Khan

**Munni Badnaam Hui
(Munni Is Infamous)**
🎤 **Singers** Mamta Sharma, Aishwarya Nigam, Master Saleem

**Humka Peeni Hai
(I Want to Drink)**
🎤 **Singers** Wajid, Master Saleem, Shabab Sabri

TANU WEDS MANU

2011

A romantic comedy, *Tanu Weds Manu* is a quirky tale about the marriage of a reserved, Non-Resident Indian and a spirited, small-town girl.

Anand Rai had already directed two films when he decided to set his next film, *Tanu Weds Manu*, in a small town in northern India. Anand's idea was to give his characters an authentic small-town feel.

Tanu Weds Manu is the story of a Non-Resident Indian man, Manu, from London, who comes to India to find a bride for himself. His parents arrange for him to meet several girls but when he meets Tanu in Kanpur, he falls for her. However, Tanu has different plans for herself, including a marriage to someone else. Manu and Tanu come across each other again at the wedding of mutual friends. Then the film goes through a series of twists and turns until she finally agrees to marry Manu.

The film has a large cast of characters, including parents, friends, and siblings, who capture the essence of small-town India—a world where marriages and family relationships are a central part of everyone's life.

◄ **Opposites attract**
The film's protagonists have very different personalities: Manu is quiet and shy, whereas Tanu is loud and boisterous.

BOLD MOVE
Anand cast Kangana Ranaut (see pp. 322–23), who had given a critically acclaimed performance in *Fashion* (see p. 299), as the leading lady of *Tanu Weds Manu*. Kangana's career was floundering at the time following a number of flops in Bollywood. However, *Tanu Weds Manu* was the perfect vehicle to showcase her terrific sense of humor, quirky personality, and fun energy on the big screen, all of which were essential to the character she played. The film was a huge success and Kangana acknowledged that the film had played a big role in turning around her career. She would later win a National Award for the film's sequel, *Tanu Weds Manu Returns*, in 2016.

Tanu Weds Manu did good business at the box office, though it received mixed reviews. Its feel-good, uncomplicated storyline drew in audiences and the film's music composer, Krsna Solo, even won the R.D. Burman award for New Music Talent given by Filmfare. Anupama Chopra, a leading Indian film critic, suggested that apart from Kangana, the film was also worth watching for the lively chemistry between the guys, Madhavan and Deepak Dobriyal, who plays Manu's friend Pappi Tiwari.

R. MADHAVAN
(b.1970)

Born to a Tamil family residing in Jharkhand, R. Madhavan initially wanted to become an electronics engineer before entering the film industry. He is one of the few actors with a pan-Indian appeal. An advertising film directed by Santosh Sivan led to an audition with Mani Ratnam, which launched Madhavan's career in Tamil films with Ratnam's *Alaipayuthey* (2000) and *Kannathil Muthamittal* (2002). Madhavan has also appeared in a number of Hindi films such as *Rang de Basanti* (see p. 288), *Guru* (see p. 341), *3 Idiots* (see pp. 302–303), and *Tanu Weds Manu Returns* (2015).

▼ **Best friend's wedding**
Punjabi singer Lehmber Hussainpuri sang the hit party song "Sadi Gali" (Our Street) in the film. Here, the effervescent Tanu performs to the upbeat music of this song at her friend's pre-wedding function.

THE RISE OF THE
SMALL TOWN

As Bollywood shifted its gaze from the city, the complex lives and characters of India's small towns hit the silver screen.

Back in the 1950s and 1960s, filmmakers visualized a simpler life outside the big cities—Raj Kapoor's *Shri 420* (1955), for instance, was an early critique of city life. Since then, however, Bollywood writers and directors, based in Mumbai, largely preferred to portray a glamorous, urban world: the job of portraying real stories—the daily struggles of the middle and lower classes—was generally left to art-house filmmakers. Bollywood continued to focus on fantasy and entertainment, full of romance, melodrama, enormous mansions, beautiful actors, and lavish song-and-dance numbers.

NEW FRONTIERS
In the early 2000s, Bollywood opened itself up to a new and young crop of writers and directors—many of whom grew up outside Mumbai, often in smaller towns and villages. These filmmakers wanted to bring the sensibilities and stories they saw around them into their scripts and films. With this, the depiction of India itself in cinema moved away from

◀ **Small town on celluloid**
In the 2007 film *Aaja Nachle* from Yash Raj Films, Madhuri Dixit's character, Dia Srivastav, returns from New York to her hometown of Shamli in Uttar Pradesh.

stories of emigrants and the diaspora to tales that were from India's villages and small towns.

For his magnum opus, *Gangs of Wasseypur* (see p. 310), which was inspired by Bihar and eastern Uttar Pradesh, Anurag Kashyap did not want gorgeous Bollywood stars to populate the film's gritty portayal of the world of coal miners, politicians, and gangsters. The authenticity of the film was appreciated with a standing ovation at the Cannes Film Festival. Similarly, for *Dabangg* (see p. 304), director Abhinav Kashyap carefully depicted small-town India through the language, costume, milieu, and politics of the fictional town of Laalgunj.

From around 2010, many such films were being made, including *Tanu Weds Manu* (see p. 305), *Raanjhanaa* (2013), and *Dum Laga ke Haisha* (2015), all set in Uttar Pradesh—a clear indication of the shift in popular Hindi cinema. Today, an increasing number of movies revolve around people and lives that are far away from the metropolises of Delhi and Mumbai.

A newfound appreciation for such subjects by a pan-Indian audience, even in big cities, prompted big stars such as Aamir Khan, Akshay Kumar, and Salman Khan to jump onto the bandwagon. This new wave of cinema was welcomed by audiences and Bollywood alike, and more realistic films now hit the theaters regularly.

"Smaller towns are now melting pots of views, aspirations, revolts and compromises ... fascinating places for storytellers."

JAIDEEP SAHNI, SCRIPTWRITER, *LIVE MINT,* DECEMBER 26, 2015

ZINDAGI NA MILEGI DOBARA

2011

When three best friends head off on a bachelor road trip to Spain, extreme sports and adventure are on the agenda. The trip will change each of their lives forever.

▼ **La Tomatina in Bollywood**
Spain's tomato-throwing La Tomatina festival was re-created on film for *ZNMD*. The three friends attend the festival in Buñol, where they meet Nuria, played by Ariadna Cabrol (far left), who falls for Farhan Akhtar's Imran (left).

Set against the stunning backdrop of Spain, with its rugged landscapes and picturesque towns, *Zindagi na Milegi Dobara* (You Won't Get a Second Life) is a feast for the eyes. Popularly known as *ZNMD*, the film seduces the audience with its beautiful locations, while engaging their emotions with a story that is essentially about the power of friendship.

ESCAPE FROM REALITY

The film opens with a proposal of marriage. Following their whirlwind romance, Kabir is getting engaged to his girlfriend Natasha. At the engagement party, Kabir announces that he is heading off on a three-week road trip through Spain for his bachelor party with his two best friends from school, Arjun and Imran.

Kabir is an architect, Arjun an investment banker, and Imran a budding writer. The three friends have a long-standing pact that on their road trip each of them will choose an adventure sport that all three of them will try. By the end of the holiday, one of the friends will have fallen in love, one will have changed the course of his career, and one will have realized he might be about to make the biggest mistake of his life.

Their trip starts with a bang in Barcelona, and then the friends head for the Costa Brava, where Kabir chooses scuba diving as their first sporting challenge. Here they meet beautiful diving instructor Laila, who helps Arjun overcome his fear of

ZINDAGI Na Milegi Dobara
15 JULY

water. There is a clear attraction between the pair, and Laila invites the group to join her and her friend Nuria at the La Tomatina festival.

Arjun's sporting challenge is skydiving, for which they travel to Seville. For the final challenge, Imran's, the boys go to Pamplona for the running of the bulls. Here the film reaches its climax, as each of the friends makes a promise that will change the course of each of their lives.

ZOYA'S BRAINCHILD

The storyline of *ZNMD*, which could have turned into a predictable take on male bonding when translated to the big screen, is given a shot of adrenaline by director Zoya Akhtar. Her deft handling of the stag trip, integrating equal parts of comedy, romance, and personal drama, drives the plot forward to its satisfying conclusion. For authenticity, she drew on her own real-life adventures while she was traveling through Spain with some girlfriends.

The filming of the movie was intense, with 107 locations scheduled for the shoot over three months. Timing was crucial, since the plot required filming the annual running of the bulls in Pamplona. The tight-knit production was very much a family-and-friends affair, which may be the reason behind the film's emotional directness and its simple, touching message about the importance of friendship. Zoya has openly admitted that she relies on her

◀ **Rugged film poster**
The three protagonists of *ZNMD* have very different personalities and approaches to life, yet they come together for one last adventure together to honor a long-standing pact.

immediate family and friends to keep her grounded, and she translates this directly into the process of filmmaking. She developed the story and co-wrote the screenplay with her friend and longtime collaborator Reema Kagti. The role of Imran was written especially for Zoya's brother Farhan Akhtar (see p. 264), who also co-produced the film along with his close friend Ritesh Sidhwani.

PICKING THE TEAM

Casting the actors for the lead roles was critical for a film that relies heavily on the chemistry between the three central figures. Zoya originally approached Imran Khan and Ranbir Kapoor (see pp. 316–17) to play Kabir and Arjun, but they turned her down in order to concentrate on their own productions.

She then managed to secure Hrithik Roshan (see p. 263), one of her favorite actors. For the final lead, she wanted someone who could hold the film together, and chose an actor with a solid reputation who was also a friend—Abhay Deol. More accustomed to acting in small, independent films, such as Reema Kagti's *Honeymoon Travels Pvt. Ltd.* (2007), Abhay had to adapt to

the different requirements of a mainstream Bollywood production, which included dancing and singing on screen for the first time.

The exuberant soundtrack of *ZNMD* was composed by Shankar Mahadevan, Ehsaan Noorani, and Loy Mendonsa, with lyrics by Zoya's father, Javed Akhtar (see pp. 138–39). The film's music also incorporated flamenco guitar to capture the atmosphere of traditional Spain.

see p. 264 · see pp. 316–17 · see p. 263 · see pp. 138–39

▶ **Seizing the moment**
Arjun, Imran, and Kabir's adventurous road trip through Spain takes them along the Costa Brava, and to Seville and Pamplona.

CAST AND CREW

★ **Hrithik Roshan** Arjun Saluja
Farhan Akhtar Imran Qureshi
Abhay Deol Kabir Dewan
Katrina Kaif Laila
Naseeruddin Shah Salman Habib
Deepti Naval Raahila Qureshi
Kalki Koechlin Natasha Arora

🎬 **Director** Zoya Akhtar
🎪 **Producers** Farhan Akhtar, Ritesh Sidhwani
🎵 **Music composers** Loy Mendonsa, Shankar Mahadevan, Ehsaan Noorani
🎼 **Lyricist** Javed Akhtar
🕺 **Choreographers** Vaibhavi Merchant, Bosco Martis, Caesar Gonsalves
📖 **Scriptwriters** Reema Kagti, Zoya Akhtar
🎥 **Cinematographer** Carlos Catalan
👔 **Costume designer** Arjun Bhasin

GANGS OF WASSEYPUR

2012

Gangs of Wasseypur is an epic saga of violence that relates the true story of blood feuds in eastern India's coal-mining industry.

Director Anurag Kashyap's magnum opus *Gangs of Wasseypur* is five and a half hours and was released in two parts. Kashyap's script was 240 pages long, and was originally supposed to be divided into three parts. He was unable to find an organic ending for each of the three sections and had to split the film into two parts.

Gangs of Wasseypur is a gangster saga spanning events from the 1940s to the 1990s, partly inspired by the US movies *The Godfather* (1972) and *Goodfellas* (1990). The film is a tale of politics and revenge between three families of Dhanbad, Jharkhand. The poor are denied their share of coal from the region's coal-rich reserves, and turn to crime as a way to fight for their rights.

Gangs of Wasseypur is also a homage to Hindi cinema, reflecting the effect of Bollywood in the everyday lives of people in India. The characters in the film live and breathe Bollywood, they dance to Bollywood songs at weddings, they go out on dates to see Bollywood movies, and they imagine themselves as characters from their favorite Bollywood films. *Gangs of Wasseypur* even features five songs that were originally performed in other Hindi films.

GOING FOLKSY

The film's soundtrack plays in the background, as opposed to the stars lip-synching to playback songs as they do in most Hindi films. However, the number of songs in the film makes

Gangs of Wasseypur the closest of all Kashyap's films to a "typical Bollywood" feature: this two-part film has 25 original songs. Many of them are traditional folk songs, some of which have strong sexual undertones. Music composer Sneha Khanwalkar traveled to Trinidad looking for traditional folk songs carried by migrant workers from India to the Caribbean island over 100 years ago.

LAUNCHPAD

The film is packed with a massive cast of some well-known Bollywood actors such as Manoj Bajpayee, and many others whose acting careers were launched in a big way through this film. These include Huma Qureshi, Nawazuddin Siddiqui, Richa Chadha, Rajkummar Rao, along with director Tigmanshu Dhulia who plays "Mafia-style" boss Ramadhir Singh in the film.

Parts one and two of *Gangs of Wasseypur* premiered at the Cannes Film Festival during the Director's Fortnight in 2012. The audience at the festival was blown away by the film and gave the director and his cast a standing ovation.

HIT SONG

Womaniya
(Oh Woman)

🎤 **Singers** Khushboo Raaj, Rekha Jha

CAST AND CREW

★ **Manoj Bajpayee** Sardar Khan
Richa Chadha Nagma Khatoon
Nawazuddin Siddiqui Faizal Khan
Tigmanshu Dhulia Ramadhir Singh
Huma Qureshi Mohsina

Director Anurag Kashyap
Producers Viacom 18 Media Pvt Ltd, Anurag Kashyap Films Pvt Ltd
🎵 **Music composer** Sneha Khanwalkar
♪ **Lyricists** Varun Grover, Piyush Mishra
📖 **Scriptwriters** Akhilesh Jaiswal, Anurag Kashyap, Sachin K. Ladia, Zeishan Quadri
Cinematographer Rajeev Ravi
👔 **Costume designer** Subodh Srivastava

◀ **Bond of hatred**
This colorful and dynamic film poster depicts the deadly blood feud, spanning three generations, between three families of the coal mafia in Dhanbad, Jharkhand.

ANURAG KASHYAP
(b.1972)

Anurag Kashyap's eventful career in Bollywood started in the late 1990s with the crime drama *Satya* (see p. 241). His first feature film *Paanch* (2003) was banned by the Central Board of Film Certification. The release of his second film *Black Friday* (see p. 340) was delayed by a court in India. It was not until *Dev.D* (see p. 342), a modern take on *Devdas*, that Kashyap actually saw box office success.

Gangs of Wasseypur, his eighth film, is the crowning example of his signature brand of gritty, violent dramas.

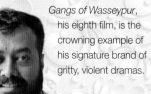

STUDENT OF THE YEAR

2012

Director Karan Johar launched the careers of three budding young actors in this stylish, entertaining Bollywood musical.

CAST AND CREW

★ **Alia Bhatt** Shanaya Singhania
Varun Dhawan Rohan Nanda
Sidharth Malhotra Abhimanyu Singh

Director Karan Johar
Producers Karan Johar,
Hiroo Johar, Gauri Khan
Music composers Vishal Dadlani,
Shekhar Ravjiani
Lyricist Anvita Dutt Guptan
Choreographers Farah Khan,
Vaibhavi Merchant, Remo
Scriptwriters Karan Johar,
Renzil, D'Silva
Cinematographer Ayananka Bose
Costume designers Manish Malhotra,
Shiraz Siddique, Archana Walavalkar

The films of Karan Johar (see pp. 248–49) are entertaining musicals with themes of love, family, marriage, and infidelity that often appeal to an older audience. Since his first hit, *Kuch Kuch Hota hai* (see pp. 246–47), in 1998, with a cast that included three of the biggest Bollywood stars of the time, Shah Rukh Khan (see pp. 214–15), Kajol (see p. 231), and Rani Mukerji (see p. 247), Karan has relied on big industry names to draw in the audiences.

However, in 2012, at the age of 40, Karan did something very different. He released a film for a younger, teenage audience with three first-time actors.

With his film *Student of the Year*, Karan launched the careers of three young actors—Alia Bhatt (daughter of producer and director Mahesh Bhatt), Varun Dhawan (son of filmmaker David Dhawan), and Sidharth Malhotra (the only lead cast member without a film family connection).

HEALTHY COMPETITION

Student of the Year is set in a private college, located on a large sprawling estate, where the scions of privileged families come to study. Things change when a new student, Abhimanyu Singh, an orphan who comes from a modest family background, joins the college. Singh's arrival triggers a competition between him and a popular student, Rohan Nanda. At first the competitiveness between the two is healthy, but it takes an ugly turn when the dean of the school announces a competition for "Student of the Year." Much of the film has the students singing, dancing, romancing, and at times competing with each other at various sports or games.

Though Student of the Year touches on the conflicts between parents and their offspring in modern-day India, it is mostly a charming entertainer with three good-looking leads. The film is packed with delightful songs composed by Vishal-Shekhar with lyrics by Anvita Dutt

Guptan, including "Ishq Wala Love" (Romantic Love) and "The Disco Song," which is a remixed version of the song "Disco Diwane" (Crazy about Disco) from the hit 1980 Bollywood film *Qurbani*.

Student of the Year was one of the first films with a non-star cast to perform exceptionally well at the box office.

DHARMA PRODUCTIONS
DHARMA PRODUCTIONS AND RED CHILLIES ENTERTAINMENT PRESENT
A KARAN JOHAR FILM
STUDENT OF THE YEAR
CASTING DIRECTOR NANDINI SHRIKENT COSTUME DIRECTOR MANISH MALHOTRA SOUND DESIGNER ALI MERCHANT CREATIVE DIRECTOR ABHISHEK VARMAN SCREENPLAY RENSIL D'SILVA DIALOGUES NIRANJAN IYENGAR LYRICS ANVITA DUTT PRODUCTION DESIGNER AMRITA MAHAL NAKAI MUSIC VISHAL & SHEKHAR EXECUTIVE PRODUCER MARLENE DSOUZA EDITOR DEEPA BHATIA ASSOCIATE PRODUCERS APOORVA MEHTA DIRECTOR OF PHOTOGRAPHY AYANANKA BOSE PRODUCED BY HIROO YASH JOHAR & GAURI KHAN DIRECTED BY KARAN JOHAR

▲ **Style statement**
The film's lead characters, played by Sidharth (left), Alia (center), and Varun (right), are young, good-looking, and fashionable students at an affluent school.

The film's three young leads have all gone on to have successful Bollywood careers.

"*Karan Johar ... creates fantastical worlds brimming with beautiful people and expensive things.*"

ANUPAMA CHOPRA, *HINDUSTAN TIMES*, 2012

◄ **Love triangle**
Rivals Rohan and Abhimanyu both fall in love with Shanaya, but she likes Rohan.

KAHAANI

A low-budget suspense thriller from the multi-talented Sujoy Ghosh, *Kahaani* became a sleeper hit and was hailed as one of the best films of the year.

CAST AND CREW

★ **Vidya Balan** Vidya Bagchi
Parambrata Chatterjee Rana
Dhritiman Chatterjee Bhaskaran
Saswata Chatterjee Bob Biswas
Nawazuddin Siddiqui Mr. Khan

🎬 **Director** Sujoy Ghosh
◻ **Producers** Vaicom 18 Media Private Limited, Pen India Private Limited
🎵 **Music composers** Clinton Cerejo, Shekhar Rajviani, Vishal Dadlani
🎵 **Lyricists** Vishal Dadlani, Anvita Dutt, Sandeep Srivastava
🎥 **Cinematographer** Satyajit Pande
📖 **Scriptwriters** Sujoy Ghosh, Suresh Nair, Advaita Kala, Ritesh Shah
👔 **Costume designers** Suchismita Dasgupta, Sabyasachi Mukherji

S et against the backdrop of Kolkata in West Bengal, the appeal of *Kahaani* (A Tale) lies in its clever, well-written script, its strong female lead, and the evocative portrayal of the city.

Kahaani opens with a dramatic poison gas explosion in the Kolkata subway, providing a chilling reminder of the ever-present threat of terrorism in the modern world. The film shifts gear and jumps forward two years, changing the focus to Vidya Bagchi, a pregnant woman who has flown to Kolkata from London during the festival of Durga Puja in search of her missing husband. As the film unfolds, the story's two threads intersect: the attack at the subway station and Vidya's mission to find her husband who has disappeared under mysterious circumstances. As Vidya follows leads, she meets the kind police officer Rana, who offers to help her with her quest. However, a series of murders complicate matters. It is not long before an intelligence officer named Khan also becomes involved in the search. He is investigating the subway attack, and Vidya's search for her husband collides with Khan's investigation. The continual twists and turns in the plot keep the audience on the edge of their seats right to the end.

SHOOTING ON THE STREETS
Director Sujoy Ghosh employed hand-held camera techniques and slick editing to create immediacy and tension in the film. In order to avoid unwanted attention and bring authenticity to the filming, the director often used a guerrilla filmmaking technique, shooting scenes quickly in real locations without any warning. Ghosh also cast several actors from Bengali films to bring integrity to the film. Kolkata-based actor Parambrata in particular gave a standout performance as the policeman who helps Vidya.

Uncredited in the cast is the city of Kolkata itself. Its bustling streets, vibrant culture, and distinctive customs are thrust to the fore in the film. The underbelly of the restless metropolis is brought to light and becomes almost a

▲ **In character**
Vidya Balan prepared for her role of a mother-to-be by spending time with pregnant women to help understand their emotional and physical challenges, as well as their superstitions.

character in its own right. Ghosh shot several scenes on location on the unadorned streets of downtown Kolkata.

WIDELY APPLAUDED
Ghosh's singular vision was rewarded with awards such as Best Screenplay and Best Story at the *Times of India* Film Awards, and the Zee Cine Critics' Award for Best Film and Best Director. The film also bagged six Filmfare Awards and three National Film Awards.

VIDYA BALAN (b.1979)

B orn in Mumbai to parents of Tamil descent, Vidya Balan made her small screen debut at the age of 16 in the sitcom *Hum Paanch*. She scored a breakthrough with *Parineeta* (2005), winning the Fimfare Award for Best Female Debut. Other roles followed, including that of a radio jockey in *Lage Raho Munna Bhai* (see pp. 286–87), a widow who uses her guile to get her way in *Ishqiya* (2010), and a south Indian actress in *The Dirty Picture* (2011). Her role in *Kahaani* established her as an accomplished actress.

OH MY GOD!

A satirical exploration of religion has been tried before—in various cultures—but this film's slick execution, witty dialogue, and charismatic leading man made it a hit.

Anyone who has argued with an insurance company over a claim will relate to this story. The film explores an atheist's struggle with religion and God via the definition of "an act of God." While the subject has been tackled before, in the Australian film *The Man Who Sued God* (2001) and the Gujarati play *Kanji Virrudh Kanji*, what makes Umesh Shukla's *Oh My God!* distinctive is its hilarious characterization and topical examination of the commercialization of religion, especially pertinent to modern-day India. *Oh My God!* touches upon a very sensitive topic—religion—but uses the everyday premise of an insurance claim to tackle the subject with humor.

"A brave and absorbing blend of satire, fable, and fantasy."

WWW.REDIFF.COM, 2012

script that includes plenty of witty one-liners. Shukla co-wrote the dialogue with Bhavesh Mandalia, and they won Best Screenplay at the 2013 National Film Awards. Bringing their words to life is Paresh Rawal's powerhouse performance as the cynical Gujarati trader, and Akshay Kumar, who plays the role of God with quiet dignity and a gentle smile.

DIVINE COMEDY

The story centers around Kanji Lalji, a shop owner at Mumbai's Chor Bazaar. Kanji dupes customers into buying fake religious relics, passing off new figurines as antiques. One day, an earthquake strikes the city, destroying his entire shop. Kanji's insurer refuses to pay for the damage because an earthquake is "an act of God" and not covered under the terms of the policy. Kanji is furious. As an atheist, he decides that since God is responsible for the disaster he will sue God. As the story in the courtroom saga progresses, Kanji comes face to face with three famous religious leaders who claim to be representing God. In doing so, he attracts the ire of various religious sects, who accuse him of mocking religion and threaten him with dire consequences. When the fanatics plot Kanji's murder, a modern-day Lord Krishna comes to his rescue, in the form of an estate agent riding a motorbike.

WINNING WORDS

Despite the fact that almost the entire action is set in a courtroom, Shukla holds the attention of the audience from start to finish with a snappy

▼ God and his disciple
Akshay Kumar plays the role of a fashionable, laptop-toting, butter-loving Lord Krishna, who comes to the rescue of Kanji Lalji, the man who sues God, played by Paresh Rawal.

SPECIAL 26

2013

Based on an extraordinary and ingenious real-life heist, this crime thriller keeps the audience riveted right up to its gripping climax with unexpected twists and turns.

CAST AND CREW

★ **Akshay Kumar** Ajay Singh
Anupam Kher P.K. Sharma
Manoj Bajpayee Waseem Khan
Jimmy Shergill Ranveer Singh
Rajesh Sharma Joginder
Kishor Kadam Iqbal

🎬 **Director** Neeraj Pandey
⬜ **Producers** Viacom 18 Media Pvt Ltd, Wide Frame Pictures, Friday Filmworks Pvt Ltd
🎵 **Music composers** M.M. Keeravani, Himesh Reshammiya, Surendra Singh Sodhi
🎼 **Lyricists** Shabbir Ahmed, Irshad Kamil
🕺 **Choreographer** Ganesh Acharya
📖 **Scriptwriter** Neeraj Pandey
🎥 **Cinematographer** Bobby Singh
👔 **Costume designer** Falguni Thakore

The film *Special 26* is based on the true story of one of the most ingenious crimes in modern Indian history. On March 19, 1987, a group of 26 men entered Tribhovandas Bhimji Zaveri & Sons, a jewelry store in the Opera House, Mumbai. The leader of the group introduced himself as officer Mon Singh from the Central Bureau of Investigation (CBI). He presented a search warrant instructing the owner, Pratapbhai Zaveri, to surrender his revolver, switch off the surveillance camera, and allow Singh's men to take samples of gold and ornaments from the store for an investigation into their quality. Singh's entourage completed the raid and left. An hour later, the suspicious owner called the Mumbai

▶ **Ace detective**
Waseem Khan, played by Manoj Bajpayee (left), is a sincere, dedicated, and tough CBI officer in the film. His officers plan to tackle Ajay's special group of 26 to apprehend the conman along with his fellow criminals.

police. Both the jeweler and police were baffled. They had been duped by a heist of breathtaking audacity—one that has not been solved to this day.

DARING HEIST
The film opens in 1987, with CBI officers interviewing suspects from the robbery. *Special 26* then rewinds to the events leading up to this moment, which are told in flashback. In the film, gang leader Ajay Singh and his aides pose as a team of CBI officers who conduct tax investigation raids on wealthy business people, and confiscate their valuable goods. After

multiple reports of this fraud, the real CBI sets out to apprehend the felons. Sub-inspector Ranveer Singh, who had unwittingly lent his officers to Ajay for support in a raid, is determined to catch the culprits, joining forces with fellow officer Waseem Khan. Aware that the authorities are onto him, Ajay plans a final heist. This will be the gang's most daring raid yet.

ACHIEVING CULT STATUS
Special 26 opened to modest audience numbers in 2013. However, as word of its enthralling plot and gripping pace spread, box office takings gradually picked up, accelerating on the back of rave reviews. Critics were especially impressed with the film's intelligent script, impressive attention to detail, and brilliant performances from its ensemble cast. By the end of the year, *Special 26* was being declared by the media as one of the best films of 2013. Neeraj Pandey, who also developed the film's screenplay, had successfully recreated the period look of 1987, with enough new flourishes to convincingly translate the real-life events onto the silver screen.

◀ **Criminal mastermind**
Akshay Kumar plays the character of conman Ajay Singh (center), who poses as a CBI official at a jewelry store with his gang of fraudsters. In the film, Ajay and his accomplices conduct a string of robberies across India.

YEH JAWAANI HAI DEEWANI

2013

A sunny, feel-good film, this romantic drama shows a youthful spirit with its glamorous cast, exotic locations, and popping dance numbers.

Life-affirming and also commercially appealing, *Yeh Jawaani hai Deewani* (The Young Are Crazy) takes all the elements of a successful blockbuster and underpins it with a heartfelt story of friendship, love, ambition, and life lessons. On one level it is a beautiful cinematic trip across the Himalayas; on another it is about the journey of self-discovery experienced by four college friends who take a trip together. Free from social constraints and the pressures of daily life, they confront their innermost emotions and finally find the courage to express their feelings.

ROMANTIC RESONANCE

The film opens on a college campus where a conscientious medical student, Naina, is studying for her degree. Although destined for a brilliant and successful career, the introvert Naina is not happy and wants more from life. She bumps into her old classmate Aditi, a bubbly girl, and decides to join her on a hiking trip to Manali in the

▶ A trip to remember
En route to Manali, Naina (left), Kabir (top), Avinash (center), and Aditi (right) get involved in a skirmish with an aggressive family and escape the melee in the melodramatic style typical of Bollywood.

Himalayas. On their way, they meet up with two of their former classmates— flirtatious, free-spirited Kabir and his best friend Avinash. By the end of the holiday, Naina has developed a strong attachment to Kabir. She is close to revealing her feelings to him when fate intervenes. It will be another eight years before the friends meet again, confront their feelings about one another, and make life-changing decisions.

YOUTHFUL ENTERPRISE

Using the theme of travel as a metaphor for personal discovery is not new to Bollywood, but *Yeh Jawaani hai Deewani* gives a fresh spin to this concept. The film is a reflection of its youthful director Ayan Mukerji, who made the film while he was still in his 20s. Perfectly channeling the anxieties, habits, and obsessions of youth, he conveys the rush and heartache of falling in love. Ayan wrote the original story, which was scripted by Hussain Dalal into snappy dialogue sequences that connect with the under-30s audience.

Ranbir Kapoor (see pp. 316–17) was the first actor to be cast in the film—he had previously starred in the director's

immensely successful *Wake Up Sid* (2009)—followed by Deepika Padukone (see pp. 328–29), who signed up for the film without even reading the script. By casting Ranbir opposite his former girlfriend Deepika, Ayan ensured sparks would fly on-screen.

Following the winning formula of *Wake Up Sid*, Ayan commissioned a cracking soundtrack for *Yeh Jawaani hai Deewani*. The film's music with its upbeat tunes, composed by Pritam Chakraborty, was an instant hit. Cinema-goers flocked to watch the film, generating the fourth biggest box office opening in the history of Indian cinema.

CAST AND CREW

★ **Deepika Padukone** Naina Talwar
Ranbir Kapoor Kabir Thapar
Kalki Koechlin Aditi Mehra
Aditya Roy Kapoor Avinash Yog

🎬 **Director** Ayan Mukerji
🎬 **Producers** Hiroo Johar, Karan Johar
🎵 **Music composer** Pritam Chakraborty
🎵 **Lyricist** Amitabh Bhattacharya
📖 **Scriptwriters** Hussain Dalal, Ayan Mukherjee
📷 **Cinematographer** V. Manikandan
👔 **Costume designers** Manish Malhotra, Samidha Wangnoo

HIT SONGS

Badtameez Dil
(This Insolent Heart)
🎤 **Singers** Benny Dayal, Shefali Alvares

Dilliwaali Girlfriend
(Girlfriend from Delhi)
🎤 **Singers** Arijit Singh, Sunidhi Chauhan

Kabira
(Wanderer)
🎤 **Singers** Rekha Bhardwaj, Tochi Raina

RANBIR KAPOOR

ACTOR b.1982

The perfect blend of looks and talent, Ranbir Kapoor has proved his mettle in Bollywood with powerful performances that show a formidable range, from comedy to drama.

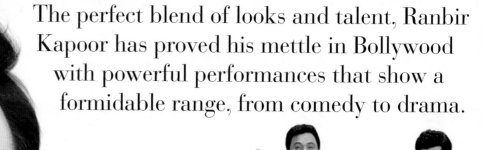

▲ A performance to remember
Rishi and Ranbir Kapoor charmed the audiences by performing together for the first time at the 13th International Indian Film Academy awards.

Being a part of the Kapoor clan—considered by many to be the first family of Bollywood—Ranbir's debut in Hindi cinema had a lot of expectations attached to it. Ranbir's great-grandfather Prithviraj Kapoor was a pioneer of the Hindi film industry, while his grandfather Raj Kapoor, an actor-director, was popularly known as "The Show Man" of Hindi cinema. His parents, Rishi Kapoor and Neetu Singh, were stars who acted in many hit films. With such a lineage it was almost inevitable that he would find his way into the movies, too.

GROWING UP
Having a famous family had its ups and downs for Ranbir. His parents Rishi and Neetu—former screen heartthrobs who had made a

successful romantic pair in the 1970s—had a troubled marriage, which had a profound impact on the young Ranbir. He recalls nights spent awake waiting for his parents to stop fighting. The experience led him to internalize his emotions, at the same time drawing him toward acting. At school, he was not a keen student and was never very interested in academic pursuits. Still, he

◀ Versatile actor
Ranbir has played serious dramatic characters in films such as *Rajneeti*, pictured here, as well as the lead in romantic films, with equal panache.

KEY WORKS

Saawariya, 2007
Wake Up Sid, 2009
Rocket Singh: Salesman of the Year, 2009
Raajneeti, 2010
Barfi!, 2012
Besharam, 2013
Ae Dil Hai Mushkil, 2016

► **A total charmer**
Ranbir's first big hit was Siddharth Anand's *Bachna Ae Haseeno* (2008), in which he played a charismatic Casanova as seen in the film's poster.

finished his pre-university education in Mumbai before moving to New York to study acting.

Very few Bollywood stars have had such thorough training in the performing arts as Ranbir. He studied filmmaking at the School of Visual Arts in New York and went on to pursue acting at the city's prestigious Lee Strasberg Theater and Film Institute. Although at that time he wasn't sure he would be able to carve out a career for himself in acting, Ranbir knew he wanted to be a part of the Hindi film industry in some capacity, be it directing or producing. As it turned out, he got the chance to work on both sides of the camera at that time, directing as well as acting: during his time in New York, he appeared in two short films, *Passion to Love* (2002) and *India 1964* (2004). However, it was not until his return to India in 2005 that Ranbir's acting career began in earnest.

ENTERING BOLLYWOOD

Back in Mumbai, Ranbir was hired as an assistant director to Sanjay Leela Bhansali (see p. 257) on the film, *Black* (2005). It proved to be a turning point, and gave Ranbir the much-needed clarity and focus to make his mark in Bollywood. Two years later, in 2007, he made his first big screen appearance in Bhansali's *Saawariya* opposite actress Sonam Kapoor. Although the film itself was not a big commercial success, Ranbir won the Filmfare Award for Best Male Debut—a promising start to his career.

> *"The characters I portray engage me, and I assume they would engage an audience."*

RANBIR KAPOOR, *INDIA TODAY*, 2013

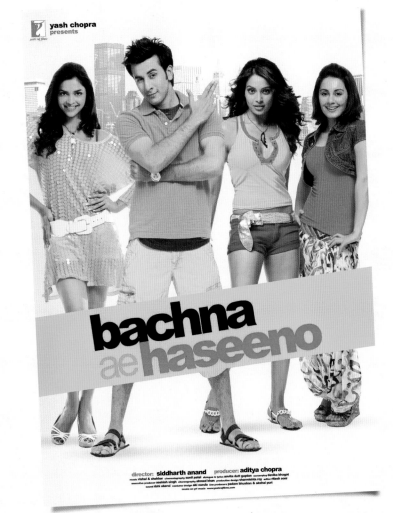

The year 2009 saw the release of three films starring Ranbir—*Wake Up Sid, Ajab Prem Ki Ghazab Kahani,* and *Rocket Singh: Salesman of the Year*. He won the Filmfare Critics Award for Best Actor for *Wake Up Sid*.

However, the best was yet to come. In the political drama, *Raajneeti*, he left a mark with his intense acting as a cunning politician. In Imtiaz Ali's *Rockstar* (2011), he portrayed the travails of a young musician—transitioning from a directionless student to a driven rockstar. His greatest performance, however, according to many critics, was his turn as a carefree deaf man in Anurag Basu's *Barfi!*. He garnered

further praise for his work in urban dramas such as *Tamasha* (2015) and *Ae Dil hai Mushkil* (2016) a year later.

PRIVATE LIFE

Ranbir's personal life has attracted substantial attention from the media. His relationship with Deepika Padukone (see pp. 328–29) was the subject of a media frenzy, from their meeting on the sets of *Bachna Ae Haseeno* to their breakup in 2009. The intense scrutiny continued with his relationship with Katrina Kaif.

Away from the bright lights of the film world and the glamour of his superstar life, Ranbir pursues his passion for football and contributes for charitable causes. He co-owns Mumbai City FC, a professional football franchise, and plays for the All Stars Football Club, a celebrity team that raises money for charity.

◄ **Comic caper**
In his role as Harpreet Singh in *Rocket Singh: Salesman of the Year* (2009), Ranbir's fans loved him for his brilliant comic timing.

HEROINE
REINVENTED

While Bollywood has always had its share of iconic female characters, a new wave of films sees women take center stage in grittier roles across a range of genres.

Actresses have played a crucial role in shaping the rich history of Bollywood, but in the past, they were mainly cast in traditional roles. Even though there were a few breakthroughs, film studios could not break free from the view that lead characters must always be male. Yet change has been on its way. A trend that had been gathering momentum since films such as *Mother India* (see pp. 56–59), *Guide* (see pp. 84–87), and *Arth* (see p. 176) has now come into its own. Many female actors feel there is no better time to be in films than today. With audiences accepting strong female leads, the Bollywood heroine is being reinvented to reflect the changing times.

MEANINGFUL CINEMA
Women in leading roles can now be seen across genres—from drama to comedy. Nagesh Kukunoor's drama *Dor* (see p. 339) shows the relationship between two different women, brought together by an act of fate. Played by actors Gul Panag and Ayesha Takia, the protagonists depict a sisterhood based on shared experiences and empathy.

Females with flair shine in the comedy-drama genre too. Kangana Ranaut (see pp. 322–23), who had impressed audiences with her acting prowess in *Tanu weds Manu* (see p.

305), had a surprise summer hit in 2014 with *Queen* (see pp. 320–21). In the film, Kangana plays a woman who is dumped the day before her wedding, and gains in confidence after traveling and meeting new people, emerging stronger for the experience.

Women also lit up the screen in action-packed thrillers. In 2014, Alia Bhatt starred in *Highway* as a girl whose kidnapping leads to her self-discovery. Anushka Sharma's *NH10* (2015) tells the violent story of honor killings—murder in the name of honor of the family or of the wider community.

Women still have some way to go to achieve parity with men in the Hindi film industry. Directors say it is harder to secure big budgets for movies carried by female leads. A recent report comparing the salaries of different actors confirmed that women still earn significantly less than their male counterparts. This is especially true with new actors. Yet the demand for better-written stories with greater variety means that actresses today will continue to break barriers with their unconventional roles.

▶ Riveting roles
In Pradeep Sarkar's action-packed *Mardaani* (2014), Rani Mukerji plays the role of a hard-as-nails policewoman who single-handedly takes on a kingpin and rescues her charge.

"We are seeing a generation of very strong women actors … who are looking to do something more."

ANUPAMA CHOPRA, FILM CRITIC, CITED IN *THE EXPRESS TRIBUNE*, AUGUST 20, 2015

QUEEN

2014

The surprise hit of 2014, *Queen* captured the hearts of audiences across India, and in the process became one of the most profitable films of the year.

HIT SONGS

London Thumakda
(Dancing in London)

🎤 **Singers** Labh Janjua, Sonu Kakkar, Neha Kakkar

O Gujariya
(O Woman)

🎤 **Singers** Shefali Alvares, Nikhil D'Souza

Taake Jhanke
(Staring and Peeping)

🎤 **Singer** Arijit Singh

Few movers and shakers in Bollywood would have predicted that a low-budget comedy-drama from a first-time director would conquer the box office. But that is just what *Queen* managed to do within a month of its release, becoming one of the highest-grossing films in the history of Indian cinema by its fourth week.

While most contemporary films rely on a large advertising and marketing budget to get audiences into cinemas, *Queen* had to rely on word of mouth. As news got out, media interest grew and rave reviews began to appear. The success of this cinematic gem is partly credited to its romantic European locations and the fresh approach of its director, Vikas Bahl. But perhaps what really makes the film shine is a clever script and the charming performance of its ensemble cast.

Queen is the story of small-town girl Rani Mehra, nicknamed Queen, who is jilted by her fiancé, Vijay, just one day before their wedding. The heartbroken Rani decides not to waste the ticket for their honeymoon, and with the blessing of her parents decides to take the journey to Europe alone. Rani had never even been on a plane before, so her bumbling behavior and previously sheltered existence leads the audience to wonder how she will handle the sophistication and potential dangers of an alien country.

JOURNEY OF DISCOVERY
Yet once she is in Paris, Rani soon meets the woman who will open her eyes to the real world—and to her true self—the Indo-French hotel maid, Vijayalakshmi, nicknamed Vijay. Having been abandoned by one Vijay, this other Vijay is just the tonic Rani

---

CAST AND CREW

⭐ **Kangana Ranaut** Rani Mehra
Rajkummar Rao Vijay
Lisa Haydon Vijayalakshmi
Mish Boyko Oleksander
Jeffrey Ho Taka
Guitobh Joseph Tim

🎬 **Director** Vikas Bahl
🎞 **Producers** Viacom 18 Media Private Limited, Phantom Films Private Limited
🎵 **Music composers** Amit Trivedi, Rupesh Kumar Ram
🎼 **Lyricist** Anvita Dutt Guptan
📝 **Scriptwriter** Vikas Bahl
🎥 **Cinematographers** Siddharth Diwan, Bobby Singh

▼ **Friends in need**
The people Rani befriends in Paris and Amsterdam, including Vijay (far left) and her roommates (right), play a pivotal role in her journey of self-discovery.

> ## "Queen *is a significant Bollywood marker, a film that is intensely local and gloriously global.*"
>
> **SHUBHRA GUPTA,** *INDIAN EXPRESS*, 2014

▲ **Lost in translation**
As someone who had never previously stepped out of India, Rani is initially daunted by the unfamiliar streets of Paris and Amsterdam.

needs. Under Vijay's influence, Rani gradually begins to let loose, shaking off her inhibitions and gaining new-found confidence and panache.

In Amsterdam, she befriends an unlikely trio of men, and takes inspiration from their courage and positive attitude. As she discovers a new world inhabited by interesting, eccentric folk, Rani also begins to explore her inner self. The plot, with its heroine traveling in a foreign environment that seems alien and unpredictable, is speculated by some critics to be loosely based on Lewis Carroll's novel *Alice's Adventures in Wonderland* (1865). Like Alice, Rani encounters curious characters who challenge her sheltered view of life. And, like Alice, she returns home having been on an incredible, life-changing journey. Rani begins the film as a jilted, virgin bride-to-be but by the end becomes a spirited woman, no longer afraid to express herself.

SMALL BUT PERFECTLY FORMED
Queen served as the perfect platform for Kangana Ranaut (pp. 322–23), which is not surprising since director Bahl wrote the script with her in mind. He went as far as to say that he would not have made the film without her. Luckily for him, mutual friend and fellow director Anurag Basu introduced him to Kangana.

It turned out to be a match made in heaven. Bold, confident, and fashion-forward in real life, Kangana was fascinated by the prospect of playing Rani, the complete opposite of her personality. Reinventing herself as the timid, insecure Rani, Kangana brought her own ideas to the film and even worked on the script with writer Anvita Dutt Guptan. She improvised on set, bringing a sense of spontaneity to all her scenes, which is just what Bahl had hoped for.

Made on a modest budget, *Queen* was definitely a no-frills production. While a big-budget film with extensive outdoor locations would normally rely on a team of more than 100, Bahl had to make do with just 25 people, filming in 145 locations in 40 days flat. The crew would film for a couple of hours at one location before lugging their equipment to the next spot. With no budget for a trailer, Kangana had to resort to changing her clothes in public toilets and restaurants; and without a dedicated catering truck, the cast and crew had to take meals at whatever eateries were closest to the spot.

RECOVERING FROM TRAGEDY
The whole production was thrown into disarray when cinematographer Bobby Singh, a veteran of the industry, tragically died from an asthma attack halfway through filming. While he genuinely mourned Singh's death, Bahl knew that he had to complete the project, and called on Siddharth Diwan to take over as director of photography. Diwan had to get up to speed quickly, and spent many hours watching the film's rushes and going over the script to organize the remaining sequences for shooting. The end result, however, gave no hint of the upheaval behind the scenes. Both cinematographers succeeded in capturing the nuances of Kangana's captivating performance.

Despite the troubles behind the scenes, Kangana and director Bahl's collaboration resulted in her winning the country's highest cinema accolades—Best Actress at both the National Film Awards and the Filmfare Awards. Bahl, meanwhile, enjoyed his own haul. He bagged the National Film Award for Best Feature Film, as well as the Filmfare Award for Best Director.

▲ **The turning point**
Rani's success in a cooking competition in Amsterdam proves to be the defining moment in her path toward self-confidence.

VIKAS BAHL
(b.1971)

Vikas Bahl earned an MBA and launched a career in advertising before finding his true calling in films. In 2011, he founded Phantom Films with directors Anurag Kashyap, Vikramaditya Motwane, and producer Madhu Mantena. The same year, he made his mark on the big screen, co-directing the kids' film *Chillar Party* with Nitesh Tiwari. Winning the National Film Award for Best Children's Film, Bahl's first effort gave him the confidence to debut as a director in his own right with *Queen*.

KANGANA RANAUT

ACTRESS **b.1987**

Daring and vulnerable on the big screen, Kangana Ranaut's ability to convey subtle emotions has earned her a rightful place as a Bollywood star.

▲ **Family bonds**
Kangana has a close relationship with her mother, Asha, and is devoted to her sister, Rangoli, who has worked as her manager. Kangana and Rangoli live together in Mumbai.

A beautiful face and a gorgeous body seem to be the requisite for any leading lady in Indian cinema, yet Kangana Ranaut delivers much more. She knows how to connect with her audience by being genuine. Her choice of challenging roles, and a desire to break boundaries and take risks, have earned her the respect of the film industry. The sincerity she projects both on- and off-screen has endeared her to the public as well. Kangana is one of the few actresses with whom leading actors openly claim they want to work. In the male-dominated realm of Hindi cinema this is quite an achievement—even more so given Kangana's unlikely start in life.

HUMBLE BEGINNINGS

Kangana was born in 1987 in the village of Bhambla, Himachal Pradesh. Her father was a contractor and her mother a school teacher. Kangana aspired to become a doctor at first, but soon realized it was not the right career choice for her. Much to her parents' surprise, she signed up with a modeling agency, and soon moved to Delhi at the age of 16 to study theater under the esteemed director Arvind Gaur, who spotted her potential for film.

Kangana soon moved to Mumbai to pursue a career in modeling. Although she had a pretty face and could work as a teen model, she was shy, did not speak English, and even struggled to express herself in Hindi. As luck would have it, at a modeling shoot she met director Anurag Basu, who auditioned her for *Gangster* in 2005, and launched her in the film in 2006. With no connections at all in Bollywood, it was miraculous that Kangana landed a lead role in a hit film. Her role as a neurotic woman in love was challenging for a young, inexperienced actress, but she rose to the occasion, winning a Filmfare Award for Best Debut Actress.

After *Gangster*, Kangana worked with Basu on two more challenging projects. She played a schizophrenic

▶ **Fashionista**
With her cascading curls and fresh, innocent face, Kangana Ranaut stands out in the sea of divas that populate Bollywood. Apart from being a remarkable actress, she is also one of the most stylish and well-dressed celebrities in India.

KEY WORKS

Woh Lamhe, 2006

Life in a … Metro, 2007

Tanu Weds Manu, 2011 (see p. 309)

Queen, 2013 (see pp. 320–21)

Revolver Rani, 2014

Rangoon, 2017

▶ Twin transformation
As shown in the film poster, Kangana plays two very different characters in *Tanu Weds Manu Returns*—fiery, seductive Tanu, and tomboy athlete Kusum—dual roles for which she won her second National Film Award.

girl in *Woh Lamhe*, and an ambitious career woman in *Life in a ... Metro*, both of which helped to build her reputation as a bold actress.

FINDING SUCCESS
The following years brought further success, with lead roles in films such as crime drama *Once Upon a Time in Mumbai* (2010), and romantic comedy *Tanu Weds Manu*, which was not only a commercial success, but also garnered critical acclaim for Kangana.

However, it was not all smooth sailing for this classy diva. Kangana appeared in several flops, including *Shakalaka Boom Boom* (2007) and *Kites* (2010), which did nothing to advance her career. She received good reviews for her role as a mutant shapeshifter in Rakesh Roshan's sci-fi blockbuster *Krrish 3* (2013) and hot on the heels of this success came *Queen*, inspiring audiences across India with its depiction of a jilted woman on a journey of self-discovery. Kangana's

heartfelt portrayal was rewarded with a Filmfare Award and a National Film Award for Best Actress in 2015.

In 2015, Kangana made film history with *Tanu Weds Manu Returns*, the sequel to the 2011 hit *Tanu Weds Manu*. In it, for the role of Kusum, Kangana had to learn the dialogues in Haryanvi (the native dialect of the Indian state of Haryana), a challenging undertaking. This was the first film with a female in the central role to make more than ₹1 billion ($16

million), and along with financial success it also earned critical acclaim.

DEDICATED PERFORMER
Kangana is known for immersing herself in the characters she plays, which is why her portrayals are so convincing. To prepare for the filming of Vishal Bhardwaj's historical romance *Rangoon* (2017), she thoroughly researched her character, which is loosely based on Bollywood stunt woman Mary Ann Evans. Although *Rangoon* received mixed reviews and was disappointing at the box office, Kangana was praised for her outstanding performance.

Regardless of whether she is appearing in blockbusters, slow-burners, or complete flops, Kangana's reputation remains untarnished. She has come a long way from the inarticulate teen who landed in Mumbai with next to nothing.

THE FIREBRAND
Labeled one of the best actresses of her generation, Kangana regularly tops the list of India's highest-paid female stars. She is also one of the few celebrities to make a strong impression off screen with her outspoken views. Kangana is critical of the male-dominated film industry and has encouraged women to be more assertive. She once told a reporter that women, "should not give in to the expectations of society that you're just a pretty little thing and you should keep your mouth shut and stay dumb because that's how you're accepted."

Leading by example, Kangana has shown that it is possible to achieve great things with determination and hard work. She aspires to write scripts and direct films in the near future; if the past decade is anything to go by, she is capable of doing anything she puts her mind to.

> "*Kangana Ranaut's confidence is not limited to her career goals.*"
>
> **KORAL DASGUPTA,** WRITER, *THE QUINT*, 2016

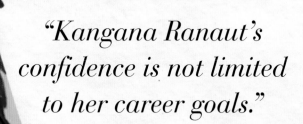

▶ Daring roles
A versatile actress, Kangana (center) studied martial arts and performed her own action stunts in *Rangoon*.

KANGANA AS RANI
MEHRA IN *QUEEN*

TIMELINE

- **March 20, 1987** Born in Bhambla, Himachal Pradesh, to Amardeep and Asha Ranaut.

- **2006** Debuts in *Gangster*, followed by a role in *Woh Lamhe*.

- **2007** Wins Stardust Award for Breakthrough Performance—Female for *Life in a ... Metro*.

- **2008** Nominated for Best Supporting Actress at the National Film Awards for her role as a supermodel with a drug problem in *Fashion*.

- **2011** Stars as a shrewd police officer in Abhinay Deo's action thriller *Game*.

- **2012** Voted "Best Dressed Personality" in *People* magazine.

- **2013** Gives an award-winning performance in *Queen*.

- **2014** Receives Indian of the Year Award in the Special Achievement category.

- **2015** Plays a dual role in *Tanu Weds Manu Returns*.

- **2015** Collaborates with leading fashion brand Vero Moda on two clothing lines.

- **2016** Walks the runway at India Couture Week for designer Manav Gangwani.

- **2016** Wins her second National Film Award in the Best Actress category.

- **2017** Receives critical acclaim for her performance in *Rangoon*.

PK

2014

The twisted tale of an alien stranded on Earth, *PK* was embraced by audiences and critics alike, propelling it to become one of the highest-grossing Indian films of all time.

▼ **The odd man out**
The alien, PK, met many people on his journey through India. He was even befriended by a bandmaster—played by Sanjay Dutt (center)—and his band.

CAST AND CREW

★ **Aamir Khan** PK
Anushka Sharma Jaggu
Sanjay Dutt Bhairon Singh
Saurabh Shukla Tapasvi Maharaj
Sushant S. Rajput Sarfaraz Yousuf

🎬 **Director** Rajkumar Hirani
🍿 **Producers** Vidhu Vinod Chopra,
Rajkumar Hirani
🎵 **Music composers** Shantanu Moitra,
Ajay–Atul, Ankit Tiwari
📖 **Scriptwriters** Abhijat Joshi,
Rajkumar Hirani
🎥 **Cinematographer** C.K.
Muraleedharan

Anyone who has seen the classic alien movie *E.T. the Extra-Terrestrial* (1982) will recognize the familiar concept of a creature from another world landing on Planet Earth and confronting human beings with their unfamiliar ways and peculiar habits. In the film *PK*, this basic idea is expanded to become a multilayered story that encompasses religious corruption, the power of friendship between strangers, and the power of love and laughter to change deep-seated preconceptions. The film becomes a funny and touching journey of discovery and enlightenment not only for the alien hero but also for the audience.

AN ALIEN COMES TO EARTH

PK is an alien who comes to Earth in human form, arriving in the north Indian state of Rajasthan to conduct a research mission. He is naked, and his only possession is the remote control for his spaceship—which is stolen by the first person he meets, triggering a series of events with enormous consequences. On the same day that PK lands on Earth, another thread of the story starts to unravel. In the Belgian city of Bruges, Jaggu and Sarfaraz, a couple in love, are being parted by fierce opposition from Jaggu's father, as Sarfaraz is Muslim. Their plan to marry is foiled, and a heartbroken Jaggu returns to India.

Meanwhile, back in Rajasthan, PK sets out to track down the thief of his remote control, but he must quickly learn how to adapt since he knows nothing of human ways. PK travels to Delhi and decides to pray for help—everyone he asked for help has told him to do so. He tries various religious traditions; in one instance he is about to steal from a collection box at a temple, when he is stopped by Jaggu, now a TV reporter. Jaggu wins PK's trust and becomes his ally and guide to the human world.

THE ILLS OF RELIGION

The film alternates between telling the story from the alien's point of view and that of the journalist Jaggu. As PK explores the land and its people, he meets Tapasvi Maharaj, a Hindu

▲ **PK's cassette player**
Posters were released showing a naked Aamir Khan covering his modesty with a Panasonic RQ-565D, which became a cult object among fans of the film.

"godman," whom he soon discovers to be a charlatan. As the plot unfolds, troubling aspects of religion are investigated through the character of PK and his journey. In the end, Jaggu, who is accompanying PK, encourages people to send in videos of their own negative experiences with religious heads of various communities.

In uncovering the corruption and self-righteousness in Hinduism and other religions, PK concludes that the real God has been obscured by the attempt of human beings to create a God that will conveniently serve their own ends.

COMIC RELIEF

Despite some of the serious issues raised in the film, *PK* is essentially a comedy. Many of the laughs come from the innocence of the main character, and his very different ways of doing things. For instance, where PK comes from, communication—and the transfer of ideas—is done by holding hands. His attempts to hold hands with complete strangers to communicate result in him being labeled a pervert. In another comical scene, when PK is taken to a brothel, he ends up holding hands with a prostitute for six hours to learn how to speak Bhojpuri from her. PK's name, too, is the result of his

▲ **Love in Bruges**
Critics praised the on-screen chemistry between Anushka Sharma and Sushant Singh Rajput. The song "Chaar Kadam" (Four Steps) featuring the pair was released a few weeks before the film.

odd and unfamiliar habits, which prompt people to ask him if he is drunk: "Pee ke ho kya?"

MIRED IN CONTROVERSY

As well as being popular, *PK* also proved to be controversial. Some Hindu commentators called for the film to be banned; others went further, demanding that the director and star be arrested, arguing for a social boycott of anyone who had worked on the film. Director Rajkumar Hirani made no apologies for his satire, which he intended to be entertaining rather than offensive. Like his other films, *Munna Bhai M.B.B.S.* (2003), *Lage Raho Munna Bhai* (see pp. 286–87), and *3 Idiots* (see pp. 302–303), *PK* is a film with a message. In *PK*, this message is that people are humans first, not Hindu or Muslim. By seeing people and their behavior through the eyes of an alien, Hirani was able to show how foolish humans can be with their superstitions and prejudices.

"You have to honestly write a story ... make it constantly entertaining. You sugarcoat your social message"

RAJKUMAR HIRANI, *DAILYO,* 2014

BAJRANGI BHAIJAAN

2015

Critics may have approached *Bajrangi Bhaijaan* with caution, as its star was better known for his action roles, but it won over audiences as a film with a heart and a message.

A touching tale of a devout man who helps a lost girl find her way back home to Pakistan, *Bajrangi Bhaijaan* has many key elements of a Hindi film—a strong man with a gentle heart, a vulnerable girl, comic supporting roles—all combined with a deft handling of border politics.

A HEARTWARMING STORY
The film revolves around a mute, six-year-old Pakistani girl, Shahida. Her mother takes her to a shrine in Delhi, hoping she will regain her voice, but the pair is separated en route. Lost in the city, Shahida spots religious devotee Pawan, also known as Bajrangi, and follows him. He takes her under his wing, and nicknames her Munni. When the local police are unable to help locate her parents, a

journey begins that leads the two into a world of adventure. Together they cross the border between India and Pakistan without a visa, face arrest, and are accused of espionage. Their story becomes an internet sensation, generating a wave of public support across both countries.

While it does tug at the heartstrings, *Bajrangi Bhaijaan* is saved from being an overly emotional melodrama by smart performances. The film also owes its success to the collaboration between writer Vijayendra Prasad, director Kabir Khan, and actor Salman Khan (see pp. 224–25).

◀ **Incredible journey**
The tale of an unlikely duo's adventures traveling from India to Pakistan proved to be a huge success at the box office.

The music album boasts of big names such as Atif Aslam, Vishal Dadlani, Adnan Sami, and Jubin Nautiyal, resulting in the year's biggest chartbusters.

REAL-LIFE INSPIRATION
Prasad took inspiration from a news article about a Pakistani couple who brought their child to Chennai for life-saving heart surgery. Much to their surprise, the hospital waived the fee,

confounding their preconceptions about India. The film that evolved from this story brings a message to the screen that people everywhere want to live in harmony.

CAST AND CREW

★ **Salman Khan** Pawan Chaturvedi
Kareena Kapoor Rasika
Harshaali Malhotra Shahida
Nawazuddin Siddiqui Chand Nawab

🎬 **Director** Kabir Khan
⬠ **Producers** Salman Khan, Rockline Venkatesh
♫ₐ **Music composer** Pritam Chakraborty
🕺 **Choreographers** Ahmeda Khan, Remo
📖 **Scriptwriter** K. V. Vijayendra Prasad
🎥 **Cinematographer** Aseem Mishra

▼ **An ardent devotee**
Salman Khan is depicted as a worshipper of the Hindu god Hanuman. The film takes its name from one of Hanuman's many names, "Bajrangi."

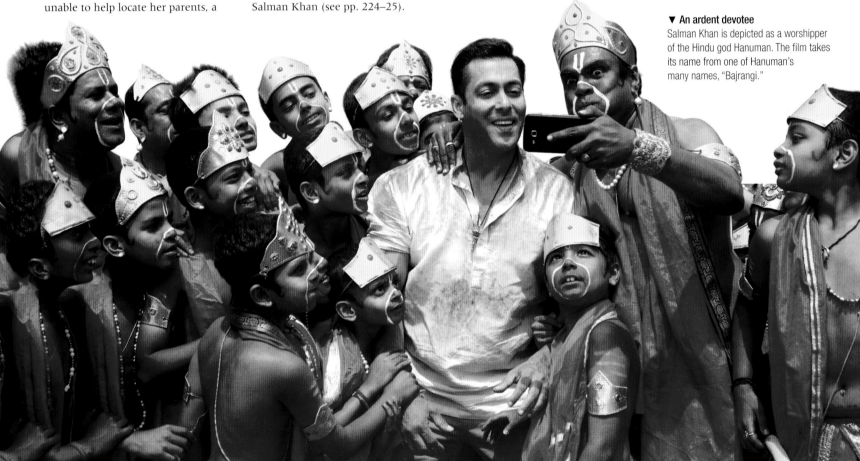

PIKU

2015

Piku is a light-hearted comedy that strips filmmaking down to its bare bones, winning over its audience with a simple story and a down-to-earth portrayal of an unusual family.

Unlike a typical Bollywood film, *Piku* has no song-and-dance routines, no grand romance, no elaborate plots, and no dramatic climax. What this film delivers instead is snappy dialogue, perfectly timed performances from the cast, and realistic execution from director Shoojit Sircar. Together these elements create an understated film that charms viewers with its emotional candor.

A FATHER–DAUGHTER RELATIONSHIP
The film centers on the relationship between an elderly father, Bhashkor, and his 30-year-old daughter Piku. This odd Bengali duo are portrayed in all their hilarious eccentricities.

Bhashkor is a hypochondriac preoccupied with his aging body, especially the movements of his bowels. This makes life difficult for his daughter Piku. As the only caretaker and companion of her father, the feisty and independent Piku constantly has to juggle her personal and professional life—a task not made easy by her loving but meddling father. In an hilarious yet oddly poignant scene in the film, Bhashkor introduces his daughter to a potential suitor at a party as a "financially, emotionally, and sexually independent, non-virgin woman."

When the pair need to take a road trip to Kolkata, they call on Rana, the quiet and unassuming owner of a taxi company that both father and daughter rely on, to drive them. This soon becomes a journey of discovery for everyone, with Rana becoming immersed in their domestic life while an unspoken romance blooms between himself and Piku.

DEPARTURE FROM THE MAINSTREAM
Quirky characters fascinate director Shoojit Sircar, who is more interested in creating independent cinema than big-budget Bollywood productions. Together with scriptwriter Juhi Chaturvedi, Sircar developed the story around a father and daughter who break many Indian social taboos—a daughter who openly discusses bowel movements with her father, and a father who is comfortable enough to have candid conversations about his daughter's sex life.

The film's characters were a hit, as was Sircar's style of filmmaking, which is bold and free of gimmicks. Like his previous films, *Vicky Donor* (2012) and *Madras Cafe* (2013), *Piku* became a commercial blockbuster.

The movie was also a critical success, and was nominated for a Filmfare Award for Best Film. For her role as Piku, Deepika Padukone won the 2016 Filmfare Award for Best Actress, while Bachchan was voted Best Actor at the National Film Awards for his portrayal of the eccentric father.

CAST AND CREW

★ **Deepika Padukone** Piku Banerjee
Amitabh Bachchan Bhashkor Banerjee
Irrfan Khan Rana Chaudhary

🎬 **Director** Shoojit Sircar
🎦 **Producers** N.P. Singh, Ronnie Lahiri, Sneha Rajani
🎵 **Music composer** Anupam Roy
🎵 **Lyricist** Anupam Roy
📖 **Scriptwriter** Juhi Chaturvedi
📷 **Cinematographer** Kamaljeet Negi
👔 **Costume designer** Veera Kapur

▲ **An eccentric trio**
A road trip from Delhi to Kolkata provides hilarious opportunities for stars Deepika Padukone, Amitabh Bachchan, and Irrfan Khan to shine.

IRRFAN KHAN (b.1967)
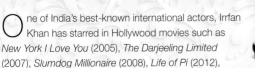
One of India's best-known international actors, Irrfan Khan has starred in Hollywood movies such as *New York I Love You* (2005), *The Darjeeling Limited* (2007), *Slumdog Millionaire* (2008), *Life of Pi* (2012), and *Jurassic World* (2015). His global success did not come overnight—he has been honing his craft since his days as a student at the National School of Drama in Delhi. After graduating he worked on soap operas such as *Banegi Apni Baat*, but his real passion has always been the big screen.

DEEPIKA PADUKONE

ACTRESS b.1986

One of the highest paid actresses in the world today, Bollywood's leading lady Deepika Padukone has won over audiences and critics alike.

◄ **Acting prowess**
Initially labeled a one-hit wonder, Deepika proved the critics wrong with her acting mettle in films such as *Goliyon Ki Raasleela Ram-Leela* (shown here) and *Piku*.

The actress who has become the darling of Bollywood could have been dismissed as just another pretty face—it was clear early in her career that the camera loved her. However, her determination to be recognized for her acting abilities eventually paid off.

EARLY START
Born in Copenhagen, Denmark, Deepika is the daughter of champion badminton player Prakash Padukone. When the family moved to Bangalore, it seemed that the young girl would follow in her father's footsteps as a sportswoman. However, while she showed great promise as a badminton player, Deepika had set her sights on a different path. She made her modeling debut at the age of eight, and by the tenth grade she had decided this was where her heart lay. She quickly found her feet in the high-pressure world of modeling. She walked the runway at India Fashion Week in 2005 and won Model of the Year at the Kingfisher Fashion Awards the same year. Her rise to

▲ **Award-winning debut**
Deepika stunned the industry with her debut film *Om Shanti Om*, bagging the IIFA Best Female Debut Award.

prominence continued in 2006 when she landed the cover of the Kingfisher Bikini Calendar. She came under the wings of model coordinator Anila Anand, who helped her get her first few advertisement campaigns.

"I am lucky to be a part of the movie business that has the power to entertain, inspire, and influence people."

DEEPIKA PADUKONE

At the age of 21, Deepika moved to Mumbai where she enrolled in an acting course at Anupam Kher's (see p. 179) film academy. Here she learned to mask her strong Kannada accent, and immersed herself in the craft she would need to take her onto the big screen.

FINDING HER FEET

Deepika made her Bollywood debut in 2007 opposite actor Shah Rukh Khan (see pp. 214–15) in director–choreographer Farah Khan's *Om Shanti Om*. A hit with audiences worldwide, the film became one of the highest grossing Indian productions ever. Deepika caught the attention of the film industry, winning awards and appreciation for her debut, including the Filmfare and the International Indian Film Academy Award (IIFA).

Despite this, in her early years in the industry Deepika battled against bad reviews and the poor commercial performance of some of her films. *Bachna Ae Haseeno* (2008) fared well at the box office, but she was criticized for lacking sparkle, while *Chandni Chowk to China* (2009) was a financial failure and earned Deepika poor reviews. However, her next film *Love Aaj Kal* (2009) was a hit and redeemed the actress in the eyes of the critics.

Meanwhile, the disclosure of her real-life romance with *Bachna Ae Haseeno* co-star Ranbir Kapoor (see

Illuminati Films and Eros International Present

C O C K T A I L

pp. 316–17) kept Deepika's name in the gossip columns. In 2010 she appeared in five films, only one of which stood out—*Lafangey Parindey*. In this touching story of a blind girl determined to win an ice skating competition, Deepika caught the public's attention starring opposite actor Neil Nitin Mukesh. However, the following year, a series of poorly reviewed films threatened to derail her career.

RISE TO STARDOM

Things turned around for Deepika in 2012, when her performance in *Cocktail* earned critical acclaim as well as nomination for Best Actress at almost all award ceremonies—winning the TOIFA (The Times of India Film Awards) for Best Actress Critics. Her star continued to climb in 2013, with roles in four of the top-grossing Indian films of the year. In particular, she shone as a Tamil girl on the run in blockbuster

◄ Turning the tide
Deepika's portrayal of the impulsive party girl Veronica in *Cocktail* was a turning point in her acting career.

action comedy *Chennai Express* and also in her gripping performance in *Goliyon Ki Raasleela Ram-Leela*, for which she won the Filmfare Award for Best Actress in 2014. In 2015, the sensational *Piku* was released, a beautifully executed father-daughter comedy drama that gave Deepika the chance to show off her acting skills. It also gave media a distraction from her romance with Ranveer Singh (see p. 330), with whom she starred in *Bajirao Mastani*, also a commercial and critical triumph.

BEYOND BOLLYWOOD

As her reputation grew, Deepika found a public voice, and decided to lend her name and face to raising awareness about an issue close to her heart—mental health. Taking inspiration from her own journey with depression, she formed "The Live Love Laugh Foundation" in 2015, and collaborated on several public health campaigns designed to support people suffering from depression. The actress has also worked for global brands with several high-profile endorsements, and she has her own fashion line. As a result, Deepika was ranked tenth on the Forbes global list of highest paid actresses in 2016. In 2017, Deepika made her first foray into Hollywood opposite actor Vin Diesel in *xXx: Return of Xander Cage*.

▼ A mixed bag
Deepika has a variety of her roles to her credit, from mainstream commercial hits such as *Chennai Express* (shown here), to offbeat films such as *Finding Fanny*.

KEY WORKS

Om Shanti Om, 2007 (see pp. 292–95)

Cocktail, 2012

Yeh Jawaani Hai Deewani, 2013 (see p. 315)

Chennai Express, 2013

Goliyon Ki Raasleela Ram-Leela, 2013

Piku, 2015 (see p. 327)

Bajirao Mastani, 2015 (see p. 330)

TIMELINE

- **January 5, 1986** Born in Copenhagen, Denmark.

- **1987** Her family relocates to Bangalore, India.

- **2005** Runway debut at India Fashion Week, a bi-annual fashion event.

- **2006** Features on the cover of the Kingfisher Bikini Calendar.

- **2006** Debuts with the Kannada film *Aishwarya*.

- **2007** Stars in her first Bollywood film, *Om Shanti Om*.

- **2008** Receives Best Female Debut Award at the Filmfare Awards and International India Film Academy Awards for *Om Shanti Om*.

- **2012** *Cocktail* marks a significant turning point in her career.

- **2013** Enjoys her most successful year, with roles in the year's highest grossing films, including *Chennai Express*, *Yeh Jawaani Hai Deewani*, and *Goliyon Ki Raasleela Ram-Leela*.

- **2014** Bags Filmfare for Best Actress for the role of a Gujarati belle, Leela, for *Goliyon Ki Rasleela - Ram Leela*.

- **2015** Receives critical appreciation for her role in *Piku*.

- **2015** Opens up about her battle with depression and sets up a foundation to create awareness about mental health.

- **2017** Debuts in Hollywood with *xXx: Return of Xander Cage* opposite Vin Diesel.

DEEPIKA'S HOLLYWOOD DEBUT WITH
XXX: RETURN OF XANDER CAGE

BAJIRAO MASTANI

2015

Hailed by critics as a masterpiece on its release, Sanjay Leela Bhansali's *Bajirao Mastani* is a romantic saga with a sumptuous look and feel.

CAST AND CREW

★ **Ranveer Singh** Bajirao I
Deepika Padukone Mastani
Priyanka Chopra Kashibai
Tanvi Azmi Radhabai
Milind Soman Ambaji Pant

🎬 **Director** Sanjay Leela Bhansali
◇ **Producers** Sanjay Leela Bhansali, Kishore Lulla
🎵 **Music composers** Sanjay Leela Bhansali, Sanchit Balhara
🕺 **Choreographers** Pandit Birju Maharaj, Ganesh Acharya
📖 **Scriptwriter** Prakash R. Kapadia
📷 **Cinematographer** Sudeep Chatterjee
👔 **Costume designer** Anju Modi

Set against the backdrop of the Maratha Empire in the 18th-century, *Bajirao Mastani* is based on the Marathi novel *Raau* (1972) by Nagnath S. Inamdar. The result of more than 10 years of meticulous planning, the film was the brainchild of director Sanjay Leela Bhansali, who had announced his intention to make the film as early as 2002, just after the release of his other movie *Devdas* (see pp. 274–77).

Bhansali had visualized Bajirao and Mastani being played by Salman Khan (see pp. 224–25) and Aishwarya Rai (see pp. 254–55), but when the real-life lovers broke up, that no longer seemed a viable proposition. After almost a decade of speculation, during which time Bhansali was busy making other films, he finally hit upon the perfect actors to play the title roles: Ranveer Singh and Deepika Padukone (see pp. 328–29), whom he had directed in *Goliyon Ki Raasleela Ram-Leela* (2013). Completing the lineup were Priyanka Chopra (see pp. 280–81) as Bajirao's first wife, Tanvi Azmi as his mother, and Irrfan Khan as the narrator.

A GRAND SAGA

The chemistry between the lead actors keeps the audience engrossed in this story of a love triangle. Bajirao is an army general, given the job of Peshwa, the equivalent of a modern-day prime minister. While on a mission, Bajirao encounters warrior princess Mastani and enjoys a brief romance with her. Once back home, he resumes his married life with Kashibai, but before long Mastani arrives to declare her love for him. So the scene is set for an enthralling plot in which love, heartbreak, betrayal, and war play out. Bhansali's sumptuous direction and music carry the film along to its dramatic conclusion.

AWARDS AND ACCOLADES

Released in December 2015, *Bajirao Mastani* was immediately hailed as a triumph. The lead actors received their share of praise, but it was the visual artistry of the film that united critics. Sudeep Chatterjee, the renowned cinematographer, won five honors, including the National Film Award and Filmfare Award for Best Cinematography. *Bajirao Mastani* scooped up all the major industry awards, winning Best Film, Best Director, Best Costume Design, Best Art Direction, Best Actor, and Best Supporting Actress at the Filmfare Awards alone.

◄ **A demanding role**
Ranveer Singh spent months mastering horse riding and learning to speak Marathi to play his character in the film. The director also asked him to put on weight and shave his head.

▲ **A love triangle**
The poster captures the film's grandeur, lush visuals, and the crackling chemistry between the lead actors. Bajirao's first wife Kashibai looks on.

RANVEER SINGH (b. 1985)

A natural showman, Ranveer Singh needed no encouragement to perform, even as a child—he often appeared in school plays, and delighted in entertaining friends. His big break came when he landed the lead role in *Band Baaja Baaraat* (2010), his magnetic on-screen presence earning him the Filmfare Award for Best Male Debut. Acclaimed roles in a string of hit films followed, including *Goliyon Ki Raasleela Ram-Leela* (2013), *Gunday* (2014), *Bajirao Mastani* (2015), and the comedy-drama *Dil Dhadakne Do* (2015).

DANGAL

2016

A quest to win gold for India at the 2010 Commonwealth Games is at the heart of *Dangal*, a film about overcoming prejudice and the power of determination and hard work.

▲ A test of strength
An ancient sport, wrestling is extremely popular in rural India. The film's story challenges the conventional notions of the male-dominated sport, showing two women wrestlers entering the arena.

CAST AND CREW

★ **Aamir Khan** Mahavir Singh Phogat
Sakshi Tanwar Daya Shobha Kaur
Fatima Sana Shaikh Geeta
Zaira Wasim Young Geeta
Sanya Malhotra Babita
Suhani Bhatnagar Young Babita
Aparshakti Khurana Omkara

🎬 **Director** Nitesh Tiwari
📀 **Producers** Aamir Khan, Kiran Rao, Kiran Roy Kapur
🎵 **Music composer** Pritam
🎵 **Lyricist** Amitabh Bhattacharya
📖 **Scriptwriter** Nitesh Tiwari
🎥 **Cinematographer** Satyajit Pande

Based on a true story about two sisters who competed as wrestlers at the 2010 Commonwealth Games, *Dangal* (Wrestling Competition) earned the admiration of cinemagoers across the nation. Although on one level the film celebrates sporting achievement, on a deeper level it delivers a message about the women's discipline and courage, and their defiance of social convention.

THE DIRECTOR'S VISION

The film tells the story of amateur wrestler Mahavir Singh Phogat, from Haryana, and his four daughters, whom he trains in the sport of wrestling. The two eldest, Geeta and Babita, show great promise and are also driven to win, but in order to fulfil their dreams and represent their country at the Games, they must challenge the unwritten ban on women competing as wrestlers. They also have to resolve personal differences with their father before they have their chance at making sporting history.

What could have been an overly sentimental drama is saved by director and scriptwriter Tiwari's talent for storytelling. By using a comical voice-over throughout the film, he creates an engaging experience that alternates between dramatic tension and humor to great effect. The narrator is Aparshakti Khurana, delivering a sterling performance as Phogat's goofy nephew.

A DREAM CAST

Casting superstar Aamir Khan (see pp. 228–29) as Phogat was an inspired masterstroke, and Tiwari made sure that he was fully prepared when he pitched the idea to the veteran actor. With the completed screenplay in hand, he spent more than three hours narrating the entire film to Khan, in a bid to lure him on board.

Khan's gruff portrayal of Phogat is the perfect foil for his two feisty female co-stars Fatima Sana Shaikh and Sanya Malhotra, who play the grown-up wrestler sisters. Stealing the first half of the film are Zaira Wasim, as young Geeta, and Suhani Bhatnagar, as young Babita. All four actresses trained six days a week for a year to prepare for their roles, while the entire cast perfected a strong Haryanvi accent to lend authenticity to their portrayal of a family from the North Indian state of Haryana.

▼ Winning the gold
The film is based on the Phogat sisters. Here, the wrestler Geeta is seen competing in the 2010 Commonwealth wrestling final.

HIT SONGS

Haanikaarak Bapu
(Harmful Father)
🎤 **Singers** Sarwar Khan, Sartaz Khan Barna, Saddy Ahmad

Dangal
(Wrestling Competition)
🎤 **Singer** Daler Mahendi

Dhakkad
(Bold and Fearless)
🎤 **Singer** Raftaar

Other movies

Organized chronologically from the late 1930s to the present day, this section lists Hindi cinema's most noteworthy and memorable movies. These films have not only done well at the box office, but have also been widely praised and loved by the audiences for their riveting themes, innovative storylines, fine cinematography, and quality entertainment.

Kisan Kanya 1937

★ **Actors** Ghulam Mohammed, Jillo, Nissar, Padmadevi

🎬 **Director** Moti B. Gidwani

🎞 **Producers** Ardeshir Irani, Imperial Pictures

🎵 **Music composer** Ram Gopal Pandey

💬 **Scriptwriter** Saadat Hasan Manto

The first Indian color film, *Kisan Kanya* (Farmer's Daughter) was produced by Ardeshir Irani and directed by Moti B. Gidwani using the American Cinecolor process. Irani was a pioneer in the field of Hindi cinema whose other notable works include *Nala Damayanti* (1920) and the country's first talkie, *Alam Ara* (see p. 20). *Kisan Kanya*, based on a novel by the Indo-Pakistani writer Saadat Hasan Manto, focused on the plight of the destitute farmers—eloquently portraying the ways in which these impoverished agrarian workers were mistreated by the landlords. A rural crime drama, it tells the story of how Ramu (Nissar), a poor peasant, is accused of murdering his cruel, exploitative landlord, Ghani.

POSTER FOR *KISAN KANYA*, THE FIRST HINDI CINECOLOR MOVIE

Aadmi 1939

★ **Actors** Shanta Hublikar, Shahu Modak, Sundarabai

🎬 **Director** V. Shantaram

🎞 **Producer** Prabhat Film Company

🎵 **Music composer** Master Krishnarao

💬 **Scriptwriter** Munshi Aziz

Aadmi (Man) was a remake of the classic Marathi film *Manoos* (1939), a melodrama that focused on social problems. It was praised by the great Charlie Chaplin. The film's protagonist is an honest policeman who falls in love with and marries a prostitute only to face the scorn and ridicule of society. Shahu Modak, the lead actor, was famous for playing the roles of many Hindu mythological characters. Music director Master Krishnarao was a modernizer and innovator and his song "Kis Liye Kal Ki Baat" (Why to Talk of Tomorrow) used six different folk styles and languages (Punjabi, Gujarati, Telugu, Marathi, Tamil, and Hindi). Today, director V. Shantaram's *Aadmi* is considered a classic, along with his other films *Duniya Na Mane* (1937) and *Padosi* (1941). It is also remembered as a reformist film that enjoyed considerable commercial success.

Aurat 1940

★ **Actors** Sardar Akhtar, Arun Kumar Ahuja, Kanhaiyalal, Surendra

🎬 **Director** Mehboob Khan

🎞 **Producer** National Studios

🎵 **Music composer** Anil Biswas

💬 **Scriptwriters** Babubhai Mehta, Wajahat Mirza

Directed by the famous Mehboob Khan, *Aurat* (Woman) was remade in 1957 as *Mother India*, one of Indian cinema's all-time greatest hits. The film's plot revolves around Radha (Sardar Akhtar), a determined mother who works herself to the bone in order to feed her children, while trying to pay off the loan of the greedy and lecherous village moneylender. In the end, the courageous mother has to decide how to deal with her own son, who has killed the moneylender and become a bandit.

NOOR JEHAN IN *ANMOL GHADI*

Anmol Ghadi 1946

★ **Actors** Noor Jehan, Suraiya, Surendra

🎬 **Director** Mehboob Khan

🎞 **Producer** Mehboob Khan

🎵 **Music composer** Naushad

💬 **Scriptwriter** Aghajani Kashmeri

Produced and directed by Mehboob Khan, *Anmol Ghadi* (Precious Moment) is remembered today for its beautiful songs composed by Naushad. Some of the unforgettable hits include "Aawaaz De Kahaan Hai" (Tell Me Where Are You), "Jawaan Hai Mohabbat" (Young Love), and "Mere Bachpan Ke Saathi Mujhe Bhool Na Jaana" (My Childhood Companion, Don't Forget Me). The film, which featured the first notable song by playback singer Mohammed Rafi "Tera Khilauna Toota" (Your Toy Broke), went on to become the highest-grossing film at the box office

in 1946. It tells the story of childhood sweethearts Chander (Surendra) and Lata (Noor Jehan), who attempt to find each other despite all odds. The plot involves a secret token, mistaken identity, sacrifice, and lost love. Since 2000, the film has been remade in a number of Indian languages.

Mahal 1949

★ **Actors** Ashok Kumar, Madhubala

🎬 **Director** Kamal Amrohi

🎞 **Producers** Ashok Kumar, Savak Vacha

🎵 **Music composer** Khemchand Prakash

💬 **Scriptwriter** Kamal Amrohi

Kamal Amrohi's directorial debut single-handedly catapulted both the leading lady, Madhubala, and singer Lata Mangeshkar (see pp. 60–61) into superstardom. The songs by Lata Mangeshkar and Rajkumari remain evergreen hits, and Lata's "Aayega Aane Waala" (Whoever Has to Come Will Come) is popular even today. Ashok Kumar plays Hari Shankar, a young man who moves into a beautiful but abandoned palace haunted by a ghostly young woman. What follows is a game of cat and mouse, with many twists and turns until the truth is revealed in the end. *Mahal* (Palace) is a groundbreaking thriller and one of the earliest films to take on the theme of reincarnation. It was also one of the biggest box office hits in 1949. Mahal has been included in the British Film Institute's list of "10 Great Romantic Horror Films." Bimal Roy, the film's editor, went on to direct *Madhumati*—which in turn inspired a host of works on the theme of reincarnation, not only in Indian cinema and television, but also perhaps in world cinema.

Samadhi 1950

★ **Actors** Nalini Jaywant, Shashi Kapoor, Kuldip Kaur, Ashok Kumar, Shyam
🎬 **Director** Ramesh Saigal
🎞 **Producer** Filmistan Pvt Ltd
🎵 **Music composer** C. Ramchandra
📖 **Scriptwriter** Ramesh Saigal

This patriotic spy thriller featuring Ashok Kumar as Shekhar in the lead role is about freedom fighter Netaji Subhash Chandra Bose's call to the Indian youth to join his Indian National Army and liberate the country from oppressive British rule. Kuldip Kaur and Nalini Jaywant play Dolly and Lilly D'Souza, sisters who are British spies. Shekhar, with whom Lilly later falls in love, eventually dies a hero's death during an operation to blow up a bridge on the Indo-Burmese border. The dialogue and confrontations between Shekhar and his elder brother Suresh (Shyam) are among the most memorable scenes. A great box office success, the film was the highest-earning Hindi film of 1950, grossing approximately ₹13.5 million (about ₹677 million / $10.5 million today).

Babul 1950

★ **Actors** Dilip Kumar, Nargis, Munawar Sultana
🎬 **Director** S.U. Sunny
🎞 **Producer** Naushad
🎵 **Music composer** Naushad
📖 **Scriptwriter** Azm Bazidpuri

Babul (Father), a classic love triangle featuring Dilip Kumar, Munawar Sultana, and Nargis, was the second-highest grossing film of 1950, earning approximately ₹12.5 million (about ₹627 million / $9.75 million today).

Two young women, Bela (Nargis) and Usha (Munawar), compete for the affection of a wealthy young postmaster whose work requires little to no effort, giving him time to indulge himself in his love for painting and music. The rich Usha finally agrees to renounce her love for the sake of her rival, Bela, but the film ends on a tragic note as Bela dies after falling from a tree. The songs of the film, written by Shakeel Badayuni, were mainly about the joys and pains of being in love, and became extremely popular. The film's most popular track, the moving "Chhod Babul Ka Ghar" (Now You Must Leave Your Father's House), is about a newly married girl leaving behind her paternal home and village.

Devdas 1955

★ **Actors** Dilip Kumar, Motilal Suchitra Sen, Vyjayanthimala
🎬 **Director** Bimal Roy
🎞 **Producer** Bimal Roy
🎵 **Music composer** S.D. Burman
📖 **Scriptwriter** Nabendu Ghosh

Based on the famous novel of the same name by Bengali writer Sarat Chandra Chattopadhyay, *Devdas* features Dilip Kumar as Devdas, Suchitra Sen as his love interest, Paro, and Vyjayanthimala as Chandramukhi, the courtesan who loses her heart to Devdas. Childhood sweethearts Devdas and Paro are cruelly separated when Paro is married off to a much older man. Devdas is unable to give up his love and begins to drown his sorrows in alcohol. Chandramukhi tries to save him from self-destruction, but his health continues to deteriorate. The film, like the novel on which it is based, is a powerful indictment of the conservative social norms prevailing

in early 20th-century Bengal. Music composer S.D. Burman drew inspiration from sources as diverse as the Baul songs of Bengal and the *thumris* (Hindustani classical music) associated with courtesan culture for the film's music.

Mr. & Mrs. '55 1955

★ **Actors** Vinita Bhatt, Guru Dutt, Madhubala, Lalita Pawar, Johnny Walker
🎬 **Director** Guru Dutt
🎞 **Producer** Guru Dutt
🎵 **Music composer** O.P. Nayyar
📖 **Scriptwriter** Abrar Alvi

A clever romantic comedy set in Mumbai (then Bombay), *Mr. & Mrs. '55* features a wonderfully naive young heiress, Anita (Madhubala), who is forced by her conniving aunt to marry Preetam (Guru Dutt), a struggling cartoonist, in a bid to save her wealth. However, after marriage Anita has a change of heart as she discovers the merits of traditional Indian values, and realizes that she is in love with Preetam. The film's memorable songs were written by Majrooh Sultanpuri and sung by Mohammed Rafi and Geeta Dutt. Cartoons by the famous humorist R.K. Laxman were featured in the film. The film has fine acting, inventive camerawork, and a witty plot—all characteristics of a Guru Dutt production. According to some sources, Madhubala's role was initially offered to Vyjayanthimala, who turned it down, regretting her decision later. However, audiences warmed to the on-screen chemistry between Dutt and Madhubala.

SUCHITRA SEN AND DILIP KUMAR IN THE 1955 VERSION OF *DEVDAS*

Jagte Raho 1956

★ **Actors** Daisy Irani, Raj Kapoor, Pradeep Kumar, Motilal, Nargis
🎬 **Directors** Amit Maitra, Sombhu Mitra
🎞 **Producer** Raj Kapoor
🎵 **Music composer** Salil Choudhury
📖 **Scriptwriters** Amit Maitra, Sombhu Mitra

Jagte Raho (Stay Awake) was produced by Raj Kapoor (see pp. 44–45), who also played the lead role. The film is about a poor peasant who arrives in the big city of Mumbai (then Bombay) looking for work, only to get caught up in a series of misadventures. Thirsty, he enters an apartment building but is chased away by the residents as they take him for a thief. He runs from one apartment to another and witnesses the many dubious activities of the "respectable" middle-class city dwellers. Apart from memorable performances by Raj Kapoor, Motilal, Daisy Irani, and Nargis in a cameo, the songs with lyrics by Prem Dhawan and Shailendra, set to music by Salil Choudhury, are particularly memorable. The film was also produced in Bengali as *Ek Din Raatre* (1956).

Tumsa Nahin Dekha 1957

★ **Actors** Ameeta, Shammi Kapoor, Pran
🎬 **Director** Nasir Hussain
🎞 **Producer** Sashadhar Mukherjee
🎵 **Music composer** O.P. Nayyar
📖 **Scriptwriter** Nasir Hussain

Scriptwriter Nasir Hussain turned director with the film *Tumsa Nahin Dekha* (Never Seen Anyone Like You). Initially planned as a vehicle to launch Ameeta into superstardom, the film instead made an overnight sensation out of the then struggling actor Shammi Kapoor (see p. 79), who took on the role after Dev Anand supposedly turned it down. This was the first film in which Kapoor's distinctive acting style and flair for musicals became evident. The plot had a bit of everything, including a murder, a love story, and a theme of mistaken identity. The music played a pivotal role in making the film a huge box office success, with songs written by Majrooh Sultanpuri and music by O.P. Nayyar.

Sujata 1959

★ **Actors** Sunil Dutt, Nutan, Shashikala
🎬 **Director** Bimal Roy
🎞 **Producer** Bimal Roy
🎵 **Music composer** S.D. Burman
📖 **Scriptwriter** Nabendu Ghosh

Based on a short story by noted Bengali writer and journalist Subodh Ghosh, *Sujata* is a sensitive portrayal of caste and caste-based discrimination in India. The filmmaker was inspired by the

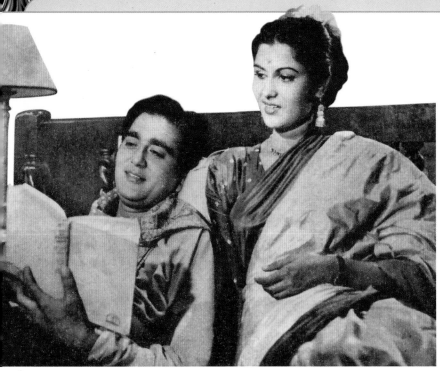

SUNIL DUTT AND SHASHIKALA IN *SUJATA*

campaign of Indian politician and social reformer Dr. B.R. Ambedkar against untouchability, and by Bengali writer Rabindranath Tagore's dance drama *Chandalika* (1938). The influence of both can be discerned in the film. The character Sujata, played by Nutan, is an untouchable woman brought up by a Brahman couple, along with their own daughter Rama, played by Shashikala. Never fully embraced by her adoptive mother, Sujata faces constant, subtle ostracism at home. Matters take a turn for the worse when a young man, Adheer (Sunil Dutt), meant as a match for Rama, instead falls in love with Sujata. Nutan's formidable performance won her the Filmfare Best Actress Award, and the film was entered into the 1960 Cannes Film Festival. Today, it is best remembered for the haunting melodies composed by music director S.D. Burman, particularly the song "Jalte Hain Jiske Liye Teri Aankhon Ke Diye" (For Whom Your Eyes Light Up) sung by Talat Mahmood.

Kanoon 1960
★ **Actors** Ashok Kumar, Rajendra Kumar, Mehmood, Nanda, Nana Palsikar
🎬 **Director** B.R. Chopra
⬠ **Producers** Anano, B.R. Chopra, Sarup Singh
🎵 **Music composer** Salil Choudhury
📖 **Scriptwriters** Akhtar-Ul-Iman, C.J. Pavri

Courtroom drama *Kanoon* (Law) was India's second songless talkie (Tamil production *Andha Naal*, 1954, had been the first). A film with a reformist agenda, it is actually a plea against capital punishment. It narrates the story of a young lawyer, Kailash (Rajendra Kumar), who suspects his

mentor, Judge Badri Prasad (Ashok Kumar), of murder. What follows is a thrilling psychological spectacle with a surprising twist in its tail. *Kanoon* won an array of awards including the National Film Award for Best Feature Film in Hindi and the Filmfare Award for Best Director. Ashok Kumar's role in the film led to an interesting legal phenomenon: any person whose true identity is unknown or must be withheld in legal action is called "Ashok Kumar" in the Indian courts.

Chaudhvin Ka Chand 1960
★ **Actors** Guru Dutt, Waheeda Rehman, Rehman, Johnny Walker
🎬 **Director** Mohammed Sadiq
⬠ **Producer** Guru Dutt
🎵 **Music composer** Ravi
📖 **Scriptwriter** Abrar Alvi

A love triangle with Guru Dutt, Rehman, and Waheeda Rehman in the lead roles, *Chaudhvin Ka Chand* (Full Moon) was produced by Guru Dutt and directed by Mohammed Sadiq. After the disastrous failure of *Kaagaz ke Phool* (see p. 65), the commercial success of this film helped to establish Guru Dutt as an actor and save his production house from ruin. The story unfolds in the city of Lucknow, where two friends (Guru Dutt and Rehman) fall in love with the same beautiful woman (Waheeda). An effervescent Johnny Walker provides much-needed comic relief in the film, while the young Farida Jalal makes her Bollywood debut with a cameo appearance. *Chaudhvin Ka Chand* also featured critically acclaimed music: Guru Dutt's favorite lyricist Shakeel Badayuni

wrote the songs and Ravi composed the music. An interesting choice was to have the title sequence in color while the rest of the film was shot in black and white.

Kabuliwala 1961
★ **Actors** Usha Kiran, Balraj Sahni, Sonu
🎬 **Director** Hemen Gupta
⬠ **Producer** Bimal Roy
🎵 **Music composer** Salil Choudhury
📖 **Scriptwriters** Vishram Bedekar, S. Khalil

Hemen Gupta's *Kabuliwala* (The Fruit Seller) is based on the popular short story of the same name by Bengali writer Rabindranath Tagore. It is a straightforward, somewhat sentimental tale of love and friendship between Abdur Rahamat Khan (Sahni), an Afghan immigrant and vendor of dry fruits, and Mini (Sonu), a little girl living in Kolkata (then Calcutta) who reminds the homesick Abdur of his own daughter in Kabul. The film's greatest strength is the sincerity of the performances by Sahni and little Sonu as Abdur and Mini. The story has a strong underlying social message too—it condemns the Indian middle-class's suspicion of foreigners. Salil Choudhury's music (sung by Manna Dey and Hemant Kumar) perfectly complements the themes of parting and longing. In addition to *Kabuliwala*, Hemen Gupta directed many other successful films, such as *Taksaal* (1956), also starring Balraj Sahni, and *Netaji Subhas Chandra Bose* (1966).

Gunga Jumna 1961
★ **Actors** Nasir Khan, Dilip Kumar, Vyjayanthimala
🎬 **Director** Nitin Bose
⬠ **Producer** Dilip Kumar
🎵 **Music composer** Naushad
📖 **Scriptwriter** Dilip Kumar

A dacoit drama that pits brother against brother, *Gunga Jumna* features Dilip Kumar as the protagonist, Gunga, with Vyjayanthimala playing Dhanno, his love interest. Dilip Kumar's real-life brother, Nasir Khan, took the part of Jumna, his brother in the film. Gunga is unjustly accused of a crime he did not commit by an evil landlord, and flees to the mountains with Dhanno, where he becomes a bandit. Years later, Jumna, now a police officer, returns to the village and demands that Gunga surrender to the law. When he refuses, his brother shoots him dead, despite the fact that it was Gunga who paid for the education that enabled him to become a police officer. *Gunga Jumna* was one of the biggest hits of the 1960s and won numerous awards in India

and abroad, including at the Boston International Film Festival. It is remembered today for its use of Bhojpuri dialect and its rustic setting. A cult classic, it is the first of many films featuring brothers on opposite sides of the law—for example, *Deewaar* (see p. 130), *Trishul*, and *Amar Akbar Anthony* (see pp. 148–49).

Bees Saal Baad 1962
★ **Actors** Biswajeet, Madan Puri, Waheeda Rehman, Sajjan, Asit Sen
🎬 **Director** Biren Nag
⬠ **Producer** Hemant Kumar
🎵 **Music composer** Hemant Kumar
📖 **Scriptwriter** Dev Kishan

Bees Saal Baad (20 Years Later) is a psychological thriller produced by Hemant Kumar, who also composed the music and sang some of the songs. A loose adaptation of the Bengali film *Jighansa* (1951), which in turn was based on Sir Arthur Conan Doyle's *The Hound of the Baskervilles* (1902), the film went on to become the biggest hit of 1962, with its haunting songs topping the charts. In fact, the song "Kahin Deep Jale Kahin Dil" (Somewhere Burns a Lamp, Somewhere a Heart), was so popular that it won Filmfare Awards for its singer, Lata Mangeshkar, and lyricist, Shakeel Badayuni.

Teesri Kasam 1966
★ **Actors** Iftekhar, Raj Kapoor, Waheeda Rehman, Asit Sen
🎬 **Director** Basu Bhattacharya
⬠ **Producer** Shailendra
🎵 **Music composers** Shankar–Jaikishan
📖 **Scriptwriter** Nabendu Ghosh

This Basu Bhattacharya drama is based on the short story *Maare Gaye Gulfam* by Hindi writer Phanishwarnath Renu, who also wrote dialogue for the film. The plot centers around Hiraman (Raj Kapoor), a simple bullcart driver from a remote village in Bihar, who falls in love with Hirabai (Waheeda), a traveling *nautanki* (folk theater) dancer considered a prostitute by the rest of the villagers. Most of the film was shot in the villages of Bihar and Madhya Pradesh, and Subrata Mitra, a cinematographer who worked with filmmaker Satyajit Ray, was part of the team. Keeping in mind the rural setting and theme of discrimination against women, Bhattacharya stuck to a realistic style throughout the film. Although the film was a commercial failure, both Raj Kapoor and Waheeda Rehman were praised for their sensitive performances, and *Teesri Kasam* (The Third Vow) won the National Film Award for Best Feature Film in 1967.

Mera Naam Joker 1970

★ **Actors** Dharmendra, Simi Garewal, Raj Kapoor, Rishi Kapoor, Manoj Kumar, Dara Singh

🎬 **Director** Raj Kapoor

🎬 **Producer** Raj Kapoor

🎵 **Music composers** Shankar–Jaikishan

📖 **Scriptwriter** K.A. Abbas

Mera Naam Joker (My Name is Joker) is supposedly based on the life of director Raj Kapoor, who took the lead role. One of the longest films (four hours) in Indian cinema, it followed Raj Kapoor's blockbuster *Sangam* (see pp. 80–81) and took six years to make. The plot follows the travails of Raju, a circus clown with a heart of gold, who always makes people laugh despite his own deep unhappiness. Apart from Raj Kapoor, the film's cast included Manoj Kumar, Simi Garewal, Dharmendra, Dara Singh, and a young Rishi Kapoor. Although the film was initially criticized for its length and experimental plot, an abridged version released in the 1980s proved to be a commercial success and today the film is viewed as Raj Kapoor's "misunderstood masterpiece." The initial box office failure of the film pushed the director into financial crisis, but he always maintained that *Mera Naam Joker* was among his favorite films.

Kati Patang 1970

★ **Actors** Bindu, Prem Chopra, Rajesh Khanna, Asha Parekh

🎬 **Director** Shakti Samanta

🎬 **Producer** Shakti Samanta

🎵 **Music composer** R.D. Burman

📖 **Scriptwriters** Vrajendra Gaur, Gulshan Nanda

Shakti Samanta's hit film was adapted by Gulshan Nanda from his novel of the same name, inspired by American novelist Cornell Woolrich's *I Married a Dead Man* (1948). Heartbroken runaway bride Madhavi (Asha Parekh) decides to impersonate her widowed friend, Poonam, but complications ensue when forest ranger Kamal (Rajesh Khanna) falls in love with her. After a murder and many twists and turns, the lovers are dramatically united just as Madhavi is about to throw herself off a cliff. *Kati Patang* (Untethered Kite) is one of a string of 17 hits delivered by lead actor Rajesh Khanna (see pp. 106–107) between 1969 and 1971. Asha Parekh's sensitive portrayal of Madhavi won

CLOWN PUPPET FROM *MERA NAAM JOKER*

her the Filmfare Award for Best Actress. The music by R.D. Burman (see p. 109) was also a hit, particularly Kishore Kumar's "Yeh Shaam Mastani" (This Evening Is Lively) and "Pyar Deewana Hota Hai" (Love Is Crazy). Another hit song, "Mera Naam Hai Shabnam" (My Name Is Shabnam), sung by Asha Bhosle, was inspired by the talk-sing style of Rex Harrison in *My Fair Lady* (1964) and is often regarded as the first Hindi rap number.

Sharmeelee 1971

★ **Actors** Nazir Hussain, Shashi Kapoor, Rakhee

🎬 **Director** Samir Ganguly

🎬 **Producer** Subodh Mukherjee

🎵 **Music composer** S.D. Burman

📖 **Scriptwriter** Gulshan Nanda

Rakhee played a dual role in Samir Ganguly's *Sharmeelee* (Shy), opposite Shashi Kapoor. A tale of love and mistaken identity, the film shows a young army captain mistakenly betrothed to the shy twin sister of the high-spirited young woman he fell in love with. The film was a hit at the box office and helped establish Rakhee as one of the top leading ladies of the 1970s. The songs, composed by S.D. Burman and sung by Kishore Kumar, Lata Mangeshkar, and Asha Bhosle, were also very popular with the audiences.

Koshish 1972

★ **Actors** Jaya Bhaduri, Sanjeev Kumar

🎬 **Director** Gulzar

🎬 **Producers** Romu N. Sippy, Raj N. Sippy

🎵 **Music composer** Madan Mohan

📖 **Scriptwriter** Gulzar

A landmark film with a strong social message, *Koshish* (Attempt) was directed by Gulzar (see pp. 142–43) and stars Jaya Bhaduri and Sanjeev Kumar as Aarthi and Hari, respectively, a deaf-mute couple struggling with life in an indifferent and insensitive society. Hari and Aarthi meet, fall in love, and have a son who dies because of Aarthi's conniving brother. However, Hari and Aarthi fight against all odds to survive this tragedy and, in time, give birth to another son, who later falls in love with a deaf girl. The film received much critical acclaim for its fresh perspective, and won National Film Awards for Best Screenplay and Best Actor. It was later remade in Tamil as *Uyarndhavargal* (1977).

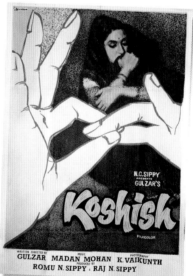

POSTER FOR *KOSHISH*

Chhoti Si Baat 1975

★ **Actors** Asrani, Ashok Kumar, Amol Palekar, Vidya Sinha

🎬 **Director** Basu Chatterjee

🎬 **Producer** B.R. Chopra

🎵 **Music composer** Salil Choudhury

📖 **Scriptwriter** Basu Chatterjee

Basu Chatterjee's quirky romantic comedy, *Chhoti Si Baat* (A Small Matter), takes us back to the Mumbai (then Bombay) of the 1970s. The film established Amol Palekar as an actor with a flair for playing a comic character that was to become his hallmark. The film also has cameo performances by popular actors such as Dharmendra, Hema Malini, and

Amitabh Bachchan (see pp. 126–27) playing themselves—a typical Basu Chatterjee feature. A commercial success when it was released, *Chhoti Si Baat* won the Filmfare Award for Best Screenplay. The music, composed by Salil Choudhury, was a great hit. The song "Jaaneman Jaaneman Tere Do Nayan" (Darling, O Darling, Your Eyes) in particular contributed to the film's success.

Parvarish 1977

★ **Actors** Shabana Azmi, Amitabh Bachchan, Shammi Kapoor, Vinod Khanna, Neetu Singh

🎬 **Director** Manmohan Desai

🎬 **Producer** A.A. Nadiadwala

🎵 **Music composers** Laxmikant–Pyarelal

📖 **Scriptwriter** Prayag Raj

A crime drama in which two brothers engage in a game of one-upmanship, *Parvarish* (Upbringing) was one of Manmohan Desai's four hit films of 1977—the others were *Dharam Veer* (see p. 150), *Chacha Bhatija*, and *Amar Akbar Anthony* (see pp. 148–49). The film tells the story of how honest cop Shamsher (Shammi Kapoor) adopts the son, Amit (Amitabh Bachchan), of a notorious bandit and brings him up along with his own son, Kishan (Vinod Khanna). Ironically, Kishan turns into a criminal, whereas Amit becomes an upright officer of the law. The film focuses on how each brother reacts to the truth when it is finally revealed. *Parvarish* marked Shammi Kapoor's entry into the kind of character roles that he would play for the next two decades. Shabana Azmi (see p. 177) and Neetu Singh play the love interests of the two brothers.

Shaan 1980

★ **Actors** Parveen Babi, Amitabh Bachchan, Sunil Dutt, Bindiya Goswami, Shashi Kapoor, Rakhee, Shatrughan Sinha

🎬 **Director** Ramesh Sippy

🎬 **Producer** G.P. Sippy

🎵 **Music composer** R.D. Burman

📖 **Scriptwriters** Salim–Javed

An action thriller about the adventures of two small-time con men, brothers Vijay and Ravi, who get caught up in the machinations of an international crime lord, Ramesh Sippy's *Shaan* (Pride) followed his blockbuster *Sholay* (see pp. 134–37). It took three years to make and drew inspiration from Cecil B. DeMille's *The Ten Commandments* (1956) and James Bond films. Sippy wanted to repeat the cast of *Sholay*, but signed Sunil Dutt, Bindiya Goswami, and Shashi Kapoor when actors Sanjeev Kumar (see p. 137), Hema

Malini (see pp. 110–11), and Dharmendra (see pp. 152–53) turned down the roles. Although it did not achieve the degree of success of its predecessor, *Shaan* was the highest-grossing Hindi film of 1980.

Kalyug 1981

★ **Actors** Raj Babbar, Shashi Kapoor, Anant Nag, Rekha
🎬 **Director** Shyam Benegal
⬡ **Producer** Shashi Kapoor
🎵 **Music composer** Vanraj Bhatia
📖 **Scriptwriters** Shyam Benegal, Girish Karnad

A modern retelling of the great Indian epic *Mahabharata* as well as a gritty crime drama, *Kalyug* (Age of Downfall) recounts the story of a conflict between two business dynasties that leads to murder and revenge within the families. Although the film's setting bears no resemblance to that of the original story, the characters and events have a striking similarity to those of *Mahabharata*, and the references to the source material are cleverly handled. Benegal assembled an excellent cast of actors for the film, which was well received by critics, who praised the ambition of the filmmaker, the complexity of the plot, the performance of the actors, and the cinematography of Govind Nihalani. The film was entered into the 12th Moscow International Film Festival. It also won the Filmfare Award for Best Film in 1982.

Naseeb 1981

★ **Actors** Amitabh Bachchan, Rishi Kapoor, Hema Malini, Pran, Reena Roy, Shatrughan Sinha
🎬 **Director** Manmohan Desai
⬡ **Producer** Manmohan Desai
🎵 **Music composers** Laxmikant–Pyarelal
📖 **Scriptwriters** Kader Khan, Prayag Raj, K.K. Shukla

Naseeb (Destiny) is a bighearted and lavishly produced action comedy. It features director Manmohan Desai's favorite star, Amitabh Bachchan (see pp. 126–27), and several other prominent actors of the time. In the film, a lottery ticket sparks off a complicated series of adventures and misadventures, creating a complex tale of deceit and revenge but also of love, friendship, and destiny. Memorable music contributed toward making *Naseeb* one of the highest-grossing films in the history of Hindi cinema. The song "John Johny Janardan," sung by Mohammed Rafi, features cameo appearances by famous actors playing themselves, including Raj Kapoor (see pp. 44–45), Shammi Kapoor (see p. 79), Rajesh Khanna (see pp. 106–107), Dharmendra (see pp. 152–53), Waheeda Rehman (see p. 85), and Sharmila Tagore (see p. 103).

Prem Rog 1982

★ **Actors** Rishi Kapoor, Shammi Kapoor, Kulbhushan Kharbanda, Padmini Kolhapure, Raza Murad, Nanda, Om Prakash, Tanuja
🎬 **Director** Raj Kapoor
⬡ **Producer** Raj Kapoor
🎵 **Music composers** Laxmikant–Pyarelal
📖 **Scriptwriters** Jainendra Jain, K.K. Singh

A poor orphan, Devdhar (Rishi Kapoor), falls in love with Manorama (Padmini Kohlapure), the daughter of a rich, orthodox Thakur (village elder). However, in accordance with her father's wishes, Manorama is married off to a rich and handsome man. When Manorama is widowed and returns to her parental home, Devdhar is determined to win her hand, but has to face the wrath of her conservative family. *Prem Rog* (Love Sickness) greatly appealed to serious lovers of cinema for taking on tough social issues—raising a voice against caste discrimination and supporting the remarriage of widows. Padmini Kolhapure's heartfelt performance as a young widow suffering from the harsh strictures of a conservative, tradition-bound Indian community won her the Filmfare Award for Best Actress. Raj Kapoor won the same award for Best Director. The film was also listed by *Cosmopolitan* magazine as one of its top 10 "Most Romantic Films Ever."

Shakti 1982

★ **Actors** Amitabh Bachchan, Anil Kapoor, Kulbhushan Kharbanda, Dilip Kumar, Smita Patil, Amrish Puri, Rakhee
🎬 **Director** Ramesh Sippy
⬡ **Producers** Mushir Alam, Mohammad Riaz
🎵 **Music composer** R.D. Burman
📖 **Scriptwriters** Salim–Javed

The first and only film in which superstar Amitabh Bachchan starred alongside legendary actor Dilip Kumar, *Shakti* (Power) is undoubtedly one of the great Indian films. An action crime drama, it has a storyline similar to the Tamil movie *Thanga Pathakkam* (1974), which went on to be remade in Hindi as *Farz Aur Kanoon* (1982). An honest police officer Ashwini (Dilip Kumar) places his principles above the life of his son Vijay (Amitabh Bachchan), who grows up with a massive grudge against his father and turns to a life of bloodshed and crime. Both Dilip Kumar and Amitabh Bachchan were nominated for the Filmfare Award for Best Actor, which was ultimately won by Dilip Kumar.

Ardh Satya 1983

★ **Actors** Sadashiv Amrapurkar, Shafi Inamdar, Smita Patil, Amrish Puri, Om Puri, Naseeruddin Shah
🎬 **Director** Govind Nihalani
⬡ **Producers** Manmohan Shetty, Pradeep Uppoor
🎵 **Music composer** Ajit Verman
📖 **Scriptwriter** Vijay Tendulkar

This landmark film is based on a short story, *Surya* (1968), by S.D. Panvalkar. Like his 1980 film, *Aakrosh*, Govind Nihalani's *Ardh Satya* (Half-Truth) is an indictment of contemporary social ills. It tells the story of Anant Velankar (Om Puri), an idealistic police officer, struggling to do his job in a world where the police, politicians, and criminals are partners in crime. The cast of talented actors, including Amrish Puri (see p. 191), Smita Patil, Naseeruddin Shah (see p. 185), and Sadashiv Amrapurkar, adds to the force of the story. The poem that gives the film its name was written by Marathi writer Dilip Chitre and features in a crucial scene in which Jyotsna (Smita Patil), Anant's love interest, gives him a poem to read. The long scene in which he is shown reading the poem aloud, his voice slowly growing more serious as its significance sinks in, is now considered a classic. *Ardh Satya* won several awards in India, with Om Puri also winning the Best Actor Award at the Karlovy Vary International Film Festival in the Czech Republic (now Czechia).

Sharaabi 1984

★ **Actors** Amitabh Bachchan, Jaya Prada, Om Prakash, Pran
🎬 **Director** Prakash Mehra
⬡ **Producer** Satyendra Pal
🎵 **Music composer** Bappi Lahiri
📖 **Scriptwriter** Lakshmikant Sharma

Prakash Mehra's sixth consecutive film with angry young man Amitabh Bachchan, *Sharaabi* (Alcoholic) is loosely based on American filmmaker Steve Gordon's film *Arthur* (1981). The neglected child of millionaire father Amarnath (Pran), Vicky (Amitabh Bachchan) grows up into an angry,

HEMA MALINI AND AMITABH BACHCHAN IN A SCENE FROM *NASEEB*

resentful, and alcoholic adult. He refuses to fall in with the dictates of his father to marry a wealthy young woman, but instead develops feelings for Meena (Jaya Prada), the daughter of a blind old man. The furious Amarnath throws Vicky out of his house, and the rest of the film is about how the inexperienced Vicky makes his way in a cruel world. The music of *Sharaabi* was a big hit, gaining a platinum disc for record sales, and both music director Bappi Lahiri and singer Kishore Kumar received Filmfare Awards for their contributions.

Salaam Bombay! 1988

★ **Actors** Anita Kanwar, Nana Patekar, Chanda Sharma, Shafiq Syed, Hansa Vithal, Raghuvir Yadav

🎬 **Director** Mira Nair

⌂ **Producers** Mira Nair, Gabriel Auer

🎵 **Music composer** L. Subramaniam

📖 **Scriptwriters** Mira Nair, Sooni Taraporevala

Mira Nair's *Salaam Bombay!* (Greetings Bombay!) chronicles the everyday lives of Krishna (Shafiq Syed), Manju (Hansa Vithal), Chillum (Raghuvir Yadav), and their friends—all street children desperately trying to survive on the streets of Bombay (now Mumbai). Most of the child actors of *Salaam Bombay!* were real-life street children who were given training at a special workshop in Mumbai before they appeared in the film. Director Mira Nair set up the organization Salaam Baalak Trust in 1989 to rehabilitate the children who acted in the film. *Salaam Bombay!* won many national and international awards, including the Golden Camera and Audience Awards at the Cannes Film Festival and three awards at the Montreal World Film Festival. It has been named in *The New York Times'* list of "The Best 1,000 Movies Ever Made."

Ram Lakhan 1989

★ **Actors** Madhuri Dixit, Dimple Kapadia, Anil Kapoor, Satish Kaushik, Anupam Kher, Amrish Puri, Rakhee, Paresh Rawal, Jackie Shroff

🎬 **Director** Subhash Ghai

⌂ **Producer** Ashok Ghai

🎵 **Music composers** Laxmikant–Pyarelal

📖 **Scriptwriter** Ram Kelkar

Subhash Ghai's *Ram Lakhan* is a crime drama with comic highlights and a distinguished cast featuring Anil Kapoor, Jackie Shroff, Madhuri Dixit, Dimple Kapadia, Rakhee, and Anupam Kher in significant roles. Ram (Jackie Shroff), an upstanding police officer, and Lakhan (Anil Kapoor), a lighthearted dreamer,

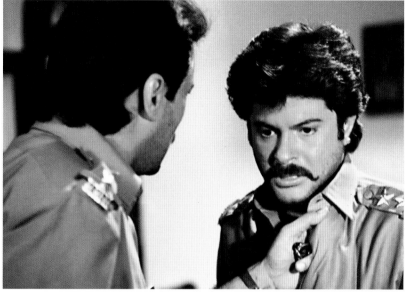

JACKIE SHROFF AND ANIL KAPOOR IN *RAM LAKHAN*

are sons of Sharda (Rakhee), whose husband has been brutally murdered by his two cousins. In time, the carefree Lakhan is seduced into a life of crime and falls out with his police officer brother. However, he soon lands in trouble and has to be rescued by Ram. Rakhee and Anupam Kher (as the father of Lakhan's love interest, Radha) shine in their respective roles and won awards for their performances. The film's popular action-comedy formula led to the making of *Ram Lakhan 2* (2018), starring Ranveer Singh and Shahid Kapoor.

Agneepath 1990

★ **Actors** Amitabh Bachchan, Mithun Chakraborty, Danny Denzongpa, Neelam Kothari, Madhavi

🎬 **Director** Mukul S. Anand

⌂ **Producer** Yash Johar

🎵 **Music composers** Laxmikant–Pyarelal, Jean-Michel Jarre

📖 **Scriptwriters** Santosh Saroj, Kader Khan

A grim gangster film with Amitabh Bachchan in the lead role, Mukul Anand's *Agneepath* (The Path of Fire) tells the story of a young man whose quest for revenge destroys his character, obliterating his ability to distinguish between good and bad. Bachchan's portrayal of the bloodthirsty Vijay Deenanath Chauhan won him his first National Film Award for Best Actor, and Mithun Chakraborty received the Best Supporting Actor Award for his role as Vijay's friend Krishnan Iyer. The title of the film is derived from a poem of the same name by Harivansh Rai Bachchan, Amitabh's father and a noted Indian poet. The poem is recited at the beginning of the movie. The film was shot extensively in Mumbai (then

Bombay) and drew positive feedback from critics for its photography. A commercial failure at the time of its release, *Agneepath* is regarded as a cult classic today and was remade in 2012 by Karan Johar.

Ek Doctor Ki Maut 1990

★ **Actors** Shabana Azmi, Anil Chatterjee, Pankaj Kapur, Irfan Khan, Deepa Sahi

🎬 **Director** Tapan Sinha

⌂ **Producer** National Film Development Corporation

🎵 **Music composer** Vanraj Bhatia

📖 **Scriptwriter** Tapan Sinha

Bengali director Tapan Sinha's award-winning film is about a junior doctor, Dipankar Roy (Pankaj Kapur), who

POSTER FOR *EK DOCTOR KI MAUT*

after years of research finds a vaccine for leprosy and becomes an overnight celebrity. However, instead of gaining respect, he falls victim to petty

professional jealousy and bureaucratic arrogance. He suffers a heart attack and is transferred to a far-off village, while two Americans receive credit for his discovery. In the end, however, Dipankar decides to continue his work of finding cures for disease. The film is based on the novel *Abhimanyu* (1982) by Ramapada Choudhury and was inspired by the life of Dr. Subhash Mukhopadhyay, an Indian physician who did pioneering work in the field of in vitro fertilization (IVF). Received well by critics, *Ek Doctor Ki Maut* (Death of a Doctor) went on to win several National Film Awards.

Saajan 1991

★ **Actors** Madhuri Dixit, Sanjay Dutt, Kader Khan, Salman Khan

🎬 **Director** Lawrence D'Souza

⌂ **Producer** Sudhakar Bokade

🎵 **Music composers** Nadeem–Shravan

📖 **Scriptwriter** Reema Rakeshnath

Lawrence D'Souza's *Saajan* (Beloved) is a romantic drama about two brothers who fall in love with the same woman. Aman (Sanjay Dutt) is a poor orphan who is adopted by the wealthy parents of Akash (Salman Khan), his friend. Pooja (Madhuri Dixit), a beautiful young woman, is enchanted by Aman's poetry and begins writing to him. Akash meets and falls in love with Pooja, but after a series of misunderstandings she is united with Aman, her true love. The film's music was a hit. All the singers were nominated for Filmfare Awards, and Kumar Sanu won Best Playback Singer for the song "Mera Dil Bhi Kitna Pagal Hai" (My Heart Is So Crazy). Other popular songs included "Dekha Hai Pehli Baar" (For the First Time I've Seen), "Jiye Toh Jiye Kaise" (How Do I Live), and "Bahut Pyar Karte Hai" (I Love You So Much). *Saajan* became the highest-grossing Bollywood film of 1991 and the fifth-highest-grossing Hindi film of the decade.

Roja 1992

★ **Actors** Madhoo, Arvind Swamy

🎬 **Director** Mani Ratnam

⌂ **Producer** K. Balachander

🎵 **Music composer** A.R. Rahman

📖 **Scriptwriter** Mani Ratnam

A Tamil romantic thriller, this audience favorite was dubbed in Malayalam, Marathi, Telugu, and Hindi. *Roja* was the first of Mani Ratnam's three films depicting human relationships against the backdrop of contemporary Indian politics (the other two were *Bombay*, see p. 338, and *Dil Se..*, see pp. 242–43). Madhoo plays Roja, a young girl from a village in Tamil Nadu who marries Rishi Kumar (Arvind Swamy), a cryptologist working with an intelligence agency. She travels with him to Kashmir, where all seems well until Rishi is abducted by terrorists. The film won several awards, including the National Film Award for Best Film on National Integration, making Ratnam an overnight star. It was re-released for international audiences in 2003, amid growing fear of terrorist attacks across the world. The soundtrack by A.R. Rahman (see pp. 244–45) is widely regarded as a masterpiece and was included in *TIME* magazine's "10 Best Soundtracks" of all time in 2005.

Hum Hain Rahi Pyar Ke 1993

★ **Actors** Baby Ashrafa, Sharokh Bharucha, Juhi Chawla, Aamir Khan, Kunal Khemu, Navneet Nishan, Dalip Tahil
🎬 **Director** Mahesh Bhatt
⬡ **Producer** Tahir Hussain
🎵 **Music composers** Nadeem–Shravan
📖 **Scriptwriters** Aamir Khan, Robin Bhatt

Rahul (Aamir Khan), a beleaguered businessman, hires the effervescent runaway Vaijayanti (Juhi Chawla) to look after his dead sister's mischievous children. Rahul and Vaijayanti fall in love, but their romance is threatened by the machinations of the scheming Maya (Navneet Nishan) who fancies herself a contender for Rahul's hand. However, all ends happily and Rahul is able to save his business and marry the love of his life. *Hum Hain Rahi Pyar Ke* (We Are Travelers on the Path of Love) bagged the National Film Award—Special Jury Award/Special Mention (Feature Film) and the Filmfare Best Film Award, while Juhi Chawla won the Filmfare Best Actress Award for her engaging performance as a young girl forced to flee her home to escape an arranged marriage.

1942: A Love Story 1994

★ **Actors** Anil Kapoor, Anupam Kher, Manisha Koirala, Jackie Shroff, Manohar Singh
🎬 **Director** Vidhu Vinod Chopra
⬡ **Producer** Vidhu Vinod Chopra
🎵 **Music composer** R.D. Burman
📖 **Scriptwriters** Sanjay Leela Bhansali, Kamna Chandra, Vidhu Vinod Chopra

A romantic drama set in the time of the British Raj with Anil Kapoor and Manisha Koirala in lead roles, this was the first ever Indian film to be given a U/A rating (subject to parental guidance for children under 12) for a scene in which the actors kiss. The film tells the story of Naren (Anil Kapoor) and

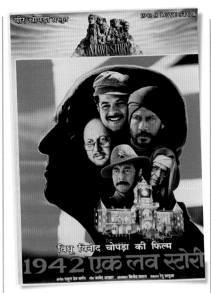

POSTER FOR *1942: A LOVE STORY*

Rajeshwari (Manisha Koirala), who fall in love with each other despite their fathers being on opposite sides of the political divide: Naren's father is a loyal British subject, whereas Rajeshwari's father is a revolutionary freedom fighter. Although its performance at the box office was average, this Vidhu Vinod Chopra feature was a hit with critics for its music, cinematography, and the performance of its leading lady. The first film in India to use Dolby stereo, *1942: A Love Story* won R.D. Burman a Filmfare Award posthumously.

Bandit Queen 1994

★ **Actors** Seema Biswas, Nirmal Pandey
🎬 **Director** Shekhar Kapur
⬡ **Producer** Bobby Bedi
🎵 **Music composers** Nusrat Fateh Ali Khan, Roger White
📖 **Scriptwriters** Ranjit Kapoor, Mala Sen

Shekhar Kapur's controversial, landmark film, *Bandit Queen*, was based on the real life of dacoit leader Phoolan Devi as recounted in the book *India's Bandit Queen: The True Story of Phoolan Devi* (1991) by Mala Sen. Seema Biswas won a National Award for her gritty portrayal of Phoolan, a woman trying to survive in a male-dominated society. The plot follows her life as a lower-caste girl from a north Indian village who is married off as a child to a physically and sexually abusive older man. Later, she is subjected to the sexual advances of upper-caste men, is raped by the police, abducted and then brutalized by a dacoit, and paraded naked before an entire village. After forming her own gang, Phoolan takes brutal revenge on her tormentors, before she finally surrenders to the law. The film received a number of awards and was

screened at Cannes and Edinburgh Film Festivals. Pakistani singer Nusrat Fateh Ali Khan composed the music for the film. Phoolan Devi, who surrendered to police in 1983 but had all charges against her dropped and was released after 11 years in prison, fiercely disputed the accuracy of the film and fought to have it banned.

Bombay 1995

★ **Actors** Manisha Koirala, Arvind Swamy
🎬 **Director** Mani Ratnam
⬡ **Producers** Mani Ratnam, Jhamu Sughand, S. Sriram
🎵 **Music composer** A.R. Rahman
📖 **Scriptwriter** Mani Ratnam

This critically acclaimed Tamil drama, dubbed and released in Hindi, stars Arvind Swamy and Manisha Koirala, and features music composed by A.R. Rahman. The film tells the story of a Hindu man and a Muslim woman from a small village in Tamil Nadu who marry in defiance of family pressure. They move to the big city of Mumbai (then Bombay). All hell breaks loose when religious tensions escalate in the city and riots erupt after the demolition of the Babri Masjid mosque in Ayodha, Uttar Pradesh, on December 6, 1992. *Bombay* was a box office blockbuster and became one of the Tamil film industry's most commercially successful films. The Hindi version earned a whopping ₹140 million (about ₹378 million / $5.8 million today). The soundtrack won A.R. Rahman his fourth Filmfare Best Music Director Award (Tamil) and sold 15 million units. Well received by critics, *Bombay* has been ranked among the top 20

Indian films by the British Film Institute (BFI). However, it was banned in Singapore and Malaysia because of its depiction of religious tensions.

Khamoshi: The Musical 1996

★ **Actors** Seema Biswas, Helen, Salman Khan, Manisha Koirala, Nana Patekar
🎬 **Director** Sanjay Leela Bhansali
⬡ **Producer** Sibte Hassan Rizvi
🎵 **Music composers** Jatin–Lalit
📖 **Scriptwriters** Sanjay Leela Bhansali, Sutapa Sikdar

The award-winning directorial debut of Sanjay Leela Bhansali (see p. 257) bagged several national awards and grossed ₹77.5 million (about ₹200 million / $3 million) in India alone. *Khamoshi* (Silence) is the story of Annie (Manisha Koirala), the daughter of a deaf-mute couple from Goa, who loves music only to have it taken away from her after the tragic death of her younger brother. However, she begins singing again after she falls in love with a Hindu boy, Raj (Salman Khan). Tragedy strikes when Annie's conservative Catholic parents turn her out of the house after she becomes pregnant with Raj's baby. The music for the film was composed by Jatin–Lalit, with lyrics written by Majrooh Sultanpuri. Popular musician Remo Fernandes composed the chart-topping songs "Shinga-Linga" and "Huiya Ho." Manisha Koirala, whose role was first offered to Madhuri Dixit (see pp. 200–201), won the 1996 Star Screen Best Actress Award for her performance. Sanjay Leela Bhansali, Seema Biswas, and singer Kavita Krishnamurthy also received Filmfare Awards for this movie.

MANISHA KOIRALA AND ARVIND SWARMY IN *BOMBAY*

Hera Pheri 2000

★ **Actors** Akshay Kumar, Paresh Rawal, Sunil Shetty, Tabu
🎬 **Director** Priyadarshan
⬠ **Producer** A.G. Nadiadwala
🎵 **Music composer** Anu Malik
▭ **Scriptwriter** Neeraj Vora

A frothy comedy that is a remake of a 1989 Malayalam film, *Hera Pheri* (Wrongdoing) was voted the best Bollywood comedy film of all time by an online poll conducted by *The Indian Express*, a leading national daily. Three down-at-heel men decide to make some money when they mistakenly receive a ransom demand for Rinku, a rich man's granddaughter. A series of comic misadventures follows. Paresh Rawal won the award for best comedian at the Filmfare, International Indian Film Academy Awards (IIFA), and Star Screen Awards, for his role as Babu Bhaiya, the hapless landlord who has to deal with tenants Raju and Shyam (Akshay Kumar and Suniel Shetty, respectively). *Hera Pheri* was such a success that Priyadarshan vowed to cast Akshay Kumar and Suniel Shetty either singly or together with Rawal in his future projects. A sequel, *Phir Hera Pheri*, was released in 2006, and *Heri Pheri 3* is anticipated.

Zubeidaa 2001

★ **Actors** Manoj Bajpayee, Lillete Dubey, Farida Jalal, Karisma Kapoor, Amrish Puri, Rekha
🎬 **Director** Shyam Benegal
⬠ **Producer** Farouq Rattonsey
🎵 **Music composer** A.R. Rahman
▭ **Scriptwriter** Khalid Mohamed

This film by Shyam Benegal is about the tumultuous life of an aspiring Muslim actress, Zubeidaa (Karisma Kapoor), who marries a Hindu Prince, Raja Hanwant Singh (Manoj Bajpayee) of Jodhpur in Rajasthan. *Zubeidaa* is the final part of a trilogy that began with *Mammo* (1994) and was followed by *Sardari Begum* (1996). With an all-star cast, the film snagged several national awards, including the National Film Award for Best Feature Film in Hindi and a Filmfare Award for Best Actress (Critics) for Karisma Kapoor (see p. 237). Audiences particularly appreciated the film's music, composed by A.R. Rahman with lyrics by writer–poet Javed Akhtar (see pp. 138–39). The extravagant jewelry worn by leading actresses Karisma Kapoor and Rekha in the film actually belonged to the royal family of Jaipur and helped to add a touch of authenticity to the production.

The Legend of Bhagat Singh 2002

★ **Actors** Raj Babbar, Ajay Devgn, Amrita Rao, D. Santosh, Sushant Singh
🎬 **Director** Rajkumar Santoshi
⬠ **Producers** Kumar Taurani, Ramesh Taurani
🎵 **Music composer** A.R. Rahman
▭ **Scriptwriter** Anjum Rajabali

Set in pre-Independence India, this film is about Bhagat Singh, an Indian freedom fighter who fought against British colonial rule. The film features Ajay Devgn in the lead role, and won great critical acclaim and two National Film Awards. The film begins with scenes where the British are trying to dispose of the body of the dead hero, so that he cannot be made into a martyr. A series of flashbacks shows how atrocities by the British Raj drove Singh and his friends to attempt the assassination of a British police officer. A sepia tint was used throughout the film to give it a period look. The film's music was well received, but the film itself failed to make a big impact with audiences.

Maqbool 2003

★ **Actors** Pankaj Kapur, Irrfan Khan, Om Puri, Naseeruddin Shah, Tabu
🎬 **Director** Vishal Bhardwaj
⬠ **Producer** Bobby Bedi
🎵 **Music composer** Vishal Bhardwaj
▭ **Scriptwriters** Vishal Bhardwaj, Abbas Tyrewala

This crime drama by Vishal Bhardwaj (see p. 289) is an adaptation of Shakespeare's *Macbeth*. With the dark Mumbai underworld as its backdrop, the film traces the tragic consequences of the growing ambition and love of Maqbool (Irrfan Khan) for Nimmi (Tabu), the mistress of his benefactor, Abba ji (Pankaj Kapur). Maqbool murders Abba ji, but both he and Nimmi are haunted by guilt and meet a tragic end. Although its performance at the box office was mediocre, the film won rave reviews from critics, and gained national and international recognition for Bhardwaj—who took on multiple tasks in the film's production as the writer, director, and music director. Kapur provides a career-best performance alongside Tabu, who shines in her complex and dark role.

HRITHIK ROSHAN WITH JAADU, THE ALIEN, IN A SCENE FROM *KOI... MIL GAYA*

Koi... Mil Gaya 2003

★ **Actors** Hrithik Roshan, Rekha, Preity Zinta
🎬 **Director** Rakesh Roshan
⬠ **Producer** Rakesh Roshan
🎵 **Music composer** Rajesh Roshan
▭ **Scriptwriters** Honey Irani, Rakesh Roshan, Robin Bhatt, Sachin Bhowmick

Bollywood's very first sci-fi film was the biggest hit of 2003 and bagged all major National Awards, including those for the Best Picture, Best Director, and Best Actor. Influenced by both Steven Spielberg's *E.T. the Extra-Terrestrial* (1982) and the 1960s story *Bankubabur Bandhu* by Satyajit Ray, *Koi... Mil Gaya* (I Found Someone) is the story of a disabled boy, Rohit (Hrithik Roshan), who comes into contact with an alien. The film was declared a blockbuster by the Indian box office, which led Rakesh Roshan to make two sequels—*Krrish* (see p. 285) and *Krrish 3*. Hrithik's convincing performance was highly praised, as was the film's music.

Veer-Zaara 2004

★ **Actors** Shah Rukh Khan, Rani Mukerji, Preity Zinta
🎬 **Director** Yash Chopra
⬠ **Producers** Aditya Chopra, Yash Chopra
🎵 **Music composers** Madan Mohan, Sanjeev Kohli
▭ **Scriptwriter** Aditya Chopra

This story of star-crossed lovers Veer and Zaara is set against the backdrop of conflict between India and Pakistan. Veer (Shah Rukh Khan), an Indian Air Force pilot, falls in love with Zaara (Preity Zinta), a girl from Pakistan. However, Veer's attempt to take Zaara home with him leads to severe consequences. The lovers are united years later after an idealistic young Pakistani lawyer, Saamiya Siddiqui (Rani Mukerji), intervenes on their behalf. *Veer-Zaara* won several national awards and became the top-grossing film of the year, earning more than ₹942 million (about ₹1.6 billion / $24.5 million today) worldwide. It was screened at multiple film festivals, including the Berlin Film Festival.

Main Hoon Na 2004

★ **Actors** Shah Rukh Khan, Zayed Khan, Amrita Rao, Sushmita Sen, Naseeruddin Shah, Sunil Shetty
🎬 **Director** Farah Khan
⬠ **Producer** Red Chillies Entertainment
🎵 **Music composer** Anu Malik
▭ **Scriptwriters** Abbas Tyrewala, Farah Khan, Rajesh Saathi

Farah Khan's directorial debut is based on a story by Anvita Dutt Guptan. It tells the story of an Indian army officer,

SHAH RUKH KHAN AND SUSHMITA SEN IN *MAIN HOON NA*

Major Ram Prasad Sharma (Shah Rukh), who gets involved in "Project Milap," an operation to release civilian captives on either side of the India–Pakistan border. *Main Hoon Na* (I Am Here) was the first film made by Shah Rukh Khan's production company, Red Chillies Entertainment, and it went on to become the second-highest-grossing Indian movie in 2004. A relatively objective take on the continuing conflict between India and Pakistan, *Main Hoon Na* included many typically Bollywood masala (see pp. 186–87) elements and is considered a thriller, musical, comedy, and action movie all rolled into one.

Black Friday 2004

★ **Actors** Pavan Malhotra, Kay Kay Menon, Aditya Shrivastava
🎬 **Director** Anurag Kashyap
☁ **Producer** Arindam Mitra
🎵 **Music composer** Indian Ocean
📖 **Scriptwriter** Anurag Kashyap

Black Friday is based on Hussain Zaidi's book *Black Friday: The True Story of the Bombay Bomb Blasts* (2002) about the bombings that killed more than 250 people on March 12, 1993, in Mumbai (then Bombay). The film focuses on the investigations into the blasts, through stories of the different people involved. It was so controversial that the Indian Censor Board did not allow the film to be released until February 9, 2007, following the verdict on the Bombay blast case by the Terrorist and Disruptive Activities court. *Black Friday* won the Grand Jury Prize at the Indian Film Festival of Los Angeles and was a nominee for the Best Film (Golden Leopard) award at the Locarno International Film Festival. The music,

particularly the song "Bandeh" (Hey, Humans), became immensely popular, and the album sold extremely well.

Lakshya 2004

★ **Actors** Amitabh Bachchan, Hrithik Roshan, Preity Zinta
🎬 **Director** Farhan Akhtar
☁ **Producer** Ritesh Sidhwani
🎵 **Music composers** Shankar–Ehsaan–Loy
📖 **Scriptwriter** Javed Akhtar

Hrithik Roshan and Preity Zinta play lead roles in this war drama about a shiftless young man who discovers his true purpose in life after becoming an officer in the Indian Army. Set at the time of the Kargil War in 1999, *Lakshya* (Objective) was shot at different locations in the mountainous state of Uttarakhand, with the Kargil scenes using the backdrop of Ladakh and Jammu and Kashmir. The scenes relating to Hrithik's military training were shot at the Indian Military Academy in Dehradun. Real-life Indian Army officers also appear in the film. *Lakshya* was not as well received as Farhan Akhtar's *Dil Chahta Hai* (see pp. 264–65). However, Hrithik's performance is regarded today as one of the actor's finest.

Paheli 2005

★ **Actors** Amitabh Bachchan, Rani Mukerji, Shah Rukh Khan
🎬 **Director** Amol Palekar
☁ **Producer** Red Chillies Entertainment
🎵 **Music composer** M.M. Keeravani
📖 **Scriptwriter** Sandhya Gokhale

An unusual and moving tale of supernatural love, *Paheli* (Riddle) is based on a short story by Rajasthani

writer Vijayadan Detha. In the film, a new bride, Lachchi (Rani Mukerji), is left alone when her husband Kishen (Shah Rukh Khan) goes off on a five-year business trip soon after their unconsummated wedding night. The next day, a ghost appears, disguised as Lachchi's husband, and voices his love for her. Shah Rukh plays the dual role of Kishen and the ghost with great sensitivity, while Rani is radiant as Lachchi. Shah Rukh decided to co-produce the film because of its feminist theme and the interesting treatment of the conflict between female desire and societal norms. *Paheli* was shot in Rajasthan in 45 days. It has achieved greater success abroad than in India and has been screened at international festivals. It was also India's official entry for the Academy Awards in 2006.

Mangal Pandey: The Rising 2005

★ **Actors** Aamir Khan, Rani Mukerji, Toby Stephens
🎬 **Director** Ketan Mehta
☁ **Producers** Bobby Bedi, Deepa Sahi, Ketan Mehta
🎵 **Music composer** A.R. Rahman
📖 **Scriptwriter** Farrukh Dhondy

Mangal Pandey is based on the real-life story of an Indian sepoy who fought against British rule in the Indian Mutiny of 1857. The film was the comeback vehicle for Aamir Khan (see pp. 228–29) after a gap of a few years (his last film had been *Dil Chahta Hai* in 2001). Although *Mangal Pandey* was only an average hit at the box office, it received positive reviews from critics who saw it as a study of oppressive imperialism and its aftermath. Nevertheless, different political parties demanded a ban on the film for its "inaccurate" and "offensive" portrayal of Pandey (one scene shows him visiting a prostitute) and there were violent protests in the district of Ballia, Uttar Pradesh, the birthplace of Mangal Pandey.

Iqbal 2005

★ **Actors** Girish Karnad, Naseeruddin Shah, Shreyas Talpade
🎬 **Director** Nagesh Kukunoor
☁ **Producer** Subhash Ghai
🎵 **Music composers** Himesh Reshammiya, Salim–Sulaiman, Sukhwinder Singh
📖 **Scriptwriter** Vipul K Rawal

Iqbal is a coming-of-age story about a young deaf-mute boy from a village who dreams of conquering obstacles and fulfilling his dream of playing for the Indian cricket team. The film was well received by both critics and audiences, and it won the National Film Award for Best Film on Other

STILL FROM THE FILM *PAHELI*

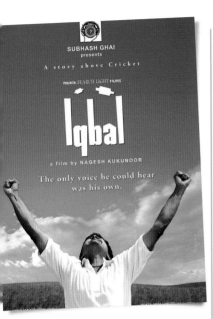

POSTER FOR *IQBAL*

Social Issues, as well as several other accolades. It was screened at the Independence Day Film Festival jointly presented by the Indian Directorate of Film Festivals and the Ministry of Defense to commemorate India's 70th Independence Day.

Bunty aur Babli 2005

★ **Actors** Abhishek Bachchan, Amitabh Bachchan, Rani Mukerji
🎬 **Director** Shaad Ali
◯ **Producer** Aditya Chopra
🎵 **Music composers** Shankar–Ehsaan–Loy
📖 **Scriptwriter** Jaideep Sahni

Shaad Ali's lighthearted crime comedy, with Rani Mukerji and Abhishek Bachchan in the lead roles, was the first film in which Amitabh Bachchan shared screen space with his son Abhishek. One of the biggest hits of 2005, *Bunty aur Babli* was inspired by the American classic *Bonnie and Clyde* (1967), but without its dark overtones. It is about the adventures of two cheerful con artists, Rakesh and Vimmi, who trick people until police officer Dashrath Singh (Amitabh) catches up with them. The music of the film was praised for its youth and novelty. An unfortunate consequence of the film was that it inspired several real-life couples to emulate the glamorous Bunty and Babli in their life of crime. On the fashion front, designer Aki Narula's *kurtis* (tunics) and *patiala salwars* (pleated trousers) for Rani sparked off a new fashion trend. The film's music is one of the highlights, with "Dhadak Dhadak" (Clattering and Whistling) and "Kajra Re" (Your Kohl-lined Eyes) the most popular songs.

Khosla ka Ghosla! 2006

★ **Actors** Parvin Dabas, Boman Irani, Anupam Kher, Vinay Pathak, Ranvir Shorey
🎬 **Director** Dibakar Banerjee
◯ **Producers** Ronnie Screwvala, Savita Raj Hiremath
🎵 **Music composers** Bapi–Tutul, Dhruv Dhalla
📖 **Scriptwriter** Jaideep Sahni

Dibakar Banerjee's low-budget comedy drama, his directorial debut, is about a simple middle-class man, Kamal Khosla (Anupam Kher), who tries to get his land back from a corrupt property dealer, Kishan Khurana (Boman Irani), with the help of his sons and their friends. The film opened to mixed reviews, but critics praised Banerjee for focusing on the common man's struggle against the rich and powerful, and for a comic verve that reminded audiences of the much-loved classics *Golmaal* (see p. 157) and *Jaane Bhi Do Yaaron* (see p. 179).

Dor 2006

★ **Actors** Girish Karnad, Gul Panag, Ayesha Takia, Shreyas Talpade
🎬 **Director** Nagesh Kukunoor
◯ **Producer** Elahe Hiptoola
🎵 **Music composers** Salim Merchant, Sulaiman Merchant
📖 **Scriptwriter** T.A. Razak

The story about a friendship between two women who come together in unusual circumstances, *Dor* (String) is a remake of the Malayalam film *Perumazhakkalam* (2004). Shreyas Talpade plays a *bahuroopiya* (mimic) who helps Zeenat (Gul Panag), an independent Muslim woman fighting to save her husband, who is on trial for murder. The *bahuroopiya* connects Zeenat with Meera (Ayesha Takia), the Hindu widow of the man who was murdered, herself from a conservative Rajasthani family. Their relationship is fraught but ultimately redemptive. Talpade studied the *bahuroopiyas* of Rajasthan for their dialect, accent, and mannerisms, for this challenging role. Despite not striking it big at the box office, *Dor* garnered rave reviews from critics for its feminist theme, engaging storyline, and cinematography.

Gangster 2006

★ **Actors** Shiney Ahuja, Emraan Hashmi, Kangana Ranaut
🎬 **Director** Anurag Basu
◯ **Producers** Mahesh Bhatt, Mukesh Bhatt
🎵 **Music composer** Pritam
📖 **Scriptwriters** Anurag Basu, Mahesh Bhatt

This action-packed love triangle about loss, betrayal, and redemption by director Anurag Basu is the story of bar girl Simran (Kangana Ranaut in her debut role), the mistress of notorious gangster Daya (Shiney Ahuja), who falls in love with Aakash (Emraan Hashmi), a singer in a restaurant. Aakash is actually an undercover detective on a mission to capture Daya. In response to rumors that the story was inspired by the romance between underworld boss Abu Salem and Bollywood actress Monica Bedi, the director has maintained that the film is not based on real-life characters or incidents. *Gangster* was a hit at the box office and its music was also very popular with songs such as "Tu hi Meri Shab hai" (You're My Night, My Day) being declared superhits within a week of the film's release. Critics were particularly impressed by Kangana, whose performance as an alcoholic woman torn between two men is refreshing. Hashmi, too, was praised for his natural, understated performance as an undercover agent.

Johnny Gaddaar 2007

★ **Actors** Dharmendra, Neil Nitin Mukesh, Vinay Pathak, Rimi Sen
🎬 **Director** Sriram Raghavan
◯ **Producer** Adlabs Films
🎵 **Music composers** Shankar–Ehsaan–Loy
📖 **Scriptwriter** Sriram Raghavan

Neil Nitin Mukesh stars as the eponymous hero in this "neo-noir" thriller, his debut film. The plot of *Johnny Gaddaar* (Johnny the Traitor) centers around a gang of five con men whose greed for money and proximity to the underworld leads to betrayal, vengeance, and murder. Inspired by English writer James Hadley Chase and Indian filmmaker Vijay Anand, *Johnny Gaddaar* contains references to both in the film—the protagonist is shown reading a novel by Chase in one scene, while in another a hotel receptionist is seen watching Anand's *Johny Mera Naam*. The sleeper hit of the year, the film was particularly lauded for the originality and verve of the music by the team of Shankar–Ehsaan–Loy, and it won the 2008 Filmfare Award for Best Sound Design.

Guru 2007

★ **Actors** Abhishek Bachchan, Vidya Balan, Mithun Chakraborty, R. Madhavan, Aishwarya Rai,
🎬 **Director** Mani Ratnam
◯ **Producers** G. Srinivasan, Mani Ratnam
🎵 **Music composer** A.R. Rahman
📖 **Scriptwriter** Mani Ratnam

The life of Gujarati business tycoon and industrialist Dhirubhai Ambani was the inspiration behind Mani Ratnam's *Guru* (Mentor). *Guru* not only chronicles the meteoric rise of an ambitious individual, it also depicts the changing face of India from Independence to the present day. Mallika Sherawat makes a guest appearance as an exotic dancer in the item number (see pp. 290–91) "Mayya Mayya" (Water). The film premiered at the Elgin Theatre in Toronto, Canada, the first mainstream Indian film to do so. Commercially, it did very well in India and abroad (particularly in the US), receiving positive reviews for the performances of its actors, and for the songs by A.R. Rahman.

AISHWARYA RAI AND ABHISHEK BACHCHAN IN *GURU*

Ghajini 2008

★ **Actors** Aamir Khan, Asin, Pradeep Rawat
🎬 **Director** A.R. Murugadoss
⌂ **Producers** Allu Aravind, Madhu Mantena, Tagore Madhu
🎵 **Music composer** A.R. Rahman
📖 **Scriptwriter** A.R. Murugadoss

Ghajini is a Hindi remake of director A.R. Murugadoss's 2005 Tamil feature of the same name. Aamir Khan plays Sanjay Singhania, a man who develops anterograde amnesia after losing his love Kalpana (Asin), a model, who has been brutally murdered by Ghajini (Pradeep Rawat), a powerful criminal. Sanjay tries to avenge her death with the help of photographs, notes, and tattoos on his body. The plot of the film was influenced by both Christopher Nolan's psychological thriller *Memento* (2000) and the peppy British comedy *Happy Go Lovely* (1951). *Ghajini* became the highest-grossing Hindi movie ever until it lost out to another Aamir Khan vehicle, *3 Idiots* (see pp. 302–303), in 2009. It even inspired a 3D video game, *Ghajini—The Game*. The film also had its share of controversy: Nolan claimed that Murugadoss had copied *Memento* without his permission, although the Bollywood director maintains *Ghajini* is not a Hindi remake of Nolan's film.

A Wednesday! 2008

★ **Actors** Aamir Bashir, Anupam Kher, Naseeruddin Shah, Deepal Shaw, Jimmy Shergill
🎬 **Director** Neeraj Pandey
⌂ **Producers** Shital Bhatia, Anjum Rizvi, Ronnie Screwvala
🎵 **Music composer** Sanjoy Chowdhury
📖 **Scriptwriter** Neeraj Pandey

An interesting storyline, provocative theme, and superb casting made this film the surprise hit of 2008. Based on the Mumbai train bombings of July 11, 2006, that killed nearly 200 people, *A Wednesday!* was a low-budget feature shot in a mere 28 days. A retiring police commissioner, Prakash Rathod (Anupam Kher), recounts a series of events that took place on a certain Wednesday involving a case that was never filed, but remained forever engraved in his memory. Director Neeraj Pandey was able to work with both Kher and Naseeruddin Shah, his favorite actors, for the leading roles. The film, grossing about ₹160 million (about ₹222 million / $3.5 million today) worldwide, was lauded by critics and won the Indira Gandhi Award for the Best First Film of a Director at the 56th National Film Awards. The film was remade in Tamil and Telugu, and it also inspired the American–Sri Lankan thriller *A Common Man* (2013).

Rock On!! 2008

★ **Actors** Farhan Akhtar, Prachi Desai, Shahana Goswami, Luke Kenny, Purab Kohli, Arjun Rampal
🎬 **Director** Abhishek Kapoor
⌂ **Producers** Farhan Akhtar, Ritesh Sidhwani
🎵 **Music composers** Shankar–Ehsaan–Loy
📖 **Scriptwriters** Abhishek Kapoor, Pubali Chaudhari

The acting debuts of Farhan Akhtar and Prachi Desai, *Rock On!!* is about a Mumbai-based rock band "Magik," formed by a group of four friends in 1998. As a band they are not able to make it big and part ways because of some differences. However, years later they come back together to achieve their dream of becoming a successful band. Despite its average performance at the box office, the film was well-received by critics and went on to win seven Filmfare Awards. The songs of the film were a hit with audiences, too. A long-awaited sequel, *Rock On!! 2*, was finally released in 2016 to mixed reviews.

Oye Lucky! Lucky Oye! 2008

★ **Actors** Neetu Chandra, Abhay Deol, Paresh Rawal
🎬 **Director** Dibakar Banerjee
⌂ **Producer** Ronnie Screwvala
🎵 **Music composer** Sneha Khanwalkar
📖 **Scriptwriters** Dibakar Banerjee, Urmi Juvekar

Dibakar Banerjee's hilarious black comedy has Abhay Deol in the lead role of a super thief, Lucky, who reflects on his spectacular life of crime, as the media speculates on how he got away with a series of daring burglaries in cities across India. *Oye Lucky! Lucky Oye!* (Hey Lucky!) is based on the colorful escapades of Devinder Singh (Bunty), a real-life burglar from Delhi. Although not very successful at the box office, the film garnered praise from critics for its novel and quirky subject—Lucky does not take to crime out of poverty, but out of boredom and the need to have fun—as well as its characterizations and tongue-in-cheek look at Delhi's seamy underbelly. It won the National Award for Best Popular Film.

Dev.D 2009

★ **Actors** Abhay Deol, Mahie Gill, Kalki Koechlin
🎬 **Director** Anurag Kashyap
⌂ **Producer** Ronnie Screwvala
🎵 **Music composer** Amit Trivedi
📖 **Scriptwriters** Anurag Kashyap, Vikramaditya Motwane

This gritty romantic comedy is set in Punjab and Delhi, and is based on the classic Bengali novel *Devdas* (1917).

Suspicion and ego drive Dev (Abhay Deol) away from his childhood sweetheart Paro (Mahie Gill), and he takes to drugs and alcohol. He meets Leni (Kalki Koechlin), a prostitute, in his attempt to get over Paro. *Dev.D* was praised for its psychedelic visual style, novel three-part structure, and quirky soundtrack. The movie includes references not only to classic films such as Sanjay Leela Bhansali's 2002 film *Devdas* (see pp. 274–77), but also to a number of recent real-life incidents that had been reported by the media—an underage sex scandal that took place in a Delhi school in 2004 and a 1999 hit-and-run case involving a prominent businessman.

Love Aaj Kal 2009

★ **Actors** Rishi Kapoor, Saif Ali Khan, Giselli Monteiro, Deepika Padukone
🎬 **Director** Imtiaz Ali
⌂ **Producers** Saif Ali Khan, Dinesh Vijan
🎵 **Music composer** Pritam
📖 **Scriptwriter** Imtiaz Ali

An old-fashioned romance, *Love Aaj Kal* (Love Nowadays) has Saif Ali Khan and Deepika Padukone (see pp. 328–29) in lead roles. Jai (Saif) and Meera (Deepika) are in love but, being a pragmatic, modern couple, decide to break up over their career aspirations, remaining good friends. Jai meets Veer Singh (Rishi Kapoor) who tells him the story of his own relationship through a series of flashbacks. Jai and

POSTER FOR *LOVE AAJ KAL*

Meera finally come to the realization that they truly love each other and are reunited. The two love stories, although belonging to different generations, end similarly—proving that love is universal and unchanging. A huge hit at the box office, *Love Aaj Kal* did not impress all critics, but director Imtiaz Ali was credited with creating a sentimental, romantic film with a young, modern feel. Pritam won his first International Indian Academy Awards (IIFA) Best Music Director trophy for the film.

Udaan 2010

- ★ **Actors** Aayan Boradia, Rajat Barmecha, Ram Kapoor, Ronit Roy
- 🎬 **Director** Vikramaditya Motwane
- ⬠ **Producers** Anurag Kashyap, Ronnie Screwvala, Sanjay Singh
- ♫ **Music composer** Amit Trivedi
- ▭ **Scriptwriters** Anurag Kashyap, Vikramaditya Motwane

Anurag Kashyap's own life was supposedly the inspiration behind this story of a young boy, Rohan (Rajat Barmecha), who is expelled from a boarding school and is forced to return home to his abusive father Bhairav (Ronit Roy) and six-year-old half-brother. A cult classic, the film was not commercially successful on its release, but it was well received by critics who praised the simple storyline and sensitive handling of the theme of teenage angst. The songs were loved by both audiences and critics for their innovative rock and grunge style. *Udaan* (Flight) was screened at several international film festivals, and in 2010 became the first Indian film to be shown in the official section at Cannes in seven years. It bagged an astounding seven trophies at the 56th Filmfare Awards in 2011 as well as several National Awards.

Anjaana Anjaani 2010

- ★ **Actors** Priyanka Chopra, Ranbir Kapoor
- 🎬 **Director** Siddharth Anand
- ⬠ **Producer** Sajid Nadiadwala
- ♫ **Music composers** Vishal–Shekhar
- ▭ **Scriptwriters** Advaita Kala, Siddharth Anand

Ranbir Kapoor and Priyanka Chopra took lead roles in this romantic drama. *Anjaana Anjaani* (Strangers) drew inspiration from the American TV series *Friends* and *Dilwale Dulhania le Jayenge* (see pp. 230–33). It depicts the story of a couple living in the US who repeatedly try to kill themselves after losing a fortune in the 2008 stock market crash. The film was shot in a variety of foreign locations, including New York City, Los Angeles, Las Vegas, and San Francisco in the US, as well as Malaysia and Thailand. It was declared a hit on the domestic circuit, and the high-octane performances of Ranbir Kapoor and Priyanka Chopra were appreciated by audiences. However, some critics panned the film for its flat, predictable storyline and lackluster script.

My Name is Khan 2010

- ★ **Actors** Kajol, Shah Rukh Khan
- 🎬 **Director** Karan Johar
- ⬠ **Producers** Gauri Khan, Hiroo Johar
- ♫ **Music composers** Shankar–Ehsaan–Loy
- ▭ **Scriptwriter** Shibani Bathija

My Name is Khan reunited old favorites Shah Rukh Khan and Kajol in the lead roles. The film tells the story of Rizvan, an autistic Indian Muslim (Shah Rukh), and his quest to meet the President of the United States in the aftermath of the attacks on September 11, 2001. In a 2009 interview, Shah Rukh described the controversial subject of the film to be "not about terrorism, or 9/11. It's about a relationship between two people, between an individual and the state, and between an individual and the country. In short, there are three important components: a love story, Islam, and a mild form of autism." *My Name is Khan* was distributed by FOX Star Entertainment, which bought the film rights for a stupendous ₹1 billion ($15 million), making it the most expensive Bollywood film of 2010. The movie became one of the highest-grossing Indian films ever overseas and broke records abroad.

Rockstar 2011

- ★ **Actors** Nargis Fakhri, Aditi Rao Hydari, Ranbir Kapoor, Shammi Kapoor
- 🎬 **Director** Imtiaz Ali
- ⬠ **Producer** Shree Ashtavinayak Cine Vision
- ♫ **Music composer** A.R. Rahman
- ▭ **Scriptwriters** Imtiaz Ali, Muazzam Beg

Rockstar tells the story of Janardhan Jhakar (Ranbir Kapoor), an innocent boy from the Jat community of north India, who lives in Delhi and dreams of becoming a rockstar like his idol and inspiration Jim Morrison. He falls in love with Heer Kaul (Nargis Fakhri), pursuing her even after her marriage. Although Janardhan succeeds in becoming the rock idol Jordan, his love for Heer ends tragically with her illness and death. The film did well at the box office, particularly with younger audiences, and both Ranbir Kapoor and music composer A.R. Rahman received National Awards for their significant contributions.

Dhobi Ghat 2011

- ★ **Actors** Prateik Babbar, Monica Dogra, Aamir Khan, Kriti Malhotra
- 🎬 **Director** Kiran Rao
- ⬠ **Producers** Aamir Khan, Dhillin Mehta, Tshephel Namgyal
- ♫ **Music composer** Gustavo Santaolalla
- ▭ **Scriptwriter** Anil Mehta

Kiran Rao's directorial debut, *Dhobi Ghat* (Washerman's Area) recounts the intersecting lives of four very different individuals in Mumbai. Arun (Aamir Khan), a professional painter, Munna (Prateik Babbar), a washerman who dreams of making it big in Bollywood, Shai (Monica Dogra), an American banker turned photographer, and Yasmin (Kriti Malhotra), a woman who records her life on home video. Tagged as an art-house feature, *Dhobi Ghat* premiered at the Toronto International Film Festival in 2010 and was longlisted for the 65th BAFTA Awards for the Film Not in the English Language category. Argentine musician Gustavo Santaolalla wrote the music, including the song "You With Me." Critics appreciated the film as a poetic tribute to Mumbai, although it failed to make an impact at the box office. The film did well in overseas markets, including the US, UK, and United Arab Emirates.

Ek Tha Tiger 2012

- ★ **Actors** Katrina Kaif, Girish Karnad, Salman Khan, Ranvir Shorey
- 🎬 **Director** Kabir Khan
- ⬠ **Producer** Aditya Chopra
- ♫ **Music composer** Sohail Sen
- ▭ **Scriptwriters** Kabir Khan, Neelesh Misra

A typical high-octane vehicle for Salman Khan (see pp. 224–25), Kabir Khan's *Ek Tha Tiger* (Once There was a Tiger) is an action-packed spy thriller about an Indian spy code-named Tiger (Salman Khan). He is sent to Dublin to observe an Indian scientist who is suspected of sharing his findings with Pakistan, but falls in love with the scientist's caretaker, Zoya (Katrina Kaif), in the course of his investigation. The film's trailer received more than a million views within the first two days of its release, which made it the most popular trailer ever produced for a Bollywood movie. Although *Ek Tha Tiger* went on to become the highest-grossing Hindi film of 2012 and the third-highest of all time, it received mixed reviews. It was not released in Pakistan following a ruling by the country's censor board that Pakistan was depicted in a negative light. A sequel to the film, *Tiger Zinda Hai*, was filmed on location in Abu Dhabi in 2017.

Barfi! 2012

- ★ **Actors** Priyanka Chopra, Ileana D'Cruz, Ranbir Kapoor
- 🎬 **Director** Anurag Basu
- ⬠ **Producers** Siddharth Roy Kapur, Syed Mehedi
- ♫ **Music composer** Pritam
- ▭ **Scriptwriter** Anurag Basu

Anurag Basu's *Barfi!* is about a cheerful deaf-mute Nepali boy from Darjeeling, Murphy "Barfi" Johnson (Ranbir), and his friendship and love for two women, the autistic Jhilmil Chatterjee (Priyanka), and Shruti Ghosh (Ileana). Critics accused Basu of plagiarism, but he defended *Barfi!* by claiming that the film was inspired by several Hollywood movies and great actors like Charlie Chaplin and Buster Keaton, and that it was an original production with a unique plot, screenplay, and characters. A great box office success both in India and abroad, *Barfi!* won a number of National Awards and was India's official entry for the Best Foreign Language Film for the 85th Academy Awards. The film's soundtrack was inspired by bossa nova, a genre of Brazilian music.

A SCENE FROM *VICKY DONOR*

Vicky Donor 2012

- ★ **Actors** Annu Kapoor, Ayushmann Khurrana, Yami Gautam
- 🎬 **Director** Shoojit Sircar
- ⬠ **Producers** John Abraham, Ronnie Lahiri
- ♫ **Music composers** Abhishek–Akshay Bann, Ayushmann Khurrana, Rochak Kohli
- ▭ **Scriptwriter** Juhi Chaturvedi

Vicky Donor is a romantic comedy centered around the controversial issue of infertility and sperm donation. Vicky Arora (Ayushmann Khurrana) is the unemployed son of a widow who is selected by Dr. Baldev Chaddha (Annu Kapoor) to supply sperm for his clinic. The plot tracks Vicky as he becomes a successful sperm donor, gets married, gives up donating sperm, and then goes back to it after discovering that

OTHER MOVIES

his wife Ashima (Yami) is infertile. Actor John Abraham, who produced the movie, said that the film was an attempt to draw attention to an issue still considered taboo in Indian society. Inspired by *Starbuck*, a French–Canadian film, *Vicky Donor* was well received by audiences and critics. It won the National Film Award for Best Popular Film Providing Wholesome Entertainment at the 60th National Film Awards.

Paan Singh Tomar 2012

★ **Actors** Mahie Gill, Irrfan Khan, Vipin Sharma, Nawazuddin Siddiqui
🎬 **Director** Tigmanshu Dhulia
◔ **Producer** Ronnie Screwvala
🎵 **Music composer** Abhishek Ray
📖 **Scriptwriters** Sanjay Chauhan, Tigmanshu Dhulia

This gritty biographical film is based on the life of athlete Paan Singh Tomar, a soldier in the Indian army and seven-time national steeplechase champion who was forced into a life of crime after retirement. Irrfan Khan plays the protagonist, with Mahie Gill, Vipin Sharma, and Nawazuddin Siddiqui in supporting roles. Director Tigmanshu Dhulia first became interested in Tomar while working on the set of Shekhar Kapur's *Bandit Queen* (see p. 338). The film was shot on a very low budget among the ravines of Chambal and in the barracks of Roorkee Cantonment where Tomar had lived. In preparation for his role, Irrfan Khan had to undergo intense physical training with steeplechase coaches. *Paan Singh Tomar* premiered at the 2010 London Film Festival and was a superhit at the box office. It received trophies for Best Feature Film and Best Actor at the 2012 National Film Awards.

Lootera 2013

★ **Actors** Ranveer Singh, Sonakshi Sinha
🎬 **Director** Vikramaditya Motwane
◔ **Producers** Vikas Bahl, Ekta Kapoor, Shobha Kapoor, Anurag Kashyap
🎵 **Music composer** Amit Trivedi
📖 **Scriptwriters** Bhavani Iyer, Vikramaditya Motwane

The second film to be directed by Vikramaditya Motwane, *Lootera* (Robber) was partly inspired by the short story *The Last Leaf* (1907) by American writer O. Henry. A period romance set in picturesque 1950s West Bengal, the film was shot in Dalhousie, Himachal Pradesh, and different parts of West Bengal, including Maoist-infiltrated rural areas in which police protection was needed for the crew. Its music by Amit Trivedi is a tribute to S.D. Burman and R.D. Burman, the celebrated Indian composers. One of its songs, "Monta Re" (My Thoughts), was inspired by the music of the Bauls, mystic minstrels from West Bengal and Bangladesh. Although *Lootera* did not achieve box office success, most critics acknowledged the quality of the period setting, old-fashioned romance, and attention to detail.

Goliyon Ki Raasleela: Ram-Leela 2013

★ **Actors** Deepika Padukone, Ranveer Singh
🎬 **Director** Sanjay Leela Bhansali
◔ **Producers** Sanjay Leela Bhansali, Chetan Deolekar, Kishore Lulla, Sandeep Singh
🎵 **Music composers** Sanjay Leela Bhansali, Hemu Gadhvi
📖 **Scriptwriters** Sanjay Leela Bhansali, Siddharth-Garima

Amid a long-running rivalry, the young heirs of two opposing families, Ram (Ranveer Singh) and Leela (Deepika Padukone), fall in love. Inspired by Shakespeare's tragedy *Romeo and Juliet* (1597), *Goliyon Ki*

SONG SEQUENCE FROM *BHAAG MILKHA BHAAG*

Raasleela Ram-Leela (A Play of Bullets Ram-Leela) narrates the tragic love story of two young lovers, doomed by the enmity between their families. The film's name was changed from *Ram-Leela* to *Goliyon Ki Raasleela* as some Hindu groups objected to the use of the first title as the movie did not have anything to do with *Ramlila*, a ritual reenactment of the life of Hindu deity, Rama. One of the box office hits of 2013, it won several National Awards. Reviewers acknowledged the chemistry between the lead actors and the lavishness of the production, characteristic of a Bhansali film, but were critical of the excesses of the plot.

Bhaag Milkha Bhaag 2013

★ **Actors** Farhan Akhtar, Sonam Kapoor, Pavan Malhotra, Meesha Shafi
🎬 **Director** Rakeysh Omprakash Mehra
◔ **Producers** Raghav Bahl, P. S. Bharathi, Maitreyee Dasgupta, Madhav Roy Kapur, Rachvin Narula, Shyam P. S, Navmeet Singh, Rajiv Tandon
🎵 **Music composers** Shankar–Ehsaan–Loy
📖 **Scriptwriter** Prasoon Joshi

The life of India's champion sprinter Milkha Singh was the inspiration behind *Bhaag Milkha Bhaag* (Run Milkha Run). Farhan Akhtar, who plays the "Flying Sikh," as Milkha Singh was popularly known, met the athlete and his family and underwent months of arduous physical training to prepare for this role. A huge success both in India and abroad, particularly in the US, the film became the sixth-highest-grossing Bollywood film worldwide in 2013, and won several National Awards. Based on Milkha Singh's autobiography, *The Race of My Life*, the film takes us through the many hardships that Milkha Singh overcame to become one of India's most successful athletes. Singh sold the book's film rights for just one rupee, but with the condition that

a share of the film's profits be given to his charitable trust, which helps underprivileged sportspeople.

The Lunchbox 2013

★ **Actors** Nimrat Kaur, Irrfan Khan
🎬 **Director** Ritesh Batra
◔ **Producers** Karan Johar, Siddharth Roy Kapur, Anurag Kashyap Films, Arun Rangachari, Vikramjit Roy, Meraj Shaikh, Danis Tanovic
🎵 **Music composer** Max Richter
📖 **Scriptwriter** Ritesh Batra

A lunchbox delivery gone wrong connects a lonely young wife, Ila (Nimrat Kaur), and a man on the verge of retirement, Saajan (Irrfan Khan). A friendship develops as they start sharing memories and events of their lives by the way of messages exchanged through the lunchbox. As they discover more about each other, they face choices that could alter their lives forever. Some of Mumbai's famous *dabbawalas* (lunch delivery men) were given minor roles in the film. *The Lunchbox* was a commercial and critical success, and it won the Critics Week Viewers' Choice Award, also known as Grand Rail d'Or, at Cannes in 2013. Ritesh Batra's screenplay also won an Honorable Jury Mention at the 2012 Cinemart at the Rotterdam International Film Festival.

Haider 2014

★ **Actors** Shahid Kapoor, Shraddha Kapoor, Irrfan Khan, Kay Kay Menon, Tabu
🎬 **Director** Vishal Bhardwaj
◔ **Producers** Vishal Bhardwaj, Siddharth Roy Kapur
🎵 **Music composer** Vishal Bhardwaj
📖 **Scriptwriters** Vishal Bhardwaj, Basharat Peer

Vishal Bhardwaj's gritty political drama, inspired by *Hamlet*, is the third part of a Shakespearean trilogy that included *Maqbool* (see p. 339) and

RANVEER AND DEEPIKA DANCING IN *GOLIYON KI RAASLEELA: RAM-LEELA*

Omkara (see p. 289). *Curfewed Night* (2008), Indian writer Basharat Peer's memoir, about the insurgency-hit Kashmir of the 1990s, provided the background for this movie about a young poet and student Haider (Shahid Kapoor) who returns to Kashmir after his father's disappearance only to be sucked into a web of intrigue involving murder and contemporary politics. *Haider* was released to worldwide critical acclaim and won several National Awards. It was also the first Indian film to receive the People's Choice Award at the Rome Film Festival. However, the movie became embroiled in controversy because of its depiction of human rights abuses by the Indian Army.

Drishyam 2015

★ **Actors** Ajay Devgn, Ishita Dutta, Shriya Saran, Tabu
🎬 **Director** Nishikant Kamat
⬭ **Producers** Ajit Andhare, Abhishek Pathak, Kumar Mangat Pathak
♫ **Music composer** Vishal Bhardwaj
▭ **Scriptwriter** Upendra Sidhaye

A remake of the Malayalam film of the same name, Nishikant Kamat's thriller *Drishyam* (The Sight) features Ajay Devgn in the role of Vijay Salgaonkar, a middle-aged man who conceals a gruesome murder to save his family from the legal consequences. What follows is a nail-biting cat-and-mouse game between Vijay and Inspector-General Meera Deshmukh (Tabu), the mother of the murdered boy. Gulzar (see pp. 142–43) wrote the songs for *Drishyam* and filmmaker Vishal Bhardwaj composed the music.

Masaan 2015

★ **Actors** Richa Chadda, Vicky Kaushal, Sanjay Mishra, Shweta Tripathi
🎬 **Director** Neeraj Ghaywan
⬭ **Producers** Sikhya Entertainment, Drishyam Films, Phantom Films, Macassar Productions
♫ **Music composer** Indian Ocean
▭ **Scriptwriter** Varun Grover

This Indo-French collaboration marks the debut of director Neeraj Ghaywan, who had earlier worked on the crime drama *Gangs of Wasseypur* (see p. 310). The film unfolds in the city of Varanasi, and involves two stories that intersect along the banks of the Ganges—that of Devi (Richa Chadda) and Deepak (Vicky Kaushal). Devi and her unfortunate father, Vidyadhar Pathak (Sanjay Mishra), are hounded by the police and socially ostracized after Devi is caught having sex with a fellow student while Deepak (Vicky

Kaushal), a low-caste boy from the Dom community in Varanasi, loses Shaalu (Shweta Tripathi), the upper-caste girl he is in love with. Critics praised the film for its soulful music and visual appeal, particularly the beautiful shots of the Ganges. *Masaan* (Crematorium) won the National Award for Best Debut Film of a Director and picked up two trophies in the Un Certain Regard section of the Cannes Film Festival in 2015.

Neerja 2016

★ **Actors** Shabana Azmi, Sonam Kapoor, Shekhar Ravjiani, Yogendra Tiku
🎬 **Director** Ram Madhvani
⬭ **Producers** Atul Kasbekar, Shanti Sivaram Maini, Fox Star Studios, Bling Unplugged
♫ **Music composer** Vishal Khurana
▭ **Scriptwriter** Saiwyn Quadras

Based on a real-life incident, *Neerja* tells the story of Neerja Bhanot, a brave flight attendant who lost her life while protecting the passengers aboard Pan Am Flight 73 that was hijacked by a Libyan terrorist group in 1986. The film did moderately well at the box office and impressed critics with its inspiring storyline and moving performances. Sonam Kapoor was particularly singled out for her assured portrayal of "an abused wife, a beloved daughter, and a flight attendant caught in her worst nightmare." *Neerja* swept the 62nd Filmfare Awards with six trophies, including Best Film (Critics), Best Actress (Critics) for Sonam Kapoor, and Best Supporting Actress for Shabana Azmi. The songs were described as moving, intimate, and a perfect complement to the narrative.

Airlift 2016

★ **Actors** Nimrat Kaur, Akshay Kumar
🎬 **Director** Raja Krishna Menon
⬭ **Producers** Nikhil Advani, Monisha Adwani, Aruna Bhatia, Madhu G. Bhojwani, Vikram Malhotra, Bhushan Kumar, Krishan Kumar
♫ **Music composers** Amaal Mallik, Ankit Tiwari
▭ **Scriptwriters** Raja Krishna Menon, Suresh Nair, Rahul Nangia, Ritesh Shah

Airlift recounts the story of Ranjit Katyal (Akshay Kumar), a well-to-do Indian businessman who assists in the evacuation of Indians living in Kuwait during its invasion by Iraq in 1990. Katyal's character, although fictional, was based on the life of Mathunny Mathews, a resident of Kuwait who actually helped evacuate about 170,000 Indians. As inspiration for his character, Akshay Kumar also cited Balraj Sahni's portrayal of Lala Kedarnath Prasanta in *Waqt* (see p. 92) in which a sudden earthquake destroys lives. The

filmmakers collaborated with Air India, which played a major role in evacuating stranded Indians during the invasion. Although *Airlift* was lauded for its taut storyline and Akshay's sincere and convincing performance, it was criticized for oversimplifying a complex operation and for portraying Indian officials in a misleading way.

Rangoon 2017

★ **Actors** Shahid Kapoor, Saif Ali Khan, Kangana Ranaut
🎬 **Director** Vishal Bhardwaj
⬭ **Producers** Viacom 18 Media Pvt Ltd, Nadiadwala Grandson Entertainment Pvt Ltd, Vishal Bhardwaj Pictures Pvt Ltd
♫ **Music composer** Vishal Bhardwaj
▭ **Scriptwriters** Vishal Bhardwaj, Sabrina Dhawan, Matthew Robbins

A romantic drama set against the backdrop of World War II, the star-studded cast of *Rangoon* includes Kangana Ranaut, Saif Ali Khan, and

Shahid Kapoor in lead roles. Kangana plays Miss Julia, a stuntwoman and an actress. The character of Miss Julia is based on Fearless Nadia, a famous actress of the 1930s who appeared in films such as *Hunterwali* (see p. 21). In the film, Julia is in a relationship with Rustom "Rusi" Billimoria (Saif), a former Indian action movie star, who now produces films. On an invitation from the British Army to perform for soldiers at the border with Burma, Julia meets Jamadar Nawab Malik (Shahid). As the attraction between Julia and Nawab deepens, Julia remains ignorant of the fact that the man she is falling in love with is a soldier who works for freedom fighter Subhash Chandra Bose's Indian National Army (INA). This complex tale of love and betrayal was shot partly in picturesque Arunachal Pradesh. *Rangoon* features memorable songs by Gulzar and Vishal Bhardwaj, including the popular "Bloody Hell."

KANGANA RANAUT AND SAIF ALI KHAN IN *RANGOON*

Index

Acknowledgments

Dorling Kindersley would like to thank the following people for their help with this book:
Editorial assistance
Suhel Ahmed, Sudeep Grover, Ashwin Khurana, Cathy Meuss, Scarlett O'Hara, Ruth O'Rourke, Georgina Palffy, Helen Ridge, and Christine Stroyan.

Proofreading: Sreshtha Bhattacharya, Rupa Rao, Suefa Lee, Vineetha Mokkil, and Dipali Singh.

Design assistance: Neetika Malik Jhingan, Shubham Rohatgi, Kanika Kalra, Suzena Sengupta, and Vikas Chauhan.

Picture research assistance: Myriam Megharbi, Nishwan Rasool, Surya Sarangi, and Surabhi Wadhwa.

DK would also like to extend special thanks to the following people for their invaluable contribution in the making of the book: Tajdar Amrohi; Arbaaz Khan at Arbaaz Khan Productions; Ashutosh Gowarikar and Laurence D'Souza at Ashutosh Gowarikar Productions Private Ltd.; Madhur Bhandarkar; Ranjit Dahiya at Bollywood Art Project; Kapil Chopra at B.R. Films; N. Chandra; Anupama Chopra, film critic and author; Mitesh Kurani at Cineyug; Marijke Desouza and Akhil Jain at Dharma Productions; Amita Naidu and Kishore Sansare at EROS International; Vikesh Bhutani and Rhea Wagh at Excel Entertainment Pvt. Ltd; Rakesh Roshan and Vasanthan Ramaswamy at Filmkraft (India) Pvt. Ltd; Shivendra Singh Dungarpur (Director), Zara Mann, Shloka Patwardhan, Jayant Patel at Film Heritage Foundation; J. Om Prakash at Filmyug Pvt Ltd.; Rajesh Gupta; Nitin at Hansa Group; Prabha Raghavan at HM Creations; Rachna Bhagat at JP Films; Boney Kapoor; Manoj Kumar and Kunal Goswami; Karishma Prakash at Kwan for Deepika Padukone; Nithya Balakirishnan at Madras Talkies; Masumeh Makhija; Manju Harmesh Malhotra; John Mathew Matthan; Ketan M. Desai at MKD Films; Urmila at Movie Tee Vee Enterprises; Sameer Farooqui at Mukta Arts; Mansoor Khan at Nasir Hussain Films; Anupama Bose and Prashanth R. at National Film Development Corporation (NFDC); G. Adiseshagiri Rao at Padmalaya Studios LLP; Kuljit Pal and Anamika Dialani; Sudhir Bhai Jain at Prakash Jha Films; Dhruv Singh at PRH; Neha Adya at Rajkumar Hirani Productions Pvt. Limited; P.K. Gupta at Rajshri Productions (P) Ltd.; Pawan Kumar at Ramayana Chitra; Geetika Hazari and Bella Mulchandani at Red Chillies Entertainment Pvt. Ltd; Mohammad Riaz; Vishwa Mehra (Mamaji) at RK Films; Rajiv Tandon at ROMP Pictures Pvt. Ltd.; Ronald Grant Archives; Aparna Desai at Salman Khan Ventures Pvt. Ltd; Ashim Samanta; M S Sathyu; Deeepesh Salgia and Vidhya Binoy at Shapoorji & Pallonji Group; Yogesh at Shemaroo; Shyam Shroff at Shringar Films; Shyam Benegal at Shyam Benegal's Sahyadri Films; Romu N. Sippy; Samir Soni; Sanjay Soni; Zehra Agha at Spice PR; Jovy Philip and Pranjal Khandhdiya at Sony Entertainment; Bhawna Kurl at Vijyata Films/Sunny Sounds, Mumbai; Chandrasekhar Tampi for *Silsila*; Prasan Kapoor at Tirupati Picture Enterprises; Rajesh Nair and Bandita Shome at Vaicom18 Media Pvt. Ltd; Girish Jain at Venus Worldwide Entertainment Pvt. Ltd; Bhavin Thakkar at Vinod Chopra Films Pvt. Ltd; Ramnarayanan and Poonam Makhecha at Yash Raj Films.

The publisher would like to thank the following for their kind permission to reproduce their photographs:

(Key: a-above; b-below/bottom; c-center; f-far; l-left; r-right; t-top)

1 Dorling Kindersley: Sameer Tawde / Courtesy of R. K. Films, Film Heritage Foundation (c) **2-3 Eros International:** Bhansali Productions / Sanjay Leela Bhansali / Chetan Deolekar / Kishore Lulla / Sandeep Singh **5 Images Courtesy of S.M.M Ausaja Pvt. Archive:** R. K. Films (br); Himanshu Rai (bl) **6 Images Courtesy of S.M.M Ausaja Pvt. Archive:** Manmohan Desai / Shemaroo Entertainment Ltd. (bl). **Rakesh Roshan and Filmkraft Team:** (br) **7 Eros International:** Bhansali Productions / Sanjay Leela Bhansali / Kishore Lulla (br). **Subhash Ghai:** (bl) **8-9 Getty Images:** Indranil Mukherjee / AFP **10-11 Alamy Stock Photo:** Laura Seoane / Ranjit Dahiya, Bollywood Art Project **12-13 Fawzan Husain 14 Images Courtesy of S.M.M Ausaja Pvt. Archive:** (bl); Dadasaheb Torne (tr) **15 Alamy Stock Photo:** Dinodia Photos (tc). **Images Courtesy of S.M.M Ausaja Pvt. Archive:** (bl); Filmistan Ltd. (crb) **16 Images Courtesy of S.M.M Ausaja Pvt. Archive:** (l) **16-35 Dreamstime.com:** Elfivetrov (Chapter Tabs) **17 Getty Images:** Universal History Archive / Dadasaheb Phalke for Phalke's Films (tl). **Images Courtesy of S.M.M Ausaja Pvt. Archive:** (cb); Dadasaheb Phalke for Phalke's Films (crb) **18-19 Image courtesy of Wirsching Archive:** Bombay Talkies **20 Film Heritage Foundation:** Imperial Movietone (bl, cr) **21 Dreamstime.com:** Kumer (Background image for all box stories across the book). **Images Courtesy of S.M.M Ausaja Pvt. Archive:** Roy Wadia / Wadia Movietone Pvt Ltd (bl, br) **22 Images Courtesy of S.M.M Ausaja Pvt. Archive:** New Theatres Ltd (bl, bc) **23 Film Heritage Foundation:** Himanshu Rai (cl). **Images Courtesy of S.M.M Ausaja Pvt. Archive:** Himanshu Rai (br) **24 Images Courtesy of S.M.M Ausaja Pvt. Archive:** (bl); Himanshu Rai (tr) **25 Film Heritage Foundation:** Himanshu Rai (ca). **Images Courtesy of S.M.M Ausaja Pvt. Archive:** Bombay Talkies (crb); Himanshu Rai (bl) **26 Images Courtesy of S.M.M Ausaja Pvt. Archive:** Prabhat Film Company (clb, cra) **27 Images Courtesy of S.M.M Ausaja Pvt. Archive:** Minerva Movietone / Sohrab Modi (b, cr) **28-29 M/S A V Damle:** Prabhat Film Company **30 Images Courtesy of S.M.M Ausaja Pvt. Archive:** Bombay Talkies (cra, bl) **31 Images Courtesy of S.M.M Ausaja Pvt. Archive:** Bombay Talkies (r, bl) **32 123RF.com:** marslander (c). **Images Courtesy of S.M.M Ausaja Pvt. Archive:** Bombay Talkies (tr, br) **33 123RF.com:** PhotosIndia.com LLC (bl). **Images Courtesy of S.M.M Ausaja Pvt. Archive:** Bombay Talkies (tr, br) **34 Images Courtesy of S.M.M Ausaja Pvt. Archive:** India Pictures / Rashid Anwar (b) **35 Images Courtesy of S.M.M Ausaja Pvt. Archive:** (br); Gemini Studios / S.S. Vasan (bl) **36-37 Getty Images:** Bloomberg / JayaHe GVK New Museum, Terminal 2, Chhatrapati Shivaji International Airport **38 Dorling Kindersley:** Sameer Tawde / Courtesy of R. K. Films, Film Heritage Foundation (tr). **Film Heritage Foundation:** R. K. Films (b) **39 Images Courtesy of S.M.M Ausaja Pvt. Archive:** (tl, cr); Prakash Pictures (bc) **40 Alamy Stock Photo:** Dinodia Photos RM / R.K. Films (bl). **Mary Evans Picture Library:** Ronald Grant Archive / R.K. Films (cra) **40-73 Dreamstime.com:** Hannu Viitanen (Chapter tabs) **41 Images Courtesy of S.M.M Ausaja Pvt. Archive:** (br); R.K. Films (t) **42-43 Images Courtesy of S.M.M Ausaja Pvt. Archive:** R. K. Films (bc) **42 Dorling Kindersley:** Sameer Tawde / R. K. Films (clb). **Images Courtesy of S.M.M Ausaja Pvt. Archive:** R. K. Films (tr, cl) **43 Images Courtesy of S.M.M Ausaja Pvt. Archive:** (tr); R. K. Films (tl). **Mary Evans Picture Library:** Ronald Grant Archive / R. K. Films (crb) **44 Image Courtesy Kamat**

Foto Flash: Mehboob Productions Pvt. Ltd. (bl); R. K. Films (r). **Images Courtesy of S.M.M Ausaja Pvt. Archive:** R. K. Films (ca) **45 Alamy Stock Photo:** Dinodia Photos RM / R. K. Films (crb). **Image Courtesy Kamat Foto Flash:** (cb). **Images Courtesy of S.M.M Ausaja Pvt. Archive:** R. K. Films (tc) **46-47 Images Courtesy of S.M.M Ausaja Pvt. Archive:** Clips from film *Aan* courtesy copyright owner Mehboob Productions Private Ltd, Mumbai, India / (Shaukat Khan) (tl, bc, tr) **47 Images Courtesy of S.M.M Ausaja Pvt. Archive:** (br) **48 Images Courtesy of S.M.M Ausaja Pvt. Archive:** R. C. Talwar (r); T.S. Muthuswamy & S.S. Palaniappan (bl) **49 Images Courtesy of S.M.M Ausaja Pvt. Archive:** Bimal Roy Productions / Bimal Roy / Rinki Roy Bhattacharya (tl); Shri Subhash Ghai / Mukta Arts (bc); Mushir - Riaz (crb) **50 Images Courtesy of S.M.M Ausaja Pvt. Archive:** (br); Bimal Roy Productions / Bimal Roy / Rinki Roy Bhattacharya (bl, tr) **51 Images Courtesy of S.M.M Ausaja Pvt. Archive:** (cr) ; Guru Dutt Films / Guru Dutt / Ultra Media & Entertainment Pvt. Ltd. (br) **52-53 Image Courtesy Kamat Foto Flash 54 Images Courtesy of S.M.M Ausaja Pvt. Archive:** Guru Dutt Films / Guru Dutt / Ultra Media & Entertainment Pvt. Ltd. (br) **55 Images Courtesy of S.M.M Ausaja Pvt. Archive:** B.R. Films (Kapil Chopra) (cla, cra) **56 Image Courtesy Kamat Foto Flash:** Clips from film *Mother India* courtesy copyright owner Mehboob Productions Private Ltd, Mumbai, India / (Shaukat Khan) (b) **57 Images Courtesy of S.M.M Ausaja Pvt. Archive:** (tr); Clips from film *Mother India* courtesy copyright owner Mehboob Productions Private Ltd, Mumbai, India / (Shaukat Khan) (tl, br) **58 Alamy Stock Photo:** Archives du 7eme Art / Photo 12 / Clips from film *Mother India* courtesy copyright owner Mehboob Productions Private Ltd, Mumbai, India / (Shaukat Khan) (bl). **Image Courtesy Kamat Foto Flash:** Clips from film *Mother India* courtesy

copyright owner Mehboob Productions Private Ltd, Mumbai, India / (Shaukat Khan) (tl, br) **59 Film Heritage Foundation:** Clips from film *Mother India* courtesy copyright owner Mehboob Productions Private Ltd, Mumbai, India / (Shaukat Khan) (c, bl). **Images Courtesy of S.M.M Ausaja Pvt. Archive:** (tc). **Photoshot:** Starstock / Clips from film *Mother India* courtesy copyright owner Mehboob Productions Private Ltd, Mumbai, India / (Shaukat Khan) (tr, crb) **60-61 Images Courtesy of S.M.M Ausaja Pvt. Archive:** (all images) **61 Alamy Stock Photo:** Kamal Kishore / Reuters (br) **62 Images Courtesy of S.M.M Ausaja Pvt. Archive:** (br); Rajkamal Kalamandir Pvt. Ltd. (all images) **63 Images Courtesy of S.M.M Ausaja Pvt. Archive:** Anoop Sharma / Shringar Films, Shyam Shroff **64 Images Courtesy of S.M.M Ausaja Pvt. Archive:** (br); Bimal Roy Productions / Bimal Roy / Rinki Roy Bhattacharya (c) **65 Images Courtesy of S.M.M Ausaja Pvt. Archive:** Guru Dutt Films / Guru Dutt / Ultra Media & Entertainment Pvt. Ltd. (br) **66-67 Images Courtesy of S.M.M Ausaja Pvt. Archive:** (all images) **67 Images Courtesy of S.M.M Ausaja Pvt. Archive:** Guru Dutt Films / Guru Dutt / Ultra Media & Entertainment Pvt. Ltd. (cb) **68-69 Shapoorji & Pallonji Group, Deepesh Salgia, Vidhya Binoy:** (all images) **69 Images Courtesy of S.M.M Ausaja Pvt. Archive:** Shapoorji & Pallonji Group, Deepesh Salgia and Vidhya Binoy (br) **70-71 Shapoorji & Pallonji Group, Deepesh Salgia, Vidhya Binoy:** (all images) **70 Dreamstime.com:** Kamensky (cr) **71 Images Courtesy of S.M.M Ausaja Pvt. Archive:** (tr) **72 Getty Images:** James Burke / THE LIFE Premium Collection (bl). **Images Courtesy of S.M.M Ausaja Pvt. Archive:** The Bombay Talkie Studios Ltd. Ashok Kumar / Savak Vacha (tr) **73 Images Courtesy of S.M.M Ausaja Pvt. Archive:** Shakti Films / Shakti Samanta (Ashim Samanta) / Pachhi / Sant Singh (tl); Anoop Sharma /

Shringar Films, Shyam Shroff (bc); K. S. Daryani (cra) **74-75 Ranjit Dahiya, Bollywood Art Project:** Sippy Films Pvt. Ltd. **76 Dorling Kindersley:** James Mann / Andrew Cluett (br). **Image Courtesy Kamat Foto Flash:** R. K. Films (tr). **Images Courtesy of S.M.M Ausaja Pvt. Archive:** V.I.P. Films / Manoj Kumar (clb) **77 Image Courtesy Kamat Foto Flash:** Nasir Hussain Films (Mansoor Khan) (t). **Images Courtesy of S.M.M Ausaja Pvt. Archive:** Rupam Pictures Pvt. Ltd. / N. C. Sippy (Romu N. Sippy) / Hrishikesh Mukherjee (bc) **78-79 Image Courtesy Kamat Foto Flash:** Hardeep / Movie Tee Vee Enterprises (l, ca) **79-119 Dreamstime.com:** Subbotina (Chapter Tabs) **79 Images Courtesy of S.M.M Ausaja Pvt. Archive:** (br) **80-81 Image Courtesy Kamat Foto Flash:** R. K. Films (b, br) **81 Images Courtesy of S.M.M Ausaja Pvt. Archive:** R. K. Films (tc) **82-83 Image Courtesy Kamat Foto Flash:** Shakti Films / Shakti Samanta (Ashim Samanta) **84 Images Courtesy of S.M.M Ausaja Pvt. Archive:** Navketan Films International / Dev Anand (Suneil Anand) **85 Image Courtesy Kamat Foto Flash:** Navketan Films International / Dev Anand (Suneil Anand) (tl, br). **Images Courtesy of S.M.M Ausaja Pvt. Archive:** (bc) **86 Alamy Stock Photo:** Courtesy Everett Collection / Navketan Films International / Dev Anand (Suneil Anand) (tr). **Images Courtesy of S.M.M Ausaja Pvt. Archive:** Navketan Films International / Dev Anand (Suneil Anand) (br) **86-87 Image Courtesy Kamat Foto Flash:** Navketan Films International / Dev Anand (Suneil Anand) (bl, bl, tr) **87 Images Courtesy of S.M.M Ausaja Pvt. Archive:** (tc) **88-89 Images Courtesy of S.M.M Ausaja Pvt. Archive:** Navketan Films International / Dev Anand (Suneil Anand) (all images) **90 Image Courtesy Kamat Foto Flash:** Guru Dutt Films / Guru Dutt / Ultra Media & Entertainment Pvt. Ltd. (bl) **91 Images Courtesy of S.M.M Ausaja Pvt. Archive:** (br); Guru Dutt Films /

Guru Dutt / Ultra Media & Entertainment Pvt. Ltd. (bl) **92 Images Courtesy of S.M.M Ausaja Pvt. Archive:** B.R. Films (Kapil Chopra) (ca, br) **93 Images Courtesy of S.M.M Ausaja Pvt. Archive:** Nasir Hussain Films (Mansoor Khan) (tl, br) **94 Image Courtesy Kamat Foto Flash:** Navketan Films International / Dev Anand (Suneil Anand) (ca). **Images Courtesy of S.M.M Ausaja Pvt. Archive:** (bc) **95 Alamy Stock Photo:** Courtesy Everett Collection / Shakti Films / Shakti Samanta (Ashim Samanta) **96-97 Image Courtesy Kamat Foto Flash:** Navketan Films International / Dev Anand (Suneil Anand) **98 Images Courtesy of S.M.M Ausaja Pvt. Archive:** (bl); Manoj Kumar / Harkishen R. Mirchandani / R. N. Goswami (br) **99 Images Courtesy of S.M.M Ausaja Pvt. Archive:** Mahmood Ali / N.C. Sippy / Rajshri Productions (P) Ltd. (cl, br) **100 Images Courtesy of S.M.M Ausaja Pvt. Archive:** (b); Seth Jagat Narain (cla) **101 Images Courtesy of S.M.M Ausaja Pvt. Archive:** (bc); S.D. Narang (tc); Kishore Kumar (cra) **102 Image Courtesy Kamat Foto Flash:** Shakti Films / Shakti Samanta (Ashim Samanta) (bl). **Images Courtesy of S.M.M Ausaja Pvt. Archive:** Shakti Films / Shakti Samanta (Ashim Samanta) (cla) **103 Images Courtesy of S.M.M Ausaja Pvt. Archive:** (cra). **The Ronald Grant Archive:** Shakti Films / Shakti Samanta (Ashim Samanta) (l) **104 123RF.com:** monthon wachirasettakul (c). **Dorling Kindersley:** Adrian Shooter (cl). **Image Courtesy Kamat Foto Flash:** Shakti Films / Shakti Samanta (Ashim Samanta) (tr, br). **Images Courtesy of S.M.M Ausaja Pvt. Archive:** Shakti Films / Shakti Samanta (Ashim Samanta) (bl) **105 Image Courtesy Kamat Foto Flash:** Shakti Films / Shakti Samanta (Ashim Samanta) (crb). **Images Courtesy of S.M.M Ausaja Pvt. Archive:** (tc). **The Ronald Grant Archive:** Shakti Films / Shakti Samanta (Ashim Samanta) (tr) **106 Image Courtesy Kamat Foto

Flash: Shakti Films / Shakti Samanta (Ashim Samanta) (r) **107 Images Courtesy of S.M.M Ausaja Pvt. Archive:** (bc); Shakti Films / Shakti Samanta (Ashim Samanta) (cla); Vinod Doshi / Shemaroo Entertainment Ltd. (cra) **108 Image Courtesy Kamat Foto Flash:** Navketan Films International / Dev Anand (Suneil Anand) (bl) **109 Images Courtesy of S.M.M Ausaja Pvt. Archive:** (bc); G. P. Sippy / Sippy Films Pvt. Ltd. (all images) **110 Images Courtesy of S.M.M Ausaja Pvt. Archive:** (r, bl) **111 Getty Images:** Yogen Shah / India Today Group (bc). **Images Courtesy of S.M.M Ausaja Pvt. Archive:** (tl); HM Creations / Hema Malini (crb) **112 Dreamstime.com:** Nikolaev (ca). **Images Courtesy of S.M.M Ausaja Pvt. Archive:** Rupam Pictures Pvt. Ltd. / N.C. Sippy (Romu N. Sippy) / Hrishikesh Mukherjee (br) **113 Images Courtesy of S.M.M Ausaja Pvt. Archive:** Shakti Films / Shakti Samanta (Ashim Samanta) (cr) **114-115 Image Courtesy Kamat Foto Flash 116-117 Image Courtesy Kamat Foto Flash:** Mahal Pictures / Kamal Amrohi (Tajdar Amrohi) (b, cra) **117 Images Courtesy of S.M.M Ausaja Pvt. Archive:** (cb, bl) **118 Image Courtesy Kamat Foto Flash:** R. K. Films (cra, bl). **Images Courtesy of S.M.M Ausaja Pvt. Archive:** R. K. Films (cla) **119 Getty Images:** Dinodia Photos (tc). **The Ronald Grant Archive:** R. K. Films (br) **120-121 Alamy Stock Photo:** Joerg Boethling / Sholay Media and Entertainment Pvt. Ltd. **122 Images Courtesy of S.M.M Ausaja Pvt. Archive:** Yash Raj Films Pvt. Ltd. (bl); Rupam Pictures Pvt. Ltd. / N.C. Sippy (Romu Sippy) / Hrishikesh Mukherjee (cr) **123 Images Courtesy of S.M.M Ausaja Pvt. Archive:** (bc); National Film Development Corporation / Devi Dutt / Shringar Films (Shyam Shroff) (tr) **124 Images Courtesy of S.M.M Ausaja Pvt. Archive:** Salim – Javed (bl) **125 Images Courtesy of S.M.M Ausaja Pvt. Archive:** (all images) **124-169 Dreamstime.com:** Irontrybex (Chapter Tabs) **126 Images Courtesy of S.M.M Ausaja Pvt. Archive:** Ramayana Chitra (Pawan Kumar) / Susheela Kamat (cra). **Mary Evans Picture Library:** Ronald Grant Archive / Manmohan Desai / Ketan M. Desai, MKD Films (l) **127 Images Courtesy of S.M.M Ausaja Pvt. Archive:** Ketan M. Desai, MKD Films (tc). **Photographs/Stills/copyrighted material et al of Film - Courtesy Sony Pictures Networks India Private Limited, Saraswati Entertainment Private Limited and Rising Sun Films Pvt. Ltd.:** (br). **Yash Raj Films Pvt. Ltd.** (bl) **128 Image Courtesy Kamat Foto Flash:** Shyam Benegal Sahyadri Films (b). **Images Courtesy of S.M.M Ausaja Pvt. Archive:** (br); Shyam Benegal Sahyadri Films (tr) **129 Rex Shutterstock:** Unit 3 Mm / Shutterstock / MS Sathyu **130 123RF.com:** prashantzi (bl). **Getty Images:** Nathan Benn (ca). **Images Courtesy of S.M.M Ausaja Pvt. Archive:** (bc) **131 Images Courtesy of S.M.M Ausaja Pvt. Archive:** B. Nagi Reddi-Chakrapani (br) **132-133 Rakesh Roshan and Filmkraft Team 134-135 Sholay Media and Entertainment Pvt. Ltd.:** G.P. Sippy (all images) **135 Images Courtesy of S.M.M Ausaja Pvt. Archive:** (br) **136-137 Sholay Media and Entertainment Pvt. Ltd.:** G.P. Sippy (all images) **137 Getty Images:** Dinodia Photos (tr) **138-139 Images Courtesy of S.M.M Ausaja Pvt. Archive:** (bc) **138 Images Courtesy of S.M.M Ausaja Pvt. Archive:** G.P. Sippy / Sippy Films Pvt. Ltd. (bl) **139 Boney Kapoor:** (tc) **140 Images Courtesy of S.M.M Ausaja Pvt. Archive:** (br); Rupam Pictures Pvt. Ltd. / N.C. Sippy (Romu N. Sippy) / Hrishikesh Mukherjee (all images) **141 Images Courtesy of S.M.M Ausaja Pvt. Archive:** Shri. J Om Prakash / Filmyug Pvt. Ltd. (all images) **142 Images Courtesy of S.M.M Ausaja Pvt. Archive:** Jai Singh (cra). **The Ronald Grant Archive:** Rupam Pictures Pvt. Ltd. / N.C. Sippy (Romu N. Sippy) / Hrishikesh Mukherjee (bl) **143 Eros International:** Kumar Mangat (crb). **Rajesh Gupta:** (bc) **144 Yash Raj Films Pvt. Ltd. 145 123RF.com:** PhotosIndia.com LLC (br). **Images Courtesy of S.M.M Ausaja Pvt. Archive:** (tr). **Yash Raj Films Pvt. Ltd.** (tl) **146-147 Yash Raj Films Pvt. Ltd.** (all images) **146 Images Courtesy of S.M.M Ausaja Pvt. Archive:** (tr) **147 Images Courtesy of S.M.M Ausaja Pvt. Archive:** (tl) **148-149 Images Courtesy of S.M.M Ausaja Pvt. Archive:** Manmohan Desai / Shemaroo Entertainment Ltd. (all images) **150 Images Courtesy of S.M.M Ausaja Pvt. Archive:** (br); Subhash Desai / Shemaroo Entertainment Ltd. (ca) **151 Images Courtesy of S.M.M Ausaja Pvt. Archive:** Suresh Shah / EROS International Pvt. Ltd. (br) **152 Sunny Sounds Pvt. Ltd.:** (l) **153 Alamy Stock Photo:** Sunny Sounds Pvt. Ltd. (br). **Images Courtesy of S.M.M Ausaja Pvt. Archive:** Sher Jeng Singh Punchee / Movie Tee Vee Enterprises (tl). **Sholay Media and Entertainment Pvt. Ltd.:** G.P. Sippy (cb) **154 Images Courtesy of S.M.M Ausaja Pvt. Archive:** (br, b) **155 Image Courtesy Kamat Foto Flash:** R.K. Films (bl). **Images Courtesy of S.M.M Ausaja Pvt. Archive:** (br) **156 123RF.com:** Narmada Gharat (ca). **Images Courtesy of S.M.M Ausaja Pvt. Archive:** (bl, br) **157 Getty Images:** Strdel / AFP (cra). **Images Courtesy of S.M.M Ausaja Pvt. Archive:** Rupam Pictures Pvt. Ltd. / N.C. Sippy (Romu N. Sippy) (all images) **158-159 Shubhash Ghai:** (all images) **159 Getty Images:** AFP (br) **160-161 Image Courtesy Kamat Foto Flash:** Boney Kapoor **162 Images Courtesy of S.M.M Ausaja Pvt. Archive:** Rupam Pictures Pvt. Ltd. / N.C. Sippy (Romu N. Sippy) / Hrishikesh Mukherjee (bl, cra) **163 Images Courtesy of S.M.M Ausaja Pvt. Archive:** (br); Basu Bhattacharya / Rinki Roy Bhattacharya (bc) **164 Image Courtesy Kamat Foto Flash:** Gul Anand / Jayshree Anand-Makhija / PLA Entertainment Pvt. Ltd. / (Masumeh Makhija) (all images) **164 Getty Images:** Hindustan Times (br) **165 Yash Raj Films Pvt. Ltd. 166- 167 Yash Raj Films Pvt. Ltd.** (all images) **168-169 Image Courtesy Kamat Foto Flash:** Muzaffar Ali (all images) **169 Alamy Stock Photo:** Dinodia Photos (tr) **170-171 Alamy Stock Photo:** Dinodia Photos **172 Images Courtesy of S.M.M Ausaja Pvt. Archive:** G. Adiseshagiri Rao / Padmalaya Studios LLP, Hyderabad (b); B. Subhash / Tilotima B Subhash / Shemaroo Entertainment Ltd. (tr) **173 Getty Images:** Yogen Shah / India Today Group (bc). **Images Courtesy of S.M.M Ausaja Pvt. Archive:** Rakesh Roshan and Filmkraft Team (tr) **174 Alamy Stock Photo:** Dinodia Photos (cl) **174-207 Dreamstime.com:** Madartists (Chapter Tabs) **175 Images Courtesy of S.M.M Ausaja Pvt. Archive:** B. Subhash / Tilotima B Subhash / Shemaroo Entertainment Ltd. (cla, b) **176 Getty Images:** Hindustan Times (br). **Images Courtesy of S.M.M Ausaja Pvt. Archive:** Kuljit Pal (tl) **177 Images Courtesy of S.M.M Ausaja Pvt. Archive:** (br); Devi Dutt / Chanda Dutt / Shringar Films / Shyam Shroff (ca, bl) **178 Images Courtesy of S.M.M Ausaja Pvt. Archive:** National Film Development Corporation (tr, br) **179 Getty Images:** Che Rosales / WireImage (br). **Rajshri Productions (P) Ltd.:** (cra,bl) **180 Images Courtesy of S.M.M Ausaja Pvt. Archive:** G. Adiseshagiri Rao / Padmalaya Studios Llp, (tr, bl) **181 Alamy Stock Photo:** Dinodia Photos (br). **Images Courtesy of S.M.M Ausaja Pvt. Archive:** Mukta Arts Pvt. Ltd. / Subhash Ghai (l) **182 Images Courtesy of S.M.M Ausaja Pvt. Archive:** (br); Tirupati Picture Enterprises / Prasan Kapoor (bl) **183 Images Courtesy of S.M.M Ausaja Pvt. Archive:** C.V. Sridhar (tl); A.S.R.Anjaneyulu / M.Arjunaraju (bc); Sunderlal Nahata / Dhoondy (cra) **184 Images Courtesy of S.M.M Ausaja Pvt. Archive:** Harmesh Malhotra / Manju Harmesh Malhotra **185 Images Courtesy of S.M.M Ausaja Pvt. Archive:** (br); Sweety Mehta / R.K. Gupta (r) **186- 187 Getty Images:** IndiaPictures / UIG / Syed Ayub / Nalini Shankar /

Deepak Adhiya **188 Image Courtesy Kamat Foto Flash:** Boney Kapoor (bl). **Boney Kapoor:** (cra) **189 Getty Images:** Gareth Cattermole (bl). **Image Courtesy Kamat Foto Flash:** Boney Kapoor (r) **190-191 Boney Kapoor:** (all images) **191 Getty Images:** Dinodia Photos (cra) **192 Shubhash Ghai:** Ashok Ghai (bl). **Boney Kapoor:** (r) **193 Alamy Stock Photo:** Entertainment Pictures / Fox Searchlight Pictures / Warner Bros. Pictures / Celador Films / Film4 (bc). **Boney Kapoor:** (cr). **Vinod Chopra Films Pvt. Ltd.:** (tc) **194 Alamy Stock Photo:** Dinodia Photos (bc). **194-195 Image Courtesy Kamat Foto Flash:** Nasir Hussain Films (Mansoor Khan) (all images) **196-197 Image Courtesy Kamat Foto Flash:** Nasir Hussain Films (Mansoor Khan) (all images) **197 Images Courtesy of S.M.M Ausaja Pvt. Archive:** (tr) **198 Images Courtesy of S.M.M Ausaja Pvt. Archive:** N. CHANDRA / Dinesh Gandhi (tr, bc) **199 Getty Images:** Gareth Cattermole / DIFF (br). **Vinod Chopra Films Pvt. Ltd.:** (bl, cla) **200 Eros International:** Bhansali Productions / Bharat Shah (r). **Images Courtesy of S.M.M Ausaja Pvt. Archive:** Rajshri Productions (P) Ltd. (cl) **201 Shubhash Ghai:** (tc); Ashok Ghai (cra). **Prakash Jha Productions:** (bc) **202 Shubhash Ghai:** (cra). **Yash Raj Films Pvt. Ltd.** (bc) **203 Images Courtesy of S.M.M Ausaja Pvt. Archive:** Jayantilal Gada / Pen India Ltd (cla, br) **204 Images Courtesy of S.M.M Ausaja Pvt. Archive:** Rupam Pictures Pvt. Ltd. (Romu N. Sippy) / Raj N. Sippy (cr). **Boney Kapoor:** (l) **205 Image courtesy of Spice PR:** Hope Productions / EROS International / Sunil Lulla / R. Balki / Rakesh Jhunjhunwala / R.K. Damani (bc). **Image Courtesy Kamat Foto Flash:** Boney Kapoor (tl). **Boney Kapoor:** (cra, br) **206 Rajshri Productions (P) Ltd.:** (br) **207 Images Courtesy of S.M.M Ausaja Pvt. Archive:** (br); Vijayta Films / Dharmendra (cr) **208-209 Getty Images:** Lonely Planet Images **210 Images Courtesy of S.M.M Ausaja**

Pvt. Archive: (br); Sudhakar Bokade / Eros International (tr); Harmesh Malhotra / Manju Harmesh Malhotra (bl) **211 Image Courtesy Kamat Foto Flash:** Rajshri Productions (P) Ltd. (t). **Images Courtesy of S.M.M Ausaja Pvt. Archive:** Image from the movie Andaz Apna Apna courtesy of M/s Vinay Pictures / Vinay Sinha (Priti Sinha) (br) **212 Image Courtesy Kamat Foto Flash:** Nasir Hussain Films (Mansoor Khan) (cr). **Images Courtesy of S.M.M Ausaja Pvt. Archive:** Nasir Hussain Films (Mansoor Khan) (clb) **212-257 Dreamstime.com:** Thomas Dutour (Chapter Tabs) **213 Yash Raj Films Pvt. Ltd. 214 Shubhash Ghai:** (cl). **Red Chillies Entertainments Pvt. Ltd.:** Gauri Khan (r) **215 Dharma Productions Private Limited:** "Images from the film "Kabhi Khushi Kabhie Gham" 2001 - Under License and permission from Dharma Productions Private Limited". (tl). **Red Chillies Entertainments Pvt. Ltd.:** (bc); Excel Entertainment Pvt. Ltd. / Ritesh Sidhwani / Gauri Khan / Farhan Akhtar (crb) **216 Images Courtesy of S.M.M Ausaja Pvt. Archive:** Ganesh Jain / Venus Worldwide Entertainment Pvt.Ltd. (b) **217 Getty Images:** Odd Andersen / AFP (br). **Images from the movie Andaz Apna Apna courtesy of M/s Vinay Pictures / Vinay Sinha (Priti Sinha):** (bl, cra) **218-219 Yash Raj Films Pvt. Ltd. 220 Image Courtesy Kamat Foto Flash:** Rajshri Productions (P) Ltd. (b). **Images Courtesy of S.M.M Ausaja Pvt. Archive:** Rajshri Productions (P) Ltd. (cla) **221 Rajshri Productions (P) Ltd.:** (tr) **222-223 Image Courtesy Kamat Foto Flash:** Rajshri Productions (P) Ltd. (all images) **222 Dreamstime.com:** Rakesh Picholiya (cb) **223 Images Courtesy of S.M.M Ausaja Pvt. Archive:** (tr). **Rajshri Productions (P) Ltd.:** (bl) **224 Alamy Stock Photo:** FotoFlirt / Arbaaz Khan Productions (r) **225 Alamy Stock Photo:** Collection Christophel / Rajshri Productions (P) Ltd. (bc). **Images Courtesy of S.M.M Ausaja Pvt. Archive:** Rajshri Productions (P) Ltd. (cra). **Boney Kapoor:** (c).

Rakesh Roshan and Filmkraft Team: (tl) **226-227 Images Courtesy of S.M.M Ausaja Pvt. Archive:** Jhamu Sughand / Ram Gopal Varma / EROS International (all images) **226 Images Courtesy of S.M.M Ausaja Pvt. Archive:** (br) **228 Alamy Stock Photo:** Dinodia Photos (r). **Images Courtesy of S.M.M Ausaja Pvt. Archive:** Nasir Hussain Films (Mansoor Khan) (ca) **229 Images Courtesy of S.M.M Ausaja Pvt. Archive:** Nasir Hussain Films (Mansoor Khan) (cra). **Rajkumar Hirani Films Private Limited.:** (bc). **ROMP Pictures Pvt. Ltd.:** Ronnie Screwvala / Rakeysh Omprakash Mehra / Zarina Mehta / Deven Khote (tl) **230 Yash Raj Films Pvt. Ltd. 231 Images Courtesy of S.M.M Ausaja Pvt. Archive:** (br). **Yash Raj Films Pvt. Ltd.** (tr) **232-233 Yash Raj Films Pvt. Ltd.** (tr, br, tr, br) **232 Dreamstime.com:** Michał Zduniak (cr) **233 123RF.com:** qpicimages (c). **Dorling Kindersley:** Royal Academy of Music (bl). **Images Courtesy of S.M.M Ausaja Pvt. Archive:** (tc) **234-235 Yash Raj Films Pvt. Ltd. 236 Rakesh Roshan and Filmkraft Team:** (all images) **237 Cineyug:** Karim Morani / Bunty Soorma / Ali Morani / Karan Soorma (all images). **Getty Images:** Milind Shelte / India Today Group (cr) **238 Alamy Stock Photo:** Dinodia Photos (br). **Getty Images:** Marwan Naamani / AFP (bl). **Images Courtesy of S.M.M Ausaja Pvt. Archive:** Rupam Pictures Pvt. Ltd. (Romu N. Sippy) (ca) **239 J.P.Dutta & J.P.Films:** (all images) **240 Shubhash Ghai:** (all images) **241 Alamy Stock Photo:** Dinodia Photos (cra). **Getty Images:** Sebastian D'souza / AFP (bl) **242-243 Madras Talkies:** (all images) **244 Alamy Stock Photo:** Jason Moore / ZUMApress.com (r). **Images Courtesy of S.M.M Ausaja Pvt. Archive:** Hansa Pictures Pvt. Ltd. (clb) **245 Getty Images:** Jonathan Alcorn / Bloomberg / © A.M.P.A.S.®" (bl); Adrian Dennis / AFP (tc). **Rex Shutterstock:** Nicholas Bailey / Shutterstock (cr) **246-247 Dharma Productions Private Limited:** "Image from the film "Kuch Kuch Hota

Hai", 1998 - Under License and permission from Dharma Productions Private Limited" (all images) **247 Getty Images:** Yogen Shah / India Today Group (br) **248 Alamy Stock Photo:** Dinodia Photos (r) **248-249 Dharma Productions Private Limited:** "Images from the film "Kabhi Alvida Naa Kehna", 2006, "My Name is Khan", 2010, "Badrinath ki Dulhania", 2017 - Under License and permission from Dharma Productions Private Limited" (all images) **249 © Viacom 18 Media Private Limited:** Flying Unicorn Entertainment / Ashi Dua (crb) **250 Images Courtesy of S.M.M Ausaja Pvt. Archive:** John Matthew Matthan (bl). **John Matthew Matthan:** (cra) **251 Shubhash Ghai:** (tr, bl) **252-253 Rex Shutterstock:** Sipa Press **254 Getty Images:** Patrick Durand / Sygma (c). **Shubhash Ghai:** (r) **255 Alamy Stock Photo:** Courtesy Everett Collection / Metro-Goldwyn-Mayer / Columbia Pictures / Robert Simonds Production (bl). **Image Courtesy Kamat Foto Flash:** Boney Kapoor (tc). **Images Courtesy of S.M.M Ausaja Pvt. Archive:** Gurinder Chadha / Deepak Nayar (cra) **256 Images Courtesy of S.M.M Ausaja Pvt. Archive:** Bhansali Productions / Sanjay Leela Bhansali / EROS International (bl) **257 Eros International:** Bhansali Productions / Sanjay Leela Bhansali (b). **Getty Images:** Ajay Aggarwal / Hindustan Times (cra) **258-259 Getty Images:** Corbis Historical **260 Eros International:** Bhansali Productions / Sanjay Leela Bhansali, Kishore Lulla (b); Firoz Nadiadwala (tr) **261 Ashutosh Gowariker Productions:** (br). **Getty Images:** Dinodia Photo (cl). **Image courtesy of Spice PR:** Excel Entertainment Pvt. Ltd. / Junglee Pictures / Ritesh Sidhwani / Farhan Akhtar (tc) **262-263 Rakesh Roshan and Filmkraft Team:** (all images) **262-331 Dreamstime.com:** Colicaranica (Chapter Tabs) **263 Alamy Stock Photo:** AF archive (cra) **264-265 Excel Entertainment Pvt. Ltd.:** (all images) **265 Getty Images:** Strdel / AFP (cra) **266 Dreamstime.com:** Gaurav Masand (bl) **267 Alamy Stock Photo:** Tim

Gainey 268 **123RF.com:** Andrey Armyagov (bl). **Alamy Stock Photo:** Shashank Mehendale / ephotocorp (br). **Getty Images:** Raj K Raj / Hindustan Times (tr) **269 Dreamstime.com:** Hilabsolution (tr). **Getty Images:** Fine Art Images / Heritage Images (br); J. Shearer / WireImage (tl) **270-271 Dharma Productions Private Limited:** "Image from the film *Kabhi Khushi Kabhie Gham*" 2001 - Under License and permission from Dharma Productions Private Limited". (bl, b) **271 Alamy Stock Photo:** The National Trust Photolibrary (tl). **Getty Images:** Chirag Wakaskar / WireImage (cra) **272-273 Eros International:** Bhansali Productions / Sanjay Leela Bhansali / Chetan Deolekar / Kishore Lulla / Sandeep Singh **274-275 Eros International:** Bhansali Productions / Sanjay Leela Bhansali / Bharat Shah (All Images) **276-277 Eros International:** Bhansali Productions / Sanjay Leela Bhansali / Bharat Shah (All Images) **277 Getty Images:** Narinder Nanu / AFP (tc) **278 Getty Images:** Gareth Cattermole (br). **Madras Talkies:** (bl) **279 Getty Images:** George Pimentel / WireImage (br). **Shubhash Ghai:** (ca, clb) **280 Eros International:** Bhansali Productions / Sanjay Leela Bhansali / Chetan Deolekar / Kishore Lulla / Sandeep Singh (r). **Shubhash Ghai:** (clb) **281 Getty Images:** rune hellestad / Corbis (cra). **Rakesh Roshan and Filmkraft Team:** (tc). © **Viacom 18 Media Private Limited:** Bhansali Productions / Sanjay Leela Bhansali (bc) **282-283 Reuters:** Stringer **284 Yash Raj Films Pvt. Ltd. 285 Rakesh Roshan and Filmkraft Team:** (br) **286-287 Vinod Chopra Films Pvt. Ltd.:** (all images) **287 Getty Images:** Milind Shelte / India Today Group (cra) **288 ROMP Pictures Pvt. Ltd.:** Ronnie Screwvala / Rakeysh Omprakash Mehra / Zarina Mehta / Deven Khote (br) **289 Alamy Stock Photo:** Max Rossi / REUTERS (br). **Eros International:** Kumar Mangat **290-291 Eros International:** Arbaaz Khan Productions **292-293 Red Chillies Entertainments Pvt. Ltd.:** (all images) **293 Getty Images:**

Prabhas Roy / Hindustan Times (crb) **294-295 Red Chillies Entertainments Pvt. Ltd.:** (all Images) **294 Getty Images:** Peter Dazeley / Photographer's Choice (crb) **295 Getty Images:** Andrew Cowie / AFP (tc) **296 Getty Images:** Yogen Shah / India Today Group (bc). **New Era High School, Panchgani:** (c) **297 Alamy Stock Photo:** Chaiwat Subprasom / REUTERS (bl). **Getty Images:** Satish Bate / Hindustan Times (br); Adam Majendie / Bloomberg (cra) **298 Getty Images:** Yogen Shah / India Today Group (br). **Yash Raj Films Pvt. Ltd.:** (bl) **299 UTV Films / Bhandarkar Entertainment 300-301 Ashutosh Gowariker Productions:** (b, cra, br) **301 Getty Images:** Matt Carr (bl) **302-303 Vinod Chopra Films Pvt. Ltd.:** (b, cb) **303 Alamy Stock Photo:** Vinod Chopra Films Pvt Ltd (tr). **Getty Images:** Parveen Kumar / Hindustan (br) **304 Arbaaz Khan Productions:** (tr). **Eros International:** Arbaaz Khan Productions (bl) **305** © **Viacom 18 Media Private Limited:** Shailesh R. Singh / Surya Sonal Singh / Vinod Bachhan (ca, b, br) **306-307 Yash Raj Films Pvt. Ltd. 308 Image courtesy of Spice PR:** EROS International / Excel Entertainment Pvt. Ltd. / Ritesh Sidhwani / Farhan Akhtar **309 Excel Entertainment Pvt. Ltd.:** (c, br) **310 Getty Images:** Manoj Verma / Hindustan Times (br). © **Viacom 18 Media Private Limited:** Anurag Kashyap Films Private Limited (c) **311 Dharma Productions Private Limited:** "Image from the film "*Student of the Year*" 2012 - Under License and permission from Dharma Productions Private Limited". (bl, tr) **312 Getty Images:** Venturelli / WireImage (bc). © **Viacom 18 Media Private Limited:** Pen India Private Limited (tr) **313** © **Viacom 18 Media Private Limited:** Dr. B. K. Modi / Grazing Goat Pictures / Playtime Creations / Ashvini Yardi / Paresh Rawal (br) **314** © **Viacom 18 Media Private Limited:** Wide Frame Pictures / Friday Filmworks Pvt. Limited (bc, tr) **315 Dharma Productions Private Limited:**

"Image from the film "*Yeh Jawani Hai Deewani*" 2013 - Under License and permission from Dharma Productions Private Limited". **316 Getty Images:** Jasjeet Plaha / Hindustan Times (cra). **Prakash Jha Productions:** (l) **317 Getty Images:** Punit Paranjpe / AFP (cra). **Yash Raj Films Pvt. Ltd.** (tc, bc) **318-319 Image courtesy of Spice PR:** Yash Raj Films Pvt. Ltd. / Aditya Chopra **320-321** © **Viacom 18 Media Private Limited:** Phantom Films Private Limited (b, tl, cra) **321 Getty Images:** Pramod Thakur / Hindustan Times (bc) **322 Getty Images:** Amlan Dutta / Hindustan Times (tl) **322-323 UTV Films / Bhandarkar Entertainment:** (bc) **323 Eros International:** Colour Yellow / Krishika Lulla / Anand L. Rai (tc). © **Viacom 18 Media Private Limited:** Nadiadwala Grandson Entertainment Private Limited / Vishal Bhardwaj Pictures Private Limited (bc); Phantom Films Private Limited (crb) **324-325 Rajkumar Hirani Films Private Limited.:** (b, tr, c) **326 Copyright protected works obtained under license from Salman Khan Ventures Private Limited:** (b, ca) **327 Getty Images:** STR / AFP (bc). **Photographs/Stills/copyrighted material et al of Film - Courtesy Sony Pictures Networks India Private Limited, Saraswati Entertainment Private Limited and Rising Sun Films Pvt. Ltd.:** (cra) **328 Alamy Stock Photo:** Chaiwat Subprasom / REUTERS (cra). **Eros International:** Bhansali Productions / Sanjay Leela Bhansali / Chetan Deolekar / Kishore Lulla / Sandeep Sing (l) **329 Eros International:** Illuminati Films / Saif Ali Khan / Dinesh Vijan (tc). **Photoshot:** Paramount Pictures / Entertainment Pictures / ZUMAPRESS.com (br). **Red Chillies Entertainments Pvt. Ltd.:** Gauri Khan / Ronnie Screwvala / Siddharth Roy Kapur (b) **330 Eros International:** Bhansali Productions / Sanjay Leela Bhansali / Kishore Lulla (bl,cr). **Getty Images:** Milind Shelte / India Today Group (bc) **331 Alamy Stock Photo:** Amit Pasricha / IndiaPicture (tr). **Getty Images:**

Raveendran / AFP (b) **332 Images Courtesy of S.M.M Ausaja Pvt. Archive:** Ardeshir Irani (clb); Mehboob Productions (cra) **332-345 Depositphotos Inc:** Gilmanshin (Chapter Tabs) **333 Images Courtesy of S.M.M Ausaja Pvt. Archive:** Bimal Roy Productions / Bimal Roy / Rinki Roy Bhattacharya (bc) **334 Images Courtesy of S.M.M Ausaja Pvt. Archive:** Bimal Roy Productions / Bimal Roy / Rinki Roy Bhattacharya (tl) **335 Dorling Kindersley:** Sameer Tawde / Courtesy of R. K. Films, Film Heritage Foundation (tc). **Images Courtesy of S.M.M Ausaja Pvt. Archive:** Rupam Pictures Pvt. Ltd. (Romu N. Sippy) / Raj N.Sippy (c) **336 Images Courtesy of S.M.M Ausaja Pvt. Archive:** Manmohan Desai / Ketan M. Desai, MKD Films (br) **337 Shubhash Ghai:** Ashok Ghai (tc). **National Film Development Corporation:** (cb) **338 Madras Talkies:** (br). **Vinod Chopra Films Pvt. Ltd.:** (tc) **339 Rakesh Roshan and Filmkraft Team:** (c) **340 Red Chillies Entertainments Pvt. Ltd.:** Gauri Khan (t, br) **341 Shubhash Ghai:** (tl). **Madras Talkies:** (br) **342 Eros International:** Saif Ali Khan / Dinesh Vijan / Sunil. A. Lulla (br) **343 Eros International:** J.A. Entertainment / Rising Sun Film Production / Rampage Motion Pictures / Sunil Lulla / John Abraham / Ronnie Lahiri (cr) **344 Eros International:** Bhansali Production / Sanjay Leela Bhansali / Chetan Deolekar / Kishore Lulla / Sandeep Singh (bl). **Image courtesy of Spice PR:** ROMP Pictures Pvt. Ltd. / Viacom18 Motion Pictures, P.S. Bharathi / Rajiv Tandon (tr) **345 Image courtesy of Spice PR:** © Viacom 18 Media Private Limited / Nadiadwala Grandson Entertainment Private Limited / Vishal Bhardwaj Pictures Private Limited (br)

Cover images: *Front and Back:* **Dreamstime.com:** Brighton bl

All other images © Dorling Kindersley For further information see: www.dkimages.com